GIRLHOOD EMBROIDERY

American Samplers & Pictorial Needlework 1650–1850

VOLUME I

Betty Ring

WITH A FOREWORD BY
ALICE WINCHESTER

ALFRED A. KNOPF   NEW YORK
1993

THIS IS A BORZOI BOOK
PUBLISHED BY ALFRED A. KNOPF, INC.

Library of Congress Cataloging-in-Publication Data

Ring, Betty.
    Girlhood embroidery : American samplers and pictorial needlework, 1650–1850 / Betty Ring. — 1st ed.
        p.   cm.
    Includes Bibliographical References and Index.
    ISBN 0-394-55009-9
    1. Samplers—United States.   2. Embroidery—United States.   I. Title.
NK9112.R57   1993
746.3973—dc20
                                                                93-6735
                                                                  CIP

Manufactured in the United States of America
First Edition

Volume I: Cover onlay. Anonymous memorial dedicated to George Washington, Boston, c.1805–1815. Silk, paint, and ink on silk; 23″ in diameter. See Figure 84.
Private collection.

Frontispiece. *ABIGAIL GOS/S,* c.1761. Silk on linen; 19¾″ x 15″. Abigail's verse by Isaac Watts would later be favored on Marblehead samplers, as would the fashion for worked black backgrounds, which was evidently peculiar to New England during the eighteenth century. At least one nineteenth-century example is known from Montgomery County, Pennsylvania (Amanda Bleyler, 1838 [Oakland Museum, H23.825]; for a piece related to Bleyler with unworked ground, see Krueger, *Gallery,* Fig. 120). Abigail Goss (1749–1801) was the daughter of Thomas Goss (1716–1780) and Abigail Wade (1717–1791). Goss was pastor of the Congregational Church in Bolton, Massachusetts, from 1741 to 1771. At age sixteen, Abigail married her former schoolmaster, Joshua Atherton (1737–1809) of Harvard, Massachusetts. In 1773 they moved to Amherst, New Hampshire, where Atherton became a prominent lawyer. Seven of their fourteen children lived to adulthood.
Private collection.

TUITION.

Mrs. Carew,

ACQUAINTS her Friends, that she proposes to open a School at her House about half way between the Town and Landing, the first of May next, for young Misses, (where a number may be boarded)—School will begin at the usual time, and open by reading, some religious passages of the best approved authors; the study of English Grammar, History, &c. Also, will be taught Cloath and Tiffina work on Sattin, with common embroidery, Tambour, and all kinds of Needle-work on Muslin, with drawing, Painting, and Figure.

Norwich, April 10, 1799.

BOARDING and DAY SCHOOL.

MISS BALCH, by the Desire of several of the Parents of her Pupils, has thought proper to alter the HOURS OF PAINTING, which has hitherto been taught from Seven to Nine in the Morning, and have it done in the usual *School Hours*, Three Mornings in a Week. Nevertheless, should any young Ladies prefer taking private Lessons, they will be attended to.

Miss BALCH assures her Employers, that she has been very fortunate in selecting Assistants, and of course thinks it in her Power to have those under her Care faithfully instructed (in Progression) from the first Elements to those Branches which will be most pleasing to their Parents or Guardians.

Her System of Education comprises Reading, Orthography, Grammar, Writing, Arithmetic, Geography, with the Use of the Globes, History and Composition, especially the Epistolary Style; Drawing, Painting, Embroidery, with all the Varieties of plain, fancy and elegant Needle Work. Likewise, Music.

The Advantages of this Seminary, it is hoped, will arise from a persevering Solicitude and constant Exertion, to improve the Morals and cultivate the Understanding in every useful Art, and in every Branch of Science to which the Attention of the Pupils may be directed.

Acknowledgments of Gratitude are due not only to the Inhabitants of this but of many other Places, for their long, constant and unceasing Patronage.

Providence, March 24, 1809.

EDUCATION.

MRS. SAUNDERS & Miss BEACH, inform their friends and the public, that they continue to receive young Ladies at their Academy, in Dorchester, for the purpose of instruction in the following branches:—Reading, Writing, Arithmetic, Ancient and Modern Geography, Astronomy, Use of Globes, Use of Maps, History, Rhetoric, Botany, Composition, English and French Languages, Drawing, Painting in Oils, Crayons and Water Colours, Painting on Velvet, Ornamental Paper Work, Drawing and Colouring Maps, Embroidery, Tambour, Plain Sewing, &c.

It is presumed that no Seminary of the kind in this Country ever offered superior advantages for the advancement of young Ladies in the accomplishments usually deemed necessary to constitute a polite education. The Pupils have access to a well chosen Library of above fifteen hundred volumes including the best Classic Authors, French and English, the use of large Maps, &c. The finest patterns for Drawing in Figures, Landscapes, Fruits, Flowers, &c. The House of Mrs. Saunders and Miss Beach is very spacious, the accommodations excellent, the situation admirable and remarkably healthy.

TERMS.

Board per quarter,	$36
Tuition from 8 to $12 per quarter,	12
Entrance for the French Language,	5
Use of Piano-forte per month,	1
Washing per doz.	50
Stationary at Booksellers prices.	
Music and Dancing by eminent Masters.	

Young Ladies who remain at the Academy one year will be boarded at $30 per quarter.

Dorchester, April 19, 1819.

Miss REA,

WOULD inform her friends and the public, that her SPRING TERM will commence on the 15th of March, in the house occupied by Mrs. M. SMITH, Exchange-street.

TUITION from $2 50 to $10 per quarter.

For Reading, Writing, Orthography, Defining, English Grammar, Geography, Arithmetic, Rhetoric, History, Chemistry, Plain and Ornamental Needle Work, Unshaded, on Cambric and Muslin,	$3 50
Drawing and Painting in Water Colors, Embroidering, Genealogies,	5 00

Oil Painting, Filagree, Embroidering on Satin, &c. from 7 to $10 per quarter.

No attention shall be wanting to give satisfaction to those who will favor her with their patronage.

Application may be made at her room in school hours, or at her boarding-house, corner of Silver and Fore Streets.

Portland, March 2, 1824.   3w*

Front endpapers:

Mary Turfrey, *The Boston News-Letter*, September 2, 1706 (the earliest newspaper advertisement for a girls' school in English colonial America).
The New-York Historical Society.

Mrs. Condy, *The Boston Evening-Post*, March 29, 1742.
American Antiquarian Society.

Elizabeth Murray, *The Boston Evening-Post*, March 26, 1753.
American Antiquarian Society.

Mrs. Jane Day, *The Boston Evening-Post*, April 30, 1759.
American Antiquarian Society.

Ame & Elizabeth Cuming, *The Boston-Gazette, and Country Journal*, April 24, 1769.
American Antiquarian Society.

Mrs. Rowson, *Columbian Centinel*, Boston, April 21, 1802.
American Antiquarian Society.

Lydia Royse, *The Connecticut Courant*, Hartford, June 17, 1799.
The Connecticut Historical Society.

John & Eleanor Druitt, *The Boston-Gazette, and Country Journal*, April 12, 1773.
American Antiquarian Society.

Mrs. Carew, *The Norwich Packet*, Norwich, Connecticut, April 10, 1799.
The Houghton Library, Harvard University.

Miss Balch, *The Providence Gazette*, March 25, 1809.
American Antiquarian Society.

Mrs. Saunders & Miss Beach, *Columbian Centinel*, Boston, April 21, 1819.
American Antiquarian Society.

Miss Rea, *Eastern Argus*, Portland, Maine, March 2, 1824.
The New-York Historical Society.

Girlhood Embroidery

ABCDEFGHIKLMNOPQRSC
DEFGHIKLMNOPQRSCDEFGHIKC

On Earth Let Me Exam
ple Shine And When I
Leave This State May
Heaven Receive This Sou
l Or Me To Bliss Div
inely Great Alsoph Cook

In loving memory
of my parents,
Nellie Fitzsimmons
and
Claude Stephen Abrego

Contents

Foreword

This book needs no foreword; its message is all here, complete and clearly told in words and full-color pictures. But I welcome the opportunity to express my admiration and affection for Betty Ring and to congratulate her on this achievement.

This book has been a long time in the making. I have followed its development through Betty's colorful accounts—sometimes discouraged, often hilarious—of her activities. What she has created is an indispensable reference work for all serious students and collectors of American girlhood embroidery.

Betty Ring's first article on the subject appeared in the October 1971 issue of *The Magazine ANTIQUES,* of which I had then been editor for over thirty years. She had been collecting for about a third of that time, and had recently launched upon the research to which she has devoted herself ever since—with the impressive results recorded in this book.

Her next article for *ANTIQUES,* "Collecting American Samplers Today," was published in June 1972—as it happened, the last issue before I retired as editor of the magazine. Since then I have had the pleasure of observing Betty Ring as she has pursued her passion for American schoolgirl needlework to the point where she has become a leading authority on the subject and an outstanding collector in this highly specialized field. It is no exaggeration to say that Betty Ring's own collecting, and her enthusiasm and research, are largely responsible for the greatly increased interest in the subject in recent years.

Betty Ring, wife of a Texas businessman, mother of seven, and grandmother of six, has become a familiar figure on the antiquarian scene. Some twenty years ago she surveyed the broad expanse of needlework, and selected the aspects that seemed to her significant and in need of further research. There had been collectors and students of the subject since the dawn of the colonial revival (about 1876), and numerous valuable books and articles had been published, as shown in her bibliography in this volume. But, as I can well remember, most collectors of early furniture or silver or other imposing examples of the decorative arts would brush aside samplers and embroidered pictures as charming or merely quaint, undeserving of scholarly research.

Now girlhood embroidery has reached a new level of appreciation. Far more than displaying a variety of stitches, it is recognized as including work of many kinds, from simple samplers showing a name and a date to elaborately composed and exquisitely worked pictures, to heraldic motifs, religious scenes, and historic personages and events, pictures from life and pictures from printed sources. And as with any subject, the more one learns about it, the more interesting it becomes. One collector may focus on techniques of stitchery, another may specialize on designs and their sources. It is a vast and varied subject.

Betty Ring approached the field with seriousness of purpose and thoroughgoing zeal. From her home in Houston she has over the years virtually commuted to the Northeast, attending antiques shows and auctions and exhibitions as well as delving in libraries. She has haunted historical societies and museums and genealogical collections and read her way through all sorts of early records. Her meticulous approach has won her the respect and assistance of local authorities, and she has produced fresh and fascinating information regarding the girls who worked early American embroideries and—especially—the women who taught them. Indeed, she was the first to call attention to mourning pictures as an expression of high fashion rather than a lugubrious task set for little girls by grieving elders.

She focused on the schoolmistresses who taught girls to do needlework, and thus added a whole new chapter to the history of female education in America. And by focusing as well on the schoolgirls, she was able to trace many a genealogical connection and to define the significance of needlework in the girls' lives. I feel that Betty sees all these antique objects in their intimate relation to people—the people who created and preserved and inherited them and who are as real to her as the people who collect them today.

Betty Ring's emphasis on regional styles and recognizable motifs in schoolgirl needlework is also of special significance, comparable to the study of regional characteristics in furniture, silver, and other decorative arts. This is shown in her geographical organization of the chapters of this book. Her discoveries regarding the work produced in Rhode Island led to a landmark exhibition held at the Rhode Island Historical Society in 1983. Betty Ring served as guest curator and wrote the catalogue, titled *Let Virtue Be a Guide to Thee: Needlework in the Education of Rhode Island Women, 1730–1830.*

While traveling about the country and pursuing her researches, Betty has become acquainted with many of the notable collections, public and private, of American needlework, and has not failed to acquire items of interest and value herself. In 1990 her collection of nearly 160 items was exhibited in New York

City by the Museum of American Folk Art. The handsome, fully illustrated catalogue, *American Needlework Treasures,* was written by Betty Ring.

Girlhood Embroidery is a comprehensive presentation of Betty Ring's knowledge and understanding of American samplers and pictorial needlework from 1650 to 1850. Her preface is a clear statement of her aims to clarify how, where, when, and *why* samplers were made and to show what can be learned from them in addition to the pure pleasure that can be derived from their artistry and skill. The book is clear and accessible, its illustrations generously provided. I am confident that this book will be welcomed by a growing and grateful public and will become an enduring classic in the library of essential books about antiques.

ALICE WINCHESTER
January 16, 1993

Acknowledgments

WRITING THIS BOOK has been an adventure, both fulfilling and frustrating. The joy has been the study of the amazing embroideries that continue to emerge and the constant encouragement of friends, but searching for the schoolmistresses responsible for this beguiling art has been the challenge—and the search was often futile! How could these women leave such splendid evidence of their skill and ingenuity, but so few facts about themselves? More often than not, they remain anonymous, but finding some of them has been a great satisfaction.

First, I want to express my appreciation to Alice Winchester, who initially encouraged my interest in this field. Her accomplishments and kindness have continually inspired me. As my interest in needlework grew, I was fortunate to find others who share my obsession with the history of the women involved in its creation, and five exceptional friends voluntarily proceeded to help me with this book, quite beyond all reasonable expectations. I cannot adequately describe the contributions of the following people, who have been my intense supporters for more than six years: Tessa Cadbury and Alison Cadbury Senter acquainted me with every aspect of Quaker history and institutions, and tirelessly assisted with research in Pennsylvania, New Jersey, and Delaware. Because of them, America's earliest dated white-work sampler came to light (Fig. 364). Dorothy McCoach, a busy textile conservator, undertook the research of Lehigh Valley schools and scholars, attended to countless tedious details on my behalf, and unfailingly made it a special treat to be in Bethlehem. Joan Stephens, who regularly contributes her textile expertise to the Smithsonian, was a wonderful comrade on many trips in search of these elusive ladies. Her cheerful diligence and reassuring optimism helped to brighten the frequent days that were fruitless. Mary Linda Zonana, an exceptional student of New York history, has worked tirelessly to solve the mystery of New York's colonial samplers, and she continues to pursue their origin and their makers with skill and relentless fervor. I am everlastingly grateful to these dedicated scholars, who have contributed so much to the fruition of this book. I fervently hope they approve of what they find here.

I am also deeply indebted to Margaret Ames, Rita Conant, Patricia T. Herr, and Sheila Rideout for generously sharing important information with me. Other kind friends have contributed to my knowledge, including Henry L. P. Beckwith, Marian S. Carson, Evelyn C. Cheney, Carl L. Crossman, Davida Deutsch, Mary Jaene Edmonds, Joanne and Theodore Foulk, Elizabeth M. Gilbert, Elton W. Hall, Joanne Harvey, Patrice G. Kleinberg, Hazel Portwood, Stephen T. Riley, Caroline Stride, Sue Studebaker, Susan B. Swan, and Louise Woodhead.

I owe special thanks to the following people for helping me in a variety of ways: Allison Eckardt Ledes, Editor of *The Magazine ANTIQUES*, and R. Scudder Smith, Editor, and Laura Beach, Associate Editor, of *Antiques And The Arts Weekly*; Nancy Druckman, William W. Stahl, Jr., and Elisabeth and Wendell Garrett of Sotheby's; Ralph Carpenter, John Hays, and Meghan Hughes of Christie's, and Jan Wurtzburger, formerly of Christie's; Merrilee J. Possner, formerly of Christie's East; Stephen L. Fletcher and Lynda A. Cain of Skinner, Inc.; also, Kenneth W. Van Blarcom; Robert C. Eldred; Mrs. Judith Webster of C. G. Sloane & Company; and George R. Hockmeyer, who drew the maps.

This book became possible because hundreds of people shared their embroideries or the resources of their institutions with me—far more than I can possibly name here. However, I must mention those who contributed significant facts or important new information. For their exceptional help, I am indebted to John F. LaBranche, Curator of the Old York Historical Society, York, Maine; Audrey G. Milne, Curator, York Institute Museum, Saco, Maine; Robert K. Weiss, Curator of Exhibitions, Essex Institute; Mrs. John P. Hunt, Jr., Executive Secretary, Marblehead Historical Society; Peter Benes, Director of the Dublin Seminar for New England Folklife; Karin C. Bengtson, Textile Department, Museum of Fine Arts, Boston, and now at the Winterthur Museum; Gary Boyd Roberts, Jerome E. Anderson, and David C. Dearborn, Librarians, New England Historic Genealogical Society; Susan E. Strickler, Director of Curatorial Affairs, Worcester Art Museum; Georgia B. Barnhill, Curator of Graphic Arts, American Antiquarian Society; Donald R. Friary, Director, Old Deerfield, Inc.; Judith N. Lund, Registrar, Old Dartmouth Historical Society, New Bedford, Massachusetts; Bertram K. Lippincott III, Librarian, Newport Historical Society; Helene Tessler, Curator, Bristol Historical Preservation Society, Bristol, Rhode Island; Elizabeth Pratt Fox, Curator, and Robert F. Trent, former Curator, Connecticut Historical Society; William N. Hosley, Jr., Curator of American Decorative Arts, Wadsworth Atheneum; and Karin E. Peterson, Coordinator of Properties and Programs, The Antiquarian and Landmarks Society, Hartford, Connecticut.

Especially helpful in the Middle States and the South were Amelia Peck, Department of American Decorative Arts, the Metropolitan Museum; Gillian Moss, Department of Textiles, the Cooper–Hewitt Museum; Elizabeth H. Moger, Librarian, Haviland Records Room, Archives of the New York Yearly Meeting of the Religious Society of Friends; Tammis Kane Groft, Curator, Albany Institute of History and Art; Patricia M. Tice, Curator of Furnishings, The Strong Museum, Rochester, New York; Suzanne C. Crilley, Curator of Cultural History, New Jersey State Museum; Rhett Pernot, Administrator, Burlington County Historical Society; Joanne L. Bradley, Curator, and Mrs. Kurt Hoelle, Librarian, Gloucester County Historical Society, Woodbury, New Jersey; Alice G. Boggs, Librarian, Salem County Historical Society, Salem, New Jersey; Elizabeth Jarvis and David Cassedy, Curators, Historical Society of Pennsylvania; Dilys Blum, Curator of Costumes and Textiles, and her Assistant, Monica Brown, Philadelphia Museum of Art; Rosemary B. Phillips, Librarian, Chester County Historical Society; Alice B. Long, Curator, Westtown School; the Reverend Vernon Nelson, Archivist, Moravian Archives, Bethlehem, Pennsylvania; Vertie Knapp, former Curator, Monroe County Historical Association, Stroudsburg, Pennsylvania; Dennis K. Moyer, Director, Schwenkfelder Museum and Library, Pennsburg, Pennsylvania; Patricia Keller, Director/Curator, the Heritage Center of Lancaster County, Lancaster, Pennsylvania; Dora M. Shotzberger, former Textile Conservator, Winterthur Museum; Sister Mary Bernard McEntee, Saint Joseph's Provincial House, Emmitsburg, Maryland; Jennifer F. Goldsborough, Chief Curator, Maryland Historical Society; Lynn Dakin Hastings, Curator, Hampton National Historic Site, Towson, Maryland; Sister Mary Leonard Whipple, Georgetown Visitation Convent, Washington, D.C.; Jean Taylor Federico and Gloria Seaman Allen, former Directors of the Daughters of the American Revolution Museum, Washington, D.C.; Barbara R. Luck, Curator, the Abby Aldrich Rockefeller Folk Art Center, Williamsburg, Virginia; Bradford L. Rauschenburg, Director of Research, Martha W. Rowe, Research Associate, and Rosemary Estes, former Archivist, Museum of Early Southern Decorative Arts, Winston–Salem, North Carolina.

I am also grateful to kind assistants abroad, particularly Margaret H. Swain of Edinburgh, Scotland; Betty Limb, Archivist, and Phyllis M. Sadler, former Archivist of the Ackworth School, Pontefract, England; and Paula Lambert of Harrogate, England, for the history of the York School.

A great many dealers have generously helped me, but I owe special thanks to Leonard and Jacqueline Balish, Ronald Bourgeault, Amy Finkel, Madeleine B. Fisher, Harry B. Hartman, Carol and Stephen Huber, and Marguerite Riordan.

Among the many fine photographers responsible for the illustrations that appear here, I must mention Arthur Vitols of Helga Photo Studio. He not only took more photographs than others, but made prolonged excursions to faraway places to accomplish this work, and was always patient, competent, and affable, for which I am most grateful.

With enthusiasm for this subject, it was Alice Quinn, formerly with Knopf, who instigated the publication of *Girlhood Embroidery*, and I have continued to enjoy her encouragement. I am most indebted, however, to Victoria Wilson, who endured the long period of preparation and made this book happen. Throughout this process, her editing and publishing expertise guided me, but she kindly permitted me a wide range of choice in determining the concept and content of these volumes. In the meantime, Antoinette White responded to my questions and soothed my worries with her reassuring buoyancy and unfailing good humor. When production finally began, I was introduced to the skills and dedication of production manager Andrew Hughes, designer Peter Andersen, and production editor Karen Leh. For their kindness and patience, as well as their abilities, they especially deserve my thanks.

Finally, but of first importance, I must gratefully acknowledge the tolerance and endearing helpfulness of my sons and daughters, and my everlastingly generous husband.

BETTY RING
Houston, March 18, 1993

Preface

It was a special recommendation to a teacher that she could make a handsome sampler. At times that was the main object in attending school.[1]

THIS TRUISM of past centuries was well known to the Westtown School instructress who wrote these words in 1875. A generation later it was largely forgotten. In the twentieth century, the schoolroom origin of samplers has never been widely understood, and is, in fact, often met with disbelief. The delightful naïveté that characterizes many American samplers is more happily attributed to the spontaneous impulses of the youthful maker, when in reality, the schoolmistress probably distributed the same pattern to her entire class.

Indeed, American samplers and needlework pictures, just as they had been in Europe, were with few exceptions the products of school instruction. Their schoolroom origin explains not only the amazing quantity of this most prevalent form of historical needlework, but why the majority of samplers were merely exercises in lettering, or a pious verse and simple motifs worked within a modest border. Until about 1840, every girl who had received the slightest education had made a sampler and was thereby prepared to mark the linens of her future household.[2] The decorative samplers and needlework pictures much admired today were made by those girls whose parents could afford a school that taught "accomplishments." Education was not free, nor was it regarded as a basic *right*. It was a privilege and often recognized as such in the sampler verses chosen by the teachers.

The primary purpose of this book is to present the most important forms of American samplers and needlework pictures now known, and to provide a refer-

---

1. Quotation from "The Sewing Room, etc., 1815–1850" by Ann Sharpless (1851–1943), a Westtown School teacher from 1872 to 1904. Manuscript bound in *Historical Essays* assembled by the Westtown Literary Union, c.1890.

2. It was also a beginner's instruction in writing, which was often denied to girls because reading schools did not necessarily teach writing. See E. Jennifer Monaghan, "Literacy Instruction and Gender in Colonial New England," *American Quarterly* 40, no. 1 (March 1988): 18–41.

ence where other pieces may be compared. Most of the embroideries have been arranged by town, county, or school within their respective states. Many examples have been illustrated so that the reader can develop a "feel" for the typical styles of specific areas. Every effort has been made to identify both the places of origin for these objects and the women responsible for their designs. I have also tried to identify the embroiderers since knowledge of their history may ultimately enable us to learn more about their teachers and other aspects of their education.

I have not focused on sampler verses, nor on stitches and textiles. The former have been well considered elsewhere. Any consistent analysis of the latter was precluded by the volume of objects in diverse places and the ownership of many pieces being now unknown. Those, in particular, I feel fortunate to include here. Frames are illustrated when they are believed to be original to the needlework and of the same period, with occasional exceptions for visual effect[3]; and all sizes are sight dimensions of the embroideries. Accession numbers have been given for pieces in institutions so scholars can easily seek more information. A key to abbreviations for institutions, publications, and auction houses appears in the back of each volume, and all publications which lack full data in the text can be found in the bibliography.

My second aim is to direct attention, by presenting tangible evidence of their endeavors, to the long-forgotten educators of one half of the population of early America. The contributions of a schoolmistress were often ignored by the local historians of her time, and therefore lost to the historians of later years. The incredible wealth of samplers known today represents only a small fraction of those that were made. Yet they attest to the number of women teaching and suggest that more girls received some sort of schooling than demographic studies indicate. Admittedly, until the mid-nineteenth century, girls were denied the academic education available to boys, but during the preceding two hundred years they created the most delightful schoolwork to survive from any era.

The history of women's education cannot be fully understood without considering what these documents convey about who was teaching girls—where, when, and for how long. When the young girl brought home her embroidery, it was proudly displayed. Even when it was unsigned, knowledge of its maker often survived with it, but the schoolmistress who provided the pattern and guided its execution was seldom known to the maker's heirs. Her identity can sometimes be gleaned from bills, receipts, or accounts of schooling that survive in the papers of the embroiderer's father or guardian. This approach identified Elizabeth Marsh, the premier schoolmistress of colonial Philadelphia; determined who taught the daughters of Governor Jonathan Trumbull of Connecticut; and proved that Susanna Condy and Eleanor Druitt taught arms embroidery in eighteenth-century Boston. Once the teacher of an important piece has been found, comparisons

---

3. Frames probably not original, or of a later date: Figures 43, 192, 193, 255, 263, 264, and 585.

make other attributions possible, and knowledge of her teaching career may be expanded.

During the period of schoolgirl "accomplishments" in America, schools that trained women to become teachers did not exist. The majority of women who taught did so out of necessity—spinsterhood, widowhood, or a need to supplement the family income—and some women kept schools while having children at regular intervals.[4] Their economic success often depended on the ability to "make a handsome sampler." It took artistry, skill, diligence, and patience to send a child home with an exceptional sampler, and many of the remarkable pieces worked by young children reflect the ability to inspire or enforce the discipline necessary for completion.

Despite the never-ending arguments on how to define folk art, the women responsible for the best examples of schoolgirl art should be included within any definition of this category. Yet these forgotten schoolmistresses have been the most neglected of American artists.

The information included here is necessarily based on the embroideries I have been able to see: published examples, collections in most of the major museums and in countless smaller ones, as well as those in private collections. Newly found pieces may alter some of my conclusions. I am confident, however, that further research and emerging embroideries will support the opening premise presented here: for the early American girl, to make a handsome sampler was "at times . . . the main object in attending school."

---

4. Among these were Leah Meguier in Harrisburg, Pennsylvania; Catharine Buchanan of Wrightsville and Marietta, Pennsylvania; and Elizabeth Folwell of Philadelphia.

Girlhood Embroidery

NEEDLEWORK IN WOMEN'S EDUCATION: ITS RISE AND FALL

SIMILE

A Sampler resembles an elegant mind,
Whose passions by reason subdu'd and refin'd,
Move only in lines of affection and duty,
Reflecting a picture of order and beauty.[1]

A girl should be taught to sew and not to read, unless one wishes to make a nun of her."[2] This early Italian proverb expressed the Western world's attitude toward female education from the dawn of Christianity until the Renaissance, and liberation from the dominance of needlework in the education of women was not fully achieved until the mid-nineteenth century. A girl's acceptable destiny, regardless of her station, was a life of domesticity, and literacy in a world of few books had little value. Sewing, however, was an essential skill as well as a respectable means of artistic expression. Therefore, from earliest recorded history until the Industrial Revolution, it was a primary subject in the education of girls, both at home and at school.

There are no records of prolonged efforts to expand women's education before the Renaissance. Sappho, the Grecian poetess (b.c.600 B.C.), is believed to have established a school for girls, but no details of this effort survive. A century later, Aspasia, the mistress of Pericles, pressed for women's intellectual emancipation. During ancient times, and throughout the Middle Ages, there were occasional movements in this direction, but the proponents of advanced education for women left no significant records until the end of the seventeenth century.

Women command little attention in the histories of the ancient and medieval Western world, but more than any other occupation, early literature refers to their involvement with textiles—their creation, their use, and their decoration.

Fig. 1. Detail from the upper left panel in the retablo of the Virgin and Saint George, late fourteenth century. Attributed to Luis Borrassá (c.1360–1424). Approximately 16¼" x 11½". *Church of San Francisco, Vilafranca del Panedés, Barcelona, Spain.*

---

1. *Simile* from Lucy Turpen's sampler of 1815, Fig. 317, Vol. II.
2. As quoted in Jarman, *Landmarks in the History of Education* (1951), 123.

Fig. 2. Queen Elizabeth of
York (1465–1503), drawn by
H. Crease from a painting
in the collection of the Earl
of Essex and engraved by
William Thomas Fry, De-
cember 1, 1815, London.
Elizabeth was the daughter
of England's King Edward
IV and Lady Elizabeth
Woodville Grey (see Fig.
416), and the mother of
Henry VIII.
British Museum, London.

Women could spin, weave, and fashion cloth into garments and a variety of household necessities, but their individual artistry could be best expressed in embroidery.

Embroidery arose before painting, probably in Asia Minor, and the ancient Phrygians became so skilled in this craft it was first known as Phrygian work. The art of embroidery also reached a high state of perfection among the Egyptians and Babylonians, from whence it spread to Greece and Rome. The Greeks ascribed its origin to Athena, their goddess of wisdom and skills. During the early Christian era, Italy became the center of fine needlework, and this art was perpetuated during the Dark Ages by the Popes of Rome, who encouraged the creation of ecclesiastical embroidery throughout Europe.

The needlework of Englishwomen, whose traditions would one day be transplanted to America, reflects the mingling of many invaders of the British Isles—the Celts, the Romans, the Anglo-Saxons, and briefly the Danes before the Norman Conquest of the eleventh century. Finally, the Conqueror was crowned William I on Christmas Day, 1066, and his reign brought feudalism to England, while opening it to Continental influences in all fields of endeavor.

Christianity had come to Britain in the seventh century,[3] and some girls of the Anglo-Saxon era had been convent-bred. The first English-educated Abbess, Hild of Hartlepool (614–680), became an outstanding female educator.[4] Following the Norman Conquest, the number of English nunneries steadily increased, and many continued to provide education for their young girl converts until the nunneries' dissolution by Henry VIII in the sixteenth century. In the meantime, girls of noble birth were gaining new opportunities for education at court. This custom no doubt spread from France and reflected the influence of Charlemagne's palace school, where his daughters, in addition to their usual instruction in needlework, received the same literary education as his sons. Here began the dominance of the needle arts in the *formal* education of English girls.[5]

The embroidery of Anglo-Saxon women, held in high esteem before the Norman Conquest, continued to flourish during feudal times when skills were developing that would ultimately characterize England's most famous needlework—*opus anglicanum.*[6] This term was applied by Continental patrons to the magnificent ecclesiastical embroideries worked by professional embroiderers from the twelfth to the fourteenth centuries.

During the time *opus anglicanum* was flowering, England also experienced an expansion in intellectual pursuits; the first universities were established, and the seeds of popular education were being sown. Again, this movement spread from France where elementary schools had existed from the beginning of the eleventh

3. Christianity had first appeared in Britain under Roman rule, but the conquered Celts did not convert the Anglo-Saxons.
4. Gardiner, *English Girlhood at School* (1929), 15–17.
5. Ibid., 21–32.
6. Wardle, *Guide to English Embroidery* (1970), 6–7.

century.[7] Instruction for girls focused, as it would for centuries, on needlework, deportment, and piety. It was, nevertheless, a beginning effort to educate English children of humble birth, and the school dame was about to enter the village scene.

In the 1400s, the educational practice of "placing out" or transferring children to the homes of others for "borde and schole" arose in England and was the forerunner of the boarding school.[8] A girl, usually between the ages of seven and twelve, was placed in another's family where she would perform certain services in return for social and practical education. She was certainly taught needlework, and other subjects as agreed upon by the adoptive family. This arrangement evolved for average children out of the custom of teaching young noblewomen at court, but foreigners regarded it as evidence of the Englishmen's indifference toward their children. Indeed, it ran the gamut from an excellent situation to a degrading one, but it continued throughout the seventeenth century in England, and to some degree in New England, although it was partly superseded by the advent of boarding schools kept by women for the instruction of girls.

The Renaissance, that great rebirth of interest in art, literature, and learning, emerged in Italy during the 1300s, and eventually it spread from Spain to England where the humanist movement lagged behind southern Europe by one hundred years until the ascension of Henry VII in 1485. Henry's victory at the Battle of Bosworth finally ended the long conflict later known as the Wars of the Roses, and the Tudor dynasty began when Henry VII, a Lancastrian, married Elizabeth of York (Fig. 2). English secular embroidery increased under the stability of their reign, and female education was soon stimulated by an accomplished young emissary of the Spanish Renaissance who was betrothed to their son, Prince Arthur.

When the sixteen-year-old Catherine of Aragon (Fig. 3) arrived in England in 1501, the working of samplers was unquestionably an established custom both in England and in Spain. Furthermore, a Spanish painting of the late 1300s suggests that samplers were commonplace during the very early years of the Renaissance (Fig. 1). Borrassá's painting was perhaps inspired by the legends of the Virgin that appeared in Greek and Latin literature between the second and ninth centuries. Beginning in the thirteenth century, various episodes from the Virgin's education were often glorified in art. This scene may relate to the Council of Priests' decree that a new veil for the Temple be worked by undefiled virgins, whereupon seven young girls, including the Child Mary, were assigned this task.[9] This story explains the traditional description of the panel as the Virgin and her friends bringing embroidered scarves to the Temple. There are, however, eight figures rather than seven and another is partly visible. Most likely the artist depicted Mary's education in a manner contemporary to his time, and the palatial setting

Fig. 3. Catherine of Aragon, c.1505, by Miguel Zittoz (1468–1525/26). Oil on panel; 11⅜″ x 8⅟₁₆″. Catherine (1485–1536) was the youngest daughter of the Spanish monarchs Ferdinand II (1452–1516) of Aragon and Isabella (1451–1504) of Castile. In 1501 she married Arthur (1488–1502), firstborn son of Henry VII (1457–1509) and Elizabeth of York (1465–1503), and in 1509, their second son, Henry VIII (1491–1547). Amiable and well educated, she delighted Henry during the early years of their marriage, which was annulled in 1533. Here her identity is partly confirmed by the letter *K* with Tudor roses in her necklace, and the pendant letter *C*. Traditionally, Catherine is remembered for her devotion to fine needlework. *Kunsthistorisches Museum, Vienna.*

7. Gardiner, *English Girlhood*, 71.

8. Ibid., 114–29.

9. Ibid., 9–12.

suggests that these are young ladies of the castle showing embroideries much like samplers to the chatelaine.

The earliest known reference to a sampler was written in the account book of Elizabeth of York on July 10, 1502, when payment was recorded for an eln of linen cloth for a sampler for the queen.[10] It is doubtful that this was intended for Elizabeth's personal use. She was then thirty-seven years old, newly pregnant with her seventh child, and mourning the recent death of her fifteen-year-old son, who had been married to Catherine of Aragon for less than six months. Other samplers in royal households remain unexplained. In 1509, the year of Catherine's marriage to Henry VIII, her elder sister, Juana, the tragic queen of Castile, owned fifty samplers that are said to have been worked in silk and gold metallic threads. Forty-three years later, the possessions of young Edward VI included thirteen samplers.[11] Unfortunately, the records of samplers belonging to the Spanish and English nobility offer no clues to their purpose. Tantalizing questions remain unanswered, including why these samplers have all disappeared.

English poet and satirist John Skelton (c. 1460–1529) left more satisfying information about a sampler when he recorded Jane Scrope's distress at the loss of her pet sparrow to a cat named Gib:

I take my sampler ones
Of purpose, for the nones,
to sewe with stychis of sylke
My sparowe whyte as mylke,
That by representacyn
of his image and facyon.
To me it might importe
Some pleasure and comforte
For my solas and sporte
But when I was sewing his beke
Methought my sparowe did speke
and opened his pretty byll
Saynge, Mayd, ye are in wyll
Agayne for me to kyll,
Ye prycke me in the head.
With that my nedel waxed red,
Methought, of phyllyps blode
My hear ryght upstode
And was in such a fray
My speche was taken away
I kest down that there was,

---

10. King, 2.
11. Ibid., 3.

> And sayd Alas, alas
> How commeth this to pas?
> My fyngers dead and colde
> Coude not my sampler holde
> My nedle and threde
> I threwe away for drede
> The best now that I may
> Is for his sowle to pray
>   A porta inferi
> Good Lord, have mercy
> Upon my sparrows soule
> Wryten in my bede roule.[12]

Jane was at school with the Benedictine nuns of Carew Abbey near Norwich, and her sampler evidently included an embroidered picture of her sparrow.

Elizabeth, Countess of Oxford, owned twelve samplers, which were a bequest to her sisters in 1537, "evinlye to be devided betwene them,"[13] and there are many references to samplers in literature of the sixteenth century. One of the most interesting is found in *Of Phylotus and Emilia,* written by Barnabe Riche in 1581:

> Now, when she had dined, then she might go seke out her examplers, and to peruse which worke would doe beste in a ruffe, whiche in a gorget, whiche in a sleeve, whiche in a quaife, whiche in a caule, whiche in a hand-carcheef; what lace would doe beste to edge it, what seame, what stitche, what cutte, what garde: and to sitte her doune and take it forthe by little and little, and thus with her nedle to passe the after noone with devising of thinges for her owne wearynge.[14]

Shakespeare also referred to a sampler in *Titus Adronicus* (1590–1592), but more descriptive are the words of Helena to Hermia in Act 3, Scene 2 of *A Midsummer Night's Dream* (1595–1596):

> . . . O! is all forgot?
> All school-days friendship, childhood innocence?
> We, Hermia, like two artificial gods,
> Have with our needles created both one flower,
> Both on one sampler, sitting on one cushion,
> Both warbling of one song, both in one key,
> As if our hands, our sides, voices, and minds,
> Had been incorporate.

---

12. *Boke of Phyllyp Sparowe* as quoted in Colby, *Samplers* (1964), 144–5.

13. Wace, "English Domestic Embroidery, Elizabeth to Anne" (1933), 13.

14. King, 3.

Fig. 4. *IANE BOSTOCKE 1598*, England. Silk, metal threads, seed pearls, and black beads on linen; 16¾" x 14". Inscribed with an alphabet minus the *J, U,* and *Z*; also, *ALICE LEE WAS BORNE THE 23 OF NOVEMBER BE/ING TEWSDAY IN THE AFTER NOONE 1596.* The upper section once included an elephant and a hare.

Victoria and Albert Museum, London, T. 190–1960.

And, late in the sixteenth century, Jane Bostocke worked the only signed and dated sampler known to survive from the reign of Elizabeth I (Fig. 4). It came to light in 1960.

Serious speculation about the origin of samplers began in the late nineteenth century, but the widespread contention that the earliest samplers must have been long, narrow ones kept on rollers is certainly subject to question. Even the origin of the belief that they were rolled up now seems impossible to trace, along with the alleged rollers for that purpose. It now seems evident that *samplers* (and the word as applied to them) first appeared during the early Renaissance, possibly in a nunnery or at court, and that they were specific accoutrements in the formal education of women. Thereafter the custom proliferated with the growth of schools for children of the middle class and was further accelerated by the craze

Fig. 5. German girls working in their garden, from the Album Amicorum of Gervasius Fabricius of Saltzburg, 1613. 5″ x 6½″. *The British Library, London.*

Fig. 6. Title page of *Schon Neues Modelbuch von allerley lustigen Modeln* by Johann Sibmacher, 1597, Nürnberg. Etching; 4¹⁵⁄₁₆″ x 6⅜″. Sibmacher's pattern book was extremely popular in seventeenth-century England and widely copied by other publishers. Many of his patterns eventually appeared on American work, especially in Pennsylvania. *Metropolitan Museum of Art, Rogers Fund, 1920.*

for embroidery that swept across Europe during the sixteenth century. It has been said that devotion to needlework soon "became a way of life among women and girls in upper class households," (Fig. 5) and this cultural phenomenon is confirmed by the great success of pattern books published in the sixteenth and seventeenth centuries (Fig. 6).[15]

Most likely samplers were always made by young people under the instruction

15. Colby, 19–20.

Fig. 7. *MARY BRAdSHAW/ HER WORK JVLY 28/ 1667*, England. Silk on linen; 33½″ x 7⅞″. Mary worked the quintessential English sampler of the seventeenth century. This style lingered into the reign of Queen Anne, even as naturalism was emerging. Both front and back are perfectly executed. *Collection of Joan Stephens.*

Fig. 8. Sampler initialed *AB/M, 1663*, Germany. Silk on linen; 9¾″ x 6⅛″. This spot motif sampler with one alphabet is characteristic of work from northern Germany of the late seventeenth and eighteenth centuries. For an early German schoolroom, see King, frontispiece. *Philadelphia Museum of Art, Whitman Sampler Collection, gift of Pet Inc., 69–288–1.*

of an experienced needlewoman. If intended as pattern records, they were no doubt favored by astute teachers as proofs of proficiency to be presented to those parents who had indulged their daughters in education. There is no convincing evidence that samplers were made by mature women other than those engaged in teaching, and the long-held belief that the fineness of early work precluded execution by children is false. Under careful guidance and the strict discipline imposed in former centuries, the steady hands and sharp eyes of children could exceed the performance of an adult—a fact later proven by the exploitation of children in intricate phases of labor.

In 1530, John Palsgrave's French grammar for English use described a sampler (which was derived from the Latin *exemplum*) as "an exampler for a woman to work by,"[16] and if first made by young girls as a reference for future use, Jane Bostocke's sampler may represent a stage in their transition from a pattern record to an exercise in embroidery technique. Unlike the long, band-pattern samplers characteristic of the seventeenth century (Fig. 7), Jane's patterns relate to those

---

16. King, 2.

Fig. 9. The top of an embroidered cabinet. England, c.1660–1680. Raised, padded, and partially detached work in silk and metal threads with seed pearls, coral, and metallic braid on silk; 9″ x 7½″. The lute player represents the sense of hearing, and panels of the cabinet depict the other senses. Similar scenes abound in framed pictures and also decorate looking-glass frames (Fig. 32). For the same lute player on a frame, see Hackenbroch, *English and Other Needlework* (1960), Pl. 68. By 1655 or earlier, embroidery of this type was being worked by girls aged ten or eleven. *Metropolitan Museum of Art, Rogers Fund, 29.23.1.*

in use in 1598. In 1799, Samuel Johnson's *Dictionary of the English Language* defined a sampler as "a pattern of work; a piece worked by young girls for improvement," and it appears that this definition was probably appropriate by the early seventeenth century.

While the scarcity of sixteenth-century samplers remains unexplained, seventeenth-century samplers from England, the Netherlands, and Germany (Figs. 7, 8) are surprisingly abundant. As the seventeenth century progressed, long, band-pattern samplers more often included alphabets, signatures, dates, and moral inscriptions, and by the reign of Charles II, some girls even named their school dame.[17] Needlework pictures in canvas work came into vogue during the reign of Charles I (1625–1649) and were followed at the mid-century by silk on silk embroideries, often with elaborate pictorial motifs in raised and padded work, now erroneously called *stump work* (Fig. 9). This form of pictorial needlework flourished despite the austerity of the Puritan Commonwealth, and reached its peak of popularity during the reign of Charles II (1660–1685). Nor were the samplers of

17. Colby, 119–22. The earliest recognized group of samplers dates from 1691 to 1710. Two pieces name mistress Judeth Hayl, while others have her initials. Recently discovered is Elizabeth Burton's, 1701 (PMA).

Fig. 10. *ELIZABETH GROOME/ AGeD TWelVe year/ July 23 16678*, England. Silk, wool, couched metallic threads, and mica on linen; 13″ x 13″. Elizabeth worked the inscription *BY THIS YOU See/ MY PARENTS TOO/K GREAT Care of me/ LOVE THE LORD anD HE/ WILL Be Tender FA/THeR UNTO THE*. This sampler, formerly in the Coe collection, was purchased in 1938. Mrs. Coe noted its "antique frame" (*Eva Johnston Coe Scrapbooks*, 366, C-H). The frame may have been original. *Cooper-Hewitt, National Museum of Design, Smithsonian Institution, 1974–42–16.*

this period all composed of repetitious band patterns; many included pictorial motifs in colored silks as well as in white work. More elaborate forms were emerging by the 1660s, and pieces like Elizabeth Groome's were probably intended for framing (Fig. 10).

Although seventeenth-century samplers survive in abundance from England, Holland, and Germany, American examples are rare, and for obvious reasons: the first settlers were necessarily absorbed in the difficulties of survival, and the majority were from the middle and lower-middle classes. It is logical, however, that the earliest needlework survives from New England, since these settlers came with their wives, often in groups who knew each other, and they quickly attempted to establish communities similar to the ones they had left behind. Coming with families and intending to stay was also typical of Pennsylvania emigrants, but they represented different nationalities, and came much later. Virginia, despite being the first English colony, was heavily populated by single men; inhabitants were widely divided, and orderly regulations were difficult to enforce. The seventeenth-century settlements in the South are unlikely to have produced samplers as early as those of New England. However, there is convincing evidence that samplers were made in Maryland, or taken there, before 1696.

The eighteenth century was the major period of colonial migration, and while little needlework is known from the seventeenth century, in the 1720s samplers were being worked in most of the major towns from Boston to Charleston (Figs. 34, 195, 348, 594). Fashions from London were the principal influence on dress and furnishings, and the widely divided colonies were often in closer touch with England than with each other. Therefore, colonial interpretations of English styles differed considerably, and by 1725 regional preferences had become evident in colonial artifacts, including samplers. Newport, Boston, and Philadelphia each produced identifiable groups of different but thoroughly English samplers during the 1720s and 1730s. With few exceptions, no striking differences between English and colonial work appeared before the third quarter of the eighteenth century, though colonial styles lagged behind those of London.

As would be expected, recognizable regional styles in colonial samplers developed only in the most densely populated areas of early America—Massachusetts, Rhode Island, Connecticut, New York, and Pennsylvania—which could support the women capable of teaching elegant needlework, and where the supplies were available.

Closely related to English embroidery are the splendid needlework pictures that developed in Philadelphia and Boston during the second quarter of the eighteenth century, and the English prototypes for Boston canvas work are decidedly obvious (Fig. 11). However, a charming, small group of Connecticut canvas-work pictures is not so easily identified with English sources, nor has the inspiration been found for coats of arms in canvas work that were made in Boston by 1740. Also, New York's earliest deeply bordered Biblical sampler, of 1746, seems to have no foreign counterparts; and the New England fashion for samplers with

Fig. 11. Bucolic canvas-work picture. England, second quarter of the eighteenth century. Wool and silk on linen; 21¾″ x 49″. Similar embroideries were worked in England at least twenty years before the "fishing lady" pictures became popular in Boston. They clearly demonstrate that Boston canvas work was purely in the English style as well as why English work may be mistaken for American embroideries. This piece has been assigned a date of 1725 or earlier (Hackenbroch, *English and Other Needlework,* 1960, Pl. 119). However, it is most likely later, for Nancy Graves Cabot found the probable source for part of its pattern in the engravings of John Boydell, 1745 (Cabot Papers, Portfolio I, Textile Department, MFA).
Metropolitan Museum of Art, Gift of Irwin Untermyer, 64.103.1355.

dramatic, solidly worked black backgrounds arose in the 1750s but was evidently unknown abroad (Frontispiece).

Between 1750 and 1775, the freedom of form and beguiling pictorial qualities characterizing the best of American samplers began to appear, particularly in New England. Also, a childlike naïveté is often found in lettering and reflects a permissiveness seldom known in England, where a child was usually compelled to correct her work until she arrived at perfection. Originality in design, with a suggestion of spontaneity, became increasingly evident in American samplers of the late eighteenth century, and reached full flower during the first quarter of the nineteenth century.

In the 1790s, girls' schools began to advertise instruction in an astonishing number of subjects. This coincided with the so-called "rise of the academies," and the number of schools available to girls was increasing dramatically. However, only a few schools had a truly expanded curriculum of academic subjects. Girls'

Fig. 12. English Girl with Her Silk Embroidery. Peter Vandyke, 1782. Oil on canvas; 23¼" x 16⅞" Delicate bouquets worked on silk became an increasingly popular form of schoolgirl embroidery in both England and America during the 1780s. For similar American work see *ANTIQUES*, February 1991, 368–9, 381.
Author's collection.

Fig. 13. *Miss GOODCHILDS first SAMPLER*. Published November 12, 1793, by Robert Sayer & Co., Fleet Street, London. A girl might work her first sampler at age five. Three samplers worked by six-year-old girls belong to the Chester County Historical Society, one of which is a fine family record worked on gauze in 1800.
The Lewis Walpole Library, Yale University.

education in general was by no means equal to that of boys', and, just as it had been a century earlier, the continuous focus on "accomplishments" was constantly criticized by the proponents of advanced education for women. Debates and discussions called attention to schools in both England and America, and schoolchildren became a popular subject for English artists (Figs. 12, 13, 15). Even charity schools received their attention (Fig. 14).

Regardless of the quality of education, more girls were attending schools than ever before, and their needles were busy. The period between 1800 and 1835 saw the greatest production of samplers in all the sampler-making countries of the Western world, and during the first thirty years of the nineteenth century, more recognizable groups of embroideries arose in New England and Pennsylvania than can possibly be included in this study. It is unquestionable that the samplers

Benevolent School

Fig. 14. *The Benevolent School,* anonymous, c.1795, England. Watercolor on paper; 15″ x 23″. This interior probably differs little from those of American charity schools in the late 1790s. A number of samplers survive from English charity schools, including a remarkable example of 1712, which names the school (Ashton, Fig. 35).
City of Bristol Museum and Art Gallery, Bristol, England.

Fig. 15. Cup decorated with a transfer print depicting a child displaying her needlework, England, c.1820–1825. Derived from an illustration in *The School-Girl in 1820* by William Upton (London 1820). The engraving was entitled *NEEDLE WORK,* with the verse

> *EMBROID'RY, flowers, and Plain work too*
> *Th' Docile maiden shews to view;*
> *In ev'ry branch a scholar true*
> *THE SCHOOL-GIRL!*

See *ANTIQUES,* March 1989, 747.
Collection of Mrs. John W. Griffith.

Fig. 16. *The SCHOOL MISTRESS.* Stipple engraving by J. Coles after Francis Wheatley; 17″ x 19¾″. Published in London, March 20, 1794, by Thomas Macklin, Poets Gallery, Fleet Street. It illustrates a passage in Shenstone's poem:

> In every village, marked with little spire
> Embower'd in trees and hardly known to fame,
> There dwells in lowly shed and mean attire,
> A matron old whom we schoolmistress name,
> Who boasts unruly brats with birch to tame.

Wheatley's painting exemplified a typical dame school kept in the home of the mistress and attended by boys and girls of about three to eight years of age. The girl at center holds her sampler with its clearly visible alphabet.
British Museum, London.

worked in this period exceed in number all the surviving pieces from previous centuries.

It was not unusual for a girl to work two samplers at a dame school between the ages of five and nine (Fig. 16).[18] Basic marking samplers would be considered "plain work," and she would definitely be learning practical stitchery. If her education continued, and her parents could afford the fees for "accomplishments," she would then undertake fancy embroidery. Even if she attended an academy for only one quarter (twelve weeks), she would surely return home with a decorative sampler or needlework picture. Often the schoolmistress would have it framed for presentation to her parents. If she remained in school until the annual examination, her work might be part of an exhibition that would be attended by local dignitaries, as well as parents and friends. Awards might be given for various categories of achievement, occasionally consisting of engraved silver medals.[19] Interested townspeople could often buy tickets to these ceremonies, where the skills of the schoolmistress in teaching needlework, painting, and penmanship would be carefully evaluated by prospective patrons.

The originality and diversity in American samplers from the Federal period is boundless in both subject matter and sayings. Exceptional pieces often appear without known counterparts or from unexpected places (Fig. 17), and others have unique touches of individuality (Fig. 18). It should be emphasized that the pat-

18. For dame schools, see Walter Herbert Small, *Early New England Schools* (New York: Arno Press & The New York Times, 1969), 162–85.

19. Silver medals are known from Susanna Rowson's Academy, 1812 (Winterthur Museum), 1817, and 1819 (Bostonian Society); from M. A. and L. Clark's Academy, Boston, 1827 (Bostonian Society); and a gold medal from Mrs. Rivardi's, Philadelphia, 1807 (Winterthur). An undated silver medal names *Miss Pagaud's* SCHOOL (private collection). Mrs. Alice Pagaud taught in Norfolk, Virginia, c. 1801–1820. Her daughter, Miss Julia, was also teaching in 1806 (Norfolk directory). Mrs. Hopkins named her recipients of silver medals in *The True American*, Trenton, on April 22, 1805. For a medal presented at this time, see the *Sunday Times-Advertiser*, Trenton, January 1, 1922, 1.

Fig. 17. *Nancy Sibley's Sampler wrought in the 10th yr of her/ age. [Grt] Barrington April 28th A.d 1808.* Silk on linen with silk, chenille, and paint on appliquéd cotton for the scene, and silk, metallic threads, and painted paper on the appliquéd black silk border; 17⅞" x 15⅜" Nancy's exceptional sampler was made in a small town in western Massachusetts, and a related example by nine-year-old Abigail Buel named *Grt Barrington* in 1807 (Krueger, *New England*, Fig. 65). The imaginative schoolmistress may have been Betsy Maria Bostwick (b.1771) who was teaching in Great Barrington in 1797 and perhaps later. Another possible teacher was Sarah Kellogg who taught there at a later date. Nancy Sibley was born October 16, 1798. Her father, Stephen Sibley (1759–1829), a clock maker, was a native of Sutton, Massachusetts. He worked in Norwich, Connecticut, before moving to Great Barrington, Massachusetts, about 1781. There he married Jemima Hopkins (1756–1836), and they had five children. This family moved to West Stockbridge about 1810, and finally to Grafton, Ohio. Nancy married the Reverend C. P. Bronson on October 4, 1826, and died shortly thereafter in Mount Vernon, Ohio.

The Minneapolis Institute of Arts, gift of Carroll Simmons, 81.91.

Fig. 18. *Martha W. Pauls Work/ 1807*, New Jersey or Pennsylvania. Silk and spangles on linen with applied painted paper and ribbon border; 22⅞" x 21¾". Sixteen-year-old Martha surrounded her watercolor miniature with shimmering gold spangles and shaped them for her name and date. Martha W. Paul (1791–1855) was the fifth child of Samuel Philip Paul (1763–1831) and Nancy Clark (1763–1845). Her father was the pioneer settler of Paulsboro, Gloucester County, New Jersey. She died unmarried. *Private collection.*

terns reflected the ingenuity of the teachers, *not* the children; this explains the repetitious designs which developed into regional styles.

While there is no question that the majority of samplers were made at schools kept by women prepared to teach needlework, there is sound evidence that samplers were occasionally worked at home. For instance, on the day after Thanksgiving in 1792, seventeen-year-old Elizabeth Fuller wrote in her diary: "I staid at home began to work me a sampler."[20] Also, nine-year-old Julia Latrobe learned needlework from her mother, and her sampler verse was composed by her famous father, the architect Benjamin Henry Latrobe (Fig. 19).[21] Although samplers worked at home were apt to be no more interesting than Julia's, some mothers and grandmothers were especially well qualified to instruct children in the family, as was Sidney Satterthwaite's grandmother, Elizabeth Claypoole (Fig. 20). Better known as Betsy Ross, she was the twenty-four-year-old widow of John Ross,

20. Francis Everett Blake, *The History of the Town of Princeton, Massachusetts* (Princeton: Town of Princeton, 1915), 1:321.

21. Entry of February 17, 1819, *The Journals of Benjamin Henry Latrobe 1799–1820, From Philadelphia to New Orleans*, Edward C. Carter II, John C. Van Horne, and Lee W. Formwalt, eds. (New Haven: Yale University Press, 1980), 3:192.

Fig. 19. *Juliana E Latrobe July 1813.* Silk on linen; 10″ x 9″. Juliana's verse was composed by her father:

> Taught by her mothers glistening/ eye/
> Her needle Julia plied/
> Uncounted flew the moments/ by/
> While grew her Samplers pride./
> Those little hands with guileless/ art/
> That wove each lettered row/
> And her bright eye and playful/ heart/
> Still gladdened oer the show

Despite her mother's guidance, Juliana worked all her *J*s backward. She was probably living in Washington, where her father served as surveyor of the Public Buildings from 1803 until 1813. Juliana Elizabeth Latrobe (1804–189?) was the daughter of Benjamin Henry Latrobe (1764–1820) and his second wife, Mary Elizabeth Hazelhurst (d.1841). She died unmarried.
Maryland Historical Society, 55.92.1.

Fig. 20. *Sidney Satterthwaite./ 1829.* Silk on linen; 16½″ x 22″. Sidney's neat sampler has many Quaker motifs and reflects capable guidance. It was worked at home under the instruction of her grandmother, Elizabeth Griscom Ross Ashburn Claypoole (1752–1836), better known as Betsy Ross. Betsy Griscom was a Quaker girl who was first taught by Rebecca Jones in Drinkers' Alley, Philadelphia. Sidney Satterthwaite (1817–1858) was the daughter of Philadelphia merchant Abel Satterthwaite and Susan Claypoole. She married Cyrus Kinsey.
Private collection.

Fig. 22. A page of embroidered patterns from *Designs in an Embroidery Book for self instruction of Women* by Johann Friedrich Netto, drawing master in Leipzig, 1795. Among the forty-eight plates, several are fully embroidered in silk and metallic threads. This book was surely known in America at an early date, especially by the Moravians. The motif in the lower left corner appears on a Salem Academy embroidery of 1805 (*ANTIQUES*, September 1974, 438).
Cooper-Hewitt, National Museum of Design, Smithsonian Institution, 1970–28–9.

Fig. 21. *Shakespeare's Tomb,* engraved by Francesco Bartolozzi (1727–1815) after a painting by Angelica Kauffmann, and published in London by Anthony Poggi, August 1, 1782; 15¾″ x 11½″. This print was among the first to be widely copied for neoclassical silk embroidery in both England and America.
British Museum, London.

and an accomplished seamstress, when she is said to have fashioned the first American flag in 1776. She was twice married thereafter, but continued to keep her upholstery shop until 1827 when she went to live with her daughter, Susan Claypoole Satterthwaite.[22] Sidney's sampler descended with the firm history of having been made under her grandmother's instruction.

The year 1800 saw a dramatic change in the focus of accomplishments at girls' schools throughout the land. Neoclassical subjects worked with silk on silk suddenly became the most fashionable expression of advanced needlework skills. Lustrous silk embroideries, in harmony with Adamesque furnishings, were already popular in England, and their compositions were often inspired by prints after paintings by Angelica Kauffmann (Fig. 21); also, similar fashions had developed on the Continent (Fig. 22). In America, however, silk on silk mourning pieces, and other subjects associated with neoclassicism, were seldom worked before 1800, although willows, weepers, and classical urns were commonly seen on a variety of objects.[23]

The death of George Washington was evidently the impetus for the sudden and overwhelming popularity of mourning embroidery, and the unparalleled expression of grief that swept the nation was quickly expressed in a wealth of memorial prints (Fig. 23). These provided excellent patterns for the schoolmistress, and some were even available on satin.[24] In addition to honoring Washington, something different immediately happened that seldom occurred abroad. American teachers devised related patterns for memorials dedicated to deceased members of the needleworker's family, and these were often carefully planned to depict the appropriate mourners. One of the earliest and most magnificent examples was

22. William D. Timmins and Robert W. Yarrington, Jr., *Betsy Ross, The Griscom Legacy* (Salem County, N.J.: Cultural and Heritage Commission, 1983), 125–58.
23. The earliest known American sampler with an urn and willow was worked in 1791 by Elizabeth Tunnecliff, probably in New York. Skinner Sale 1120, November 1, 1986, Lot 220; now at the Winterthur Museum.
24. *ANTIQUES*, February 1977, 325, Fig. 2.

Fig. 23. *The Tears of America.* Early nineteenth-century imported cotton handkerchief, probably from Glasgow; 20″ x 20″. The monument and figures in this Washington memorial print were widely copied on mourning embroideries. Its basic elements appear in reverse on a relatively crude Washington memorial print published by Pember and Luzarder in Philadelphia in 1800. Their rendition may have been inspired by this elegant composition, which was probably first engraved on paper. Their print was no doubt less expensive and more available to schoolteachers. See Deutsch, "Washington Memorial Prints" (1977), 326.

The Elizabeth Day McCormick Collection, Museum of Fine Arts, Boston, 50.2418.

worked in 1800 by Lucretia Carew, shortly after the death of her younger sister (Fig. 24).

Although some mourning pieces were worked immediately following a death, the majority appear to have been made as a record and a decoration, rather than an expression of current grief, and they were the result of fashion rather than melancholy. Throughout the sampler-making era in America, women's letters and diaries reflect a widespread apprehension of death, but there is nothing to indicate that an intensified preoccupation with death led to the popularity of mourning embroidery. Instead, its delicacy and symbolism were associated with refinement and the ennobling culture of antiquity.

Print work was perhaps the most demanding form of pictorial silk embroidery, and it appeared in America by 1801, if not earlier. This tedious needlework in imitation of engraving was popular in England by 1783,[25] but it evidently had limited appeal for American schoolgirls. It was mentioned in school advertisements throughout the country between 1799 and the mid-1820s, but only two recognizable groups of print-work embroideries are presently known. Both are mourning pieces, and they were worked with a high degree of skill in Albany and Providence.

Neoclassical silk embroidery was the last important type of needlework to de-

---

25. Hughes, *English Domestic Needlework 1660–1860* (1961), 91.

velop during the schoolgirl needlework era, and it was a new challenge for the schoolmistress as well as her scholars. Some young teachers were ill prepared to undertake this newly popular embroidery, but sought to satisfy their fashion-conscious patrons. Bathsheba Whitman was teaching at Sandwich Academy in Massachusetts when she wrote to a friend on August 15, 1805: "I must some way or other contrive to send to Boston . . . for Satins and silks for my scholars, for there is no such thing here." In a letter of October 16th, she said: "I have twelve pieces of embroidery, and here I *am* Mrs. Cushing daubing on satin *without knowledge* and *without confidence. . . .*" In April of 1806, at the age of twenty-eight, Bathsheba was attending Susanna Rowson's school in Newton where she was improving her skills in painting on silk. She found that many of the scholars were nearly of her own age, but they were not congenial, and she vowed to her friend that this "is the last excursion of this kind I will ever make, if I can live through these three weeks for not a moment longer do I intend to stay."[26] Thereafter, she taught school until 1845.

Although procedures for silk embroidery differed, the design was customarily sketched on the silk, worked, and then painted. The teacher may have designed the piece, directed the student's work, and then painted the silk herself; or she may have engaged a professional artist to draw the pattern. If so, he would need to return to add the final painting. Such work was widely solicited by miniature painters and drawing masters. Among them was John Roberts (1768–1803), who advertised in the *Portland Gazette* (Maine) on March 14, 1803, and offered to paint "all kinds of FANCY and EMBROIDERY WORK for schools and individuals." In 1807, New York miniaturist Philip Parisen was also prepared to do "all kinds of drawing on silk for needlework."[27] John C. Bell of Baltimore advertised miniature painting in 1814 and mentioned "The Faces, & c. of Needle Work colored," while a Louisville, Kentucky, newspaper proprietor advertised fancy printing in 1817, including "Mourning Pieces and Registers, on SILK or SATIN."[28] This small sampling of available services in widely divided places offers some idea of the many artisans who became involved with the needlework of the schoolgirl, in addition to the frame maker.

Girlhood embroidery became a boon to the frame-making business in the second quarter of the seventeenth century when girls began making needlework pictures for purely decorative purposes. By the mid-seventeenth century, extravagant raised work was set in panels for looking-glass frames which often had protective cases, as did cabinets with raised and padded work (Fig. 31). When parents began framing their daughters' samplers is unknown, but it was probably earlier than

---

26. Bathsheba Whitman in Sandwich to Mrs. Nathaniel Cushing in Pembroke, August 15, 1805; October 16, 1805; and April 24, 1806; Whitman Letters, in the Nathaniel Cushing Papers, 1776–1827, MHS. Bathsheba Whitman (1777–1864) was born in Bridgewater and died in Lexington, unmarried.
27. *Commercial Advertiser*, New York, June 30, 1807.
28. *American & Commercial Daily Advertiser*, Baltimore, March 29, 1814; *Louisville Correspondent*, Kentucky, June 28, 1817.

Fig. 24. *Lucretia Carew 1800* inscribed on the original glass (now replaced). Silk, appliquéd silk, cotton, and other trimmings with paint and ink on silk; 20½″ x 26¼″. Inscribed on the plinth *In Memory of/ Mrs Lucy Tillinghast/ Born July 11,th 1783—Died August 27,th 1800./ And her Son/ Joseph Elisha,/ Born August 23,/d 1800, Died September 6th/ Early, Bright, Transient, Chast, as Morning Dew/ She sparkled, was exhal'd, and went to Heaven.* The figures represent Lucretia Carew with her parents and brother at the tomb of her younger sister. The painted faces are miniatures of the mourners and have been attributed to John Brewster, Jr. (1766–1854) by Davida Deutsch (*The Clarion,* Fall 1990, 46–50). Lucretia's work is the most elaborate personal mourning embroidery presently known. As yet, no related pieces have appeared, although this was no doubt worked at the school kept by Lucretia's mother in her Norwich, Connecticut, home which was "about one mile from the Court-House, on the road leading from the town to the Landing." Mrs. Carew gave this location when she announced the opening of her boarding school for "young Misses" in the *Norwich Packet* of April 3, 1798. A year later she offered instruction in "work on Sattin . . . Tambour, and all kinds of Needle-work on Muslin, with drawing, Painting, and Figure." (Ibid., April 10, 1799; see front endpapers.)

Probably Lucretia was also teaching, and her embroidery was perhaps planned to demonstrate the ultimate ability of the schoolmistress. Her inscription "Early, Bright, Transient . . ." is typical of memorials from Mary Balch's school in Providence, as is the decorative detail worked on the temple, but there similarity ends. Delicate appliqué of garments was favored at Lydia Royse's school in Hartford, but Lucretia's exquisite appliqué is much more elaborate. Lucretia may have attended both schools, although her childhood sampler (Fig. 232) was unquestionably worked in Norwich. It is also possible that her mother kept a school long before advertising a boarding school, and she may have been responsible for samplers like Lucretia's, which reflect the earlier Norwich style. A painted mourning locket with gilded paper and hair work on the reverse is dedicated to Lucy Tillinghast and attributed to Lucretia (Pike and Armstrong, *A Time to Mourn,* [1980], Fig. 97). She also made an intricate picture in filigree dated 1811 (Museums at Stony Brook). Lucretia Carew (September 30, 1778–August 19, 1862) was born in Norwich to Daniel Carew (1747–1813) and Lucy Perkins (1758–1832). She died unmarried.

The Museums at Stony Brook, Stony Brook, New York, 00.1704.

Fig. 25. *Jessie W. Briscoe/ Ursuline Convent/ Galveston Texas/ Finished August 20ᵗʰ/ In memory of my/ school days. 1860.* Wool on linen; 12½" x 11". The Ursulines opened their school in Galveston in 1847 and it continued until 1968. Instruction in sewing began at age five. Jessie Wade Briscoe (1845–1920) was born in Harrisburg, Texas (annexed to Houston in 1926). She was the daughter of Andrew Briscoe (1810–1849) and Mary Jane Harris (1819–1903). Her father was a signer of the Texas Declaration of Independence and the first judge of Harris County. In 1873 she married Milton Grosvenor Howe (1834–1902), and they had one son.
Collection of Harris Milton Howe and Dorothy Knox Howe Houghton.

previously suspected, since the 1696 appraisal of the estate of Maryland's David Richardson included "4 needlework flowers & 4 wooden frames with pictures & one frame Sampler . . . 00 05 00."[29]

The custom of framing samplers appeared in Philadelphia at an early date, as proven by original frames on samplers from the 1720s (Fig. 347). Samplers were usually framed in modest walnut, mahogany, or ebonized frames that covered the edges of the embroidery. These frames were relatively inexpensive, but when silk embroideries became fashionable, the framing of needlework became a substantial part of the frame-makers' business. Neoclassical silk embroideries made in America before 1800 usually had simple frames (Fig. 176) or were surrounded by gilded and sanded mats, as often found on paintings and prints of the 1790s (Fig. 406). It seems to have been precisely in 1800 that reverse-painted black glass mats became an almost standard embellishment for lustrous embroideries on silk, and they were usually surrounded by elegant gold frames in the neoclassical taste. Some frame makers decorated glass in distinctive styles, particularly John Doggett of Roxbury, Massachusetts (Figs. 101, 104), and William T. Grinnell of Providence (Fig. 212). Elegant silk embroideries of Boston and Hartford often had glass mats with interesting patterns in the spandrels (Figs. 87, 244), and Philadelphia was noted for deeply coved, gilded moldings filled with heavy carving (Figs. 408, 418). So popular were glass mats for elegant embroideries of this period that they were occasionally simulated in needlework for samplers.[30] For the most part, this type of framing continued through the 1820s and was followed by heavy, mahogany-veneered Empire frames.

By the 1830s, the war against "accomplishments" in female education was beginning to make definite progress. The zealous crusade of reformers such as Catherine Beecher, William Woodbridge, and Emma Willard, combined with the social upheaval of the Industrial Revolution, finally led to the demise of ornamental needlework as a primary subject in the education of women. In most larger cities, this centuries-old custom ended abruptly between 1835 and 1840.[31] Portland, Maine, and parts of Pennsylvania were notable exceptions, while Catholic schools (Fig. 25) and towns along the frontier were among the last to relinquish the old traditions.[32] Coarse samplers, often on Berlin-work canvas, and wool-work knicknacks on Bristol board were occasionally made by schoolgirls during the late nineteenth century. They were outside the tradition of earlier

29. *Maryland Prerogative Court, Inventories and Accounts,* 1694–1696, 13:125, as recorded at MESDA.

30. There are examples at the Jackson Homestead, Newton, Massachusetts, and at Gore Place, Waltham, Massachusetts; also, a recognizable group, c. 1818–1830, from Upper Providence, Montgomery County, Pennsylvania, and probably made under instruction of Elizabeth Robinson (1778–1865). See B&C, Pl. LXXVIII and Rumford, *American Folk Paintings* (1988), 338.

31. At about this time, public education began in a number of states and caused private schools to decrease in number.

32. Traditional embroidery was also taught at Indian mission schools. Samplers are known to name the *Cherokee Mission School Dwight/Arkansas/1828* (Edmonds, 149–153) and the *Choctaw Mission school/Mayhew* [Mississippi] *1830* (private collection).

work, however, and did not reflect similar aims and attitudes, as demonstrated by the definition of a sampler in *McGuffey's Fifth Eclectic Reader* of 1879: "a needle-work pattern; a species of fancy work formerly much in vogue." Of course, schoolroom instruction in sewing was not abandoned (Fig. 26), and neat little booklets with samples of plain sewing survive in considerable numbers from the nineteenth and early twentieth centuries.

In the meantime, while Victorian trivia was still in vogue, discerning collec-tors began to appreciate the incomparable samplers of the colonial and Federal periods. It soon became evident that the endless diversity and extraordinary visual appeal of American schoolgirl embroidery surpassed that of other nations, there-fore provoking serious study by 1920. In writing *American Samplers* (1921), Ethel Stanwood Bolton and Eva Johnston Coe left a priceless legacy for which all sub-sequent samplers scholars owe them tribute.

Fig. 26. The sewing lesson at a village school. This print appeared as the frontispiece in *The Work-woman's Guide* by a Lady (London: Simpkin, Marshall & Co., 1838). During the Victorian period, instruction in plain needlework and knitting was particularly stressed at charity schools, and in general, it continued to be regarded as one of the most essential preparations for a girl's adult life. *The New York Public Library, Astor, Lenox and Tilden Foundations.*

Fig. 27. Sampler worked by Loara Standish, c.1640–1650. Silk on linen; 23″ x 7″. Signed *Loara Standish is my name,* and in a variety of upper- and lowercase letters (several of which are backward and others missing), is a longer than average verse for this period: *Lorde gvide my hart that/ I may doe thy will also fill/ my hands with svch c/onvenient skill as may/ condvce to vertue void of/ shame and I will give/ the glory to thy name.* The Standish family lived in Duxbury during the 1640s. Loara may have been "placed out" with a Plymouth family when she worked her sampler. *Pilgrim Hall Museum, Plymouth, Massachusetts, 108.*

NEEDLEWORK OF
MASSACHUSETTS

The Pilgrim Century

NEW ENGLAND received less than one third of the sixty thousand Englishmen who left the Old World for the New between 1620 and 1642, but the
Colony of Massachusetts Bay was destined to exceed in importance the West Indian settlements favored by the majority of English immigrants during the reign
of Charles I. Those who went to New England braved the Atlantic Ocean for both
economic and religious reasons, but their success in the colony depended on con-
forming to the code of behavior decreed by its Puritan leaders, who established
the civic and cultural traditions of their homeland, including an equal degree of
religious intolerance. In 1636 they founded Harvard College to train their ministers, and the customary patterns of primary education in England were transplanted to New England shores as soon as an orderly lifestyle prevailed. Small
boys and girls first learned to read and spell, and the girls to sew, in the home
of a local school-dame. These private elementary schools in seventeenth- and
early eighteenth-century Boston were generally called "reading schools."[1]

Despite Puritan sumptuary laws, which sought to reduce the type of finery that
ornamental needlework made possible,[2] Massachusetts produced the only American samplers and pictorial embroideries that have survived from the seventeenth
century. If fortuitous, it is also wonderfully appropriate that the earliest surviving colonial sampler was worked by Loara Standish, only daughter of the famous
Myles (c.1584–1656) (Fig. 27). Loara's sampler is undated, and her exact life span
is unknown. Her existence was recorded only by her sampler and her father's
wish "to bee layed as neare as Conveniently may bee to my two Daughters Lora
Standish my Daughter and Mary Standish my Daughterinlaw."[3] It is therefore evi-

---

1. Seybolt, *The Private Schools of Colonial Boston* (1935), 9.
2. Townsend, "Notes on New England Needlework before 1800" (1944), 5.
3. Will of Myles Standish, *The Mayflower Descendant, A Quarterly Magazine of Pilgrim Genealogy and History* 3 (1901), 153.

Fig. 28. Sampler initialed *MA* and attributed to Mary Attwood of Plymouth, c.1650–1660. Silk on linen; 22″ x 5½″. Mary worked nineteen band patterns and two alphabets. She was born between 1637 and 1645 and died January 6, 1714/15. Mary was the daughter of John Attwood (d.1675/76) and Sarah Masterson, and the eldest of nine children. In 1661 she married the Reverend John Holmes of Duxbury (d.1675), and second, William Bradford (1624–1703/4). She had seven children. Mary's sampler remained with her descendants until 1988. *Collection of The Examplarery.*

dent that she predeceased him, as did a young daughter-in-law, and a nineteenth-century investigation revealed that he was, indeed, buried between two teen-aged girls.[4]

Standish's first wife came with him on the *Mayflower,* but died of "the sickness" during her first year in Plymouth. Loara's mother, Barbara, of unknown surname, arrived on the *Anne* in July or August of 1623. Myles Standish and Barbara had three sons before May 22, 1627. In unknown order, Loara and three other sons were born after this date; but in 1651, only four sons survived. Loara unquestionably died between the ages of fourteen and twenty, so she was evidently born between 1628 and 1636. She is said to have had "a splendid coil of light colored hair and perfect teeth."[5]

With Barbara, on the *Anne,* were the wives and children of some of the earlier settlers. Only seven of the twelve children who came on the *Mayflower* survived the first winter, but at least sixty children, or young people, were in Plymouth by 1627.[6] Little is known of their daily life and since no records of a school survive, it has often been assumed that none existed in Plymouth during the mid-seventeenth century.[7] Yet Loara's incredibly intricate sampler and a contemporary example (Fig. 28) are sound evidence that a capable woman was teaching Plymouth girls in the customary English manner. This schoolmistress was probably Mrs. Margaret Hicks, who came on the *Anne* with her children in 1623.[8] She was the wife of Robert Hicks, fellmonger from Southwark, who arrived in Plymouth on the *Fortune* in 1621.[9] When the respected Pilgrim Dr. Samuel Fuller died in Plymouth in 1633, he left the following instructions for his executors: "My will is that when my daughter Mercy is fit to goe to scole that Mrs. Heeks may teach her as well as my son."[10] Fuller's reference to Mrs. Hicks indicates that she was

4. E. J. V. Huiginn, *The Graves of Myles Standish and Other Pilgrims* (Beverly, Mass.: published by the author, 1914), 118–29.

5. Ibid., 140–5. The descent of Loara's sampler: her brother Josiah Standish; Mary Standish Carey; James Carey; Sarah Carey Barrell; Sarah Barrell Alden; Sarah Alden Tolman; Pilgrim Hall Museum, 1844. See Marcus Alden Tolman, "Lora Standish's Sampler," *Wide Awake* 34, no. 6 (May 1892): 581–2. This was called to my attention by Joanne Harvey.

6. Frederick A. Noble, *The Pilgrims* (Boston: The Pilgrim Press, 1907), 354.

7. Demos, *A Little Commonwealth* (1970), 143.

8. Francis Baylis, *An Historical Memoir of the Colony of New Plymouth* (Boston: Wiggin and Lunt, 1866), 1:263.

9. *NEHGR* 18:364, 368.

10. *The Mayflower Descendant* 1 (1899), 24–8. Fuller's will reveals that the custom of "placing out" was definitely practiced in Plymouth, for both Elizabeth Cowles and George Foster "being placed with me," he di-

Fig. 29. *MARY HOLINGWOR/TH*, c.1665. Silk on linen; 24¾" x 7½". Mary Hollingsworth (1652–1694) was the daughter of William Hollingsworth and Eleanor Story (d.1690) of Salem. She married Philip English (c.1650–1735), a very successful Salem merchant, on July 1, 1675. In 1692 Mary and Philip were accused of witchcraft and imprisoned, but escaped to New York. Eventually exonerated, they returned to their plundered Salem property. This incident, however, is believed to have caused Mary's early death. During Mary's absence, four of her children stayed with Mrs. Holyitt in Boston, and Susannah, the youngest, boarded with Mary Turfrey in Boston, where she remained until she was eighteen. Bentley describes an elaborate "Specimen of her employment at School" (*Diary* vol. 2 [1962], 23–6). Madame Turfrey (d.1717) placed the first advertisement for a girls' school in an American newspaper (*Boston News-Letter*, September 2, 1706). See front endpapers.
Essex Institute, bequest of George Rea Curwen, 1900, 4234.39.

an esteemed schoolmistress. Robert Hicks died in 1647, but Margaret Hicks lived until 1665 and may have taught for twenty or thirty years.

One other seventeenth-century sampler survives from a well-known family (Fig. 29). Mary Hollingsworth was the only child of a wealthy Salem merchant, and she is said to have studied with "Madame Piedmonte . . . a celebrated instructress of that day in Boston."[11] In 1793, Salem diarist William Bentley noted that she "had the best education of her times. Wrote with great ease & has left a specimen of her needlework in her infancy, or Youth."[12]

Occasionally samplers were described in seventeenth-century wills and inventories.[13] They were also mentioned, along with the heroic women of Boston, by New England's native-born schoolmaster poet Benjamin Tompson in 1676:

ON A FORTIFICATION
At Boston begun by Women
Dux Femina Facti

A Grand attempt some Amazonian Dames
Contrive whereby to glorify their names,
A Ruff for Boston Neck of mud and turf,
Reaching from side to side from surf to surf,
Their nimble hands spin up like Christmas pies,

rected that they be returned to their parents. References to children being placed with Samuel or Bridget Fuller have led to the belief that she was a schoolmistress (Robert M. Bartlett, *The Faith of the Pilgrims* [New York: United Church Press, 1978], 95). It is far more likely that children were "placed out" with the wealthy Fullers who then supervised their education and engaged appropriate teachers. Nineteenth- and twentieth-century historians have seldom understood the early custom of "placing out" (Demos, *A Little Commonwealth*, 73–4). Samuel Fuller (1580–1633) of Harleston, Norfolk County, England, went with the Pilgrims to Leyden, Holland, in 1609. There he married his third wife, Bridget Lee (d. after 1664). In 1641, she married Henry Sirkman.

11. *EIHC* 1:158–9.
12. Bentley, *Diary* (1905–1914; reprint, 1962), 2: 24.
13. Townsend, "New England Needlework," 6; Swan, *Plain & Fancy*, 52.

Opposite:

Fig. 30. *Rebeckah Wheeler/ Ye month May 1664* is worked on the blue velvet backing of this embroidery of Queen Esther and King Ahasuerus. Wool, silk, silver metallic threads, and beads on linen; 12¾″ x 18¼″. Rebeckah's work is the earliest signed and dated pictorial embroidery of unquestionable American origin. Two of the four episodes from the Book of Esther (Esther Receiving the Sceptre and Haman's Fall) were derived from engravings by Nicolas Visscher after Maerten van Heemskerck (*Concord Antiquarian Museum Newsletter* [October 1982], 5). Rebeckah Wheeler (September 6, 1645–February 20, 1718) was the daughter of Joseph Wheeler and Sarah Merriam of Concord. In 1667 she married Peter Bulkeley (1641–1688), and, in 1689, Jonathan Prescott.

Concord Museum, Concord, Massachusetts, T-100.

Their pastry by degrees on high doth rise.
The wheel at home counts it an holiday,
Since while the Mistress worketh it may play.
A tribe of female hands, but manly hearts
Forsake at home their pasty-crust and tarts
To knead the dirt, the samplers down they hurl,
Their undulating silks they closely furl.
The pick-axe one as a Commandress holds,
While t' other at her awkness gently scolds.
One puffs and sweats, the other mutters why
Can't you promove your work so fast as I?
Some dig, some delve, and others' hands do feel
The little wagons weight with single wheel.
And least some fainting fits the weak surprise,
They want no sack nor cakes, they are more wise.
These brave essays draw forth Male stronger hands
More like to Dawbers than to Martial bands:
These do the work, and sturdy bulwarks raise,
But the beginners well deserve the praise.[14]

As with English literary references to samplers, it remains doubtful that the author had a clear concept of women's needlework. However, if his wife, Susanna, assisted him in teaching, Tompson may have been familiar with groups of young girls working samplers.

Pictorial embroideries, like samplers, were surely made by seventeenth-century colonial schoolgirls, but only two authentic examples are known.[15] Rebeckah Wheeler worked her Biblical picture (Fig. 30) when she was eighteen. Three years later she married Peter Bulkeley, the grandson and namesake of the founder of Concord, Massachusetts. Unlike the majority of English embroideries of this date, her ground material is linen rather than silk, suggesting that her pattern may have been drawn in Boston. Also, the work is predominantly in wool rather than silk, and there is little raised work. Rebeckah's needlework appears in the 1747 inventory of the estate of her daughter, Rebeckah Bulkeley Whiting.

---

14. Howard Judson Hall, ed., *Benjamin Tompson . . . His Poems* (Boston: Houghton Mifflin Co., 1924), 191. Benjamin Tompson (1642–1714) was born in Quincy, Massachusetts, graduated from Harvard in 1662, and taught in Quincy, Boston, Charlestown, Braintree, and Roxbury (*Sibley's Harvard Graduates, 1659–1677* [1881], 2:103–10).

15. Unpublished is a pictorial embroidery of wool, silk, metal, and mica on greenish-blue wool; approximately 17¼″ x 24⅜″. It features a couple in seventeenth-century dress beside the Tree of Life and a rendition of the prodigal son amid many birds, beasts, and flowers. Inscribed on the reverse: "This picture was wrought at a boarding school in Boston by Miss Sarah Phillips daughter of Rev. Sam. Phillips." Sarah Phillips (1656–1706/7) was born in Rowley to Samuel Phillips (1625–1696) and Sarah Appleton (c.1628–1714). In 1680 she married Stephen Mighill (1651–1687) and second, Robert Greenough. This fully documented and wonderfully colorful piece was loaned to the MFA in 1946. (Nancy Graves Cabot, photograph files, Textile Department, MFA.)

It was described as "the Effiges of King Ahasueres and Queen Esther," but with no evaluation. In 1861, it was given to the Concord Antiquarian Museum by Rebeckah Whiting's great granddaughter Mary Minot.[16]

Traditionally, it is believed that two daughters of John Leverett, Governor of Massachusetts, worked the cabinet in Figure 31, although the exact origin of this attribution is now unknown.[17] Leverett married his second wife, Sarah Sedgwick, in 1647, and in 1655 the family went to England where Leverett represented the

---

16. Information and references to print sources (Fig. 30) provided by Peter Benes, former Education Director of the Concord Antiquarian Museum (letter of April 11, 1986).

17. Donor documentation which probably accompanied the cabinet has disappeared. Gertrude Townsend, in charge of textiles at the MFA from 1919 until 1959, attributed its origin to Leverett's first and third surviving daughters, Elizabeth and Mary ("New England Needlework," 7), and this has been often repeated (Fairbanks, *New England Begins*, vol. 3, Fig. 389, and elsewhere). Townsend first saw the cabinet at the Essex Institute on January 11, 1934, and noted that the makers were "Mary and Elizabeth daughters of Governor John Leverett" (Gertrude Townsend, "American Embroidery" Notebook II, Textile Department, MFA). The donor, Mrs. Justin Whittier, née Elizabeth Wise Farley (1854–1927), was a direct descendant of Governor Leverett through his son Hudson (1640–1692) and grandson John Leverett (1662–1724), president of Harvard College. References to "Mary and Elizabeth" by Miss Townsend could reflect donor confusion about the identity of Mary Leverett, only daughter of Hudson by his first wife, Sarah Payton (1643–1679), and his step-daughter Elizabeth Tay Myham, who were both mentioned in Hudson Leverett's will (Frederick W.

Fig. 31. Embroidered cabinet with original wooden case. New England or England, c.1657–1685. Silk, linen, metallic threads, and metallic braid on silk; 12″ x 10⅞″ x 7½″. The embroidery is attributed to one or more of the daughters of Governor John Leverett, a tradition supported (although not conclusively) by the use of New England white pine (*pinus strobus*) for its case. In the typical manner, the front of the case is hinged at the base and folds down for easy removal of the cabinet. Nearly identical silk and paper linings and trim are known on English embroidered cabinets of the 1660s. It is possible, however, that Boston teachers were capable of providing these materials, and the cabinet could have been worked by any of the six daughters of John Leverett (1616–1679) and Sarah Sedgwick (1629–1704): Elizabeth (1651–1715) married in 1668 Elisha Cooke (1637–1716); Ann (1652–1717) married in 1671 John Hubbard (1648–1710); Mary (1656–1699) married in 1675 Paul Dudley, and second, Penn Townsend; Hannah (1661–1732) married in 1690 Eleazar Allen; Rebecca (1664–1739) married in 1691 James Lloyd; Sarah (1673–1730) married in 1718 Nathaniel Byfield.
Essex Institute, gift of Mrs. Justin Whittier, 1925, 118, 284a.

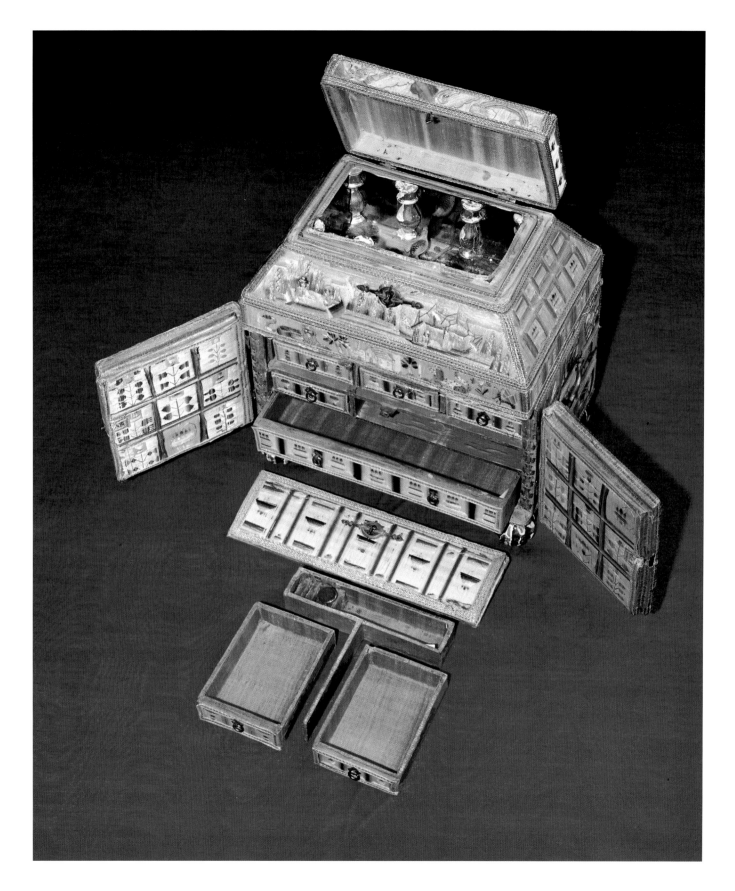

Fig. 31a. Leverett cabinet with front panel removed to reveal a nest of hidden drawers. The secret ring receptacle holds Governor Leverett's gold and carnelian ring bearing the Leverett arms (gift of Mrs. William West, 1928). The dome contains a mirrored and painted garden with gilded columns and below it is a writing compartment fitted with seal boxes, ink bottles, and various vials.

Essex Institute.

Colony at the English court. They did not return to Boston until after the birth of their ninth child in August of 1661. With them was Leverett's eldest daughter Hannah (April 16, 1643–December 9, 1657), who was born in Boston and died during their sojourn in England.[18] Perhaps the fourteen-year-old Hannah worked the cabinet in 1657, since it descended in the family of Hudson Leverett (1640–1692), her full brother, rather than with the heirs of her half sisters.

It is also possible that Elizabeth (b.1651) or Ann (b.1652) began work on the cabinet in England when they were about ten or nine years old, respectively, for English girls of this age are known to have worked similar pieces.[19] It could, however, have been worked in Boston by any of the six Leverett daughters who were born between 1651 and 1673. The great similarity of the cabinet to many English examples is convincing evidence that their patterns and materials were professionally prepared for working, and the experienced English schoolmistress on either side of the Atlantic could no doubt procure them for the daughters of wealthy patrons.

According to the Reverend William Bentley of Salem, a more intricate example of raised work was made by one of the Leverett daughters, and it may be the looking glass given to the Museum of Fine Arts, Boston, by Mrs. Philip Leverett Saltonstall in 1913 (Fig. 32). On June 20, 1810, in describing a visit to Ipswich, Bentley noted that "This Mrs. Perkins was a Philips & is descended from Gov. J. L. and the Cooke's. . . . She shewed to us . . . the work of a Dressing Glass. It was done by a d. of Gov. Leveret. It was very highly raised. It exhibited K[ing] W[illiam] & Q[ueen] M[ary] dressed in pearls & had a rich profusion of other figures."[20]

Although Bentley was confused about the identity of Mrs. Perkins,[21] and the embroidered figures were more likely intended to be Charles II and Catherine of

---

Wead, "The Second Wife of Hudson Leverett," *American Genealogist* 25, no. 3 [July 1949]: 160–1). The cabinet may have been the work of Elizabeth Leverett Cooke (1651–1715), who had only one son and a very young granddaughter at the time of her death. She may have given the cabinet to either of her half brother Hudson's granddaughters: Sarah Leverett (1700–1727), who died the year after her marriage to Edward Wigglesworth, or Mary Leverett (1701–1756), who married John Denison in 1719 and was the great, great, great grandmother of the donor. If given to Mary, it would have been another opportunity for the names Mary and Elizabeth to be associated with the cabinet. Its original case, although catalogued in 1925, has heretofore been unnoticed. A nearly identical case for a similar cabinet of definite English origin (collection of Margaret B. Schiffer) is made of Scots pine (pinus sylvestris), which suggests that imported New England white pine was not normally used for such utilitarian objects in seventeenth-century England. Wood from the Leverett and Schiffer cases was analyzed by Bruce Hoadley, Professor, Wood Science and Technology, the University of Massachusetts at Amherst. I am indebted to Mr. and Mrs. Schiffer for making this comparison possible.

18. John Leverett (1616–1679) was born in Boston, England, and arrived in Boston, New England, in 1633. In 1639 he married Hannah Hudson (1621–1646). Two of their four children survived infancy: Hudson (1640–1692) and Hannah (1643–1657). Leverett was governor of the Colony from 1673 until his death. For his own record of his children, see Bentley, *Diary* 3 [1962], 177–8.

19. See Jennifer Harris, "Hannah Smith's Embroidered Casket," *The ANTIQUE COLLECTOR*, July 1988, 49–55; also, Levey, "English embroidered cabinets of the seventeenth century" (June 1991), 1130–9.

20. Bentley, *Diary* 3 [1962], 524–5.

21. Elizabeth Leverett Cooke's granddaughter Sarah Cooke (1710–1740) married in 1732 John Phillips, a

Fig. 32. Dressing glass with embroidered frame, New England or England, c.1657–1685. Raised, padded, and partially detached work of silk, wood, metallic wire and foil, mica, pearls, glass beads, feathers, and iridescent insect parts decorate the silk ground which surrounds the original beveled mirror; 22½″ x 22″ x ½″. The back is covered with peach-colored plush, including its easel. Both are edged with metallic braid, and the recess for the easel is lined with marbled paper. At least until 1913 it survived in its original silk-lined leather case which is now unknown. Traditionally in the Leverett family in America for at least seven generations, the donor believed it came to America with the first Leverett in 1633, a date too early for its origin. It descended to Philip Leverett Saltonstall (b.1867), the great, great, great, great grandson of Elizabeth Leverett Cooke (1651–1715), daughter of Governor John Leverett. Probably it is the raised work "Dressing Glass" shown to William Bentley in 1810 by Elizabeth's childless great granddaughter-in-law Mary Calef Phillips Perkins (1737–1830), from whom it went to the descendants of her first husband's aunt, Mary Cooke Saltonstall. Like the cabinet (Fig. 31), it is possibly the work of Hannah Leverett (1643–1657), Elizabeth Leverett (1651–1715), or another daughter of Governor John Leverett.
Museum of Fine Arts, Boston, gift of Mrs. Philip Leverett Saltonstall, 13.384.

Braganza rather than William and Mary, he probably saw the Saltonstall looking glass in 1810. The frame of the "Dressing Glass," as he quite properly called it, could have been the work of a daughter or a granddaughter of Governor Leverett, since this type of embroidery continued to be made during the first decade of the eighteenth century, although its peak of popularity in England was between 1660 and 1690.[22]

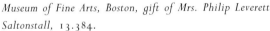

merchant of Boston, and their son William Phillips (1736–before 1793) married Mary Calef (1737–1830), whose second husband was James Perkins (1736–1818) of Ipswich. Mrs. Perkins was evidently in possession of her first husband's Leverett heirlooms, which were later a gift or bequest to the Leverett descendants of his mother's sister, Mary Cooke Saltonstall (1723–1804).
22. Swain, 65.

Boston Embroideries in the Eighteenth Century

It is doubtful that any town of comparable size, at any time in history, produced more impressive schoolgirl art than the "accomplishments" made at Boston schools during the eighteenth century. The early fashions for filigree, wax work, and painting on glass were soon overshadowed by a wealth of pictorial and heraldic embroidery in styles that remained unique to eastern Massachusetts. Like English furniture forms, English needlework patterns found fresh interpretation in Boston, while pictures solidly stitched on black silk and decorative armorial embroidery appear to have developed without foreign counterparts.

ADAM AND EVE SAMPLERS

Boston's first important group of samplers emerged in the 1720s. The earliest recorded example is dated 1724 (Fig. 34). Unlike the stylized band patterns with newly fashionable borders that characterized Newport and Philadelphia samplers of this decade, Boston work retained the form and techniques of the seventeenth century and continued the charming pictorial naïveté of the Stuart period.

The Adam and Eve samplers worked in Boston between 1724 and 1744 (Figs. 34–36, 39), and several closely related pieces (Fig. 37), are startling in their similarity to an English sampler of 1654, although the band patterns of the early example are more exquisitely and intricately worked (Fig. 33). Why a Boston schoolmistress favored a mid-seventeenth-century pattern in the 1720s remains unexplained. In any case, the pictorial motifs she chose are nearly identical to their 1654 prototype, and the lacy, partly detached embroidery and lift-up fig leaves echo the seventeenth-century style.[1]

The hexagonal band pattern, which appears to be exclusive to the Boston region, is found on a band sampler worked by Lydia Hart in 1731,[2] and it is first known to be coupled with Adam and Eve in the 1734 work of Ann Peartree (Fig.

---

1. Two other recognizable groups of Boston samplers that are more contemporary with English work appeared by 1739 and 1747. See the former in Krueger, *New England*, Fig. 12, and Ring, *Treasures*, Fig. 5. For the latter, see Hannah Church, 1747 (Krueger, *Gallery*, Fig. 17); Hannah Storer, 1747, in the MHS (*A&AW*, January 25, 1991, 38); Sarah Lowell, 1750 (Fawdry and Brown, 61); Sarah Erving, 1750 (Peabody Museum of Salem, acc. no. 24, 426); Sarah Henshaw, 1750 (privately owned).
2. Probably this was Lydia Hart, born September 12, 1719, to Elias and Lydia Hart of Boston. Her sampler belongs to the NHHS.

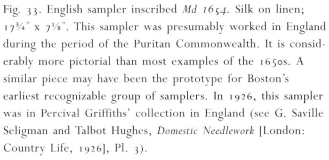

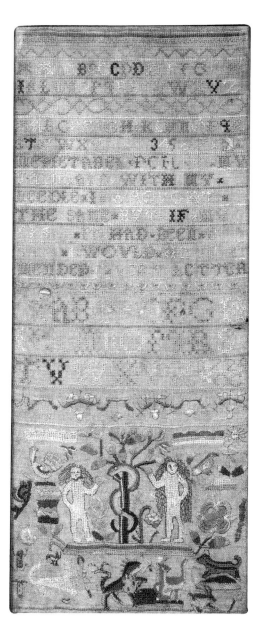

Fig. 33. English sampler inscribed *Md 1654*. Silk on linen; 17¾″ x 7⅛″. This sampler was presumably worked in England during the period of the Puritan Commonwealth. It is considerably more pictorial than most examples of the 1650s. A similar piece may have been the prototype for Boston's earliest recognizable group of samplers. In 1926, this sampler was in Percival Griffiths' collection in England (see G. Saville Seligman and Talbot Hughes, *Domestic Needlework* [London: Country Life, 1926], Pl. 3).
M. and M. Karolik Collection, Museum of Fine Arts, Boston, 43.275.

Fig. 34. *Mehetabel Done [is] my/ name and with my/ needle I wrovght/ the same bvt if my/ ski[ll] it had been b[ett/er] I wovld ha[v]e/ mended e very letter/ 1724.* Silk on linen; 18½″ x 7½″. Mehetabel's sampler is now the earliest known example of Boston's Adam and Eve samplers. Her pictorial motifs are remarkably similar to those in Figure 33, although the figures of Adam and Eve are reversed. Despite some thread loss in the surname, it has definitely been determined that the maker's name was Mehetabel Done. Mehetabel, born in Boston on April 4, 1715, was the daughter of John Done (1690–1723) and Abiah Callender (b.1690), who were married by the Reverend Cotton Mather on June 23, 1714. Her grandfather Ellis Callender became pastor of Boston's First Baptist Church in 1708. On April 13, 1736, Mehetabel was married, by her uncle the Reverend Elisha Callender, to John Cowley. They had two sons and two daughters.
Collection of Mr. And Mrs. S. P. Keller.

Fig. 35. *Martha Bvtler/ is my name and with my/ needle I wrovght the/ same and if my skill it/ had been better I wovld/ have mended every letter/ AV the 19 day 1729 in th/ 12 year of my age.* Silk on linen; 18½″ x 8⅛″. Martha's Garden of Eden is much like that of Mehetabel Done, but she added lift-up fig leaves to the formerly unclad Adam and Eve. Martha (b.c.1718) may have been the daughter of Peter Butler and Martha Wharton, who were married in Boston on February 8, 1717. A Martha Butler married Peter Jenkins in Boston on September 9, 1742.
Cooper-Hewitt, National Museum of Design, Smithsonian Institution, bequest of Rosalie Coe, 1974-42-5.

Opposite:
Fig. 36. *Ann Pear/tree Her/ Work 173/4.* Silk and metallic threads on linen; 14½″ x 11¼″. Ann worked her scene above an early rendition of the Boston band pattern, which appeared on samplers of this region from 1731 until the 1820s, but this design seldom occurred elsewhere in a simple band-pattern form. Ann Peartree was the daughter of a now-unknown father and Katherine Peartree, who lived on Middle Street in Boston and was licensed to sell "Strong Drink" at retail on October 13, 1740. (*Report of the Record Commissioners of the City of Boston 1742/43–1753* [Boston: Rockwell and Churchill, 1887], 78). On April 22, 1742, Katherine Peartree married William Taylor. Ann died of smallpox, probably in December 1743 and Katherine was a widow by January 31, 1744, when she was granted the administration of Ann's estate. She also died before February 25, 1744, and Ann's uncle William Tadcar, a tailor, was then named administrator of the estate (Suffolk County Probate No. 8203).
Cooper-Hewitt, National Museum of Design, Smithsonian Institution, bequest of Gertrude M. Oppenheimer, 1981-28-157.

36). Another Lydia Hart worked an exceptionally elaborate example in this style in 1744 (Fig. 39). Otherwise the Adam and Eve patterns appear to have been simplified by 1739 when Ruth Rogers worked her sampler, probably at a different school (Fig. 38).[3] No facts are available concerning the leading schoolmistress of Boston during the 1720s, but there is little doubt that she taught between 1724 and 1744, or that the patterns she favored were carefully copied by others. A

3. Samplers similar to Figure 38: B&C, Pl. XV; SPB, Garbisch I, Sale 3595, January 24, 1974, Lot 200, and Garbisch II, Sale 3637, May 8, 1974, Lot 50; Krueger, *New England*, Fig. 21, and *Gallery*, Fig. 18; also Ring, *Treasures*, 5.

likely possibility is Mrs. Susanna Hiller Condy (1686–1747), who was born in Boston to Joseph Hiller and Susanna Dennis. Her father, a tinplate worker, tavern keeper, and occasionally an agent for London clients, was quite prosperous until his new home in Cornhill burned in 1711.[4] On November 1, 1706, Susanna married Jeremiah Condy (1682–1741), who in 1719 became master of the public writing school at the north end of town. They lived on Prince Street where they owned a home and a slave named Jack who added to their income by working as a chimney sweep. Susanna's brother graduated from Harvard in 1705, and in 1722, with the help of the Reverend Elisha Callender, her son Jeremiah (1709–1768) entered Harvard with a Hollis fellowship.[5] Susanna and her family had joined Callender's First Baptist Church about 1720, and surely she would have been acquainted with his sister, Abiah Callender Done, who also lived in the north end of town and was the mother of Mehetabel (Fig. 34). With the contacts of her English immigrant parents, and a brother who had traveled to London, Susanna was well aware of English goods and fashions, and in 1736, she advertised for sale a "fine Fustian Suit of Curtains . . . drawn in London, one Frame full already worked."[6] Two years later she described "*Patterns from* London, *but drawn by her much cheaper than English drawing.*"[7] She never specifically mentioned a school until the following advertisement appeared in *The Boston Evening-Post* of March 15, 1742 (see front endpapers for a slight variation of two weeks later):

> Mrs. *Condy* opens her School next Week, and Persons may be supplyed with the Materials for the Works she teaches, whether they learn of her or not. She draws Patterns of all sorts, *especially*, Pocket-Books, House-Wives, Screens, Pictures, Chimney-Pieces, Escrutoires, & c. for *Tent-Stitch*, in a plainer Manner, and cheaper than those which come from *London*.

The somewhat casual reference to opening "her School next Week" suggests that it was so well known as to need no further description. By this time Susanna was a widow and her son Jeremiah had become pastor of the First Baptist Church.

On September 24, 1747, Susanna Condy wrote her will and divided her considerable property between her two surviving children, Jeremiah and Elizabeth Russell, and her granddaughter Susanna Jarvis. She specifically devised £80 to her daughter "to fit her children up to follow me to the grave" and £20 "to put my Granddaughter Susanna Jarvis in mourning." She also ordered "that my Negro Woman named Flora shall be sold for the most she will fetch."[8] Her son was to be her sole executor, and in the presence of Joseph Clarke, her brother Joseph

---

4. *Sibley's Harvard Graduates, 1701–1712* (1937), 5:263–5.

5. *Sibley's Harvard Graduates, 1726–1730* (1951), 8:20–30. Jeremiah was the second of eight children.

6. *The Boston Gazette*, May 17/24, 1736.

7. *The Boston Weekly News-Letter*, April 27/May 4, 1738.

8. Boston's earliest newspaper advertisements are dominated by Negroes for sale. In the 1760s, Susanna's son Jeremiah Condy, then a bookseller and pastor of the First Baptist Church, owned two slaves.

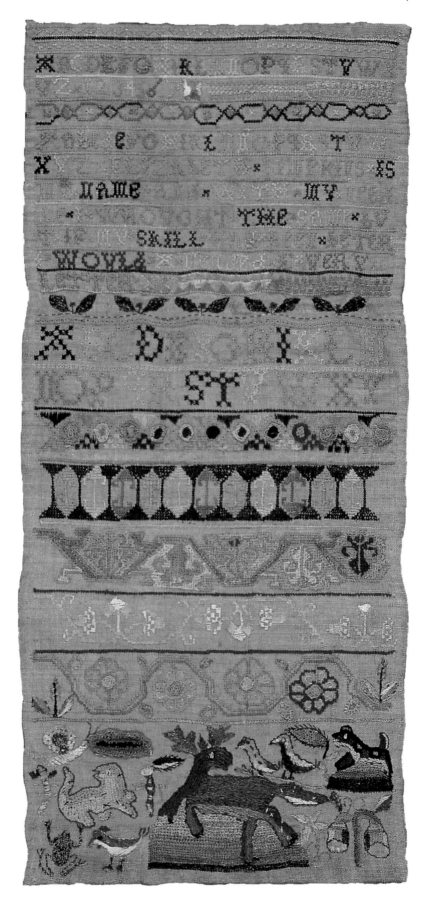

Fig. 37. *Elizabeth Simpkins is/ my name and with my need/le I wrovght the same bv/t if my skill had been beter/ I wovld a mended e very/ letter,* c.1736. Silk on linen; 17½" x 8". Although Adam and Eve were omitted, Elizabeth's sampler definitely belongs within this group. This probably was the Elizabeth Simpkins born in Boston to goldsmith William Simpkins (1704–1780) and Elizabeth Simms on January 7, 1726. Her classmate must have been Frances Pinckny (1726–1777), who worked a nearly identical undated sampler now at Gore Place. Frances married heraldic painter and shopkeeper John Gore and became the mother of Governor Christopher Gore. It was probably a younger sister of Elizabeth (Katharine, b.1736, or Mary, b.1744) who worked the arms of Simpkins and Symmes now in the Winterthur Museum (Swan, *Guide,* 136). *Private collection.*

Fig. 38. *Rvth/ Rogers Ended/ the/ sample/ in the/ 8 year/ of her/ age/ 1739.* Silk on linen; 18¼" x 9". Ruth worked the most commonly found form within Boston's Adam and Eve group. The signature inscription is crowded on the outer edges beside the figures. The first four band patterns occur in the same order on at least five other examples dating from 1741 to 1749 (see footnote 3). This girl may have been Ruth Rogers (1731–1749), the daughter of Stephen Rogers (b.1693) and Mary of Newbury. She died unmarried.
Metropolitan Museum of Art, bequest of Barbara Schiff Sinauer, 1984.331.6.

Hiller, and his wife Abigail, the sixty-year-old Susanna signed her will with a steady hand; it was presented for probate on November 4.[9]

Unfortunately, no inventory of Susanna's estate has been found, but within a month of her death her daughter was dismantling her household. The following advertisement appeared in *The Boston Gazette, or Weekly Journal* of December 15, 1747:

> A Variety of very beautiful Patterns to draw by, of the late Mrs. *Susannah Condy*, deceas'd, any Gentlewoman or others disposed to improve and purchase the same, which will be very much to their Advantage, may inquire of *Elizabeth Russell*, Daughter of the deceas'd, near the DrawBridge.

Quite possibly Susanna's sister-in-law, Abigail Stevens Hiller, was prepared to continue with Susanna's former scholars, for *The Boston Evening-Post* carried this advertisement on February 1, 1748:

> This may inform young Gentlewomen in Town and Country, That early in the Spring, Mrs. *Hiller* designs to open a Boarding-School at the House where she lives, in *Fish-Street*, at the the North End of *Boston*, next Door to Doctor *Clark's*, where they may be taught Wax-Work, Transparent and Filligree, Painting upon Glass, Japanning, Quill-Work, Feather-Work and embroidering with Gold and Silver, and several other sorts of Work not here enumerated, and may be supplied with Patterns and all sorts of Drawing, and Materials for their Work.

Abigail Hiller also advertised her boarding school in April of 1753, June of 1754, and May of 1756.[10] In the 1940s, this series of advertisements convinced textile scholar Nancy Graves Cabot that Susanna Condy was the woman responsible for initiating Boston's most famous form of colonial embroidery, the pastoral pictures in canvas work. The dispersal of her patterns would also account for the repetition of designs that continued in the 1750s.[11] More recent evidence tends to support her conclusions.

---

9. Suffolk County Probate No. 8871.
10. *The Boston Evening-Post*, April 9, 1753; *The Boston Gazette, or Weekly Advertiser*, June 11, 1754; and *The Boston-Gazette, and Country Journal*, May 24, 1756.
11. *ANTIQUES,* December 1941, 367–9.

Fig. 39. *Lydia Hart May the 28 1744*. Silk on linen; 11½″ x 9″. Lydia worked the most elaborate and fully embroidered example within the Boston Adam and Eve group, and the only known piece to have a border. As in the English version of 1654, Adam still has a goatee, and elements of the earlier pattern also appear on Sarah Silsbee's sampler, which named *Boston* in 1748 (Krueger, *Gallery*, Fig. 18). Lydia has not been identified.

Private collection.

Fig. 40. Chimney piece attributed to Eunice Bourne, c.1748. Wool, silk, metallic threads, and beads on canvas; 20½″ x 43½″; original frame that first had three-part glass (see *ANTIQUES,* August 1923, 71). A supreme example, and one of the best preserved, of the fishing lady pictures. The small pole vaulter (beneath the man with a pack), the three sheep at left, the horseman, the lady drop-spinning, the man with the pack, the stag chased by hounds, and the house with a picket fence at the far right are images found on many other pieces in this group. Eunice Bourne (1732–between 1773 and 1781) was the daughter of Sylvanus Bourne (1694–1764) and Mercy Gorham (c.1696–1782) of Barnstable. She married Captain John Gallison (1731–1786) of Marblehead in 1754, and they had thirteen children. Eunice no doubt worked her chimney piece at a Boston boarding school in company with Sarah Warren (1730–1797) of Barnstable, who signed a very similar piece and dated it 1748. Also dated 1748 is an anonymous chimney piece of nearly identical design (*ANTIQUES,* July 1941, 28, and December 1941, 367).
Museum of Fine Arts, Boston, Seth K. Sweetser Fund, 21.2233.

FISHING LADY PICTURES

Throughout the seventeenth and eighteenth centuries, the elite of New England sent their daughters to Boston to finish their education. In the twentieth century, the strongest evidence of this custom is a group of mid-eighteenth-century pastoral embroideries called the "fishing lady pictures." This name was derived from an article entitled "The Fishing Lady and Boston Common," which appeared in the magazine *ANTIQUES* of August 1923, wherein the author, Helen Bowen, called attention to seven idyllic embroidered landscapes featuring the same fishing lady (Fig. 40). In 1941, Nancy Graves Cabot determined that the fishing lady pictures were the products of Boston boarding schools, and the name was soon applied to related Boston needlework, with or without the fishing lady (the second most commonly found female is a reclining shepherdess as in Fig. 41). The fishing lady group now includes a variety of pastoral compositions in canvas work or crewels on linen, and they may appear on sconces, screens, pictures, chimney pieces, chair seats, valances, samplers, the tops for card tables, or even petticoat borders.[1]

Bucolic scenes in canvas work became fashionable in England during the first quarter of the eighteenth century, and they were in harmony with the literature of the period by poets such as James Thomson and Ambrose Philips. Pictorial canvas work appeared in Boston by the early 1730s,[2] but with the exception of Norwich, Connecticut, there is no evidence that it became popular in the other American colonies.[3]

The fishing lady pictures fall into several major groups worked in similar styles, and a number of subgroups. Most numerous and cohesive are examples featuring the fishing lady or the motifs that surround her in a variety of different combinations and worked primarily with crewel yarns in tent stitch (Figs. 40–45). Occasionally these pieces have painted faces or applied paper faces. Most of Boston's canvas-work chimney pieces fall within this group, and Nancy Cabot found many of their figures in early prints, but the source for the famous fishing lady is still uncertain.[4]

The scene in Figure 46 represents another group worked in a similar technique but very different style. These pieces are more linear, with delicately worked fig-

Fig. 41. Needlework picture by Susannah Heath, c.1774. Wool and mica on linen canvas; 16½" x 20½". Susannah's classmate and future sister-in-law, Hannah Goddard (1759–1786), worked a virtually identical piece (*ANTIQUES*, July 1941, 30) and Esther Stoddard (1738–1816) used a similar pattern in the 1750s (*The Great River* [1985], 399–401), as did Priscilla Rice (b.1741) of Sturbridge (Skinner Sale 1014, January 4, 1985, Lot 245). Other examples are in the Concord Museum and Historic Deerfield's collection. Susannah Heath (1758–1787) was the daughter of John Heath (1732–1804) and Susannah Craft (1738–1808) of Brookline. She was first among the four wives of Dr. John Goddard (1756–1829) of Brookline, who became an apothecary in Portsmouth, New Hampshire. For an article about her remarkable tune book, see *Proceedings of the American Antiquarian Society* 84, pt. 1, 1974. An account of her wedding appears in *The Crafts Family* by James M. and William F. Crafts (Northampton, Mass., 1893), 694. *Museum of Fine Arts, Boston, 41.559.*

---

1. Cabot, "The Fishing Lady and Boston Common" (1941), 28–31. Nancy Graves (1889–1969) was born in Newburyport and married Samuel Cabot (1884–1967) of Boston in 1909.

2. A small canvas-work picture with birds in a tree is dated 1734 and said to be by Jane Pierce of Newburyport (NHHS). Another, depicting a hunter, stag, and hounds bears the initials of Mary Cooke (1723–1804), daughter of Elisha Cooke, Jr. (1678–1737) and granddaughter of Elizabeth Leverett Cooke (Fig. 31). Photographs are in the Cabot Papers, Textile Department, MFA.

3. Several small pieces are known from Philadelphia. See the works of Hannah Reeve, 1733, and Martha Gray, 1779 (*ANTIQUES*, July 1930, 47, and February 1974, 357). The work of Mary or Martha Bulyn, 1730, is said to be from Pennsylvania (B&C, Pl. XII).

4. Cabot, "Engravings and Embroideries" (1941), 28–31; also, A. Hyatt Mayor, "The Hunt for the Fishing Lady," *ANTIQUES*, July 1977, 113.

Fig. 42. *ANN PEARTREE 1739* worked below the picture. Wool and silk on linen; 10¾" x 9". Ann's tent-stitched allegorical picture has survived in all its glorious if illogical color. Her work is Boston's earliest signed and dated canvas-work picture, and smaller than her sampler of 1734 (Fig. 36). *Museum of Fine Arts, Boston, bequest of Elsie T. Friedman, 59.22.*

Fig. 43. *PRISCILLA ALLEN DAUGHTER TO MR BENJAMIN ALLEN AND MRS/ ELIZABETH ALLEN BOSTON July THE 20 1746.* Wool on linen canvas; 21" x 15⅜". The figures were derived from *LeSoir*, an engraving by Bouzonnet after Jacques Stella. An almost identical anonymous piece is privately owned, and the woman with the basket is the central figure in a chimney piece at the Historical Society of Old Newbury. These figures and the couple on the right in Eunice Bourne's chimney piece (Fig. 40) also occur on English embroideries of 1762 and 1769 which name *Mrs Rosco's Boarding School* in Bristol (Skinner, Sale 1389, June 15, 1991, Lot 273; Ring, "For Persons of Fortune Who Have Taste" [1977], 8). Priscilla's work is the only known fishing lady picture to name *Boston*. Priscilla Allen (1728–1785) was the daughter of the Reverend Benjamin Allen (1689–1754) and Elizabeth Crocker (1688–1762). Her father graduated from Yale in 1708; Priscilla was probably born in Bridgewater, Massachusetts, and the family moved to Cape Elizabeth, Maine, in 1735. Of their eleven children, five died there of diphtheria in 1738. Priscilla married Caleb Upham, who graduated from Harvard in 1744. He was the Congregationalist minister in Truro, Massachusetts, for thirty years. They had one son and adopted their niece, Achsah Jordan (c.1745–1801), who married the Reverend Enos Hitchcock in 1771.

Winterthur Museum, 62.588A.

Fig. 44. Chimney piece by Mary Pickering, c.1748. Wool on linen canvas; 13" x 36¼". The mounted sportsman on the right appears on many related embroideries as do the stag and hounds. Mary Pickering (1733–1805) was the daughter of Timothy Pickering (1703–1778) and Mary Wingate (1708–1784) of Salem. She married the Reverend Dudley Leavitt (1720–1762) in 1751, and second, Nathaniel Peaslee Sargent (1730–1791). Her embroidery still hangs in the house that received it on her return from boarding school.
Private collection.

Fig. 45. Anonymous needlework picture, c.1750–1760. Wool and silk on linen canvas; 25" x 29½". This unfinished embroidery reveals the sparse drawing of the pattern. Clearly these were worked under the close supervision of the schoolmistress or by an advanced student. For a similar work attributed to Jane Tyler (b.c.1733), see *ANTIQUES*, June 1944, 300–1; also, Skinner Sale 584, September 22, 1978, Lot 117. For related work on samplers, see Ring, "Schoolgirl Embroideries" (1981–82), 18–21.
Philadelphia Museum of Art, 49-12-1.

Fig. 46. Anonymous needlework picture, c.1750–1760. Wool and silk on linen canvas; 23¾" x 24½". This is the most elaborate example belonging to a different school of work within Boston's fishing lady group. The scene at the backgammon table is from an engraving by N. de Larmessin after Nicholas Lancret (1690–1743). See Cabot, "Engravings as Pattern Sources," *ANTIQUES* 58, no. 6 (1950): 479. Elements in this embroidery also occur in others (Swan, *Plain & Fancy*, 106–7). *Museum of Art, Rhode Island School of Design, gift of Mrs. Jessie H. Metcalf, 23.075.*

ures on a smaller scale; the women often have vertically striped dresses, particularly a tall shepherdess in a rather stiff pose with somewhat scrawny sheep.[5]

Boston's most remarkable canvas-work picture is by Hannah Otis (Fig. 47), and it appears to be a unique, realistic view of Boston Common for which no prototypes have been found. It was inherited by Harrison Gray Otis, Hannah's nephew, who was the mayor of Boston in 1829, and he left this account of it:

> A view of the Hancock House, and appendages, and of the Common, and its vicinity, as they were in 1755–60. It was the boarding school lesson of Hannah Otis, daughter of the Hon. James Otis of Barnstable, educated in Boston. It was considered a chef d'oeuvre, and made a great noise at the time. The science of perspective was not worthy of Claude Lorraine, but perhaps not behind that of some who since then have had the care of the Common.[6]

Because Hannah's work is known to have been made at a Boston boarding school, it is very likely that related pieces by other girls still exist.[7]

---

5. No signed pieces are known. For other examples: Wheeler, *The Development of Embroidery in America* (1921), opp. 56; *The Bulletin of the Metropolitan Museum of Art* 35, no. 2 (February 1940): 43; also, MFA *Bulletin* 62, no. 328 (1964): 77–8.

6. As quoted by Cabot, "The Fishing Lady," 29.

7. An exceptional canvas-work picture of 1756 appears to depict a contemporary event, but it is not certain if the design was original or inspired by a print. See Fairbanks et al., *Paul Revere's Boston* (1975), 86. For another realistic scene see Schiffer, "American Needlework" (1969), 111.

Fig. 47. Chimney piece by Hannah Otis, c.1750. Wool, silk, metallic threads, and beads on linen; 24¼″ x 52¼″. Hannah's recognizable view of Beacon Hill, the 1737 Hancock House, and Boston Common is unique among Boston canvas-work pictures. Although worked at a boarding school, it descended with the tradition that it was Hannah's original design. The couple at left may represent Thomas Hancock (1703–1764) and his wife, Lydia Henchman (1714–1776), while the horseman could be their nephew John Hancock (1737–1793), the future governor. Hannah Otis (1732–1773) was the daughter of Colonel James Otis (1702–1778) and Mary Alleyne (1702–1767) of Barnstable. She died unmarried.
Museum of Fine Arts, Boston, loan of Miss Mary Otis, 23.54.

Two other types of fishing lady pictures are generally described as crewel embroidery on linen. One has bold designs with a central figure of a shepherdess seated stiffly at the foot of a tree with a rather reticent shepherd in a large black hat. These usually have one or two other figures amid a variety of birds and beasts (Fig. 48).[8] A second crewel-work form was more precisely designed and beautifully executed (Fig. 49).[9]

During the 1760s, particularly in the 1770s, and occasionally as late as the 1790s, Boston samplers also included motifs that are typical of the fishing lady

8. See Swan, *Guide*, 82–3; Nancy Jo Fox, *Liberties with Liberty* (New York: E. P. Dutton, 1985), 34; others are in the Amherst Historical Society, Amherst, Massachusetts; the Colonial Williamsburg Foundation; and the MFA.

9. Probably of Boston origin is a chimney piece featuring Adam and Eve and worked in this technique (*ANTIQUES*, July 1980, 23). In *The Boston-Gazette, and Country Journal,* of May 23, 1757, auctioneer Samuel Smith described "*a Chimney Piece imitating Adam and Eve in Paradise, wro't with Needle after the best Manner . . .*"

Fig. 48. Needlework picture attributed to Polly Burns, c.1768. Wool and silk on linen; 15⅞″ x 24″. Pieces within this group are worked primarily in Roumanian couching (also called New England laid stitch). The same bold upright shepherdess is the dominant figure in five anonymous examples that have all survived with excellent color (see footnote 6). Polly Burns was probably Mary Burns (1753–1794), the daughter of Francis Burns (c.1723–1800) and Margaret (c.1716–1794), who are said to have lived in the Fountain House in Medford, Massachusetts. Mary married Samuel Buel (c.1758–1813) of Litchfield, Connecticut, on December 25, 1783. *Museum of Fine Arts, Boston, loan of Maria Wait, 93.44.*

pictures (Fig. 51).[10] Figure 50 seems to display one step in the transition of the reclining shepherdess to the sampler form, which is complete in Figure 51.

No one knows who initiated Boston's pastoral scenes in canvas work. Susanna Condy continues to be the most likely originator of both the fishing lady pictures and Boston's heraldic embroidery, although she died just as these fashions were reaching full flower. Quite possibly Susanna instructed Ann Peartree to work her

10. Zebiah Gore's sampler in B&C, Pl. XXXVIII; Elizabeth Richards' nearly identical work in Swan, *Plain & Fancy*, 80; Anna Pope, 1796, in Ring, *Treasures*, 6.

Fig. 49. Needlework picture by an unknown girl of the Chandler family, 1758. Wool and silk on linen; 15″ x 23″. This scene is beautifully worked, primarily in Roumanian couching. For others of this quality see Skinner Sale 1000, October 27, 1984, Lot 208; also, Mary Taylor Landon and Susan Burrows Swan, *American Crewel Work* (New York: Macmillan Co., 1970), 42. The embroideress placed her date above the door but failed to sign her work.
Private collection; photograph courtesy of the Worcester Art Museum.

sampler in 1734 (Fig. 36) and then directed the embroidery of her small canvas-work picture in 1739 (Fig. 42). Only two coats of arms are reliably attributed to Susanna Condy's school (Figs. 64, 305), but her charges to Rufus Greene indicate that she was concentrating on teaching the most costly accomplishments.

The account books of Greene,[11] a Boston silversmith, record school expenses for his eight children from 1736 until 1770,[12] and particularly for his eldest child,

<hr />

11. Rufus Greene Account Book 1728–1746 and Rufus Greene Expence Book 1747–1774. Manuscripts, MHS.

12. A series of teachers included Mrs. Allen, Mrs. Swett, Mrs. Dyer, Sarah Goodwin, and Mrs. Hannah Simpson; also, John Leddell, Richard Green, Richard Pateshall, Mr. Holbrook, and Master Lovell in 1770.

Katharine, whom he called Caty. During the 1740s, Greene included the following expenses specifically for Caty:

April 19 1741	To Cash for Entrance of Caty D School	£ 2 — 0 — 0
July 26	To 1 Quarter School for Caty	3 — 0 — 0
Oct 21	To one Quarter Schooling for Caty	3 — 0 — 0
Oct 4 1744	To Cash paid Mrs. Cunday for Caty	6 — 6 — 0
Apr 25	Paid Mr. Brimmer for Caty's Stays	6 — 0 — 0
Dec 3 1745	To Cash paid William Price for my Daughters 13 pictures	22 — 11 — 0
Dec 17	Cash paid Mr. Deblois for teaching my daughter Caty 4 months	8 — 0 — 0
Jan 4 1746	Cash paid Mrs. Susanna Condy	23 — 1 — 0
Nov 20	Mr Deblois for teaching Caty D/24/—	12 — 0 — 0
Dec 10	Cash paid for my daughter Catys pair of Sconces to Madam Condy	39 — 0 — 0
Nov 18 1748	paid Mrs Crab for teaching Caty	10 — 0 — 0

Caty's 1745 coat of arms was surely among the "13 pictures" framed by William Price, but no one knows what the others depicted, or where they are now; and whether the sconces were canvas work, filigree, or wax work is a tantalizing question.

Fig. 50. Anonymous needlework picture, c.1760–1770. Silk on linen; 13¾″ x 13⅝″. In a typical reclining-shepherdess setting, this awakened shepherdess has been joined by the pole vaulter that appears on the Bourne embroidery (Fig. 40). The trio of sheep in the center (one black and two white ones) occurs in identical form on the 1748 anonymous chimney piece that closely resembles the Bourne example (see caption, Fig. 40). The vine with strawberries on either side would soon become the characteristic framing border on a group of pastoral samplers.
Cooper-Hewitt, National Museum of Design, Smithsonian Institution, 1970-28-2.

Fig. 51. *Mary Welsh Her Sampler Wrought In The 12 Year Of/ Her Age*, c.1772. Silk on linen; 21″ x 15″. Mary may have worked this sampler in the company of the girl who made the piece in Figure 50. The same border appears on pastoral samplers by Sarah Doubt, 1765 (Christie's, October 21, 1987, Lot 132); by Rebecca Leach, 1768 (Richard A. Bourne Co., Inc., August 23, 1983, cover and Lot 104); and by Sarah Diamond, 1770 (*ANTIQUES*, February 1974, 358). Mary Welsh (September 9, 1760–1820) was the daughter of Boston jeweler John Welsh (c.1730–1812) and Mary Parker (1733–1803). She died unmarried. For other fishing lady samplers, including a magnificent example by Mary's sister, Grace Welsh (1762–1827), see B&C, Pls. XIX, XXV, XXVI, and CVI.
Colonial Williamsburg Foundation, Williamsburg, Virginia, 1962–309.

As Nancy Graves Cabot observed in 1941, it may have been Susanna Condy's sister-in-law, Abigail Hiller, who took over Susanna's scholars and continued the use of her patterns. Possibly she directed the work of Eunice Bourne (Fig. 40) and others whose pictures are strikingly similar to Priscilla Allen's embroidery of 1746 (Fig. 43) and to some with figures derived from the same print. No other likely teachers advertised in the 1740s, but in the 1750s and 1760s, a growing number of women offered instruction in every variety of needlework. They produced a fascinating wealth of fishing lady pictures, embroideries on silk, and elegant coats of arms.

The costliness of this Boston education is well revealed in charges to Rufus Greene and others, and when girls returned home, the "accomplishments" were the property of their parents. Eunice Bourne's chimney piece (Fig. 40) remained in her mother's household after her marriage and was eventually willed to her daughter, and "a work called the Coat of Arms" left to Mercy Bourne Jordan was probably of her making.[13] In his will of 1774, James Otis made various bequests to his daughter Hannah and added, "I also give her both her patch work Counterpens that she made herself . . . and a Chimmy piece . . ." (Fig. 47).[14] Richard Derby's will of 1783 included major bequests of money, land, and slaves, but the balance of his estate went to two sons and the heirs of a third son.[15] Consequently, a canvas-work chimney piece attributed to Sarah Derby descended through the heirs of her brother, Elias Hasket Derby, rather than through her children.[16]

13. C. F. Swift, ed., *Genealogical Notes of Barnstable Families, being a reprint of the Amos Otis Papers* (Barnstable, Mass., 1888), 1, 117.
14. Copy of the Otis will in Harrison Gray Otis Papers, SPNEA Library.
15. Perley Derby, "Genealogy of the Derby Family," *EIHC* 3 (1861): 163–4.
16. *ANTIQUES*, August 1923, 73, Fig. 7.

Fig. 52. The Death of Absalom by Faith Trumbull, c.1753. Silk, gold and silver metal, metallic cord, fringe, and threads, and painted paper on black silk; 18¾" x 18⅝". In 1950, Nancy Graves Cabot examined this embroidery with Sarah Henshaw's (Fig. 54) and found them so alike "as to bespeak a common origin" (*ANTIQUES*, December 1950, 476). Probably they were both worked under the instruction of Elizabeth Murray (Fig. 53). Faith Trumbull (1743–1775) was the daughter of Jonathan Trumbull (1710–1785) and Faith Robinson (1718–1780) of Lebanon, Connecticut. Her father was governor of Connecticut from 1769 to 1783. Faith married Jedediah Huntington (1743–1818) of Norwich, Connecticut, on May 1, 1766.
Lyman Allyn Museum, New London, Connecticut, 1950.5.

SILK EMBROIDERIES OF COLONIAL BOSTON

Contemporary with the fishing lady pictures is a small but impressive group of pictorial embroideries on silk worked in Boston during the 1750s and 1760s. Four of the surviving examples, of which three are shown here, were worked by Faith, the eldest daughter of Governor Jonathan Trumbull of Lebanon, Connecticut (Figs. 52, 56, 57). Her younger brother, the artist John Trumbull, remarked in his autobiography that his two sisters "had completed their education in an excellent school in Boston, where they both had been taught embroidery."[1] Also, correspondence in the Jonathan Trumbull papers reveals that in 1753 Faith Trumbull was instructed by Elizabeth Murray and thereby offers clues to the type of needlework taught by one of the most interesting and successful women teaching in mid-eighteenth-century Boston (Fig. 53).[2]

Elizabeth Murray was twenty-three years old in 1749 when she arrived in Boston from Scotland, with sufficient goods to open a dry goods shop and considerable skills as a needlewoman. On March 25, 1751, she placed the following advertisement in *The Boston Evening-Post*: "ELIZABETH MURRAY, *Next Door to Deacon Bouteneau's in Cornhill*, Boston, TEACHES *Dresden*, and other kinds of Needle Works, likewise accommodates young Ladies with Board, and half Board, at a reasonable Price . . ." and this was followed by a long list of items for sale. Dur-

---

1. Theodore Sizer, ed., *The Autobiography of Colonel John Trumbull* (New Haven: Yale University Press, 1953), 5.
2. For a full account of her life see Mary Beth Norton, "A Cherished Spirit of Independence: The Life of an Eighteenth-Century Boston Businesswoman," in Berkin and Norton, eds., *Women of America* (1979), 48–65.

ing the next two years she ran a number of ads as a milliner with descriptions of the goods she sold but no references to teaching. She was at the same address on March 12, 1753, when she again offered instruction and board to young ladies.[3] Within a few years she had evidently established a secure business, and judging by her charges for materials and tuition, she had the wealthiest of New Englanders for her patrons.

Faith Trumbull entered Elizabeth Murray's school at the age of ten in the summer of 1753 and Jonathan Trumbull's itemized receipt for her expenses survives. Tuition for one quarter and one month was £6-5, and thirty-five other items made a total bill of £60-1-6. Most charges were for a variety of sewing materials; also, "paid for drawing your picture £2-5."[4] The latter may have pertained to the picture in Figure 52.

In the fall of 1754, Faith and Mary Trumbull, then eleven and nine years old, boarded with Mrs. Mary Willis in Boston, and she wrote to their father concerning their progress and various expenses on November 4:

> Honored Sir
>
> These come to inform you I recived your kind leter and am sorry the ladys were not redy to come when so good an opportunity presented. Ladys they are all ways when they come from dancing scool. . . . I have done all I could to make them eseey an comfortable an contented, & your worthy daughter I think has been very well dissposed and they have been kept very constante at school. . . . Thay have cleared with Mr. Pelham for 4 months scoling. . . . We have sent but have not got Mrs Morrays account yet an dread to set it. But Mr. Dennys is come. . . .[5]

Evidently the girls took dancing lessons from Charles Pelham, and they continued to study with Elizabeth Murray. On November 22, 1754, Mrs. Willis wrote to Jonathan Trumbull concerning the transportation of Faith's "picture," which was not yet ready to send home. In December she sent David Mason's receipt for the purchase of its frame.

> Boston Dec[r] 4 1754
> Rec[d] of Mrs Willis thirteen pound
> Old Tenner in full from a
> Large frame & Glass
>   David Mason[6]

Fig. 53. Mrs. James Smith, née Elizabeth Murray (1726–1785), by John Singleton Copley, 1769. Oil on canvas; 49½″ x 40″. Elizabeth was born in Scotland and visited North Carolina as a young girl before becoming a Boston schoolmistress and a shopkeeper. In 1755 she married ship captain Thomas Campbell; then, in 1760, James Smith; and finally, in 1771, Ralph Inman (1718–1788). There were no children. She devoted herself to nieces and nephews and was the much respected aunt of Providence businessman John Innes Clark (1745–1808). For his daughters' school experiences, see Ring, *Virtue*, 93–5, 209–11. *Museum of Fine Arts, Boston, gift of Joseph W. R. and Mary C. Rogers, 42.463.*

3. *The Boston Evening-Post.* See front endpapers for entry of March 26, 1753.

4. Receipt of July 2, 1754 (Trumbull Papers, CHS); see back endpapers. Elizabeth Murray arrived in London on February 10, 1754, after a journey of six weeks (letter to James Murray from London, April 2, 1754, Murray Papers, MHS). She returned to Boston in May or June 1754.

5. Trumbull Papers, CHS. Charles Pelham (1722–1793) was a son of the engraver Peter Pelham (1697–1751). He advertised his dancing school in *The Boston Evening-Post* of October 17, 1754.

6. Ibid. David Mason (1726–1794), japanner, advertised all sorts of painting as well as "Coats of Arms, Drawings on Sattin or Canvis for Embroidery, also Pictures fram'd after the neatest Manner" in *The Boston-Gazette, and Country Journal* of December 18, 1758.

Fig. 54. The Death of Absalom, a chimney piece, and scratched on the glass (although not originally), "Wrought by Sarah Henshaw Boston A.D. 1753." Silk, gold and silver metal, metallic cord, fringe, and threads, beads, and painted paper on silk; 22½″ x 54¼″. See Sarah's coat of arms (Fig. 68). In 1750 she also worked a fine sampler (privately owned). It is much like the work by Sarah Lowell, 1750, in Fawdry and Brown, 61. Possibly of Boston origin is another Death of Absalom chimney piece on black silk in the Currier Gallery of Art, Manchester, New Hampshire. Sarah Henshaw (1736–1822) was the daughter of Boston merchant Joshua Henshaw (1703–1777) and Elizabeth Bill (1712–1782). She married her first cousin Joseph Henshaw (1727–1794) in 1758. They were childless.
Museum of Fine Arts, Boston, Otis Norcross Fund, 41.815.

This is believed to be the frame on Faith's embroidery in Figure 56.

On June 29, 1761, Faith Trumbull was again in Boston and assured her parents that she was "very well contented with my Situation at Mr. Lovells . . . I am treated with the greatest pleasantness and generosity. . . . I Believe I shall not get ready to go to School till next week & then I must be as diligent as a bee." She expressed her eagerness to "see any Body that comes from Connectticut" and signed her name "Faith Trumble Junr."[7] Where Faith studied in Boston in 1761 and how long she stayed there are now unknown. She was then eighteen, and during this sojourn in Boston she is believed to have worked the chimney piece in Figure 57.

It is unlikely that Elizabeth Murray was still teaching at this time, since in 1760 she married her second husband, James Smith, a wealthy Boston distiller twice her age. She probably would have recommended Jannette Day's school, although Mrs. Lovell may also have been influential in the choice of Faith's teachers. Faith

---

7. Ibid.

was evidently boarding with John Lovell, master of the South Grammar School, and his wife, Ann Dudley Lovell.[8] In any case, Faith must have returned home with her elegant chimney piece unframed, for when writing to his son, Joseph, in London, on May 28, 1764, Jonathan Trumbull reminded him that "Your sister sent by you for Frame & Glass to her Picture 4 feet 4 Inches in length & 1 foot 7 Inches in Width."[9] These dimensions match the size of the frame on Faith's embroidery (Fig. 57).

The history of the origin of the three embroideries here attributed to Faith Trumbull became confused between 1950 and 1975. In 1950, two of Faith's embroideries (Figs. 52, 57) were mistakenly attributed to her mother, Faith Robinson Trumbull (1718–1780), and to her niece, Faith Trumbull (b.1769), the daughter of her brother, the second Governor Jonathan Trumbull. Her chimney piece in Figure 56 then belonged to descendants of her sister, Mary Trumbull Williams, and descended through Mary's daughter, Faith Williams McClellan (1775–1838), to George E. McClellan (b.1869), whose family correctly attributed it to its true maker.[10] However, when this piece was acquired by the Connecticut Historical Society in 1974, it was erroneously attributed to Mary Trumbull because it had descended in her family. The Trumbull house in Lebanon is still standing and these embroideries must have been impressive decorations over the

Fig. 56. Chimney piece by Faith Trumbull, Boston, 1754. Silk, mica, and paint on blue silk; 20¼″ x 51″; frame attributed to David Mason. Nancy Graves Cabot found the print sources for the figures in this composition, Figure 57, and another embroidery by Faith Trumbull, c.1754 (*ANTIQUES*, December 1950, 476–8). Faith is believed to have worked this embroidery while attending Elizabeth Murray's school during the fall of 1754 when she was eleven years old.
The Connecticut Historical Society, 1974-99-0.

8. Schoolmaster John Lovell (1710–1778) was a Loyalist and died in Halifax, Nova Scotia; his wife died in 1775. It is unlikely that Faith boarded with their son James Lovell (1737–1814) and his new wife, Mary Middleton (c.1736–1817), although James attended Harvard with her brother, Joseph. James Lovell was an ardent patriot. *Sibley's Harvard Graduates, 1726–1730* (1951), 8:441–6, and *1756–1760* (1968), 14:31–48.
9. Trumbull Papers, CHS.
10. *ANTIQUES*, December 1950, 476–9. Faith's other chimney piece (Fig. 57) descended in the Huntington family and went to the CHS in 1925.

Fig. 57. Chimney piece by
Faith Trumbull, Boston,
c.1761–1763. Silk and paint
on black silk; 18¼″ x 51¼″.
The ground is completely
embroidered except for the
birdcatcher's hat, pants, and
shoes. The frame is believed
to have been purchased in
London by Faith's brother,
Joseph, in 1764. It has been
refinished. The same milk-
maid (from Cornelis Viss-
cher's engraving after
Nicolaes Berghem) appears
on both of Faith's chimney
pieces, and suggests that
they were drawn by the
same professional pattern
drawer, possibly David
Mason. Another Boston
chimney piece entirely
embroidered over black silk
is dated 1766 (Fairbanks et
al., *Paul Revere's Boston*
[1975], 83).
*The Connecticut Historical
Society, 1925-1-3.*

fireplaces in the relatively small principal parlors. They probably remained there during the lifetime of Jonathan Trumbull, who reared Faith's only child, Jabez Huntington, after his mother's tragic death.[11]

The likelihood of Faith Trumbull's attendance at Jannette Day's school in 1761 is supported by the fact that Mrs. Day was teaching Sally Derby in 1763. Sally also worked an impressive chimney piece on black silk (Fig. 58).[12] On October 31, 1763, Jannette Day wrote a receipt to Captain Richard Darby [sic] for £72-18. This included "Miss Sallys Board 10 weeks at £5 per week"; also for "128 skens shade silk . . . 22-8" and 10 shillings for "Making a Hatt."[13] While no later bills for Sally's tuition have been found, it is likely that she continued to study with Mrs. Day, at least intermittently, until she was eighteen or nineteen years old. Her silk-embroidered chimney piece was probably framed by Salem's Samuel Blythe, Junior, since on May 18, 1767, he billed Captain Richard Derby for "Framing & Gilding Sallys Picture £14-0-0."[14]

Sally Derby is also credited with a canvas-work chimney piece framed in the manner of Eunice Bourne's (Fig. 40), and said to have been worked by a Miss Derby in 1765.[15] That embroidery can be traced to the Derby family,[16] and if

---

11. Faith became depressed after witnessing the Battle of Bunker Hill, and despite every effort of her concerned family and doctors, she hung herself. The British seized on this tragedy for propaganda and described her suicide as a martyr's protest against her family's support of the Revolution. *Sibley's Harvard Graduates, 1761–1763* (1970), 15:410.

12. Gertrude Townsend, Curator of Textiles, MFA, noticed similarities in the Trumbull and Derby silk embroideries (Gertrude Townsend to Charles F. Montgomery, February 6, 1950, in Winterthur acc. file 57.1030).

13. Derby Family Papers (Mss37/B15/F4), EI. See the receipt in the back endpapers.

14. Ibid. (Mss37/B16/F1), EI.

15. *ANTIQUES*, August 1923, 73, Fig. 7; with date, dimensions, and former owner in *Old-Time New England, Bulletin of SPNEA* (July 1920): inside back cover.

16. Elias Hasket Derby (b.1739) to Ezekiel Hersey Derby (b.1772), to his wife's niece and adopted daugh-

worked in 1765, Sally was the only Derby daughter young enough to have made it. However, the source of the date is unknown, and it may have been worked by one of her sisters, Mary (b.1737) or Martha (b.1744).

No canvas work can be assigned with certainty to Jannette Day's school, but on September 2, 1761, she charged Samuel Phillips Savage £53-9 for various materials, "Drawing 7 Chairs," and "3 months Schooling."[17] Jannette Day probably perfected her teaching skills under the direction of her benefactress, Elizabeth Murray. She was a destitute unwed mother when Elizabeth Murray (then Campbell) helped her to open a school, become self-supporting, and regain her self-respect.[18] Jannette (also Jean or Jane) Day advertised her school in *The Boston-Gazette, and Country Journal* of May 23, 1757, and in Boston and Newport papers in the spring of 1759.[19] During the 1760s, she was teaching the daughters of prestigious New Englanders, but she returned to her native Scotland in the spring of 1768, where she married a Mr. Barclay. He died before May 1770 and Jannette Day Barclay died about 1771.[20]

---

ter, Mrs. Hepsibah Jones Fitch Hall (b.1790), to her step-son and nephew Dudley Cotton Hall (b.1818), to his daughter Mrs. Grace Mary Hall Wainwright (b.1859), to the collector Dwight M. Prouty, to Wanamaker's Antiques, to Miss Clara Fichter of Ambler, Pennsylvania, in 1921. Said to be destroyed (Nancy Graves Cabot to Dean A. Fales, Jr., August 6, 1959, in Winterthur acc. file 57.1030). Family descent determined by genealogist Gary Boyd Roberts.

17. Manuscripts, MHS. Charges must have been for his daughter Faith Savage (1744–1769).
18. Norton, *Liberty's Daughters* (1980), 54–5, 150.
19. *The Boston Evening-Post*, April 30, 1759, and *Newport Mercury*, May 8, 1759.
20. J. M. Robbins Papers, MHS.

Fig. 58. Chimney piece by Sarah Derby, Boston, c.1763–1766. Silk and paint on black silk; 18⅜" x 54"; original frame with original glass in center panel. As in the Trumbull embroidery (Fig. 57), the black silk is intentionally visible in several places. In 1959, Nancy Graves Cabot discovered that this composition was derived from an etching by Jean Le Pautre (1617–1682), *Women Dancing in an Arcadian Landscape* (Oeuvres de Jean Le Pautre, Album I, 61, Prints Department, MFA, and Cabot Papers, Portfolio I, Textile Department, MFA). Sarah Derby (1747–1774), called Sally, was the youngest child of Richard Derby (1712–1783) and Mary Hodges (1713–1770) of Salem. She married Captain John Gardner and had three children. This embroidery descended to her great, great grandson, Benjamin P. Ellis. *Winterthur Museum, 57.1030.*

Fig. 59. The Wyllys hatchment, 1720. Oil on panel with applied frame; 24″ square. Inscribed on the back "For Hezki[ah] Wyllys Esqr/ in Hartford/ 1720." The Wyllys family of Connecticut could rightfully bear these arms. George Wyllys was Secretary of the Colony from 1642 until 1645 and his grandson Hezekiah Wyllys (1672–1741) held this office between 1712 and 1734. The hatchment was sent to Hezekiah Wyllys from New York with the following comments from Samuel Belknap: "S[r] I have sent you y[r] Coate of Armes which if you please to Except shall be my satisfaction, indeed it unhappely fell out that I did not lite on so Good a work man as wisht I had done which was because my not being aquanted, for I had it drawn as sone as Ever I Receaved y[r] plate . . . New Yorke July 26 1720."
The Connecticut Historical Society, 1972-7-0.

EMBROIDERED   COATS   OF   ARMS

Boston's embroidered coats of arms are the most unique, personal, and richly worked evidence of schoolgirl skill to survive in large numbers from eighteenth-century America—and they are the most misunderstood embroideries collected today. They have been mistaken for hatchments throughout most of the twentieth century,[1] although there is no evidence that they were ever associated with mourning rituals in the long-established European tradition of painted hatchments. The majority of embroidered arms, like pastoral embroideries in canvas work, were created as elegant and prestigious domestic decorations by young girls who were finishing their education in Boston. The confusion concerning their purpose no doubt arose because coats of arms were often, although not exclusively, worked in the traditional hatchment shape, and after 1750, silk on black silk became the most popular materials for arms embroidery in Boston. The word "hatchment" (derived from achievement) properly applies to a coat of arms painted diagonally against a black background on a square panel and hung from one corner (Fig. 59).[2] As a symbol of mourning, it was customarily placed above

---

1. This error has persisted despite the protests of heraldic authorities such as Howard Millar Chapin (1887–1940), Harold Bowditch (1883–1964), and currently, Henry L. P. Beckwith.

2. Hatchments are generally described as being in lozenge shape (four equal sides with two obtuse angles). However, surviving American hatchments and embroidered arms in hatchment shape are usually square.

Fig. 60. *A Prospective View of part of the Commons*, engraved by Sidney L. S. Smith after a watercolor by Christian Remick dated October 1768; 11″ x 15¾″. Published by Charles Goodspeed, Boston, 1902. Behind the encampment of the 29th Regiment is the Thomas Hancock house with a hatchment hanging between the center dormer window and the second story. Remick presumably painted the house as he saw it in 1768, and the hatchment evidently remained there from the time of Thomas Hancock's death in 1764. *Concord Museum, Concord, Massachusetts.*

the entrance to the home of the deceased and later moved to the family's house of worship. Although hatchments were used in New England during the seventeenth and eighteenth centuries (Fig. 60),[3] they were generally referred to as "escutcheons" or "coats of arms" and the contemporary use of the word "hatchment" by New Englanders was uncommon.

America's earliest embroidered arms, as well as decorative painted ones, appear to date from the 1740s (Figs. 63–68),[4] but armorial insignia were not eschewed by the Puritans of earlier days, and men of substance displayed their coats of arms as status symbols without hesitation. When discussing hatchments in *ANTIQUES*, October 1929, Howard M. Chapin candidly explained the attitudes of the first Englishmen who migrated to America:

> Brought up in the environment of Stuart England, with no conception of that unattainable (and, indeed, perhaps undesirable) social equality, which the hypocrisy of our present phase of civilization seeks to glorify, our early settlers not only recognized but emphasized the inequalities inherent in the political, religious, and social life of humankind.

---

3. At least forty hatchments were used in the Boston area before 1725. (Donald R. Friary, *The Use of Heraldry as a Status Symbol in Colonial Boston* [manuscript, Historic Deerfield, Inc., 1963], 3, 15.)

4. Thomas Johnston (or Johnson) painted the earliest documented New England arms on paper (12″ square) in or before 1740 and signed it "T Johnson fecit" (*ANTIQUES*, April 1992, 626).

Fig. 61. Filigree arms of Foster initialed *L H* and dated *1737*. Red, gold, and green rolled paper work, with gold leaf, mounted against mica on a greenish-blue paper liner within an ebonized shadow box frame; 14″ square. Inscribed on the back "Worked by Lydia Hutchinson who died at 25 sister of Elizabeth . . . Rev Nathan Robins of Milton." Lydia Hutchinson (1722/23–1748) was eleventh among the thirteen children born in Boston to Edward Hutchinson (1678–1752) and Lydia Foster (1686–1748), and the third named Lydia. She made this coat of arms at the age of fourteen. Of her twelve siblings, three survived her, but only the youngest, Elizabeth, wife of Reverend Nathan Robins, had issue. Lydia was the first cousin of Governor Thomas Hutchinson.
Museum of Fine Arts, Boston, gift of Miss Lois Lilly Howe, 57.714.

Despite the stated ideals of their Puritan lifestyle, and the sumptuary laws that sought to enforce them, studies of recent years have clearly revealed the extravagant tastes of successful New Englanders during the seventeenth century. By the early eighteenth century, a rising merchant aristocracy was willingly served by craftsmen who could decorate silver, bookplates, coaches, hatchments, and tombstones with their coats of arms, or supply them with appropriate designs if theirs were lacking.

By 1730 heraldic painters had access to a number of publications that illustrated coats of arms, and they could provide the schoolmistress with a pattern for a girl's family arms just as they did the silversmith or the stone cutter. Notable among these men in Boston was Thomas Johnston (1708–1767), whose painted arms of 1740 and 1744 (Fig. 63) are among the few surviving examples in hatchment shape and with a full mantling as found in the embroideries, for the majority of decorative painted arms are vertical rectangles. He also left a rare and informative reference to a hatchment. Johnston's bill to "The Estate of the Honble Anthony Stoddard Esqr" included the following charges for "Feb^{ry} 10 1747/48":

To Sundries for his Wifes Funeral &	
To a Hatchment for the House	£36
To inside and outside frames for ditto	5
To iron doggs for and putting up ditto	2
To painting Ten Silk Escutcheons at 100/p^r Agreement,	
Mr Stod.	50
To 2 Yards of Taffety at 72/	7 – 4
Cr By an Old Hatchment frame	5[5]

---

5. Thomas Greenough Papers, MHS.

The reference to "inside and outside frames" for a hatchment may explain how arms painted on canvas could have served as hatchments, a possibility that has been debated.[6]

The fashion for embroidered arms was preceded by one for coats of arms in filigree, some of which were in hatchment shape (Fig. 61).[7] Although instruction in "filigrew" was first advertised in 1714,[8] Boston's golden age of filigree (or quill-work) as a schoolgirl accomplishment was between 1720 and 1740, and sconces are the most familiar surviving form. It is likely that Susanna Condy was involved in the teaching of this craft in the 1720s and 1730s, since her daughter Elizabeth (b.1710) was later noted for her exceptional skill in the art of filigree.[9] Although coats of arms in filigree were popular in England during the late seventeenth and early eighteenth centuries, there appear to be no prototypes for New England's heraldic embroidery of either the eighteenth or the early nineteenth centuries, and there is no evidence that it was popular elsewhere in colonial or Federal America.

Who initiated this enduring fashion in Boston remains unknown. No schoolmistress of the 1740s advertised instruction in working coats of arms. The small, silk-worked Southworth coat of arms is probably among the earliest examples (Fig. 64).[10] Also, the format found in Figure 62 may reflect the earliest experimentation with arms embroidered for domestic decoration, but at present only two examples are known and their exact dates of execution are uncertain. The earliest dated example of 1740 is canvas work in hatchment shape (Fig. 65), and it appears to have been copied from a vertical painting since the corners are filled with flowers unrelated to the mantling. It includes the name of the maker and her father, as do Katharine Greene's (Fig. 66) and Mary Ellery's embroideries, both dated 1745 (Figs. 66, 305). Because Susanna Condy unquestionably instructed Katharine Greene, this unusual combination of names suggests that she also taught Rachel Leonard in 1740, and possibly drew the patterns for the arms of 1745. Their basic shapes for framing the shield, their motto ribbons, and their mantling were more gracefully interpreted by 1750, and thereafter this became the dominant style for Boston's heraldic needlework (Figs. 69–73). If not the first

---

6. Nora M. Davis, "Colonial Hatchments in America," *Year Book, City of Charleston, S.C.* (Charleston, 1946), 183.

7. The hatchment-shaped filigree arms of the Dering family of Boston, dated 1731, is here attributed to Elizabeth (b.1715) or Mary (b.1717), daughters of Henry Dering (b.1684) and Elizabeth (Illustrated in *Bulletin of the MMA* 33 [December 1938]: 267). Probably the earliest-documented American arms in filigree is a vertical rectangle of the Appleton arms. It was made c.1719–1720 by Margaret Appleton (1701/2–1740), daughter of John Appleton (1652–1739) and Elizabeth Rogers (1663–1754) of Ipswich. In 1725 she became the second wife of the Reverend Edward Holyoke (1689–1769), president of Harvard, 1737–1769 (EI). A sconce of filigree and wax includes the arms of Emerson, dated 1737 (MFA; *ANTIQUES*, December 1960, 564–5.)

8. School in the house of James Ivers (*Boston News-Letter*, April 12, 1714).

9. John Russell Bartlett, *Genealogy of the Russell Family* (Providence, 1879), 22.

10. The long-held belief that the Southworth coat of arms was a "crest" listed in the 1657 inventory of Governor William Bradford was dispelled in 1943 (McClure Meredith Howland, "A Report on Research into the English Background of the Southworth Family of Plymouth Colony," *NEHGR* 97 [1943]: 359). Bowditch also attributed the Southworth arms pattern to Johnston, and considered Lucy Howland (1726–1803) a likely embroiderer (*NEHGR* 109 [1955]: 314).

Fig. 62. The arms of Foxcroft and Coney, c.1740–1760. Silk, highly raised gold and silver metallic threads, and paint on silk; 31½″ x 28½″. This exceptionally large and impressive embroidery may represent an obscure practice of placing husbands' and wives' arms on a horizontally divided shield. The only stylistic counterpart for its needlework is found in the arms of Salter and Bryan made by Mary Salter (1726–1755) and illustrated in Earle, *Home Life in Colonial Days* (1898), opp. 266. Its size and present location are unknown. This embroidery descended in the family of Phebe Foxcroft (1743–1812), the youngest daughter of Francis Foxcroft (1694–1768) and Mehitable Coney (1703–1782) of Cambridge. In 1768 it was the "Worked Picture Coat of Arms" that hung in "the best Room" of the Foxcroft home, and "a Picture of the Coat of Arms on Parchment" was upstairs in "the Green Chamber" (Inventory of Francis Foxcroft, Middlesex County Probate 8408). Phebe married Samuel Phillips (1752–1802), the founder of Phillips Academy. Phebe may have worked the arms, but considering its similarity to the Salter arms, it was probably worked by one of her sisters, Mehitable (1723–1770) or Elizabeth (1725/6–1757), who were closer contemporaries of Mary Salter.
Addison Gallery of American Art, Phillips Academy, Andover, Massachusetts, gift of Mr. C. Lloyd Thomas, 1962.6.

Fig. 63. *BY THE NAME OF BARTON* inscribed on the motto ribbon, c.1744. Oil on canvas; 32½" x 32¼". Attributed to Thomas Johnston (or Johnson) of Boston. This painting and an earlier watercolor arms by Johnston indicate that the Southworth arms (Fig. 64) was derived from a Johnston painting or pattern, as was the canvas-work Cross arms at the Historical Society of Old Newbury; also, the canvas-work Chandler arms by Katherine Chandler (1735–1791) at the MFA.
Essex Institute, 125,000.

Fig. 64. The Southworth arms with the name inscribed on the motto ribbon, c.1740. Silk tent stitch on linen with the ground worked in pale yellowish green; approx. 12" square. (See footnote 10.) It is most likely that this coat of arms was worked by Lucy Howland Hammatt (1726–1803), from whom it descended to the last known owner. Lucy was the daughter of Consider Howland (1700–1775) and Ruth Bryant (1709–1775) of Plymouth. Her father was the grandson of Joseph Howland (1639–1736) and Elizabeth Southworth (1645–1717). Working arms of a great grandparent seems unusual, but Lucy may have worked Howland and Bryant arms as well; or the Southworth arms may have been the only family arms with a proper image available to copy.
Location unknown; photograph courtesy of The Magazine ANTIQUES.

Fig. 65. *RACHEL•LEONARD/ AGED:13:1740./*
GEORGE•LEONARD/ AGED 42 worked on the motto ribbon
beneath unidentified arms, although traditionally known as
Leonard. Wool on canvas; 11½″ square; original frame with
later paint. Rachel worked the earliest signed and dated coat
of arms as well as the earliest signed and dated Dresden work
now known to have been made in America (Fig. 368). The
Leonards were large landowners in Norton, Massachusetts,
and lived much like the English nobility. Rachel Leonard

(1727–1805) was the daughter of George Leonard
(1698–1778) and Rachel Clapp (1701–1783). She married the
Reverend David Barns (1732–1811) of Scituate in 1756, and
they had three children. One of their daughters, either Rachel
(b.1757) or Ann (b.1765), is believed to have worked the
accurate rendition of the Leonard arms in the Gore pattern
(*ANTIQUES*, January 1992, 105).
Private collection.

Fig. 66. *RUF^S GREENE/ KATH GREENE/ 1745* worked on the ribbon beneath the shield, and inscribed on the back "the work of Mrs. Catharine Amory daughter of Mr. Rufus Greene done at the age of 14, 1745." Silk, wool, and beads (for the stags' eyes) on linen; 19⅜" x 18⅛". Katharine Greene (1731–1777) was the daughter of Boston silversmith Rufus Greene (1707–1777) and Katharine Stanbridge (1709–1768). She worked the earliest coat of arms that can be attributed to a specific school. Her father's account book reveals that she was instructed by Susanna Condy in 1744 and 1745, and this was evidently one of her "13 pictures" framed by English-born cabinetmaker and merchant William Price (1684–1771) in the fall of 1745. Katharine married John Amory (1728–1805) on January 16, 1751, and they had nine children. Amory was a Loyalist and in May of 1775, Katharine bid farewell to her children and sailed for England on the *Minerva* out of Marblehead. She died in England. Her husband was permitted to return in 1784.

M. and M. Karolik Collection, Museum of Fine Arts, Boston, 39.243.

Fig. 67. Katharine Greene Amory by John Singleton Copley (1738–1815), c.1764. Oil on canvas; 49½" x 40". M. and M. Karolik Collection, Museum of Fine Arts, Boston, 37.36.

Fig. 68. The arms of Henshaw and Bill. Inscribed on the back "wrought by Sarah Henshaw in the year 1748." Silk, metallic threads, appliquéd wool, spangles, and ink on silk; approx. 18″ square. Sarah's work is now the earliest-dated Boston arms worked on silk, and on a cream color in harmony with canvas-work arms of the 1740s, which usually have solidly worked colored grounds rather than black. See her silk embroidery and portrait, Figures 54 and 55.
Collection of Judith and John Herdeg.

to teach arms embroidery in Boston, Susanna Condy was surely in the vanguard of a trend that would escalate dramatically after her death.

Sarah Henshaw's embroidery of 1748 (Fig. 68) is now the earliest-known coat of arms on silk in hatchment shape. In the early 1750s, arms worked on black silk with elegant metallic embellishments became the overwhelmingly popular style for arms embroidery (Fig. 69), and arms in canvas work made after the 1750s are uncommon.

In addition to Susanna Condy, six teachers are known to have taught arms embroidery in Boston, and there were no doubt many others. The first advertisement for armorial embroidery was placed in *The Boston Evening-Post* of April 7, 1755, by "ELEANOR PURCELL, in Milk-Street," who described "Pictures and Coats of Arms embroidered on Satten" as well as "Coats of Arms, and all Sorts of Flowers in Shell-Work." In 1757, Jannette Day also advertised instruction in "Coats of Arms,"[11] and she was still teaching a decade later when fifteen-year-old Ann Grant left East Windsor Hill, Connecticut, to study in Boston. Ann had already attended Mrs. Mary Langwell's boarding school in Hartford, and her bill reveals that she studied "ye art of wax work."[12] Although Jannette Day offered boarding, Ann was "placed in a family" and in the usual manner of Boston boarders, she attended more than one school. Ann was noted for diligence, and she is said to have had "her embroidery sent home at night that she might work before the writing school in the morning."[13] That work is now unknown, although a bill of September 28, 1767, headed "Miss Grant to Jannette Day," reveals that she owed £41 for three months schooling and a variety of costly materials for needlework.[14]

Ann Grant evidently worked her coat of arms (Fig. 70) under the instruction of the Misses Cuming, who took over Jannette Day's school upon her departure for England. This transition was announced in *The Massachusetts Gazette And Boston News-Letter* of April 15, 1768:

Mrs. DAY'S School
For young Ladies being discontinued,
A School on the same Plan will be opened on the first Monday in *May*, by
Ame and Elizabeth Cuming,
at their House opposite to the Old Brick Meeting, where Embroidery, all sorts of coloured Work and Dresden will be taught, and the Materials furnished. Young Ladies may be also boarded with them.

---

11. *The Boston-Gazette, and Country Journal*, May 16, 1757.
12. France H. Judd, "Ebenezer Grant Mansion" (typescript, CHS), 38. See Ann's home in *The Great River* (1985), 84, 85.
13. Ibid.
14. Henry R. Stiles, *The History and Genealogies of Ancient Windsor* (Hartford: Lockwood & Brainard Co., 1892), 2:311.

Fig. 69. Pickering arms inscribed on the motto ribbon *PICKERING 1758*. Silk and silver metallic threads on silk; 18″ x 18″. Attributed to Elizabeth Pickering whose work is the earliest-known dated instance of Boston's dominant arms pattern on silk. It was used in 1750 for the canvas-work Quincy/Sturgis arms (*ANTIQUES*, April 1992, 622) and in 1796 by Sarah Peirce on cream-colored silk (EI). Each of the eight earliest examples among sixty pieces with this pattern have flowers on the sides of the shield where the majority have leafy scrolls (Figs. 70–73). An exception is the Fowle arms, believed to be c.1783. See the incompletely worked pattern drawn with white on black silk for Jerusha Pitkin (1736–1800) in *The Great River* (1985), 405. Elizabeth Pickering (1737–1823) was the daughter of Timothy Pickering (1703–1778) and Mary Wingate (1708–1784) of Salem. She married John Gardner (1731–1805). Elizabeth's sister Mary worked the chimney piece in Figure 44 and her sister Sarah's canvas-work Pickering arms is signed and dated 1753 (Fig. 306).

Private collection.

Like Jannette Day, the Misses Cuming were befriended by Elizabeth Murray (Fig. 53). About 1764, she financed the opening of a small shop for these orphaned sisters, and she no doubt advised them when they assumed the school of her protégé.[15] The Cuming sisters advertised instruction in "coats of arms" in April of 1769,[16] and their bill of the following September reveals that Ann must have worked the Grant arms while boarding with them for a period of seventeen weeks. Among the variety of goods she purchased during this sojourn were "Black satin for a Skreen 8/8" and "Black satin for Cot of Arms 7s 4d."[17] Ann's return to East Windsor was no doubt timely, for pre-revolutionary violence was mounting in Boston. Young Betsy Cuming witnessed an alarming skirmish the month of Ann's departure, and shortly thereafter, she and her sister were harassed for selling imported goods. When the British army left Boston in 1776, the Cuming sisters moved to Nova Scotia.[18]

Nearly a contemporary of the Cuming sisters was schoolmistress Sarah Hill Oliver, who was the last Boston teacher to mention armorial embroidery in an advertisement. Sarah became the second wife of schoolmaster Nathaniel Oliver (1713–1769) in 1763 and taught with him until his death.[19] Thereafter she advertised her school in greater detail, and in the spring of 1774, she informed "the young Ladies both in Town & Country, That she still continues teaching Embroidery, Queen, Tenth and Irish Stitching, Coats of Arms, Marking and plain Sewing."[20] Sarah probably taught throughout the 1770s. She died in 1784.

Twenty-five years after Elizabeth Pickering completed the Pickering arms (Fig. 69), Elizabeth Cutts worked her coat of arms in essentially the same design (Fig. 71), and before commencing it, she sought advice from her father about the proper arms for her family. She wrote from Boston on April 22, 1783:

> Hon[rd] Papa,
>
>   I have been to get the Coat Arms prepared for working, and Mr. Gore shewed me two Arms by the name Cutts, the one belonging to a Family from London, and the other from Chelsey, both Arms different; and Papa as you chuse I should work your Arms I should be fond of making no mistake & of working the right, if your business permitted your letting me know by name the right one, it would be sufficient, without further trouble, as my utmost abilities shall be exerted to please Mama & yourself sir in the working.[21]

---

15. Mary Beth Norton, *Liberty's Daughters* (1980), 150.

16. *The Boston-Gazette, and Country Journal*, April 24, 1769; see front endpapers.

17. September 28, 1769. Judd, "Ebenezer Grant Mansion," 38.

18. Norton, *Liberty's Daughters*, 157.

19. *Sibley's Harvard Graduates, 1731–1735* (1956), 9:314–8.

20. *The Boston-Gazette, and Country Journal*, April 11, 1774. Portsmouth widow Sarah Winkley and her daughter Elizabeth Hill are the only teachers known to have advertised instruction in coats-of-arms embroidery outside of Boston (*The New-Hampshire Gazette*, Portsmouth, May 24, 1774).

21. George Addison Emery, *Colonel Thomas Cutts* (Saco, Me., 1917), 15. This letter was the first clue to the origin of Boston's dominant pattern for embroidered arms. It was discussed and first published in Sprague, *Agreeable Situations* (1987), 240.

Fig. 70. The Grant arms worked by Ann Grant at the Misses Cuming's school in 1769. Silk with gold and silver metals and metallic threads on silk; 21″ square. Ann was probably the classmate of Mary Cheever, whose similar piece is signed *MC 1769* (SPNEA). Ann Grant (1748–1838) was the daughter of Ebenezer Grant (1706–1797) and Ann Ellsworth (1712–1783). Her father was one of the leading citizens of East Windsor, Connecticut. Ann, known as Miss Nancy, was a pretty, vivacious girl with sparkling black eyes. In 1775 she married the Reverend John Marsh (1742–1821), pastor of the First Church of Wethersfield (Fig. 261). They had seven children, six of whom lived until their eightieth birthday or longer.

Historic Deerfield, Inc., 1391.

Fig. 71. Milward arms by Elizabeth Cutts, who worked *THE/ NAME OF/ CUTTS* on the motto ribbon, 1783. Silk, metallic threads, and spangles on silk; 20″ x 20″. Heraldic painter Samuel Gore supplied Elizabeth's pattern and she unknowingly worked the Milward arms rather than the arms of Cutts. She was instructed by Eleanor Druitt, as was her sister Sarah (1774–1845) in 1792. Sarah's unidentified arms are inscribed *THE/ NAME/ SCAMMAN* (private collection). Both arms have the same distinctive helmet and lettering and they were framed alike. Elizabeth Cutts (1766–1810) was third among the eight children of Thomas Cutts (1736–1821) and Elizabeth Scamman (1745–1803). Her father was the most prominent citizen of Saco, Maine. Elizabeth married Richard Foxwell Cutts (1757–1830) in 1785. They lived in Berwick, Maine, and had ten children. For the Dover, New Hampshire, sampler of her daughter, Elizabeth Cutts (1787–1882), see Krueger, *Gallery*, Fig. 43.
York Institute, Saco, Maine, gift of George Addison Emery, 0000.23.

Elizabeth had consulted Samuel Gore (1750/51–1831) at the "Sign of the Painter's Arms" in Queen Street where his father, John Gore (1718–1796), kept a color shop for many years. Both father and son were heraldic painters, and John was noted for designing coats of arms for the New England gentry. However, as a Loyalist, he left Boston in 1776 and was not permitted to return until 1785.[22] Samuel Gore probably showed Elizabeth Cutts "the two Books of Heraldry the old manuscript and Guillium [sic]," which John Gore had taken with him in 1776 and sent back to Boston in 1779.[23] Despite her query, Elizabeth did not copy the Cutts arms but worked the Milward arms, which appears on the same page as the Cutts arms in John Guillim's *A Display of Heraldry*.[24]

Assuming that Samuel Gore provided Elizabeth's complete pattern, the dominant design for Boston coats of arms is now explained. The Gores probably had stencils for their standard shield and its surrounding design and needed only to

22. Charles A. Hammond and Stephen A. Wilbur, *Gay and Graceful Style, A Catalogue of Objects Associated with Christopher and Rebecca Gore* (Waltham, Mass.: Gore Place Society, 1982).

23. John Gore, London, to Dear Child (evidently Samuel in Boston), September 15, 1779. *John Gore's Letter Book, November 20, 1773–July 22, 1780* (manuscript, Bostonian Society). The "old manuscript" was probably William Smith's *PROMPTVARIVM ARMORVM* (compiled 1602–1616) and containing 4,500 painted "Coates and Creasts." This may have been where Elizabeth Cutts saw Cutts arms from London and Chelsey, for only one arms for Cutts appears in Guillim, and the image was later confused with the illustration of the Milward arms.

24. John Guillim, *A Display of Heraldry*, 6th ed. (London: printed by T. W. for R. and J. Bonwicke and R. Wilkin and J. Walthoe and Tho. Ward, 1724), 356.

Fig. 72. The arms of *Babcock and Howe* with an old paper label inscribed "Wrought by Hannah Babcock at/ Mrs Snows school, Pemberton Hill,/ Boston, 1785." Silk on silk; 20⅝" x 20⅝". Hannah's embroidery emerged in 1983 and called attention to Deborah Snow's previously unrecognized school. Hannah Babcock (1770–1856) was eldest of the eleven children of Joseph Babcock (1746–1813) and Hannah Howe (d. 1794) of Milton, Massachusetts. In April of 1794 she was married in Boston to Samuel Fiske (1769–1842) of Waltham, and they later moved to Claremont, New Hampshire. Fiske was a brother of William Fiske (b. 1770), the Boston cabinet-maker, and should not be confused with Samuel Fiske (1764–1834), a lawyer (Harvard, 1793), who also lived in Claremont.

The Bayou Bend Collection, Museum of Fine Arts, Houston, B.84.7.

add the crest and the proper emblazonment within the shield. The Gores would have been capable of supplying such a pattern for fully half a century.

There is convincing evidence that Elizabeth Cutts worked her coat of arms at Eleanor Druitt's school. Although her only surviving letter from Boston does not mention her teacher, her sisters were taught by Mrs. Druitt between 1779 and 1798.[25] Arms by Elizabeth and Sarah Cutts reveal that Eleanor Druitt favored very highly raised work in brilliant gold and silver, but most distinctive are their motto ribbons. Often edged with minute spangles, they are solidly worked from side to side in fine metallic threads (usually silver) with inscriptions stitched over them in tiny, upright black silk cross-stitches. Also, these pieces generally have helmets with worked gorgets and visors but unworked crowns, which are delimited by the mantling.[26]

Eleanor Druitt announced the opening of her school near the Quaker Meeting House in *The Massachusetts Gazette and The Boston Weekly News-Letter* of October 17, 1771, and in 1773 and 1774 John and Eleanor Druitt ran lengthy advertisements to describe their school in Hanover Street.[27] Before 1789 they moved to Court

---

25. Letters reveal that Mary (1763–1796) and Sarah (1774–1845) attended Eleanor Druitt's school in 1779 and 1792, and there is an undated bill for Eunice Cutts (1782–1853) (Emery, *Cutts*, 15–16).

26. Now attributed to the Druitt School are the arms of Fisk and of Peirce (EI), Lloyd (Historic Deerfield, Inc.), and Heard (Ipswich Historical Society).

27. Seybolt, *The Private Schools of Colonial Boston* (1935), 72–3. Mrs. Druitt also proposed opening a boarding school in Portsmouth, and her advertisement reveals that she came from abroad (*The New-Hampshire*

Street and Eleanor continued teaching there after John's death on December 29, 1790. Directories listed her boarding school through 1798. On January 13, 1800, Eliza Kneeland wrote from Boston to her former classmate Eunice Cutts with the news that "Mrs. Druitt has resigned school keeping, and I hear is going to be married, but fancy it is only a report."[28] This was perhaps a premature rumor, but an Eleanor Druitt was married to Michael Collins by the Reverend Thomas Baldwin on August 19, 1802. Nothing more is known of this union, and "Eleanor Druitt" appeared as a "retailer No 26 Middle St" in the Boston directory of 1803. No record of her death has been found.

Schoolmistress Deborah Snow never advertised, but Hannah Babcock's coat of arms reveals that she was teaching elegant embroidery on Pemberton Hill in the 1780s (Fig. 72). Boston directories listed her "boarding school for Young ladies" on Green Street from 1796 through 1803, and she was probably boarding eight or ten girls in 1790 when the census recorded one boy and eleven females in her household. It must have been a crowded situation. The house she occupied was a two-story frame dwelling with 750 square feet on 4,850 square feet of land and was owned by Tuttle Hubbard.[29] Mrs. Snow may have been Deborah Cook of Eastham, Massachusetts, who was married there to Sylvanus Snow on November 11, 1761. She was possibly the Deborah Snow who died in Watertown, aged seventy-three, in September 1812.[30] At present, Hannah Babcock's arms, one small embroidered wreath,[31] and the directory listings are the only evidence of her teaching, which was probably continuous for at least eighteen years.

Many embroidered arms survive in extraordinarily handsome frames, but the arms of Williams and Bell (Fig. 73) have the most elaborate frame known on American needlework, and it may be the latest extant work of Boston carver John Welch.[32] Henry Howell Williams of Roxbury married Elizabeth Bell in 1762, and they lived sumptuously on Noddle's Island in Boston Harbor until 1793. A coat of arms "work'd on Satten with Silver & Gold thread" in a "Mahogy Gilt Frame" was hanging in the front hall of their mansion house in 1775 when it was among the property destroyed "in consequence of the landing of a detachment of the American army."[33] This was probably the girlhood work of Elizabeth Bell. Her daughter Martha's standard Boston pattern (Fig. 73) has interlaced silver in a style

Gazette, April 21, 1775). Cutts correspondence indicates that the Druitts taught in Newburyport in November 1779 (Emery, *Cutts*, 16). Patrons of their Boston school were merchant Isaac Smith in 1773 and General Henry Knox in 1784 (bills for tuition in the MHS); also, Rebecca Rice of Pownalborough, Maine, who was pleased with her school and mistress in 1797 (Isabel Erskine Brewster, *Recollections* [Concord, N.H.: Rumford Press, 1934], 63–6).

28. Cutts collection, No. X.468D.8, Item 10, manuscripts, Dyer Library, Saco, Maine.

29. *A Report of the Record Commissioners of the City of Boston containing the Statistics of the U.S. Direct Tax of 1798* (Boston: Rockwell and Churchill, 1890), 266.

30. *Columbian Centinel*, Boston, September 19, 1812.

31. *The Decorative Arts of New Hampshire* (1973), Fig. 142.

32. Luke Beckerdite, "Carving Practices in Eighteenth-Century Boston," *Old-Time New England, Bulletin of SPNEA* 72(1987): 123–62.

33. Williams' Declaration of Losses, March 10, 1787. Noddle's Island Papers, 1775–1814 (MHS). Williams was suspected of Loyalist leanings, and his house was burned.

Fig. 73. The arms of Williams and Bell, c.1784. Silk and metallic threads on silk and retaining the maker's needle; 18¼″ x 18¼″. Original gilded white pine frame with carving attributed to John Welch (1711–1789). This embroidery further attests to the Gores as the provider of this pattern because a record of arms painted by John Gore, and known as "The Gore Roll of Arms," appears to have been the only possible source for the Bell arms shown here. Attributed to Martha Williams (1768–1828), the second daughter of Henry Howell Williams (1736–1802) and Elizabeth Bell (d.1820). Martha married Daniel Sigourney (1769–1818) in 1798, and her coat of arms belonged to her great, great, great grandson in 1926.
Collection of Mr. and Mrs. George M. Kaufman.

common to several examples of the 1780s, but more often found on work of the 1760s (Fig. 70), and the school Martha attended remains unknown.

There is no evidence that these elegant status symbols were favored primarily by New England Tories during the Revolutionary period, for they were worked in about equal numbers by the daughters of American patriots as well as by the daughters of Loyalists. They were, however, unquestionably peculiar to the families of wealth and prominence and were probably the most costly embroideries undertaken by American schoolgirls.

Very few of the most prestigious New England families were actually entitled to bear arms, and embroidered arms seldom adhere to the rigid rules of heraldry. They rarely include mottos, and many have names incorrectly placed on their motto ribbons. The basic elements of their compositions, however, were usually derived from recognized heraldic sources, and complete fabrications were uncommon.

Although the working of arms in the hatchment shape was generally abandoned by 1800,[34] armorial embroidery continued to thrive in New England and was inspired by a new wealth of painted arms.[35] During the first decade of the nineteenth century, embroidered arms were worked in Salem, Gloucester, Newburyport, Providence, and Hartford. Occasionally they appear on samplers. Surprisingly, no Boston coats of arms characteristic of this period have been discovered.

---

34. Exceptions were made in Gloucester at Mrs. Judith Foster Saunders' school, c.1802 (*ANTIQUES*, August 1976, 302; Christie's, October 10, 1987, Lot 105).
35. According to Bowditch, "1790 to 1830 was the period of mass production of painted arms in Boston" ("Early Water-Color Paintings of New England Coats of Arms," 175).

Fig. 74. *millisent connor her work aged ten boston 1799.* Silk on linen; 16¼" x 21⅛". The normal perspective of Millisent's layered format was very much altered by her long green lane running upward. Her sampler belongs to a small Boston group that may be recognized by their distinctive clouds. See Eliza Whitman's 1796 sampler in Krueger, *Gallery,* 34; also *ANTIQUES,* January 1960, 93. *Metropolitan Museum of Art, gift of Edgar William and Bernice Chrysler Garbisch, 1974.42.*

Boston and Its Suburbs
in the Federal Period

A remarkable number of women advertised schools in Boston newspapers during the early nineteenth century; yet relatively few recognizable groups of samplers are known from Federal-period Boston, and rarely can they be assigned to specific schools. A small group with very consistent patterns names *Mrs. Dobel's school,*[1] and another appealing form can now be identified because Millisent Connor named *Boston* (Fig. 74). There are, however, two large and easily recognized groups of samplers from this region, although the originators of their styles are unknown. They appear with considerable variations, and the family tree form was worked at two or more schools in Boston or in nearby towns.

The earliest of these two types are attractive samplers usually in vertical form, with wide, deeply arcaded borders at the top and sides, and a saw-tooth border which encloses a center section that often includes one alphabet and a verse above

---

1. B&C, Pl. LXXXVI and Fairbanks et al., *Paul Revere's Boston* (1975), 174. Directories list Mary Doble, schoolmistress in 1796, and at 40 Middle Street, 1798–1822 (except 1800 and 1805). She advertised her exhibition at the North School House in the *Columbian Centinel,* August 28, 1811.

Fig. 75. *Anna Brown's Work Wrought in / the Thirteenth Year of her Age 1797.* Silk on linen; 22" x 18". At least eighteen similar versions of Anna's pattern are known, as well as variant examples. The majority of their makers lived in Middlesex County in the vicinity of Cambridge, West Cambridge (Arlington), Waltham, Lexington, and Concord. Probably they attended a boarding school. In 1795 Nabby Townsend of Waltham worked the closest counterpart to Anna's sampler, although on a wool ground (Baltimore Museum of Art, 1973.76.351). Sukey Foster named *Cambridge* on her work of 1803 (National Museum of American History, Washington, D.C., 1980.0849.01). Anna Brown (July 31, 1784–1843) was the youngest child of Amos Brown (1737–1812) and Anna Sanderson (1739–1823) of Waltham. In 1815 she married Amos Harrington (b.1780). Only one daughter survived her.
Collection of Mrs. Theodore H. Kapnek, Sr.

a variety of pictorial elements (Figs. 75, 76). A house is most common, but there may be figures, trees, flowerpots, or various combinations of motifs. Nevertheless, they can be easily recognized by their typical borders and similar workmanship. Many pieces are undated, and although earlier dates have been suggested, it now appears that this style emerged about 1790, was worked steadily until at least 1805, and occasionally occurred much later.[2]

Family records in the form of fruit-laden trees also appeared in this region during the 1790s and remained popular until about 1825. Similar compositions were being embroidered on silk, or painted on silk or paper by both schoolgirls and various ornamental artists.[3] A print probably inspired this version of a long-established genealogical concept (Fig. 77), but no example with the characteristic arrangement of interlocked hearts at the base of the tree has been found. The majority of embroidered family trees were worked by girls who lived in Middlesex County, and Figures 78 and 79 represent the most typical form. Related to the tree embroideries is a group of family record samplers featuring a similar heart arrangement (Fig. 80).[4]

---

2. In B&C, Pl. XXVII and Krueger, *New England,* Fig. 17, Betsy Adams' undated sampler is incorrectly given a date of 1773. See also Figures 16, 18, and 19. Possibly a forerunner of this form was worked by Ann McKay in 1784 (SPB Sale 3760, May 15, 1975, Lot 137). Hannah Child's related sampler is dated 1805. (*Witness to America's Past: Two Centuries of Collecting by the Massachusetts Historical Society* [Boston: MHS and MFA, 1991], Fig. 127.) Hannah W. Jackson's similar work names *Newton . . . 1827* (Jackson Homestead, Newton).
3. For an extensive study of these pieces, see Benes, *Families and Children* (1987), 91–145; also, Allen, *Family Record,* cover, 10–11, 44–5.
4. Benes lists all except the work of Catharine D. Gardiner, 1833 (private collection) and Julia Knox, 1837 (*MAD,* January 1992, 21-A). The Gardiner sampler was called to my attention by Mary Jaene Edmonds.

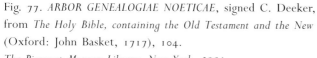

Fig. 76. *Hannah Cutters Work Wrought/ in the ninth Year of her Age*, c.1798. Silk on linen; 21⅝″ x 17″. Hannah's central pot of flowers is an image that occurs repeatedly on samplers within this group, as do the houses, the figures, and the border surrounding the signature. The girl was probably Hannah Cutter (1790–1842), the daughter of Ammi Cutter and Hannah of Cambridge. She married Thomas Gibson in 1808 and died in Ashby. It is also possible that she was the Hannah born on December 29, 1782, to Richard Cutter, Jr., and Meriam Brown of Cambridge, which would make the date of this sampler 1791. Its closest counterpart was worked by Dorcas Stearns, c.1792 (Krueger, *New England*, Fig. 18).
Cooper-Hewitt, National Museum of Design, Smithsonian Institution, 1941-69-2.

Fig. 77. *ARBOR GENEALOGIAE NOETICAE*, signed C. Deeker, from *The Holy Bible, containing the Old Testament and the New* (Oxford: John Basket, 1717), 104.
The Pierpont Morgan Library, New York, 2901.

Fig. 78. *Dorcas Munroe s work*, c.1800. Silk on linen; 16⅞″ x 12⅜″. Like the majority of New England family record samplers, this type records only the maker's parents and siblings. One unusual example by Mary Munroe Smith records the family of her maternal grandparents rather than the children of her parents (Lexington Historical Society). This sampler is strikingly similar to an example by Lorenza Fisk (b.1796) of Lexington (Benes, *Families and Children* [1987], 92, 111). Dorcas Munroe (b.1788) was the eighth child of Nathan Munroe (1748–1829) and Elizabeth Harrington (1750–1812) of Lexington. She married Leonard Brown of Boston in 1810.
Fine Arts Museums of San Francisco, gift of Mrs. Jessie Allard Kline, 78.19.1.

Fig. 79. *Family Record/ Susan Garfield,* c.1825. Silk on linen; 21″ x 16¼″. Susan's sampler and the record in Figure 78 belong to the largest and most closely related group of family tree samplers. They were probably made under the same instructress between the years 1800 and about 1825. For other examples embroidered entirely over the ground, see Edmonds, Fig. 21; and Sotheby's Sale 6075, October 20, 1990, Lot 174. Susan Garfield (b.1811) was the daughter of Joseph Garfield (1761–1824) and Susanna Hagar (b.1769) of Waltham.

Collection of Mr. and Mrs. James F. Miller.

Fig. 80. *Family Record/ Lucy Ann Williams Charlestown Nov 19 1830 aged 14 years.* Silk on linen; 17″ x 17″. The heart motif found on this and a related group of samplers shows kinship to the family trees. They may have replaced the earlier type at the same school. Six pieces belonging to this group date from 1824 to 1837 and five name *Charlestown.* For examples of 1824 and 1831, see Schaffner and Klein, *Folk Hearts* (1984), 42–3; also Sotheby's Sale 4590Y, April 30, 1981, Lot 680. Lucy Ann Williams (b.1816) was the youngest child of John Williams (1773–1828) and Abigail Corey (b.1776). Lucy was probably the Lucy A. Williams of Charlestown who married Joseph W. Gliden on August 23, 1834.

Location unknown; photograph courtesy of Sotheby's.

In the Federal period, as in the colonial period, Boston's most glorious school-girl embroideries were needlework pictures. Pictorial embroidery on silk was moderately popular in Boston before the Revolution, but except for coats of arms it was seldom worked during the balance of the eighteenth century.[5] The taste for neoclassicism brought about its strong revival in 1800, and one of America's most magnificent groups of silk embroideries survives from Boston. As with the Folwell group from Philadelphia, Boston origin can often be recognized by the style of the artist who painted figures and backgrounds on the silk, and while many pieces were worked in the same manner and can be attributed to one school, it is obvious that the painter was employed by more than one schoolmistress.[6] Only one piece within this group has survived with a reference to an artist painting it, but the "celebrated school in Boston" where it was made, and the "limner" were unnamed (Fig. 83).

It now appears likely that the Boston "limner" was the Boston portrait painter John Johnston (1753–1818), youngest son of the heraldic painter and engraver Thomas Johnston.[7] During the first fifteen years of the nineteenth century, when the embroideries were painted, Johnston was a recognized portraitist, but it is entirely logical that he would also have done this work. His training began when he was apprenticed to John Gore in 1767. In 1773 he began work as an ornamental artist in partnership with his brother-in-law, Daniel Rea, II. After the Revolution, he continued with Rea until 1789 when he confined his career primarily to portrait painting. Faces on some of the memorials attributed to him appear to be miniatures of family members, and he probably drew the patterns for highly personalized pieces such as the memorial to Robert Haswell (Fig. 96). A consistent style is easily recognizable in Figures 81 through 88, 96, and 97, and he may have painted Figures 89 and 95.

Many other ornamental artists were busy in Boston. While their work has not been individually identified, it is evident that someone was painting in the Boston limner's style, which is occasionally found on Boston work of 1819 or later.[8]

---

5. Exceptional is a 1785 embroidered bouquet on black silk from the Misses Sutherland's school (*ANTIQUES*, February 1991, 368–9). The Misses Sutherland opened their school on Hanover Street in 1784 (*The Boston-Gazette, and Country Journal*, September 6, 1784). They did not appear in the first directory of 1789, or in later editions.

6. Similar painting appears on "Hector and Andromache," formerly owned by Sheila Rideout and naming Mrs. Ball's school. Possibly this is the Maria V. Ball, schoolmistress, in Boston directories of 1800–1813. Another "Hector and Andromache" by Caroline Williams (1789–1825) of Newburyport names the *Berry Street Academy* kept by William Payne, 1799–1809 (EI). Probably the same hand painted a piece naming Miss Calder's school in Quincy (collection of Joan Stephens). Ann Calder (b.1795 in Charlestown) taught in Roxbury in 1819 and in Providence from 1820 to 1827.

7. "The New Fashion for Mourning in the Decorative Arts," a lecture by Davida Deutsch at the Forty-second Williamsburg Antiques Forum, February 4–9, 1990. Her conclusions concerning Johnston's painting on embroideries will soon be published.

8. An example is the memorial to John T. Prentice of Boston, d. July 18, 1819 (Deborah A. Young, *A Record for Time*, exhibition catalogue [Halifax: Art Gallery of Nova Scotia, 1985], cover, 37).

Fig. 81. *Act I, Scene II./ Shakespeare's Tempest/ Caroline Blaney* inscribed on the glass, c.1812. Silk and paint on silk; 23½″ x 26″. Jane Nylander discovered that this composition was derived from the print entitled *The Enchanted Island: Before the Cell of Prospero*, engraved by Jean Pierre Simon after Henry Fuseli, and published by John and Josiah Boydell, London, 1797. Caroline's sister, Mary Zeigler Blaney, also worked a scene from *The Tempest* that was painted by the same hand

(*ANTIQUES*, August 1976, 300). The painting on these pieces represents the "Boston limner" at his best. Caroline Blaney (d.1834) and Mary Zeigler Blaney (c.1801–1835) were the daughters of Henry Blaney (b.1770) and his second wife, Caroline Blaney (b.1772) of Roxbury. Caroline, Mary, and their sisters Eunice and Margaret all died between 1834 and 1836.
Private collection.

Fig. 82. Mourning piece attributed to Mary D. Brown, c.1803. Silk, paint, and ink on silk; 17⅜″ x 24¼″. Inscribed on the plinth *Dedicated to the/ Memory of/ John Ball Brown/ Aet 6 years 10 mo.* On the back, the embroiderer is identified as "Mary D. Brown, the daughter of Dr. Jabez Brown." Like Mary Lyman's memorial (Fig. 83), this example has solidly worked dark embroidery behind much of the willow's foliage, and the painting was by the same hand. The scene evidently depicts the parents and their surviving child as they would have appeared in 1777. Mary Dexter Brown (December 13, 1787–September 1, 1849) was the youngest child of Dr. Jabez Brown (1742–1830) and Anna Ball (1749–1823) of Wilmington, Middlesex County. The memorial is dedicated to their first child, who was born on December 14, 1770, and died on October 16, 1777. John Ball Brown 2nd was born in 1784. Mary's oldest sister, Anna, called Nancy (1775–1855), and pictured here, married the Reverend Freegrace Raynolds; but Mary died unmarried in Wilmington.
Concord Museum, Concord, Massachusetts, T-701.

Opposite: Fig. 83. Mourning piece by Mary Lyman, c.1804. Silk and paint on silk; 26½″ x 21″. On August 5, 1805, schoolmistress Abby Wright of South Hadley wrote the following to her half-sister:

> We called at the Rev. Mr. Howard's [in Springfield] . . . to see a piece of needlework lately executed at a celebrated school in Boston. . . . The piece I refer to was wrought by a Miss Lyman in memory of both her parents. . . . The expense of drawing and painting the faces was eight dollars and six months spent in Boston in working it. Comparing this with the labor of six or eight weeks in the country by a country girl without the assistance of a limner we might expect as great a contrast as we find. ("Abby Wright Allen: A Record of Her Letters, etc., 1795–1842," 76–7. Mount Holyoke College Library, South Hadley, Massachusetts.)

This letter confirms the fact that it was not a talented schoolmistress painting the impressive Boston silk embroideries but a professional artist. Closely related in style to this memorial are three others, and in each case, dark embroidery surrounds part of the tree trunk as seen here. The faces appear to have been painted by the same hand (Ring, *Treasures,* 64; *ANTIQUES,* March 1986, 600, Pl. X; and PB, Haskell V, Sale 613, December 8, 1944, Lot 576). Mary Lyman (1786–1826) was the daughter of Mary Pynchon (c.1752–1802) and the Honorable Samuel Lyman (1749–1802), a United States congressman from Massachusetts, 1795–1800. She married Robert Emery (1773–1841) and had five children.
Society for the Preservation of New England Antiquities, gift of Miss Isabelle Robinson, 1917.284.

Fig. 84. Anonymous Washington memorial, Boston, c.1805–1815. Silk, paint, and ink on silk; 23½″ in diameter. This memorial has essentially the same composition as Fig. 86. However, the miniature portrait of Washington is very different and relates more closely to that in Figure 85. A partly legible name, possibly *C R Hall* or *Hale*, is inscribed on the gun stock above the eagle's head. This could be the embroiderer's.
Private collection.

Fig. 85. Anonymous Washington memorial, Boston, c.1805–1815. Silk and paint on silk; 17½″ x 14¾″. This unusual composition, with the focal point of the picture seemingly sliced off, has not been altered. A nearly identical composition, but with the ground completely embroidered, is in the MHS.
The Bayou Bend Collection, Museum of Fine Arts, Houston, gift of William James Hill, B.86.13.

Fig. 86. Anonymous Washington memorial, Boston, c.1805–1815. Silk, metallic threads, and paint on silk; 23″ in diameter. The basic composition of this memorial relates to the memorial engraving *Pater Patriae* by Enoch G. Gridley after a now-lost painting by John Coles, Jr. The plinth was derived from John James Barralet's *Apotheosis of Washington* and includes the same incorrect death date (for these prints of 1800 and 1802, respectively, see *ANTIQUES*, February 1977, 325, 329). The source for the figure of Columbia with the eagle is unknown. Quite possibly this complete composition occurs in an undiscovered print. *Author's collection.*

Fig. 83a. Detail of the Lyman memorial. Inscribed on the urns *M L* and *S L* and on the plinth *M. Lyman/ Obt Oct. 23/ 1802* and *S. Lyman/ Obt June/ 1802*. The figures no doubt represent Mary Lyman with her older brother, Charles P. Lyman, and her younger brother, Samuel Lyman. The painting of these faces as well as the embroidery style and lettering on the plinth show kinship to the Washington memorial in Figure 86.

Fig. 88. Anonymous mourning embroidery, Boston, c.1805. Silk, paint, and ink on silk; 15¾" x 13⅛". Dedicated to *E BACON/ OB 23 Oct'/ 1800/AE23* and *E B Gleason/ OB 28 Dec'/ 17??/ AE 1 Year*. This belongs to a group of six similar memorials, and four have the same angel on the plinth. For the earliest dated piece of 1802, see Sotheby's Sale 5810, January 27, 1989, Lot 1114, and another is Lot 1115. One is illustrated in Ring, *Treasures*, 63. One belongs to the Historical Society of Old Newbury.
Collection of Shirley E. Gibson.

Fig. 87. *Wro'. By Miss ANN VOSE 1807.* Inscribed on the glass, and on the monument *IN MEMORY OF/ MRS MARY VOSE./ WHO DIED JULY 22D/ 1807/ AGED 38 YEARS.* Silk, paint, and ink on silk; 17⁷⁄₁₆" x 15⅜". The painting and the embroidery of Ann's memorial bear kinship to those of both the Washington and the Tempest embroideries (Figs. 81, 84, 86). Ann Vose (1797–1861) was the daughter of Boston cabinetmaker Isaac Vose (1767–1823) and Mary Bemis (1769–1807). She married her cousin, Charles Bemis (1789–1874), in 1815. He was a lawyer of Watertown. They had three children.
The Bayou Bend Collection, Museum of Fine Arts, Houston, B.70.51.

Fig. 89. *THE WASHINGTON FAMILY/ Wrought by Nancy H. Lincoln, 1815* inscribed on the glass. Silk and paint on silk; 22⅛″ x 25½″. Nancy's embroidery was faithfully copied from the engraving in Fig. 90. It is far rarer than Boston embroideries depicting *The Washington Family* after the engraving by Edward Savage. For an 1807 example of that type, probably painted by the same hand, and of the engraving, see *ANTIQUES*, February 1981, 404. Nancy Howe Lincoln (b. February 22, 1800) was the daughter of Hawkes Lincoln (1769–1829), a shipwright born in Hingham, and Mary Howe (1771–1828), born in Boston. They lived in Boston and Hingham. On January 25, 1828, Nancy became the third wife of Captain Jacob Woodbury (1782–1841), originally of Jaffrey, New Hampshire. They lived in Beverly.
The Jackson Homestead, Newton, Massachusetts, 79.8066.

Left: Fig. 90. *The Washington Family*, mezzotint engraving by Edward Bell of London after a painting by Jeremiah Paul, Jr., of Philadelphia. Published December 1, 1800, by Atkins and Nightingale, No. 143 Leaden Hall Street, London, and No. 35 North Front Street, Philadelphia 18″ x 23⅞″.
The Bayou Bend Collection, Museum of Fine Arts, Houston, B.65.5.

S U S A N N A   R O W S O N ' S   A C A D E M Y

Fig. 91. Miniature of Susanna Haswell Rowson (1762–1824) by William M. S. Doyle (1769–1828), c.1810. Susanna was born in Portsmouth, England, to William Rowson (d.1805) and Susanna Musgrove (d.1762).
Location unknown; photograph courtesy of the American Antiquarian Society.

Boston's most celebrated girls' school of the Federal period was opened in 1797 by Susanna Haswell Rowson (Fig. 91), an English-born novelist, playwright, and actress who performed with her husband in several American cities before retiring from the stage at the age of thirty-five.[1] Despite the disadvantage of a recent career in the theatre, this clever and hard-working woman quickly gained respect as a teacher, and her school was well patronized until her retirement in 1822.

Where Susanna Rowson received the education required for a literary and teaching career remains unclear.[2] But her school became noted for the public performances of its students and the exhibitions of their work, and her pen was never idle. She wrote novels, plays, poetry, and textbooks, and contributed steadily to a number of periodicals. Even so, she supervised every aspect of her school and endeared herself to her students. In 1798, Eliza Southgate wrote happily to her father of being "under the tuition of an amiable lady, so mild, so good, no one can help loving her; she treats all her scholars with such a tenderness as would win the affection of the most savage brute. . . . I have described one of the blessings of creation in Mrs. Rawson. . . ."[3] Susanna personally reviewed the progress of each girl and distributed written comments every Saturday.[4] Her school was among the few girls' schools of this period to bestow silver rewards of merit for exceptional performance (Fig. 93).

Mrs. Rowson taught in Boston from 1798 until 1800 when she moved her school to Medford. In June of 1803 she commenced teaching in Newton, where in June of 1805 she was joined by her half-brother's widow, Mary Cordis Haswell. By May of 1807, they had returned to Boston and were located on Washington Street, near Roxbury. Susanna's husband, William Rowson, was a clerk in the Custom House, but by 1809, the success of Susanna's seminary had enabled him to purchase a house on Hollis Street and in 1811 it became the final home of the Rowson school. Mary Haswell opened her own school in Charlestown on October 1, 1809, and in 1811 she moved her school into the Washington Street house formerly occupied by the Rowsons.[5]

Mrs. Rowson's many school advertisements described the needlework and other accomplishments she was prepared to teach, but the style and quality of embroideries from her school vary greatly, and heretofore, no unique trait or technique has made the identification of unsigned pieces possible. Most often at-

1. For a detailed account of her life and extracts from her writings, see Nason, *A Memoir of Mrs. Susanna Rowson* (1870).

2. From 1766 until 1778 she lived in Nantasket, Massachusetts, with her father, a British naval officer, his American-born wife, Rachel Woodward, and three half-brothers. The family was forced to return to England in 1778.

3. Bowne, *A Girl's Life Eighty Years Ago* (1888), 17.

4. Nason, *A Memoir,* 105–6.

5. *Columbian Centinel,* September 2, 1809, and March 30, 1811. Mary Cordis Haswell (1781–1868) married John Lemist (1785–1840) of Roxbury in 1816.

Fig. 92. One of a pair of pastoral scenes worked by Mary Brown at Mrs. Rowson's Academy in Medford, 1802. Silk and paint on silk; 9¾″ x 7⅜″. Mary's work survived with her silver reward of merit (Fig. 93). A number of similar small embroideries, very much in the English style, are known from the Rowson school (see Ring, *Treasures*, Fig. 102; *A&AW* [August 22, 1986], 24, for an example at Deerfield; SPNEA owns a printwork piece made in Medford by S. White). Attributed to Mary Brown (1787–1860), the daughter of Francis Brown (1753–1790) and Judith Burnham (c.1760–1834) of Ipswich. She died unmarried.
Ipswich Historical Society, gift of Roxana C. Cowles, 3.

tributed to her teaching are renditions of *Columbus* like Figure 95. This is nearly identical to two documented embroideries, and all three were probably painted by John Johnston.[6] However, because of their repetitious interpretation of an unknown print (Fig. 97),[7] it is now possible to assign a group of memorials to her school. They also provide the clue for attributing Mary Lyman's work (Fig. 83) and other related silk embroideries to her teaching. Although Eliza Adams' embroidery of about 1810 (Fig. 97) was done considerably later than Mary Lyman's and Mary D. Brown's (Figs. 82, 83), they share a peculiar treatment of their trees. On these and a number of related pieces, including the Tempest embroidery by Caroline Blaney's sister, Mary (see caption, Fig. 81), the background between the branches and leaves of the trees has been partly worked in dark colors that do not blend with the painted background. The reason for the working of these areas is

Fig. 93. Silver medal engraved on the front *BEST/ MB/ EMBROIDERY/ 1802* and on the reverse *MRS ROWSONS/ ACADEMY/ MEDFORD*; actual size.
Ipswich Historical Society, gift of Roxana C. Cowles.

6. A similar composition from the Edwin print was worked on silk in 1816 by Catharine Fager at the school of Mrs. Nancy Anthony, who taught in Harrisburg, Pennsylvania, at least from 1814 through 1823. It belongs to the Dauphin County Historical Society, Harrisburg.

7. See a similar watercolor example by Laura S. Bartlett in *The Decorative Arts of New Hampshire, A Sesquicentennial Exhibition* (Concord, N.H., NHHS, 1973), 44. Laura is listed among Susanna Rowson's students in Nason's *Memoir*.

Fig. 94. *BOSTON HARBOUR/ Workd/ by/ SALLY DODGE/ at/ Mrs Rowsons/ Medford/ Feby 27/ 1800*. Silk and paint on silk; 23″ x 19″. The source for Sally's map was published in the *Pennsylvania Magazine* of June 1775, and first recognized by Jane Nylander, who illustrated a nearly identical embroidered map of 1799 in *ANTIQUES*, September 1970, 437. Mrs. Rowson did not specifically advertise the working of maps, but she introduced map embroidery into her curriculum at an early date. Evidently it did not become popular in Boston since only two examples are known. However, Mrs. Rowson emphasized the study of geography and published *Youths' First Steps in Geography* in 1818. Several girls named Sally Dodge lived in and near Boston at this time. *Private collection.*

unclear since in some instances there would have been ample space to paint the openings in the same manner that surrounded the trees. This peculiarity is not found on every example from Mrs. Rowson's school, but it is apparent on Eliza Adams' memorial (Fig. 97), and even more conspicuous on two unsigned pieces that are nearly identical to it.

This treatment on Mary Zeigler Blaney's work also makes Caroline Blaney's *Tempest* embroidery (Fig. 81) attributable to the Rowson school. The style of the Blaney pictures and their exquisite needlework add to the possibility that the Rowson school produced the spectacular Washington memorials as well (Figs. 84–86). The dates of these embroideries also support the logic of a Rowson attribution. Few Boston schools are known to have produced this type of needlework from 1802 until 1815. The latter date is based on the fact that Mary Zeigler Blaney was born around 1801 and would normally have been at least twelve or

Opposite:
Fig. 95. *Landing of Columbus* inscribed on the glass, c.1800–1802. Silk and paint on silk; 21½″ x 14⅜″. Derived from *The Landing of Christopher Columbus*, engraved by David Edwin (1776–1841) after a painting by Edward Savage, and published by Savage in Philadelphia, January 1, 1800. This anonymous embroidery is attributed to Susanna Rowson's school because it is nearly identical to the same subject worked by Rowson student Margaret Mitchell (1784–1867) of Peterborough, New Hampshire (illustrated with the print in *ANTIQUES*, August 1976, 293–4); also to another piece inscribed on the glass *wrought by Miss Abbey Low, at Mrs. Rawson's Academy* (see *ANTIQUES*, October 1992, 421). *Collection of Mrs. Robert S. Ames.*

Fig. 96. Mourning piece by Mary Haswell inscribed *SACRED/ TO THE MEMORY OF CAP^{T}N/ ROB . . . HASWELL/ Who was lost on the Voyage to the. . . ./ A. D. 1801 AE 33 yrs/ His daughter Mary inscribes this as a tribute . . .* , and with the ship *LOUISA* pictured on the monument, c.1808. Silk and paint on silk; 19⅞″ x 14⅞″. The figures represent Haswell's widow, Mary Cordis Haswell, and his daughters, Mary and Rebecca. It was probably made at the Rowson and Haswell Academy on Washington Street, or possibly at Mrs. Mary Haswell's school in Charlestown between 1809 and 1811. Mary Haswell (b.c.1798) married George Murdock of Boston in 1819, and they had two daughters.
Private collection.

Fig. 97. *Wrought by MISS. ELIZA ADAMS AT MRS. ROWSON'S ACADEMY* inscribed on the glass, c.1810. Silk and paint on silk; 18″ x 13¼″. A similar piece dedicated to *Bezaleel Woodward Esq.* is at Dartmouth College. Another counterpart dedicated to twins *M & E Coolidge* was sold at Christie's East on April 26, 1989, Sale 6805, Lot 487. Eliza Adams also worked a companion mourning piece with a different composition. Both of her memorials and the Woodward piece have dark colors among the leaves and branches, while the Coolidge memorial has solidly worked dark brown between the branches much like Mary Lyman's embroidery (Fig. 83). Eliza Adams (1795–1881) was the daughter of Zabadiel Adams (1767–1820) and Rachel Lyon (1772–1809) of Roxbury. On December 6, 1821, she married watch and clockmaker Simon Willard, Jr. (1795–1874). They had seven children but three died in infancy and only two survived them. Eliza probably attended the Rowson Academy with Catherine Gates Willard (b.1794), the daughter of clockmaker Aaron Willard (1757–1844). Catherine's calligraphic work on paper named the Rowson Academy in 1810. It is also at the Willard House.
Willard House and Clock Museum, Grafton, Massachusetts, 333.

Fig. 98. *WROUGHT at M^s ROWSON'S ACADEMY by MARY ANN BARRY,/ 1812* inscribed on the glass and dedicated to two infants both of whom were named Lucretia Thayer Barry and who died in 1810 and in 1811. Silk, paint, and ink on silk; 17½" x 12½". The pattern for this mourning piece was evidently favored at Mrs. Rowson's school. For a similar embroidery, see Sotheby's Sale 5282, February 1, 1985, Lot 373. Mary Ann Barry (1798–1866) was the daughter of James Barry (c.1768–1834) and Mehitable Crane (c.1772–1838). Barry was a cooper, and they resided on Washington Street. Mary Ann married Ephraim Potter (1784–1826) in 1816, and they moved to Concord. She married Richard Hall Messer (1803–1863) in 1834.
Concord Museum, Concord, Massachusetts, T-1200.

older when she worked an embroidery of this type. Her work and its related technique suggest a likely date for the anonymous Washington memorials (Figs. 84–86), and Nancy Lincoln's needlework is evidence that these large silk embroideries were still fashionable in Boston in 1815. However, the Washington memorials may have been worked much earlier, especially since the plinths in Figures 83 and 86 have such similar lettering.

Susanna Rowson's school was actually in Newton when Mary Lyman's embroidery is said to have required six months "spent in Boston in working it." To the residents of Springfield or South Hadley, it was probably considered a Boston school because of Mrs. Rowson's high profile in the city. When her school was in Medford in 1802, the October examination took place in Boston's Franklin Hall, and it was described in the *Boston Weekly Magazine*. Mrs. Rowson was also the editor of this publication from 1802 until 1805.[8]

Because of declining health, Susanna Rowson announced her forthcoming retirement in the *Columbian Centinel* of April 3, 1822. She was relinquishing "her duties in the school . . . to her adopted daughter, Miss Mills, and her niece, Miss Johnston." She died on March 2, 1824, and was eulogized in Boston newspapers to an unusual extent for a woman of this period. Her husband survived her and within the year he married Hannah S. Bancroft.

---

8. Nason, *A Memoir*, 114.

MRS. SAUNDERS' AND MISS BEACH'S ACADEMY, DORCHESTER

Judging by the well remembered symmetrical lives of several aged gentlewomen of Kittery, Maine, and Portsmouth, N.H., who had their early training at "Clifton Hill Academy, Dorchester, Mass.", under the care and tuition of Mrs. Saunders and Miss Beach, it may be safely noted that this school was a model in every essential particular. . . .[1]

Mrs. Judith Foster Saunders was already noted for teaching fine needlework in her native Gloucester when she was joined by the English-born Clementina Beach (Fig. 100),[2] and they opened a young ladies' academy in Dorchester in February of 1803.[3] In June of the following year they purchased a newly built house, near the First Parish Church on Dorchester's Meeting House Hill (Fig. 99), where they kept one of New England's most elite boarding schools for more than thirty years.[4] Many of their scholars were from the prominent families of Maine and New Hampshire.[5]

Silk embroideries from this school were finely worked with meticulous skill and a conspicuous lack of chenille. They can often be recognized by the flawlessly embroidered inscriptions beneath the pictures (Figs. 101, 102). These teachers patronized the Roxbury framer John Doggett, and elegantly inscribed glass mats from his shop usually name the embroiderer together with *Mrs. Saunders' and Miss Beach's Academy, Dorchester* (Figs. 101, 104).[6] Newspaper advertisements mentioned the school's fine library and collection of drawings,[7] and a number of print sources for their needlework patterns have been recognized. Judith or Clementina probably drew the patterns and painted the figures on the silk, and later pieces were most likely painted by Clementina, who is said to have studied with the artist Gilbert Stuart.[8]

In 1804, there were thirty-six boarders attending the school, which was also called the Ladies Academy or Clifton Hill Seminary. The majority of the girls were from New England and ranged in age from six to eighteen years.[9] There

1. Miss Harriet H. Shapleigh to Joseph Foster (undated), as quoted in Joseph Foster, *Colonel Joseph Foster, His Children and Grandchildren* (Hartford, Conn.: edition of four copies, 1935), 180.

2. "Capt. Gibaut dined with me & assured me that a Mrs. Saunders keeps a school in Gloucester for young ladies, where needle work will bear comparison with any of the work of our Schools not excepting Mrs. Rogers of Salem" (Bentley, *Diary* [1905–1914; reprint, 1962], entry of July 26, 1802, 2:441). Judith (b. 1772) was separated from her husband, Thomas Bradbury Saunders (1770–1810); Clementina never married.

3. *Columbian Centinel,* Boston, February 5, 1803.

4. From October 1822 until May 1825, they taught at three different rented locations in Boston. See their advertisements in the *Columbian Centinel* for November 9, 1822; March 22, 1823; February 24, 1824; and April 16, 1825.

5. Sprague, *Agreeable Situations* (1987), 101, 228, 242–3, 268–9.

6. For more about Doggett, see *ANTIQUES,* March 1929, 196–200, and May 1981, 1183.

7. *Columbian Centinel,* Boston, March 21, 1827.

8. George C. Mason, *The Life and Works of Gilbert Stuart* (New York: Burt Franklin Reprints, 1972), 136.

9. Sarah Ripley's Diary, June–August 1804 (Stearns Collection, Arthur and Elizabeth Schlesinger Library,

Fig. 99. The house of Mrs. Saunders and Miss Beach, Meeting House Hill, Dorchester, c.1925. It was new when purchased by Clementina Beach for $4,500, and they moved the school there on June 7, 1804. In 1810 it housed forty-one people, including thirty-six young lady boarders. In the rear is the 1817 addition. It still stands at the corner of Adams and East Streets, although considerably altered.
The Bostonian Society, Old State House, Boston.

Fig. 100. Clementina Beach (1774–1855) by Gilbert Stuart, c.1824. Oil on panel; 26″ x 21″. Miss Beach, with her father, William Beach, and her sister Eliza, came from Bristol, England, to Gloucester about 1793, and in 1799, the Salem diarist William Bentley described her as "a young lady of accomplishments."
Author's collection.

Fig. 101. *Wrought by Mary Beach, At Mrs Saunders & Miss Beach's Academy Dorchester* inscribed on the glass, c.1804. Silk and paint on silk; 16″ x 16½″. Mary's composition was copied from a stipple engraving by Francesco Bartolozzi (1727–1815) after a painting by Angelica Kauffmann. Entitled *Cornelia Mother of the Gracchi*, it was published in London in 1788 (*ANTIQUES*, August 1976, 296). Although John Doggett's account book does not mention framing Mary's embroidery, the white glass mat and border decoration are typical of his shop, and this may be the frame with painted glass and lettering that was sold to Mrs. Saunders and Miss Beach for $5.50 on June 6, 1805. Mary Beach (1786–1843) was the daughter of John Beach (c.1747–1819) and Mary Pearce (1763–1794) of Gloucester, and the first cousin of schoolmistress Clementina Beach. With her sister Elizabeth, Mary was a boarder at the Academy in 1804, and possibly in 1805. She married Thomas W. Penhallow of Portsmouth, New Hampshire, on April 9, 1809.

Location unknown; photograph courtesy of Sotheby's.

were also twenty day scholars. Among the Academy's first students was Anne Jean Robbins (1789–1867) of Milton who entered in 1803. Her biographer described the following incidents:

> Her room-mate at this school was a sweet, attractive, refined little girl, two years younger than herself, named Elizabeth Beach. When they went to their room the first night of their companionship, the little girl looked at her elder acquaintance with a dawning respect, as she was so large and tall, and, to her eyes, almost a woman. "Which side of the bed shall I sleep, Miss Robbins?" she said deferentially. "Oh! It's perfectly immaterial to me which side you sleep," said Anne in her clear ringing voice, "for I *always* sleep in the middle."
>
> The next morning, when seated around the breakfast-table, the other girls eating with pewter spoons, which were thought good enough for boarding-

Radcliffe College, Cambridge, Mass.). Nancy Lee, aged sixteen, was from Georgetown, Maryland. For her silk embroidery, see *ANTIQUES,* August 1976, 303, Pl. III. St. Croix's Ruth Smith was twelve years old; her now-unknown "Picture" was framed by John Doggett for $6.00 (entry of October 3, 1807, *John Doggett's Book*, December 4, 1802–December 8, 1809, now in the Joseph Downs Manuscript Collection, Winterthur Museum).

Fig. 102. *WROUGHT by EUNICE BENT/ At Mrs SAUNDERS & MISS BEACH'S ACADEMY DORCHESTER* inscribed on the glass, c.1805. Silk and paint on silk; 21¼" x 15". Embroidered on the silk: *And God heard the voice of the Lad; and the Angel of God called unto Hagar out of Heaven/ and said unto her, what aileth thee Hagar? fear not; for God hath heard the voice of the Lad/ where he is./ Genesis Chap XXI ver. 17.* Although in reverse, the composition was evidently derived from the engraving in Figure 103, which was discovered by Margaret Swain. Four other embroideries from the Academy depict this scene. For Patty R. Zeigler's, see *ANTIQUES,* August 1976, 307. An unsigned example appears in Ring, *Treasures,* 73. Mary Ann Huntting's version is in the MFA. For Elizabeth Sumner's, see Christie's, October 1, 1988, Lot 259. Eunice Bent (1790–1857) was the daughter of Joseph Bent (1762–1849) and Sarah White (1769–1857) of Milton; she died unmarried. Her sister Sally (1787–1829) also worked an embroidery at the Academy in 1804 (*ANTIQUES,* August 1976, 309). *Collection of Bertram K. and Nina Fletcher Little.*

Below:
Fig. 103. Engraving of Hagar and Ishmael, from *THE HOLY BIBLE containing the Old Testament and the New* (Oxford: John Baskett, 1717). *The Pierpont Morgan Library,* New York, 2901.

school children of that day,—and really were so,—Anne cheerfully pulled a bright *silver* spoon out of her pocket, and began to eat her breakfast. "As long as there are *silver* spoons in the world," she said in an under-tone, "I shall eat with one; and, when there cease to be, I will put up with some inferior metal."[10]

The spirited Anne Jean Robbins married Judge Joseph Lyman (1767–1847) of Northampton in 1811 and became the adored mother of five children and six step-children. She was the great niece of another high-spirited woman, the Boston schoolmistress Elizabeth Murray Smith (Fig. 53).

Sally Ripley of Greenfield was eighteen years old when her father took her to the Saunders and Beach Academy on May 17, 1804.[11] Her diary mentions the school's move to the new house on June 7, and on June 29, "Mrs. Saunders and Miss Beach gave an elegant ball; there was a large collection of Ladies and Gentlemen, among them were two ministers of the Gospel. The room was hand-

10. Susan I. Lesley, *Memoir of the Life of Mrs. Anne Jean Lyman* (Cambridge, Mass., 1876), 12–13; as quoted in Foster, *Colonel Joseph Foster,* 182–3. Anne Jean Robbins was the daughter of Edward H. Robbins (1758–1829) and Elizabeth Murray.
11. Sarah Ripley's diary.

Fig. 104. *WROUGHT By MEHITABLE NEAL AT Mrs. SAUNDERS AND Miss BEACH'S ACADEMY* inscribed on the glass, c.1807. Silk and paint on silk; 21¼″ x 25″. Mehitable pictured *CYMBELINE* in a manner very similar to that of embroideries from Susanna Rowson's school (*ANTIQUES*, August 1976, 295). Surely this is one of the three embroidery frames with glass that were billed to Mrs. Saunders and Miss Beach by John Doggett "for Miss Mehitable Neall" on September 11 and October 3, 1807, at a total cost of $17.50. This student was probably Mehitable Neal (1786–1856), the daughter of Jonathan Neal (1759–1837) and Mehitable Eden (1760–1786) of Salem. In 1833, she became the second wife of Amos Choate (1775–1844), who was for many years the Register [*sic*] of Deeds for Essex County.
Collection of Joan Stephens.

somely ornamented, The entertainment splendid and brilliant, but I did not enjoy myself very much." On August 7, Sally "paid $50 dollars on my bill, the whole was $69.41 including the frame for my piece. . . ." The next day Sally "left the academy . . . and I do not depart without regret. Mrs. Saunders and Miss Beach have been very kind to me. . . ."[12]

Judith Saunders died in 1841. Clementina Beach sold the Dorchester property in 1846, and spent the rest of her life at a niece's home in Hingham.[13]

---

12. Ibid.
13. Her niece was Amelia Beach Fudger Loring, wife of Hingham merchant Thomas Loring. For more about the Saunders and Beach Academy, see *ANTIQUES,* August 1976, 302–12; and for other embroideries, Ring, *Treasures,* 70–5.

Fig. 105. *Wrought by Clarissa D Wentworth at Mrs. Saunders & Miss Beachs/ Acd^Y Dorchester* inscribed on the glass, c.1813. Silk, paint, and ink on silk; 14½″ x 11⅜″. Inscribed on the monument: *IN MEMORY of/ ANDREW WENTWORTH Esq/ who departed this life March 17th 1813/ Aged 48 years.* A similar watercolor memorial was painted at the Academy by Sarah Ann Holmes (*A&AW,* January 29, 1988, 138); for another, probably from this Academy, see SPB Sale 4478Y, November 21, 1980, Lot 808. Clarissa D. Wentworth (1797–1865) was the daughter of Andrew Wentworth (1764–1813) and Mary Rollins (1769–1842) of Salmon Falls, New Hampshire. She married John Samuel Hayes Durell (1798–1862) in 1845 and they lived in Dover, New Hampshire. Probably classmates of Clarissa were Lucy and Lydia Jackson of Plymouth, who attended the Academy in 1812 and 1813. Lydia (1802–1892) became the second wife of poet Ralph Waldo Emerson (1803–1882) in 1835. *Collection of Mr. and Mrs. George P. Valluzzo.*

Fig. 106. Needlework picture by Anstiss Crowninshield, c.1740. Silk on silk; 10¼" x 15". For a related but anonymous piece that is perhaps earlier, see *MAD*, January 1991, 44-C. Anstiss Crowninshield (1726–1768) was the daughter of John Crowninshield (1696–1761) and Anstiss Williams (1700–1773) of Salem. She married Christopher Babbidge, Jr. (c.1718–1751), a mariner, on September 27, 1749, and had one daughter. In 1760, she married William King (c.1729–1773) and had three children. Her sister Elizabeth (1735–1799) married Elias Hasket Derby (1739–1799). *Essex Institute, 124.820.*

Embroideries of Essex County

Essex County, Massachusetts, became both populous and prosperous during the seventeenth century, and by 1700 it was among the most densely inhabited areas within England's American colonies. Toward the mid-eighteenth century, this fostered a number of private schools for girls, and some of the most exciting groups of American embroideries were worked in Salem, Danvers, Marblehead, and Lynn; also, in Newbury, Newburyport, and Haverhill.

SILK EMBROIDERIES AND SAMPLERS OF SALEM

The needlework of eighteenth-century Salem schoolgirls rivaled the work from Boston, and can generally be recognized by the presence of crinkly silk worked in uncouched satin stitches of exceptional length, often in diagonal directions. This unusual technique was evidently initiated around 1740 by a Salem schoolmistress with fresh ideas and considerable talent and was continued by her successors until the close of the century.

Pictorial embroideries on black silk were the first to exhibit this Salem style. They were made from the 1740s through the 1770s while closely related scenes also appeared on Salem samplers. The work of Anstiss Crowninshield is perhaps

Fig. 107. Needlework picture by Love Rawlins Pickman, c.1745. Silk on silk; 12″ x 17⅝″. This is one of a set of six pictures worked on black silk by Love Pickman in the 1740s and framed alike. Four are in the MFA; for another, see *ANTIQUES*, May 1989, 1001; one is unlocated. Love Rawlins Pickman (1732–1809) was the daughter of Benjamin Pickman (1706–1773) of Salem and Love Rawlins (1709–1786) who was born in Boston. As a Salem merchant, Love's father amassed a large fortune, became a Colonel in the Essex Regiment, and was active in civic affairs. In 1751, Love married Peter Frye (1723–1820), who opened a school for girls in Salem in 1743 and also taught the town grammar school before joining his father-in-law in business. They had eight children. As a Tory, Frye left for England in 1775 without his wife, and he never returned. Love did not remarry.
M. and M. Karolik Collection, Museum of Fine Arts, Boston, 39.241.

Below:
Fig. 108. *ELIZABETH HERBERT/ Her Sampler/ Aged Twelve/ 1764.* Silk and metal on linen; 17¾″ x 14½″. Elizabeth's sheep, hillocks, and leopard are very similar to those worked on a pair of black silk embroideries by Mary Ingersoll of Salem in 1750 (recorded in the Cabot Papers, MFA). Dorothy Ashton must have been Elizabeth's classmate, for they made nearly identical samplers in the same year (Krueger, *New England*, Fig. 23). Elizabeth Herbert (1751–1767) was the daughter of Benjamin Herbert (1709–1761) and Elizabeth Fowler (1717–1772) of Salem.
Peabody Museum of Salem, M19027.

the earliest of the Salem silk embroideries known today (Fig. 106). The bold figures and the leaves of the trees in her embroidery relate to the work of Love Rawlins Pickman and Elizabeth Herbert (Figs. 107, 108), which suggests that the same instructress was active from about 1740 through 1764. In quite a different style, an unknown girl worked the scene in Figure 109, which bears a definite relationship to the sampler of Susannah Saunders (Fig. 110) and to Mary Jennison's embroidery (Fig. 113). This teacher probably taught music as well, and the engravings from her songbooks may have inspired her embroidery patterns (Figs. 111, 113).[1]

1. Nancy Graves Cabot believed these music book illustrations were probably the inspiration for the couples in Figures 109 and 110 (Cabot Papers, MFA).

Fig. 109. Anonymous
needlework picture at-
tributed to a Salem girls'
school, c.1760–1770. Silk
on silk; 17½" x 17⅝".
Notice the similarity of the
couple at left to the figures
on Susannah Saunders'
sampler (Fig. 110). Possibly
both were inspired by the
print in Figure 111.
Ipswich Historical Society, 554

Little is known about the Salem teachers of the colonial period. The widow
Catherine Hodges Dealland (b.1664) was teaching in the town school in 1712, but
it is doubtful that she taught elaborate embroidery. The widow Abigail Fowler
(c.1701–1771), who taught in Salem for most of her adult life and was later described as a "noted school dame,"[2] is the more likely originator of Salem's long-
stitch style. Also teaching during this period were the spinster sisters Margaret
(1713–1764) and Anstis Phippen (1724–1782);[3] and Susannah Becket Babbidge
(1714–1804) kept a "famous private school for fifty years," after the death of her
husband in 1745. Her unmarried daughter Lydia (1733–1800) is believed to have
taught accomplishments to young ladies in later years.[4] The duration of Elizabeth
Gaudin's boarding school on Derby Street is unknown. It was opened in 1773,
and she taught plain sewing, marking, tent and Irish stitch.[5]

---

2. Joseph B. Felt, *Annals of Salem* (Salem: W. & S. B. Ives, 1845), 1: 442–50.
3. Margaret and Anstis Phippen were the daughters of Salem cooper Nathaniel Phippen (1687–c.1757) and
Margaret Palfrey. They were the great aunts of Polly Phippen and Prisce and Betsey Gill, who worked samplers at Sarah Stivours' school. Miss Rebecca Phippen owned "two pieces of embroidery of their workmanship" in 1848 (George Dean Phippen, *Phippen Genealogy,* 1848. Manuscript, EI).
4. James Duncan Phillips, *Salem in the Eighteenth Century* (Salem: Essex Institute, 1937; reprint, 1969), 345.
5. Felt, *Annals,* 1: 451.

Fig. 110. *Susannah Saunders Wrought Th/ is In The 12 th year of her Age/ june The 23 1766.* Silk and metal on linen; 16″ x 18½″. Rebekah White (1753–1823) of Salem worked a very similar sampler in the same year (Krueger, *New England*, Fig. 26). Also, in 1765, a closely related piece was made by Rebekah's sister Abigail (b.1751); it is recorded in the Cabot Papers, MFA. Susannah Saunders (1754–1838) was the daughter of Salem merchant John Saunders (b.1724) and Susannah Barrett. On March 17, 1771, Susannah married her schoolmaster, Daniel Hopkins (1734–1814), a Yale graduate of 1758. From 1778 until his death, Hopkins was pastor of the Third Church in Salem. Susannah and Daniel Hopkins had six children.
Author's collection.

Fig. 111. "The Rapture," in *Calliope, or English Harmony*, vol. 1, engraved and sold by Henry Roberts, London, 1739; illustration: 1⅞″ x 4⅝″.
Boston Public Library.

Fig. 112. Needlework picture inscribed on paper glued to the backboard "Mary Jennison born [Oct] 13, 1755/ This piece was embroidered by her while at a boarding school in Salem Mass. 1773." Silk and metallic threads on silk; 8″ x 13″. Inscribed on the inside of the backboard "& two for/ this/ S Blyth," indicating that Samuel Blythe framed Mary's picture. The couple in this embroidery may have been derived from the print in Figure 113. The Winterthur Museum owns four other Salem embroideries on black silk. Two are illustrated in Swan, *Guide*, 91, and *Plain & Fancy*, 64. Another of probable Salem origin, by Mary Adams (b.1755), belongs to the Marblehead Historical Society. Mary (Polly) Jennison (1755–1812), born in Mendon, was the daughter of Dr. William Jennison (1732–1798) and Mary Staples. Mary's aunt, Mary Jennison Giles (d.1784), lived in Danvers and may have been responsible for Mary attending a school in Salem. On December 25, 1777, Mary was married in Douglas to Jonathan Whipple (c.1752–1839) of Mendon. They lived in Uxbridge and had many children.
Winterthur Museum, 55.137.

Fig. 113. "A New Song," in *Clio and Euterpe, or British Harmony*, vol. 2, engraved by Henry Roberts, London, 1758; illustration: 1⅞″ x 4⅜″.
Boston Public Library.

Fig. 114. *HANNAH/ BATCHELDER/ HER SAM-PLER/ WROUGHT 1780* and beneath the verse *SARAH STIVOURS SCHOOL/ MISTRESS.* Silk on linen; 18¼″ x 15¼″. The ten-year-old Hannah often reversed the letters *S* and *C*. Her sister, Joanna (b.1765), worked a very precise and different type of sampler in 1779 (private collection). Hannah Batchelder (1770–1805) was the daughter of Josiah Batchelder, Jr. (1737–1809), and Hannah Dodge (1740–1797) of Beverly. Her father was a wealthy sea captain, an influential citizen, and very active in the patriot cause. In 1794, Hannah married John Lovett (1769–1805), also of Beverly. Hannah's sampler belongs to her great, great granddaughter.
Collection of Mrs. Thomas W. Storrow.

SARAH STIVOURS' SCHOOL AND SALEM SAMPLERS

One teacher stands out, however—Sarah Stivours, the first American schoolmistress to have her name worked on a distinctive group of samplers.[1] She was Sarah Fiske (1742–1819), the daughter of Samuel Fiske (1689–1770), a native of Braintree, who became a schoolmaster and a minister in Salem. After seventeen years as pastor of the First Church in Salem, he was dismissed in 1735. Four years later, at the age of fifty, he married Anna Gerrish (1712–1761) of Wenham; three of their five children died young. Their son John Fiske (1744–1797) commanded a privateer during the Revolution and became an eminent merchant of Salem, but except for her name on four samplers, no reference to their daughter's teaching career has been found.

On December 19, 1771, Sarah Fiske married Jacob Stivours, and the only comments concerning her life were written by William Bentley at the time of her

---

1. She first received recognition in B&C, wherein the authors assigned four samplers to her school with the implication that her name appeared on each one. Their attributions may have been based on the Peele sampler (their Pl. XC). The Witt sampler (their Pl. XCI) does not name her school, and the Woodbridge and Ives samplers have not been located.

Fig. 115. *BETSE[Y] GILL HER/ SAMPLER WROUGHT/ 1781 IN THE 12/ YEAR OF HER AGE.* Silk on linen; 17½″ x 16⅜″. Betsey's figures resemble those on two nearly identical samplers that named Sarah Stivours' school in 1778 (B&C, Pl. XC, and Krueger, *Gallery*, Fig. 24). Her sister, Prisce Gill, worked a similar sampler in 1782, and it is the only Stivours example to name *SALAM* (Skinner Sale 1156, June 6, 1987, Lot 208). Betsey (1770–1814) and Prisce (1772–1818) were the daughters of John Gill (d.c.1785) and Priscilla Phippen (c.1742–1826), who was a Salem schoolmistress during her widowhood. Betsey married merchant Samuel Brooks (c.1758–1805) on December 21, 1791, and they had five children.
Author's collection.

death. He described Stivours as a baker from Holland and stated that Sarah was "not one year in married life." Also, that "Her Husband from a transaction in his business long since was obliged to withdraw after he had obliged her to alienate her patrimony. . . . Aunt Stivers . . . has lived on the bounty of friends. . . . Was a woman of rude deportment & died in great obscurity."[2] One can only suspect that Bentley knew little about her early life and formed this opinion after old age and hardships had taken their toll.

Samplers that name Sarah Stivours' school (Figs. 114, 116) and pieces that may be attributed with confidence to her teaching offer sound evidence that she taught from 1778 through 1794, presumably in Salem. Prisce Gill named Salem on her sampler of 1782, and the sampler makers all lived in Salem with the exception of Hannah Batchelder (Fig. 114) of Beverly and Sally Witt who lived in Lynn. Other samplers in the Salem long-stitch style have occasionally been attributed to her school, such as Mary Richardson's and Mary Austin's (Figs. 117, 118), but these attributions are questionable.

A number of capable women were teaching in Salem during the last quarter of the eighteenth century; they, too, were probably influenced by those who taught Elizabeth Herbert (Fig. 108) or Susannah Saunders (Fig. 110) and they could have continued the "Salem style" in a variety of ways. In 1798, Bentley reported that Salem had "four public Schools & three Houses, four private Schools, Women's

---

2. "Bentley's Record of Deaths," *EIHC* 19:179; Bentley, *Diary* (1905–1914; reprint, 1962), 4:600. There is conflict concerning Sarah's age. Bentley records death at seventy. Frederick Clifton Pierce (*Fisk & Fiske Family* [Chicago: published by the author, 1896], 82) records birth in 1742; also *Vital Records of Salem,* 1:303 and 6:251.

Fig. 116. *SALLY RUST/ HER SAMPLER WROUG/HT 1788 IN THE 13/ YEAR OF HER AGE*, and stitched below the verse *SARAH STIVOURS SCHOOL*. Silk on linen; 21¼″ x 20½″. Notice that the Stivours samplers are signed in a consistent manner. The latest example attributed to this school was made by Hannah Hunt in 1794 and is exceptionally large (Gore Place Society, Waltham, Massachusetts). Sally Rust (1776–1803) was the tenth child of Salem cabinetmaker and merchant Henry Rust (1737–1812) and Lydia Janes (1740–1808). She married, as his third wife, John Deland (1767–1842), on December 28, 1801, and had one son. In 1786, Sally Rust's first cousin, Sally Witt of Lynn, worked a similar sampler but without the Stivours name (B&C, Pl. XCI).
Collection of Mrs. William Russell Burns.

schools for needle work, four well known in addition to the great number for reading only, or common work."[3]

Mehitable Robie Higginson (1723–1818) was surely among the "well known" teachers. She was born in Salem and married John Higginson (1720–1774) in Boston in 1755. Mrs. Higginson was a staunch Loyalist, and during the Revolution she lived in Halifax and supported her daughter by teaching. Upon her return to Salem in 1782, she opened a school that Bentley described as "the school of fashion for many years.[4] Miss Hetty Higginson (1764–1846) continued teaching after her mother's death and was much beloved by her pupils."[5] Another important schoolmistress was Abigail Dodge Rogers (c.1764–1817), the wife of schoolmaster Nathaniel Rogers (1762–1799). They came from Ipswich and were both teaching in Salem by 1793. Bentley said she "has had the greatest applause in the education of our daughters, of which she has instructed sixty at one time." Her school was especially noted for fine needlework.[6] Priscilla Phippen Gill (1742–1826) was also a Salem schoolmistress of the 1790s (Fig. 115), but exactly who the "four well known" needlework teachers were is unknown now.

---

3. Bentley, *Diary*, entry of May 25, 1798, 2: 270.

4. Ibid., entry of Jan. 20, 1818, 4:496. Girls such as the daughters of John Innes Clark and Robert Sterry of Providence attended this school in 1794 (Ring, *Virtue*, 95).

5. For an account of her school, see Silsbee, *A Half Century in Salem* (1887), 48–51.

6. Bentley, *Diary*, entry of July 2, 1793, 2: 30–1. Abigail Rogers was much admired, but her husband lost his teaching position in Salem in 1796. In 1797, they proposed opening a school in Newburyport (*Newburyport Herald and Country Gazette*, November 3, 1797). Nathaniel Rogers died in Biddeford, Maine, in July 1799, and Abigail, with her children, returned to Salem (Bentley, *Diary*, entry of July 18, 1799, 2:315; July 26, 1802, 2: 441). There is a list of forty-one girls who attended her school in 1800 (EI).

Fig. 117. *Mary Richardson/ This I Did In The 12 Year Of My AGE 1783*. Silk on linen; 20″ x 20½″. Mary's work is perhaps the best-preserved example of Salem's most elaborate sampler style of the 1780s. Many related pieces are known, including Figure 118, and a striking counterpart made by Sally Bott in 1785 (Krueger, *New England*, Fig. 24). The dominant Salem sampler styles of the 1780s did not end abruptly but occasionally lingered into the nineteenth century. See Sally Oliver's sampler of 1801 in Skinner Sale 756, June 26, 1981, Lot 244. Mary Richardson (1772–1824) was the only daughter of Captain Addison Richardson (1739–1811) and Mary Greenleaf (1734–1799) of Salem. She married shipmaster Penn Townsend (1772–1846) on December 1, 1793. They had two daughters.
Essex Institute, 123,559.

Fig. 118. *Mary Austin Her Sampler/ Work In The 12 Year Of/ My Age Salem 1784.* Silk on linen; 12½" x 10". While a degree of crudeness might fit Mary Austin's sampler into the group from Sarah Stivours' school, the difference in the dominant alphabet, the manner of signing it, and the absence of diagonal stitches raises doubt that she was the teacher. Mary's work is one of the few examples of this type to name *Salem.* Mary Austin (b.1773) was the daughter of Jonathan Austin. Possibly she was the Polly Austin who married Dudley Porter (b.1771) of Gloucester on April 6, 1793.

Metropolitan Museum of Art, gift of Mrs. Screven Lorillard, 53.179.14.

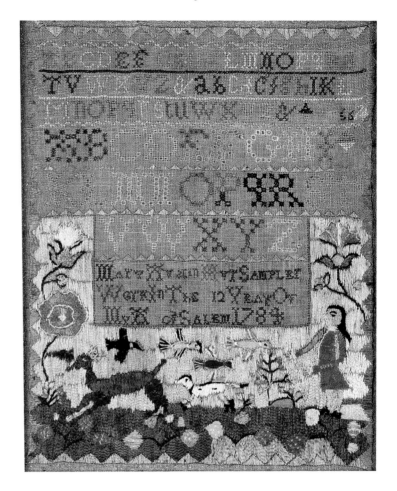

SALEM, DANVERS, AND LYNN

Distinguishing between the samplers of Salem and Danvers is difficult, and logically so, since the part of Salem known as Salem Village became the town of Danvers in 1752. Eighteenth-century samplers with appealing scenes beneath lines of inscriptions filled out with small motifs were generally made by Danvers girls (Fig. 120), but Rebekah Hacker of Salem worked this type in 1786, although her pictorial elements remain typical of Salem (Fig. 119). Other Danvers girls worked line-end designs with a central rose tree and stubby side trees, as in Figures 120 and 121, although with flowing borders and pineapple-like motifs in the corners, as in Figure 122.[1] Similar patterns without line-end designs were also made by girls of Lynn.[2] A great many samplers from this region may be recognized by their combinations of these motifs.

Lydia Stocker and Sally Breed (Figs. 123, 124) both lived in Lynn, as did Sarah Newhall who worked a similar sampler and named *Lynn* in 1798. Content Phillips

———

1. For 1774 and 1788 samplers with pineapple corner motifs see *ANTIQUES*, July 1941, 31, and Swan *Guide*, 14. Abigail Purintun, who worked the 1788 sampler, was born in Danvers on March 3, 1778 (not Reading, as captioned).

2. See *ANTIQUES*, September 1978, 541, for the 1789 sampler of Lydia Burrill, who was born in Lynn.

Fig. 119. *Rebekah Hacker Is My Name And With My/ Nedle I work The Same In The 10 Year Of My age/ 1786.* Silk on linen; 16″ x 13″. A sampler in this style was worked by Mary Purintun, a Quaker girl of Danvers, in 1767 (PMA), but this was made by a Salem girl. Rebekah Hacker (1777–1799) was the daughter of Isaac Hacker (1750–1818) and Anna Estes (1754–1802). For twenty-nine years her father was the writing master of the West School in Salem; he retired in 1814.
Allentown Art Museum, gift of Mrs. William P. Hacker, 78.80.3.

Fig. 120. *Lucy Low Her Sampler Aged 12 1776.* Silk on linen; 14½″ x 11⅜″. Lucy Low continued the earlier borderless format, but her solidly worked scene introduces a central rose tree and stubby side trees, which often reoccur on work from this area. Lucy Low (1764–1842) was the daughter of Caleb Low (1739–1810) and Sarah Shillaber (1739–1815) of Danvers. She married John Frost (1758–1829) in 1781. They lived in Danvers and had at least seven children.
Private collection.

Fig. 121. *Mary Shillaber Her Sampler Aged 14 1776*. Silk on linen; 15¼" x 15". Mary worked figures identical to those of her first cousin, Lucy Low (Fig. 120), but she failed to finish the solidly worked background that was begun in the left corner. Another first cousin, Elizabeth (Betsey) Shillaber, also worked this pattern in 1776 (Skinner Sale 1332, June 16, 1990, Lot 81). She was the mother of Betsey Daniels (Fig. 122). Mary Shillaber (1762–1796) was fourth among the eleven children of William Shillaber (1734–1804) and Mary Waters (b.1735) of Danvers. She married Joseph Osborne, Jr. (1757–1829), in 1785 and died following the birth of her fifth child.

Collection of Madeleine Bond Fisher.

Fig. 122. *Bestey Daniels is my Name and with my hand/ I have Wroght the same in the 12 year of/ My age Danvers January 1 1800*. Silk on linen; 26" x 23¾". The composition and lustrous colors of Betsey's sampler are nearly identical to those in a sampler by Elizabeth Briggs, who signed her work in exactly the same manner and used the same verse, but named *Salem* in 1806 (EI). The teacher may have moved, or they named their home towns, but these girls unquestionably had the same instructress. In 1808, Betsey attended Bradford Academy in Bradford, Massachusetts (Catalogue of Bradford Academy, 1803–1853, at the AAS). Betsey Daniels (b.1788) was the daughter of David Daniels (1757–1827) and Betsey Shillaber (1763–1831). She married Jonathan Howard (d.1825) of Salem in 1810.

Danvers Historical Society, 85.19.1.

Fig. 123. *Lydia Stocker aged 13 1798*. Silk on linen; 17″ x 16″. Closely related samplers were worked by Sally Breed (Fig. 124) and Sarah Newhall (b.1789), both of Lynn, and it now appears likely that these samplers were worked in Lynn. Lydia Stocker (1785–1841) was the daughter of Joseph Stocker (d.1795) and Mehitable Norwood (d.1793) of Lynn. In 1806 she married Nathaniel O. Gowdy (d.1825), a shoemaker. They had seven children.
Cooper-Hewitt, National Museum of Design, Smithsonian Institution, 1970-28-3.

(b.1794) of Lynn also made a related example.³ Lydia Stocker's work has long been associated with Salem samplers, but no evidence of her schooling beyond the town of Lynn has been found.⁴ It now seems evident that these pieces were worked under a schoolmistress in Lynn. She may have been Sarah Sargent, who was instructing the daughter of Nathaniel Collins in 1801.⁵

Many women were teaching in Salem and the surrounding towns during the first quarter of the nineteenth century, and the characteristic styles of specific towns therefore became more diffuse. A growing preference for samplers worked on a green ground (usually linsey-woolsey) became noticeable at the turn of the century. They appeared in Boston as early as 1788,⁶ and later throughout New England; occasionally they occur in the Middle States, and more rarely in the South (Fig. 590). They were especially popular in the coastal region from the northern shore of Massachusetts to southern Maine. Flowing borders growing from cornucopias were much favored in the Salem area (Fig. 125), although certainly not exclusive to it,⁷ while distinctive styles on green grounds developed in Marblehead (Figs. 157–159) and Portsmouth (Figs. 275–277), and the most charming of pictorial pieces are known in small numbers from Connecticut.⁸

——————

3. Sarah Newhall's sampler is privately owned; Content Phillips' is illustrated in B&C, Pl. LV.

4. This research was described in Margaret Vincent's lecture "Names on Samplers and Genealogical Research" at the Cooper-Hewitt Museum's Sampler Day on April 19, 1984.

5. Bill from Sarah Sargent to Nathaniel Collins for instruction of his daughter in 1801 (Lynn Historical Society).

6. The 1788 sampler of Slowi Hays (1779–1836) is in the Smithsonian Institution, Washington, acc. no. 75–122.

7. For samplers representing two recognizable groups from Lynn, see Allen, *Family Record*, Figs. 62, 72.

8. The sampler of Charlotte Porter, Middletown, 1810 (Christie's, January 23, 1982, Lot 205); Sina Hall named *Wallingford* in 1811 (Skinner Sale 1174, October 31, 1987, Lot 105); Nancy Stanton (1790–1879), aged nine, worked a fine example now in the Adam Stanton House, Clinton, Connecticut.

Fig. 124. *Sally Breed 1798 age 11.*
Silk on linen; 14½″ x 17½″. Why
Sally left one border unfinished is
unexplained, but being incomplete,
her sampler survived unframed and
therefore unfaded. In 1801 she
completed a large sampler with a
solidly worked central scene, two
deer in the same shape as seen
here, and a similar motif in the
upper border (John Paul Jones
House, Portsmouth). Sally Breed
(1787–1853) was the daughter of
Frederick Breed (1755–1820) and
his second wife, Sarah Mansfield
(1746–1803), of Lynn. She married
James Burrill on January 5, 1806.
The samplers of Sally's mother, her
sister Mary, and her two daughters
also belong to the Lynn Historical
Society.
Lynn Historical Society, 5388.

Fig. 125. *Sarah G. Tate/ Aged 12 1809.* Silk
on green linsey-woolsey; 20″ x 17″. Several
samplers by Salem girls were obviously made
under Sarah's instructress (see Skinner Sale
1186, January 16, 1988, Lots 200, 201). The
relatively uncommon shape of Sarah's cursive
letter *O* often appears on samplers from this
area, including an 1810 example by Hannah
Phillips, which names Miss Upton's school,
Lynn (Lynn Historical Society); and the
Salem sampler of Mary Southward, 1807
(Krueger, *New England*, Fig. 72). Sarah G.
Tate (1797–before 1843) was born in Salem
to Thomas Tate (d.1838) and Elizabeth
(c.1769–1839). She married Malachi Wilson
(b.1785) in Lynnfield on January 30, 1823.
They lived in Danvers and had seven chil-
dren. In 1843, Malachi married Mary Tate.
*Philadelphia Museum of Art, Whitman Sampler
Collection, gift of Pet Inc., 69.288.96.*

Fig. 126. *Anna Fowler Born March 2 1739 this/ Sampler I did the year 1754.* Silk on linen; 18¾″ x 12¼″. Within a trefoil border Anna worked conventional band patterns and a multicolored, checkered sawtooth above and below her principal motif. Most unusual is the invasion of the major band pattern into the surrounding border. Anna Fowler (b.1739) was the daughter of Samuel Fowler, a Quaker of Newbury, and Abigail. She married blacksmith Samuel Jackman (b.1738) on August 5, 1772, and they lived in Boscawen, New Hampshire.
Collection of Jean and Joseph Andress.

EMBROIDERIES OF NEWBURY AND NEWBURYPORT

In 1635, English planters settled at the junction of the Merrimack and Quascacunquen rivers, and this was the beginning of Newbury. Originally an agrarian community, it gradually developed a prosperous maritime trade, and in 1764 this mercantile district, often referred to as the waterside, officially separated from the old town and was known thereafter as Newburyport.[1]

In the 1750s, if not earlier, a skilled embroideress was teaching in Newbury, and during the next sixty years Newbury and Newburyport girls produced an extraordinary number of handsome samplers. Usually their work can be recognized by a series of repetitious motifs that endured, in modified ways, from the colonial period until the early nineteenth century.

In 1754, Anna Fowler worked a bordered band sampler without pictorial motifs (Fig. 126), but two years later Sarah Toppan added to hers a fruit tree surrounded by birds, beasts, and bugs, and these reoccur on many later examples (Fig. 127). Both girls featured the same stylized floral band pattern that appeared on English work in virtually identical form by 1704 and perhaps earlier. It was also worked on Newport's earliest group of samplers during the 1730s and 1740s (Figs. 196, 197), often in combination with the trefoil border that remained popular in Newbury throughout the eighteenth century.[2]

In addition to fruit trees and animals, flowers in blue vases became a favorite motif in the 1770s and remained popular well into the nineteenth century (Figs. 128, 136). Other enduring Newbury/Newburyport motifs were sawtooth borders in checkered form (Figs. 126–129, 131, 132); multicolored parrots, often with little long-tailed black birds (Figs. 129–131); tiered trees that would also appear on Canterbury, New Hampshire, samplers by 1787 (Fig. 268), and in other New Hampshire towns slightly later; and a stylized carnation motif that had appeared on Boston samplers in the 1730s, and eventually lost its identity, but continued as a shaded clump on a stem (Fig. 129) or a shaded rock, and appears on New Hampshire and Maine samplers well into the 1820s (Figs. 273, 274). It seems certain that the patterns of Newbury and Newburyport also had considerable influence on later samplers of the Piscataqua region.

The earliest Newbury piece that can be attributed to a specific teacher was worked by Elizabeth Coffin in 1784 (Fig. 130), and related work suggests that schoolmistress Ann Waters continued to teach after her marriage to John Woodman, Jr., of Newburyport on December 5, 1787. Although Sarah Anna Emery mentioned numerous teachers in her delightful *Reminiscences of a Nonagenarian,* it is impossible to associate any of those teachers with specific samplers.[3]

---

1. Benes, *Old-Town and the Waterside* (1986), 7–28.
2. Huish, Fig. 32; Ring, *Virtue,* 64, 66–7; the same motif appeared in Dighton, Massachusetts (Krueger, *New England,* Fig. 20), and it was worked in Weare, New Hampshire, in 1817 (*MAD,* October 1986, 28-D) and in 1822 (private collection).
3. Emery, *Reminiscences of a Nonagenarian* (1879), 222–3. Emery praised schoolmistress Mary Ann Coleman

Important among the women teaching in Newburyport during the eighteenth century were the three spinster daughters of Bulkeley Emerson (1732–1801) and Mary Moody (1730–before 1777). Their father was a bookbinder, stationer, and Newburyport's first postmaster, and his only daughters, Mary (1753–1815), Elizabeth (1760–1833), and Martha (1764–1827), devoted their lives to keeping a private girls' school. They may have been teaching by the 1780s, and quite possibly they continued to use the patterns favored by their own girlhood instructress of the 1760–1780 period. Because of their family connections and lengthy careers, it is likely that they were responsible for some of Newburyport's most noteworthy samplers.

The Emersons were, in fact, themselves in their prime when the town's most famous samplers flowered (Figs. 133–135). These spectacular samplers of 1799–1806 are generally known as the "shady bower" group since ten out of eleven examples have the following verse:

> Here in this green and shady bower
> Delicious fruits and fragrant flowers
> Virtue shall dwell within this seat
> Virtue alone can make it sweet

The first and most extraordinary example to emerge was worked by Sally Johnson in 1799 (Fig. 133), and, as yet, no others like it have appeared. However, the samplers in Figures 134 and 135 are unquestionably related to it, and five similar pieces are dated between 1800 and 1803; two are undated, and another piece, without people, was worked in 1806.[4]

A major group of mourning embroideries from this area can be easily recognized by starfish-shaped leaves on the ground (Fig. 137), which are often beneath willow trees having solidly worked diamond-shaped leaves (Fig. 138), and combined with a small repertoire of figures and monuments. It now appears that at least one type within this group was made at Byfield Academy. The history of the school in Byfield is somewhat confusing, but there is reason to believe that similar embroideries were being worked there from 1807 through 1812, and from the summer of 1818 until the fall of 1821.

Deacon Benjamin Coleman, a shoemaker, lived nearly opposite the Congregational Meeting House in Byfield (a part of Newbury), and in the winter of

Fig. 127. *Sarah Toppan Born May 16 1748 This Samplar I did/ The Year 1756.* Silk on linen; 19¼" x 13⅜". A very similar piece, no doubt earlier, was worked by Sarah Sawyer of Newbury who included her birthdate of March 25, 1740 (Skinner Sale 1265, June 10, 1989, Lot 161). In 1760, Mary Starker (b.1749) named *Newbury* on a closely related sampler and added two blue vases shaped like those in Mary Batchelder's piece in Figure 128 (*MESDA Journal* 16, no. 2 [November 1990]: 42). Sarah Toppan (1748–1823) was the daughter of cabinetmaker Edward Toppan (1715–1795) and Sarah Bayley of Newbury. She married Josiah Little (1747–1830) on March 23, 1770. In 1762, Sarah's sister Mary worked a sampler that is described in B&C, 80. It belongs to the Historical Society of Old Newbury. *Location unknown; photograph courtesy of* The Magazine ANTIQUES.

(b.1792), who continued a school begun by her father, Samuel Coleman (1762–1810). Her school was advertised in the *Newburyport Herald* from 1812 to 1818. Also mentioned was "Marm" Dod or Miss Dod, who was probably Mary Thurla Dodd (1776–1824), the widow of Andrew Dodd. She advertised the continuance of her school in the *Newburyport Herald* of April 17, 1812. Emery did not mention Miss Gould (variously named Sally, Ann, or Hannah F.), who advertised from 1803 until 1813. They were probably sisters.

4. For shady bower samplers, see the following: Abigail Prince, 1801 (Ring, *Treasures,* 12); Mary Ann Perkins, 1802 (Stevens-Coolidge Place, North Andover, Mass.); Elizabeth Thurston, 1802 (Skinner Sale 1222, October 29, 1988, Lot 207); Mary Todd, who worked a different verse in 1803 (*ANTIQUES,* September 1978, 545); Sarah Frost Blunt, undated (*A&AW,* October 21, 1983, 44); Dolly Johnson, 1806 (Benes, *Old-Town,* 174); an unsigned example (at SPNEA); unlocated is Mary Little, 1800 (described in B&C, 189).

Fig. 128. *Mary Batchelder Was Born June The 13ᵗʰ 1757 Wrought this/ Sampler 1773.* Silk on linen; 16½″ x 11″. Lucretia Little (1759–1851) of Newbury worked a smaller but closely related sampler in 1773 (Benes, *Old-Town* [1986], Fig. 47). This vase appears on Newbury/Newburyport samplers well into the nineteenth century. For an example of 1799, see Skinner Sale 1098, May 30, 1986, Lot 159. Lucy Lakeman worked one in 1807 (Historical Society of Old Newbury). Mary Batchelder's identity has defied discovery.

Cooper-Hewitt, National Museum of Design, Smithsonian Institution, 1941-69-166.

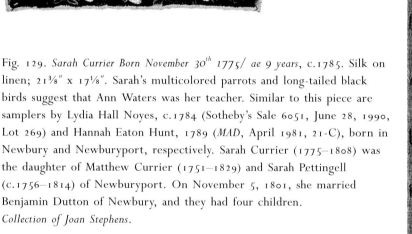

Fig. 129. *Sarah Currier Born November 30ᵗʰ 1775/ ae 9 years*, c.1785. Silk on linen; 21⅜″ x 17⅛″. Sarah's multicolored parrots and long-tailed black birds suggest that Ann Waters was her teacher. Similar to this piece are samplers by Lydia Hall Noyes, c.1784 (Sotheby's Sale 6051, June 28, 1990, Lot 269) and Hannah Eaton Hunt, 1789 (*MAD*, April 1981, 21-C), born in Newbury and Newburyport, respectively. Sarah Currier (1775–1808) was the daughter of Matthew Currier (1751–1829) and Sarah Pettingell (c.1756–1814) of Newburyport. On November 5, 1801, she married Benjamin Dutton of Newbury, and they had four children.
Collection of Joan Stephens.

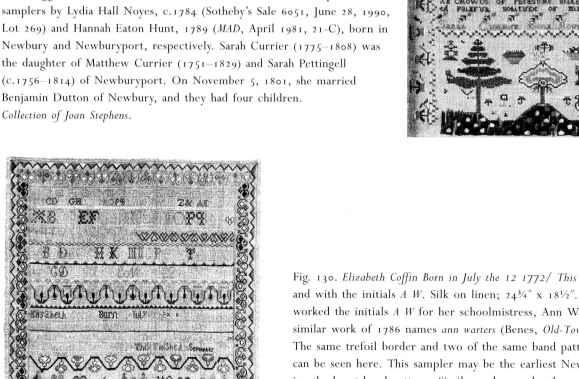

Fig. 130. *Elizabeth Coffin Born in July the 12 1772/ This Finished September 1784* and with the initials *A W*. Silk on linen; 24¾″ x 18½″. Elizabeth no doubt worked the initials *A W* for her schoolmistress, Ann Waters. Her sister Sarah's similar work of 1786 names *ann warters* (Benes, *Old-Town* [1986], Fig. 138a). The same trefoil border and two of the same band patterns used in the 1750s can be seen here. This sampler may be the earliest Newbury example containing the heart band pattern. Similar and more handsome samplers with paired parrots were worked by the sisters Sarah (b.1782) and Abigail Brown (b.1787) in the 1790s (Benes, *Old-Town*, Figs. 48a, 48b). Elizabeth Coffin (1772–1808) was the daughter of the Newbury mariner Abel Coffin (1741–1791) and Anna Gardner Brewer (1738–1825). She married Joseph Hoyt 3rd (1765–1834) on November 14, 1799. In 1810 he married her sister Sarah (1775–1849).
Society for the Preservation of New England Antiquities, Coffin House Collection, gift of Lillian Hale Fay, 1942.814.

Fig. 131. *Jane Herbert Was born May 10 1784 did/ this Work April 1796*. Silk on linen; 21½″ x 19″. Jane included two traditional band patterns and added the heart band pattern. Her more naturalistic floral border also includes the earlier checkered sawtooth design, and her parrot suggests Ann Waters' influence. However, her duck pond anticipates the forthcoming shady bower patterns (Fig. 135). Jane's twin sister, Molly, worked an identical sampler that evidently had its date altered in later years (Christie's, January 30, 1980, Lot 611). Jane Herbert (b.1784) was the daughter of Charles Herbert (c.1757–1808) and Molly Butler of Newburyport. She married David Parker (b.1784) in 1812. *New Hampshire Historical Society, 1925.8.1.*

Fig. 132. *Mary Wiggin her Sampler Wrought in the Year 1797*. Silk on linen; 18″ x 22″. Mary included many typical Newburyport motifs and gave them striking emphasis against a solidly worked black background. Here is the stylized bouquet of earlier years between perfect examples of the "Newbury" fruit tree and bordered with a stunning rendition of the checkered sawtooth motifs. No close counterpart to this sampler has been found, but there is little doubt that it reflects the tuition or influence of Newbury/Newburyport teachers. This sampler maker was most likely Mary Wiggin (b.1780), the daughter of Andrew Wiggin (1752–1836) and the only child of his first wife, Mary Brackett (1754–1786). They lived in Stratham, New Hampshire. Mary married George Hilton (1765–1821) of New Market, New Hampshire, in July 1803, and they had one child. This sampler was recorded in B&C and was said to be from New Market, but no other Mary Wiggin of this period was found to have any connection with New Market. Mary's father was a prosperous and influential citizen of Stratham, who probably sent his eldest daughter to boarding school while rearing his five younger children. *Philadelphia Museum of Art, Whitman Sampler Collection, gift of Pet Inc., 69.288.18.*

Fig. 133. *Sally Johnson/ AE 12/ 1799.* Silk on linen; 19″ x 27″. Each line of Sally's verse begins with a capital letter and ends on the line above. Her remarkable sampler was the first of the shady bower group to be published (B&C, Pl. CVI), and its complex pattern surpasses its closest counterparts (Figs. 134, 135). Sarah (Sally) Johnson (1787–1868) was second among the eight children of Nicholas Johnson (1752–1825) and Mary Perkins (c.1755–1829). Her father was among the richest men of Newburyport and active in civic affairs. Sally married John Chickering (c.1784–1845) on January 30, 1812. They were childless.
Milwaukee Art Museum, M1991.403; photograph courtesy of Skinner, Inc.

Fig. 134. *Sarah Bartlett/ AE 12 Augᵗ 26/1800.* Silk on linen; dimensions unknown. Unlike the majority of shady bower samplers, Sarah's work has no arbor, duck pond, or lady beneath an umbrella. Sarah Bartlett (1788–1822) was the daughter of Richard Bartlett (1762–1810) and Ann Moody (1765–1831) of Newburyport. She married William Gage on May 31, 1809. *Location unknown; photograph courtesy of Sotheby's.*

Fig. 135. *Mary Coffin AE. 10. 1801.* Silk on linen; 15″ x 20½″. Mary's sampler is a typical example of the shady bower group, and, like Jane Herbert's work (Fig. 131), it bears kinship to a forerunner of this style made by Tabby Russell in 1789 (Sotheby's Sale 6149, February 1, 1991, Lot 781). Mary Coffin (1790–1864) was the daughter of Newburyport mer-

chant David Coffin (1763–1838) and Elizabeth Stone (1767–1811). When she was fifteen, in 1806, Mary attended Bradford Academy. She married Nathaniel Noyes, Jr. (1791–1864), on November 12, 1815, and they had seven children.

Location unknown; photograph courtesy of Robert C. Eldred Co., Inc.

Fig. 136. *Hannah Bartlet born Sept[r] 26 1791 AE 13 Years 1804/ NEWBURY/PORT Novem/ber 1804.* Silk on linen; 21″ x 16½″. Hannah included many motifs found on earlier work, including a cow and a black dog with white spots that seems to have a horse's head, as often found on Haverhill samplers. Her sheep resemble those of Sarah Bartlett (Fig. 134). There are the familiar blue vase, heart and trefoil band patterns, and the same verse worked by Mary Todd on her shady bower sampler of 1803. Hannah Bartlett (b.1791) was the daughter of Richard Bartlett (1763–1832) and Hannah Pettingell (1764–1836). In 1822 she married Nathaniel Hodge (1794–1859). They had three children.
Historical Society of Old Newbury, 335.

1806–1807, he moved the old Slade Meeting House to a nearby property and prepared it for a school building. On April 10, 1807, the *Newburyport Herald* published the prospectus for Byfield Academy, which was to open on the second Wednesday in May for both sexes and under "an able Preceptor and Preceptress." Subjects included "Drawing, Painting, Embroidery, and all kinds of fine Needle Work." The building was described as "large, the situation healthy and pleasant, in the centre of the parish, near the elegant country seat of Ebenezer Parsons, Esq." Applicants were to contact "BENJAMIN COLEMAN, Agent of the Proprietors."

This school was advertised regularly through April 1812, but the preceptress was never named. Actually its series of teachers were mostly young women who had belonged to the first class at Bradford Academy when it opened in 1803. They were Rebecca Hardy (b.1786) from Pelham, New Hampshire; Rebecca Hasseltine (b.1782) of Bradford, assisted by her sister Ann (b.1789); Mary Atwood (b.1789) of Haverhill; and finally Eliza Tuck and Mary Adams, who were not Bradford alumna.[5] Sarah Emery recalled that there were usually forty or fifty scholars attending the Byfield Academy. They were "young ladies from the wealthier families in the neighborhood and surrounding country, with others from places more

---

5. Pond, *Bradford, A New England Academy* (1930), 77.

Fig. 137. Mourning embroidery dedicated on the plinth to *The Rev Ariel Parish/ Obt May 20 1794 AE 30/ By his daughter Amelia*, c.1808. Silk and paint on silk; 11½" x 12". Attributed to the Byfield Academy because of a nearly identical piece known to have been worked there in 1808 under the instruction of Mary Atwood (Benes, *Old-Town* [1986], Fig. 196). A piece worked by Catharine Pearson in 1807 is also nearly identical (Northeast Auctions, Hampton, New Hampshire, April 30, 1989, Lot 564). Amelia Parish (September 18, 1794–1859) was born in Manchester after the death of her father, the Reverend Ariel Parish (1765–1794), who married Hannah Chute (1765–1842) of Rowley in 1792. Amelia's uncle, Elijah Parish (c.1762–1825), was the much respected minister of the Congregational Church in Byfield. Probably she lived with his family while attending Byfield Academy, as did a number of other students. Amelia married the Reverend Ebenezer Perkins (1794–1861) of Royalston in 1819 and had seven children.

Location unknown; photograph courtesy of Sotheby's.

remote. . . . The Misses Hazeltine and some half dozen of the pupils boarded with Dr. Parish. . . ."[6]

According to an inscription on a mourning embroidery that is nearly identical to Figure 137, "Miss Atwood" was the preceptress in 1808.[7] Rebecca Hasseltine may also have been there at this time, and her sister Abigail, later the much respected Principal of Bradford Academy, is said to have taught there for one summer. In January of 1810, Rebecca Hasseltine married, as his third wife, the Reverend Joseph Emerson (1777–1833) of Beverly.

No references to the closing of the Byfield Academy have been found, but on March 24, 1818, the *Newburyport Herald* devoted four full columns to the Seminary in Byfield that was to open under the direction of the Reverend Joseph Emerson, noting that he had purchased "the house in which the Female Academy was kept several years." Emerson was well known for his ideas on advanced education for women, and though he taught in Byfield for less than three years, the school is remembered for such scholars as Zilpah Grant and Mary Lyon.[8] Emerson's wife Rebecca, his active assistant, no doubt taught embroidery with the recognizable motifs of earlier work, for certainly the unusual starfish leaves known to have been worked in Byfield in 1808 (Fig. 137) appeared again in 1819 (Fig. 138). Rebecca Hasseltine may have originated the solidly worked, diamond-shaped willow leaves when she first taught in Byfield, and these leaves also occur on later Newburyport samplers.[9]

It is equally possible, however, that these motifs originated at Bradford Academy and were developed in various ways by a number of its students who

6. Emery, *Reminiscences,* 98.

7. Inscribed on the reverse. Benes, *Old-Town,* Fig. 196. Contrary to the caption, Mary Atwood, not Harriet, was the preceptress. Harriet Atwood (1793–1812) may have attended the Byfield Academy when her sister taught there.

8. Portland schoolmistress Alma Cross also attended the Byfield Seminary. Emerson moved his school to Saugus in November 1821, and to Wethersfield, Connecticut, in 1824.

9. Benes, *Old-Town,* Fig. 153; Allen, *Family Record,* Fig. 77.

Fig. 138. Mourning piece inscribed on the plinth *Memento/ Mori./ Children of Theop & Sarah/ Jaques/ Sarah born March 6th 1796. Obt. April 26, 1802 AE 5 yr/ Paul T. born June 27th 1796 Obt. in Batavia Sep 25th 1818 AE 31 yr/ This piece was done by the hand of their sister Mary AE 20 yr*, c.1819. Silk and paint on silk; 13″ x 15¾″. Mary worked the Newburyport region's most familiar form of mourning embroidery, probably at the Byfield Seminary under the instruction of Rebecca Hasseltine Emerson. It is likely that Mary would have attended Emerson's school where a number of older girls were enrolled. She was probably the Mary Jacques listed in the 1813 class of Bradford Academy. A very similar Dodge/Coleman family memorial belongs to Old Sturbridge Village; a nearly identical piece dedicated to Bayley family members was sold in Skinner Sale 1126, January 2, 1987, but not shown in the catalogue. For a related watercolor memorial and another embroidery, see SPB, Garbisch III, Sale 3692, November 12, 1974, Lots 29, 67. Mary Jaques (b.c.1799) was the daughter of Theophilus Jaques (1765–1840) and Sarah Wood (1763–1837) of Newburyport. She married Nathaniel Woodman in 1832. *Historical Society of Old Newbury, gift of the estate of Willard Hale, 1266.*

Fig. 139. Embroidered arms inscribed on the motto ribbon *BY THE/NAME OF/ LITTLE* and on the reverse of the original frame *Wrought by Abigail Little*, c.1801. Silk on silk; 18″ x 13″. Abigail's pattern was probably derived from painted arms by John Coles, Sr. (1749–1809). She also worked the Dummer arms in the style of a different heraldic painter and added her embroidered signature (Little, *Little by Little* [1984], Fig. 186). Abigail's work may represent the type of arms made at Mrs. Katherine Brown's school in Newburyport, since she is known to have taught heraldic embroidery. Abigail Little (1787–1871) was the daughter of Moses Little (1767–1857) and Elizabeth Dummer (1763–1840). She spent her life in Newbury and died unmarried, aged eighty-four.
Collection of Bertram K. and Nina Fletcher Little.

taught in the region. A watercolor painted by Nancy Hildreth at Bradford in 1805 has a shepherdess in a pasture with a suggestion of the starfish leaves seen in Figures 137 and 138,[10] and among Nancy's classmates were Mary Atwood and the Hasseltine sisters. Some of the family names found on the memorials also appear in early Bradford enrollment records,[11] and Sophia Hayes, a student of 1807, recalled that work on satin was much in vogue.[12] Yet it is still impossible to associate any group of embroideries with Bradford Academy.

Sarah Anna Emery mentioned the silk embroideries worked at Mrs. Brown's school and also coats of arms "embroidered on white satin with colored silk."[13] Quite possibly Abigail Little worked her arms at this school (Fig. 139). Mrs. Brown was Katherine Wigglesworth Jones, the daughter of Nathaniel Jones and Katherine Wigglesworth of Ipswich, who were married in Newbury in 1762. Katherine married the sea captain William Brown (1768–1799) in 1793, and they had three children. He was lost at sea, and in the *Newburyport Herald* of September 5, 1800, she announced the opening of her school for young ladies. In later advertisements, she usually offered board, and in March of 1813 she mentioned "plain Needlework, Embroidery of all kinds, painting on wood, silk or paper, Flowers, figures, landscapes, transparencies and the new and much admired art of drawing and shading in durable ink."[14] According to Emery, she was later "the Principal of a flourishing seminary in Georgetown, D.C."[15]

---

10. Illustrated in Pond, *Bradford,* opp. 70. Harriet Webster (1785–1807) of Bradford was preceptress at Bradford Academy in 1805–1806.

11. *Semi-Centennial Catalogue of the Officers and Students of Bradford Academy, 1803–1853* (1853).

12. Wyatt, *Autobiography of a Landlady of the Old School* (1854), 47–8. Sophia Cushing Hayes was a young widow and had already kept a school in Dover, New Hampshire.

13. Emery, *Reminiscences,* 223.

14. *Newburyport Herald,* March 23, 1813.

15. Emery, *Reminiscences,* 222.

S A M P L E R S   O F   H A V E R H I L L

The town of Haverhill was established beside the Merrimack River in 1640 and named for the English hometown of its minister, the Reverend John Ward, who was instrumental in its settlement.[1] Well over a century later, the population of Haverhill was still under two thousand, but samplers reveal that a capable woman was teaching Haverhill girls during the second quarter of the eighteenth century. Probably before 1730, Anna Pecker worked her birthdate of *January 3, 1715* and the following verse on her borderless band sampler: *Anna Pecker it is/ my name NewEngland/ is my nation Haverhil/ is my Dweling Place/ and Christ is my/ exaltation.*[2] In 1738, sixteen-year-old Hannah Cogswell completed a more skillfully worked version of essentially the same pattern and used the standard *Salvation* rather than *exaltation* in the familiar verse.[3]

The existence of the earlier Haverhill samplers supports the likelihood that Elisabeth Pecker worked her splendid sampler of 1750 in her hometown rather than in a Boston boarding school (Fig. 140). The basic format of Elisabeth's sampler, with trees and animals below band patterns, also occurs on early Newbury/ Newburyport samplers (Fig. 127), but the fruit trees as well as the animals are worked differently. However, Haverhill's typical motifs of the donkey-headed, spotted black dog and the long-legged bird looking backward are occasionally found on later Newburyport samplers, including several belonging to the shady bower group. If the Misses Emerson of Newburyport were responsible for those patterns, it may be significant that their mother, Mary Moody (b.1730) was a native-born Haverhill girl and a contemporary of Elisabeth Pecker. In any case, the motifs worked in the 1750s reappeared with remarkable fidelity on Haverhill samplers of the 1780s and 1790s (Figs. 141, 142). This suggests the enduring influence of a respected schoolmistress.

Unlike Newburyport samplers, early Haverhill examples are relatively rare. However, a new horizontal Haverhill style appeared in 1801, and at least twelve pieces, signed *HAVERHILL COUNTY ESSEX*, were worked in a consistent style until 1810 (Figs. 143, 144). They retain the geometric side borders of earlier Haverhill samplers, but their grassy knolls are without animals or people. Their greatest charm lies in the wide, leafy outer borders found on the best examples. Elizabeth Ayer worked one of the finest pieces within this group in 1801 and named *Miss Parker's School* (Fig. 143),[4] as did Ruth Emerson on a similar but un-

1. *Vital Records of Haverhill to the end of the year 1849* (Topsfield, Mass.: Topsfield Historical Society, 1910), 1:4.

2. Anna Pecker (1715–1778) of Haverhill married the Reverend Samuel Chandler (1713–1775) of Gloucester. Her sampler is in the EI.

3. Hannah Cogswell (1722–1761) was the daughter of John Cogswell (1699–1780) and Susanna Low (1698–1784). They moved to Haverhill from Marblehead. Hannah married Dr. James Pecker of Haverhill. Her sampler belongs to the Quabog Historical Society, West Brookfield, Massachusetts.

4. Others were worked by Hannah Gale, 1801 (Fawdry & Brown, 102); Mary Hazen Bradley, 1807 (*MAD*, August 1979, 29-C); Mary Davis, 1807 (North Andover Historical Society); Harriot W. Hildreth, 1807 (Ed-

Fig. 140. *Elisabeth Pecker/ Born July 31/ in the year/ of our Lord 1733/ ELISABETH PECKER IS MY NAME AND WI/TH MY NEEDLE I WROUGHT THE SAME 1750*. Silk, wool, hair, metal-wrapped silk, and woven fabric on linen; 20″ x 15¾″. Elisabeth worked one of the earliest Massachusetts samplers with appliqué and an elaborate pastoral scene. Her scroll pattern at the top, the square and hexagonal pattern, and the triangular one, appear on early Boston samplers as well as on Hannah Cogswell's Haverhill sampler of 1738. Elisabeth worked typical Haverhill fruit trees with trunks splitting into two major branches separated by a bird on a stubby center branch. The white-bellied deer, the white-spotted black dog with a donkey-shaped head, the bird looking backward, and the multicolored bird at the far right are found on other Haverhill samplers (Figs. 141, 142). Elisabeth Pecker (1733–1803) was the daughter of John Pecker (1687–1756) and Hannah (Redford) Wainwright of Haverhill. She died unmarried.
Cooper-Hewitt, National Museum of Design, Smithsonian Institution, 1970-28-15.

finished sampler of 1802. Circumstantial evidence indicates that Miss Parker was Anne (b. August 5, 1759), the daughter of the Reverend Benjamin Parker (1718–1789) and Elizabeth Fletcher (1728–1759). Benjamin Parker was born in Bradford, graduated from Harvard in 1737, and received his M.A. degree in 1740. In 1744 he was ordained the first minister of Haverhill's East Congregational Church and began a somewhat stormy career as pastor of the East Meetinghouse where he struggled to maintain his family on an exceedingly meager income. When he was finally dismissed in January of 1777, his church became extinct, and he retired to a small farm.[5] Anne was the youngest of his six children by his first wife. He later had daughter Lucy (1761–1837) by Lucy Ruggles, whom he married in 1760.

Because of the financial difficulties of this well-educated family, it is likely that they turned to teaching to supplement their income. Parker's second child, Daniel (1751–1821), graduated from Harvard and was for many years a schoolmaster in Haverhill. By 1793, when the other Parker children had died or moved

monds, Fig. 16); Mary Swett, 1808 (private collection); and Abigail Ayer (see Fig. 143). Four others are described in B&C, 126, 140, 165, 219. Ruth Emerson's is in a private collection.
5. *Sibley's Harvard Graduates, 1736–1740* (1958), 10:220–2.

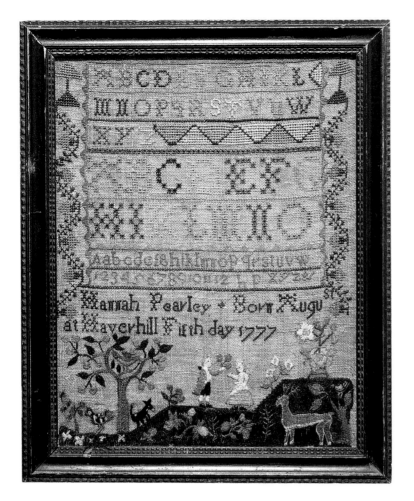

Fig. 141. *Hannah Pearley Born Augu*ˢᵗ/ *at Haverhill Fifth day 1777*, c. 1789. Silk on linen; 13″ x 10″. About forty years after Elisabeth Pecker worked her sampler (Fig. 140), Hannah Pearley stitched a very similar fruit tree, deer, dog, and multicolored bird, and ended her first alphabet with the same triangular pattern. Hannah was the daughter of John Pearley (1746–1778) and Hannah Green (1747–1846) of Haverhill. Her father was a farmer and a tailor, and fought at the battle of Lexington. He died of small-pox before Hannah was two years old and his brother Benjamin became the guardian of his children. Hannah married Moses Payson.

Location unknown; photograph courtesy of C. G. Sloan & Company, Inc., North Bethesda, Maryland.

Fig. 142. *Haverhill August the 11 Sally Aye*ʳ/*Born in the year of our Lord 1780/ This wrought in the 11 Year of age*, c.1790. Silk on linen; 17″ x 13″. Sally's sampler bears kinship to both earlier and later Haverhill work. Between typical sawtooth and strawberry side borders she added the unique geometric border that characterizes the nine-teenth-century Haverhill samplers attributed to Miss Parker's school. For this border on Sarah Swett's sampler, c.1783, see Ring, *Treasures*, 12. Sally Ayer (1780–1802) was the daughter of Moses Ayer (1747–1820) and Martha Kimball (c.1749–1805) of Haverhill. She died of consumption on April 7, 1802.

Collection of Madeleine Bond Fisher.

Fig. 143. *ELIZABETH AYER*
Born August 11ᵗʰ 1789
wrought/ this in Miss
PARKER'S School 1801
HAVERHILL/ COUNTY
ESSEX. Silk on linen; 16½"
x 20¾". Miss Parker was
probably Anne (Nancy)
Parker (1759–after 1840),
and she may have instructed
Sally Ayer (Fig. 142).
Elizabeth's work belongs to
a group of thirteen closely
related samplers, but only
one of the other makers
named her mistress. Elizabeth Ayer (b.1789) was the
daughter of Obadiah Ayer
(c.1751–1823) and Elizabeth
Whittier (1755–1818) of
Haverhill. In 1808, Elizabeth's sister Abigail (b.1795)
worked a similar and equally
beautiful sampler (Sotheby's,
Kapnek Sale 4531Y, January
31, 1981, Lot 43).
Collection of Timra and Mark
Freedman.

elsewhere, Daniel, Anne (usually called Nancy), and Lucy Parker sold the homestead inherited from their father—one piece of property adjacent to the meetinghouse and another by the great pond.[6] Daniel later moved to Salem where he
was master of the Public Latin School from 1798 until 1810. He was also librarian of the Philosophical Society (which became the Salem Atheneum) and the
clerk of Saint Peter's Church.[7] By about 1800, the spinster sisters Nancy and Lucy
Parker were the last of their family in Haverhill. They may have taught school
with their brother in earlier years, and after selling the homestead, they probably moved into town and opened a girls' school, although no deeds or other
records have been found to confirm this. The census reveals that Nancy Parker
was living in Haverhill until after 1840, but the date of her death is unknown, and
no family graves are marked except Nancy's mother's grave.

The Misses Parker, either Nancy or Lucy, could have been teaching around
1783 when Sarah Swett worked a sampler suggestive of the later Haverhill style.
If the Miss Parker of 1801 was not responsible for Sarah Swett's or Sally Ayer's
samplers (Fig. 142), she may have been taught by their instructress. Surely she
was aware of their patterns since she adopted their geometric side border, which
was worked on all the samplers of the Haverhill group from 1801 through 1810.

6. Essex County Deeds, Book 157, 55.
7. "Recollections of Benjamin F. Brown," *EIHC* 5:199–200.

Fig. 144. *LYDIA TEEL SOUTHER, wrought this in 1810./ AGED. 10 HAVERHILL COUNTY ESSEX.* Silk on linen; 15½″ x 17½″. Lydia Teel Souther (1800–after 1882), the daughter of Samuel Souther, Jr. (1756–1813), and Sarah Wilson (c.1760–1850), was born in Amesbury. She married Paul Dole (d.1836) in Haverhill on August 28, 1831. *Collection of Timra and Mark Freedman.*

Other characteristic motifs and a remarkably similar technique appear in Martha Ayer's sampler and suggest that Miss Parker was still teaching in 1827 (Fig. 146).

Variations of the nineteenth-century Haverhill format were also used by another instructress in 1808 and 1815 (Fig. 145). Both pieces were probably made under the tuition of Elizabeth White Plummer (1789–1830), a teacher who may have been a former pupil of Miss Parker. She was the daughter of Haverhill's Thomas Plummer (1756–1836) and Elizabeth Chandler (1761–1839). At present, only the samplers of the Kimball sisters can be attributed to her instruction, but they indicate that she kept her school for at least seven years. She died unmarried.

In the meantime, the Misses White opened a boarding and day school in Haverhill in the spring of 1809, which offered "different varieties of Fancy Needle Work," and they were still teaching in 1811.[8] Atkinson Academy in nearby Atkinson, New Hampshire, also advertised various accomplishments in 1810.[9] These schools were in competition with Bradford Academy, where "Samplers, fine muslin embroidery and lace making" are said to have been taught for many years,[10] but no samplers from Haverhill, Atkinson, or Bradford have yet rivaled the output of the elusive Miss Parker.

---

8. *Merrimack Intelligencer,* Haverhill, May 5, 1809, and March 16, 1811.
9. Ibid., April 28, 1810.
10. Pond, *Bradford* (1930), 63.

Fig. 145. *MARY G KIMBALL wrought this in E. PLUM-MER'S School in the/ 11th year of her age HAVERHILL 1808.* Silk on linen; 12½" x 17". Mary's sister Caroline worked a related sampler and named *Haverhill Massachusetts* in 1815 (PMA). Mary Graves (b.1797) and Caroline (b.1802) were the daughters of Solomon Kimball (1773–1825) and Polly Shepard (c.1771–1830). Mary married James W. Ayer, 2nd, on March 29, 1826.
Collection of Robert W. Roth-bard.

Fig. 146. *MARTHA KIMBALL AYER born/ Dec. 8th 1818. Wrought this in 1827.* Silk on linen; 15½" x 17½". In the manner of eighteenth-century Haverhill samplers, Martha gave her full birth-date. She also recorded the deaths of her father and grandfather. Martha Kimball Ayer was the daughter of Joseph Kimball Ayer (1792–1820) and Sally Sargent of Haverhill. Sally Ayer (Fig. 142) was her father's older sister. On May 7, 1839, Martha married Samuel C. Sawyer of Bradford.
Author's collection.

Fig. 147. *RUTHY ROGERS,* c.1789. Silk on linen; 10½" x 9". Ruthy's captivating composition above the simplicity of her balanced signature creates a sampler of extraordinary appeal. Lydia Boden worked a close counterpart with the figure in profile (*ANTIQUES,* September 1987, 382). Ruthy Rogers (1778–1812) was the daughter of Marblehead tailor William Rogers (1747–1835) and Ruth Vickery (b.1751). Ruthy married shipmaster Benjamin Andrews, Jr. (1775–1821), on June 28, 1799, and died of consumption, aged thirty-four. Her husband drowned in Sumatra by "Overseting the Boat" (*Vital Records of Marblehead,* 2:476). Her sampler descended with this note: "The sampler was made by your great great grandmother in the 1700's somewhere . . . she was my great grandmother, grandfather Andrews first wife—Dec. 25, 1923." *Private collection.*

MARBLEHEAD: ITS MAGNIFICENT SAMPLERS AND EMINENT SCHOOLMISTRESS

The incomparable samplers of Marblehead have no foreign counterparts and represent American girlhood embroidery at its best. Their lively designs (as in Figs. 147, 152) and perky verses (Figs. 148, 149) captured the spirit of optimism in the new nation as well as the climate of their town, which was described by William Bentley, with a touch of disdain, as "the singular freedom of speaking & acting that characterizes Marblehead."[1]

The existence of Marblehead samplers as a group was unknown before 1980, but they now compose one of the most spectacular recognizable groups of New England needlework. In their diversity and the charm of their compositions, they rival the work from Mary Balch's school in Providence. However, unlike the wealth of history and interesting anecdotes concerning Mary Balch's school, scarcely a shred of evidence confirms the existence of the Marblehead schoolmistress responsible for these masterpieces, and the town of their origin was decidedly different from Providence.

The rocky reef that is Marblehead was a rugged fishing village by 1633, and in 1634, its "good harbor for boats and safe riding for ships" was described by William Wood in *New England's Prospect*.[2] On August 14, 1766, John Adams observed that "Marblehead differs from Salem. The streets are narrow and rugged, and dirty, but there are some very grand buildings,"[3] and the prosperous fishermen who lived in the "grand buildings" were sending their children to a respectable school kept by Hannah Pickering Collins (b. 1708), the widow of Adoniram. She taught there during the 1760s and 1770s, and her influence possibly contributed to the samplers considered here. Hannah recorded the names of 130 children who attended her school between 1759 and 1763, as well as a number from the 1770s.[4]

Marblehead's remarkable samplers appeared in the 1780s when the local economy was suffering from the aftermath of the Revolution. Upon visiting there in 1789, George Washington said, "About 5000 souls are said to be in this place, which has the appearance of antiquity; the Houses are old; the streets dirty; and the common people not very clean."[5] In 1750, Francis Goelet had complained about "the Stench of the Fish," and in 1796, the Duke De La Rochefoucault-Liancourt observed that "All the men are so entirely occupied in fishing, that the town, to a stranger who passes through the streets, appears to be solely inhabited

---

1. Bentley, *Diary* (1905–1914; reprint, 1962), entry of January 13, 1806, 3:211.
2. William Wood, *New England's Prospect*, Alden T. Vaughn, ed. (Amherst, Mass.: University of Massachusetts, 1977), 64. First published in London in 1634.
3. George Francis Dow, "Essex County in the Massachusetts Bay Colony as described by early Travelers," *The Historical Collections of the Topsfield Historical Society*, (1921), 26:15–16.
4. *EIHC* 56 (1920): 283–7.
5. Dow, "Essex County," 95.

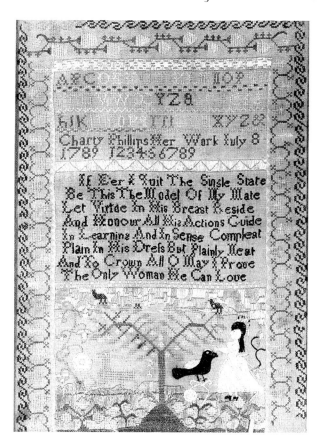

Fig. 148. *Charty Phillips Her Work Iuly 8/ 1789.* Silk on linen; 14″ x 10″. Charity's work is the earliest dated example of the piquant people form, and she worked an unusual verse:

> If E'er I quit The Single State
> Be This The Model Of My Mate
> Let Virtue In His Breast Reside
> And Honour All His Actions Guide
> In Learning And In Sense Compleat
> Plain In His Dress But Plainly Neat
> And To Crown All O May I Prove
> The Only Woman He Can Love

Charity's sampler evidently descended with a sampler of 1770 worked by an earlier Charity Phillips (born to John and Charity in 1751) and sold at Sotheby's Sale 4785Y, January 27–30, 1982, Lot 960. The Charity of this sampler has not been found.
Location unknown; photograph courtesy of Sotheby's.

Fig. 149. *Hannah Stacy Her Work November 8 89.* Silk on linen; 14¼″ x 13⅜″. Hannah's deeply arcaded border is the most elaborate within this group. Her verse is also unusual:

> Why should I make a man my trust
> Princes must die and turn to dust
> Their breath departs their pomp and po/wer
> And thoughts all vanish in an hour

It is impossible to identify Hannah, since girls named Hannah Stacy were born in Marblehead in 1778, 1779, and 1780.
Hagley Museum and Library, Wilmington, Delaware, 70.25.87.

Fig. 150. *LOIS HOOPER*, c.1790. Silk on linen; 10¾″ x 8¼″. Like Ruthy Rogers, Lois worked a forward view of the typical wasp-waisted lady and added a man to her composition. A similar man with a lady in side view, and both wearing hats, was worked by Rebecca Dixey (*ANTIQUES*, July 1989, 70). Its composition and border closely resemble the work of Betsy Gail (Ring, *Treasures*, 11). This girl was probably Lois Hooper (1780–1872), the daughter of Luther Hooper (1746–1831) and Phebe Washburne (1761–1827) of Bridgewater, Massachusetts. On April 12, 1801, she married Avery Fobes (1770–1845). Lois and Sukey Smith (Fig. 153) are the only sampler makers within this group whose parents were not residents of Marblehead, but they unquestionably worked these samplers there.
Private collection.

Fig. 151. *Hannah Nimblett Her Work/ aged 13 Years,*
c.1795. Silk on linen; 10⅜″ x 7¼″. Hannah's work
appears to be a forerunner of a number of Marblehead
samplers featuring facing couples. Her figures have hats
somewhat larger than those worked by Rebecca Dixey on
her piquant people sampler, c.1790. Very similar people
were placed against a solidly worked background by
twenty-five-year-old Sally Brown and within a border like
Mary Follet's (Fig. 154) but undated (privately owned).
Hannah Nimblett (b.1782) was the daughter of Robert
Nimblett and Hannah Dodd of Marblehead. Her sampler
was found in Marblehead's John Rockwood house, built
in the 1730s.
Collection of Joan Stephens.

by women and children, all of whom have a most miserable and wretched appearance."[6]

But the Marblehead samplers attest to the presence of a grace and culture in
Marblehead that eluded these passing travelers, and working among the people of
quality was a woman who must have seen majesty, rather than danger, in the
wave-washed rocky shore. Her sunlit schoolroom was surely drenched in the per-
fume from her garden—not the stench of drying fish; and despite a life of hard-
ship and widowhood, she approached teaching with fresh ideas and a cheerful
enthusiasm. How else could she have envisioned such winsome figures in exuberant floating landscapes (Figs. 152–155), or placed such piquant people amid giant
flowers and inquisitive birds (Figs. 147–151)? There is no question that the products of her teaching were admired in her time, and she became known as "an eminent schoolmistress" in an age when men's accolades for women were not
carelessly bestowed.[7]

---

6. Ibid., 4, 109.

7. Martha Barber was described as "an eminent schoolmistress for many years" by Reverend John Bartlett,
whose private death records comprise part of the *Vital Records of Marblehead, Massachusetts to the End of the
Year 1849* (Salem: Essex Institute, 1904), 2: 480.

Fig. 152. *Hannah Hooper Work^d in the 12th year,* c. 1790. Silk and metal on linen; 16¼″ x 21″. Many motifs in Hannah's sampler relate to others within this group, including the earliest example. "Work'd by Mary Russell in 1784," and Mary Trail's sampler of 1791 (B&C, Pls. CIX, XLIV). Hannah Hooper (1778–1855) was the daughter of Robert Hooper

(1741–1814), a wealthy merchant of Marblehead, and Mary Ingalls (1740–1807). On November 13, 1800, she married William Reed (1776–1837), a merchant in partnership with her brothers and a representative to Congress, 1811–1815. *Collection of William Hooper.*

Fig. 153. *Sukey Jarvis Smith Workd in the year 1791*. Silk on linen; 19¼″ x 21½″. This is perhaps the most skillfully worked of the solidly stitched black background samplers. Sukey was seventeen or eighteen years old when she made it. Susan Jarvis Smith (1773–1809) was the daughter of Stephen Smith (1741–1799), a wealthy citizen of Bristol, Rhode Island, and Mary Gorham (1743–1785). She evidently worked this sampler while visiting her sister Hannah, the wife of Dr. John Drury of Marblehead. On January 7, 1797, Sukey was married in Bristol to shipmaster Edward Spalding, Jr. (1767–1804), son of the Providence clockmaker. They had two daughters. Although previously assigned to a Bristol, Rhode Island, school along with Mary Russell's sampler of 1791 and Figure 154 (Ring, *Virtue,* 224–7), there is now sound evidence that these were worked in Marblehead. *Private collection.*

Fig. 154. *Mary Follet Her Work/ aged 12 years 1802*. Silk on linen; 21″ x 16½″. Mary's sampler provides a convincing link between the different styles employed at Martha Barber's school. The flowers of her border are similar to those in Betsy Gail's sampler (belonging to the piquant people group), and it is clearly related to Sally Butman's border (Fig. 156).

Its central scene continues the patterns of the 1780s and 1790s. Mary Follet (b.1789) was the daughter of Thomas Follet (b.1758) and Mary Blaney of Marblehead. She married Samuel Collins, Jr., of Lynn on November 24, 1811.
Cooper-Hewitt, National Museum of Design, Smithsonian Institution, bequest of Gertrude M. Oppenheimer, 1981-28-132.

On the strength of circumstantial evidence, the Marblehead schoolmistress is here identified as Martha Tarr Hanover Barber, who was baptized in Marblehead on March 2, 1734/35. Her father was Richard Tarr from Gloucester, who married Sarah Beal (b.1697) on September 29, 1719, and Martha was the third of their four children. On February 2, 1759, Martha married Marblehead cordwainer Samuel Hanover (1734–1772), and between November 1759 and September 1765, they had four children—Othniel Beal, Martha, Sarah, and John Beal. Martha was a thirty-nine-year-old widow when on June 30, 1774, she married John Barber (Barbier, Barbet). He was the widower of her deceased husband's sister Miriam, by whom he had ten children. Martha and John Barber had Miriam, born April 9, 1775, and by 1780, Martha was again a widow.[8] Possibly she opened her school shortly thereafter. A spectacular sampler of 1784 belongs to the Marblehead group,[9] but the greatest period of productivity during the eighteenth century seems to have been between 1789 and 1791.[10] Martha Barber died intestate on January 23, 1812, and her death was attributed to "old age." She was seventy-seven. For at least thirty-two years Martha had been a widow, and probably the school was her principal means of support. Her daughter Sarah Hanover Wooldridge (1763–1823), then forty-nine years old and a widow, was the administratrix of her estate, with Nathan Bowen, Esq., and Sarah's son-in-law Josiah P. Creesey as sureties.[11] Martha left a house at the head of Pond Street, valued at $545, and personal belongings worth $69.03. Listed among her heirs were Captain Thomas Cloutman and his wife, Hannah Butman Cloutman (they deeded their interest in the house on Pond Street to Martha's schoolmistress daughter, Miriam Barber). Other heirs were John Beal Hanover and Samuel Blackler Hanover, children of her son John Hanover and Rebecca Blackler.[12]

Her daughter Miriam Barber continued the school until shortly before her death on January 20, 1830. The Reverend Bartlett described Miriam as "a noted School Mistress."[13] Martha and Miriam Barber were the only schoolmistresses to receive any comment in his records.

In 1907 two samplers were loaned by Thomas Doliber (1837–1912) to an exhibit held at the Marblehead Historical Society with the following descriptions:

Sampler, dated 1807, wrought by Miss Miriam Barbier. She kept a private school for girls in her home on Green Street.

---

8. Essex County Deeds, Book 137, 40; "Martha Barber, widow" to Jeremiah Gatchel, March 29, 1780.
9. Sampler of Mary Russell, 1784 (B&C, Pl. CIX). This sampler, the "star" of the Hodge Collection in 1921, was sought by Nancy Cabot for an exhibition in the 1940s, but could not be found. It reappeared in a Florida antiques shop in 1972, but in badly deteriorated condition. It has since been in a private collection.
10. Although many are not dated, identity of the makers reveals at least twelve surviving pieces date from 1789 to 1791.
11. Essex County Administration No. 1640.
12. Martha's connections to the Cloutman, Butman, and Blackler families increase the likelihood that the samplers of Sally Butman (Fig. 156) and Sally H. Cloutman were made at her school; also, the sampler by Betsy Gail (b.1781) whose mother was Mary Blackler (1742–1829).
13. Bartlett, *Vital Records*, 2:480.

Fig. 155. *Susanna H. White Her/ Work in The Thirteenth/ Year of her Age 1806*. Silk on linsey-woolsey; 19″ x 14½″. Susanna included a floating landscape with a number of motifs from earlier work and enclosed them in an exceptional lacy border. Susanna Haskell White (1794–1819) was sixth among the eight children of John White (1756–1833) and Ruth Haskell (1757–1808) of Marblehead. She married John Peach (1795–1821) who died in Calcutta two years after her death. *Location unknown; photograph courtesy of Skinner, Inc.*

Fig. 156. *Sally Butman her work in the/ 11ᵗʰ year of her age 1801.* Silk on linen; 12½″ x 10⅜″. Sally worked this verse:

> On Earth let my example shine
> And when I leave this State
> May heaven receive this Soul of/ mine
> To bliss divinely great

It appears on at least six other examples, including Rebecca Dixey's sampler, c.1790, and Figure 157. This basic pattern was worked by Rebeckah Roundey in 1800 (Krueger, *New England,* Fig. 33) and Sally H. Cloutman in 1807 (PMA). Sally's work was identified as a Marblehead sampler and illustrated in *The Essex Antiquarian* of September 1899. Sally Butman (b.1790) was the daughter of Benjamin Butman (d.1830) and Sarah Cloutman (b.1760). She was the sister of Hannah Butman who married Thomas Cloutman, and they were among the heirs of schoolmistress Martha Barber. Sally Butman married Joseph Millet (b.1787) on February 26, 1809. *Private collection.*

Fig. 157. *Salley Bridgeo/ Her sampler/ wor.d in the/ 12 year/ of Her/ age,* c.1802. Silk on linen; 21″ x 15½″. A related sampler, but without figures, was worked on green linsey-woolsey by Margaret D. Thompson in 1806 (PMA, 69-288-230). See Ruth Homan's, c.1806, in *MAD,* January 1984, 25-B. Salley Bridgeo (b.1791) was the daughter of Philip Bridgeo (1759–1820) and Hannah Knight (c.1758–1845) of Marblehead. In 1816, she married Robert Bray Chinn (1786–1846).
Marblehead Historical Society, 1970.3.

Sampler dated 1829. Wrought by Sarah E. Homan of Marblehead, aged 11 years, while a pupil of Miss Miriam Barbier's private school.[14]

If these samplers could be found, they would probably prove the attribution of the Marblehead samplers to the school of Martha and Miriam Barber.

No published histories of Marblehead mention a schoolmistress of the 1780–1800 period. The town's prominent citizens established Marblehead Academy, which opened on April 5, 1788, and continued until it was superseded by public high schools. There is, however, no evidence that its succession of preceptresses were responsible for the samplers considered here. No woman is known to have taught there before Miss Mary Lamb, who boarded with Rebecca Stacy in 1795 and 1796. Miss Ann Dowse was employed in 1804 and Miss Sara Dana was preceptress nearly every year between 1808 and 1818; Miss Abigail Dana taught in 1812; Rebecca Kimball in 1820; and Phillippa Call from 1821 to 1822.[15]

---

14. Thomas Doliber, Brookline, Massachusetts, July 25, 1907, to the Marblehead Historical Society.

15. Marblehead Academy records, Marblehead Historical Society. A sampler by Hannah Cash, aged eleven, named *Marblehead Academy* in 1806, but it is unrelated to those shown here (EI).

Fig. 158. *Sally/ M/ Bowen/ her sampler/ Work.d in the/ year*, c.1800. Silk on linen; 20⅛″ x 16¼″. Sally's work may be the earliest example of the last distinctive sampler style to develop at Martha Barber's school. It was probably Sally who removed the date. Sally Martin Bowen (b.1789) was the daughter of Nathan Bowen (1752–1837) and Elizabeth Martin (1761–1797) of Marblehead. Her father assisted in the administration of Martha Barber's estate in 1812 and witnessed the will of schoolmistress Miriam Barber in 1830. Sally married Isaac Story, Jr., on April 7, 1813, and they had at least twelve children.

Essex Institute, gift of Frederick W. Story, Sr., 1981, 135, 370.

Fig. 159. *Mary Sparhawk her/ Work aged 9 years/ MARBLE-HEAD/ AD 1807.* Silk on linsey-woolsey; 22⅝" x 15½". A closely related sampler was worked by Mary LeFavour in 1804 (Ring, *Treasures,* 11). Mary Sparhawk (b.1797) was the daughter of John Sparhawk (b.1770) and Emma Martin (b.1767). She married Arnold Martin 3d on February 6, 1820.
Collection of Mrs. Norris Bull.

A recognized Marblehead school of the early nineteenth century was kept by the sisters Betsy (b.c.1786) and Lydia Wilson (b.1790) in a building next to their parents' home on Washington Street, and their afternoon sessions are said to have been devoted to needlework. They were the daughters of Customs Collector Joseph Wilson who came from Bath, Maine, to Marblehead and married Lydia Waitt in 1786.[16] The Misses Wilson commenced teaching about 1810 or later, so they could not have contributed to the samplers considered here.

If Marblehead's magnificent samplers continue to emerge at their recent rate, positive documentation that Martha and Miriam Barber were responsible for them should soon appear. Meanwhile, the opening plea of their favorite sampler verse has been fulfilled: *On earth let my example shine.*[17] Two hundred years later, the samplers they originated are shining examples of the best in American schoolgirl art.

---

16. *Marblehead Messenger,* June 19, 1969.

17. The verse, as quoted in the caption of Figure 156, is from Isaac Watts, "Hymn for his 39th sermon, verse 6." It appears on a Dorchester, Massachusetts, sampler by Margaret Breck, 1741, and also on the Marblehead sampler of Jean Elkins, 1796 (B&C, 33, 43, 279).

Fig. 160. *Lydia Nobles Sampler / aged Seven Years 1793*. Silk on linen; 10″ x 8″. Lydia worked the same border found on a family record sampler made by a daughter of Azariah Mosely, c.1788 (*The Great River* [1985], No. 270). Seven-year-old Lucy Fowler also worked the same pattern with a dark ground for the border and a light field for the alphabet (*A&AW* [December 23, 1988], 97, now at the Westfield Athenaeum). Lydia Noble (b.December 28, 1785) was the daughter of Solomon Noble (1760–1786) and Lydia Sacket (c.1764–1838) of Westfield. She married Daniel Mosely.
Collection of The Examplarery.

Work from Western Massachusetts

WESTFIELD

Two easily recognizable groups of samplers originated in western Massachusetts in the late eighteenth century. Probably the earliest are the solidly worked samplers of Westfield (Figs. 160–162), which show a closer kinship to those from Norwich, Connecticut, than to the styles of coastal Massachusetts. Westfield samplers are usually small and vertical. They were entirely worked over the linen ground by girls who were between the ages of seven and eleven years. At present they date from 1788 through 1796, but no appropriate Westfield instructress of this period has been identified. A Miss Lucy Mosley was teaching in Westfield in April 1799,[1] but whether she taught earlier is unknown. Three of the Westfield sampler makers had a parent named Mosley, and one married a Mosley.

The fathers of several of the sampler makers were original trustees of Westfield Academy, which opened January 1, 1800. By 1802, Miss Parnell Fairchild was preceptress at the Academy, and she was followed by Miss Elizabeth Sumner

---

1. John H. Lockwood, *Westfield and Its Historic Influences, 1669–1919* (printed by the author, 1922), 181.

Fig. 161. *Cynthia Mosley Samp aged/ Nine Years Worked August 1793,* and inscribed beneath the shield *by/ the Name of MOSLEY.* Silk on linen; 17¾" x 10½". Cynthia worked the only coat of arms found within this group. She was born on August 30, 1783; perhaps she worked on this all year and completed it just before her tenth birthday. Cynthia was the daughter of David Mosley and Lydia Gay. She married Henry Chapin (1781–1865) on October 12, 1803, and had two daughters before her death on January 16, 1807, in Canandaigua, New York.
Private collection.

Fig. 162. Record of the family of Stephen Sacket and Eunice Lovering, initialed *S S* and attributed to Sally Sacket, c.1796. Silk on linen; 17" x 10⅝". A similar record of the Enoch Loomis family was probably worked by the youngest daughter, Polly Loomis, who was also born in 1786 (Skinner Sale 1060, November 2, 1985, Lot 199J). Sally Sacket was the daughter of Stephen Sacket (1748–1830) and Eunice Lovering (1752–1842). Sally reversed her parents' birthdates.
Cooper-Hewitt, National Museum of Design, Smithsonian Institution, 1941-69-46.

Fig. 163. *Marietta Stebbin/ AE 10 1801*. Silk on linen; 12⅞″ x 10½″. In 1798, nine-year-old Caroline Stebbins of Deerfield, a first cousin of Marietta, worked an almost identical sampler. Both girls were enrolled at Deerfield Academy in 1805–1806. The black and white cross-stitched doves appear in this identical form on related samplers until 1826, as well as the border and many similar motifs (see *Encyclopedia of Collectibles, Radios to Signs* [Alexandria, Va.: Time-Life Books, 1980], 94–5). Marietta Stebbins (1791–1820) was the daughter of farmer and miller Asa Stebbins (1767–1844) and Emilia Harvey (c.1769–1841) of Deerfield. She married Dr. William H. Williams in 1813.
Historic Deerfield, Inc., 86.86.

in 1803. Many of the young girls who worked typical Westfield samplers probably continued their education at the Academy. Miss Emma Hart, better known as Mrs. Emma Willard, also taught there during the school's early years, but no identified needlework from Westfield Academy has been found. Around 1889, Westfield Academy and the Westfield High School were merged into one school.[2]

WHITE DOVE SAMPLERS OF THE DEERFIELD AREA

The so-called white dove samplers of the Deerfield area are known today in greater numbers than the Westfield samplers. These pieces can be identified by pairs of black-outlined white birds hovering over a few commonplace motifs that are often in balanced arrangements beneath alphabets and within a three-sided border. The sampler by Marietta Stebbins illustrates their most typical form (Fig.

---

2. Ibid., 218–21.

163). Less common are pieces with the birds outlined in black and blue as worked by Persis Dana (Fig. 164). These samplers range in date from 1791 until 1826 or later, and a remarkably consistent style was maintained from 1798 until 1826.[1] Their great uniformity suggests that they were worked under the same instructress, but where she taught is unknown. A very typical sampler was worked by Marian Childs, who named *Shelburne* in 1820,[2] but since she was the daughter of Israel Childs, a schoolmaster of Shelburne, Massachusetts, she probably named her hometown.

---

1. An unsigned family register, with the latest birthdate of 1818, has the conventional border as in Figure 163. It records the family of Scotto Clark of Conway. An atypical example by Eunice Nash, aged fourteen, of Plainfield, has a more elaborate border and a five-bay fenced mansion; it is said to have been worked in 1830 (both at the Northampton Historical Society).
2. Historic Deerfield, Inc., acc. no. 63-330.

Fig. 164. *Persis K Dana In Her 10th Year/ 1795*. Silk on linen; 11¾″ x 11⅝″. A borderless, balanced example was worked by Molly Billings in 1791 (*A&AW* [September 16, 1988], 152). Celendai Cram worked a pattern very similar to this one in 1805 (author's collection). Persis Kibbe Dana (b.1786) was the daughter of the Honorable Daniel Dana (1760–1839) and Persis Kibbe (1769–1835). Persis was born in Enfield, Connecticut. In 1797, her family moved to Guildhall, Vermont, where she married Thomas Carlisle (1781–1844). They lived in Lancaster, New Hampshire. *Author's collection.*

Nantucket Samplers

Traces of Quaker influence are apparent on a number of nineteenth-century samplers from Plymouth and Darmouth, Massachusetts,[1] but the Friends' schools in Nantucket appear to have produced a distinctive motif of their own during the late eighteenth century. An unknown schoolmistress favored rows of fat little trees on her sampler patterns, which are now used to identify one group of Nantucket samplers worked between 1797 and about 1808 (Figs. 165–167).[2]

Quakers are said to have arrived on the island of Nantucket in 1659.[3] By 1711 the Friends were sufficiently established to build their first meeting house.[4] Without question Nantucket Quakers instructed their children using George Fox's primer, but plans for schools under the direction of the Monthly Meetings did not commence until 1795.[5] In 1797, a schoolmaster was appointed, and in March of that year Phebe Folger was engaged to teach for one quarter. She may have continued until Abiel Hussey became the schoolmistress. The Monthly Meeting Minutes of November 1, 1797, reveal that Abiel "was to keep another quarter" and was willing to take thirty scholars; also that "sewing and Nitting be admitted into the Exercises of the School when requested by the Parents."[6] In 1799 Elizabeth Brown taught for one quarter, and Lydia Gardner was the teacher in 1801.[7] This was probably the same Lydia who taught in 1808 (Fig. 166).

It is evident that decorative embroidery was not taught at the Friends' school during its first session. Polly Coffin's sampler of 1797 (Fig. 165), and the early pieces related to it, were probably made at a private school kept by a Quaker woman. Eventually this teacher may have become an instructress at the Friends' school, or she may have instructed the women who taught there during the school's first decade. However, the woman most likely responsible for Nantucket's interesting samplers was the artistic Phebe Folger who taught the first class at the Friends' school in the spring of 1797. The Friends probably chose her because she was twenty-five years old and experienced. During that same year, Phebe compiled, or began compiling, a remarkable copybook that clearly reveals her artistic

1. See Figures 188–190 and *Images of Childhood* (1977), 49–51.

2. In 1831 Sophia A. Ray knitted a splendid pincushion with a similar row of trees (Nantucket Historical Association).

3. Zora Klain, *Educational Activities of New England Quakers* (Philadelphia: Westbrook Printing Co., 1928), 115.

4. R. A. Douglas-Lithgow, *Nantucket, A History* (New York: G. P. Putnam's Sons, 1914), 119–21.

5. Klain, *Educational Activities*, 115, 117.

6. Ibid., 119, 125.

7. Ibid., 121–2.

Fig. 165. *Polly Coffin Born march The 16 1786/ Markt This In april 1797.* Silk on linen; 14½″ x 13″. Polly worked characteristic rows of "Nantucket trees" at the top and bottom of her sampler as well as a strong but slightly modified version of the Boston band pattern. For three related examples with similar trees, see Carpenter and Carpenter, *The Decorative Arts and Crafts of Nantucket* (1987), 95–6. Polly (Mary) Coffin (b.1786) was the daughter of Joseph Coffin and Elizabeth of Nantucket. She married Theodore Fish on October 5, 1812. *Nantucket Historical Association, 87.10.*

ability (Fig. 169) and leaves no doubt that she was capable of designing original patterns for her students' needlework.

Phebe Folger (October 11, 1771–1857) was the daughter of Walter Folger (1735–1826) and Elizabeth Starbuck (1738–1821) of Nantucket, and the sister of Walter Folger, Jr. (1765–1849), an inventive craftsman who built a now-famous Nantucket clock. Phebe may have left her post at the Friends' school to prepare for her marriage to Samuel Coleman (1771–1825) in 1798. Four of their five daughters were born in Nantucket before they moved to Ghent, New York, about 1808. Phebe was evidently keeping a private school in Nantucket in 1800, for on February 9, 1800, she wrote a newsy letter to her absent husband and mentioned that "I have kept school Days and evenings ever since the 16th of the 12th mo. and have about thirty schollars belonging to my school the business is fatiguing but [torn] . . . am willing to contribute my mite to accellerate that happy period when we shall not be obliged to separate."[8] Phebe was perhaps teaching Sally Barker whose sampler of 1800 (Fig. 168) is very similar to three others made that year, each with this aphorism:

> To no peculiar lot of life
> Is happiness confind
> But in a self approving heart
> And firm contented mind

---

8. Coleman Family Papers, Collection no. 107, Folder 17, Nantucket Historical Association.

Fig. 167. *Sally Starbuck Finished this Sampler in the/ tenth year of her age/ Nantucket Friends School 3ᵐᵒ Second 1808.* Silk on linen; 16⅜" x 16⅜". Sally worked seven alphabets in the standard American styles for this period but featured a bold rendition of the Roman alphabet often favored by Quaker teachers (although it diverts from the standard capital Q). She then worked a family record and ended her sampler with two flowers and three Nantucket trees. Sarah B. (Sally) Starbuck (1799–1883) was the younger sister of Mary Starbuck (Fig. 166). She married Isaiah Folger (b.1795) on June 10, 1824. *Nantucket Historical Association, 52-97a.*

Fig. 166. *Mary Starbuck born/ 10ᵐᵒ third 1796/ Finished this Sampler in/ the 12ᵗʰ year of her age/ 1808/ Friends School kept by Lydia Gardner/ Nantucket 2ᵐᵒ 17ᵗʰ 1808.* Silk on linen; 14½" x 13½". Mary worked one row of trees and two trees in the center of her sampler. Her clear lettering and style of dating is more in the acceptable Quaker manner than the earlier Nantucket work. Mary Starbuck (1796–1887) was the daughter of Kimbal Starbuck (b.1771) and Mary Coffin (1770–1847). Kimball Starbuck was the first cousin of schoolmistress Phebe Folger. Mary married Shubael Allen (b.1795) on January 5, 1818. *Nantucket Historical Association, 52-97b.*

Phebe's daughter Eliza was born the following October, and it is not known if she taught thereafter.

Because of the number of Lydia Gardners in Nantucket, the Lydia who was teaching in 1801 or 1808 cannot be identified (Fig. 166). Possibly it was she who was responsible for Nantucket's important samplers from this period. A small sampler with only an alphabet and numerals reveals that typical Quaker lettering, like the major alphabet in Figure 167, continued in Nantucket until at least 1830.[9]

---

9. Krueger, *New England*, Fig. 93.

Fig. 168. *Sally Barker is my/ name/ At 12 years old i mark/ the same/ 1800.* Silk on linen; 13½" x 12¾". Sally's sampler belongs to a group of four very similar Nantucket samplers dated 1800. However, hers is the only one to have an acrostic verse worked with the first eight letters of the alphabet. Sally Barker (b.1787) was the daughter of Josiah Barker, Jr. (1765–1803), and Elizabeth Hussey (d.1805). *Nantucket Historical Association, 2563.*

Fig. 169. Title page of *Un Recueil/ Containing/ Painting, Penmaship, Algebra/ and Pieces selected from various Au-/ thors in Prose and Verse; with a few/ Pieces in French with their Translation/ by/ Phebe Folger of Nantucket/ MDCCXCVII;* 12¾" x 8"; suede bound; 155 pages. Phebe's miscellany of 1797 includes no sampler patterns but reveals her good education, artistic skill, and wide span of interests.
Houghton Library, Harvard University.

Fig. 170. Sarah Langlee
Hersey Derby (1714–1790).
Nineteenth-century copy of
a now-unknown portrait,
c.1772. Oil on canvas; 49½″
x 39½″. Sarah Langlee was
born in Hingham, the
daughter of shipwright John
Langlee (1676/77–1738) and
Hannah Vickery
(1686–1769). In 1738 she
married Dr. Ezekiel Hersey
(1709–1770), a Harvard
graduate of 1728. He left
£1,000 to establish a chair
for a professor of Anatomy
and Physic at Harvard
College. In 1771, Sarah
married Richard Derby
(1712–1783), whose name,
although not his fortune,
was applied to Hingham's
enduring school. In her will
of 1789, Sarah Derby
requested that her portrait
and her new clock be
placed in the Derby School.
Derby Academy.

The Derby School in Hingham

A newly established coeducational school in the small town of Hingham appears to have produced New England's first cohesive group of neoclassical silk embroideries, as well as the earliest group of mourning pieces made in America. Signed needlework pictures naming the *Derby School* in Hingham are dated 1796, and an example from 1795 was unquestionably made there (Figs. 171, 172).[1] In May of 1791, Lucy Lane, a twenty-five-year-old native of Hingham, became the school's first preceptress and she taught until May of 1796.[2] Where she was educated is now unknown, but she was definitely a few years ahead of the women who were keeping New England's best-known girls' schools, such as Mary Balch in Providence and Sarah Pierce in Litchfield.[3] Lucy's students were working scenes on silk that were copied from prints before they became popular elsewhere in Federal America, and her successor continued this practice.[4]

The small, unpainted scenes worked by Lucy Lane's pupils can be recognized by trees worked in long, vertical satin or whip stitches with prickly edges and lighter dots in the mass of their foliage (Fig. 174). In the summer of 1796, Elizabeth Dawes replaced Lucy as the school's preceptress and taught until 1804. Trees on the needlework continued to be a distinctive feature during her tenure, but instead of being spotted and spiked, their foliage was softly shaded in horizontal layers (Figs. 175, 176). In 1797, the Derby School officially became Derby Academy, and this name appeared on the school's earliest mourning embroideries of 1799 (Fig. 176).

Bolton and Coe recorded the earliest-known Derby School embroidery when they listed the sampler of Lydia Loring who worked her birthdate of August 31, 1781, and named *Derby School* in 1794. Two girls of the Jacob family worked samplers naming *Hingham* in 1809 (Fig. 178). Possibly they were worked at the Academy under the direction of Betsy Cushing who followed Elizabeth Dawes as

---

1. Philadelphia's typical Folwell silk embroideries emerged in the 1790s, but they were seldom signed or dated.
2. Lucy Lane (b.1765) was the fifth child of shipmaster George Lane (1731–1790) and Elizabeth Thaxter (1732–1801). In later life George Lane taught in Hingham's public school. Lucy's uncle John Thaxter, Sr., was an original trustee of the Derby School. On May 30, 1796, Lucy married master mariner Ephraim Andrews (1759–1820), and they had four children.
3. Silk embroideries of the 1790s occasionally appear from other New England schools. Rebecca Rice of Pownalborough, Maine, attended Eleanor Druitt's school in Boston in 1797–1798 and worked a vase of flowers on white satin. It is illustrated in Isabel Erskine Brewster, *Recollections* (Concord, N.H.: Rumford Press, 1934), 261. This was called to my attention by Sheila Rideout.
4. If the 1796 Quincy arms (Fig. 177) were worked at the Derby School, it is impossible to know if Lucy Lane or Elizabeth Dawes taught Joanna Loring. They bear no resemblance to those worked in Salem, Newburyport, Providence, or Hartford between 1800 and 1810.

Fig. 171. *Nabby Fearing/ 1795* embroidered beneath the picture. Silk on silk; 8¼" x 10⅞". Nabby's work is now the earliest-known pictorial embroidery attributed to the Derby School. Although copied from a foreign print, her spotted and spiky trees are typical of the instruction of Lucy Lane. For another castle scene worked at the Derby School, by Deborah Briggs of Scituate in 1796, see Ring, *Treasures,* 61. Abigail Fearing (1781–1850) was the daughter of Thomas Fearing (1749–1820) and Lydia Ripley (1753–1815) of Hingham. In 1803, she married David Whiton (1775–1843), a flour and grain dealer of Hingham. They had five children. *Collection of a great, great granddaughter of Nabby Fearing.*

preceptress in 1804. Like the early mourning pieces, these samplers have monuments with inscriptions in a black reserve on the plinth, but their Derby School origin is unconfirmed, since no enrollment records predate 1831.[5]

The Derby School came into existence by the beneficence of a childless widow, Sarah Langlee Hersey Derby (Fig. 170), who wanted the wealth of her first husband directed toward a worthy cause in his native town. In 1771, she was a widow of fifty-seven when she married the enormously wealthy widower Richard Derby (1712–1783) of Salem; but after his death, she accepted little from his estate and returned to Hingham to plan the disposition of the Hersey fortune.

With the help of the Reverend Ebenezer Gay (1696–1787) and others, a board of trustees was appointed for the proposed Derby School, and it was incorporated on November 11, 1784.[6] Extensive plans were formulated, with the stipulation that the school would not open until after the death of Sarah Derby. Unlike other New England schools, the Derby School was to offer boys both general and vocational courses as well as college preparatory instruction for those who sought

5. The school of the Misses Cushing also flourished in Hingham in the early nineteenth century. They were the daughters of David Cushing (1727–1800) and Mabel Gardner. Miss Christiana Cushing (1775–1822) was teaching in 1821 and a list of her scholars for that year is in the MHS.

6. When the school was first considered in 1784, Hingham's population was two thousand, and there was widespread financial depression in Massachusetts (Roscoe, *History of Derby Academy 1784–1984* [1984], 11).

Fig. 172. *Sukey Wilder Aged 15, 1796 Derby School, Hingham* embroidered beneath the picture. Silk on silk; 11¼" x 16". Sukey evidently worked this before her sixteenth birthday on February 26, 1796, and the composition was derived from the print in Figure 173. As in other embroideries made under the instruction of Lucy Lane, no ink or paint was used. Sukey

(Susa) Wilder (1780–1857) was the daughter of Isaiah Wilder (1757–1843) and Susa Leavitt (1760–1840) of Hingham. In 1799 she married Epalet Loring (1774–1852), a tanner and farmer, and they had thirteen children.
Hingham Historical Society, TE32.

Fig. 173. *View of the Seat of the Hon. MOSES GILL Esq. at Princeton in the County of Worcester, Mass[ts]*, engraved by Samuel Hill, State Street, Boston, and used as the frontispiece for *The Massachusetts Magazine,* November 1792, with a lengthy description of the plate. The house of Moses Gill (1734–1800) was on a farm of more than 3,000 acres. He married Sarah Prince (c.1728–1771) and later, Rebecca Boylston (d.1798); both were childless. This source for the embroidery was discovered by Jane Nylander.
American Antiquarian Society.

Fig. 174. *Rachel Thaxter aged 12 years 1796* embroidered beneath the picture. Silk on silk; 8″ x 10⅛″. The style of the signature and the similarity of the trees to those in Figures 171 and 172 leave no doubt that Rachel worked this at the Derby School. Rachel Thaxter (b.1784) was the daughter of Jacob Thaxter (b.1746) and Rachel Lincoln (1751–1836). They lived on Main Street near the Meeting House in Hingham. Rachel married a Mr. Jenkins of Scituate. *Winterthur Museum, 64.841A.*

it, and also advanced education for girls. Thirty girls and forty boys were to be admitted, and the entire facility was principally intended for the children of Hingham's North Parish.[7] Girls could enter at the age of nine and boys at twelve. College preparatory students were considered at earlier ages. Sarah Derby specified that "the females" should be taught "writing in the English and French languages, arithmetic and the art of needlework in general" and that the preceptress should be a "sensible, discreet woman skilled in the art of needlework."[8]

Sarah Derby died on June 17, 1790, and the Derby School officially opened on April 5, 1791. Abner Lincoln (1766–1826), a Harvard graduate of 1788, became the first preceptor and served for fourteen years. Derby Academy has been in continuous existence since its opening, and while it was not the earliest, it is now the oldest independent coeducational school in New England.[9]

---

7. Embroideries worked by girls of Scituate and Cohasset reveal that girls from other towns were soon admitted. The 1796 work of Betsey Turner of Cohasset belongs to the Cohasset Historical Society. A recognizable group of samplers was worked in Scituate, c.1804–1830. For their typical form see Krueger, *Gallery,* Figs. 51, 54.

8. Francis H. Lincoln, *History of the Town of Hingham* 1, pt. 2 (Hingham, 1893), 119.

9. Roscoe, *Derby Academy,* 90–2.

Fig. 175. Needlework picture by Lydia Cushing, c. 1798. Silk and paint on silk; 16″ x 22″. Here the trees reflect the instruction of Elizabeth Dawes, and the sky is very lightly tinted. This embroidery descended with the tradition that it depicts the Boston Common, John Hancock's house, and the Park Street Church in Boston. Lydia Cushing (1784–1803) was the daughter of Thomas Cushing (1753–1832), a farmer, and Elizabeth Lincoln (1761–1797). For an embroidery with a similar avenue of trees, elegant house, and tinted sky, see SPB, Garbisch I, Sale 3595, January 23, 1974, Lot 41. *Hingham Historical Society, TE 26.*

Fig. 176. Anonymous mourning embroidery with the following embroidered inscription beneath the picture: *In Memory of Mrs. Rachel Lincoln, who died July 13th 1797, in the 42d year of her age. Hingham. Derby Academy 1799.* Silk and metallic threads on silk; 9½″ x 13″. For a closely related memorial, also of 1799, see *ANTIQUES*, June 1979, 1243. Others are in the Hingham Historical Society. See also Rumford, *American Folk Paintings* (1988), 418. This memorial was probably worked by a daughter of Mrs. Lincoln—either Charlotte (1785–1862) or Rachel (1787–1864). *Hingham Historical Society, TE 1.*

Fig. 177. *BY THE NAME OF QUINCY/ Joanna Q. Loring/ 1796.*
Silk on silk; 11⅜″ x 10¼″. Probably this coat of arms was
worked at the Derby School, but, as yet no similar pieces
have appeared. Joanna Quincy Loring (b.1782) was the
daughter of Hingham merchant Thomas Loring (1755–1828)
and Joanna Quincy Thaxter (1757–1836). She married Perez
Lincoln (1777–1811) in 1808. During their brief marriage he
was a minister in Gloucester; they were childless. Joanna's
brother, Thomas Loring (1789–1863), married Amelia Fudger,
the niece of schoolmistress Clementina Beach, who died at
their home in Hingham in 1855 (see Fig. 100).
Hingham Historical Society, TE 1A.

Fig. 178. *Lucy Jacob Aged 11ʸᵀˢ Hingham 1809.* Silk on linen;
16″ x 22⅜″. Another Hingham family record sampler with a
similar monument was worked by Lucy's first cousin Mary J.
Jacob in 1809 (Allen, *Family Record,* Fig. 56). They were most
likely made at the Derby Academy when Betsey Cushing was
preceptress. A sampler of 1801 that names Derby Academy is
described in Davidson, *Plimoth Colony Samplers* (1974), 28–9.
Lucy Jacob (1798–1878) was the daughter of Jotham Jacob
(1775–1852) and Grace Tower (1777–1852). He was a blacksmith and farmer of Hingham. Lucy married Silas Chipman in
1818.
Hingham Historical Society, TE 47.

Fig. 179. Anonymous mourning embroidery, c.1804. Inscribed on the plinth *C. Chapin/ Died Jan.ʸ: 12th 1799/ Aged 37 years*; and on the side of the plinth *Be ye not/ slothful but/ Followers of/ Those who/ thro' Truth/ & Patience/ inherit the/ Promised Land*. Silk, silver metallic thread, wool, and paint on silk, with ink on paper; 17″ x 13″. Typical of Abby Wright's school are the wispy willow trees, plants surrounded by minute seed stitches, the silver-trimmed urn, and applied paper for the inscriptions. The weeper, characteristic of early examples, more commonly wears a black striped dress, as in Figure 181, and backgrounds typically include the same mansion and meetinghouse. The painted face of the mourner is often found on early pieces, but two later styles of painting are also repetitious (Figs. 183, 184). This embroidery is dedicated to Chloe Lombard, who married Captain Israel Chapin of Springfield, Massachusetts, on June 26, 1788, and it is attributed to Harriet Chapin (1789–1818), the first of their seven children.

Private collection; photograph courtesy of Sotheby's.

Silk Embroideries of South Hadley

"Perhaps in no period of a woman's life is her conduct more criticized and her actions more liable to censure than when attending a boarding school," said schoolmistress Abby Wright to her young lady students. She went on to express her "desire to promote the happiness of my pupils, to lead them in the paths of rectitude and virtue, that they may establish an unblemished reputation and become ornaments to society."[1] So began one of the many lectures Abby would deliver to her students during the six and one half years that she guided classes of forty or fifty girls along the paths of propriety and piety, and helped them create the needlework pictures that have established her lasting fame. Some of the most beautiful and easily recognized New England silk embroideries were made at Abby Wright's school in South Hadley from 1803 until 1811. These pieces are characterized by a variety of materials, exquisite stitchery, and the technique of surrounding small shrubs or plants with minute seed stitches to define their shapes against background embroidery in similar colors.[2]

Abby Wright attended Westfield Academy when she was twenty-six years old and commenced teaching in South Hadley in the spring of 1803,[3] but where she learned to work elaborate silk embroidery is unknown. She grew up in Pittsfield with the seven younger children of her mother and stepfather Josiah Goodrich, and there is no evidence that she ever visited a town larger than Springfield before she opened her girls' school. The velvet appliqué and the lavish use of metallic threads on her students' embroideries suggest that she was familiar with Hartford silk embroideries. Her mother was from Wethersfield and Abby may have attended school in that area of Connecticut or visited in Hartford before the beginning of the letters and memoirs that record much of her life. However, the Hartford embroideries that could have influenced her teaching are not known to predate 1800.

Residents of South Hadley urged Abby to open a girls' school in their town, and because of her dedication, it quickly became a success. She spent seven or

---

1. "Abby Wright Allen: A Record of Her Letters, etc., 1795–1842," 222, 224. The microfilm of this manuscript is in the Mount Holyoke College Library.

2. For typical urns but different ground treatment, see the memorial by Maria Hulbert in Sotheby's Sale 4709Y, October 24, 1981, Lot 309. Divergent examples with silver urns are a memorial by Betsy Wright at the Windsor (Conn.) Historical Society and a memorial to Mrs. Betsey Robeson (d.1806) at the Wadsworth Atheneum in Hartford. For typical pieces without metallic urns, see the memorial to Edward Chapin in *MAD*, September 1982, 2-C, and that to Mrs. Experience Parson in the Northampton Historical Society.

3. Abby taught district schools for several summers before she attended Westfield Academy in the fall and winter of 1800–1801. She wrote that Peter Starr, the first preceptor, "is an agreeable man and takes the greatest pains to instruct his pupils. He says 'Very Well' one hundred times a day." (Abby to her half-sister Sophia, October 22, 1800, "Abby Wright Allen," 25).

Fig. 180. Portrait of Abigail (Abby) Wright Allen (1774–1842), artist unknown, c.1810. Pastel on paper; 26½" x 22½". Abby, born in Wethersfield, Connecticut, was the only child of Levi Wright and Abigail Wolcott (1752–1832). She married Peter Allen (1764–1848), originally of Enfield, Connecticut, but they lived in South Hadley and were survived by two sons, Peter and Levi Wright Allen.
Mount Holyoke College Art Museum, gift of Mrs. Elbert S. Pratt, in 1956.

Fig. 181. *Embroidered at South Hadley in the Summer of 1805: by - Nancy Hastings AE 17: under the Instruction of Miss Abby Wright* inscribed on paper beneath the embroidery. Silk, wool, heavy chenille, silver metallic thread, velvet appliqué, and paint on silk; 16½" x 17". Nancy left her monuments uninscribed, but her additional inscription offers irrefutable proof that this frequently found form of memorial originated at Abby Wright's school, an assumption that has heretofore been based on circumstantial evidence. Nancy Hastings (1787–1849) was the daughter of farmer and blacksmith Elijah Hastings (1753–1803) and his first wife, Jerusha Billings (1763–1798), of Amherst, Massachusetts. This was probably intended as a memorial to Nancy's parents, and the figures were meant to represent, from left to right, Nancy, her brother Elijah (b.1791), and her sisters Lydia (1786–1872) and Lucinda (1784–1856). In 1807, Nancy married Dr. Isaac Guernsey Cutler (1782–1834). They had eight children.
Jones Library, Special Collections, Amherst, Massachusetts.

Fig. 182. Liberty and cornucopia worked by Sarah White, c.1805. Silk, silver and gold metallic threads, and paint on silk with a painted paper face; 16″ x 13¼″. Sarah's border is almost identical to the borders on two other Liberty embroideries attributed to Abby Wright's school (*ANTIQUES*, September 1986, 488–9). Another was auctioned by Richard W. Withington, January 5, 1991 (*MAD*, January 1991, 20-E). Sarah White (1789–1855) was the daughter of South Hadley farmer and innkeeper Joseph White (1754–1829) and Sally Yeomans (1759–1840). Abby Wright was intimately acquainted with this family and in 1804 a number of her students boarded with them. In 1814, Sarah White married Andrew Henry (c.1788–1821), and in 1828, Dr. William F. Sellon (c.1786–1842). This embroidery was given to the Amherst Historical Society in 1915 by Sarah's granddaughter, Miss Helen F. Pray.
Amherst Historical Society, Amherst, Massachusetts, 73.87.

more hours each day in the classroom, and most of her time at home was consumed with preparing the schoolwork. Some of her students were local girls of no more than ten or eleven years, but the majority were from fourteen to twenty-one years old and upward, and many who came from other towns boarded with South Hadley families. However, by the fall of 1804, Abby lamented that it was "almost impossible" for those from afar "to get boarded."[4] This situation was finally relieved when her widowed mother joined her in South Hadley, and they acquired a house large enough to accommodate boarders.

Abby's letters seldom mention the needlework that she taught, nor do they disclose where she bought the materials necessary for her students' embroidery. Probably she shopped in Springfield or Northampton. Her school was advertised in Springfield's *Hampshire Federalist* and Northampton's *Hampshire Gazette*,[5] and several embroideries by her students have Northampton framers' labels. It was January of 1806 before Abby made her first trip to Boston, and she wrote a letter to her sisters, lest they might "never have the honor of receiving one from the

---

4. Abby Wright to her mother, September 24, 1804, "Abby Wright Allen," 73.
5. *Hampshire Federalist*, March 17, 1808; *Hampshire Gazette*, March 16, 1808, and at other times.

Fig. 183. Anonymous mourning embroidery inscribed on the plinth *IN MEMORY of/ M.ʳ Thomas Bliss,/ Died Augˢᵗ 15ᵗʰ 1806. AE: 64.* Silk, silver metallic thread, and paint on silk, with ink on paper; 14¼″ x 12″. The silver-trimmed urn is a conspicuous characteristic of Abby Wright's school, but by 1807, the figures were often entirely painted as seen here. For a closely related piece dated 1807, see *ANTIQUES,* September 1986, 486. Thomas Bliss (1742–1806) was a Revolutionary soldier of Brimfield, Massachusetts, who married Sarah King (1748–1839) of Palmer in 1765. This memorial is attributed to Mary Bliss, the youngest of their eleven children, born November 25, 1791. She married Alban Janes of Brimfield on April 12, 1812. *Old Sturbridge Village, 20-8-9.*

Fig. 184. Anonymous mourning embroidery, c.1809. Inscribed on the plinth *Sacred/ to the memory of/ JONATHAN PRATT,/ Born July 14.ᵗʰ 1801./ Died August 22.ᵈ 1803/ Aged 2 years.* Silk, silver metallic thread, paint, and ink on silk; 15⅛″ x 12⅝″. The name *Harriet* is written on a silk spandrel of this embroidery, and it is attributed to Harriet Pratt (b.1797), the daughter of Nahum Pratt (1770–1837) and Abigail of Oxford, Massachusetts. Harriet pictured her parents, herself, and her sister Lucy (b.1799) as they would have appeared when her brother died. She married William Dana (b.1785) on July 12, 1812. Two other Oxford girls, Mary Elizabeth Blount Stone (b.1794) and Hannah Kingsbury (b.1797), worked embroideries at Abby Wright's school (private collections). For a close counterpart to Harriet's work, and with golden urns on the plinth, see *ANTIQUES,* September 1986, 486.
Collection of Joan Stephens.

Fig. 185. *Wrought by Polly Rice* inscribed on the glass, c.1809. Silk, chenille, mica, and paint on silk; 16″ x 13″. Hillside houses painted in this manner often appear on embroidered pictures worked at Abby Wright's school. The face is painted in the style of the Bliss memorial (Fig. 183). Polly Rice may have been one of three girls who were born in nearby Massachusetts towns: the daughter of Freeman Rice of Hardwick born in 1790; the daughter of Benjamin and Lovenia Rice of Greenfield born in 1793; or the daughter of William Newton Rice of Rutland, born in 1793.
Collection of Virginia and Leonard Marx.

grand capital of New England," although she had doubts about its grandeur. She described the congested streets where people "who can afford it ride in coaches, others in cutters and sleighs but the multitude go on foot, just as country people do. . . . Sometimes it is with difficulty that one can pass in the streets without jostling against a shoulder of mutton, a leg of pork or a basket of Poultry." She purchased some necessary articles for her school, but did not "covet the happiness of residing continually in the metropolis."[6]

In the fall of 1809, after sixteen years of teaching all or part of a year, Abby's career ended with her marriage to Peter Allen, a prosperous merchant and brewer of South Hadley. Her half-sister took over her school and her mother continued to manage their boarding facility, at least until 1811. Exactly when or why the school was discontinued is unknown. In later years, Abby Wright Allen became South Hadley's "acknowledged leader in all benevolent enterprises."[7]

6. Abby Wright to her half-sisters Sophia and Harriet, January 29, 1806, "Abby Wright Allen," 92–3.

7. Kathryn Kish Sklar, "The Founding of Mount Holyoke College," in Berkin and Norton, *Women of America, A History,* 196.

Fig. 187. *JOSEPH'S DREAM* inscribed on the glass at center, and at left *LUCY DEXTER, AE. 14 1809*. Silk, chenille, silver metallic thread, and paint on silk; 24″ x 31″. The garland above the scene is embroidered, but the flowers below it are painted. Here several interesting plants are surrounded by seed stitches as well as the sheaves of wheat. The center tree has grape-like clusters of foliage similar to a tree in Figure 186. Lucy Dexter has not been identified. For a companion piece by Almira Dexter and another version of *Joseph's Dream*, see *ANTIQUES*, September 1986, 487, 491.
National Museum of American History, Smithsonian Institution; gift of Eleanor and Mabel Van Alstyne, 261195.

Opposite:
Fig. 186. *Hadassah Moody* signed with ink on the linen beneath the picture, c.1805. Silk, chenille, pencil, and paint on silk; 15⅝″ x 12⅝″. Hadassah or one of her sisters worked a memorial to their sister Keziah, who also attended Abby Wright's school and died on July 6, 1803 (*ANTIQUES*, September 1986, 485). Hadassah Moody (b.1787) was fifth among the thirteen children of Seth Moody (1752–1839) and Mary Pomeroy (1761–1832) of South Hadley.
Abby Aldrich Rockefeller Folk Art Center, Williamsburg, Virginia, G 1971-1756.

Fig. 188. *Executed by Caroline R. Dunham of Plymouth agd 12/ AD 1816. Silk on linen; 17" x 17¼".* Caroline's sampler is an early example of the developing Plymouth style. By 1818 her square field with rounded corners had become a true oval and by 1822 a well-defined octagon. Caroline R. Dunham (b.1803) was the daughter of Robert Dunham, Jr. (1778–1833), and Sarah Barnes Goddard (c.1775–1831). She married William H. Gardiner in Boston in December 1838. *Philadelphia Museum of Art, Whitman Sampler Collection, gift of Pet Inc., 69-288-295.*

Samplers of Plymouth

From the time of Loara Standish, samplers were surely stitched by the schoolgirls of Plymouth, but it was not until the early nineteenth century that a recognizable school of work emerged in this first New England town. A clearly cohesive group of Plymouth samplers now dates from between 1816 and 1845, although positive evidence that they were produced under the same instructress is still lacking.

The earliest forerunner of the typical form includes a meandering, flowering-vine border enclosing a square field with rounded corners, which contains ligatures, three alphabets, and the period's most popular sampler verse beginning "Jesus permit thy gracious name to stand/ As the first efforts of an infant's hand . . ." (Fig. 188). Plymouth samplers of 1818 and 1819 have the same rounded field with embroidered landscapes beneath similar ligatures, alphabets, and verses.[1] Although there were relatively few Quakers in Plymouth, the samplers' ligatures and bold Roman alphabets reflect unmistakable Quaker influence, and they appear on samplers within this group at least through the year 1824

---

1. Betsey T. Harlow's sampler of 1818 belongs to the Middleborough Historical Association; for the 1819 sampler of Betsey C. Battles, see Skinner Sale 1146, March 21, 1987, Lot 46; another of 1819 was made by Sally H. Tribble (private collection).

Fig. 189. *Wrought by Nancy Holmes/ Aged 15 years 1823.* Silk and paint on linen; 18″ x 18″. At present Nancy's sampler is the most elaborate example within this group and the only one with a recognizable scene. Her view of Mount Vernon was derived from an aquatint engraving by Francis Jukes (1774–1812) after a drawing by Alexander Robertson (1772–1841). Entitled *Mount Vernon in Virginia/ The Seat of the late Lieu.t General George Washington,* it was issued in London on March 31, 1800, and it was widely copied for schoolgirl art. For a closely related sampler of 1822, see Ring, *Treasures,* Fig. 21. Nancy Holmes (b.1807) was the daughter of Bartlett Holmes (c.1784–1861) and Betsy Paty (b.c.1786) of Plymouth. She married shoemaker Harvey Bartlett in 1828, and they had eight children. Her sampler descended to her great granddaughter.

Collection of Mrs. F. Jane Baker.

(Fig. 190). By 1822, a clearly octagonal enclosure was defined by bands of cross-stitches within a floral border, and beneath the alphabets and a verse, a scene was both worked and painted on the linen (Figs. 189, 190, 192). With slight variations, this style continued through 1835, although pieces with an octagonal field containing only inscriptions and flowers were also made in the 1830s,[2] as well as others with the painted scenes below genealogical records.[3] Lucy Lanman's sampler of 1845 (Fig. 193) bears a remarkable resemblance to earlier pieces although its linen ground is typical of Victorian Berlin work, and no paint was added to its landscape.

There is no positive evidence concerning the schoolmistresses who initiated and continued this Plymouth style. However, in 1975, Plymouth sampler scholar Mary M. Davidson presented her belief that it originated under the direction of Maria deVerdier Turner.[4] More recent study supports her conclusion. This group was most likely the product of a private girls' school kept by the sisters Sarah (1795–1878) and Deborah L. Turner (1797–1857), with the early assistance of their foreign-born sister-in-law Maria Turner (1789–1838).[5]

It was during the troubled years of the War of 1812 that shipmaster Lothrop Turner, Jr., brought his Swedish bride to Plymouth. The artistic and well-educated Maria deVerdier Turner was acquainted with aristocratic social circles in her native Sweden as well as in Copenhagen, but was only beginning to learn English when she arrived in Plymouth. Nevertheless, within a short time, she became involved in the affairs of the community as well as the girls' school kept by her Turner sisters-in-law, and she is believed to have introduced ornamental needle-work, painting, and music into their curriculum by 1813.[6] The most skillfully worked and painted Plymouth samplers, such as Figures 189 and 190, may reflect her instruction, and she had ample time to teach, for her eighteen-month-old daughter died in 1815, and her husband was often at sea. However, the painted samplers reveal a consistent style, and more likely Maria taught one of her sisters-in-law to prepare these patterns and skillfully combine the paint and embroidery. Lothrop Turner, Jr., died in Havana in the spring of 1824. Thereafter, Maria Turner taught in both Boston and New York and published instructions for "Drawing and Shadowing Flowers" and "The Young Ladies' Assistant in Drawing and Painting." She also visited in Sweden but returned to Boston where she died of consumption in 1838.[7]

---

2. Skinner Sale 1174, October 31, 1987, Lot 209; and Edmonds, Fig. 20.

3. Ring, *Treasures*, 14–15.

4. Davidson, *Plimoth Colony Samplers* (1974), 34–5.

5. Their sister Susan Turner (1793–1847) was probably involved in the school although her name is absent from the meager evidence of the school's existence.

6. William T. Davis, *Memories of an Octogenarian* (Plymouth, Mass. 1906), 336. Sarah Sturtevant's sampler of 1813 has ligatures and a Roman alphabet and was probably among the first pieces directed by Maria Turner. See Davidson, *Samplers*, 35, 37.

7. Davis, *Memories of an Octogenarian*, 337. There has been speculation about her possible involvement in teaching the sisters Lucy D. and Emeline B. Stickney whose Charlestown samplers have beautifully painted scenes on linen. For Lucy's work of 1830 see B&C, Pl. LI, now at the C-H.

Fig. 190. *Wrought by Eliza-beth Drew Aged 13 AD 1824.* Silk and paint on linen with ink on paper; 20½″ x 19½″. The monuments are dedi-cated to two infants, Charles and Charles S. Drew, who died in Decem-ber 1821 and January 1825. Either the monument on the right was planned for another family member and the applied paper was changed in 1825, or Eliza-beth dated her sampler well before its completion. Elizabeth Drew (1810–after 1850) was the daughter of William Drew, Jr. (1784–1829), and Sarah Holmes (1785–1861) of Plymouth. On November 10, 1835, she married Isaac W. Proctor (1812–1848) of Washington, New Hamp-shire. They lived in Fram-ingham, Massachusetts. *Collection of Mary Jaene Edmonds.*

In 1826, the then-mature Turner sisters were evidently expanding their school's curriculum when their only detailed advertisement appeared in Plymouth's *Old Colony Memorial* of April 15 (Fig. 191).[8] At this time there appears to have been no other well-established private girls' schools in Plymouth, although there was much nearby competition. Miss Deborah Sampson was keeping a young ladies' school in Kingston, Miss Bathsheba Whitman was the preceptress at the East Bridgewater Academy, and Bridgewater Academy advertised an "experienced" but unnamed instructress to replace Miss Sarah M. Shaw, who taught there in 1825.[9] Peirce Academy in Middleborough, Bristol Academy in Taunton, and Derby

8. It is uncertain whether "Miss Turner" was Sarah or Deborah at this time. They are believed to have taught together.

9. *Old Colony Memorial*, April 8, 1826; April 15, 1826; May 13, 1826; April 16, 1825. A recognizable group of mourning embroideries survives from Bridgewater Academy, and dates from about 1802 to 1805. Typi-cal is a rising sun at far left; some are ovals within dark sawtooth borders; others have figures after Kauff-mann (Fig. 21). Olive Sanger's work of 1804 is in the Concord Museum.

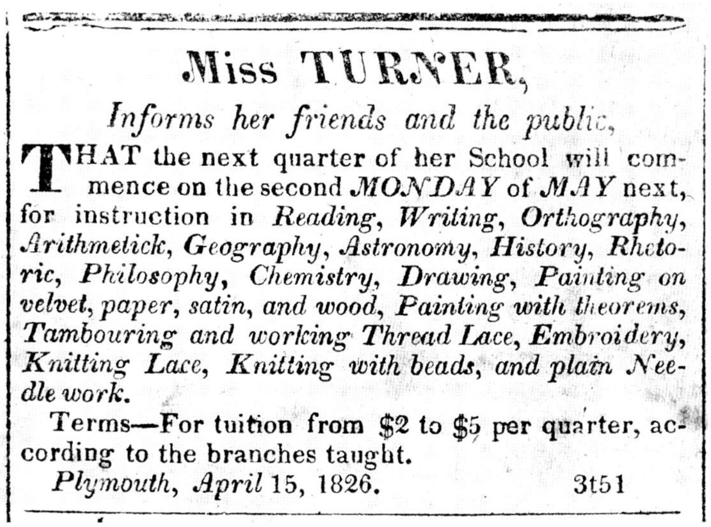

Miss TURNER,

Informs her friends and the public,

THAT the next quarter of her School will commence on the second *MONDAY* of *MAY* next, for instruction in *Reading, Writing, Orthography, Arithmetick, Geography, Astronomy, History, Rhetoric, Philosophy, Chemistry, Drawing, Painting on velvet, paper, satin, and wood, Painting with theorems, Tambouring and working Thread Lace, Embroidery, Knitting Lace, Knitting with beads, and plain Needle work.*

Terms—For tuition from $2 to $5 per quarter, according to the branches taught.

Plymouth, April 15, 1826.   3t51

Fig. 191. The wording of this announcement in Plymouth's *Old Colony Memorial* suggests that Miss Turner's school was a well-established institution. *American Antiquarian Society.*

Academy in Hingham were all including accomplishments in their curricula. Miss Laura Dewey (1807–1833) opened a girls' school in Plymouth in 1827, and she also advertised in the spring of 1828.[10] Her school may have continued until her marriage to Andrew Leach Russell in 1832.

The *Old Colony Memorial* of March 29, 1828, included a notice that "The Spring Term of Miss Turner's School will commence on the 14th of April" and a similar announcement about the spring term of "Miss D. L. Turner's school" appeared on April 13, 1833. No other contemporary references to the Turner school have been found. In his voluminous histories of the town, William T. Davis mentioned many Plymouth teachers, although without dates. Included is the statement that "Miss Lucy Bagnall and Sarah Turner at the foot of Leyden Street, will be recalled with both sad and pleasant memories."[11] This tantalizing comment is unexplained.

Deborah L. Turner wrote her will on August 22, 1848, and she expressed affectionate regard for her brothers David (1803–1869) and Eleazar (b.1805), and for the children of her deceased half-sister, Betsey M. Turner Jackson, but she devised all her possessions to her sister Sarah.[12] At the time of her death in 1857, the settlement of her estate revealed that she was a milliner when she died and was living in one-half of a house on Main Street, which she had purchased with her sisters Susan and Sarah in earlier years.

Today the three unmarried Turner sisters rest in Plymouth's Oak Grove Cemetery beside their more adventurous sister-in-law, Maria deVerdier Turner, who is revered as the founder of the Plymouth Fragment Society, a charitable organization that has functioned continuously since 1818.

---

10. Ibid., July 7, 1827; March 8, 1828.

11. William T. Davis, *Ancient Landmarks of Plymouth* (Boston: Damrell & Upham, 1809), pt. 1, 120. Also, in describing the hall above David Turner's shop, Davis mentioned that "one of David Turner's sisters and Miss Louisa S. Jackson taught school there for a time." This followed a reference to a school of 1832 (Davis, *Memories of an Octogenarian*, 54).

12. Plymouth County Probate Records No. 21325.

Fig. 192. *Wrought by Betsey Ellis Hutchinson/ Aged 9 Years 1831.* Silk and paint on linen; 17″ x 16½″. For an almost identical sampler worked in 1832 by Susan Stephens Lapham, aged eight, see *ANTIQUES,* April 1979, 672. Betsey Ellis Hutchinson (b. September 22, 1822) was the daughter of an Irish seaman, Robert Hutchinson (1788–1868), and his second wife, Deborah Brewster of Plymouth. Betsey married Plymouth carpenter Thomas Rider (b.1821). *Pilgrim Society, Plymouth, Massachusetts, 1019.*

Fig. 193. *Wrought by Lucy A. Lanman Aged 11/ 1845.* Silk on linen; 15¾″ x 16¾″. Lucy framed her field in the same shaded border that characterized this group of samplers by 1822. Her first and third alphabets are also worked in the identical style used by Nancy Holmes for her first and fourth alphabets in 1823. Lucy Ann Lanman (b.c.1834) was the daughter of Plymouth carpenter Nathaniel Cobb Lanman (b.c.1793) and Nancy Ellis Bagnall. She married Eleazar Thomas, and second, Alanson Thomas. *Plymouth Antiquarian Society, Plymouth, Massachusetts. 85.1920.*

NEEDLEWORK OF RHODE ISLAND

Newport Samplers

RHODE ISLAND was settled in 1636 by religious dissidents from Massachusetts who sought the separation of church and state. In 1663 their several communities became known as the Colony of Rhode Island and Providence Plantations under a charter from Charles II.[1] With its magnificent harbor and vigorous, diverse population, William Coddington's town of Newport would become one of England's major eighteenth-century maritime centers. Its prosperity and liberal atmosphere fostered creativity in craftsmanship, and some of America's colonial furniture forms reached their greatest perfection there. Newport was also the birthplace of extraordinary sampler styles, which spread to other Rhode Island towns with Newport-born teachers.

Newport's earliest group of samplers has recently been found to predate the first groups made in Boston and Philadelphia. Anne Chase's sampler of 1721 (Fig. 195) is the earliest among several similar pieces made by Newport girls,[2] and it is also among the first American samplers to have a surrounding border. Even English samplers rarely had borders at this early date.[3] Virtually nothing is known of the women who were teaching girls in Newport during the first quarter of the eighteenth century, but the schoolmistress who instructed Anne Chase was teaching purely in the English tradition.

Despite Newport's prosperity and sophistication during the mid-eighteenth

Fig. 194. *Hannah Taylor/ Born December 17/ 1763 and made/ this August 18 1774/ at Newport/ Rhodisland/ 1774.* Silk on linen; 18″ x 13″. Hannah's sampler is the most striking and well-preserved Newport sampler of the eighteenth century. A similar blue house is found on many related examples, and reflects the taste for blue houses in Newport of this period. Hannah Taylor has not been identified. *American Museum in Britain, Claverton Manor, Bath, 59.180.*

---

1. Roger Williams (c.1603–1683) founded Providence in 1636; the Antinomians John Clarke (1609–1676), Anne Hutchinson (1591–1643), and William Coddington (1601–1678) established Portsmouth in 1638. Coddington moved and settled at Newport in 1639. Samuel Gorton (1592–1677) founded Warwick in 1643.
2. Mary Taylor, 1740 (Baltimore Museum of Art); Phebe Bull (b.1738), 1750 (MacPheadris-Warner House, Portsmouth, N.H.); and the work of Elizabeth Lindy (1738–1824) is recorded at the New Brunswick Museum, St. John. Elizabeth married John Forrester, Jr., and they went to New Brunswick as Loyalists.
3. In 1901, the earliest-recorded English bordered sampler was dated 1726 (Huish, 21, 76). In 1921, B&C recorded an example of 1721 (Pl. XI). In 1939, an English bordered sampler of 1709 was described by Payne in *Guide to the Collection of Samplers and Embroideries* (1939), 29.

Fig. 196. *ABIGAIL PINNIGE/R/ HER/ SAMPLE/R/ MAID/ IN/
1730.* Silk on linen; 16″ x 9¾″. The bold, central motif of
Abigail's second band (possibly a stylized Tudor rose) is found
on several pieces within this early Newport group, including
Ann Almy's of 1733 which is misdated in B&C, Pl. CXII. It
often occurs on English work as well as eighteenth-century
Newburyport samplers (Figs. 126–128, 132), and occasionally
on other American work of the nineteenth century. See a
Weare, New Hampshire, example dated 1817, in *MAD*,
October 1986, 28-D. Abigail's opening maxim, *LOVE THOU
THE LORD AND HE WILL BE A TENDER FATHER UNTO THEE*,
was a favorite on Rhode Island samplers but not exclusive to
this region. Abigail Pinniger (1715–1779) was the daughter of
William Pinniger and Abigail Moon. She married Joseph
Thurston (1706–1758) at Trinity Church in Newport on April
8, 1733; they had nine children.
*Museum of Art, Rhode Island School of Design, gift of Miss Susan
B. Thurston, 14.060.*

Fig. 195. *Anne Chase Made This Sampler In/ The Thirteenth Year
Of Her Age 1721.* Silk on wool; 12″ x 8¼″. Anne's sampler is
one of two recorded American examples that were worked
with a surrounding border in 1721 (B&C, Pl. XI). Her bold
central band pattern, also on Abigail Pinniger's sampler (Fig.
196), appeared on Boston samplers by 1750 (Fawdry and
Brown, 61). Anne's upper lily-and-bird band pattern was
worked by Ann Bowers (Fig. 197). Anne Chase, the daughter
of James Chase (1685–1728/29) and Rachel Browne
(1687–1741), was born in Martha's Vineyard on April 22,
1709. About 1712, her family moved to Newport where she
married Timothy Folger (1706–1749/50) of Nantucket on
December 5, 1733. They lived in Nantucket and had five
children.
Private collection.

Fig. 197. *Ann/ Bowers [Her] Sampler Made In The 13/ Year Of Her Age*, c.1746. Silk on linen; 16″ x 9½″. Ann's major band patterns are seen in Figures 195 and 196, and her first band patterns, and the row of queen-stitched strawberries below, appear on the 1738 sampler of Sarah Baley (Ring, *Virtue*, 66). Ann Bowers, a Quaker girl, was born in Newport on January 18, 1734. She was the daughter of Jonathan Bowers (d.1775), a Newport boat builder, and Mary Boss. In 1780, she moved with her mother to Swansey, Massachusetts.
Collection of the Examplarery.

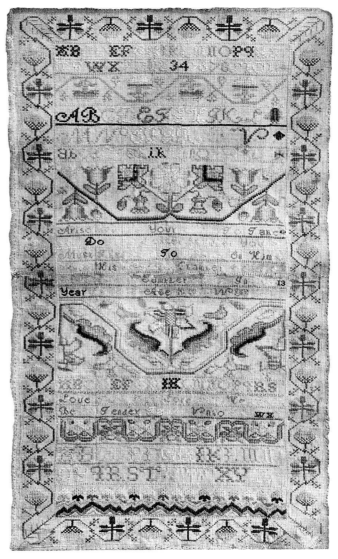

Fig. 198. *Sarah/ Johnson/ Ne[wport]/ Rhodisland/ 1769.* Silk on linen; 9″ x 16″. Sarah also signed her work *Salle Johnson Born/ May 4 1757 and made/ this May 8 1769 in my 13 year.* This is now the earliest sampler to name *Newport*; Sarah Feke named *Rhodisland* in 1762 (Ring, *Virtue*, 80); it is also the second fully developed piece within the frolicking people group (see Lydia Rider's sampler of 1767 in Ring, *Virtue*, 69). Sarah's parents and birth record have not been found. She was probably the Sarah Johnson who married the blacksmith Jeremiah Hill (d.1800) on March 2, 1788, at the Second Baptist Church in Newport, and died in Providence, August 1821. Her age was reported as sixty-five but was probably meant to indicate her sixty-fifth year.
Private collection.

Fig. 199. Mary Balch/ Born February/ 9 1762 and made/ This March 24/ Newport in/ Rhodisland/ 1773. Silk metallic threads and metal on linen; 14½" x 11". With its metal-decorated figures and solidly worked vignettes in the upper border, Mary's sampler is the most elaborate Newport example presently known. Above the sentinels that flank her cartouche is the suggestion of a streaky sky that appeared later on Bristol, Rhode Island, samplers (Figs. 221, 222). The building on her sampler was also worked by students at her Providence School in 1785, and she became Rhode Island's most famous schoolmistress. Mary Balch (1762–1831) was the daughter of Timothy Balch (1725–1776) and Sarah Rogers (1735–1811). She was born in Newport and moved with her family to Providence in 1776. *Rhode Island Historical Society, gift of Forrest Tobey Choate in memory of Berkeley Greene Tobey, 1979.30.1.*

Fig. 200. *Sarah E./ Pope Her Work/ Wrought in the/ eleventh year/ of Her Age/ 1773.* Silk on linen; 13¾" x 11". Sarah worked the earliest fully developed example within Newport's elegant house group. Characteristic is the mansion behind a fence with an intricate gate, and with balanced motifs and inscriptions. Sarah Experience Pope (1762–1845) was the daughter of Ezra Pope and Sarah Freeman, who were married in Sandwich, Massachusetts, and later moved to Newport. Sarah, an only child, died unmarried. *Newport Historical Society, 01.135.*

Fig. 201. Sarah Osborn (1714–1796) taught in Newport for more than forty years, but this was her only advertisement. It appeared in Newport's recently launched *Newport Mercury* on December 19 and 26, 1758, and January 2, 1759. In May of 1759, she had ten young lady boarders and more than sixty day scholars. She reduced the size of her school when she became increasingly involved as a religious activist. *Rhode Island Historical Society.*

SARAH OSBORN, Schoolmiftrefs in Newport, propofes to keep a

Boarding School.

ANY Perfon defirous of fending Children, may be accommodated, and have them inftructed in Reading, Writing, Plain Work, Embroidering, Tent Stitch, Samplers, &c. on reafonable Terms.

century, many families sent their daughters to Boston boarding schools.[4] At this time, Boston schools were producing magnificent coats of arms and silk and canvas-work pictures, and there is only slight evidence that Newport women offered similar instruction.[5] However, their incomparable sampler patterns were evolving. The transition from stylized patterns to naturalistic ones occurred during the 1750s, and two recognizable styles were fully developed by the 1770s:[6] the so-called "frolicking people" group with a layered format, luxuriant floral side borders, and figures in random arrangement (Figs. 194, 198, 199), and the "elegant house" samplers, which are somewhat more formal (Figs. 200, 202). These patterns most likely developed at two different schools.

Circumstantial evidence suggests that the frolicking people samplers were worked under the instruction of Mrs. Sarah Haggar Osborn, a notable Newport woman who taught boys and girls from 1734 until 1776 or later. From 1758 until about 1764, she had both a boarding and day school (Fig. 201).

The most respected Newport girls' school of the revolutionary period was kept by Mrs. Abigail Brenton Wilkinson (1735–1809) who was patronized by Rhode Island's leading patriots even though several of her brothers were staunch Loyalists. John and Nicholas Brown of Providence sent their daughters to her school during the early 1780s, and Rebecca Carter's sister Ann started working a sampler there in 1779 (Fig. 208). It is doubtful that Abigail Wilkinson was teaching early enough to have originated either of Newport's typical sampler styles, but she and her several school-teaching nieces, the Misses Brenton, probably perpetuated the established Newport patterns, which were continued, often in modified form, well into the nineteenth century.

Fig. 202. *Mary/ Anthony her/ work made in/ her 11th year/ 1783.* Silk on linen; 16¼" x 15". Mary's sampler is typical of Newport's elegant house group of the 1780s, and very similar houses were worked on Newport samplers until 1835. Above Mary's house is an unmistakable rendition of the same stylized lily motif seen in Figures 195 and 197. Mary cannot be identified because there were a number of Mary Anthonys in and near Newport who were ten years old in 1783. *Michigan Historical Museum, Lansing, Michigan, SM-299-78.*

4. Among them was Penelope Bowler (b. 1753), daughter of Metcalf Bowler (Fig. 214) and Anne Fairchild (1732–1803), who died while at school at Boston. Boston schoolmistress Jane (Jannette) Day solicited Newport patronage in the *Newport Mercury* of May 8, 1759.

5. Sarah Osborn first advertised her boarding school in Newport in 1758. However, in 1751, she was boarding Mary Fish (1736–1818) and wrote to the Reverend Joseph Fish (1706–1781) with reference to materials and patterns for chair seats, probably for his daughter to work (Osborn Letters, 1747–1769, AAS). Mary and Rebecca Fish (1739–1783) were there in 1754 (Joy Day Buel and Richard Buel, Jr., *The Way of Duty* [New York: W. W. Norton, 1984], 18–20). Mary Wright of Middletown, Connecticut, is said to have made canvas-work pictures of the seasons at a Newport school in 1753 and 1754 (Krueger, "Mary Wright Alsop" [1992], 142–51).

6. For the earliest-known transitional pieces and 122 illustrations of Rhode Island work, see Ring, *Virtue*; also, *ANTIQUES*, April 1975, 660–71, and September 1983, 500–7.

Fig. 203. *Nancy Winsor's Work/ Providence Dec. 4 1786*. Silk, brass metal, and silver metallic threads on linen; 14¾″ x 14½″. Eight-year-old Nancy worked *Honour and Renown; shall the ingenious crown*, which was a favorite maxim at Mary Balch's school, and named her impressive vessel *ship/ Nan/cy* with a backward *N*. Although Nancy's sampler is closely related to the work of her classmates, her nautical scene appears to be unique. Nancy Winsor (1778–1850) was the daughter of Providence merchant Olney Winsor (1753–1837) and Freelove Waterman (1755–1783). Nancy did not marry and in later life she lived at 22 Angell Street in Providence with her unmarried half-sister, Susan Jenckes Winsor (1789–1879), whose Balch-school mourning piece also survives (*ANTIQUES*, October 1972, 511).
Private collection.

Mary Balch's School in Providence

Samplers from Mary Balch's school in Providence were the first American embroideries to receive wide recognition as a distinctive group from a specific school, and they continue to be the most renowned samplers made under an identified instructress. A variety of patterns for both samplers and silk embroideries were used at this school, but no significant examples actually name the teacher. Many name *Providence* (Figs. 203, 206, 209) but most pieces reveal their origin through typical motifs or a characteristic technique that relates to documented examples. Most extraordinary are those with recognizable renditions of important Providence buildings (Figs. 204, 205, 207, 208).

Mary Balch (1762–1831), often called Polly, was the daughter of the Newport tailor Timothy Balch (1725–1776) and Sarah Rogers (1735–1811). She spent her childhood in Newport during the final years of its pre-revolutionary grandeur, and in some unknown school she developed the skill most necessary for her future success as a schoolmistress—she became an artist with her needle (see her sampler, Fig. 199). Her parents moved to Providence on the eve of the British occupation of Newport in 1776, and her father died within the year, leaving Sarah with four children and an insolvent estate. To help her mother support the family, Mary probably began teaching before she was twenty in 1782. She was definitely teaching in March of 1785 when the earliest sampler attributed to her school was dated.[1] Her career continued in the same town for forty-five years, spanning the entire Federal period, and the surviving embroideries from her school mirror the taste of the young republic during this era.

Some years ago, there was doubt that Mary Balch personally directed the embroidery of her students,[2] but this question was resolved by a 1787 letter from Olney Winsor directly to Mary Balch, wherein he recommended that his daughter Nancy work the Providence State House on her sampler.[3] This was after the completion of Nancy's "Ship" sampler (Fig. 203). The most spectacular samplers from Mary Balch's school were worked while Mary was teaching in a rented house on Constitution Hill, and there is no evidence that she had any assistants other than her mother and her brother Timothy, who were involved with Mary's

---

1. For this sampler by Abija Hall and extensive information on Mary Balch's school, see Ring, *Virtue*, 97–203.

2. *ANTIQUES*, July 1928, 43–4, and April 1975, 660.

3. "I wrote to Polly Balch that I could not send a draft of a suitable building to put in Nancy's sampler for we had none here, and advised to have the State House in Providence put in, for it is the best proportioned building I have seen," wrote Olney Winsor to Hope Thurber Winsor, February 22, 1787 (Winsor Letters, 1786–1788, Virginia State Library). The significance of this letter in respect to Mary Balch's school was first recognized by Swan in *Plain & Fancy*, 57, 59. Nancy's "State House" sampler is unknown.

Fig. 204. *Loann/ Smith born/ September 27/ 1772, and made/ this july 25/ 1785.* Silk on linen; 15" x 12". Loann's sampler is one of five examples that are dated 1785. It depicts the same building found on Mary Balch's childhood sampler and many other similar motifs (Fig. 199). A notable addition is the college edifice of Rhode Island College in the upper right corner, which is known today as University Hall of Brown University. Loann Smith (1772–1799) was the daughter of Providence chaisemaker Noah Smith (c.1746–1815) and Hannah Healey (1751–1814). She married cabinetmaker Stephen Olney (1770–1841), and after having three children, she died when she was twenty-six (see Fig. 215). *Museum of Art, Rhode Island School of Design, gift of Mrs. Gustav Radeke, 15.160.*

Fig. 205. *Mary Tillinghast 1796 / Aged 10 years.* Silk on linen; 17⅜" x 17¾". Mary pictured the First Baptist Meeting House in Providence, which was completed in 1775 and is still in use. The delicacy of this composition departs from the earlier "building" patterns and reflects the trend toward neoclassicism. Sally Davis, aged eleven, also worked this pattern in the same year (Cabot Papers, MFA). Mary Tillinghast (1786–1867) was the daughter of shipmaster and merchant Joseph Tillinghast (1734–1816), who was a member of the First Baptist Church, and Mary Earle (1753–1797). She married, first, Benjamin Thurber Chandler (1783–1815) and had Elizabeth Ann (1813–1858); and second, John Gladding (1777–1851). Of their five children, only Benjamin reached adulthood. *Collection of Barbara Gladding Babcock Johnson.*

Fig. 206. *MARY GREENMAN'S WORK PROVIDENCE/ 1796.*
Silk on linen; 13″ x 9½″. Mary's archway form was one
of the most popular patterns at Miss Balch's school and
was worked from 1785 until at least 1797. Mary Greenman (1785–1863), born in Providence, was the daughter
of Jeremiah Greenman, Jr. (1758–1828), and Mary Eddy
(1759–1839). In 1805 she married William Williams
Dunham (1783–1833), and they had six children. This
family moved to Marietta, Ohio, and then to
Waynesville, Illinois, where Mary died.
Collection of Mr. and Mrs. William Appenzeller.

Fig. 207. *Polly Spurr 1796.* Silk on linen;
17³⁄₁₆″ x 16³⁄₄″. Polly was ten years old when
she worked this exquisite rendition of the
First Congregational Church in Providence,
which was built in 1795 and destroyed by
fire in 1814. She was no doubt a classmate
of Mary Tillinghast, and their samplers were
framed in identical frames. Abby Bishop
worked a sampler much like this in the same
year and it also has the same frame. Polly
Spurr (1785–1805) was the daughter of John
Spurr (1749–1822) and Sally West
(1760–1820) of Providence. Her father was a
Major in the Revolution and a member of
the Society of the Cincinnati. Polly died
unmarried.
*Museum of Art, Rhode Island School of Design,
gift of Miss Ellen D. Sharpe, 49.368.*

Fig. 208. *Rebecca/ Carters/ work made/ AD 1788.* Silk, metallic threads, and hair on linen; 19¼" x 13½". Rebecca worked a narrowed version of the 1762 five-bay Providence State House and gave her seven figures real blond hair. In later life, she wrote the following inscription on the back of the frame, and provided the clue that led to the rediscovery of Abigail Wilkinson's Newport School:

> This sampler was begun by my eldest sister the late Mrs. Ann Brown Wife to the Honorable Nicholas Brown, while she was at school in Newport at Mrs. Wilkinson, (I think.) She was then about 9 years old. Finish'd by me at Miss Balches school when I was about 10 years; . . . when this was finished my late honoured Father, John Carter Esq. employed Mr. John Carlile to frame it—immediately he was much pleased with it. The above information tho' by no means important is written for my beloved absent children; one at Marietta, & one at N. York.
> Rebecca C. Jenckes
> 1825 June 8th

Rebecca Carter (1778–1837) was sixth among the twelve children of John Carter (1745–1814) and Amy Crawford (1744–1806). Her father was a bookseller and publisher of the *Providence Gazette*. She married Amos Throop Jenckes (1778–1809) in 1801. She was a widow at the age of thirty-one and only two of her five children lived to adulthood. *Private collection.*

Fig. 209. *Betsy Manchesters work/ Providence July 31/ 1793*. Silk on linen; 14¼″ x 10½″. Betsy worked a particularly graceful version of the undulating border found on this and four other samplers from Mary Balch's school. Elizabeth (Betsy) Manchester (1782–1847) was the daughter of John Manchester (d. before 1818) and Elizabeth Potter (c.1754–1818). She married Israel Arnold (1776–1861) on May 29, 1800. They had four children. *State Historical Society of Wisconsin, 44.994.*

school until their deaths.[4] Her adopted daughter, Eliza Walker, may also have been living with the family in this house, later known as 429 North Main Street. Eliza was born around 1783, and under Mary's direction, she did most of the embroidery on a banner commissioned by the Mechanics' and Manufacturers' Association in 1800.[5]

On August 10, 1801, Mary opened a boarding school in her own newly built house on George Street, and there her curriculum soon expanded, with Eliza Walker as a full-time assistant. At this time, silk embroidery on silk was the most popular needlework for advanced students (Figs. 210–216). Miss Balch also employed both a writing and a music master and engaged a hall for dancing classes. Various teachers and students from Rhode Island College (Brown University after 1804) taught special subjects when needed. Rising competition, particularly the arrival in Providence of schoolmistress Rhoda Remington,[6] evidently caused Mary

---

4. Timothy Balch (1769–1822); Mary's brother Joseph Balch (1766–1845), noted for his penmanship, also taught school at various times; John (1772–1848), her youngest brother, was a bookkeeper.

5. *Providence Gazette*, April 19, 1800.

6. Rhoda Bullen (b.1774) was the daughter of Samuel Bullen and Elizabeth of Medway, Massachusetts. She married merchant William Remington, of New York, in Providence on March 19, 1796. She advertised a school in Dedham, Massachusetts, in 1806, opened an academy in Providence in November 1808, and departed one year later. She kept a boarding and day school in Hallowell, Maine, from 1810 until about 1814 and is unknown thereafter (Emma Huntington Nason, *Old Hallowell on the Kennebec* [Augusta, Me.: Press of Burleigh & Flynt, 1909], 219–20). This publication was called to my attention by Sheila Rideout.

Fig. 210. Pictorial embroidery, initialed *EA*, c.1800. Silk on silk; 9¼″ x 10⅝″. By 1800, delicate silk embroideries in the neoclassical taste had supplanted samplers in importance at Mary Balch's school. This bowl of fruit appears in samplers of 1799 and on silk embroideries with urns of flowers similar to the one in Figure 211.
Baltimore Museum of Art, gift of Mrs. Frances White from the collection of Mrs. Miles White, Jr., 73.76.322.

Fig. 211. *Wrought by Maria Turpin 1802* embroidered on the silk. Silk and chenille on silk; 19¼″ x 16¾″. Typical of the earliest pictorial embroideries from Mary Balch's school is Maria's blue and white flower-filled urn on a chenille mound beneath a garland, and with an embroidered signature. For a related piece of the same year, see Rumford, *American Folk Paintings* (1987), 160–1). Maria Turpin was the daughter of Providence tanner and currier Banjamin Turpin (c.1763–1826) and Lydia Wheaton (c.1770–1843). She was married in Providence to John McNamara (d.1826) of Boston on November 10, 1813.
Collection of Jean and Joseph Andress.

Fig. 212. *BY THE NAME OF RUSSELL* worked
on the motto ribbon, with *Amey Russell*
inscribed on the gold band of the glass
(lower right), and on the reverse, the label
of William T. Grinnell, Providence, dated
1809. Silk, gold and silver metallic threads
and cords, and gold glitter on silk; 19″ x
17″. Amey's coat of arms displays a distinctive style worked at Mary Balch's school,
with raised work akin to Hartford embroidery (Figs. 235–238). For others, see B&C,
Pl. CXXIII; Ring, *Treasures*, 90; and
Christie's, October 24, 1992, Lot 65.
Amey's sampler and mourning piece are
illustrated in Ring, *Virtue*, 189–90. Amey
Russell (1796–1881) was the daughter of
William Russell III (1764–1833) and his
second wife, Ruth Akin (1771–1799), of
New Bedford, Massachusetts. Amey married
Oliver Swain in 1819.
*Old Dartmouth Historical Society, New Bedford,
Massachusetts, 00.50.1.*

Balch to begin a steady program of advertising her school in 1808. Despite some
success, Mrs. Remington departed Providence for Hallowell, Maine, in 1809, but
Miss Balch continued advertising through the year 1826. In 1821, hers was unquestionably the best-attended private school in Providence with an enrollment of
one hundred thirteen students—eighteen small boys and ninety-five girls between
the ages of six and twenty.[7]

Mary Balch was a shrewd, independent, and self-respecting businesswoman
whose abilities were coupled with grace, prudence, and propriety. She was unfailingly solicitous of her family and was noted "for her tender feeling toward all
in distress"; her youngest brother considered her "a pattern of all the amiable
qualities of her sex."[8] Mary was respected by her patrons and lovingly revered by
her students, many of whom remarked upon her admirable qualities in later life.[9]
Unlike her contemporaries Sarah Pierce and Susanna Rowson, she has received no
recognition in the histories of American education or the annals of notable American women, but in the field of American decorative arts she has a secure fame.

7. "Return of the Private Schools in Providence," No. 0038444, RIHS Library.
8. Tribute to Mary Balch by John Rogers Balch, November 6, 1831, in the Balch Family Bible, RIHS Library.
9. *Providence Journal*, July 1 and 24, 1883; also Scrapbook No. 42, 92, RIHS Library.

Fig. 213. *Wrought by Ann Lovett, Jan. 1801.* Silk and chenille on silk; 20″ x 27½″. An absence of paint and weepers is typical of the first mourning pieces from Mary Balch's school. The satin-stitched willow leaves have a shimmering effect and the lettering is flawlessly worked. The monument is inscribed *James Lovett/ was born April/ 6th 1733 died/ April 12th 1800.* Ann (called Nancy) Lovett (b.1785) was the daughter of James Lovett (1733–1800) and Ruth Whipple (1740–1827) of Cumberland, Rhode Island. Members of this family moved to New York City and Schenectady. *Schenectady Museum, gift of Mrs. Helen VanEps Hatcher, 68.207.4.*

Fig. 214. Mourning embroidery inscribed *Metcalf Bowler, died Sept. 19/ 1789 AEta (t) 63 years/ Samuel B. Bowler died in St./ Eustatia May 13 1790 AEtat 25.* c.1800. Silk on silk; 13¼″ x 14¼″. Metcalf Bowler was a wealthy Newport merchant and Rhode Island statesman. After the Revolution he moved to Providence. Attributed to Almy Harris Bowler (1789–1870), the granddaughter of Metcalf Bowler, and the daughter of Samuel B. Bowler (1764–1790) and Abigail Lee of Providence. She married Henry Hoppin in 1810 and had ten children. *Metropolitan Museum of Art, Rogers Fund, 41.16.*

Fig. 215. Anonymous mourning piece inscribed on the monument *Mrs. Loanna Olney/ died Jan. 29th 1799. In the 27th/ year of her age./ Mr. Paschal Paoli Smith/ died March 2d, 1802. In the/ 19th year of his age.* c.1809. Silk, chenille, and paint on silk; 15¾" x 13¼". About 1806, patterns for mourning embroideries changed at Mary Balch's school. The earlier delicacy gave way to larger monuments, heavier trees, partly painted figures, and painted backgrounds, but the inscriptions continued to be embroidered. Prudence W. Simmons (1798–1861) worked a similar pattern in 1809 (SPB Sale 3834, January 31, 1976, Lot 630). This was probably worked by Alice Olney (1796–1870), the eldest daughter of Loann Smith Olney, in memory of her mother and her uncle, or perhaps by one of Loann's several sisters who were born in the 1790s (see Fig. 204).
Private collection.

Fig. 216. *Sophia Ellsworth 1812* inscribed on the glass. Silk and paint on silk; 15⅞" x 21⅜". Sophia's memorial is typical of print work from Mary Balch's school, and similar pieces were made between 1811 and about 1820. Particularly characteristic is the foliage of the tree at right and the embroidered inscriptions. Sophia dedicated the monuments to her father and two sisters. Sophia Ellsworth (b.1794) was the daughter of Daniel Ellsworth (1757–1798) and Mary Abbott (1758–1835) of Ellington, Connecticut. Her widowed mother married Ebenezer Scarboro and moved to Brooklyn, Connecticut, in February 1809. Frances Williams, also of Brooklyn, worked a print-work memorial at Miss Balch's school in the same year. (Ring, *Treasures*, 93).
The Connecticut Historical Society, 1987–38.0.

Fig. 217. *Patty Davis/ born December 4/ 1771 at Newport/ Wrought at/ Warren/ February the 12 AD 1793*. Silk on linen; 17½″ x 13″. Martha (Patty) Davis (1771–1850) was the second daughter of Newport mariner John Davis (1740–c.1774) and Martha Pease (c.1743–1806). Patty was twenty-one years old when she worked her sampler, and she may have been teaching with her mother. In 1794, she married sea captain John Carr (1771–1815), and they had eight children.
Rhode Island Historical Society, bequest of Charlotte Greene, 1981.39.1.

Warren Samplers and Schoolmistress Martha Davis

A group of samplers made in Warren, Rhode Island, between 1793 and 1803 are strikingly similar to those from Providence. Except for their characteristic acrostic verses, they have essentially the same pattern worked by Polly Turner at Mary Balch's school in Providence in 1786.[1] It is possible that Polly's sampler or a similar one inspired their patterns. It is also conceivable, however, that both the Providence and Warren samplers developed from earlier Newport work that was known to both Mary Balch and Martha Pease Davis.

The Warren samplers are attributed to the instruction of Mrs. Martha Pease Davis because she is known to have been a schoolmistress, and both her daughter (Fig. 217), her granddaughter Anna Sanders, and her students worked similar samplers proclaiming that they were *Wrought at Warren* (Figs. 218, 219).[2] Martha Pease Davis (1743–1806) was a near contemporary of Sarah Rogers Balch, the

---

1. Polly Turner's sampler is illustrated in Ring, *Virtue,* 140; also in Fawdry and Brown, 65.
2. For Sanders and related samplers, see Ring, *Virtue,* 214–15, 228–32.

mother of Mary Balch, and the pattern of her life has close parallels. She was born in Newport, married John Davis at Newport's First Congregational Church in 1763, and became a widow before 1775. Like the Balch family, she fled war-torn Newport and supported herself and her two small daughters by teaching school, in her case in Rehoboth, Massachusetts. After her daughter Nancy married a Warren, Rhode Island, mariner in 1788, she moved to Warren with her younger daughter, Patty, and she probably taught school there until her death at the age of 63.

Fig. 218. *Joanna Maxwell/ born May the 8/ A D 1782 at Warren/ Wrought at/ Warren/ September/ the 12 A D 1793.* Silk on linen; 16½″ x 13″. Eleven-year-old Joanna worked the identical pattern chosen by the twenty-one-year-old daughter of her schoolmistress and showed nearly an equal degree of skill. Consistently dark silk makes the lettering of her acrostic verse more legible than the one by Patty Davis (Fig. 217). Joanna Maxwell (1782–1847) was the daughter of Warren sea captain Level Maxwell (b.1754) and Abigail Hill (b.1757). Joanna lived with her father and step-mother, Henrietta Smith Maxwell, in a mansion built by her grandfather, the Reverend Samuel Maxwell, and now owned by the Warren Historical Society. She died unmarried.
Private collection.

Fig. 219. *This Work/ Wrought at Warren/ By Nancy Baker/ July the 25 1803.* Silk on linen; 19″ x 16″. Nancy's central scene adheres to the earlier Warren style, except for the change in fashionable clothing, but her bird-capped pillars and broad arch lack the harmony found in the Davis and Maxwell patterns. Her distinctive border relates her work to other examples probably made under the instruction of Martha Davis (Ring, *Virtue*, 230–2; Sotheby's Sale 6051, June 28, 1990, Lot 275). Nancy's uncle Luther Baker wrote the acrostic verse worked by Martha Davis' granddaughter Anna Sanders in 1801, and probably for Martha's other students as well. Nancy Baker (1795–1837) was the only daughter of Warren shipmaster Jesse Baker, Jr. (1768–1846), and Hannah Smith (1767–1819). Nancy married George Leonard Horton (1797–1866) of Rehoboth and died after the birth of her seventh child.
Author's collection.

Samplers of Bristol

In 1790, Jemima Gorham worked a sampler that is clearly akin to Newport work (Fig. 220). It depicts a man with a walking stick and a lady in a flowered dress that suggest the frolicking people samplers of Newport, with a blocked cartouche resembling the elegant house form. Also in typical Newport fashion, there is a flowing floral border, and Jemima gave her birthdate; but she added something unknown on other Rhode Island samplers: the words *made this sampler in Bristol 1790 at Mrs Ushers School*. Thereby she provided a clue for the rediscovery of an important eighteenth-century schoolmistress, and probably a key to the origin of other samplers that name *Bristol New E* (Figs. 221, 222).

The Newport influence apparent in Jemima's work is not surprising. Anne Bowman Usher (1723–1793) was baptized at Trinity Church in Newport and married Hezekiah Usher there in 1750. By 1774, if not earlier, the childless Ushers were keeping a respected girls' boarding and day school on the southeast corner of Hope and State streets in Bristol. It was diagonally opposite the residence of Jemima Gorham's prosperous uncle, Stephen Smith. By his first wife, Mary Gorham, Stephen Smith had seven daughters born between 1764 and 1776, and like Jemima, they probably attended Anne Usher's school and made similar samplers. The school was also patronized by important Providence families, and its activities were particularly well described by the daughters of John Innes Clark.[1]

Four other samplers that name Bristol have been attributed to Anne Usher's school or to her successor's. They name *Bristol* and give birthdates of their makers but no dates of execution. These extraordinarily appealing samplers have been an unprecedented enigma. Their format suggests Newport influence, and there is a hint of their streaky sky in Mary Balch's sampler (Fig. 199). Their borders, with queen-stitched carnations and the outlining of tulip petals, resemble those in Jemima Gorham's sampler (Fig. 220); their makers, like Jemima Gorham, worked atypical alphabets with the *V* preceding the *U*. Yet their principal scenes, with worked black backgrounds, are filled with characteristic Marblehead, Massachusetts, motifs. No other major groups of American samplers from widely divided places are known to share such an array of distinctive pictorial patterns, except stereotypes derived from prints. It is illogical to conclude that the girls who named Bristol on their samplers would have worked them in Marblehead. However, Marblehead samplers with black backgrounds and similar birds, animals, and people survive in far greater numbers and cover a longer time span

---

1. For excerpts from their correspondence and more about Anne Usher's school, see Ring, *Virtue*, 208–14.

Fig. 220. *Jemima/ Gorham born/ August 28 1775/ made this sampler/ in Bristol/ 1790/ at Mʳˢ Ushers/ School*. Silk on linen; 13″ x 10⅞″. Jemima's work reflects Newport and Providence influences. Her motifs resemble Newport patterns, including a typical cartouche for the maker's name, while her verse was a favorite at Mary Balch's school in Providence. Jemima (1775–1798) was the eldest child of sea captain Isaac Gorham (1747–1795) and Sarah Thomas (d. 1835). She was a boarder at Mrs. Usher's school from April 12 until mid-November 1790. On October 1, 1797, she married, as his second wife, Nicholas Peck (1762–1847) and died shortly after the birth of her only child. *National Museum of American History, Smithsonian Institution; gift of the Misses Edith C. and Annette Everett Long, 113420*.

(1784–1802) than is indicated by the birthdates on the Bristol samplers (1777–1780).

A logical solution to the Bristol-Marblehead mystery has recently surfaced. Among the seven daughters of Mrs. Usher's prosperous neighbors Stephen (1741–1799) and Mary Gorham Smith (1743–1785) was Hannah (1768–1810), who married Dr. John Drury (c. 1760–1823) of Marblehead on May 24, 1787. Drury, a native of Grafton, Massachusetts, lived in Bristol from 1786 until 1788, when he settled in Marblehead,[2] where he became a respected physician and merchant. John and Hannah Drury maintained close contacts with friends and family in Bristol, and their two infant sons were baptized at Saint Michael's Church in Bristol on May 2, 1790. Hannah's sister Sukey Jarvis Smith was seventeen years old on May 26, 1790, and it is now reasonable to assume that she was living with the Drurys in Marblehead in 1791 when she worked the sampler in Figure 153.[3] Sukey was definitely with Hannah in 1793, and there were no doubt earlier visits. On July 21, 1792, her sister Mary wrote to Hannah: "Suky in particular sends her love to you and the Doctor . . . she has been quite affronted at your not writ-

---

2. Sukey Jarvis Smith to Hannah Drury in Marblehead, December 20, 1788 (John Drury Papers, EI).

3. Sukey was among the nine children of Mary Gorham Smith, who died when Sukey was eleven years old. Her father married Ruth Bosworth on December 1, 1785, and they had five children. In 1790 his household consisted of four males, six females, and three slaves.

Fig. 221. *Patty Coggeshall Born/ Feb 15th 1780 Bristol New E.* c.1792. Silk and metal on linen; 20½" x 16⅝". Many of the motifs in Patty's upper border and central scene are similar to those in Sukey Smith's sampler (Fig. 153), and she also worked a black background. The facing couples in tall hats occur also on Providence work. The alphabet and the flowers of her border strongly suggest that she worked this at Mrs. Usher's school. Patty Coggeshall (1780–1797) was the daughter of William Coggeshall (1719–1796) and his second wife, Margaret Munroe (1744–1809). They lived in Bristol. Patty's sister Polly (b. December 5, 1777) worked a very similar sampler (see Ring, *Virtue*, 222).
Metropolitan Museum of Art, Rogers Fund, 1913, 14.26.

ing to her. She grows a very good girl every day and we all love her more than ever."[4]

When John and Hannah Drury moved to Marblehead, the samplers being worked at Martha Barber's school were at their peak, and judging by Martha's other patrons, Sukey was probably happy with the opportunity of attending her school. When she returned to Bristol with her spectacular sampler, its size, sprightly composition, and dramatic black background must have created a sensation among her friends and neighbors.[5] Sukey was then eighteen years old or older, and she may have become an assistant at Mrs. Usher's school.[6] Her sampler could easily have been the prototype from which the duck pond, hunter, courting couple, musician, Venus drawn by doves, long-tailed birds, and black background were derived and incorporated into the basic Rhode Island format worked by Patty Coggeshall, Peggy Ingraham, and at least two other Bristol schoolgirls.

---

4. Mary Smith Fales to Hannah Smith Drury, July 21, 1792 (Drury Papers, EI).

5. The Bristol-Marblehead connection continued for the Smith and Drury families. In 1811, John Drury married Hannah's sister Sally (1776–1820), the widow of Dr. Luther Andrew Crossman (d.1804). Two of John and Hannah's sons married their first cousins, daughters of Hannah's sisters Lydia and Sally, and they lived in Bristol.

6. Mrs. Usher died December 14, 1793. In a letter of February 22, 1801, Mary Fales told Hannah Drury that she was keeping a school (Drury Papers, EI).

Fig. 222. *Peggy Ingraham Born/ May 18th 1778 Bristol*, c.1792. Silk on linen; 15½" x 12½". Peggy's long-tailed birds, the musician, and the partly worked black background are the most striking evidence of Marblehead influence. She also worked Mary Balch's favorite maxim. Her border and alphabet are related to Jemima Gorham's (Fig. 220). Peggy's classmate was probably Fanny Moor (1779–1797) of Bristol, who worked *Bristol New E* on her sampler. She centered the same house amid various figures on a light field within a black border (see PB, Haskell, Part 5, Sale 613, December 9, 1944, Lot 778). Margaret Ingraham (1778–1818) was the daughter of Providence housewright Simeon Ingraham and Elizabeth Granger (c.1753–1803). She married sea captain Charles Spooner (c.1769–1809) on June 19, 1796.
Metropolitan Museum of Art, bequest of Barbara Schiff Sinauer, 1984.331.12.

Fig. 223. *MARY WILLIAMS/ 1744/ THE QUEEN OF SHEBA ADMIRING THE WISDOM OF SOLOMON.* Wool and metallic threads on linen; 17¼″ x 21½″. Eleven-year-old Mary worked five houses and thirty-eight people on her masterpiece and enlivened her picture with a lavish use of silver metallic thread. Mary Williams (1733–1793) was the sixth child of the Reverend Solomon Williams (1701–1776) and Mary Porter (1703–1787) of Lebanon. She married the Reverend Richard Salter (1721–1787) of Mansfield, whose first wife was Mary Williams of Wethersfield. Their three children all died in infancy. Mary's brother William, "The Signer," married Mary Trumbull, the sister of Faith (Figs. 52, 56, 57).

National Museum of American History, Smithsonian Institution; gift of Dr. and Mrs. Arthur M. Greenwood, 182022.

NEEDLEWORK OF CONNECTICUT

Embroideries of New London County

THE MOST IMPORTANT Colonial samplers and needlework pictures of Connecticut were made by girls of New London County, probably in Norwich, which was the commercial center of eastern Connecticut in the mid-eighteenth century. This town began as an agricultural community in 1660, and it was fourteen miles from the sea. Nevertheless, its location at the junction of three rivers led to ship-building and a lucrative trade with the West Indies. In 1742, Norwich had the highest tax assessment in the Colony of Connecticut. Eventually the towns of Bozrah, Franklin, Sprague, Jewett City, and parts of Preston and Poquetannock developed within the nine square miles of the original Norwich deed and remained a part of the town until their division in 1786.[1] Also, just on its fringe was Lebanon, a community of exceptional men and of much activity during the pre-revolutionary period.[2]

NORWICH CANVAS WORK

During the prosperous years of the 1740s, a talented woman was teaching the daughters of prominent Norwich and Lebanon families. Possibly she was Mrs. Hall, née Pierce, who died in New London in 1752, having been a "Celebrated School-mistress who Taught Reading writing & Arithmetick & the Needle to ye female. She belonged to the Church of England. aged 60 odd."[3] In any case, a

---

1. Joan Nafie, *To the Beat of the Drum, a History of Norwich, Connecticut, during the American Revolution* (Norwich, Conn.: Old Town Press, 1975), 2.

2. A charming group of samplers, dated 1830–1834, name *Lebanon* and two teachers, Ann Beaumont and Lydia L. Scovell. See Krueger, *New England*, 39–40, Figs. 87, 88; also DAPC, no. 81.2076.

3. *Diary of Joshua Hempstead of New London, Connecticut* (New London: The New London County Historical Society, 1901), 584–5. Robert Trent kindly brought this to my attention.

Fig. 224. Needlework picture initialed *M W*, c.1744. Wool on linen; 17½″ x 21½″. Although it lacks metallic threads, this embroidery's relationship to the work of Mary Williams (Fig. 223) and Elizabeth Lothrop (Fig. 225) is unmistakable. It descended in a Connecticut family with some genealogical background, but an appropriate M W has not been found. *Lyman Allyn Museum, New London, gift of Mrs. Edith Chappell Sheffield, 1974.94.*

Fig. 225. *ELIZABETH LOTHROP 1745.* Wool and metallic threads on linen; 10⅜″ x 12⅞″. Elizabeth used silver threads in the manner of Mary Williams (Fig. 223). Also surviving is an Irish-stitched chair seat signed on the chair rail *N°. 3 June 17th 1756 Elizabeth Lothrop* (see *Connecticut Historical Society Bulletin 50*, no. 4 [Fall *1985*]: 93, Fig. 14). Elizabeth Lothrop (1733–1763) was the daughter of Colonel Simon Lothrop (1689–1775), who married his first cousin Martha Lothrop (1696–1775) in 1714. Elizabeth was the eighth child of this wealthy and influential Norwich family; she died unmarried.
The Leffingwell Inn, The Society of the Founders of Norwich, Connecticut, Inc., 305.

Fig. 226. *CHRISTIAN WILLIAMS/ 1751*. Wool and metallic threads on linen; 16½″ x 21½″. There is little in Christian's picture that relates closely to her sister's work (Fig. 223) except the tree at right and her name worked in silver. The date was painted over at a later time. Christian Williams (1738–1816) was eighth among the eleven children of the Reverend Solomon Williams of Lebanon, who was one of the most respected and influential ministers in New England and the first cousin of the Reverend Jonathan Edwards. Christian was named for her grandmother, Christian Stoddard Williams. She married John Salter (1725–1795) of Mansfield, the brother of her sister Mary's husband. She was the grandmother of Christian and Harriet Salter (Figs. 248, 246). *Winterthur Museum, 65.3080.*

teacher in or near Norwich produced the only colonial canvas-work pictures that rival the fishing ladies of Boston (Figs. 223–226). Unlike Boston teachers, who usually followed the English fashion for glorified pastoral scenes inspired by prints, this schoolmistress, or the person who drew her patterns, portrayed Biblical subjects with colonial people, and other varied activities in a quite different but delightful manner.

NORWICH SAMPLERS

An enduring sampler style emerged in Norwich in the 1760s, if not earlier, and vestiges of its early motifs lingered on into the nineteenth century. The earliest pieces are small, nearly square samplers crowded with roses, tulips, carnations, and stylized trees against solidly stitched black backgrounds (Figs. 227, 228). In 1765, Esther Copp, a Stonington girl, worked a more open sampler pattern with similar motifs,[4] quite possibly in the school where Naby Lord worked her sampler in the same year. In 1766, two sheep were added to Nabby Fitch's pattern (Fig. 228), and below the letter *H* in her alphabet she worked an upright and inverted heart motif that would expand into a central design on Norwich samplers of the 1770s and 1780s (Fig. 229)[5]; it was used on simple samplers of this region as late as 1807.[6] The samplers of the 1760s and 1770s also included small sections of a Greek key pattern (Figs. 227–230), and this later became an enveloping border (Fig. 232).

---

4. See Krueger, *New England*, Fig. 6.

5. This motif appears as a flower on Boston samplers of 1739 (Ring, *Treasures*, 4), and, in more geometric form, it appears in European pattern books of the sixteenth century (*ANTIQUES*, February 1991, 370).

6. It appears on the 1807 sampler of Abbey Story, who stitched the following: *Love is folly, Beauty is a blast. Virtue is a flower That will always last.* (Allentown Art Museum, 79.80.47).

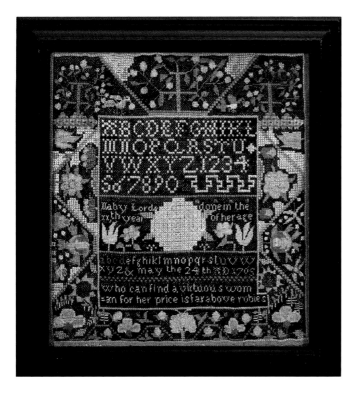

Below:
Fig. 228. *Nabby Fitch her sampler made in the 9th year of her age/ July 1766.* Silk on linen; 10½″ x 9¹⁵⁄₁₆″. The relationship of Nabby Fitch's sampler to Naby Lord's (Fig. 227) is evident, and many of her motifs are found on later Norwich samplers. Similar tulips and carnations appear in Figure 230, where the Greek-key pattern grew larger, and eventually became a framing border (Fig. 232). See also Ruth Huntington's sampler of 1787 (SPB Sale 3720, January 31, 1975, Lot 425). Nabby Fitch (August 4, 1757–March 1798) was fourth among the eleven children of Eleazer Fitch (1724/25–1797) and Mary Huntington (b.1728) of Norwich. She married John Post on March 13, 1788, and they had three sons and one daughter.
Private collection.

Above:
Fig. 227. *Naby Lords done in the/ 11ᵗʰ year of her age/ May the 24th A D 1765.* Silk and metal on linen; 11¼″ x 10″. Naby extended her border to accommodate the last line of her inscription. Her younger sister Elizabeth (1757–1805) completed a nearly identical sampler in 1764 (Ring, *Treasures*, 22). Abigail (Naby) Lord (1754–1821) was the daughter of tavern keeper Eleazar Lord, Jr. (1729–1809), and Elizabeth Lord (1729–1803) of Norwich. She married, as his second wife, Mundator Tracy (1749–1816) on May 4, 1786.
Author's collection.

Fig. 229. *Elizabeth Tracy aged twelve years/ 1774.* Silk on linen; 14¾″ x 12½″. Elizabeth's pattern is closely related to the work of Esther Copp, 1765, and beneath her inscriptions, she worked the Greek-key design used by Nabby Fitch (Fig. 228). Her central motif is also found on Norwich samplers of the 1780s (see Lucy Coit, 1785, and Martha Avery, 1786, both naming *Norwich*, in Edmonds, Figs. 9, 10). Elizabeth boldly stitched *GOD SAVE THE KING*. In 1776, Betsy Lathrop of Norwich worked a similar pattern with *God save America* (privately owned). Also, in 1798, Eunice Birchard worked an alphabet sampler with the heart motif (as in Fig. 228) and *GOD SAVE AMERICA* (Allentown Art Museum, 79.80.46). Elizabeth Tracy (August 16, 1762–March 9, 1782) was the daughter of Isaac Tracy, Jr. (b.1731), and Elizabeth Rogers of Norwich. She died unmarried.
Private collection; photograph courtesy of Kenneth W. Van Blarcom Auctioneers.

Fig. 230. *Alice Mather her Sampler made in the/ twelvth year of her age july* [th]/ *8 AD 1774.* Silk on linen with a printed chintz border; 13¾" x 11½". Alice worked a blue house reminiscent of earlier Norwich canvas work and she chose the same truism stitched by Naby Lord (Fig. 227). Alice Mather (October 4, 1762–1842) was the daughter of Samuel Mather (1742/43–1834) and Alice Ransom (1761–1805). Her father was a doctor in Lyme, New London County. In 1783 she married Dr. William Ely (1762–1829) of Pleasant Valley, New York. One of their four children survived them.
Private collection; photograph courtesy of Christie's.

Another Norwich teacher no doubt drew Hannah Lord's elegant pattern with its splendid naturalistic vine border in 1770 (Fig. 231), but the dramatic effect of a solidly worked black background prevailed. Toward the close of the eighteenth century, a solidly worked ground was still favored by a very imaginative woman who opened a school in Norwich, or in that part of Norwich that had become Franklin. Three remarkable samplers reflect her instruction from 1797 until 1803 (Figs. 233, 234).

Although Frances Manwaring Caulkins wrote a superb *History of Norwich, Connecticut,* in 1866, with a chapter on schools and academies, she offered no specific facts on women who taught in the eighteenth century. In 1745, the town maintained eight schools that were open for several months of the year. It was noted

Fig. 231. *Hannah Lord 1770*, with the initials *I B*, probably for her teacher. Silk on linen; 16¼" x 13¼". For a classmate, Hannah had Abigail Burnam (1757–1820) of Norwich, who worked a closely related sampler on a natural ground in the same year (*ANTIQUES*, February 1974, 357). Hannah Lord (1760–1836) was the daughter of Asa Lord (1736–1766) and Abigail Mumford (1737-1762) of Norwich. On March 1, 1781, she married Rufus Avery (1758–1842) of Groton and had five children. Hannah was the first cousin of Naby Lord (Fig. 227).
Lyman Allyn Museum, New London, Connecticut, 33.33.

Fig. 232. *Lucretia Carew 12*, c.1791. Silk on linen; 16¾" x 11¾". Lucretia did not date her sampler nor did two other girls who worked closely related patterns. One was signed by Mary Ayres who was probably born in 1774 to Joseph Ayres and Mary of Norwich (see Sotheby's Sale 5680, January 30, 1988, Lots 1538, 1539). Lucretia's upper band pattern and Greek-key border also occur on a solidly worked pictorial sampler made by Eunice Brewster Crary of Preston in 1814 (private collection). Lucretia Carew (September 30, 1778–August 19, 1862) was the daughter of Daniel Carew (1747–1813) and Lucy Perkins (1758–1832) of Norwich. She died unmarried. See her magnificent memorial (Fig. 24).
Slater Memorial Museum, Norwich, Connecticut, 250.E.207.

Fig. 233. *Fanny Smith/ her Sampler A/ug 23 AD 1797/ in the 14 year of her ᵃᵍᵉ*. Silk on linen; 17″ x 16¼″. Each vignette on Fanny's sampler probably had a significance that is unknown now. Fanny Smith (b. March 25, 1784) was the daughter of Andrew Smith (b.1754) and Alice Baker (b.1753) of Norwich. *Private collection; photograph courtesy of Stephen and Carol Huber.*

Fig. 234. *Laura Hyde/ her sampler AE/ 13 June 27 1800*. Silk and metallic threads on linen; 13¼″ x 13″. In Figure 233, Fanny Smith seems to picture an episode in America, but Laura Hyde features a harem scene beside the Bay of Bengal, although she added an American eagle. In 1803, Anna Huntington portrayed scenes of Jerusalem and the Levant (Krueger, *New England*, Fig. 64). Laura Hyde (1787–after 1857) was the daughter of Joshua Hyde (1756–1830) and Cynthia Tracy (1758–1829) of Norwich. They later moved to Franklin. Laura married Burrell Woodworth (1784–1849) in 1810. They had five children.
Metropolitan Museum of Art, Rogers Fund, 44.113.

that if any of the schools was kept by a woman, it could remain open twice as long, for "the pay of the mistress was but half that of the master."[7] It is unlikely that one of these schools introduced the town's enduring sampler styles, since they were taught primarily by men, and the women responsible for the extraordinary Norwich needlework of the eighteenth century remain unknown.[8]

Emerging embroideries should eventually lead to more information concerning the Norwich school kept by Lucy Carew, who was probably assisted by her daughter Lucretia (see Fig. 24).

---

7. Caulkins, *History of Norwich, Connecticut* (1866; reprint 1976), 275.

8. The *Norwich Packet* began publication on October 1, 1773, but no significant schools were advertised until the 1790s. Thomas Leffingwell's Account Book of 1753–1774 and Andrew Huntington's Ledger of 1780–1794 (both at the Leffingwell Inn, Norwich) record only brief instances of women teaching very young children.

Fig. 235. *THE WATSON ARMS* inscribed in ink beneath the shield and *HARRIET WATSON.* on the glass, c.1802. Silk, gold and silver metallic threads, gold metallic cord, spangles, and ink on silk; 17½″ x 14¼″; glass replaced. Harriet's embroidery is the only example presently known to use an American flag for a crest, as found on many painted arms by John Coles, Sr. (c.1749–1809), heraldic painter of Boston. His painted arms evidently inspired the basic compositions for arms worked at the Patten school. For a painted coat of arms by Coles and the Bliss arms worked by Harriet's sister Sally, see Ring, *Treasures*, 83. The Watson girls' coats of arms are atypical because of their inked inscriptions. Harriet Watson (1786–1866) was the daughter of John Watson (1744–1824) and Anna Bliss (1751–1827) of East Windsor. She married James Killam (c.1787–1863) in 1826.
Author's collection.

Connecticut Silk Embroideries

Many of New England's most exquisite neoclassical silk embroideries originated at three girls' schools in central Connecticut. The styles and standards they maintained appear to have influenced other schools of the Connecticut River Valley from Deerfield to coastal Connecticut,[1] and perhaps even farther afield. These long-lasting institutions were taught by the Misses Patten and Mrs. Lydia Royse in Hartford, and by Miss Sarah Pierce in Litchfield. The work of their students is often so similar that definitive attribution to a specific school may be impossible. However, in recent years, several characteristic techniques from the Patten and Royse schools have been identified, although they do not occur on every example from either school.

THE MISSES PATTEN

The most easily recognized Connecticut needlework has the highly raised and padded metallic embroidery favored by the Misses Patten during the first decade

---

1. For pieces belonging to a recognizable group of Washington memorials from the Clinton-Westbrook area, and not included here, see *ANTIQUES*, February 1981, Pl. 6, 409; Sotheby's Sale 4785Y, January 30, 1982, Lot 904; Nancy Jo Fox, *Liberties with Liberty* (New York: E. P. Dutton, 1985), 36, Fig. 34.

of the nineteenth century[2] but seldom used elsewhere by American schoolgirls except on eighteenth-century Boston coats of arms.[3] At the Patten school, pictorial subjects or coats of arms were often surmounted by a gold or silver raised-work eagle above a swagged garland suspended from spangled bow knots in the upper corners. The central motif was often partly encircled by palms or fronds with golden, bearded ears of wheat (Figs. 235–237). It also appears that certain allegorical or Biblical subjects were favorites of the Misses Patten, particularly views of Charity (Fig. 238) after the Stampa print (Fig. 239) and depictions of Moses in the Bulrushes (Fig. 241).[4] Rarer, but still recognizable, are other combinations of the typical motifs, as seen in Figure 240. Contemporary with these embroideries is a large group of painted coats of arms with patterns identical to the worked ones.

A large and somewhat later group of pictorial embroideries, mourning pieces, and painted memorials are also now attributed to the Patten school (Figs. 241, 242, 244). The needlework memorials usually have fully painted rather than embroidered figures. There is occasionally an appliquéd hat or shawl (Fig. 242), willow trees have drooping clumps of foliage with some inner branches visible, a small clump of leaves or flowers often nestles in the chenille-worked foreground, and some examples have an unusual rounded variety of palm tree (Fig. 244), which is also known on several views worked beneath the traditional eagle and swag.[5]

Only nineteenth-century work has been identified from the Misses Pattens' school, although Miss Sarah Patten first began teaching at her mother's Hartford home in November 1785, and this soon led to a successful family enterprise that continued until 1825. Sarah (1761–1843), Ruth (1764–1850), and Mary Patten (1769–1850) were the daughters of the Reverend William Patten (1738–1775) and Ruth Wheelock (1740–1831), and the granddaughters of Eleazer Wheelock (1711–1779), the founder of Dartmouth College. Their father entered Harvard at the age of twelve; he was ordained a minister before his nineteenth birthday, and he died at the age of thirty-six, leaving his thirty-four-year-old widow with six children between the ages of two and fourteen. Ruth Patten did not remarry, but she managed to keep her family together and attended to much of their education herself. Her son William recalled that his sisters also attended schools in Hart-

---

2. The first to identify a typical embroidery from the Patten school was Elisabeth Donaghy Garrett when she was the Director/Curator of the DAR Museum (*ANTIQUES*, February 1974, 359, 363).

3. Similar raised work in gold metallic thread is found on an 1809 coat of arms from Mary Balch's school in Providence (Fig. 212). See also, Baltimore samplers, Figures 568 and 569.

4. Mary Hathaway's *Charity* is at the New-York Historical Society; Sarah Marshall's of 1806 is at the DAR; Aurelia Palmer worked one in 1806 (privately owned; recorded at the Wadsworth Atheneum, Hartford); *Charity*, evidently in this form, was Lot 943 in the Alexander W. Drake Sale at the American Art Galleries on March 12, 1913; see also, Skinner Sale 1362, January 12, 1991, Lot 151. For a watercolor example, see Sotheby's Sale 4211, February 2, 1979, Lot 704. Also attributed to the Patten school are a patriotic embroidery at Historic Deerfield, Inc., and a related example, with the typical rounded palm tree (*ANTIQUES*, August 1976, 254, and March 1991, 500).

5. See an example with *The Holy Family* in *ANTIQUES*, April 1941, 193.

Fig. 236. The arms of *BUTLER* with the embroidered motto *SPERO ADVERSIS/ MUTEO SECUNDIS* and gold wrought monogram *M P B.*, c.1804. Silk, gold and silver metallic threads, and gold metallic cord on silk; 17¼″ x 14″. Worked by Mary Porter Butler (1788–1832), the daughter of Frederick Butler (1766–1843) and Mary Belden (1770–1811) of Wethersfield. Either Mary or her sister, Charlotte (1790–1858), may have been the "Miss Butler" responsible for Wethersfield's distinctive samplers, which incorporate paper eagles holding floral swags and are reminiscent of the Patten school (see Figs. 264, 265). For Charlotte's arms of the Belden family, now at the Norwalk Historical Society, see PB Sale 1521, May 13, 1954, Lot 215.
The Brooklyn Museum, 54.121.

Fig. 237. The arms of *HUMPHREY* with the motto *Fear GOD/
In Life* worked beneath the shield, and initialed in embroidery
NH., signed on the glass *N. HUMPHREY*, c.1804. Silk, chenille, gold and silver metallic threads, and spangles on silk;
16⅝″ x 13 ¾″. The festoon of flowers below the monogram is
found on many related pieces, both worked and painted on
silk or paper. See the embroidered arms by Jerusha Williams
in *The Great River* (1985), 406. The line decoration surrounding the inner gold band on the glass mat suggests that this
was framed by Ruggles and Dunbar, working in Hartford,

1804–1806. Similar decoration appears on a labeled frame in
Ring, *Treasures*, 81. Most likely, N. Humphrey was either
Nancy (1786–1823), the daughter of David Humphrey, Jr.
(1758–1831), and Lucy Marshall of Goshen, Connecticut, or
Nancy (1791–1822), the daughter of Colonel Jonathan
Humphrey (1744–1812) and Lydia Griswold Phelps
(c.1764–1828) of Simsbury. Both died unmarried.
*Baltimore Museum of Art, gift of Mrs. William C. Whitridge,
70.54.*

Fig. 238. *ELIZA STONE* inscribed on the glass mat above the picture and the title *CHARITY* below, c. 1808. Silk, chenille, gold and silver metallic threads, and paint on silk; 19″ x 25¼″. Eliza Stone and Louisa Bellows, both of Walpole, New Hampshire, worked nearly identical embroideries. For Louisa's *Charity*, see *Art & Auction*, January 1988, 105. Eliza Stone married lawyer William G. Field in 1816. He kept school between 1820 and 1831 and was preceptor of the Walpole Academy in 1825. They later moved to Greene County, Ohio. *Cincinnati Art Museum, 1914.327.*

Fig. 239. *CHARITY*, mezzotint engraving *Publish'd Sept.ʳ 20 1802, by P. Stampa, 74, Leather Lane, London;* 11″ x 9″. There is little doubt that the embroideries of *Charity* from the Patten school were inspired by this print. *Daughters of the American Revolution Museum, Washington, D.C.*

ford "which were well supplied with excellent teachers in reading, writing, arithmetic, lessons in music, and now and then some ornamental works, which were profitable to assist in supporting the family, as no goods of these kinds were imported in war time."[6]

Either their mother or some unknown Hartford schoolmistress imparted to the Patten sisters their extraordinary skill in needlework. Ruth Wheelock Patten (Fig. 243) is said to have received a superior education at the Windsor, Connecticut, home of the Reverend Timothy Edwards, where two of his daughters kept "a select school for needlework, composition, and various branches of mental and moral improvements. . . ."[7] She later presided over morals, manners, and religious instruction at her daughters' school, but who drew the patterns for needlework or instigated the working and painting of coats of arms remains unknown. Letters of 1806 from Miss Ruth Patten to Providence student Susan Jenckes Winsor suggest that miniaturist Gerrit Schipper was painting figures on the embroideries in 1805 and again in 1807.[8] However, his residence in Hartford was brief and he could not have contributed a consistent style to their work.[9]

By about 1800, the Misses Pattens' school had "attained great celebrity," and at times there were more than two hundred scholars, with thirty or forty as boarders.[10] Although it was a girls' school, a small boy with an older sister was occasionally admitted. In the 1880s, one such pupil had happy memories of his experience there:

6. Ruth Patten, *Interesting Family Letters of the Late Mrs. Ruth Patten, of Hartford, Conn.* (1845), 17.

7. William Patten, *Memoirs of Mrs. Ruth Patten, of Hartford, Conn. with Letters and Incidental Subjects* (1834), 9.

8. Ruth Patten to Susan J. Winsor, January 20, 1806, and December 13, 1806 (CHS). The former is partly quoted in Krueger, *New England*, 29.

9. Gerrit Schipper (1775–c.1830) advertised in Boston's *Columbian Centinel and Massachusetts Federalist* on October 19, 1803, and April 21, 1804; in the *Salem Gazette*, Salem, Massachusetts, on June 4, 1804; in the *Albany Centinel* of January 4, 1805; he married in Amsterdam, New York, in October 1806; and advertised in Hartford's *Connecticut Courant* on March 18, 1807. Shortly thereafter he moved to England.

10. William Patten, *Memoirs*, 72.

R. GREEN.   "AND SHE HAD COMPASSION ON HIM." EXOD. CH.2.V.6.

Right:
Fig. 240. Washington commemorative embroidery, anonymous, c.1800. Silk, gold and silver metallic threads, and printed paper on silk; 18½″ x 16½″. The floral garlands and golden, bearded ears of wheat relate this embroidery to others from the Patten school. A similar piece, with the same aquatint engraving of Washington by Edward Savage, is said to have been "Worked about 1799 by Col. Beach Daughter." (*MAD*, August 1987, 10-D.) An oval embroidery with a similar cascade of flowers, and entitled *The Royal Psalmist*, was worked by Rhoda Newbury (1786–1874) of Windsor, Connecticut, in 1800 (Sotheby's Sale 5282, February 1, 1985, Lot 357). For a more typical Patten composition with a different Savage engraving of Washington, see *ANTIQUES*, February 1981, 406.
Western Reserve Historical Society, Cleveland, Ohio, gift of George W. Bierce, 72.21.1.

Fig. 241. *R. GREEN . . . "AND SHE HAD COMPASSION ON HIM." EXOD. CH. 2. V. 6.* inscribed on the glass, c.1805. Chenille, applied painted paper, and paint on silk; 16⅝″ x 19¼″. Here only the tree at right is worked. The large leaves in the foreground at left, the formation of the willow tree, and the tilted conifers are all characteristic of embroidered and painted pictures and memorials from the Patten school. For related examples, see the work of Lucretia Colton (b. December 29, 1788, in Longmeadow) in Harbeson, opp. 83; also Rumford, *American Folk Paintings* (1987), Fig. 199. Ruth Green (1791–1851) was from New Haven. In 1827, she became the second wife of John Warner Barber (1798–1885), the noted engraver and historian. *The Connecticut Historical Society, A-2100.*

Mrs. Patten did not engage in teaching at the time [about 1822 when he attended]. . . . Even her daughters were well advanced in years. But I well remember their gentleness and gentility and a certain combination of cheerfulness and sobriety which characterized them. Their long service in the trying profession of teaching had not soured them. . . .[11]

11. Thomas A. Thatcher (1815–1886) as quoted in J. Hammond Trumbull, ed., *The Memorial History of Hartford County, Connecticut, 1633–1884* (Boston: Edward L. Osgood, 1886), 1:635.

Fig. 242. *ELIZA DURNFORD* inscribed on the glass above the memorial and on the plinth *SACRED/ to the Memory/ of the Honourable/ ANDREW DURNFORD/ departed this life/ Sept. 10ᵗʰ 1798/ Aged 53*, c.1805. Silk, chenille, appliquéd lace shawl, and paint on silk; 20½″ x 18″. Elizabeth Durnford (1789–1847) was the eldest of six children born in Bermuda to British officer Colonel Andrew Durnford (1744–1798) and Elizabeth Lucas (d.1834), who was presumed to be his wife. However, his death revealed that his legal wife and children were in England. Durnford came to America in 1776 and served in Georgia, Florida, and Nova Scotia, before he was appointed Surveyor General of Bermuda in 1788. With Eliza, beside the monument, are her mother and surviving siblings, John, Henry, and James Andrew Durnford. Her mother was probably an American. In any case, Eliza Durnford attended the Patten school and her painted arms of *DURNFORD* descended with her embroidery. She was married in Hartford to Thomas M. Skinner on October 29, 1817. *Location unknown; photograph courtesy of Sotheby's.*

Fig. 243. Ruth Wheelock Patten (1740–1831) from a lithograph by D. W. Kellogg & Co., of Hartford, used as the frontispiece for William Patten's *Memoirs of Mrs. Ruth Patten*, published in 1834. Ruth Wheelock was the daughter of Eleazer Wheelock (1711–1779) and Sarah Davenport (1702–1746). She was born in Lebanon, Connecticut, and married William Patten (1738–1775) on June 9, 1758. Three of their eight children died young. Her son William (1763–1839) was pastor of the Second Congregational Church in Newport, Rhode Island, 1786–1833. He was the only child to leave issue.
American Antiquarian Society.

Along with the girls, this little boy learned to sew patches together and knitted a pair of garters.[12]

In the closing years of her career, Miss Ruth Patten remarked that Miss Catherine E. Beecher and her sister, Mrs. Mary Perkins, attended to only the "solid branches" at their newly established school in Hartford.[13] Had the Patten sisters done the same, they would now be forgotten. Instead, "Each young lady had a handsome framed piece on their return home, to present to their parents,"[14] and after more than a century of oblivion, the "framed" pieces have brought new recognition to the Misses Patten for their exceptional contributions to America's decorative arts. Their skills were further perpetuated by their students who became teachers: Jerusha Mather Williams (1783–1844), of Longmeadow, Massachusetts, attended their school around 1800 and taught similar needlework as the preceptress of Deerfield Academy from 1806 until 1811;[15] and either Mary Porter Butler, or her sister Charlotte, was probably responsible for the eagle and garland designs that later appeared on Wethersfield samplers.

---

12. Ibid.
13. Ruth Patten, *Family Letters*, 215.
14. Ibid., 19.
15. Suzanne L. Flynt, *Ornamental and Useful Accomplishments: Schoolgirl Education and Deerfield Academy 1800–1830* (1988), 17–30. Jerusha was the daughter of Mrs. Patten's first cousin Samuel Williams.

Fig. 244. *E. COLT* inscribed on the glass above a mournful verse, c.1807. Silk, chenille, and paint on silk; 26½" x 24¼". Inscribed on the plinth *The Tribute of an/ Affectionate Daughter,/ In Memory of/ Mrs. REBECCA Colt,/ Who died May 27, 1806./ Aged 38 Years./ and/ SALLY COLT,/ Who died August 29, 1798/ Aged 10 Months*. This typical memorial from the Patten school has figures that are fully painted. The willow tree has clumps of drooping foliage with rounded tops and some exposed branches. Sprigs of a small plant are in the foreground. The tiered, rounded palm tree appears to be a unique style of this school. For three closely related memorials, see Ring, *Treasures*, 86–8; also, Sotheby's Sale 6075, October 20, 1990, Lot 120. Similar examples painted on silk are illustrated in *Art in America*, May 1954, 136–7. Elizabeth Colt (c.1792–1812) was the daughter of Elisha Colt (1758–1827) and Rebecca Butler (c.1768–1806) of Hartford. Her father was comptroller of the State of Connecticut, 1806–1818. Elizabeth married Marcus Bull (1787–1851) on November 29, 1810, and died less than two years later. *Private collection; photograph courtesy of Sotheby's.*

Fig. 245. Pictorial embroidery by Rebecca Butler, 1805. Silk, chenille, velvet, and wool appliqué, with paint on silk; 25½″ x 25½″. Inscribed on the back: "This embroidery was done in the summer of 1805 finished early September, 1805 at Lydia Royses' school, needlework by Rebecca Butler (dau. of Patty & Norman Butler) and the ptg by Eliza Lydia Butler." Assuming that this information is basically accurate, Rebecca's embroidery is now an important key for identifying work from Lydia Royse's school. It includes a tree with unusual star-shaped leaves worked in chenille, garments of sheer appliquéd wool on the figures, and appliquéd velvet in the foreground with embroidered sprigs of flowers. Also, the ribbon-like, upright bank of the stream appears on other scenes from this school. The painting was surely by Lydia Royse, rather than her daughter, Eliza Lydia Butler, as stated in the inscription, for Eliza Lydia was eight years old on September 23, 1805. Rebecca Butler (1788–1849) was the daughter of Normand Butler (1763–1838) and Patty Olcott (1763–1806). She died unmarried.

Butler-McCook Homestead, The Antiquarian and Landmarks Society, Inc., Hartford, Connecticut, 1981.6.371.

MRS. LYDIA ROYSE

The school which attracted most attention and educated a large number of girls, before 1820, was established by Mrs. Lydia Bull Royse, about 1800.[1]

Superb needlework pictures and mourning embroideries survive from Lydia Royse's school in Hartford. They can often be identified by the characteristic appliquéd garments on the figures,[2] or by velvet appliqué in the foreground of scenic compositions,[3] and occasionally they have trees with peculiar star-shaped, chenille-worked leaves (Figs. 245, 246, 248). Although this school opened after the Misses Pattens' school, it appears to have been widely patronized from the time that it commenced, perhaps because it was frequently advertised.

As with the Patten sisters, there is no record of the woman who taught Lydia Bull Royse during her girlhood in Hartford. She is said to have studied art with

1. J. Hammond Trumbull, ed., *The Memorial History of Hartford County, Connecticut, 1633–1884* (Boston: Edward L. Osgood, 1886), 1:645.

2. A smaller group of Connecticut memorials has quite similar appliquéd garments but very different painting and embroidery. The school of their origin is undetermined. See Ring, *Treasures*, 85; Schorsch, *Mourning Becomes America* (1976), No. 48/170; and *The Connecticut Historical Society Bulletin* 25, no. 2 (April 1960): 56–7.

3. Schoolmistress Abby Wright of South Hadley, Massachusetts, also used velvet appliqué. See Figure 181.

Fig. 246. *LIBERTY GUIDED BY THE WISDOM OF '76* and *HARRIET M. SALTER* inscribed on the glass, c.1807. Silk, chenille, gold metallic thread, velvet appliqué, and paint on silk; 17″ x 17″. Harriet's embroidery reveals that like the Patten sisters, Lydia Royse was skilled in the use of metallic threads. An almost identical anonymous embroidery, with the same title on the glass, has the label of Hartford framer Nathan Ruggles that came into use after April 1806 (see Dean A. Fales, Jr., *The Furniture of Historic Deerfield* [New York: E. P. Dutton, 1976], 281). Harriet Maria Salter (1792–1846) was a sister of Christian Salter (Fig. 248). She married, as his second wife, Herman Ely (1775–1852), on August 20, 1828, and moved to Elyria, Ohio. They had one son.
National Museum of American History, Smithsonian Institution; gift of Dr. and Mrs. Arthur M. Greenwood, 182022.

Fig. 247. Mrs. Lydia Bull
Royse (1772–1832), c.1810.
Watercolor on ivory; 2⁹⁄₁₆″
x 2¹⁄₁₆″. This anonymous
miniature may be a self-
portrait. A portrait and
several watercolors in the
Butler-McCook Homestead
are attributed to Mrs.
Royse.
*Butler-McCook Homestead, The
Antiquarian and Landmarks
Society, Inc., Hartford, Con-
necticut.*

John Trumbull,[4] but this assertion has not been confirmed. In any case, she enjoyed painting, and presumably it was she who painted all the embroideries attributed to her school, for they appear to be the work of one hand. As with most
teachers, her patterns were often inspired by prints, and the subjects she favored
for embroidery were *Cybele*, *Ruth and Naomi*, the *Arch of Titus*, *The Parting of Hector and Andromache*, and *The Romps* (a charming household scene after a painting
by W. R. Bigg).[5] Mrs. Royse did not include terms for tuition in her advertisements, but a bill to Miss Ursula Wolcott's father gives an idea of the charges in
1813.

Major Woolcott	To Mrs. Royse, Dr.
For Miss Ursula Woolcott—Tuition 14 weeks	$7.62
Drawing Picture, 6/—Stationery, 3/9—Medicine, 3/	2.12½
30 & ¼ Silks @ 10¹⁰⁰, 18/2—33 yds.	
Chenille @ 4½d., 12/4	5.09
	14.83
Painting Picture included	5.50
Board, 12 weeks, @ 13/6	27
	41.83
	5.50
	47.33

Rec'd Payment,   Lydia Royse
Hartford, April 8th, 1813.[6]

Ursula Wolcott worked *The Parting of Hector and Andromache*, and the cost of the
materials, with the drawing and painting of the picture, exceeded eleven dollars.
Her embroidery was no doubt similar to the example in Figure 250, since among
her classmates at Mrs. Royse's school were her cousins Helen Wolcott and
Frances and Maria Bissell.[7]

Considerable rivalry existed between the Patten and Royse schools, and com-
paring their enrollment and the work of their students were topics of local interest. In recalling her youth, one elderly lady declared that Mrs. Royse's school
was "far ahead of the Misses Pattens."[8] Also, in 1804, Nancy Francis wrote from
Hartford to her friend Ruth Pease in Blandford, a former Patten scholar, with the
comment that "Miss Smith spends the winter at Miss Pattens, they have but a few
boarders & think it probable they will have quite a thin school this season."[9] Nev-

4. Written on the reverse of a portrait of her son-in-law that is attributed to her (Butler-McCook Homestead, Hartford).
5. Trumbull, *Memorial History*, 646. For an engraving of *The Romps*, see *ANTIQUES*, December 1947, 399.
6. Trumbull, 646. Calculations here are confusing. Board appears to have been $2.25 per week.
7. Ibid. The Wolcott and Bissell girls were not sisters, but all four were related to each other as first
cousins.
8. Ibid., 647.
9. Nancy Francis to Ruth Pease, November 24, 1804 (collection of Historic Deerfield, Inc.). Ruth's wonderful copybooks from the Patten school, August 1804, are also in this collection.

Fig. 248. *INNOCENCE* and *CHRISTIAN W. SALTER* inscribed on the glass, c.1805. Silk, chenille, velvet, and wool appliqué, with paint on silk; 21″ x 20″. Christian's composition is much like Rebecca Butler's (Fig. 245). Christian Williams Salter (1790–1856) was a daughter of John Salter (1769–1831) and Mary Williams (1769–1850) of Tolland, Connecticut. She was named for her grandmother (Fig. 226). She died unmarried.
Location unknown; photograph courtesy of Sotheby's.

ertheless, a wealth of elegant embroidery offers ample evidence that both schools were well patronized by the leading families of the Connecticut Valley.

Lydia Bull Royse (1772–1832), born in Hartford, was first among the six children of Hartford tavern keeper and merchant Frederick Bull (1753–1797) and Lydia Griswold (1753–1811). At the age of twenty in 1792, she was married in New York City to John Royse (1772–1798), the son of Thomas Royse and Elizabeth Forder. They lived in New York and Richmond, Virginia, before he died of yellow fever in New Bern, North Carolina, leaving Lydia with their fourth and only surviving child, Eliza Lydia.[10]

Lydia returned to Hartford where her recently widowed mother had opened a boarding house, and in May of 1799 they advertised that "The widows LYDIA BULL and LYDIA ROYCE" offered to accommodate six boarders.[11] The first advertisement for Lydia's school appeared in the *Connecticut Courant* on June 17, 1799, and ran through August 5 (see front endpapers):

> A SCHOOL is opened in Front-Street by LYDIA ROYSE, where young Ladies may be instructed in Reading, Writing, Plain Work, Tambour do, Embroidery, Cotton and Dresden Work, Drawing, & c — Young Ladies from the country may be accomodated with board in the same house on reasonable terms.
>
> Hartford. June 17.

10. Trumbull, *Memorial History*, 645.
11. *Connecticut Courant*, Hartford, May 6, 1799.

By June of 1803, the school was located "a little south of the Baptist Church,"[12] and Lydia Royse was assisted in teaching by her widowed sister, Martha Chenevard.[13] Before 1806, she moved to Burr Street and taught there until 1811 when she announced her location in "the north part of the city—where she hopes to establish her school permanently."[14]

Lydia evidently closed her school when her daughter married George Sheldon in January 1816, for Eliza Sheldon later recalled that "whilst she had a home with us [she] pursued her favorite occupation of teaching drawing and painting to a few pupils."[15] This pleasant situation ended with George Sheldon's sudden death in 1817, and Lydia Royse attempted to re-establish her school. She advertised in May and November of that year and advised that "scholars may be accommodated with board in the family by Russell Bull."[16] For unknown reasons she abandoned teaching in 1818, and her daughter opened a school with a Mrs. Grosvenor while Lydia cared for her child. In 1820, Mrs. Grosvenor and Mrs. Sheldon advertised their school in Boston's *Columbian Centinel*, explaining that they were "Only one days ride from Boston."[17] Their partnership continued at least until 1824.[18] Thereafter, Lydia and her daughter invested in a Ladies Warehouse where they sold piece goods, notions, etc., while continuing to teach music and drawing to a few young ladies.[19] Thereby they managed to eke out a living, but when Lydia Royse died in 1832, her estate was insolvent.

In 1837, at the age of thirty-nine, Eliza Royse Sheldon married John Butler (1780–1847), a prosperous Hartford bachelor, and finally she had a secure future. Eliza Sheldon Butler was born in 1840, and in 1858 Eliza Royse Sheldon Butler (b.1797) died in Paris, France, while on an extended European tour with her daughters Mary Eliza Sheldon (1816–1887) and Eliza Sheldon Butler (1840–1917). The Butler home continued to be occupied by their descendants until 1971, and it is now the property of the Antiquarian and Landmarks Society of Connecticut.[20]

---

12. Ibid., June 8, 1803.

13. Eliza Lydia Royse Sheldon Butler to Mrs. C. Scott, February 27, 1855 (transcription, Butler-McCook Homestead). Martha Bull (1775–1832) married J. Michael Chenevard (1771–1801) in 1794.

14. *Connecticut Courant*, April 9, 1806, and March 20, 1811.

15. Butler letter to Mrs. Scott (Butler-McCook Homestead). There is a group of large, many-peopled Connecticut memorials that are painted on silk or paper and with monuments much like the one in Figure 252. Their origin is undetermined. Possibly they are late pieces painted under Lydia Royse's instruction about 1815–1817. See Schorsch, *Mourning*, No. 37/127; Pike and Armstrong, *A Time to Mourn* (1980), 155; also, Christie's, January 20, 21, 1989, Lot 392.

16. *Connecticut Courant*, May 6 and November 18, 1817. Russell Bull (1772–1835) married Lydia Royse's sister, Clarissa Bull (b.1784), in 1810.

17. *Columbian Centinel*, Boston, April 12, 1820; also, *Connecticut Courant*, March 27, 1821.

18. Trumbull, *Memorial History*, 647.

19. Butler letter to Mrs. Scott (Butler-McCook Homestead).

20. "Butler-McCook Homestead" in Reynolds, *Images of Connecticut Life* (1978), 83–93.

Fig. 249. Allegorical embroidery known on a similar piece as *Wisdom Directing Innocence to the Temple of Virtue*, c.1806. Silk, chenille, metallic threads, spangles, and paint on silk, and silk on velvet; 17″ x 21⅜″. An example by Elizabeth T. Smith, with the above title, is illustrated in Rumford, *American Folk Paintings* (1987), 384. The theme is the same on an embroi-

dery from Sarah Pierce's school (Fig. 255), but evidently from a different print source. Here the embroidered velvet foreground is a strong clue to Lydia Royse's instruction as well as the style of painting.

M. and M. Karolik Collection, Museum of Fine Arts, Boston, 67.1170.

Fig. 250. *The Parting of Hector and Andromache/ M. Bissell, 1810* inscribed on the original glass mat (now replaced). Silk, chenille, gold metallic thread, velvet appliqué, and paint on silk; 17¼″ x 22⅜″. The figures in this composition were probably derived from *The Parting of Hector and Andromache* engraved by W. Durrell, New York, 1808, and used as the frontispiece in *The Iliad of Homer*, vol. 2, translated by Alexander Pope (Boston: Hastings, Etheridge, and Bliss, 1808). It is illustrated in Ring, *Virtue*, 198. For a very similar piece, here attributed to Lydia Royse's school, see Sotheby's Sale 5282, February 1, 1985, Lot 370. Maria Bissell (1793–1848) was a daughter of Aaron Bissell (1761–1834) and Naomi Tudor (1764–1847). Her father owned Bissell's Tavern in East Windsor. She died unmarried.

The Connecticut Historical Society, 1934-6-1.

Fig. 251. *MARY TREADWELL* inscribed on the glass above the embroidery and below it *WE MOURN BUT NOT WITHOUT HOPE*, c.1805. Silk, chenille, paint, and ink on silk with appliquéd silk and velvet; 23½″ x 23″. Inscribed on the plinth *In Memory/ of/ A Sister/ LUCY JEROME/ Ob Sept^br 26th 1804/ AE 23 years*. Typical of mourning pieces from Lydia Royse's school are the appliquéd garments of the female weepers, the somewhat thin, wispy willow trees, and the appliquéd velvet in the foreground. Many examples include the kneeling figure, who is believed to represent the needleworker. An almost identical memorial was worked by a girl of the Abbe family; only the figures between the mother, at left, and the urn are different (DePauw and Hunt, *Remember the Ladies* [1976], 42). Mary Treadwell (b.1786) was the daughter of John Treadwell (1745–1823) and Dorothy Pomeroy of Farmington. John Treadwell served in the Continental Congress and was governor of Connecticut (1809–1810). In 1814, Mary married Erastus Perry.
Private collection.

Fig. 252. *CATHERINE BUTLER* inscribed on the glass and dedicated on the plinth to *Henry Butler Jun*^r/ *ob Sept*^{br} *24th 1804 AEt 19*^{yrs}, c.1809. Silk, chenille, paint, and ink on silk with silk, wool, and velvet appliqué; 21″ x 20¼″. For a similar example, see Laura Hadley Moseley, *The Diaries of Julia Cowles* (New Haven: Yale University Press, 1933), frontispiece. The decoration on the plinth is characteristic of Lydia Royse's school and lends credence to the belief that later painted memorials reflect her instruction. Compare the memorial by Sarah Turney (b.1801) in Pike and Armstrong, *A Time to Mourn* (1980), 155. Its monuments and house in the background are strikingly similar to the ones on this example. For another Royse type, see the Bidwell and Matson memorials in

Ring, *Treasures*, 84, and Groft, *The Folk Spirit of Albany* (1978), 67. Catherine Butler (b.1792) was the daughter of Henry Butler (1765–1830), a Hartford merchant, and Chloe Hinsdale (1768–1824). Her brother Henry, Jr., died at Martinique on September 24, 1805, according to Hartford's *American Mercury* of October 24, 1805. The discrepancy in the date on the plinth is unexplained. By 1809, Catherine had five younger brothers (another Henry was born in 1806; Daniel in 1808). The young lady behind the kneeling Catherine is unidentified. Catherine married Miles Beach, Jr. (1789–1820), of Hartford in 1816. She married twice thereafter and lived in Columbus, Ohio.

Winterthur Museum, 58.2876F.

Fig. 253. Sarah Pierce
(1767–1852), c.1830.
Watercolor on ivory; 3¼″ x
2⅞″. She was a small,
slender woman with fair
skin, blue eyes, and a
cheerful, lively disposition.
On October 11, 1811,
Meroa Robbins wrote from
Litchfield to her brother
Amatus in Colchester:
"Could I imitate the virtues
of my beloved instructress,
or attain half the knowledge
she possesses, I should think
myself wise." (Robbins
Letters, CSL.)
*The Litchfield Historical
Society, 1941-02-2.*

SARAH PIERCE'S LITCHFIELD ACADEMY

The history of Sarah Pierce's school in Litchfield is probably better known than
that of any other American girls' school of the Federal period, because Emily
Noyes Vanderpoel (1842–1939), an enthusiastic historian, published voluminous
chronicles about Sarah Pierce and her pupils in 1903 and 1927.[1] This author zeal-
ously sought information when elderly former students were still able to supply
it, and her books are filled with fascinating anecdotes relating to school life in
Litchfield. This respected institution existed under Miss Pierce's direction from
1792 through 1833, and it became known for its advanced curriculum. Ornamental accomplishments were not abandoned, however, as evidenced by the embroideries illustrated here. Still, no distinctive body of work is associated with the
school, although documented examples reveal that its needlework adhered to the
dominant trends of this region, for in style and subject matter it is closely akin
to Hartford embroidery. At least two thousand girls attended the Litchfield
Academy, so it is still possible that some repetitious form of embroidery will
emerge and provide clues for the recognition of many unidentified Connecticut
pieces.

Sarah Pierce (1767–1852) was youngest among the seven children of John
Pierce (1730–1783), a Litchfield potter, and his first wife, Mary Paterson
(1731–1770). After her father's death, her eldest brother headed the family, and,

1. Vanderpoel, *Chronicles of a Pioneer School from 1792 to 1833* (1903), and *More Chronicles of a Pioneer School
from 1792–1833* (1927). See also Lynne Templeton Brickley's essay on Sarah Pierce's Academy in Mary An-
toine de Julio, *"What a Rich Reward": Betsey Reynolds Voorhees and the Collection of Her Handiwork* (Fort Johnson, N.Y.: Montgomery County Historical Society, 1986), 60–5.

with her sister Nancy, Sarah was sent to school in New York "with the express purpose in view of their opening a school in Litchfield."[2] Where she attended school earlier is unknown, but quite possibly she was instructed in Hartford by the same unknown woman who taught her close contemporaries the Misses Patten and Lydia Bull Royse. She was about twenty-five years old when she began teaching in the dining room of the Pierce home, and journals of her early scholars reveal that her program was rather erratic and their attendance somewhat casual. Often the daily entries say "Miss Sally did not keep school," generally with no reasons given. Nevertheless, by 1798, the school had achieved such prominence that the town fathers provided a building for its use. It was thereafter known as the Female Academy.[3]

Catherine Beecher attended Miss Pierce's school after her father became the pastor of Litchfield's Congregational Church in 1810. She remembered Miss Pierce as "a woman of more than ordinary talent, sprightly in conversation, social and full of benevolent activity." She continued with the following details:

> Her school was a small building of only one room, probably not exceeding 30 ft by 70, with small closets at each end, one large enough to hold a piano, and the others used for bonnets and over garments. The plainest pine desks, long plank benches, a small table and an elevated teacher's chair, constituted the whole furniture. When I began school there, she was sole teacher, aided occasionally by her sister in certain classes, and by her brother-in-law in penmanship. At that time 'higher branches' had not entered female schools. Map drawing, painting, embroidery and the piano, were the accomplishments sought, and history was the only study added to geography, grammar and arithmetic. In process of time her nephew, Mr. John Brace became her associate and introduced a more extended course.[4]

Miss Pierce is said to have had little talent or taste for needlework.[5] Instead, she wrote plays for her students to perform, stressed the study of history and geography, and published a well-received history textbook. Nevertheless, either she or her sister must have supervised the work of Nancy Hale and her classmates (Fig. 254). When writing to her family in 1802, Nancy commented on her embroidery and Miss Pierce:

> I spend my time very agreeably am very much engaged about my Picture. C [Cyrinthia] Smith began one when she first came here like mine but I have got some ways before her I shall endeavor to be as diligent as possible. . . . Besides Embroidering I study Geography and write Composition I get my lessons in Evening. She does not allow any one to Embroider without they

---

2. Vanderpoel, *Chronicles*, 5.
3. Ibid., 19.
4. Ibid., 179.
5. Brickley in de Julio, *"What a Rich Reward,"* 63.

Fig. 254. *NANCY HALE* inscribed on the silk and on the glass *THE COTTAGE GIRL*, 1802. Silk, gold metallic thread, paint and ink on silk; 22″ x 19″. The format of this embroidery appears on four pieces worked in 1802. Cyrinthia Smith's nearly identical work (but without metallic threads) is dated *1802* (Litchfield Historical Society). Esther Lyman (c.1785–1816) of Middlefield, Connecticut, depicted *The Return from Egypt* within her oval (Vanderpoel, *More Chronicles*

[1927], opp. 224); and Melissa Hays featured an unidentified female figure (Salmon Brook Historical Society, Granby, Connecticut). Nancy Hale (c.1786–1808) was the youngest daughter of Gideon Hale (c.1737–1812) and Mary White (c.1741–1820) of Glastonbury, Connecticut. She died unmarried.

The Connecticut Historical Society, 1956-63-9.

Fig. 255. Allegorical embroidery, c.1800. Silk and paint on silk with the silk ground surrounding the picture painted black; 13½″ x 14½″. This embroidery was derived from the engraving in Figure 256, and it has survived with a matching watercolor. It is attributed to Lucretia Champion (1783–1882), who is believed to have attended the Pierce Academy. She was the daughter of Epaphroditus Champion (1756–1834) and Lucretia Hubbard (1760–1836) of East Haddam, Connecticut. In 1806, she married Asa Bacon, a young lawyer who had moved to Litchfield in 1803 and formed a partnership with James Gould. The pictures were given to the Litchfield Historical Society in 1919 by Lucretia Champion Bacon's only grandchild, Mrs. Katherine Bacon Trowbridge (b.1844), whose mother, Elizabeth Sheldon Dutcher Bacon, also attended the Litchfield Female Academy. Another accurate needlework rendition derived from the same print is in the collection of the Tryon Palace Restoration Complex, New Bern, North Carolina. It is signed on the glass *A. Johnson*, and it may have been worked by Antonette Johnson of Bristol, Connecticut, who attended the Pierce School during the summer of 1827.
The Litchfield Historical Society, 1919-26-0.

Fig. 256. *INNOCENCE protected by WISDOM, in her Road to the Temple of Virtue*, engraving, etching, and stipple on paper, by James Thackara (1767–1848); 4⅞″ x 6⅞″ plate. Published as the frontispiece to *The Literary Miscellany*, vol. I, 1795, by T. Stephens, No. 60 South Second Street, Philadelphia. This print was the design source for Figure 255.
The John S. Phillips Collection, The Pennsylvania Academy of Fine Arts, 1984.258.

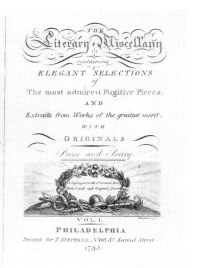

attend to some study for she says she wishes to have them ornament their minds when they are with her.[6]

In later years, it was probably a capable assistant who instructed Frances Ann Brace to embroider with gold, in the manner of earlier Hartford work (Fig. 257), and reminiscences of another student reveal that teaching ornamental needlework continued. Harriet Wadsworth described the graduation ceremonies of 1830–1831: "The closing exercises of the academy were held at the Court House. Paintings and needlework by the young ladies were hung on the walls. The pupils were dressed in white and were given diplomas. Singing and recitations were part of the exercises."[7]

During the first quarter of the nineteenth century, girls came to Sarah Pierce's school from nearly every state in the Union as well as from Canada and the West Indies. There is no doubt that the fame of Tapping Reeve's Litchfield Law School contributed to the knowledge of the Pierce school and its popularity.[8] Throughout the Academy's existence, out-of-town girls were boarded with Litchfield families, and although Miss Pierce strictly supervised their conduct, students from the two schools enjoyed an active social life. At least fifty-eight law scholars are known to have married Academy girls.[9] In 1827, the school was incorporated as The Litchfield Female Academy and under the direction of the trustees, a "large and commodious building" was erected "with suitable apartments for every branch of study appropriate to such an institution."[10] At that time, both schools in Litchfield were flourishing, but the decline would soon commence. In 1832, John Pierce Brace, Miss Pierce's associate principal, accepted a teaching position in Hartford and cited the Academy's declining enrollment, which he attributed to the growing number of rival academies and the inaccessibility of Litchfield.[11] Miss Pierce retired in 1833, and Miss Henrietta Jones, a former scholar, became the principal, but the heyday of this institution was over. By 1844 the Academy property was used by the Normal School, and in 1856 the trustees sold the school building and its land to Miss Mary Pierce for $900.[12]

––––––––––

6. Nancy Hale to her Dear Sisters, September 1802, as quoted in B&C, 371. "C Smith" was Cyrinthia Sacretia Smith (1788–1864) of Glastonbury, who attended the school with her sister Laurilla Aleroyla (1789–1857) in 1802. They were sisters of the suffragist activists Abby and Julia Smith. See Pamela Cartledge's essay on the Smith Sisters of Glastonbury in *The Connecticut Historical Society Bulletin* 52, no. 1 (Winter 1987): 14–43. Another student, Mary Ann Bacon (b.1787), wrote in her journal on August 11, 1802, ". . . Miss Pierce drew my landscape . . ." (Vanderpoel, *Chronicles*, 69).

7. Vanderpoel, *Chronicles*, 286.

8. Tapping Reeve (1744–1823) opened his law school in 1784. After his death it was continued by James Gould (1770–1838).

9. Brickley in de Julio, *"What a Rich Reward,"* 62.

10. Vanderpoel, *Chronicles*, 264.

11. Ibid., 306. John Pierce Brace (1793–1872) resigned after eighteen years at the Pierce school and became principal at Catherine Beecher's Hartford Female Seminary. He later became editor of the *Hartford Courant* and retired in 1861.

12. Ibid., 268. Mary Pierce (1780–1863) was Sarah Pierce's half-sister, the daughter of her father's second wife, Mary Goodwin (c.1734–1803).

Fig. 257. Pictorial embroidery by Frances Ann Brace, c.1823. Silk and metallic threads on silk; 18″ x 16¾″. The delicacy of this embroidery and its gold metallic threads are reminiscent of pieces made by Nancy Hale and her contemporaries twenty years earlier (Fig. 254). Frances Ann first attended Miss Pierce's school in the summer of 1821. When writing home in 1822, she explained that we "lose a certain number of credit marks if we do not sew or write while we are reciting our lessons, . . ." (Bunce-Brace Correspondence, 1813–1859, CHS). Frances Ann Brace (1808–1838) was the daughter of Thomas Kimberly Brace (1779–1860) and Lucy Mather Lee (c.1785–1837) of Hartford. Her father was president of the Aetna Insurance Company, 1819–1857, and Mayor of Hartford, 1840–1843. Frances Ann married James Marvin Bunce (1806–1859), and they had three children.
The Connecticut Historical Society, 1984-42-1.

Fig. 258. Diploma, 1824. Printed on silk with the inscription *Litchfield Female Academy Miss Frances A Brace has completed with honour/ the prescribed course of Study/ Grammar, Geography, History, Arithmetic, Rhetoric, Natural and Moral Philosophy, Chemistry & Logic*; 7½″ x 7½″. Many years later, Miss Pierce's nephew and assistant, John Pierce Brace (who was not related to Frances Ann Brace), recalled that "She was an excellent scholar, and what is better, a most estimable girl, upright, amiable, intelligent. . . ." (Vanderpoel, *More Chronicles* [1927], 160).
The Connecticut Historical Society.

Wethersfield Samplers

During the first twenty years of the nineteenth century, when fabulous silk embroideries were the fashion in Hartford, a group of exceptional samplers were created in the village of Wethersfield. This riverside community was established in 1635, and with Hartford and Windsor, it belonged to the trio of founding towns that composed the Connecticut Colony, but no characteristic eighteenth-century schoolgirl work from this region of Connecticut has been identified. However, the state's largest recognizable group of samplers is of Wethersfield origin.[1] It consists of extraordinarily appealing pieces portraying scenes and townscapes that are occasionally embellished with paint and applied paper. Known examples date from 1804 until about 1821,[2] and while there is a kinship between the earlier and later pieces, the guidance of two teachers seems apparent. The samplers dated 1804 (Figs. 259, 260) and 1809 are decidedly more naïve than those worked between 1816 and 1821 (Figs. 262–266). Circumstantial evidence now suggests that the earlier pieces within this group were worked under the instruction of spinster schoolmistress Abigail Goodrich, and that the later samplers were made under the tuition of one of the five daughters of schoolmaster Frederick Butler.

Abigail Goodrich (1762–1829) was the eldest among the seven children of Elizur Goodrich (1730–1785), a mariner who died in the French West Indies, and Abigail Deming (c.1733–1813). She is known to have kept a private school in Wethersfield,[3] and on April 10, 1810, she billed Frederick Butler for "schooling" his youngest children, Elizabeth, Julia, and Thomas, for seventeen weeks.[4] It is likely that Abigail, then forty-eight years old, had also taught Butler's older daughters, Mary, Charlotte, and Abigail, and probably their contemporaries Hope Moseley and Sarah Robbins, who worked the samplers in Figures 259 and 260.

In 1819, Anna Stillman worked a sampler that was exhibited in Hartford in 1924 and was said to have been worked at "Miss Butler's School, Wethersfield." It was described as having "Letters and numbers, garlands held by a paper eagle

---

1. In the 1830s a group of mourning samplers was worked in nearby Glastonbury at Miss Cornwall's school. See Benes, *Two Towns,* 164; Howard Williston Carter, *Carter Genealogy* (Norfolk, Ct., 1909), op. 88; and *MAD*, October 1981, 37-C.

2. A sampler by Sarah Roberts Weeks (b.1809) has been dated c.1827 (Benes, *Two Towns* (1982), 162). It was probably worked about 1821 and death dates added to the monument at a later date. Another example, c.1820, by Hannah Boardman (1807–1901), is at the CHS. The original paper eagles are now missing from these samplers.

3. Henry R. Stiles, *The History of Ancient Wethersfield, Connecticut* (New York: Grafton Press, 1904), 2:385.

4. Personal Papers of Frederick Butler, Wethersfield, Connecticut, 1756–1834, Manuscripts, CSL.

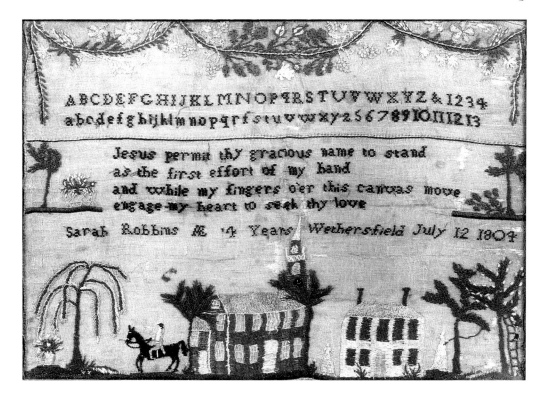

Fig. 259. *Sarah Robbins AE 14 Years Wethersfield July 12 1804.* Silk and wool on linen; 12¼″ x 16¾″. The meetinghouse on this and other Wethersfield samplers is thought to represent the First Church in Wethersfield (Fig. 261) although the interpretations vary considerably. Sarah Robbins (1789–1869) was the daughter of Elisha Robbins (1763–1844) and Sarah Goodrich (1766–1853) of Wethersfield. She married Daniel Pettis (d.1828) of Hartford in 1813, and Horace Savage in 1833. *First Church of Christ in Wethersfield, no acc. no.*

Fig. 260. *Hope Mosely AE 9 Years Nov. the 2 1804.* Silk and wool on linen; 11¾″ x 15″. Cornelia Fuller's 1809 sampler has similar flowers at the top but a much more elaborate townscape beside the river (*The Great River* [1985], 412–13). Hope Mosely (1794–1806) was the daughter of Dr. Abner Mosely (1766–1811) and Eunice Welles (1767–1811) of Wethersfield. Her sister Eunice worked a related sampler, but its whereabouts are now unknown. *Private collection.*

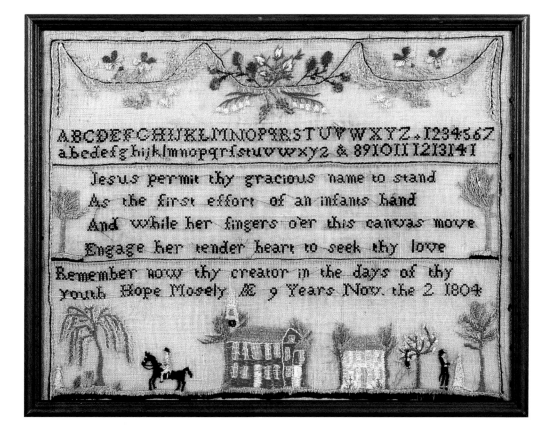

CONGREGATIONAL CHURCH, WETHERSFIELD, CT.

may·ye·6
1761
Inscription on Corner Stone.

Fig. 261. The First Church of Christ in Wethersfield, which was constructed in 1761–1764, is the third meetinghouse on this site. (The earliest Congregational Church, a log structure, was built here in 1645.) This was the only brick meetinghouse built in Connecticut during the colonial period. Exactly when it was first painted is unknown, but the samplers suggest that this occurred in the early nineteenth century. The pastor of the church during the sampler-making period was the Reverend John Marsh (1742–1821) who served from 1774 until 1821. His wife was Ann Grant (Fig. 70). It cannot be determined if the building usually pictured beside the meetinghouse was intended to be the Marsh house where she lived for sixty-one years. For other views of the meetinghouse, see Benes, *Two Towns* (1982), 144–5. *First Church of Christ in Wethersfield.*

above; below, the 'Finding of Moses' embroidered, painted paper and tinsel. 21″ x 25½″," and it belonged to "Miss Alice W. Stillman."[5] There is little doubt that its garland and paper eagle were like those in Figures 264 and 265, and its "Finding of Moses" may have been similar to the favorite Moses scene from the Patten school (Fig. 241). Certainly Wethersfield's most likely "Miss Butler" was one of the two eldest daughters of Frederick Butler, Mary Porter (1788–1832) or Charlotte (1790–1858), who had attended the Misses Pattens' school in Hartford where they worked elegant coats of arms with similar swags and eagles (Fig. 236).

Frederick Butler (1766–1843) was graduated from Yale in 1785, married Mary Belden (1770–1811) in 1787, and they had eight children between 1788 and 1806. Butler spent most of his life in Wethersfield, but in the 1790s he was also involved in a business in Hartford that ended in dismal failure. Disaster befell him in 1811. In January, his wife died, and the following September he filed for bankruptcy.[6] Butler was essentially a scholarly man and an avid historian,[7] and sometime after the year 1811, he opened a private school in the Academy building in Wethersfield.[8] Butler's older daughters were single and in their early twenties when he faced financial ruin, and most likely they also commenced teaching at about this time. They may have taught with their father at the Academy,[9] or in company with Abigail Goodrich, with whom they had almost certainly studied during their childhood.

It seems logical that the Butler sisters would have combined elements from both their Wethersfield and Patten school experiences when designing sampler patterns. Except for the sampler naming a "Miss Butler's School," it might be assumed that Abigail Goodrich was responsible for the entire group of Wethersfield samplers and that she had been influenced by needlework brought from Hartford. Certainly there is no doubt that she was well acquainted with the Butler family. On April 16, 1829, Frederick Butler witnessed her will, and he was among those who presented it for probate. In 1830, Ebenezer Stillman (the father of sampler maker Anna Stillman) and Leonard Welles (the father of Sarah, Fig. 266) ap-

5. List of samplers in an exhibit at the Morgan Memorial from November 21 to December 21, 1924 (CHS). Anna Stillman (July 6, 1805–1892) was the daughter of Deacon Ebenezer Stillman (1776–1854), a Wethersfield shoemaker, and Rhoda Francis (c.1779–1833). She died unmarried and her sampler descended to her niece, Alice Webster Stillman (b.1852), the daughter of her brother Henry Allyn Stillman (b.1815). Its present location is unknown.

6. Butler Papers, CSL.

7. Between 1817 and 1828, he wrote a number of history books (Stiles, *Ancient Wethersfield*, 190). For a sketch of the Butler home in Wethersfield, see Benes, *Two Towns*, no. 68.

8. Stiles, *Ancient Wethersfield*, 1:380. Frederick Butler billed James Francis on August 18, 1817, "To 12 weeks Tuition of your daughter." Francis Papers XVIII (CHS). Francis had daughters Pamela (b.1793), Clarissa (b.1798), and Maria (b.1801).

9. The Academy building on Main Street was built with public funds and by subscription in 1804. Butler's school was among its early occupants. The Reverend Joseph Emerson moved his female seminary from Saugus, Massachusetts, to this building in 1824. It continued there until his death in 1833, and it was carried on in his widow's home for some years thereafter. The Old Academy now houses the Wethersfield Historical Society.

Fig. 262. *Elizabeth Cooke Crittenton Aged 12 years/ July 24 1818*. Silk and paint on linen; 16½″ x 22½″. Elizabeth worked the most commonly found form of Wethersfield sampler. Others of 1816 and 1818 are in Benes, *Two Towns* (1982), 91, 153; also, B&C, Pl. LXVIII (contrary to their caption, there is no reason to believe that Sophia Stevens Smith [1804–1881] worked a view of North Branford). In 1826, Elizabeth Cooke Crittendon (1806–1885) was married in Wethersfield to Chauncy Wright (1798–1854) of Hartford.
Collection of Dr. and Mrs. I. Mandelbaum.

praised her estate, which consisted of a dwelling house with land, and furnishings that included "7 large pictures."[10]

There is also a possibility that the later Wethersfield samplers were made under the instruction of Abigail Porter Butler (1798–1832), or perhaps all three of the oldest Butler sisters were teaching for a livelihood. Abigail married James Bidwell in 1824 and moved to Utica, New York. She may have been teaching there when she met him. If so, it might explain a sampler typical of Wethersfield that was worked by Mary Millerd of Aurelius, New York, in 1823.[11] It was probably Abigail who sent a prospectus for an infant school in Utica to her younger sister Elizabeth in 1820.[12] It specified the requirements for a preceptress they sought to hire, and possibly Elizabeth considered this position, but there is no evidence that she applied. Abigail Butler Bidwell died in 1832, as did her sister Mary, and Elizabeth died in 1833. Only Charlotte and Julia Ann (1804–1889) survived their father, with their brothers Roswell (1795–1884), and Thomas Belden (1806–1873), a distinguished lawyer, who became the Chief Justice of the Supreme Court of Connecticut in 1870.

---

10. Hartford County Probate Records, CSL.

11. This sampler, much like the one in Figure 262, is privately owned. It was called to my attention by Claire Gonzales, former Curatorial Assistant at the Michigan State Museum.

12. Butler Papers, CSL.

Fig. 263. *Katharine D Hurlbut AE 8 Years Feb 25 1819*. Silk on linen; 26″ x 27″. Katharine's horseman and meetinghouse relate to those in Figures 259 and 260, while other elements are similar to those of the most common Wethersfield form (Fig. 262). Katharine D. Hurlbut (1810–1892) was the daughter of ship owner and West Indies trader James Hurlbut (1773–1852) and Wealthy Griswold (1779–1864) of Wethersfield. In 1869, she married Merritt Butler (c.1795–1891) of Springfield and they lived on Main Street in Wethersfield. *Private collection.*

Fig. 264. *A. Hurlbut*, c.1819. Silk, paper, and paint on linen; 17″ x 20½″. The floral swag and painted paper eagle of this sampler fit the description of an 1819 sampler by Anna Stillman that was exhibited in Hartford in 1924 and said to have named *Miss Butlers School* in Wethersfield. The eagle and garland pattern supports the belief that either Mary or Charlotte Butler was the teacher, since they worked similar motifs on silk embroideries at the Misses Pattens' school (see Fig. 236). Abigail Hurlbut (1808–1891), the sister of Katharine (Fig. 263), died unmarried. *Private collection.*

William	Talcott		Born	Nov 2	1771
Amelia	Hanmer		Born	Dec 18	1775
Married				July 31	1800
Amelia	Hanmer	Talcott	Born	July 2	1801
Celia	Talcott		Born	Feb 1	1804
William	Talcott		Born	Sep 22	1806
Sarah	Treat	Talcott	Born	July 21	1809
Francis Hanmer	Talcott		Born	April 19	1812
William	Talcott		Died	June 28	1813

Celia Talcott

Fig. 265. *Celia Talcott*, c.1818. Silk, paint, and painted paper on linen; 21½″ x 27½″. Celia's silvery-colored paper eagle does not conform to the space originally sketched on the linen but it grasps the garland in the same manner, although in reverse, as the eagles on needlework from the Misses Patten's school. Another very large, scenic embroidery, with painted people, was worked by Mehitable Griswold in 1819 (PMA). Celia Talcott (1804–1886) was the daughter of Wethersfield druggist William Talcott (1771–1813) and Amelia Hanmer (1775–1837). She married Henry Robbins (1793–1864), the brother of Sarah Robbins (Fig. 259). *Collection of Lucille A. LeClair.*

Fig. 266. *S. Welles Sept 11 1818.* Silk, printed paper, and paint on linen; 16¼″ x 22⅜″. Sarah's large family record retains the familiar beribboned swag, but her scene with the paper-faced people may represent an historic or fictitious episode that is now unrecognized. The faces appear to depict seventeenth-century people. Sarah Welles (b.1806) was the daughter of Leonard Welles (1765–1835) and Prudence Robbins (1767–1840) of Wethersfield. Sarah kept the school at the North Brick School House in Wethersfield in 1826 and 1827. *Windsor Historical Society, 86.758.2.*

Fig. 267. *Hannah Foster her sampler wrought/ in the Twelfth year of her age AD 179*. Silk on linen; 15⅛″ x 14⅝″. Hannah's sampler of 1795 is one of the most beautiful examples within this group, but excellent workmanship continued in the nineteenth century. About 1820, twelve-year-old Eliza Peverly of Sanbornton worked the background of her border in queen stitch (private collection), while her sister Harriet worked a handsome example in 1826 (Krueger, *New England*, Fig. 62). Hannah Foster (1784–1873) was the daughter of Captain Jonathan Foster (1747–1815) and Lucy Rogers (1748–1830) who was descended from the Reverend John Rogers (1629/30–1684), president of Harvard College. In 1815, Hannah married Joseph Moody (1788–1879), a farmer. *New Hampshire Historical Society, 1940.2.*

NEEDLEWORK OF NEW HAMPSHIRE

English settlements near the mouth of New England's Piscataqua River were established by 1631, and the port that developed there soon became known as Strawbery Banke. It is said to have been "accidentally soe-called by reason of a banke where straberries was found."[1] In 1653, the growing seaport assumed the more dignified name of Portsmouth, and in the following years it became an important center of shipbuilding. It was particularly known for providing the masts essential to His Majesty's Navy, and like other New England ports, it prospered with the growing triangular trade of slaves, sugar, and rum.

The New-Hampshire Gazette commenced publication in Portsmouth on October 7, 1756, and 1765 saw the beginning of a continuous series of advertisements for the education of girls. On June 14, 1765, the widow Sarah Winkley offered "Boarding and Schooling for Young Ladies" and in 1770, Ruth Jones would teach "all the various Branches of Needlework on Lawn, Flowering with cruel, Working Pocket Books with Irish Stitch. . . ." By 1774, Elizabeth Hill and her mother, the Widow Winkley, advertised instruction in the "Working of Samplers, Pictures, Coats of Arms, & c."[2] Anna Green named *Piscataqua* on a borderless band sampler of 1741,[3] and in 1765 another girl included *Portsmouth* in a popular sampler verse:

---

1. William G. Saltonstall, *Ports of the Piscataqua* (New York: Russell & Russell, 1941), 11.

2. *The New-Hampshire Gazette,* February 16, 1770, and May 24, 1774. Schoolmistress Sarah Wade Winkley, born in 1701 in Berwick, was the daughter of the Reverend John Wade (1674–1703) and Elizabeth Gerrish. She married Captain Nicholas Winkley (d.1739); her daughter Elizabeth married William Hill of Portsmouth.

3. Winterthur Museum. Anna Green (d.1816) was the daughter of Joseph Green (1703–1765) and Anna Pierce. She married, in 1759, her cousin Joshua Winslow (1727–1801) and was the mother of Anna Green Winslow (1760–1779) whose delightful *Diary of Anna Green Winslow, a Boston Schoolgirl* was edited by Alice Morse Earle (1894). Susan B. Swan kindly called this relationship to my attention.

Fig. 268. *Polly Foster her sampler wrought in the thirteenth year/ of her age A D 1787.* Silk on linen; 16¼″ x 15¼″. The leafy green plume above Polly's basket is a distinctive motif within this group of samplers and sometimes occurs twice, as in an exquisite example worked by Apphia Woodman (1773–1842) of Sanbornton in 1787 (B&C, Pl. CXIII). Mary (Polly) Foster (1774–1869) was seventh among the nine children of the Reverend Abiel Foster (1735–1806) and the second child of his second wife, Mary Rogers (1745–1813). Her father resigned from the ministry of Canterbury's First Church in 1779 and later served in the Continental Congress and as a United States Congressman. Polly married Henry Gerrish, Jr. (1772–1862), of Boscawen. They had seven children. *New Hampshire Historical Society, 1944-5-1.*

Sarah Sherburne is my name
England is my nation
Portsmouth is my dwelling place
and Christ is my salvation[4]

Lydia Peirce worked *Portsmouth* on a green linsey-woolsey ground in 1792,[5] and this material became especially popular for sampler embroidery in this region. However, none of these samplers can be assigned to a specific school, nor has a recognizable Portsmouth style emerged from the eighteenth century.

The Bird and Basket Samplers of Canterbury

A rural area along the Merrimack River appears to have produced New Hampshire's earliest, largest, and most enduring sampler style—the bird and basket samplers of Canterbury. These pieces have the principal motifs outlined in black, and they usually include a leafy green plume, which seems to be exclusive to the samplers of Canterbury and its environs (Figs. 267–272). While some variations developed in the nineteenth century (Figs. 270, 271), the basic Canterbury patterns remained essentially the same for at least forty-four years (Fig. 272), and

---

4. Portsmouth Historical Society.
5. Macpheadris–Warner House Association, Portsmouth.

Fig. 269. *Ruthy Foster her sampler wrought/ in the twenty fist year of her age 18/ A d*, c.1800. Silk on linen; 16¾" x 16¾". Ruthy Foster (September 14, 1779–1858) was the ninth child of Daniel Foster (1737–1833) and Hannah Kittredge. Ruthy did not marry, and she was a schoolmistress for much of her adult life. She may have been the principal teacher to perpetuate Canterbury's bird and basket patterns during the first thirty years of the nineteenth century.
Private collection.

Fig. 270. *Susanna N. Knapp's sampler* Wrought in the/ thirteenth Year of her Age. A.D. 1812. Silk on linen and entirely embroidered over the ground; 24½" x 21". Susanna shaped a modified version of the typical green plume into a leafy cartouche and stitched *Drawn/ by/ Abigail Abbott.*, who was probably her teacher. A related example was worked by Anna Lyford (b.1793) of Northfield in 1806 (*ANTIQUES*, February 1974, 362–3). Susanna Newman Knapp (1799–1876) was the daughter of Benjamin N. Knapp (1776–c.1814) of Sanbornton and Elizabeth Hancock (1780–1859) of Northfield. She died unmarried. Abigail Abbott may have been the Abigail Abbott (1783–1864) who was born in Concord, New Hampshire, to Elias Abbott (1757–1847) and Elizabeth Buswell (1761–1832). Her family moved to Northfield in 1801.

Plymouth Antiquarian Society, Plymouth, Massachusetts, 1956.86.

the sampler makers who can be identified were all residents of the Merrimack Valley in the vicinity of Canterbury, Loudon, Northfield, and Sanbornton.

The charter for the town of Canterbury was dated 1727. At least thirty families had settled in Canterbury by 1750, and in 1761, the man who would become the town's most distinguished citizen was ordained the second minister of Canterbury's First Congregational Church. This was the Reverend Abiel Foster (Harvard, 1756), and he was soon joined by his father, Asa Foster, and brothers Asa, Daniel, David, and Jonathan, who left their native Andover, Massachusetts, and moved to Canterbury.[1]

Four samplers worked by daughters of the Foster brothers are known today. The earliest was made in 1786 by Asa Foster's fourteen-year-old daughter Mehitable,[2] and her cousin Polly's is dated 1787 (Fig. 268). Polly was a double cousin of Hannah, who obviously had the same teacher in 1795 (Fig. 267), and their cousin Ruthy worked a related pattern in 1799 or 1800 when she was twenty-one years old (Fig. 269). Ruthy no doubt continued the bird and basket pattern during a quarter century of teaching in Canterbury, as did other teachers who maintained the initial compositions with varying degrees of faithfulness (Figs. 270, 271).

---

1. *Sibley's Harvard Graduates, 1756–1760* (1968), 14:15–19.
2. Edmonds, Fig. 8.

It appears likely that a member of the Foster family was instrumental in the origin of the Canterbury sampler pattern, but no conclusive evidence concerning the schoolmistress of the 1780s has been found. As suggested in Edmonds, the ingenious teacher was perhaps the widow Hannah Wise Rogers (b.1719), who kept a respected girls' school in Ipswich during the 1770s and early 1780s.[3] Possibly she moved to Canterbury to be with daughters Mary and Lucy, the wives of Abiel and Jonathan Foster. Also, her sister Lucy Rogers Wise (1723–1787) was the second wife of the family patriarch, Asa Foster (1710–1787). When Hannah may have moved to Canterbury is uncertain. John Heard of Ipswich recorded charges for repairs to her house in September 1786, but in March 1791, her account with Heard was managed by Major Charles Smith.[4] The place and date of her death are unknown. Hannah's daughter Lucy and various granddaughters taught in Canterbury's town schools from the 1780s through the 1830s.[5]

No work from Hannah Rogers' Ipswich school is known, nor has a characteristic group of Ipswich samplers been identified. At present, the most closely related forerunners of the Canterbury motifs appear on the samplers of Newburyport. The Foster cousins worked undulating, flower-strewn hillocks and black-outlined birds beside central bouquets reminiscent of Mary Batchelder's 1773 sampler (Fig. 128). Also, checkered sawtooth borders and tiered trees characterize Newburyport work of the 1780s (Fig. 129).

3. Ibid., 40. The Ipswich school of "Madame Rogers, . . . a singularly intellectual and cultivated woman," was attended by wealthy girls from Boston, Salem, Newburyport, and Portsmouth, as well as Ipswich. *Ipswich Antiquarian Papers* (February 1884), 179.

4. John Heard Papers, AC-2. *Journal 1783–1788*, 106–7. Baker Library, Harvard Business School. Hannah Rogers sold her property to John Heard in 1784 (recorded January 15, 1786) but reserved "the use & improvement of the . . . premises during her natural life." Essex County Deeds, Book 145:50. A copy of this deed was kindly provided by Mary Jaene Edmonds.

5. See *Lessons Stitched in Silk: Samplers from the Canterbury Region of New Hampshire*, exhibition catalogue (Hanover, N.H.: Hood Museum of Art, Dartmouth College, March 10–May 13, 1990).

Fig. 273. *Lydia Cogswell born May *th*30 in 1793/ Aged 11 Years Dover August*th *4 1804.* Silk on linsey-woolsey; 27″ x 23½″. Lydia worked the most elaborate sampler within this group. Her painted mourning picture also survives with the Portsmouth label of framer B. Cermenati, dated 1812. Lydia Cogswell (1793–1872) was the daughter of Amos Cogswell (1752–1826) and Lydia Baker (1759–1828) of Dover. She married Paul Wentworth (1782–1855) in 1814. *Privately owned.*

Fig. 274. *Jane Margaret Andrews Sampler/ Aged 8th January 2d 1800*, c.1808. Silk on linsey-woolsey; 22″ x 17¼″. Unlike her older classmates, Jane neglected to explain that 1800 was her birthdate. For others from the same Dover school, see the sampler of Elizabeth Cutts (daughter of Elizabeth Cutts, Fig. 71) in Krueger, *Gallery*, Fig. 43; Skinner Sale 809, April 30, 1982, Lot 128; *MAD*, March 1986, 20-C. Jane Margaret Andrews was born in Dover to George Andrews and Ann Neil. In 1831 she married James Bartlett at Dover's First Unitarian Church.
Location unknown; photograph courtesy of The Magazine ANTIQUES.

Samplers of Dover

At the turn of the new century, a stunning group of samplers was worked in Dover by local girls as well as several who lived just north of the Piscataqua River (Figs. 273, 274). All known examples (nine, at present) are on green linsey-woolsey and date from 1800 through 1804 and 1808 through 1810. Each sampler maker customarily included her birthdate and her age, and the examples made in 1804 also have the date of execution and name *Dover*.[1] The tiered trees and shaded central motifs of these samplers echo the earlier patterns of Newburyport (Fig. 129), and they appear on all but one example within this group.[2]

---

1. Rita Conant has identified the Dover schoolmistress, and her studies will soon be published.
2. Harriot Boardman's sampler, 1804, in Krueger, *New England*, Fig. 2.

Fig. 275. *Deborah Laighton Worked at Mary Ann Smiths School Portsmouth October 15 1818* (or 1819). Silk on linsey-woolsey; 17½" x 22¾". Deborah worked a pattern that had appeared in Portsmouth by 1818 and was continued in modified forms until 1840 (part of the last digit of her date is now missing). Probably from the Misses Smiths' school are similar samplers naming *Portsmouth, 1822*, by Maria Wiggin, on green, and Elizabeth Dore, on a natural linen (see the *Ellis Memorial Antique Show Catalogue*, Boston [October 26–30, 1983], 29, and Edmonds, Fig. 30). Deborah Laighton (1805–1820) was named for a sister who died in 1803. She was the daughter of Portsmouth mast and sail maker Luke Mills Laighton (1766–1834) and Elizabeth Mendum (1767–1854).
Location unknown; photograph courtesy of The Magazine ANTIQUES.

The House and Barn Samplers of Portsmouth

The largest recognizable group of Portsmouth samplers appeared about 1818, and it seems to have originated simultaneously at two different schools kept by the Misses Smith and the Misses Walden. Why they chose patterns essentially alike is unexplained, but these young pairs of sisters were about the same age and may have attended the same Portsmouth school a few years earlier. At least one sampler with the dominant pattern includes the names of each of the sisters.

The earliest-known dated example within this group was made by Priscilla Hall Badger (1805–1842), and she named *Elizabeth S Smith's School Portsmouth April 28th 1818.*[1] Except for a gable-end view of the house, her work is nearly identical to Deborah Laighton's sampler (Fig. 275) naming *Mary Ann Smiths School Portsmouth October 15 1818* (or 1819). Elizabeth Salter Smith (1798–1884) and Mary Ann Smith (1799–1827) were the daughters of Portsmouth joiner Isaac Smith (c.1774–1827) and Elizabeth Leigh (c.1772–1840). Elizabeth Smith was listed as

---

1. Krueger, *New England*, Fig. 73.

Fig. 276. *Caroline Vaughn Aged 10 Worked at Mary Waldens School October 28, 1818.* Silk on linsey-woolsey; 16¾″ x 19″. Unlike the Misses Smith, the Misses Walden did not have their pupils name Portsmouth on their samplers, and the enclosures for their signatures are not as well defined as those from the Smith school. The Baltimore Museum owns another example worked on green by Margaret Lowd in 1822, but without a teacher's name. Caroline Vaughn (1808–1849) was the daughter of packet master Michael Vaughn and Polly Moore of Portsmouth.
Baltimore Museum of Art, gift of Mrs. Francis White from the collection of Mrs. Miles White, Jr., 73.76.387.

a schoolmistress on Vaughn Street in the Portsmouth directory of 1821, but in December of 1822, she married shipmaster John S. Davis (1798–1874). Her sister Mary Ann died of consumption at the age of twenty-eight.

The house and barn samplers naming the Smith school have the verse that begins, "How blest the maid whom circling years improve," while the Walden sisters favored the verse beginning "Jesus permit thy gracious name to stand." Caroline Vaughn named *Mary Waldens School October 28 1818* (Fig. 276) and Adaline M. Ferguson worked her sampler at *E Waldens School March 23. 1822* (Fig. 277). Evidently one of these sisters advertised Miss Walden's "Drawing School" in

Fig. 277. *Adaline M. Ferguson Aged 13 years Worked at E Waldens School March 23. 1822*. Silk on linsey-woolsey; 16″ x 17¾″. Three men named Ferguson appear in the Portsmouth direc-

tory of 1821—a mariner, a blacksmith, and a joiner—but no trace of Adaline has been found.
Author's collection.

Fig. 278. *Ann Elizabeth Ham Aged 11 Portsmouth New Hampshire Marked at Miss Ann L C Jones 1826.* Silk on linen; 19⅝″ x 26⅝″. The composition of Ann's sampler reflects the influence of earlier work, and possibly Miss Jones attended the Smith or Walden schools. Schoolmistress Ann L. C. Jones, daughter of the mariner William Jones, married William J. Southerin, a merchant, in December 1826. Ann Elizabeth Ham (1815–1899) was the daughter of William Ham and Ann Nancy Green. In 1836, she married Portsmouth stonemason Allen Treat (1812–1874), and they had eight children. *Private collection.*

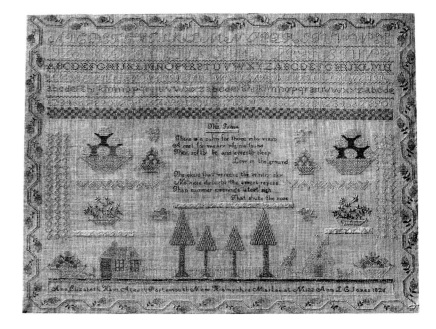

March 1821.[2] Mary Walden (1799–1885) and Elvira Walden (1802–1883) were the daughters of Jacob Walden and Abigail. In June of 1821, Mary married stage-coach proprietor Willis Barnaby (c.1789–1862), and they had five children. Elvira married tavern keeper Oliver Potter (1800–1870) in 1823.[3]

Obviously the Smith and Walden sisters kept day schools of short duration,[4] but their patterns were adopted by other Portsmouth teachers. Ann Elizabeth Ham worked a new version in 1826 (Fig. 278). Mary Ann Marden worked the earlier style and named the *M F S Hall School* in 1828,[5] while a handsome example true to the original pattern was made in 1835 (Fig. 279). Also, a house and barn reminiscent of earlier examples appears on Portsmouth samplers of 1839 and 1840.[6]

Another group of samplers worked from about 1812 until at least 1832 is represented here by the work of Harriet Ann Dockum (Fig. 280). These pieces often have town houses or civic buildings finely worked in tent stitch with stubby trees in hexagonal shapes and a unique border of hexagons divided by delicate flower sprigs.[7]

2. *Portsmouth Oracle*, March 24, 1821.

3. I am deeply indebted to Rita Conant and John F. LaBranche for sharing research on the identity of teachers and sampler makers from their forthcoming publication on Portsmouth samplers.

4. All samplers naming their schools, or attributed to them, were made by Portsmouth girls, excepting Adaline M. Ferguson whose identity is undetermined.

5. *A&AW*, January 4, 1991, 112.

6. Sampler by Sarah E. Gerrish, 1839, in a sampler exhibit at the Wenham, Massachusetts, Historical Society in 1980; sampler by Sarah Emily Currier, 1840, in the John Paul Jones House, Portsmouth.

7. This border appears on an 1812 band sampler by Mary Cleaves, of Biddeford, Maine (Brick Store Museum, Kennebunk, Maine). She may have gone to a Portsmouth school before attending the Misses Martin's school in Portland and the Saunders and Beach Academy in Dorchester. For her other work, see Sprague, *Agreeable Situations* (1987), 228.

Fig. 279. *Martha Jane Fowler Worked this in the 14 year of her age born March 22ⁿᵈ/ 1822 October 21 1835 Portsmouth N H.* Silk on linen; 21″ x 17½″. Martha Jane's instructress drew an elegant version of the house and barn pattern, with the principal elements of earlier work, and a border like Caroline Vaughn's (Fig. 276). Martha Jane Fowler was the daughter of Portsmouth joiner Paul Fowler and Phebe.
Location unknown; photograph courtesy of Sotheby's.

Fig. 280. *Harriet Ann Dockum aged 10 years October 22ᵗʰ/ 1825.* Silk on linen; 25½″ x 21″. Harriet's sampler is closely related to a sampler by Sally Wildes LeFavour, 1827 (private collection), and another by Ann M. Gerrish, 1832, which names *Portsmouth*. All three have interesting white-work embroidery between the hexagonal motifs of their borders. Also, the similarity of the first two band patterns on this sampler relate it to another Portsmouth type with solidly worked scenes. See the work of Ann M. Gerrish and Harriet Biron Reding in Ring, *Treasures,* 21. Harriet Ann Dockum (b.1815) was the only child of Portsmouth cabinetmaker Samuel M. Dockum (1792–1872) and Lucy Norton. She married Dr. John T. G. Pike on December 6, 1837. They had one daughter. *Private collection.*

Fig. 281. *Betsey Fay/ 1818*. Silk, chenille, metal, and painted paper on linen; 20¾″ x 20¾″. Betsey Fay (1802–1828) was the twelfth child of John Fay (c.1756–1839) and Lovina Brigham (c.1760–1840) who moved from Marlboro, Massachusetts, to Fitzwilliam in 1783. Betsey's younger sister, Orpha, married Samuel G. Bowker, Laura's first cousin. Betsey died unmarried.
Private collection.

Fig. 282. *Laura Bowker aet 11./1817.* Silk, chenille, metal, painted paper, and kid on linen; 17″ x 21½″. A variety of luxuriant flowers grow on the vine of Laura's border, and the Johnny-jump-ups appear consistently except on the work of Rebeccah Thomas (see footnote 25). Laura Bowker (1805–1843) was the daughter of Charles Bowker (c.1758–1839) and Beulah Stone (1767–1836) of Fitzwilliam. She married Ebenezer Roby (1802–1848) of Cambridge, Massachusetts, on December 19, 1826. They had four children.
Cooper-Hewitt, National Museum of Design, Smithsonian Institution, 1941-69-98.

Pictorial Samplers of
Southern New Hampshire

Just as a cluster of small towns saw the origin of New Hampshire's most important samplers of the eighteenth century, so too did the state's most appealing pictorial samplers emerge near a trio of small communities just north of the Massachusetts border. Between 1817 and 1821, girls of Fitzwilliam and Rindge placed paper-faced ladies in elegant pastures surrounded by luxuriant floral borders (Figs. 281–283). Their samplers have an interesting variety of materials and their paper-faced people and consistently worked flowers unquestionably relate them to a later example naming *Jaffrey Aug. 6 1829* (Fig. 284), as well as to more modest family record samplers of Jaffrey.[1]

As yet, there is no evidence of the schoolmistress responsible for these patterns, but she was probably familiar with slightly earlier samplers worked in Leominster and Lancaster, Massachusetts. Less pictorial, but with heavy floral borders containing some of the same flowers, is a group of samplers made in Leominster, and it maintained nearly identical patterns from 1806 until 1817.[2] More closely related to the New Hampshire pieces are the Lancaster samplers. Their floral borders also have blue and white pinwheel flowers, johnny-jump-ups,

---

1. Allen, *Family Record*, Figs. 108, 109.
2. Krueger, *Gallery*, Fig. 52; Israel Sack, Inc., Brochure No. 26, October 1, 1974, 43; Skinner Sale 631, July 27, 1979, Lot 114.

Fig. 283. *Nancy S. Perkins/ Agd 14 1821.* Silk, chenille, and metal, with painted and pricked paper on linen; 17″ x 18″. Nancy S. Perkins (1807–1875), born in Jaffrey, was the daughter of Robinson Perkins (1766–1847) and Peddy Shephardson (1771–1838). Perkins was a prosperous clockmaker and silversmith who moved to Fitzwilliam in 1810. In 1831, Nancy married Dr. Gideon C. Noble (1803–1879), and they had five children.

Museum of Art, Rhode Island School of Design, gift of Miss Edith M. Noble, 37.034.

Fig. 284. *Mary J Perkins aged/ 13 ys. Jaffrey Aug. 6 1829.* Silk and chenille with painted and ink-inscribed paper on linen; 17½″ x 18¾″. Mary dedicated her monument to three siblings who died between 1810 and 1827. She pictured her parents and seven surviving children born between 1810 and 1821, although by 1829, the older children were adults and some had married. Mary Jane Perkins (1815–1885) was the eighth child of Edward Perkins (1773–1856) and Ruth Gordon (1777–1860) of Jaffrey, and the first cousin of Nancy Perkins (Fig. 283). She married first, Jabez Morse, second, Jesse Adams (1796–1863), and third, Hale.
Private collection; photograph courtesy of Sotheby's.

and other similar blossoms framing central scenes with painted or paper-faced figures.[3] A number of families from this region of Massachusetts moved into southern New Hampshire during the early Federal period, and contact was no doubt continued with friends and relatives in their former hometowns.

Hannah Brigham (b.1777) and her sister Anna (1782–1860) are said to have been popular teachers in Fitzwilliam, but they were too early for this group of samplers.[4] *The History of Fitzwilliam* names a Betsy Bowker and a Betsy Wright who taught there at an unknown date,[5] and this may refer to Laura Bowker's sister Betsy (1795–1880), who married Lyman Wright (1793–1886) in 1817. However, the relationship of the Perkins girls (Figs. 283, 284) suggests that Mary Jane Perkins and her older sisters (Hannah, b.1806, and Ruth, b.1809) went to the same school attended by Nancy Perkins, although Nancy's family moved from Jaffrey to Fitzwilliam in 1810. Because Mary Ann Wilder, the maker of a similar sampler in 1817, lived in Rindge, as did Rebeccah Thomas,[6] it is unlikely that these girls walked to a day school. Possibly they boarded in Jaffrey and attended school during the summer months as did many of the girls who went to Abby Wright's school in South Hadley.

---

3. Krueger, *Gallery*, Fig. 66; B&C, Pl. XLIX. Sophia Emerson's is in the C-H, 1974-42-22; Polly Warner's of 1816 is in the Lancaster Library.

4. John F. Norton, *The History of Fitzwilliam, New Hampshire* (New York: Burr Printing House, 1888), 320. Hannah married William Fisher Perry (1776–1871); Ann married Timothy Kendall (1782–1851) and lived elsewhere between 1815 and 1845.

5. Ibid.

6. A sampler signed *Mary Ann Wilder born April 1, 1806 Wrought 1817* was at the Pine Cupboard Antique Shop in Franklin, New Hampshire, in October 1968; a divergent example signed *Rebeccah Thomas born August 4th 1803* (in Rindge) is erroneously dated 1807. This piece has no metal embellishments or applied paper (the face is painted on the linen) and there is no variety of flowers in its border (Edmonds, Fig. 29).

Fig. 285. *Eliz. Abigail Leavitt Portland 1823* inscribed on the glass. Silk, chenille, pencil, paint, and ink on silk; 20 ¾″ x 24¼″. Although her figure is larger than average, Abigail Leavitt worked the most familiar composition found on Maine memorials, either worked, or painted on silk, paper, or velvet, and known to date from 1821 until about 1827 (for a velvet example, see SPB, Sale 4529Y, January 30, 1981, Lot 1114). Abigail, an only child, was twenty-six years old when she worked this memorial to her parents with its poignant verse about the orphan's loss, which appears on a number of related embroideries, including Fig. 295. Her swirling painted sky is also found on other Portland pieces. Elizabeth Abigail Leavitt (b.1797) was the daughter of Benjamin Leavitt (1766–1821) and Abigail Hersey (c.1772–1819). She died unmarried.

Hingham Historical Society, Hingham, Massachusetts, TE 6.

NEEDLEWORK

OF MAINE

THE ENGLISH had settled in the vicinity of Falmouth by the mid-seventeenth century, and by 1669, the Province of Maine was governed by the Puritans of Massachusetts. There were worrisome Indian conflicts, backed by the French, until after the mid-eighteenth century, when Falmouth, with its superb natural harbor, began to prosper; but progress ended abruptly with the British bombardment of 1775. Recovery from the Revolution finally came in the 1790s, and within a few years, Portland (a part of Falmouth until 1786) became the commercial center of the province.

Portland has produced the largest and most important groups of Maine embroideries, and striking samplers appeared there long before this part of Massachusetts became the state of Maine in 1820. Very shortly thereafter, Portland schools originated spectacular groups of silk embroideries, and one of these groups continued until a later date than any comparable work made in New England.

The samplers and needlework pictures of Portland are easily recognized, and both forms reflect the extraordinary interest in genealogies that endured in this region throughout the first forty years of the nineteenth century. A basic conformity appears in a wealth of Portland samplers worked between 1803 and about 1820, but there is little doubt that they were made at several different schools, for genealogies naming the *School of the Miss Mayo's*, in 1817, and *Eliza^{th} Hussey's school*, in 1818, each have headings and borders much like those in Elizabeth Mountfort's work (Fig. 288).[1] The earliest samplers belonging to this group, with either genealogical data or alphabets and verses, have a stylized, queen-stitched rose-vine border with pictorial vignettes or solidly worked scenes in their lower

---

1. The Mayo sampler is illustrated in *ANTIQUES*, September 1988, 515; the Hussey sampler is privately owned.

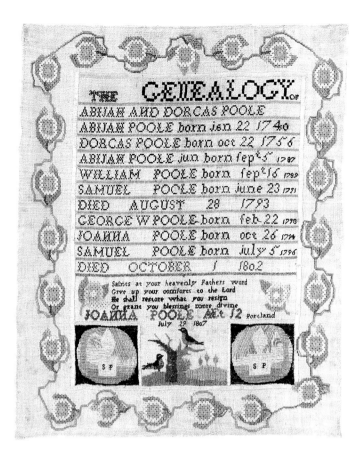

Fig. 286. *JOANNA POOLE AEt 12 Portland/ July 29 1807.* Silk on linen; 21″ x 17″. Joanna's genealogy is a typical early example within the best-known group of Portland's family record samplers. For another example of 1805, see Christie's, January 21, 1989, Lot 384. Joanna Poole (1794–1864) was the daughter of Portland bricklayer Abijah Poole (1740–1820) and Dorcas Tucker (1756–1824). She died unmarried.
Maine Historical Society, gift of Mrs. Alfred Haskell, 1936, A86-584.

sections (Figs. 286, 287). While other details remained the same, the borders became naturalistic rose vines by about 1815, and this style prevailed until about 1826.[2]

The inspiration for these samplers may have come from earlier work made under the instruction of two little-known women who were teaching in Falmouth during the eighteenth century. Sarah Jenkins Price (1730–1824) and Rachel Hall Neal (1769–1849) commenced teaching in 1772 and 1794, respectively, and they were still listed among Portland teachers in 1810.[3] However, their careers, and those of about sixteen other Portland teachers, had no doubt been overshadowed by Maine's most prestigious young ladies' academy, which was opened in Portland by the Misses Martin in 1804 and flourished until 1834. These women were Eliza, Catherine, and Penelope (Fig. 289), the daughters of William and Elizabeth Galpine Martin (Fig. 290), who immigrated to Boston in 1783. This English family moved to North Yarmouth, Maine, in 1788, and finally settled in Portland after financial reverses necessitated the opening of a school, in which they all participated. Penelope and Eliza were the principal teachers, and Catherine was the household supervisor.[4] They conducted their school entirely in the English man-

---

2. There are exceptions. Abigail Dodge worked a genealogy above a solidly worked scene with three houses and a queen-stitched border in 1818 (privately owned), while Mary Owen worked an alphabet and verse above a scene with a naturalistic rose-vine border in 1815 (Skinner Sale 1246, March 25, 1989, Lot 67). Examples worked after 1820 usually have no pictorial elements.

3. *Portland Gazette & Maine Advertiser*, April 16, 1810.

4. Their school first opened in North Yarmouth in 1803. In Portland the Misses Martin continued to live with their parents and brother. Their father was active in civic affairs and was a Trustee of Bowdoin College from 1794 until 1813, but both parents and their brother assisted in the school. In 1806–1807 they had between twenty-eight and thirty-three boarders, but they later reduced this number to about fifteen or

Fig. 288. *Elizabeth I Mountfort/ AE 14 years Portland July/ 27 1820*. Silk on linen; 28½″ x 17½″. Lettering in Holbein stitch, like Elizabeth's signature, is common to this group; for a similar example of 1817 with two verses from the same poem, see Sprague, *Agreeable Situations* (1987), 247. Elizabeth Isley Mountfort (1806–1876) was the daughter of Daniel Mountfort (1762–1822) and Elizabeth Isley (1768–1852). She died unmarried.

Collection of Mrs. Bradbury Bedell.

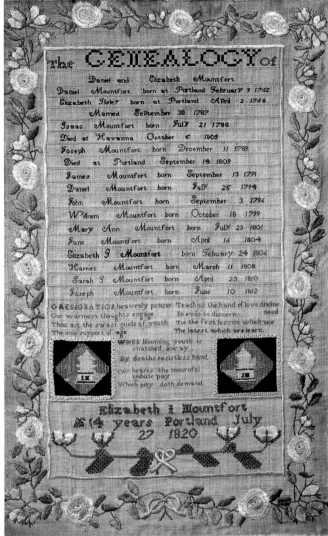

Fig. 287. *MARY RICHARDS AEt 13 years Portland/ July 13 1808*. Silk on linen; 21″ x 19″. Portland samplers often have genealogies or alphabets with verses above a solidly worked townscape as seen here. This type had appeared by 1803 and continued at least until 1820 (B&C describes Eliza Harden's 1803 sampler, 168). By 1815, the border was often a naturalistic rose vine as in Figure 288; see also Krueger, *Gallery*, Fig. 81. A related piece naming *Cape Elizabeth* is illustrated in Sprague, *Agreeable Situations* (1987), 246. Mary Richards (b.1795) was the daughter of Jesse Richards and Elizabeth of Portland. Probably she was the Mary Richards who married William Warner in Portland in 1815.

Cooper-Hewitt, National Museum of Design, Smithsonian Institution, 1941-69-13.

Right:

Fig. 289. Miniature of Penelope Martin (1773–1859), London, c.1787. Watercolor on ivory. Penelope Martin was the principal preceptress of the Misses Martin's school in Portland. When her family left for New England in 1783, she remained in England to complete her education at the genteel London boarding school kept by her aunt Catherine Galpine Low. Her eldest brother, William Clark Martin (1763–1849), joined their parents in 1784 and Penelope arrived in 1790. *Portland Museum of Art, bequest of William Martin Payson in memory of the Martin family, 1921.19.2.*

Far right:

Fig. 290. Miniature believed to be of Elizabeth Galpine Martin (1739–1829), London, c.1780. Watercolor on ivory. In Nottingham, England, in 1762, Elizabeth Galpine married, as his second wife, William Martin (1733–1814). They had nine children, six of whom eventually became residents of Maine, but only their sons Samuel and Nathaniel had issue. Elizabeth Martin assisted her daughters with their school until her death. *Portland Museum of Art, bequest of William Martin Payson in memory of the Martin family, 1921, 19.1.*

ner, and both their gentility and their advanced curriculum attracted patronage from a wide area. Few silk embroideries from the Misses Martin's school have been identified, but the similarity of three pieces is conspicuous (Figs. 291, 292), and the boldness of their oversized floral motifs may have influenced Portland's larger and later groups of pictorial embroideries and watercolors.

In the early 1820s, two Portland girls' schools introduced wonderfully bold and exuberant groups of silk embroideries, and their refreshing naïveté is far removed from the typical neoclassical style so often copied from prints. More colorful and generally larger in size than their earlier New England counterparts, these pieces also reflect the greater focus on painting that characterized the last years of the schoolgirl needlework era. Both groups of Portland silk embroideries are largely composed of mourning pieces, and their gigantic monuments have long epitaphs printed with type on the main body of the silk, revealing that they were carefully planned, sketched, printed, worked, and then painted. It is possible that a professional artist drew the patterns, and generally the schoolmistress or an ornamental artist would have added the painting. However, because many of the Portland pieces are entirely painted on silk or paper and proudly signed by the schoolgirl, it seems evident that the charcoal-sketched compositions of the Portland pieces were both worked and at least partly painted by the student.[5]

The earliest dated embroidery within Portland's first and largest group was worked in 1822 (Fig. 293), and it was preceded by a closely related scene that

twenty, and in 1812 they admitted day scholars. In 1832, an inheritance from their cousin, Miss Galpine, enabled them to retire in comfort. See Edward C. Cutter, "Misses Martin," *The Christian Mirror,* Portland, February 7, 1860; also, *NEHGR* (January 1900) 54:27–31. Penelope Martin's *Manuscript,* 1821–1825, with recollections of the seminary, is in the Maine Women Writers Collection, Abplanalp Library, Westbrook College, Portland, Maine. This was called to my attention by Sheila Rideout.

5. For enlightening facts about school procedures in respect to drawing and painting, see *ANTIQUES,* March 1989, 616, 620, 624.

Fig. 291. *Holy Family, By Mary L. Ingraham* inscribed on the glass, c.1822. Silk and paint on silk; 15⅜″ x 17¼″. Mary Little Ingraham (b.1806) and her sister Anne (1802–1844) appear in the Misses Martin's list of day scholars. They were the daughters of silversmith Joseph Holt Ingraham (1752–1841) and his third wife, Anna Tate (1767–1844). Their father was an enterprising merchant and land developer of Portland whose mansion of 1801 still stands. In 1834, Mary married Daniel Brazier (c.1809–1849), a Portland tailor.
Abby Aldrich Rockefeller Folk Art Center, Williamsburg, Virginia, 35.601.1.

Fig. 292. Pictorial embroidery initialed *S. O. P.* (on second page of book in the picture), c.1817. Silk and paint on silk; 12″ x 14½″. Attributed to the Misses Martin's school on the basis of its similarity to Figure 291 and to another example from the school (*ANTIQUES*, September 1988, 516). For Nancy Myrick's pictorial embroidery from the Misses Martin's school, c.1820, see Rumford, *American Folk Paintings* (1987), Fig. 328. *Private collection.*

was painted on paper and dated 1821.[6] Both the school that produced these and the artist who drew them are undetermined. Almost invariably they have a charming seacoast village in the background with giant embroidered flowers in the foreground, and beguiling figures that were obviously drawn by a confident and facile hand (Figs. 285, 293, 295). The winged cherubs that appear on the monuments are sometimes found in the sky,[7] or on related samplers (Fig. 294), and they are almost like a signature of the artist. The majority of pieces were not dated by their makers, but March 4, 1826, is the latest death date found on a memorial within this group,[8] and it appears that this type ceased to be made about 1826. However, because samplers like that in Figure 294 continued to be made without the background drawing or the winged cherubs, it is possible that the artist became unavailable even though the school continued.[9]

There were a number of Portland boarding schools that may have produced these embroideries and watercolors.[10] However, the most logical place of their origin was the school of the Misses Mayo for it is the only Portland school of this period known to have been "celebrated for exquisite needle-work, both plain and ornamental."[11] Martha Merchant (c.1756–1831), of Boston, married Simeon Mayo (1745–1813), originally from Portland, in 1778, and in 1800 they were living in Portland. In 1810, the census found Simeon living alone, while Martha resided with their six daughters. All the Mayo sisters remained single except Martha, the eldest, who married the Reverend Thomas B. Ripley when she was forty-five years old in 1827, and they soon left Portland. If the Mayo school produced these embroideries and Martha was their designer, then her marriage would explain their abrupt end. The Misses Mayo's boarding school was still listed in the Portland directory of 1847–1848.

The other school that spanned the period of Portland's "winged cherub" embroideries and watercolors was kept by the Misses Paine from 1821, or earlier, until about 1839.[12] In 1821, Charlotte (1794–1857) and her sister Sarah Paine (1795–1880) were prepared to board girls from the country "on the most reasonable terms," and they unquestionably taught elegant accomplishments, for a school advertisement of 1827 mentioned "needlwork, lace work, embroidery and

6. *The Old Print Shop Portfolio* XI, no. 2 (October 1951):30.

7. For a cherub in the sky with a painted paper face glued to the silk, see Ring, *Treasures*, 78.

8. *ANTIQUES*, October 1971, 491.

9. Related samplers without penciled columns or winged cherubs were made by Sarah Skillin in 1835 and Mary C. Plumer in 1837 (Allen, *Family Record*, Figs. 100, 104).

10. Elizabeth C. Thaxter, the former Mrs. Moody, was teaching in 1821, if not earlier, and kept a boarding school from about 1823 until after 1824 (*Eastern Argus*, Portland, June 26, 1821; March 19, 1822; March 16, 1824). Mrs. Abigail Murray opened a boarding and day school in 1822, which continued at least through 1827 (Ibid., July 2, 1822; February 21, 1826; March 6, 1827). Miss Alma Cross opened a day school in January 1822 and a boarding school with her sister Rebecca in 1827; it continued until after 1859 (see an account of their school in *The Portland Transcript*, February 5, 1896).

11. Edward H. Elwell, *The Schools of Portland* (Portland: William M. Marks, Printer, 1888), 33.

12. The Paine sisters were the daughters of Dr. James Paine (1759–1822), born in Eastham, Massachusetts, and Sarah Wingate (d.1838) of Biddeford, Maine. He practiced in Limeric and Windham, Maine, before moving to Portland.

Fig. 293. *By Harriet Whitney. 1822* inscribed on the glass. Silk, chenille, pencil, paint, and ink on silk; 16¼″ x 21¼″. Harriet was twenty-one years old when she worked one of Portland's most beautiful "winged cherub" mourning pieces and dedicated it to her mother. For her sister's sampler and watercolor memorial from the same school, see *ANTIQUES*, September 1988, 515, 518. Harriet Whitney (1801–1843) was the daughter of William Clark Whitney (1765–1859) and his first wife, Sophia Fuller (1779–1813). Her father was a prominent landowner in Hebron, Maine. In 1827, Harriet married Dr. Solomon Paddleford Cushman (1801–1844) of Brunswick, Maine, and they had five children.

Collection of Mrs. Thomas Ridgway.

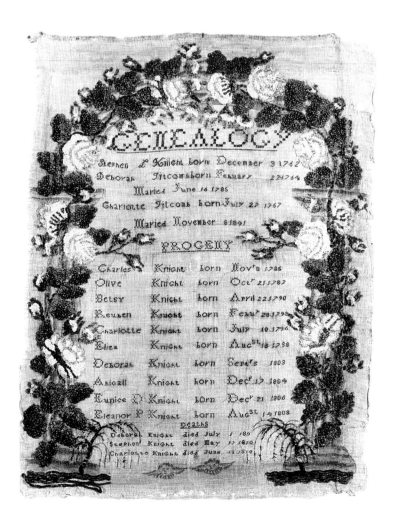

Fig. 294. Genealogical sampler for the family of Stephen L. Knight, c.1825. Silk, chenille, pencil, and paint on linen; 23¼″ x 17¼″. The drawing of the columns and the winged cherubs' heads relate this sampler to the silk embroideries in Figures 293 and 295. A similar genealogy of the Bryant family is in the Maine Historical Society. Stephen Longfellow Knight (1762–1810) of Falmouth, Maine, married, first, Deborah Titcomb (1764–1801) and second, her sister Charlotte Titcomb (1767–1810). This sampler is attributed to one of Charlotte's daughters, either Eunice (b.1806) or Eleanor (b.1808), who probably could not remember their parents.

Maine Historical Society, A86-549.

Fig. 295. Anonymous mourning embroidery with a monument dedicated to *MRS. ABIGAIL GAGE,/ WHO DIED MARCH 12, 1807, AGED 24 YEARS*, c.1823. Silk, pencil, and paint on silk; 17½″ x 22½″. The memorial verse begins *Here let the orphan drop the filial tear/ O'er the frail casket of a mother dear.* The embroidery is attributed to one of the two daughters (appropriately pictured here) of Richard Gage (b.1781) and Abigail Wheelock (1782–1807) of Bridgeton, Maine. They were Martha Maria (b.1804) and Abigail Wheelock Gage, who was born March 12, 1807, the day her mother died. Richard Gage married his deceased wife's sister, Martha, and they had four children.

The Fine Arts Museums of San Francisco, gift of W. M. Streehy, 49410.

Painting."[13] The Paine sisters, including their sister Phebe (1802–1872), later lived in Carlisle, Pennsylvania, and died there.[14]

Portland's second group of silk embroideries is equally impressive although the patterns were drawn by a less fluid hand and the figures are somewhat awkward (Figs. 296, 297, 300, 301). The embroideries are most unusual for their occasional depictions of identifiable buildings, and in some cases, for their extraordinarily large sizes. Similar scenes were entirely painted rather than worked (Fig. 298) and also occur on samplers (Fig. 299). These pieces date from 1824 to 1842, and they were made under the instruction of Miss Mary Rea, who announced the opening of her school in the *Eastern Argus* of March 18, 1823. The following year she specifically offered instruction in "Embroidering Genealogies," and her tuition ranged from $2.50 to $10 per quarter.

> For Reading, Writing, Orthography, Defining, English Grammar, Geography, Arithmetic, Rhetoric, History, Chemistry, Plain and Ornamental Needle Work, Unshaded, on Cambric and Muslin $3.50
> Drawing and Painting in Water Colors, Embroidering Genealogies $5.00
> Oil Painting, Filagree, Embroidering on Satin, & c. from 7 to $10 per quarter.[15]

In an advertisement of 1826, she mentioned that "A few young ladies who cannot attend as regular scholars may receive instruction in Writing, Drawing, painting, working Lace, & c. on Wednesday and Saturday afternoons."[16]

Mary Rea (1787–1846) was born in Windham, Maine, to Dr. Caleb Rea, Jr. (1758–1796), and Sarah White (1758–1836). She was evidently living with her widowed mother in Windham in 1821,[17] and she probably moved to Portland after her younger brother, Dr. Albus Rea (1795–1848), took his medical degree from Bowdoin and opened his practice in Portland about 1822. Mary seems to have kept her day school in various rented rooms, and her name did not appear in Portland directories until 1841. She was last listed as a teacher on Green Street in 1846, and she died in Portland on November 1, 1849. The attribution of these embroideries to Mary Rea's school rests on a 1916 bequest from Mrs. Julia Crockett Rumery to the Maine Historical Society. The works of Sarah Jane Moore (Fig. 301) and her sister came with the notation that "When these pictures were made the girls were at Miss Rea's school in Portland. Miss Rea was the sister of Dr. Rea, the father of Mrs. Dr. Burr." Mrs. Rumery was the daughter of Sarah Jane Moore. The Moore embroideries are now the latest dated works of this type that are known to have been made in New England.

---

13. *Eastern Argus*, June 26, 1821, and March 9, 1827.

14. Phebe may have been the Phebe Paine named among the day scholars in the Misses Martin's list of students from 1804 through 1829. The list is in the Maine Historical Society, but it is known to be incomplete.

15. *Eastern Argus*, March 2, 1824. See front endpapers.

16. Ibid., February 26, 1826.

17. H. K. Treadwell, Salem, Massachusetts, to Mrs. Sarah Rea and Mary in Windham, June 27, 1821 (Maine Historical Society).

Fig. 296. Anonymous mourning embroidery dedicated to *SARAH D. KNAPP,/ WHO DIED FEBRUARY 14, 1824 AGED 9 YEARS AND 3 MONTHS*, c.1824. Silk, pencil, paint, and ink on silk; 17″ x 21″. This embroidery is typical of the early memorials worked at Miss Mary Rea's school. Attributed to Hannah Morrill Knapp (1809–1832), the sister of Sarah Davenport Knapp (1814–1824), to whom this is dedicated. They were the only daughters among the seven children of Anthony Knapp (1778–1851) and Dolly (Dorothy) Morrill (1781–1879). He was a Portland caulker, and they lived on Deer Street. Hannah married Charles Thomas in 1828 and died when she was twenty-two.
Private collection.

Fig. 298. Anonymous memorial dedicated to the infants Emeline and Sarah Brackett, c.1824. Watercolor and ink on paper; 17″ x 22″. In the background is the domed roof of Boston's Massachusetts General Hospital; for its print source, see *ANTIQUES*, September 1988, 523. It also appears in a mourning piece worked by Sarah E. Sawyer (Skinner Sale 1196, March 26, 1988, Lot 101), and in an anonymous embroidery dedicated to Mrs. Harriet H. Lewis (*MAD*, August 1991, 27-E). Emeline and Sarah Brackett, who died in 1810 and 1811, were the first children and only daughters of Zachariah Bangs Brackett (1789–1840) and Abigail Reed (1789–1847). This memorial is typical of Mary Rea's school and was probably painted by Abigail Brackett's sister, Mary Ann Reed (b.1806), when she was studying there in 1824 (Fig. 297).

Portland Museum of Art, 1974.14.

Opposite:

Fig. 297. *By Mary A. Reed 1824* inscribed on the glass. Silk, pencil, and paint on silk; 17¼″ x 21½″. The episode depicted here is not clear, but the busy townscape is typical of embroideries from Mary Rea's school. The major trees, flowers in the foreground, windows of the houses, and flags on the ships are embroidered, but painting predominates. For another scene attributed to Miss Rea's school, see Swan, *Guide*, Fig. 69. Mary Ann Reed (b.1806) was the daughter of Jonathan Reed (b.1752) and Dorothy Blake of Westbrook. In 1828, she married Dr. Cornelius Thompson Springer Brackett (d.1839).

Author's collection.

Fig. 299. *GENEALOGY WT 1824.* Silk, pencil, and paint on linen; 22¼″ x 18¼″. A record of the family of the Reverend James Carruthers (1772–1857) and Robina Johnston (1774–1834) who were born in Scotland. The Reverend Carruthers was educated in Glasgow and became pastor of Portland's Second Parish Church. Attributed to Mary Rea's school and Janet Carruthers (b.1809), the only surviving daughter of appropriate age to have worked this in 1824. Janet was teaching girls in the 1830s (Edward H. Elwell, *Schools of Portland* [Portland: William M. Marks, Printer, 1988], 20). She died unmarried. *Maine Historical Society, A86-551.*

Fig. 299a. Detail of the painted and embroidered memorial on the Carruthers genealogical sampler. Its little boats and buildings are clearly related to the silk embroideries from Miss Rea's school.

Fig. 300. *By Cordelia Knight.* inscribed on the glass and *GENEALOGY* printed on the silk, c.1835. Silk, pencil, paint, and ink on silk; 27¾″ x 18¾″. The monument is dedicated to seven of the fifteen children of Benjamin and Mary Knight who died between 1806 and 1832. The following inscription appears on the paper backing:

> The painting and hand embroidery on this Geneal-
> ogy was done by my mother, Cordelia Knight
> Adams—wife of Elijah Adams 2d Portland
> Maine—about 1835. The old brick house in the
> foreground was her home—on Deer St—near Fore
> St—on the water front—and was destroyed in the
> fire of 1866. On the right is Portland Head
> Light—In the center—the Old Second Parish
> Church on Middle St—opposite Church St. This
> also was destroyed in the fire of 1866—on its left
> The Portland Observatory on Monjoy Hill.
> (signed) Ella L. Adams Farrington, Portland,
> Maine 1925

Cordelia Knight (1818–1853) was the eleventh child of Portland merchant Benjamin Knight (1780–1860) and Mary Hutchison (1782–1861). She married Elijah Adams in 1844. Her sister Harriet Eliza Knight (1811–1832) also worked a memorial at Miss Mary Rea's school (*ANTIQUES*, September 1988, 520–1).
Maine Historical Society, A86-718.

Fig. 301. *By Sarah J. Moore, August 1838* inscribed on the glass. Silk, pencil, paint, and ink on silk; 33½″ x 35¾″. Flowers, shrubs, grass beneath the monument, and foliage of the tree at right are embroidered. The monument is dedicated to two infants who died in 1817 and 1829. At far left is the Portland Observa-tory; the three-story mansion left of the monument is the Jones Boarding House on the corner of Park and Congress streets; on the far right is the Portland Head Light. Sarah Jane Moore (1818–1881) was the daughter of prosperous Portland merchant James B. Moore (1791–1883) and Sally Plumer (b.1791). She married John R. Crockett (c.1817–1845) in 1840. Sarah's sister, Ellen P. Moore, worked a family register, dated 1842 and much like Figure 300 (*ANTIQUES*, September 1988, 524).
Maine Historical Society, A86-719.

Fig. 302. *BY THE/ NAME LYNDE/ AND BOWLES* painted on the ribbon worked in metallic threads; silk, gold and silver metallic threads, one bead, and blue paint on black silk; 17⅛″ x 17⅛″. Inscribed on the back: "This coat of arms was worked by Miss Lydia Lynde Salem 1762 Saved from the fire in Newburyport August 19, 1820 Was regilt and glazed by Pierce and Smith, Boston Aug 5, 1832." This pattern and the frame are much like those of the Gardner arms. Lydia Lynde (1741–1798) was the daughter of Benjamin Lynde, Jr. (1700–1781), and Mary Bowles (1709–1791) of Salem. In 1766 she married the Reverend William Walter (1737–1800). *Privately owned.*

Appendix I

Each entry in this list represents an embroidered coat of arms believed to have been worked in New England during the eighteenth century. Included are pieces known today and those for which some image exists. References to the arms and crests are included if they are identified, or a description is given. Monochrome reproductions and badly faded embroidery have prevented positive identification of the arms in some cases. Also, examples known only from photographs often lack dimensions and materials may be unclear. Pattern sources, makers, and schools are named if known, as well as sound attributions. An illustration is cited when possible. All dimensions are sight measurements of the needlework; hatchment shapes are measured by equal sides rather than diagonally. Not included here are two coats of arms in the Gore pattern but probably worked at a later date: the Curwen & Russell arms (EI, 4134.90) and the Gore arms (Gore Place Society, T-137-G). A supplemental list includes examples of unknown appearance that were described by Charles Knowles Bolton in *Bolton's American Armory* of 1927.

Abbreviations for frequently cited people, publications, and institutions that do not appear in Appendix II:

Bolton	Bolton, Charles Knowles. *Bolton's American Armory*. Boston: F. W. Faxon Co., 1927.
Burke	Burke, Sir Bernard. *The General Armory of England, Scotland, Ireland and Wales comprising a Registry of Armorial Bearings from the Earliest to the Present Time*. London, 1884.
Fairbairn	Fairbairn, James. *Fairbairn's Book of Crests of the Families of Great Britain and Ireland*. Edited by A. C. Fox-Davies. London, 1905. Reprint. Baltimore: Heraldic Book Company, 1968.
Gore	John and Samuel Gore, pattern drawers.

Gore Roll	Gore, John. *The Gore Roll of Arms*. Manuscript. Boston: New England Historic Genealogical Society.
Guillim	Guillim, John. *A Display of Heraldry*. 6th ed. London: printed by T. W. for R. and J. Bonwicke and R. Wilkin and J. Walthoe and Tho. Ward, 1724.
NEHGR Roll	"The Roll of Arms." *The New England Historical and Genealogical Register,* Vol. 82–125 (1928–1971). Boston: New England Historic Genealogical Society.
Papworth	Papworth, John W. *Papworth's Ordinary of British Armorials.* 1874. Reprint. London: Tabard Publications, 1961.
CF	The Chipstone Foundation, Milwaukee, Wisconsin.
CW	Colonial Williamsburg Foundation, Williamsburg, Virginia.
HD	Historic Deerfield, Inc., Deerfield, Massachusetts.
HSON	Historical Society of Old Newbury, Newburyport, Massachusetts.
SHM	Sargent House Museum, Gloucester, Massachusetts.
WM	Henry Francis du Pont Winterthur Museum, Winterthur, Delaware.
Yale	Yale University Art Gallery, New Haven, Connecticut.

Fig. 303. The Cobb arms, c.1760–1765. Silk, gold and silver metallic threads, beads, and one spangle on black silk; 18″ x 15¼″. This composition also appears on the Ingersoll canvas-work arms of 1758 and relates to painted arms by Christian Remick (b.1726), as well as to the later work of Newburyport heraldic artists George Searle and Edward Bass. Attributed to Sally Cobb (1744–1816), the daughter of Thomas Cobb (1705–1779) and Lydia Leonard (c.1707–1762) of Taunton, Massachusetts. In 1770 she married Robert Treat Paine (1730/31–1814), a signer of the Declaration of Independence. *Massachusetts Historical Society, 1420.*

ANDREWS

Inscribed: *BY THE/ NAME OF/ ANDREWS*

Reference: Bolton, 4; Burke, 18. Crest unidentified: lion, tiger, or catamount (wild cat) rampant.

Shape: vertical rectangle; 21″ x 19″.

Materials: silk and metallic threads on black silk.

Pattern: similar to PARKER & FREEMAN.

Maker: Hannah Andrews (1747–1831), daughter of Benjamin Andrews and Hannah Holland of Boston. Married 1770 Samuel Breck (1747–1809) of Boston. They moved to Philadelphia.

PMA, 56–68–42.

BABCOCK & HOWE 1785

Reference: BABCOCK (variant arms): three bars, the center one charged with three cocks. HOWE: Guillim, 193. Crest: dove with olive branch, unknown for BABCOCK or HOWE.

Illustrated: Fig. 72.

The Bayou Bend Collection, Museum of Fine Arts, Houston, B.84.7.

BARTLETT

Inscription: illegible.

Reference: Bolton, 10.

Shape: lozenge hatchment.

Materials: silk and metallic threads on black silk.

Pattern: Gore.

Maker: Katherine Bartlett of Charlestown in 1769 (according to exhibition record, Cabot Papers, MFA).

Illustrated: Fig. 306.

Owner unknown.

BECK (traditionally) 1768

Inscribed: *BY THE NAME OF BECK/ 68.*

Reference: arms unidentified: gules a cross (moline?) between four lions rampant (gold?). Crest: a tyger's? head gules razed collared vair. See CROSS.

Shape: hatchment; 14¾″ sq.

Materials: crewels on canvas.

Maker: possibly Mary Beck (b.1749), daughter of Jonathan Beck and Joanna Daniel (d.1761) of Newburyport, Mass.

HSON, 2033A.

BILLINGS 1796

Inscribed: *Arms to the Name of Billings 1796.*

Reference: Bolton, 15; Fairbairn, 53.

Shape: vertical rectangle; 10″ x 8″.

Materials: silk on canvas.

Maker: Eunice Minot (1781–1863), daughter of George Minot (1755–1826) and Eunice Billings (1760–1849) of Dorchester, Mass. Married in 1807 Ezra Glover (1770–1847).

WM, 59.3764A.

BLANCHARD & HUNT c.1765

Inscribed: *By ye NAME/ of BLANCHARD/ & HUNT.*

Reference: dexter arms unidentified—silver a chevron between three cross crosslets fitchy sable, impaling HUNT, Guillim, 263. Crest: a lion's head party per fess razed.

Shape: hatchment; 18⅝″ sq.

Materials: silk and metallic threads on black silk with gray paint edging some motifs.

Maker: Elizabeth Blanchard (1749–1804), daughter of Joshua Blanchard, Jr. (c.1717–1785), stationer of Boston, and Elizabeth Hunt (c.1723–1807). Unm.

MHS, gift of Clara B. Winthrop, 1924, 1016.

BLYTHE

Reference: Papworth, 784. Crest: Fairbairn, 58.

Shape: hatchment; 18⅛″ sq.

Materials: silk on black silk.

Pattern: Gore.

MFA, 27.63.

BOWEN c.1788

Reference: Guillim, 156. Crest: Fairbairn, 67.

Shape: hatchment; 19¼″ sq.

Materials: silk and metallic threads on black silk.

Pattern: Gore.

Maker: probably Mary Bowen (1772–1793), daughter of Jabez Bowen (1737–1815) and Sarah Brown (1742–1800) of Providence, R.I. Unm.

Illustrated: *A&AW,* August 3, 1984, 42.

CF, 1984.1.

BOYD & BREWSTER c.1790

Inscribed: *SUBMIT BOYD.*

Reference: Bolton, 20; Burke, 21. Crest unidentified (bird preying?).

Shape: lozenge hatchment; 17¾″ x 17¾″.

Materials: silk and metallic threads on black silk.

Pattern: Gore.

Maker: Submit Boyd (1774–1803), daughter of George Boyd (c. 1733–1787) and Jane Brewster (c. 1737–1800) of Portsmouth, N.H. Married 1791 John Samuel

Married 1791 John Samuel
Sherburne (1757–1830).
Illustrated: Sotheby's Sale
5357, June 28, 1985, Lot
244.
*The Dietrich Americana Foun-
dation, 4.5.1248.*

BRADSTREET C.1766
Inscribed: *BY THE/ NAME
OF/ BRADSTREET/ R B.*
Reference: Bolton, 21.
Shape: lozenge hatchment;
18⅛″ x 18⅛″.
Materials: silk and metallic
threads on black silk.
Pattern: Gore.
Maker: Rebecca Bradstreet
(1750–1824), daughter of
the Reverend Simon
Bradstreet (1709–1771),
and Mary Strahan
(1718–1768) of Marble-
head. Married 1771 the
Reverend Isaac Story
(c.1749–1816).
Illustrated: *ANTIQUES,* May
1959, 408.
CF, T1959.14.

BROWN 1758
Inscribed: *1758./ JANE
BROWN/ AET. 15.*
Reference: Guillim, 432.
Shape: hatchment; 17⅛″ sq.
Materials: wool on canvas.
Maker: Jane Brown.
Illustrated: Swan, *Plain &
Fancy,* 156.
WM, 59.2851C

BROWN
Inscribed: *Elizabeth Gerrish.*
Reference: Guillim, 121.
Crest: Burke, 134.
Shape: vertical rectangle.
Materials: silk on black silk.
Maker: probably Elizabeth
Gerrish (1769–1825),
daughter of William
Gerrish, Jr. (1730–1801),
and Mary Brown
(1733–1803) of Newbury,

Mass. Married 1792
Benjamin Peirce
(1769–1831) of Newbury-
port.
Illustrated: Fig. 306.
Owner unknown.

CABOT & FITCH
C.1765
Reference: CABOT: correct
source unknown. FITCH:
Guillim, 260.
Shape: hatchment; 17½″ sq.
Materials: silk (and metallic
threads?) on black silk.
Maker: attributed to Mary
Cabot (1749–1771),
daughter of Francis Cabot
(1717–1786), merchant of
Salem, and Mary Fitch
(1724–1756). Unm.
Illustrated: Little, *Little by
Little* (1984), 137.
*Collection of Bertram K. and
Nina F. Little.*

CARPENTER
Reference: Guillim, 194.
Crest unidentified: falcon
silver rising on branch
leafed proper.
Shape: lozenge hatchment;
17¾″ x 17⅝″.
Materials: silk and metallic
threads with raised work
on black silk.
Pattern: Gore.
Illustrated: Christie's Sale,
October 19, 1990, Lot
145.
*Layton Art Collection, Milwau-
kee Art Museum, gift of
Collectors' Corner,
M1990.114.*

CHANDLER C.1750
Reference: Bolton, 32.
Shape: hatchment; 13¾″ sq.
Materials: silk, wool, and
silver threads on linen
ground worked in green.
Pattern: probably Thomas
Johnston.

Maker: Katherine Chandler
(1735–1791), daughter of
John Chandler
(1693–1762) and Hannah
Gardiner (1699–1739) of
Worcester, Mass. Married
Levi Willard (1727–1775).
Illustrated: Edwin J. Hipkiss,
*Eighteenth-Century American
Arts: The M. and M. Karolik
Collection* (Cambridge,
Mass.: Harvard University
Press, 1941), 278.
MFA, 39.244.

CHANDLER
Reference: Bolton, 32.
Shape: hatchment; 18½″ sq.
Materials: silk and metallic
threads on black silk.
Pattern: Gore.
*Collection of Mr. and Mrs. E.
Victor Milione.*

CHANDLER C.1790
Reference: Bolton, 32.
Shape: hatchment; 19½″ sq.
Frame labeled by Joseph
Stokes, Milk Street,
Boston.
Materials: silk and metallic
threads on black silk.
Pattern: Gore.
Illustrated: *ANTIQUES,*
February 1993, c-2.
Israel Sack, Inc.

CHANDLER 1797
Inscribed: *Anna Maria Chan-
dler/ 1797.*
Reference: Bolton, 32.
Shape: hatchment; 17⅜″ sq.
Materials: silk and metallic
threads on black silk.
Maker: Anna Maria Chandler
(1778–1823), daughter of
John Chandler
(1736–1796) and Mary
Chandler (1738–1816).
They lived in Newtown,
Connecticut, and moved
to Peacham, Vermont, in
1796. Chandler family

correspondence of August 1796 (Bailey/Howe Library, University of Vermont) suggests that Anna Maria then had the pattern for her coat of arms and may have completed it in Peacham. Her arms and the CRAFTS arms by her first cousin definitely had a common origin.
Illustrated: Sotheby's Sale 5680, January 30, 1988, Lot 1568.
Private collection.

CHEEVER 1769
Inscribed: *M C 1769.*
Reference: Bolton, 33.
Shape: lozenge hatchment; 17¾″ x 17¾″.
Materials: silk and metallic threads on black silk; one bead and one spangle.
Pattern: Gore.
Maker: Mary Cheever.
School: probably the Misses Cuming.
Illustrated: Fig. 306.
SPNEA, 1985.660.

CHESTER
Reference: *The Heraldic Journal* 2 (1866), 44.
Shape: hatchment; 18″ sq.
Materials: silk and metallic threads on black silk; similar to GRANT and CHEEVER.
Pattern: Gore.
Privately owned but since destroyed in a fire.

CLOPTON (traditionally CLAPP)
Reference: Guillim, 62.
Shape: hatchment; 19″ sq.
Materials: silk on black silk.
Pattern: Gore.
Illustrated: *ANTIQUES,* June 1980, 1332.

Yale University Library, Manuscripts and Archives Collection, no acc. no.

COBB c.1760
Reference: Bolton, 36.
Illustrated: Fig. 303.
MHS, 1420.

CRAFTS 1795
Inscribed: *QUO/ FATA/ VOCANT/ Augusta Crafts/ 1795.*
Reference: arms unidentified: sable a chevron ermine between three bulls' heads gold. Crest: a standing unicorn (churning?).
Shape: hatchment; 16¼″ sq.
Materials: silk and metallic threads on black silk.
Maker: Augusta Crafts (1773–1861), daughter of Ebenezer Crafts (1740–1810) and Mehitable Chandler (1741–1812) of Sturbridge, Mass. Moved to Craftsbury, Vermont, in 1791. Married 1796 Dr. James Paddock (c.1765–1809); Dr. Ephraim Brewster (d.1812); Benjamin Clark (d.1838).
Illustrated: Nancy Price Graff, ed., *Celebrating Vermont: Myths and Realities,* exhibition catalogue (Middlebury, Vt.: Middlebury College, 1991), 128–9.
Private collection.

CROSS (traditionally) c.1740–1750
Reference: arms unidentified: a cross moline between four lions rampant. Crest: gules a tyger's head razed collared vair.

Shape: hatchment; 12¾″ sq.
Materials: wool and silk canvas work with cream-colored ground.
Pattern: Thomas Johnston.
HSON, 935.

CUSHING
Inscribed: *THE/ CUSHING/ NAME.*
Reference: Gore Roll, 86.
Shape: hatchment; 11¼″ sq.
Materials: silk and metallic threads on white silk.
Mrs. Charles S. Lowry.

CUSHING
Inscribed: *THE/ CUSHING/ NAME.*
Reference: Gore Roll, 86.
Shape: hatchment; 18″ sq.
Materials: silk and metallic threads on white silk.
Pattern: Gore.
Illustrated: Ronald Bourgeault, *Northeast Auctions,* August 4–5, 1990, Lot 433.
Mr. and Mrs. Stanley P. Sax.

CUSHING c.1750
Reference: Gore Roll, 86.
Shape: hatchment; 20″ sq.
Materials: silk and metallic threads on linen; ground worked in green; very similar to QUINCY & STURGIS arms.
Pattern: Gore.
Illustrated: Little, *Little by Little* (1984), 137.
Collection of Bertram K. and Nina Fletcher Little.

CUSHING c.1778
Reference: Gore Roll, 86.
Shape: hatchment; 17¾″ sq.
Materials: wool and silk canvas work.
Maker: Deborah Cushing (1762–1845), daughter of Thomas Cushing (1725–1788) and Deborah

Fletcher (c.1727–1790).
Married 1781 Henry
Newman (c.1755–1811).
SPNEA, 1923.469.

CUTTS
Reference: Guillim, 356.
    Crest unidentified: a bird
    rising.
Shape: hatchment; 18⅜″ sq.
Materials: silk and metallic
    threads on black silk, and
    appliquéd white silk for
    helmet and ribbon.
Illustrated: Fig. 306.
SPNEA, 1985.659.

DAVIS 1753
Inscribed: *Amy Davis 1753/*
    The Arms of Eᵈ Davis/ And
    is the Paternal Coat Armour
    of the Right Honorable
    Thomas Davis Kt Lord/
    Mayar of London/ Anno
    1677.
Reference: Guillim, 104.
    Crest: Fairbairn, 154.
Shape: hatchment; 8½″ sq.;
    framed as a miniature fire
    screen.
Materials: canvas work in
    wool and metallic threads.
Maker: Amy Davis.
Illustrated: Fig. 306 and B &
    C, Pl. CXXIV.
HSON, 2230.

DIX
Reference: dexter arms
    unidentified: a chevron
    between three lions'
    heads; sinister arms and
    crest are DIX, Bolton, 49.
Shape: hatchment; 19″ sq.
Materials: silk and several
    beads on black silk.
Pattern: Gore.
Illustrated: Fig. 306.
Worcester Historical Museum,
    no acc. no.

DIX & PHILLIPS quar-
    tered, impaling LEM-
    MON

Reference: Bolton, 49;
    PHILLIPS and LEMMON:
    Gore Roll, 63 and 38.
Shape: hatchment; 17¼″ sq.
Materials: silk and metallic
    threads on black silk.
Pattern: Gore.
Maker: Mary Dix
    (1776–1852) born in
    Worcester, Mass., to Dr.
    Elijah Dix (1747–1809)
    and Dorothy Lynde
    (c.1746–1837), whose
    mother was Mary Lem-
    mon. Her filigree arms of
    Lemmon, 1735, is de-
    scribed in Bolton, 101.
    Mary Dix married 1795
    the Reverend Thaddeus
    Mason Harris
    (1768–1842).
Illustrated: *Architectural*
    Digest, May 1984, 205.
Private collection.

DUNCAN &
    (PHILLIPS?) impaling
LEMMON
Reference: Bolton, 52;
    PHILLIPS and LEMMON:
    Gore Roll, 63 and 38.
Shape: hatchment; 17⅞″ sq.
Materials: silk and metallic
    threads on black silk.
Pattern: Gore.
Private collection.

FISK c.1784
Inscribed: *THE/ NAME OF/*
    FISK.
Reference: Bolton, 60.
Shape: hatchment; 18⅜″ sq.
Materials: silk, raised metal-
    lic work, and spangles on
    black silk.
Pattern: Gore.
Maker: Lydia Fiske
    (c.1768–1785), daughter
    of John Fiske (1744–1797)
    and Lydia Phippen
    (1747–1782) of Salem.
School: attributed to Eleanor
    Druitt.

Illustrated: *ANTIQUES,* April
    1992, 629.
EI, 112,131.

FITCH & HALL
c.1773
Reference: Guillim, 139,
    260.
Shape: lozenge hatchment.
Materials: silk and metallic
    threads on black silk.
Pattern: Gore.
Illustrated: Fig. 306.
Owner unknown.

FLETCHER c.1745
Reference: Guillim, 429.
    Crest: Burke, 361.
Shape: hatchment; 16″ sq.
Materials: wool on canvas
    ground worked in blue.
Pattern: vertical format
    within hatchment-shaped
    frame and with unworked
    side corners; composition
    much like INGERSOLL
    and COBB.
Maker: Mary Fletcher
    (1730–1797), daughter of
    William Fletcher
    (1688–1745) and Margaret
    Cushing (1696–1747) of
    Beverly, Mass. Married
    1763 Nathaniel Balch.
Beverly Historical Society, no
    acc. no.

FOWLE c.1783
Inscribed: *BY/ THE NAME*
    OF/ FOWLE.
Reference: Bolton, 62.
Shape: hatchment.
Materials: wool canvas work.
Pattern: Gore.
Maker: Margery Fowle
    (1767–1799), daughter of
    Josiah Fowle (1731–1805)
    and Margery Carter
    (1730–1812) of Woburn,
    Mass. Married 1791 (as
    his second wife) Colonel
    Loammi Baldwin
    (1745–1807).

Fig. 304. *BY THE/ NAME/ OF NOR/ WOOD* inscribed on the motto ribbon, c.1755. Silk on black silk; 21½" x 19¼". Worked by Judith Norwood (1738–1762), the daughter of William Norwood (1708–1781) and Judith Woodbury (1710–1775) of Gloucester. In 1761 she married David Plumer (1738–1801). *Sargent House Museum, Gloucester, Massachusetts, 701.*

Illustrated: Eugene Chalmers Fowle, comp., *Descendants of George Fowle (1610/11–1682) of Charlestown, Massachusetts* (Boston: New England Historic Genealogical Society, 1990), cover. *Private collection.*

FOXCROFT & CONEY
c.1740–1760
Reference: BOLTON, 62; Burke, 220, 373.
Illustrated: Fig. 62.
Addison Gallery of American Art, Phillips Academy, Andover, Mass., 1962.6.

GARDNER
Reference: Guillim, 65.
Shape: hatchment; 18" sq.

Materials: silk and metallic threads on black silk.
Maker: Lois Gardner (1741–1819), daughter of Samuel Gardner (1712–1769) and Esther Orne (1714/15–1756) of Salem, Mass. Similar to the LYNDE & BOWLES arms and possibly worked in Salem. Lois married 1773 the Reverend Thomas Barnard (1747/48–1814).
Illustrated: Harrison Ellery and Charles Pickering Bowditch, *The Pickering Genealogy* 1 (Cambridge, Mass.: Cambridge University Press, 1897), 91. *EI, 135,124.*

GERRISH
Inscribed: *THE/ NAME OF/ GERRISH/ ELIZABETH GERRISH.*
Reference: Bolton, 66.
Shape: vertical rectangle.
Materials: silk on black silk?
Maker: Elizabeth Gerrish (see BROWN).
Illustrated: Fig. 306.
Owner unknown.

GRAFTON 1747
Reference: Burke, 417.
Illustrated: Fig. 307.
Mr. and Mrs. Stanley P. Sax.

GRANT
Inscribed: *TANQUAM/ DESPICATUS/ SUM VINCO.*
Reference: Guillim, 182.
Shape: hatchment.

Materials: silk on black silk?
*Photograph in Gertrude
    Townsend's papers, MFA.*

GRANT 1769
Reference: Guillim, 182.
Crest: Fairbairn, 237.
Illustrated: Fig. 70.
HD, 1391.

GRAY & LEWIS
Reference: Bolton, 70, 102.
Shape: hatchment.
Materials: silk and metallic
    threads on black silk.
Pattern: Gore.
Maker: Elizabeth Gray
    (c.1745–1779), daughter
    of Harrison Gray
    (1711?–1794) and Eliza-
    beth Lewis. Married 1764
    Samuel Alleyne Otis
    (1740–1814).
Illustrated: B&C, Pl.
    CXXVI.
Owner unknown.

GREENE
Reference: Guillim, 157.
Shape: hatchment; 18¾″ sq.
Materials: silk and metallic
    threads on black silk.
Pattern: Gore.
*DAR Museum, Washington,
    D.C., 86.32.1.*

GREENE 1745
Reference: Guillim, 157.
Illustrated: Fig. 66.
MFA, 39.243.

HALL & BRADSHAW
Reference: Guillim, 139;
    Burke, 114.
Shape: hatchment; 18″ sq.
Materials: silk and metallic
    threads on black silk.
Pattern: Gore.
Maker: Abigail Hall
    (b.c.1772), daughter
    of Nathaniel Hall
    (1735–1809), a merchant
    of Chelsea, Mass. and

Mary Bradshaw
    (c.1735–1804).
*Colonial Society of
    Massachusetts, no acc. no.*

HALL quartering
    (HALL?)
Reference: Guillim, 139;
    Bolton, 74.
Shape: hatchment; 17½″ sq.
Materials: silk and metallic
    threads on black silk.
Pattern: Gore.
Illustrated: Swan, *Guide,*
    135.
WM, 58.1524.

HEARD c.1790
Inscribed: *BY THE/ NAME
    OF/ HEARD.*
Reference: Bolton, 87.
Shape: hatchment; 18⅝″ sq.
Materials: silk and metallic
    threads on black silk;
    some motifs very highly
    raised.
Pattern: Gore.
Maker: one of the daughters
    of John Heard
    (1744–1834) and Elizabeth
    Ann Story (c.1746–1775)
    of Ipswich; probably Mary
    (1773–1795).
School: attributed to Eleanor
    Druitt.
*John Heard House, Ipswich
    Historical Society.*

HENSHAW & BILL
    1748
Reference: Bolton, no. 79;
    Burke, 82; *NEHGR* 107,
    (1953), 193, 365.
Illustrated: Fig. 68.
*Collection of Judith and John
    Herdeg.*

HODGES & KING
Inscribed: *BY THE NAME OF
    HODGES AND KING.*
Reference: Bolton, 82, 96.
Shape: hatchment; 17½″ sq.

Materials: silk and metallic
    threads on dark brown
    silk.
Pattern: possibly James
    Turner of Marblehead.
Maker: possibly Hannah
    Hodges (1779–1792),
    daughter of shipmaster
    Benjamin Hodges
    (1754–1806) and Hannah
    King (1755–1814) of
    Salem, Mass.
Illustrated: Alice Winchester,
    ed., *The Antiques Treasury*
    (New York: E. P. Dutton
    & Co., 1959), 31.
WM, 67.1393.

HOSKINS
Reference: Guillim, 387.
Shape: hatchment; 19″ sq.
Materials: silk and metallic
    threads on black silk.
Pattern: Gore.
*Yale, bequest of Josephine
    Setze, 1982.61.3.*

HULBERT & CLARK
    c.1785–1795
Inscribed: *HULBERT AND
    CLARK.*
Reference: Guillim, 390,
    436.
Shape: vertical rectangle;
    15¼″ x 11½″.
Materials: silk on black silk.
Maker: possibly one of the
    daughters of Hezekiah
    Hulbert (1749–1800) and
    Hannah Clark
    (1753–1796): Hannah
    (b.1771), Anna (b.1780),
    or Elizabeth (b.1782).
    This Middletown, Conn.,
    family moved to Holland
    Patent, N.Y., in 1797.
*Collection of Bernard and S.
    Dean Levy.*

HUNT
Inscribed: *BY THE/ NAME
    OF/ HUNT/ Mary Hunt AE
    15.*
Reference: Guillim, 263.

Shape: vertical rectangle;
  18″ x 17³⁄₁₆″.
Materials: silk, paint, and
  ink on black silk.
Maker: Mary Hunt.
Illustrated: Skinner Sale
  1246, March 25, 1989,
  Lot 170.
Owner unknown.

INGERSOLL 1758
Inscribed: *BY THE/ NAME
  OF/ INGERSOLL/ Anne
  Ingersoll aD 1758.*
Reference: Bolton, 88.
Shape: vertical rectangle;
  18¾″ x 16⅜″.
Materials: wool canvas work.
Pattern: possibly Christian
  Remick.
Maker: Anne Ingersoll
  (b.1737), the daughter of
  Thomas Ingersoll
  (1692–1748) and Sarah
  Dewey (1696–1778) of
  Westfield, Mass. Married
  Colonel Sluman of the
  British Army.
Private collection.

IVES
Reference: Guillim, 251;
  Bolton, 89.
Shape: vertical rectangle.
Materials: silk on black silk.
Pattern: unknown but
  similar to COBB and
  INGERSOLL.
Maker: Rebecca Ives
  (1745–1823), daughter of
  Benjamin Ives
  (1720–1757), master
  mariner, and Elizabeth
  Hale (b.1725) of Beverly,
  Mass. Married 1763
  Joseph Gilman
  (1738–1806), who was
  appointed Judge of the
  Northwest Territory by
  George Washington.
Illustrated: Fig. 306.
Owner unknown.

JACKSON
Inscribed: on the glass, *BY
  THE NAME OF JACKSON*
Reference: Bolton, 90
  (variant: 3 suns).
Shape: hatchment; 23½″ sq.
Materials: silk and metallic
  threads on black silk.
Illustrated: John A. H.
  Sweeney, *The Treasure
  House of Early American
  Rooms* (N.Y. Viking Press,
  1963), 98.
WM, 64.617.

JONES c.1762–1768
Inscribed: *BY THE/ NAME
  OF/ JONES.*
Reference: Guillim, 156.
Shape: lozenge hatchment;
  17¼″ x 17¼″.
Materials: silk and metallic
  threads on black silk.
Pattern: Gore.
Maker: Mary Jones
  (1748–1830), daughter of
  Colonel Elisha Jones
  (1710–1775) and Mary
  Allen (b.1714) of Weston,
  Mass. Married 1772 the
  Reverend Asa Dunbar
  (1745–1787), and in 1798
  Jonas Minot (1735–1813).
Illustrated: Benes, *Two Towns*
  (1982), 160; also Fig. 306.
Concord Museum, T-900.

JORDAN
Reference: Guillim, 275.
  Variant crest: dove with
  olive branch.
Shape: hatchment; 18¼″ sq.
Materials: silk and metallic
  threads on black silk.
Pattern: Gore.
Shelburne Museum, 8.3-64.

LEONARD 1740
Reference: arms unidenti-
  fied: azure three lions
  rampant gold.
Illustrated: Fig. 65.
Private collection.

LEONARD
  c.1772–1780
Reference: Guillim, 128.
Shape: hatchment; 17¾″ sq.
Materials: silk and metallic
  threads on black silk.
Pattern: Gore.
Maker: probably a daughter
  of the Reverend David
  Barns (1732–1811) and
  Rachel Leonard
  (1727–1805) of Scituate,
  Mass., either Rachel
  (1757–1808) or Anna
  (1765–1794).
Illustrated: *ANTIQUES,*
  January 1992, 105.
private collection.

LLOYD
Inscribed: *THE/ NAME/
  LLOYD.*
Reference: Guillim, 272.
Shape: hatchment; 18″ sq.
Materials: silk, two beads,
  and highly raised metallic
  work on black silk.
Pattern: Gore.
School: attributed to Eleanor
  Druitt.
Illustrated: *ANTIQUES,* May
  1966, 732.
HD, 63.154.

LYNDE & BOWLES
  1762
Reference: Bolton, 107;
  Guillim, 311.
Illustrated: Fig. 302.
Privately owned.

MACKAY
Reference: Burke, 642.
Shape: hatchment.
Materials: silk on black silk.
Pattern: Gore.
Illustrated: Fig. 306.
Owner unknown.

MASON
Inscribed: *MASON* (center of
  motto ribbon).
Reference: Bolton, 110.

Shape: hatchment; 18¼″ sq.
Materials: silk and metallic threads on black silk.
Pattern: Gore.
Illustrated: Ronald Bourgeault, *Northeast Auctions*, August 4–5, 1990, Lot 432.
Mr. and Mrs. Stanley P. Sax.

MAY & WILLIAMS
c.1785
Reference: Burke, 673; Bolton, 181.
Shape: hatchment; 20⅝″ sq.
Materials: silk on black silk.
Pattern: Gore.
Maker: Mary May (1769–1853), daughter of Samuel May (1723–1794) and Abigail Williams (1733–1811). Married Isaac Davenport (1754–1828). Mary's sister Catharine (1757–1788) worked a "fishing lady" sampler in 1770 (recorded in the Cabot Papers, MFA).
School: probably Deborah Snow.
Illustrated: Fig. 306.
Collection of Mary May Binney Wakefield.

MEERS & RIVERS
Reference: Guillim, 353; Burke, 859. Variant crest: a garb gold.
Shape: hatchment; 19″ sq.
Materials: silk on black silk.
Pattern: Gore.
SPNEA, 1962.20.

MILWARD (traditionally CUTTS) c.1783
Reference: Guillim, 356.
Illustrated: Fig. 71.
York Institute Museum, Saco, Maine, 0000.23.

MOSLEY 1793
Reference: Bolton, 119; used as a quartering by Mosley; crest correct.

Illustrated: Fig. 161.
Private collection.

NORWOOD
Reference: Guillim, 53.
Illustrated: Fig. 304.
SHM, 701.

PARKER & FREEMAN
Inscribed: *THE ARMS/ OF PARKER AND/ FREEMAN.*
Reference: Guillim, 160; Bolton, 63.
Shape: vertical rectangle; 19½″ x 17⅛″.
Materials: silk, metallic threads, and beads on black silk.
Maker: probably one of the daughters of Samuel or Joseph Parker of Brewster and Falmouth, Mass., who married the sisters Desire and Rebecca Freeman. Samuel's daughter Temperance possibly worked a canvas-work "Reclining Shepherdess" now in the WM. A sampler by Peggy Parker, 1774, is nearly identical to Pl. XXV in B&C (recorded in the Cabot Papers, MFA).
MFA, 44.618.

PEIRCE 1796
Inscribed: *THE NAME/ OF/ PEIRCE.*
Reference: Guillim, 223.
Shape: hatchment; 17⅜″ sq.
Materials: silk, spangles, and highly raised metallic threads on cream-colored silk.
Pattern: Gore.
Maker: Sarah Peirce (1780–1835), daughter of Jerathmiel Peirce (1747–1827) and Sarah Rogers (1752–1796) of Salem. Married in 1801 George Nichols (1778–1865).
School: attributed to Eleanor Druitt.

Illustrated: Harrison Ellery and Charles Pickering Bowditch, *The Pickering Genealogy,* vol. 1 (Cambridge, Mass.: Cambridge University Press, 1897), opp. 225.
EI, no acc. no.

PENHALLOW & KNEELAND
Reference: PENHALLOW: "Roll of Arms," *NEHGR* 86, no. 135; quartered with Penwarne: Burke, 791; KNEELAND: Gore Roll, 96. Variant crest: a lion rampant (buff colored).
Shape: hatchment; 19½″ sq.
Materials: wool and silk canvas work with ground worked in brown.
Pattern: Gore.
Maker: possibly Prudence Kneeland (1733–1810), only daughter of John Kneeland of Boston by his second wife, Prudence Clark. Married in 1749 Samuel Penhallow (c.1720–1813). They lived in Portsmouth, N.H., and were childless. This may have been worked for Prudence by an older or younger half-sister, Dorcas (1727–1755) or Mary (b.1740).
Illustrated: John A. H. Sweeney, *The Treasure House of Early American Rooms* (N.Y.: Viking Press, 1963) 29.
WM, 53.171.

PICKERING 1753
Inscribed: *1753 SARAH PICKERING.*
Reference: Guillim, 177. Crest consistently absent.
Shape: hatchment; 17″ sq.
Materials: wool canvas work.
Maker: Sarah Pickering (1730–1826), daughter of

Timothy Pickering
(1703–1773) and Mary
Wingate (1708–1784) of
Salem, Mass. Married
John Clark (c.1718–1801).
Illustrated: Fig. 306.
Privately owned.

PICKERING 1758
Inscribed: *PICKERING 1758.*
Reference: Guillim, 177.
Illustrated: Fig. 69.
Privately owned.

PICKMAN
Inscribed: *ELIZABETH
DELHONDE.*
Reference: Gore Roll, No.
76. Crest: dove?
Shape: hatchment; 16⅛″ sq.
Materials: silk and metallic
threads on black silk.
Pattern: Gore.
Maker: Elizabeth Delhonde
(1742–1834), daughter of
John Delhonde (b.1716)
and Elizabeth Pike
(1717–1793). Married
1762 Samuel Grant
(1740–1794). The arms of
Pickman were possibly
substituted inadvertently
for those of Pike.
Illustrated: Little, *Little by
Little* (1984), 137.
*Collection of Bertram K. and
Nina Fletcher Little.*

PIERPONT
Inscribed: *MARY/ PIER-
PONTS/ WORK.*
Reference: Guillim, 276.
Shape: hatchment; 17¾″ sq.
Materials: silk, raised metal-
lic work, and spangles on
black silk.
Pattern: Gore.
Maker: Mary Pierpont.
School: probably Eleanor
Druitt.
MHS, no acc. no.

PITKIN
Reference: Bolton, 132.
Shape: hatchment; 17¾″ sq.

Materials: unfinished; partly
worked in silk on black
silk.
Pattern: Gore.
Maker: Jerusha Pitkin
(1736–1800), daughter of
Joseph Pitkin (1696–1762)
and Mary Lord
(1702–1740) of Hartford,
Conn. Married 1760 John
Willis (1730–1801).
Illustrated: *ANTIQUES*, April
1975, 723.
CHS, 1935-10-1.

PORTER
Reference: Guillim, 308;
Bolton, 133.
Shape: hatchment; 19¼″ sq.
Materials: silk and metallic
threads on black silk.
Pattern: Gore.
Illustrated: *ANTIQUES*,
March 1953, 266.
CW, 51.77.

PRESCOTT &
LAWRENCE
Reference: Guillim, 221;
Bolton, 134.
Shape: lozenge hatchment;
18¼″ x 18¼″.
Materials: silk and metallic
threads on black silk.
Pattern: Gore.
Maker: Susanna Prescott
(1757–1832), daughter of
James Prescott
(1721–1800) and Susanna
Lawrence (1726–1806) of
Groton, Mass. Married
1779 the Reverend Daniel
Chaplin (1743–1831).
Illustrated: Fig. 306.
*Groton Historical Society,
1602.*

QUINCY 1796
Reference: Bolton, 135.
Crest unidentified: a
crown.
Illustrated: Fig. 177.
*Hingham Historical Society, TE
1A.*

QUINCY & STURGIS
1750
Inscribed: on the back
"Arms of the Quincy &
Sturgis families embroi-
dered by Hannah Quincy
. . . in 1750. . . ."
Reference: Bolton, 135.
Crest unidentified: a wing.
Shape: hatchment; 19½″ x
19¾″.
Materials: silk tent stitch
and metallic threads on
linen ground worked in
green.
Pattern: Gore.
Maker: Hannah Quincy
(1736–1826), daughter of
Josiah Quincy
(1709–1784) and Hannah
Sturgis (c.1712–1755).
Married 1758 Dr. Bela
Lincoln (1734–1773) and
second, Ebenezer Storer,
Jr. (1729–1807).
Illustrated: *ANTIQUES*, April
1992, 622.
SPNEA, 1972.39.

RIDGEWAY
Inscribed: *BY THE/ NAME
OF/ RIDGEWAY.*
Reference: Guillim, 216;
Bolton, 139.
Shape: hatchment; 18⅛″ sq.
Materials: silk and metallic
threads on black silk.
Pattern: Gore.
School: attributed to Eleanor
Druitt.
Private collection.

ROSS c.1768
Reference: Guillim, 182;
Bolton 142.
Shape: hatchment; 18″ sq.
Materials: silk and metallic
threads with some raised
work on black silk;
technique similar to
GRANT arms.
Pattern: Gore.
Maker: attributed to Eliza-
beth Ross (1751–1831),
only child of Alexander

Ross and Elizabeth Duguild of Falmouth, Maine. Married 1769 William Tyng (1737–1807). The arms, long thought to be those of Tyng, descended to the heirs of their adopted daughter, Eliza Heddle (c.1775–1837) who married 1801 the Reverend Timothy Hilliard (1776–1842). John Singleton Copley's portrait of Elizabeth Ross, c.1767, is in the M. and M. Karolik Collection, MFA.
School: possibly the Misses Cuming.
HD, 58-234.

SALTER & BRYAN c.1742–1748
Reference: Guillim, 67, 366.
Shape: vertical rectangle.
Materials: silk and metallic threads on black silk.
Maker: Mary Salter (1726–1755), daughter of William Salter (1696–1753) and Jerusha Bryan (1697–1769) of Boston. Mary's sampler saying *Boston is my dwelling place* was dated 1735. She married 1749 Henry Quincy (1727–1780) whose sister Dorothy married John Hancock.
Illustrated: Earle, *Home Life in Colonial Days* (1898), opp. 266.
Owner unknown.

SALTONSTALL, WINTHROP, DUDLEY, & ROSWELL
Reference: SALTONSTALL: Gore Roll, 24; WINTHROP: Gore Roll, 1, 10, 41; DUDLEY: Gore Roll, 60, 72;

ROSWELL: Gore Roll, 82.
Shape: hatchment; 19¼″ sq.
Materials: silk and metallic threads on black silk.
Pattern: Gore.
Maker: Henrietta Saltonstall (b.1750), daughter of General Gurdon Saltonstall (1708–1785) and Rebecca Winthrop (1713–1776) of New London, Conn. Married 1772 John Still Miller (1746–1824).
Illustrated: *Journal of the New Haven Colony Historical Society* 7, no. 4 (Dec. 1958): cover.
New Haven Colony Historical Society, 1977.310.

SALTONSTALL, WINTHROP, DUDLEY, & ROSWELL
Nearly identical to the above; dimensions: 18⅜″ sq.
Maker: one of the daughters of General Gurdon Saltonstall and a sister of Henrietta, probably Mary (b.1744) or Martha (b.1748). Descended in the family of their brother Winthrop Saltonstall (b.1737) to the donor, Miss Ella Winthrop Saltonstall (b.1876).
MFA, 43.75.

SARGENT & COIT (QUOYS) 1745
Reference: Gore Roll, 5, 13, 31; Burke, 834.
Illustrated: Fig. 305.
SHM, 726.

SCAMMAN (traditionally)
Inscribed: *THE/ NAME/ SCAMMAN.*
Reference: arms unidentified: a bend ermine

between two eagles. Crest: an eagle.
Shape: hatchment; 21⅛″ sq.
Materials: silk with highly raised metallic work on black silk.
Pattern: Gore.
Maker: Sarah Cutts (1774–1845), daughter of Thomas Cutts (1736–1821) and Elizabeth Scamman (1745–1803) of Saco, Maine. Married 1793 Thomas Gilbert Thornton (1768–1824).
School: Eleanor Druitt.
Illustrated: *ANTIQUES,* October 1946, 242.
Private collection.

SEWALL
Inscribed: *THE/ NAME/ SEWALL.*
Reference: Bolton, 147.
Shape: hatchment; 18½″ sq.
Materials: silk with highly raised gold metallic work on white silk.
Pattern: Gore.
School: attributed to Eleanor Druitt.
Illustrated: *MAD,* April 1989, 11-A.
Mr. and Mrs. Stanley P. Sax.

SIMPKINS & SYMMES
Inscribed: *Simpkins/ And/ Symmes.*
Reference: SIMPKINS unidentified: between two cinquefoils a bend charged with three cross crosslets fitchy overall a quarter ermine. SYMMES: Guillim, 91. Crest: head and shoulders of a Turk.
Shape: vertical rectangle; 20¼″ x 17¼″.
Materials: canvas work in wool and silk; ground worked in blue.
Maker: probably one of the five daughters of Boston

Fig. 305. The arms of Sargent and Coit (or Quoys), 1745. Silk and wool canvas work with a cream-colored ground; 17⅞" square. Inscribed on the motto ribbon *Nathaniel and/ Mary Ellery/ Anno Dom 1745.* Attributed to Mary Ellery (1723–1766), the daughter of Nathaniel Ellery (1683–1761) and his second wife, Ann Sargent (1692–1782) of Gloucester. Her paternal grandmother was Mary Coit. In 1748 Mary married the Reverend John Rogers (c.1719–1782) of Gloucester. Mary's pattern and inscription relate to the work of Katharine Greene (Fig. 66), and her arms are attributed to the school of Susanna Condy.

Sargent House Museum, Gloucester, Massachusetts, 726.

goldsmith William Simpkins (1701–1780) and Elizabeth Symmes (c.1705–1794) who were born between 1726 and 1744.
Illustrated: Swan, *Guide,* 136.
WM, 57.1395.

SOUTHWORTH
Reference: *NEHGR* 97 (1943): 359.
Illustrated: Fig. 64.
Owner unknown.

STARR 1790
Inscribed: *The Arms of/ The Family of/ STARR/ Sarah Starr her Sampler Mark'd This in The Thirteenth year of her Age Dec/ 10 1790.*
Reference: Bolton, 156.
Shape: horizontal rectangle; 16" x 22¼".
Materials: silk on linen.

Maker: Sarah Starr.
MMA, bequest of Barbara Schiff Sinauer, 1984.331.21.

STEDMAN
Reference: Bolton, 156.
Shape: hatchment; 18½" sq.
Materials: wool, silk, and metallic threads on black silk.
Pattern: Gore.
HSON, 963.

STODDARD
Inscribed: *Stoddard.*
Reference: Gore Roll, 28.
Shape: hatchment; 19½" sq.
Materials: silk and metallic threads on black silk with three spangles and one bead.
Pattern: Gore.
Maker: attributed to Esther Stoddard (1738–1816), daughter of John Stoddard (1682–1748) and Pru-

dence Chester (1699–1780) of Northampton, Mass. Unm.
Northampton Historical Society, 17.119.

STODDARD
Reference: Gore Roll, 28.
Shape: hatchment; 19" sq.
Materials: brilliant gold metal covering shield and bordered with silver, surrounded with embroidery in silk and metallic threads. Technique similar to that of GRANT arms.
Pattern: Gore.
HD, 56-538.

THOMAS c.1786
Inscribed: *BY THE/ NAME OF/ THOMAS.*
Reference: Guillim, 96; Bolton, 163.
Shape: hatchment; 18" sq.

Fig. 306. One segment of a loan exhibition of needlework held at the Women's Educational and Industrial Union, 264 Boylston Street, Boston, October 25–30, 1937. It was organized by the Union's needlework committee under the direction of Mrs. Samuel Cabot (Nancy Graves) and consisted of eighteenth-century New England needlework of every description as well as some early English and French embroideries. Fifteen of the arms displayed can be identified. Nine are in the Gore pattern and five are in lozenge shape. Arms and lenders: *left to right, top row*: CUTTS (Mrs. Henry W. Montague); FITCH/HALL (Miss Margaret Cushing); CHEEVER (Miss Amelia Peabody); *second row from top*: MAY/WILLIAMS (Mrs. Henry P. Binney); unknown arms impaling DIX (Mrs. Ernest Tappen); IVES (Mrs. Robert Bancroft); PRESCOTT/LAWRENCE (Groton Historical Society); BARTLETT (lender unknown); *third row from top*: MACKAY (Mrs. M. B. L. Bradford); on stand DAVIS (Glenn Tilley Morse); JONES (Concord Antiquarian Society); TRACY (Miss Esther Jackson); *bottom row*: BROWN and GERRISH (Mrs. Gordon Prince); PICKERING (Mrs. John W. Pickering).

The Women's Educational and Industrial Union; photograph courtesy of the Museum of Fine Arts, Boston.

Materials: silk on black silk.
Pattern: Gore.
Maker: Mary Ann Thomas
(b.1772), daughter of
Boston printer Isaiah
Thomas (1749–1831) and
Mary Dill. Married 1792
James R. Hutchins; 1797
Samuel Mather; 1805, Dr.
Levi Simmons (divorced
Mather and Simmons).
School: probably Deborah
Snow.
Illustrated: Harbeson,
American Needlework
(1938), opp. 103.
MMA, 36.28.

TRACY
Reference: Bolton, 166.
Shape: lozenge hatchment;
18″ x 18″.
Materials: silk, metallic
threads, and spangles on
black silk.
Pattern: Gore.
Illustrated: Fig. 306.
EI, no acc. no.

WALLEY
Reference: Bolton, 173.
Shape: hatchment; 18½″ sq.
Materials: silk and metallic
threads with raised work
on black silk.
Pattern: Gore.
WM, 59.2850.

WENDELL & OLIVER
c.1740
Inscribed: *WEN/DELL AND/
OLIVER.*
Reference: Bolton, 123, 177.
Shape: hatchment; 13″ sq.
Materials: silk and wool
canvas work with paint;
ground worked in black.
Pattern: Thomas Johnston.
Maker: one of the five
daughters of Jacob Wen-
dell (1691–1761) and
Sarah Oliver (1696–1762)
who were born between

1719 and 1726, possibly
Mary (1724–1746), who
married Samuel Sewall
and died childless. It
descended in the family of
their brother, Oliver
Wendell (b.1733) to his
grandson Oliver Wendell
Holmes.
*MFA, bequest of Mrs. Edward
Jackson Holmes, 64.2045.*

WICKHAM
Reference: Bolton, 180.
Shape: hatchment; 18⅛″ sq.
Materials: silk (other embel-
lishments?) on black silk.
Pattern: Gore.
Illustrated: (faintly) Marvin
D. Schwartz, *American
Interiors 1675–1885* (New
York: Brooklyn Museum,
1968), 44.
*The Brooklyn Museum, 44.197-
1 (presently unlocated).*

WILLARD c.1794
Inscribed: *BY THE/ NAME
OF/ WILLARD.*
Reference: Bolton, 180.
Shape: hatchment; 20⅜″ sq.
Materials: silk, metallic
threads, and spangles on
black silk.
Pattern: Gore.
Maker: Mary Willard
(1778–1860), daughter of
Joseph Willard
(1738–1804), President of
Harvard, and Mary Sheafe
(1753–1826). Unm.
SPNEA, 1926.50.

WILLIAMS c.1767
Reference: Guillim, 391.
Shape: hatchment; 19⅝″ x
18⅞″.
Materials: silk, metallic
threads, and beads on
black silk.
Pattern: Gore.
MMA, 1971.82.

WILLIAMS & BELL
c.1784
Reference: WILLIAMS:
Bolton, 181. BELL: Gore
Roll, 99.
Illustrated: Fig. 73.
*Collection of Mr. and Mrs.
George M. Kaufman.*

WRIGHT
c.1790–1800
Inscribed: *BY THE/ NAME
OF/ WRIGHT.*
Reference: arms unidenti-
fied: a chevron between
three leopards' faces.
Crest: a lion rampant
(issuing from a coronet?).
Shape: hatchment.
Materials: silk and metallic
threads on cream-colored
silk.
Illustrated: Christie's Joynt
Collection, January
19–20, 1990, Lot 419.
Owner unknown.

UNKNOWN ARMS
Reference: (silver?) three
(coots?) sable impaling
sable a chevron gold
between three (pine
cones? ears of wheat or
rye?) gold garnished
silver. Crest: a (dove?)
sable holding in its beak
an (olive sprig?) gold.
Shape: vertical rectangle.
Materials: silk and metallic
threads on black silk;
pattern and work very
similar to COBB.
Illustrated: Israel Sack, Inc.,
Brochure no. 22 (Novem-
ber 1, 1972), 21.
Private collection.

Fig. 307. *By The Name of Grafton/ Wrought in/ 1747* inscribed with ink on the motto ribbon; wool and silk on linen; 13″ square. The pattern was evidently drawn by Thomas Johnston or copied from a Johnston painting (see Fig. 63). Attributed to a daughter of William Parker (1703–1791) and Elizabeth Grafton of Portsmouth, probably Zerviah (1728–1750) or perhaps Elizabeth (1734–1814). It descended through their sister Sarah Parker (1746–1837), who married Christopher Toppan (1735–1818) of Hampton, New Hampshire. See the maker's canvas-work hunting scene in *Northeast Auctions*, November 8, 1992, Lot 572.
Collection of Mr. and Mrs. Stanley P. Sax; photograph courtesy of Ronald Bourgeault.

CHECKLIST SUPPLEMENT
Unknown arms and their owners as described in *Bolton's American Armory*, 1927.

BLAYNEY
Owned by Dr. William Cogswell, Haverhill, Mass.

CARY
Owned by Mrs. Robert H. Russell, Boston.

CHARNOCK impaling KING
Maker: Elizabeth Charnock (b.1707), daughter of John Charnock and Mary King of Boston. Married Thomas Lee in 1727.

CHEEVER
Inscribed: *By the name of Cheever/ E C.*
Owned by Mrs. Alexander Whiteside, Boston.

DAWES impaling (MAY?)

Owned in 1924 by Arthur Holland, Concord, Mass.

DOANE impaling RICH
Maker: Hope Doane (1750–1830), daughter of Isaiah Doane and Hope Rich of Cape Cod. Married Samuel Savage.

DUNCAN
Maker: Isabella Duncan, daughter of Mrs. Isabella Caldwell Duncan.
Owned by Mrs. Richard Morgan, Plymouth, Mass. (Isabella's canvas-work picture and her portrait by Joseph Badger are in the MFA.)

ELLIS
Maker: Elizabeth Ellis

(b.1732), daughter of Dr. Edward Ellis of Boston.
Owned by Henry W. Montague, Boston (unframed, on table in Fig. 306).

FORBES
Maker: Mary Forbes Coffin (b.1774); married Henry Phelps, 1795.
Owned by Mrs. Charles C. Goodwin, Lexington, Mass.

SELBY
Sampler, 1678.
Owned by Mrs. Eugene Hale, Ellsworth, Maine.

WILLIAMSON
Embroidery 11¾″ x 9″.
Owned by Mrs. Henry H. Edes, Cambridge, Mass.

Appendix II

INSTITUTIONS

AARFAC	The Abby Aldrich Rockefeller Folk Art Center, Williamsburg, Virginia.
AAS	American Antiquarian Society, Worcester, Massachusetts.
CCHS	Chester County Historical Society, West Chester, Pennsylvania.
C-H	Cooper-Hewitt, National Museum of Design, Smithsonian Institution, New York, New York.
CHS	The Connecticut Historical Society, Hartford, Connecticut.
CSL	Connecticut State Library, Hartford, Connecticut.
DAPC	Decorative Arts Photographic Collection, Winterthur Museum, Winterthur, Delaware.
DAR	Daughters of the American Revolution Museum, Washington, D.C.
EI	Essex Institute, Salem, Massachusetts.
HSP	Historical Society of Pennsylvania, Philadelphia, Pennsylvania.
MESDA	Museum of Early Southern Decorative Arts, Winston-Salem, North Carolina.
MFA	Museum of Fine Arts, Boston—Boston, Massachusetts.
MHS	Massachusetts Historical Society, Boston, Massachusetts.
MMA	Metropolitan Museum of Art, New York, New York.
NHHS	New Hampshire Historical Society, Concord, New Hampshire.
NYHS	New-York Historical Society, New York, New York.
PMA	Philadelphia Museum of Art, Philadelphia, Pennsylvania.

RIHS   Rhode Island Historical Society, Providence, Rhode Island.
SPNEA   Society for the Preservation of New England Antiquities,
                        Boston, Massachusetts.

PUBLICATIONS

Allen, *Family Record*   Allen, Gloria Seaman. *Family Record: Genealogical Watercolors
                        and Needlework*. Washington, D.C.: DAR Museum, 1989.

ANTIQUES   *The Magazine ANTIQUES*. New York: Brant Publications.

A&AW   *Antiques And The Arts Weekly*. Newtown, Conn.: The Bee
                        Publishing Company.

Ashton   Ashton, Leigh. *Samplers, Selected and Described*. London &
                        Boston: The Medici Society, 1926.

B&C   Bolton, Ethel Stanwood and Eva Johnston Coe. *American
                        Samplers*. Boston: Massachusetts Society of the Colonial
                        Dames of America, 1921.

The Clarion   *The Clarion, America's Folk Art Magazine* (The Museum of
                        American Folk Art quarterly). New York: The Museum
                        of American Folk Art. Renamed *Folk Art*, fall 1992.

Colby   Colby, Averil. *Samplers*. London: B. T. Batsford, 1964.

Edmonds   Edmonds, Mary Jaene. *Samplers & Samplermakers*. New
                        York: Rizzoli/Los Angeles County Museum of Art, 1991.

EIHC   *Essex Institute Historical Collections* (Essex Institute quarterly).
                        Salem, Mass.: Essex Institute.

Fawdry and Brown   Fawdry, Marguerite and Deborah Brown. *The Book of Sam
                        plers*. New York: St. Martin's Press, 1980.

Harbeson   Harbeson, Georgiana Brown. *American Needlework*. New
                        York: Coward-McCann, 1938.

Huish   Huish, Marcus B. *Samplers and Tapestry Embroideries*. 2nd
                        ed. London: Longmans, Green, and Co., 1913.

IGI   *International Genealogical Index of the Church of Jesus Christ of
                        the Latter Day Saints*. Salt Lake City, Utah.

King   King, Donald. *Samplers*. London: Her Majesty's Stationery
                        Office, 1960.

Krueger, *Gallery*   Krueger, Glee F. *A Gallery of American Samplers: The
                        Theodore H. Kapnek Collection*. Exhibition catalogue. New
                        York: E. P. Dutton in association with the Museum of
                        American Folk Art, 1978.

Krueger, *New England* Krueger, Glee. *New England Samplers to 1840*. Sturbridge,
                        Mass.: Old Sturbridge Village, 1978.

MAD   *Maine Antique Digest* (a monthly newspaper). Waldoboro,
                        Maine: Maine Antique Digest, Inc.

NEHGR *The New England Historical and Genealogical Register* (New England Historic Genealogical Society quarterly). Boston, Mass.

NYGBR *The New York Genealogical and Biographical Record* (The New York Genealogical and Biographical Society quarterly). New York.

PGM *The Pennsylvania Genealogical Magazine* (The Genealogical Society of Pennsylvania biannual). Philadelphia. Issues irregular between 1895 and 1948 and known as *Publications of the Genealogical Society of Pennsylvania.*

PMHB *The Pennsylvania Magazine of History and Biography* (The Historical Society of Pennsylvania quarterly). Philadelphia.

Ring, *Treasures* Ring, Betty. *American Needlework Treasures: Samplers and Silk Embroideries from the Collection of Betty Ring*. New York: E. P. Dutton in association with the Museum of American Folk Art, 1987.

Ring, *Virtue* Ring, Betty. *Let Virtue Be a Guide to Thee: Needlework in the Education of Rhode Island Women, 1730–1830*. Exhibition catalogue. Providence: The Rhode Island Historical Society, 1983.

Schiffer Schiffer, Margaret B. *Historical Needlework of Pennsylvania*. New York: Charles Scribner's Sons, 1968.

Swain Swain, Margaret H. *Historical Needlework: A Study of Influences in Scotland and Northern England*. London: Barrie & Jenkins, 1970.

Swan, *Guide* Swan, Susan Burrows. *Winterthur Guide to American Needlework*. A Winterthur Book/Rutledge Books. New York: Crown Publishers, Inc., 1976.

Swan, *Plain & Fancy* Swan, Susan Burrows. *Plain & Fancy: American Women and Their Needlework, 1700–1850*. New York: Holt, Rinehart and Winston, 1977.

AUCTION HOUSES

Christie's Christie, Manson & Woods International, Inc., New York.
Christie's East A division of Christie, Manson & Woods, Inc., New York.
PB Parke-Bernet Galleries, Inc., New York.
Skinner Skinner, Inc., Bolton, Massachusetts.
Sotheby's Sotheby's, New York.
SPB Sotheby Parke Bernet Inc., New York.

All auction house publications cited are for Americana sales.

Back endpapers:

Receipts for Schooling

Elizabeth Murray to Colonel Jonathan Trumbull, July 2, 1754 (third page). See Fig. 52.
   Trumbull Papers, Connecticut Historical Society.

Eleanor Druitt to Isaac Smith, Boston, March 8, 1773.
   Smith-Carter Papers, Massachusetts Historical Society.

Judith Foster Saunders and Clementina Beach to Thomas Gilbert Thornton upon the enrollment
   of Ann Thornton, May 28, 1822. Ann was a niece of Elizabeth Cutts (Fig. 71) and the
   daughter of Sarah Cutts Thornton. See arms checklist (Appendix I) for SCAMMAN.
   Thomas G. Thornton Papers (Mss98/II/B1/4), The New England Historic Genealogical Society.

Jannette Day to Richard Darby (Derby), Boston, October 31, 1763. See Fig. 58.
   Derby Family Papers (Mss37/B15/F4), Essex Institute.

Mary Balch to the Reverend Enos Hitchcock, January 1800.
   Hitchcock Papers (RHi/X3/6819), Rhode Island Historical Society.

Brought over ..... 52..12..3

Scholling ↓ qr 1 month 6..5..—

½ ⅛ yd black sattin

@ 4..10 ... — — — — — — 2..16..3

                    £61..13..6

Miss has paid for

a crown & flower ..... 1..12..—

                    £60..1..6

Received the above
        in full Eliz Murray

Mr Smith to Eleanor Druitt Dr

1773

To one Quarter Instruction of Miss Smith at
~ Needle work ended the 27th October Last — £ ..18..—
To Drawing — — — — — — — — ..2..8
                                £1..—..8

Received the Contents of the above Acct and in full of all
Demands this 8th day of March 1773

                            Eleanor Druitt

Received
account of

ALSO BY BETTY RING

Let Virtue Be a Guide to Thee

American Needlework Treasures

Needlework: An Historical Survey

Girlhood Embroidery

GIRLHOOD EMBROIDERY

American Samplers & Pictorial Needlework 1650–1850

VOLUME II

Betty Ring

ALFRED A. KNOPF   NEW YORK

1993

THIS IS A BORZOI BOOK
PUBLISHED BY ALFRED A. KNOPF, INC.

Library of Congress Cataloging-in-Publication Data

Ring, Betty.

  Girlhood embroidery : American samplers and pictorial needlework, 1650–1850 / Betty Ring. — 1st ed.

    p.   cm.

  Includes Bibliographical References and Index.

  ISBN 0-394-55009-9

  1. Samplers—United States.   2. Embroidery—United States.   I. Title.

NK9112.R57   1993

746.3973—dc20

93-6735
CIP

Manufactured in the United States of America
First Edition

Volume II: Cover onlay. Anonymous memorial dedicated to George Washington, Philadelphia, c.1800–1805. Silk, paint, and ink on silk; 21½″ x 27⅝″. Attributed to the School of Samuel and Elizabeth Folwell. See Figure 409.
National Museum of American History, Smithsonian Institution, gift of Eleanor and Mabel Alstyne.

Frontispiece. *Maria Boswell/ Aged 12 years the'/ 4ᵗʰ of April/ 1812/ Washington City Augˢᵗ th' 18ᵗʰ 1812.* Silk and chenille on linsey-woolsey; 18″ x 18″. Maria Boswell (1800–1868) was the daughter of Washington carpenter Clement Boswell and Eleanor Collard. About 1817 she married an unidentified Mr. Boswell.
Private collection.

Contents

Girlhood Embroidery

QUAKER SAMPLERS
IN AMERICA

Reason's whole pleasure, all the joys of sense,
Lie in three words, health, peace, and competence.
But health consists with temperance alone;
And peace, oh, virtue! peace is all thy own.[1]

T HE E UROPEANS who came to the American colonies, and later to the United States, represented different religious persuasions, but their needlework styles generally reflected the national traditions of their homelands. It was only in the Federal period that the Religious Society of Friends introduced sampler motifs that were purely their own, and these were maintained over a wide area throughout the last forty years of the schoolgirl needlework era. Therefore, the most typical Quaker styles cannot be assigned to a specific state. In keeping with their number, the Quakers' strongest impact was definitely in the Delaware Valley, but they also developed distinctive subgroups in New York, and their plain alphabet and characteristic motifs were being worked from Massachusetts to Virginia.

To some degree, their preference in patterns reflected the Society's theology, which arose in England along with Puritanism during the early seventeenth century. The ideology of George Fox (1624–1691), founder of the Society of Friends, favored plainness, pacifism, and confidence in God-given inspiration (or the inward light) independent of clergy or ceremonious rituals.[2] In 1672, Fox visited the American colonies where a number of Quakers had sought refuge from persecution in England. Except in Rhode Island, however, they continued to meet with intolerance. Four Friends were hanged on Boston Common in 1661, and one

Fig. 308. *Martha M. Bishop/ 1824.* Silk on linen; 25½" x 21¼". Martha's work is characteristic of the large, decorative samplers made by Quaker girls of the Delaware Valley during the 1820s and 1830s. Within a typical Burlington County, New Jersey, border, she stitched a recognizable rendition of the Friends' Westtown Boarding School in Chester County, Pennsylvania. Her unknown schoolmistress was probably a former Westtown student. Her unusual deer were worked with Westtown School in 1806 (B&C Pl. XCIII). Martha Moore Bishop (1813–1891) was the ninth child of Timothy Bishop (1765–1853) and Sarah Fenimore (1771–1860). Her father was a farmer of Willingboro Township, Burlington County, New Jersey. Martha died unmarried.
Author's collection.

---

1. From the sampler of *RACHEL JAMES/ 1811/ NORTH-SCHOOL*, Philadelphia (Krueger, *Gallery*, 47). Rachel (1802–1825) was the daughter of John James and Mary Drinker, who belonged to the Northern District Monthly Meeting, which administered the North School. Rachel married William J. Yardley three months before her death.
2. The term *inner light* was not used by seventeenth- and eighteenth-century Friends as it is today. See Frost, *The Quaker Family in Colonial America* (1973), 15.

Fig. 309. Title page of the third edition of John Woolman's *A First Book for Children*, c.1774. First published in Philadelphia in 1768. Original size: 4¾" x 3¹⁵⁄₁₆". This is the best available photograph (with wide margins cropped) of the only known copy of Woolman's book. The resemblance of its bold Roman alphabet to the many sampler renditions is conspicuous.
Library of the Religious Society of Friends, London.

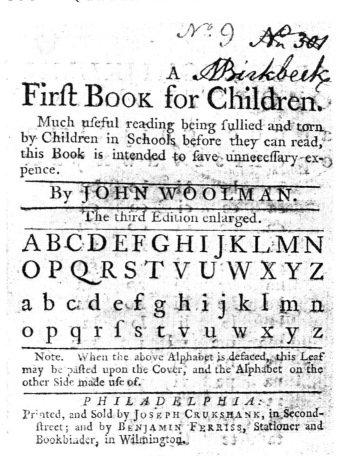

died of cruel treatment in Virginia. But within a few years they would have a major stronghold in the Delaware Valley, where the Quaker Proprietor, William Penn, established his City of Brotherly Love in 1682. He considered his colony of Pennsylvania a "Holy Experiment" with religious tolerance as its keystone.

Before Penn's arrival, Newport, Rhode Island, had been the dominant Quaker settlement, and during the colonial period there were six Yearly Meetings in America: New England, New York, Philadelphia, Maryland, Virginia, and South Carolina. Yet only in Philadelphia was there a sufficient concentration of Quakers to support the establishment of an enduring school at an early date. The Philadelphia Yearly Meeting established a Latin School under a charter from the Proprietor in 1689, which still exists as the William Penn Charter School.[3] During the eighteenth century, a network of Friends' schools sprang forth in Philadelphia and occasionally they were blessed with exceptional teachers. Notable among these was Francis D. Pastorius whose primer of 1698 was the only textbook by an American Quaker until John Woolman's *First Book for Children* appeared in 1768 (Fig.

---

3. The earliest-known Philadelphia schoolmistress was Olive Songhurst, teaching at the Friends' School in 1701. The second-oldest long-lasting Friends' school within the Philadelphia Yearly Meeting was the Byberry School, which existed from 1720 or earlier until 1918. (Woody, *Early Quaker Education in Pennsylvania* [1920], 54, 74; see also *Friends Intelligencer,* June 24, 1918. This Hicksite weekly was published in Philadelphia, 1844–1965.)

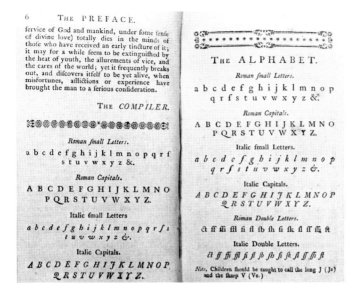

Fig. 310. Alphabets in the second edition of *The Pennsylvania Spelling-Book* compiled by Anthony Benezet, Philadelphia, 1779. Pages 6½″ x 3¾″. While the *U* and *J* were often omitted from samplers and were generally interchangeable with the *V* and *I* in the eighteenth century, early textbooks consistently included the full alphabet. This same Roman alphabet appears in a George Fox spelling book that was reprinted in Philadelphia in 1702 (Library Company of Philadelphia).
Friends Historical Library of Swarthmore College, Swarthmore, Pennsylvania.

Fig. 311. Sampler letters as they appear in the sixth edition (1801) of *The Pennsylvania Spelling-Book* compiled by Anthony Benezet. Pages 6½″ x 3¾″. In the uppercase alphabet, three versions of the letter *I* are included and two versions of the letter *U*, but no recognizable *J*. In the lowercase alphabet the *J* is also omitted. Absence of the letter *J* and use of a long *s* occasionally occur on samplers well into the nineteenth century. Therefore, on undated work, this should not be regarded as proof of eighteenth-century origin. Notice the small crown occasionally seen on samplers.
Friends Historical Library of Swarthmore College, Swarthmore, Pennsylvania.

309). More beneficial for girls was the career of the compassionate schoolmaster Anthony Benezet (1713–1784) who devoted himself to an advanced girls' school almost continuously from 1754 until 1782.[4] His school, kept only in the mornings, was administered by the Society of Friends, and prominent Quaker families were represented by students such as Ann Emlen, Sally Wister, and Deborah Norris. He also taught Rebecca Jones, who was destined to become the best-known Quakeress in early America. To facilitate his labors, Benezet wrote *A First Book for Children* and *The Pennsylvania Spelling-Book,* which included the standard Roman alphabet and also a sampler alphabet (Figs. 310, 311). The girls in his school were probably taught needlework in the afternoon, and Ann Marsh was surely one of their teachers (Figs. 353, 354).

Although the Friends recognized the importance of education for both boys and girls, they distrusted institutions of higher learning. Consequently no young college graduates were available to teach their children, as they were in New England, and in both colonial and Federal America, a lack of qualified Quaker

---

4. Woody (1920), 217. Benezet undertook the girls' school after twelve years of teaching at the William Penn Charter School. Ill health forced his retirement from 1755 to 1757 and 1766 to 1767 (Brookes, *Friend Anthony Benezet* [1937], 37–45).

Fig. 312. *Margaret Boxall/ Ackworth/ School/ 1799.* Silk on linen; 10″ x 10½″. Inscribed on a paper backing: "Such girls as choose to have one of these Darns, work them in play hours . . . as it is thought it would take up too much Time to do them in School, having other Pieces to work, as well as their own and the Household linen to make and mend." Margaret Boxall from Godalming was number 1469 at the Ackworth School. She entered in 1793 and departed in 1799.
Ackworth School, Yorkshire, England.

teachers hindered their efforts to maintain schools taught by members of their faith. The Quaker approach to education was also different. Quakers did not train their children to adjust themselves to society, but to stand apart from it when conscience required.[5] Basic reading, writing, and cyphering were considered desirable but not at the risk of corrupting specific restrictions concerning dress, speech, and silence. Therefore, during their early years in America, only the larger Quaker settlements were able to offer adequate education under the jurisdiction of Friends, and parents were cautioned to teach their children at home rather than expose them to the influence of outsiders. This may explain the lack of recognizable Quaker samplers from the eighteenth century, but more likely no policy concerning needlework instruction or approved patterns had been formulated.

Many of the most beautiful samplers and pictorial embroideries that survive from colonial Philadelphia were worked by Quaker girls, and certainly under Quaker instruction, but they conform to the mainstream of elegant English fashion. There is no evidence that the Friends' policy of plainness was applied to exercises in decorative needlework, and pieces in their original period frames reveal that they were proudly displayed.

In the absence of documentation, it may be assumed from surviving samplers that efforts toward conformity in Quaker samplers followed the founding of the Ackworth School in 1779.[6] This large boarding school for boys and girls in York-

---

5. Howard H. Brinton, *Quaker Education in Theory and Practice* (Wallingford, Pa.: Pendle Hill, 1940), 69.
6. English Quakers had boarding schools in the seventeenth century. Schools for girls were in Warrington and Brighton in 1671, and many others were coeducational. (Gardiner, *English Girlhood at School* [1929], 223–4.)

Fig. 313. *YORK SCHOOL/ Hannah Lamb 1791.* Silk on wool; 11″ x 12½″. Hannah worked six flawless alphabets within an oval, a pattern that would be worked at the Westtown School in Pennsylvania by 1800 (Krueger, *Gallery*, Fig. 41). Hannah Lamb lived in London. She was number 95 at Esther Tuke's York School, which she entered in 1790.

The Mount School, York, England, N 10.

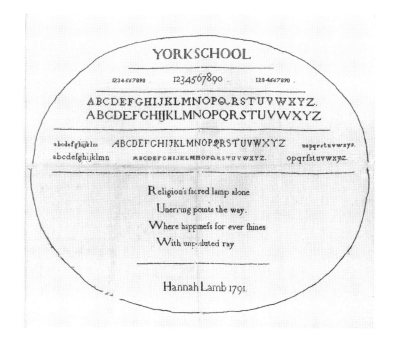

shire, England, was administered by the London Yearly Meeting, and it was intended primarily for the underprivileged children of the Society. The emphasis placed on teaching practical stitchery was commonplace at all girls' schools, but at Ackworth even a difficult darning sampler was considered a special diversion (Fig. 312). Whether worked during class or play hours, a number of late-eighteenth-century samplers survive from the Ackworth School, and they display the three most recognizable traits that characterize English and American Quaker samplers of the early nineteenth century.

Similar patterns also survive from the girls' boarding school in York, England (Fig. 313), which was independently established by Esther Tuke and a committee of Quaker women in 1785; it continued for twenty-nine years.[7] Among Friends' schools in England, this school became exemplary because of the lofty aims and lovable personality of its foundress. While a "guarded education" was stressed in the school's prospectus, the girls were taught "accomplishments," such as French and elegant penmanship; they also learned geography by working "wonderful maps" with silk and chenille upon white satin.[8] Philadelphia's former teacher and traveling minister, Rebecca Jones, visited York and observed that "Friends here seem more attentive to their daughters' education than in some parts of our country."[9]

After four years in England, Rebecca Jones returned to Philadelphia in 1788, just as the rise of the academies was about to begin in the United States. Zeal for education was also growing in Quaker communities, and schools under the juris-

---

7. Sturge and Clark, *The Mount School, York, 1785–1814, 1831–1931* (1931), 3–6.
8. Ibid., 11.
9. Ibid., 12.

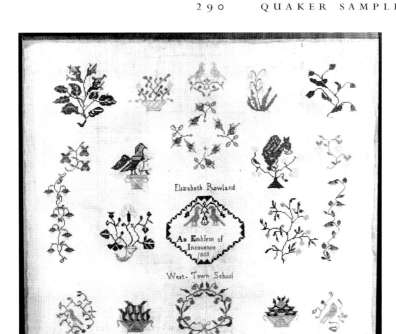

Fig. 314. *Elizabeth Rowland/ An Emblem of/ Innocence/ 1803/ West-Town School.* Silk on linen; 13⅞" x 13¼". Elizabeth worked a typical Quaker sampler of the Delaware Valley. Many of the same motifs appear on English Quaker work and were also worked as far south as Virginia (*ANTIQUES*, February 1974, 360, Fig. 7). Elizabeth Rowland (b.1789) of Camden, Delaware, entered Westtown School at the age of fourteen in January 1800. She re-entered in April 1803 and October 1807. In 1803, she also worked an alphabet sampler and an "Extract" piece, similar to Figures 428 and 429.
Chester County Historical Society, NS 81.

diction of the monthly meetings became far more commonplace. Suddenly, between 1800 and 1803, almost identical alphabets and designs were being worked at Quaker schools in widely divided places. No specific records or surviving patterns explain how these consistent styles were introduced or maintained. There was, however, much travel between Quaker communities, and it is evident that America's most prominent Quakers were acquainted with each other.

The most pervasive and easily recognizable evidence of Quaker instruction is bold renditions of the Roman alphabet in both uppercase and lowercase forms, and frequently with the inclusion of ligatures. This exceedingly legible alphabet was published in schoolbooks during the seventeenth century and throughout the eighteenth century, but at present, Ackworth School seems to have been the first place where it was stitched on samplers. It is seldom found on American samplers worked before 1800, and thereafter it appears to have been worked only under Quaker instruction or influence. The majority of non-Quaker samplers have lettering worked in the style printed in the Benezet book of 1801 (Fig. 311), and this alphabet often appears on Quaker samplers in combination with the Roman alphabet. Almost the same alphabet as Benezet's, and equally difficult to read in embroidery, it was printed in George Fisher's *The Instructor: or, Young*

A Bunch of Pinks

Rose Bud

Johnny jump up

Cornucopiæ

Fig. 315. *ACKWORTH/ SCHOOL/ 1790/ M Wigham.* Silk on linen; 12″ x 13″. Mary Wigham's work is the earliest sampler with geometric motifs in the collection of the Ackworth School. Mary lived in Pontefract. She entered the school in 1788 and left in 1791.
Ackworth School, Yorkshire, England.

Man's Best Companion and was included specifically for guidance "in marking linen." This book was frequently reprinted from the mid-eighteenth century until the early nineteenth century in both Britain and America.[10]

The most commonly found Quaker motifs are cross-stitched sprays or sprigs of flowers, particularly a rose, rosebuds, lilies of the valley, an iris, bunches of Indian pinks, and Johnny-jump-ups as reproduced below;[11] also a swan, a squirrel, a bird, a circular wreath, and paired doves within saw-toothed octagons that enclose the inscription *An Emblem of Innocence* or *An Emblem of Love* (Fig. 314). The Quaker preference for the legible Roman alphabet is in keeping with their quest for plainness, and the simple cross-stitched motifs bespeak peace and serenity.

---

10. Krueger, *New England,* 8, 9, and Figs. 4, 5.
11. Reproduced by Alison Cadbury Senter from a sampler signed *Ann D C Elkinton Philadelphia 1818* and rare for its worked descriptions of the floral motifs (private collection).

A Jessamine   A French Pink   Lily of the Valley   A Rose

Fig. 316. Sampler initialed *MW* and *L/W/G, 1775.* Wool and silk on linen; 12″ x 7¾″. Here is the earliest known instance of Quaker geometric motifs on a sampler with a reliable American provenance. It descended in a Chester County family, with a history of having been worked in Philadelphia by Lydia Walter, the great, great grandmother of the donor. *Daughters of the American Revolution Museum, Washington, D.C., gift of Josephine M. Cathcart, 1935, 2671.*

They are often combined, however, with bold geometric medallions or half medallions, which also designate unmistakable Quaker instruction. Yet neither the origin, the significance, nor the enduring Quaker preference for these motifs has been explained. They were used at the Ackworth School by the 1790s (Fig. 315), and it would seem that they spread from there to America.

Recently, however, two unmistakable half medallions have been found on a Philadelphia girl's sampler of 1775 (Fig. 316). A related piece of unknown origin is owned in Nantucket,[12] and a New Jersey girl's work of 1788 has many similar designs (Fig. 317). Early snowflake designs on eighteenth-century Friesland samplers have been considered a possible source from which these patterns evolved.[13] They may have been taken to England by Quakers who traveled on the Continent, and brought to America at about the same time, but why Quakers chose these motifs and clung to them remains a mystery. Though absent from clothing and

---

12. Signed *MN 1775* (Nantucket Historical Association, 18D).
13. For Frisian motifs, see Meulenbelt-Nieuwburg, *Embroidery Motifs from Old Dutch Samplers* (1974), 162–70.

Fig. 317. *Sybil Tatums 1788.*
Wool and silk on linen;
25¾" x 26". At present no
other embroidery like Sybil
Tatum's is known. It is
unusual for its large size as
well as its use of geometric
half medallions in 1788.
Many of its flower motifs
are known on Delaware
Valley samplers of this
period. Under careful
examination it appears to be
genuine and unaltered, and
its seven-year-old maker left
it unfinished. Sybil Tatum
(August 20, 1781–1821) was
born in Woodbury, New
Jersey. She was the daughter
of John Tatum and his
second wife, Elizabeth
Cooper (1751–1814). Her
embroidery descended
directly to her great granddaughter, Sybil Tatum Jones
(d. 1946), with her mother's
sampler of 1763 and her
daughter's sampler of 1816.
They were all Quakers.
*Gloucester County Historical
Society, Woodbury, New Jersey,
37.1886.*

household textiles, they were favored in Quaker sampler embroidery for more than thirty years.[14]

The majority of American darning samplers also reflect Quaker instruction. Elaborate darning samplers embellished with floral bouquets and various insignia were popular in England and on the Continent,[15] but they were virtually unknown in America. Instead, modest and practical pieces related to early Ackworth examples (Fig. 312) survive in considerable numbers, particularly from the Delaware Valley (Figs. 425, 546).

---

14. Although Quaker geometric motifs are seldom found in New England, a sampler with the Roman alphabet and one definite Quaker geometric motif was worked by Clara Gillet in 1810, and it names *Colchester Ct* (Governor Jonathan Trumbull House, Lebanon, Connecticut).

15. For a Dutch darning sampler of 1699 and many later ones, see Schipper-van Lottum, *Over Merklappen Gesproken* (1980), 241–6.

Fig. 318. *Elizabeth Lamb her Work/ Aged 11 Years 1746*. Silk and metallic thread on linen; 18″ x 17¼″. Three of Elizabeth's Biblical scenes represent passages from Genesis: Adam and Eve, the Sacrifice of Isaac (center right), and Jacob's ladder (lower right). At top left is the Sower (Matt. 13) and at lower left Christ rests beside a cormorant as he prepares to feed barley-loaves and fish to the multitude (John 6). (The Sacrifice of Isaac and episodes from the New Testament were identified by textile conservator Dorothy McCoach.) The same rendition of Adam and Eve persisted on New York samplers throughout the sampler-making era, and Christ and Jacob's ladder were worked in the lower corners of related pieces during the entire eighteenth century (Fig. 324). It is highly probable that these simplified Biblical pictures were derived from scriptural tiles, from which the Dutch are said to have taught their children the parables. Elizabeth Lamb (1735–1804) was the daughter of noted New York instrument maker Anthony Lamb (1698–1784) and Cornelia Ham. Elizabeth married Joseph Willson (b.1731) in 1754 and had two daughters. In 1761 she married Loyalist Samuel Hallett (b.1726) in New York's Trinity Church, and they moved to St. John, New Brunswick, in 1789. Elizabeth and Samuel had ten adult children when he wrote his will in 1795.

The New Brunswick Museum, St. John, New Brunswick, 63.100c.

NEEDLEWORK OF
NEW YORK

HENRY HUDSON was employed by the Dutch East India Company in 1609 when he discovered the great river that now bears his name. Thereafter, the Dutch laid claim to the vast but vaguely defined territory between the Connecticut and Delaware rivers, calling it the province of New Netherland. In an effort to duplicate the great financial success of the East India Company in the Orient, the Dutch West India Company undertook the settlement of this region. In 1624 they sailed up the Hudson River and established Fort Orange, which later became Albany. By 1626, about 270 colonists were located on the East River near the lower tip of Manhattan Island. They clustered their homes around Fort New Amsterdam, which soon became the company's major stronghold in the province. However, despite a thriving business in furs, the company did not prosper, nor were the inhabitants happy with its paternalistic policies in governing the colony.

In 1647, Peter Stuyvesant, the company's sixth and last director general, arrived in New Amsterdam. He adamantly opposed all immigration except by members of the Dutch Reformed Church, but the company finally overruled him in its eagerness to increase the size of New Amsterdam. The colony was also plagued by vicious Indian attacks between 1655 and 1664, and the declining fortunes of the West India Company were approaching bankruptcy. It is little wonder that Stuyvesant had no course but surrender when an English squadron seized the city in August of 1664, and on August 29, it was decreed that the city would henceforth be known as New York.

This abrupt change was accepted with remarkable equanimity by the inhabitants, who already included a number of Englishmen, and their community of about 1,500 people grew to nearly 5,000 by the 1690s. In 1692, the Englishman, and later the mayor, Charles Lodwick lamented that "Our chiefest unhappiness here is too great a mixture of nations, and English the least part. The French Protestants have in the late king's reign resorted hither in great numbers proportionably to the other nations' inhabitants. The Dutch are generally the most frugal and laborious, and consequently the richest, whereas most of the English are the contrary."[1] Nevertheless, despite much incompetency in English rule, the city became increasingly cosmopolitan and prosperous during the eighteenth century, and before the Revolution New York's population of 20,000 people surpassed that of Boston.[2] Therefore, its small volume of colonial needlework is particularly baffling.

The working of samplers at school was a deeply rooted custom in the Netherlands by the beginning of the seventeenth century, just as it was in England, and the Dutch were devoted to the education of girls as well as boys. It is therefore surprising that no samplers made by either Dutch or English girls of New York are known to have survived from the seventeenth century, especially since this commercially motivated colony was populated by a goodly number of prosperous people. Colonial New York samplers of the eighteenth century are also decidedly rare,[3] and even from later years, only six groups of easily recognized New York embroideries have been identified.[4] Quite inexplicably, many nineteenth-century samplers that name New York could otherwise be mistaken for English pieces, and while a number of New York samplers name a school or an instructress, they have not yet developed into significant groups.

The Biblical Samplers of
Colonial and Federal New York

Throughout most of this century, no characteristic group of colonial New York samplers was known. Finally, in 1983, it became evident that early Biblical samplers in six different collections were very similar (Figs. 318–321), and that they shared motifs with later samplers that named *New York* (Figs. 322, 323, 324). The six closely related examples date from 1746 to 1768, and all but one (Fig. 319) consist of four to six Biblical scenes worked within a deeply arcaded, tripartite border. They are solidly worked over the entire ground, mostly in cross stitches,

---

1. Patterson, *The City of New York* (1978), 37.

2. Ibid., 45.

3. The B&C compilation of 938 eighteenth-century samplers included a likely place of origin for 509 pieces, but only 18 were assigned to New York, with 5 from the colonial period (Sally Sacket's Westfield, Massachusetts, sampler, Fig. 162, was mistakenly placed in Long Island). Interesting and possibly related samplers were worked by Ealli Crygier in 1734 (Krueger, *Gallery*, Fig. 14) and Margaret Grant in 1737 (C-H). For other colonial New York needlework, see Swan, *Guide*, Figs. 31, 32.

4. In addition to the five forms illustrated here, a recognizable group of memorials was made in the 1820s, probably in New York City (Ring, *Treasures*, Fig. 155; Harbeson, Fig. 4, opp. 82; also, Schorsch, *Mourning Becomes America* [1976], Pl. 7/136). For a potential group, see Mary Green's silk embroidery in the *Worcester Art Museum Journal* 5 (1981–82): 24–31; and Sotheby's Sale 6149, February 1, 1991, Lot 747.

Fig. 319. *ELIZABETH KORTRIGHT S/ WORK IN/ THE YEA/R OF OVR/ LORD 1757 AG.* Silk on linen; 9″ x 9⅛″. Elizabeth's small sampler has lost half of its border and was left unfinished, for only part of the ground is solidly worked. She may have removed the numerals of her age and half of the word *AGED.* Nevertheless, her modest work provides a key to the origin of the Adam and Eve samplers. In 1758, Elizabeth was attending a French boarding school in New Rochelle, and she probably worked this sampler there during the previous year. Elizabeth Kortright (b.1745) was youngest of the seven children of New York merchant Cornelius Kortright (1704–1745) and Hester Cannon, who descended from an early Huguenot family of Staten Island. In 1765 Elizabeth married William Ricketts Van Cortland (b.1742) and they had four children. Elizabeth's niece, Elizabeth Kortright, became the wife of James Monroe (fifth President of the United States), and her great niece, Eliza Kortright, made the embroidery in Figure 489. *Historic Hudson Valley, Tarrytown, New York, VC.81.9.*

and four have queen-stitched inner and outer borders. Their compositions and bold, wide borders are unusual for the 1740s, and they appear to have no foreign counterparts. Renditions of their principal motifs are nearly identical, and four examples have the letter *Y* worked backward.[5] It is reasonably certain that these samplers had a common origin.

Shortly after the New York colonial samplers were recognized, an astonishing number of related pieces from the Federal period also appeared, and the Adam and Eve samplers of New York now represent the most enduring sampler style made in America. The motifs of the earliest examples were continued into the nineteenth century with amazing fidelity. In 1833, Judith Van Pelt worked an enormous sampler with Biblical motifs,[6] among them the typical Adam and Eve in tutus with Eve's hair swinging below her uplifted arm, and she also included the quotation *Abraham, Abraham, here am I,* as seen in Figure 323. In addition to the consistency of the major motifs within this group, it is surprising to find that Dutch motifs become increasingly evident in many of the crowded renditions of the late eighteenth and early nineteenth centuries. The fruit tree in the center of the Lamb sampler (Fig. 318) is the most conspicuous Dutch (or German) motif in the early examples, but Adam and Eve stand beneath a decidedly Dutch tree in Figures 323 and 325, and Dutch furniture motifs appear on other examples.[7]

5. Figures 318, 320, 321, and the sampler of Mary DeGrushe, 1765 (Ring, *Treasures,* 30); also, the closely related sampler of Hannah Pritchet, 1777 (SPB Sale 3947, January 26–29, 1977, Lot 815).

6. Staten Island Historical Society, 1033.

7. SPB Sale 4663Y, July 10, 1981, Lot 360. See also Sotheby's Sale 6269, January 25, 1992, Lot 815.

Fig. 320. *ElizaBeth ELmendorPh Her Work Aged 10 Years/ 1766.* Silk and metallic threads on linen; 12½″ x 18⅜″. In a different format, Elizabeth worked five of the scenes and the identical fruit tree that appear in Elizabeth Lamb's sampler (Fig. 318). The closest counterpart to this example was made by Mary DeGrushe in 1765 (Ring, *Treasures,* Fig. 47). Eleven-year-old Ann M. Donnell worked the same vignettes and dated her sampler *ST THE 19 1768,* but she did not include the queen-stitched inner and outer borders or the metallic cloud, and her inscription has no backward letters (private collection). Similar to Ann's sampler in arrangement is the undated work of Magdalen Gombauld, aged ten (*A&AW,*

March 1, 1991, 107). Elizabeth's sampler illustrates a consistent peculiarity of this colonial group: the makers gave as their age the year they were in, rather than the number they had attained. Elizabeth Elmendorph (b. January 24, 1757) was the daughter of Peter Edmund Elmendorph (1715–1765) and Maria Crook (b.1721) of Kingston. Letters of Elizabeth's younger brother, Peter, reveal that she was with him at a school in New York in 1774, but where she studied in 1766 is undetermined. Elizabeth married New York merchant Cornelius Ray (d.1834), and they had eight sons and two daughters but few survived them.
Winterthur Museum, 58.968A.

Fig. 321. *Mary OGilVie her Work AGed 9 Years/ 1768.* Silk and metallic threads on linen; 15⅜″ x 16½″. In the identical manner of Elizabeth Lamb and Elizabeth Elmendorph (Figs. 318, 320), Mary used silver threads for a cloud band at the top of Jacob's ladder, and every leaf on her fruit tree matches Elizabeth Lamb's. Mary Margaret Ogilvie (bapt. February 8, 1760, in Schenectady) was the only daughter of the Anglican minister John Ogilvie (1722–1774) and Catherine Susanna Symes. Her father became the assistant pastor of Trinity Church in New York City in 1764. An engraving of Ogilvie's 1771 portrait by Copley was commissioned by Anthony Lamb, the father of Elizabeth (Fig. 318). On October 17, 1777, Mary Ogilvie was married to Barent Roorbach (b.1745) at Trinity Church. Roorbach was a Loyalist who fought in Canada during the Revolution, but in 1790 they lived in Schenectady, and later in New York City. They had seven children. *Colonial Williamsburg Foundation, Williamsburg, Virginia, G1979.57.*

As in the other American colonies, knowledge of girls' schools of the mid-eighteenth century in New York is also scant. The majority of women who advertised instruction in needlework before 1776 were "lately" from Great Britain. In December of 1731 Martha Gazley offered to "Teacheth the following curious Works, Viz. Artificial Fruit and Flowers, and other Wax-work, Nuns-work, Philligree and Pencil Work upon Muslin, all sorts of Needle-Work, and Raising of Paste, as also to Paint upon Glass, and Transparant for Sconces, with other Works...."[8] She was followed by a series of women who often combined teaching with dressmaking and professional embroidery, but it is unlikely that any of these Englishwomen were responsible for the colonial Adam and Eve samplers, despite their English inscriptions. The closest counterparts to their motifs are found on Dutch and German samplers, although no prototype whatever has been found for their borders.

Circumstantial evidence now indicates that the Biblical samplers originated at one of the French boarding schools for girls in New Rochelle, which were first

---

8. *The New-York Gazette,* December 13/21, 1731.

Fig. 322. *LATICIA TERHUNE HER WORK AGED/ 9 YEARS NEW YORK JULY 24 1773.* Silk on linen; 16¼" x 17½". Along with many of the earlier motifs, Laticia depicted Moses receiving the tablets with the Ten Commandments (Exodus 31:18). The division of the three central motifs supports the likelihood that scriptural tiles were their sources of design. Laticia (Letitia) Terhune (1762–1833) was the daughter of Stephanus Terhune (1730–1784) and his second wife, Letitia Bergen. They lived in New York City until about 1777 and later in New Jersey. Laticia married Jacobus Housman (b.1757) in 1782 and her sampler descended in her family. The discrepancy of her age with the date on her sampler is unexplained. *Mr. and Mrs. Larry Flory.*

described by Helen Evertson Smith in 1900.[9] Since early French samplers are unknown, this might seem unlikely. However, many of the Huguenots who came to New York had previously made their homes in Holland.[10] As mentioned earlier, French Huguenots immigrated to New York in considerable numbers during the seventeenth century, and in 1685 the town of New Rochelle was established in what is now Westchester County. A prominent citizen was the Reverend Pierre Stouppe who served as pastor of New Rochelle's Trinity Church from 1724 until 1760 and also kept a boarding school for boys in his parsonage. Much of his fame rests on the achievements of his best known scholars, for he instructed General Philip Schuyler (1733–1804) and statesman John Jay (1745–1829) in their boyhoods.

The illustrious families of this region were soon sending their daughters as well

---

9. Smith, *Colonial Days and Ways* (1900), 161–3.

10. Among them were the De la Maters (La Fayette De La Mater, *Genealogy of the Descendants of Claude Le Maitre* [Albany: Joel Munsell's Sons, 1882], 3).

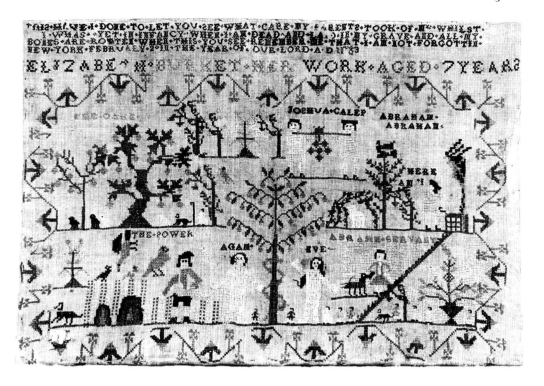

Fig. 323. *ELIZABETH BUR-KET HER WORK AGED 7 YEARS/ NEW YORK FEBRU-ARY 20 IN THE YEAR OF OUR LORD A D 1783.* Silk on linen; 16⅞" x 23⅝". Elizabeth identified *THE SOWER, ADAM* and *EVE, JOSHUA* and *CALEB,* and above a rendition of Abraham and Isaac, she quoted from Genesis, Chapter 22, Verse 11, *ABRAHAM, ABRA-HAM, HERE AM I.* At the top of her sampler she also worked verses often found on related pieces: *THIS HAVE I DONE TO LET YOU SEE WHAT CARE MY PAR-ENTS TOOK OF ME WHILST/ I WAS YET IN INFANCY WHEN I AM DEAD AND LAID IN MY GRAVE AND ALL MY/ BONES ARE ROTTEN WHEN THIS YOU SEE REMEMBER ME THAT I AM NOT FORGOTTEN.* For a similar sampler with more Dutch motifs, see SPB Sale 4478Y, November 21, 1980, Lot 791. Elizabeth has not been identified; since her sampler descended in a Nova Scotia family, it is likely that her father was a Loyalist who left New York after the British evacuation of 1783.
Historic Parks and Sites, Southwestern Nova Scotia, BA43.1.1.

as their sons to New Rochelle. The French opened respected boarding schools for girls in the 1730s, which were eagerly patronized by prosperous Dutch and English families. Music, dancing, French, embroidery, and painting were taught, and in the late nineteenth century Helen Smith saw paintings in Nova Scotia from the schools of New Rochelle, including a watercolor signed "Eleanora Morris, Pension de Demoiselles de Madame De la Vergne, La Nouvelle Rochelle, Province de New York, 1736." She also described "exquisite embroideries on the most delicate of muslins, as well as remnants of laces which are known to be the handiwork of some of Mme. De la Plaine's or Mme. De la Mater's pupils."[11] The Biblical samplers are believed to have originated in New Rochelle because Elizabeth Kortright (Fig. 319) attended a boarding school there in July 1758, and most likely during the previous year when she worked her sampler.[12]

Correspondence in the Sanders Papers introduces the name of a French schoolmistress of the 1760s, who possibly studied or taught in New Rochelle before opening a school in New York. Robert Ray of New York City wrote the following to John Sanders of Schenectady on July 15, 1765:

I have applied to Mrs. Blanche Boyeau concerning your brothers daughter Catherine: who we cannot prevail on at present to take, as she says she has now 14 boarders and that is as many as she can possibly entertain; but in the Spring she says she is willing to take her: as there will then be a vacancy:

---

11. Smith, *Colonial Days,* 162–3.
12. Barrett, *The Old Merchants of New York City* (1885), 29–30.

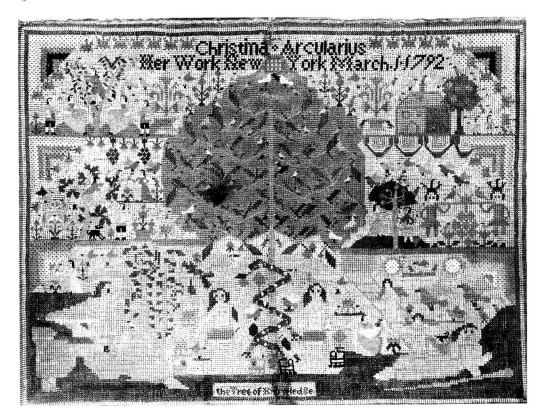

Fig. 324. *Christina Arcularius/ Her Work New York March 1 1792,* and inscribed below *The Tree of Knowledge.* Silk on linen; 16½″ x 22¼″. Christina worked a confusing array of motifs and twenty-two figures of varying scale amid a solidly worked background in the manner of the colonial pieces. Adam and Eve, Jacob's ladder, and the figure of Christ are much like earlier examples (Figs. 318–321), and the other motifs appear in various combinations on early nineteenth-century New York samplers. *New York* was also named on a related but less intricate sampler of 1789 (Kassell, *Stitches In Time* [1966], 11). Christina Arcularius (1777–1860) was the daughter of German baker Philip Jacob Arcularius and Elizabeth Grimm. She married Samuel Barker Harper in 1799, and they had eight children.
The New-York Historical Society, 54436.

her price is £40 a year however if the child has a mind to come and you choose to send her; I can get her boarded in a very good family till spring at the rate of £25 or £30 a year: and then she can go to school to Mrs. Blanches immediately and she shall be under our care and direction and be as tenderly used as at home. . . ."[13]

This letter may be a clue to New York City's most fashionable girls' school of the pre-Revolutionary period. It is now impossible to know if Mrs. Boyeau was responsible for any of the samplers considered here, but it appears evident that Frenchwomen were keeping the schools patronized by the elite. Young Peter Ed-

---

13. Sanders Papers, Box 12, NYHS.

Fig. 325. *armenia lyon her Work aged 8/ years in the year 1805 finished in 1806.* Silk on linen; 16″ x 19½″. Armenia named *the sower* and her Adam and Eve are like those worked by Elizabeth Lamb sixty years earlier, as are Eliza Turnbull's of 1819 (Krueger, *Gallery,* Fig. 76). Probably this sampler maker was Armenia Lyon (b.c.1797), the daughter of New York cooper and merchant Nicholas B. Lyon (1773–1839) and Rachel. She married Richard Kain (d.1824).
Collection of Lewis Bunker Rohrbach.

mundus Elmendorph continually referred to "the Madams" when writing from the New York school where he studied with his sister Betsy (Elizabeth, Fig. 320) in 1774.[14] Whether it was one of the Frenchwomen of New Rochelle or not, the instructress who initiated New York's Biblical sampler style taught for at least twenty-two years, and her powerful influence prevailed in this region until the sampler-making era was over.[15]

In 1800, New York had a population of 60,515 and a number of artists and museums, but there is little identifiable New York needlework from the early Federal period other than a number of samplers related to the Biblical group. Prominent among teachers at this time was Mrs. Isabella Marshall Graham, a Scotswoman who opened a school in October 1789 and met with immediate success. She was honored with Washington's patronage, and she continued teaching until 1798.[16] No dominant group of silk embroideries like those of Boston and Philadelphia has been found. Yet many women advertised girls' schools, and di-

14. Peter Edmundus Elmendorph, New York, to Mrs. Mary Elmendorph in Kingston, February 11, 1774, and others. Elmendorph Papers, Box 1700–1779, Folder 1774, NYHS.
15. I am deeply indebted to Mary Linda Zonana, who has shared her extensive research on New York sampler makers and colonial girls' schools. Her studies will soon be published.
16. Bethune, *The Life of Mrs. Isabella Graham* (1839). In 1792, Eliza Sanders of Schenectady worked silk maps for a pair of fire screens at Mrs. Graham's School (*ANTIQUES,* February 1971, 220).

Fig. 326. *ELIZABETH VAN KLEECK M E & A SKETCH/LEYS HAERLEM LANE N. Y. 1805* inscribed on the silk beneath the oval (the city directory shows them at 103 Harman). Silk, chenille, paint, and ink on silk; 19¼″ x 17½″. Elizabeth's work is characteristic of embroideries from the Sketchley school. A nearly identical but undated piece was worked by Margaret McKay (Smithsonian). For a different composition within an oval of 1806, see Wheeler, *The Development of Embroidery in America* (1921), opp. 54. Elizabeth van Kleeck (1788–1846) was born in Poughkeepsie and had a twin brother. She was the daughter of Lawrence Van Kleeck (1770–before 1815) and Charity Warner. In 1809 she married Dr. Peter Wendell (1786–1849) of Albany, and they had eleven children.

Israel Sack, Inc.

rectories show that some taught over long periods of time. Among them were the following, with their listings of 1804 and their years of inclusion:

> Isabella Ball, boarding school, 38 Partition: 1798–1813.
> Victoire Bancel, boarding school, Harrison: 1795–1812.
> Eliza Dunscomb, ladies school: 1792–1805.
> Mrs. Finlay, boarding school, 95 Greenwich: 1801–1821.
> Mrs. Heffernan, misses academy, 105 William: 1794–1807.
> Elizabeth Ledyard, teacher, 23 Fair: 1790–1806.
> Henry Priest, young ladies academy, 16 Cedar: 1799–1812.
> Mary Pringle, teacher of needlework, etc., 19 Division: 1803–1829.
> Violetta R. Taylor, boarding school, 34 Fair: 1796–1814.
> S. Woofendale, ladies' seminary, 141 Pearl: 1804–1849.

As yet, no embroideries can be associated with these schools,[17] and silk embroideries from specific New York City schools are rare (see footnote 16), except for work naming the Sketchleys, who appeared in the city in 1805 (Fig. 326). The name of their school was usually worked on the silk embroideries of their students. These pieces have elegant scenes in the neoclassical taste, but they lack distinctive qualities to help in the identification of unsigned work, which could easily be confused with English embroideries. Certainly their instruction reflected no particular regional style, for the Sketchleys moved frequently.

"Mesdames M. E. & A. Sketchley" advertised their "MONTREAL BOARDING SCHOOL/ For Young Ladies/ Removed to Lansingburgh" in the *Northern Budget* of Troy, New York, on February 19, 1799, and cited their twelve years' experience. They must have had little encouragement, for they soon moved to Poughkeepsie and described their girls' boarding school at length in the *Poughkeepsie Journal* of February 4, 1800. The Sketchleys evidently remained in Poughkeepsie for several years, for Mary Hoyt, the mother of William Tecumseh Sherman, named their school on a silk embroidery of about 1802.[18] After five years in New York City, they taught in various Virginia and North Carolina towns until at least 1815,[19] but no needlework from this period has been found.

---

17. Elizabeth Ledyard was teaching in 1784. See Earle, *Child Life in Colonial Days* (1899), 115–16; also, Ring, "Schoolgirl Embroideries" (1981–82), 27–8.

18. Sotheby's Sale 5215, June 30, 1984, Lot 155. Now in the Sherman House, Lancaster, Ohio.

19. *Alexandria Daily Gazette,* Virginia, January 31, 1811; *Norfolk Gazette and Public Ledger,* October 18, 1811; *Norfolk Herald,* June 28, 1814, and September 6, 1815 (MESDA records).

Nine Partners' Boarding School
in Dutchess County

New York, 9 mo. 2d, 1800

My Dear Mary,

   Thy letter of the 29 of last month came safe to hand and I am . . . pleased that thee is engaged in making a sampler which I desire thee to execute with great neatness and accuracy as a specimen of the needle work of the boarding school.[1]

When Mary Collins received this letter from her mother, she had already worked one of the earliest samplers known to survive from the Nine Partners' Boarding School. Her sampler of 1798 contained alphabets and a verse worked in colored silks above queen-stitched strawberries.[2] Her work of 1799 includes the earliest known instance of "the rule to mark napkins," which appears to be peculiar to New York Quaker schools (Figs. 328–330, 332). Mary Collins, with two brothers and a sister, was among the first scholars at the first successful coeducational boarding school founded by the Religious Society of Friends in the United States.[3]

"A religious and guarded education of our youth" was of serious concern to the Friends who convened at the New York Yearly Meeting in May of 1794, and a committee was then appointed to consider a boarding school.[4] Less than three years later, the Nine Partners' Boarding School in the village of Mechanic, Dutchess County, was established.[5] It opened on "the 20th of the 12th month,

---

1. *Reminiscences of Isaac and Rachel (Budd) Collins with an account of some of their descendants* (Philadelphia: J. B. Lippincott Co., 1893), 60.

2. *MAD,* January 1986, 33-C. Ann Burling worked a very similar sampler in 1798 (private collection). Both pieces name the school but neither have recognizable Quaker motifs.

3. Benjamin (1784–1857), Isaac (1787–1863), and Mary Collins (1789–1865) were enrolled on January 29, 1797 (*Nine Partners' School Journal 1795–1804,* 12, in the Haviland Records Room, Archives of the New York Yearly Meeting of the Religious Society of Friends, New York City). A boarding school was opened in Portsmouth, Rhode Island, by the New England Yearly Meeting in 1784, but it closed in 1788.

4. Katharine E. Cook, "Oakwood Seminary—Union Springs, New York" (typescript at Oakwood Seminary, the Friends' successor to Nine Partners' School), 1–2. Advising the school committee in 1796 was Martha Winter Routh (1743–1817), an English Quaker minister who formerly kept a girls' school in Nottingham. With Esther Tuke, she was among the nine women who planned the York School in 1785. Contact with her and her continuing interest in Nine Partners may have influenced the designs of the sampler patterns. (Frank Hasbrouck, ed., *The History of Dutchess County, New York* [Poughkeepsie: S. A. Mathieu, 1909], 488.)

5. The school took its name from its location in the Great Nine Partners' Patent, which was a tract of land granted to nine Englishmen by William III in 1697. Early Dutchess County historians locate the school in the village of Mechanic, although after 1788, the post office was called Washington. (Philip H. Smith, *General History of Dutchess County from 1609 to 1876* [Pauling, N.Y., 1877], 426.)

Fig. 327. *old Nine Partners School House* by Jonathan Thorne, 1816. Watercolor on paper; 8″ x 9½″. A similar watercolor is owned by the Oakwood Seminary in Union Springs, New York, and more detailed student views of about the same period are in the Haviland Records Room, Archives of the New York Yearly Meeting of the Religious Society of Friends, New York City. Jonathan Thorne (1801–1884) was the son of Samuel Thorne and Phebe Dean of Mechanic, and he studied at the district school kept by Lydia Treadwell before he entered the Nine Partners' School. In 1823 he married Lydia Ann Corse (1805–1872), and they had eleven children.
Friends Historical Library of Swarthmore College, Swarthmore, Pennsylvania.

1796,"[6] with seventy boys and thirty girls in attendance. They were housed in a large edifice on ten acres of land that was purchased in May 1795 from Joseph S. Mabbett for £1,600 (Figs. 327, 333). Essential wood for heating the school became available when fifty-six acres of woods were added to this property in 1796. By 1798, 138 children had been admitted to the school and 100 attended regularly. They could enter at the age of seven, and girls were allowed to continue until they were fourteen, boys until they were fifteen.

Joseph Talcott and his wife served as the first administrators until 1801. Alexander and Phebe Brown next held this position, and they were succeeded by Isaac and Ruth Hallock in December 1802. Esther Hallett also taught there from 1800 until 1803 when she married Joseph Townsend of Baltimore, having met him when he enrolled his four motherless children. Deborah Rogers, a former student, was the girls' head teacher when Lucretia Coffin (1793–1880), the school's most famous alumna, was enrolled about 1806. Lucretia was born in Nantucket, but her parents moved to Boston about 1804, and Lucretia and her younger sister were sent to the Nine Partners' Boarding School. After four years' attendance, Lucretia became a teacher there, and in 1811 she married fellow instructor James Mott. In later life she became famous as an abolitionist and women's suf-

---

6. Cook, "Oakwood Seminary" (n.d.), 2.

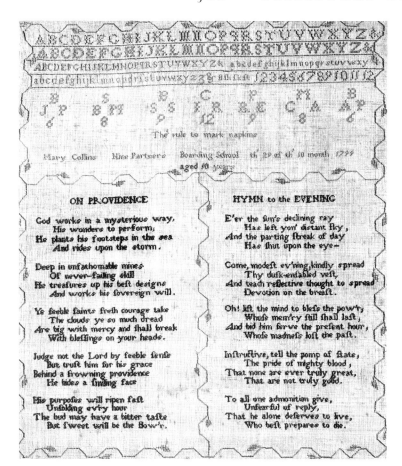

Fig. 328. *Mary Collins Nine Partners Boarding School th' 29 of th' 10 month 1799/ aged 10 years.* Blue and black silk on linen; 17½" x 15". Mary's sampler demonstrates *The rule to mark napkins.* It was customary to work the surname initial above the given name initials of husband and wife and give a number to each napkin within a set. Here Mary's parents' initials are in the center. The other initials are probably for aunts and uncles. Mary's verse *On Providence* was worked by Hannah Wigham at the Friends' Ackworth School in England in 1786 (Ackworth School). Mary Collins (b. July 27, 1789) was the twelfth child of the respected Quaker printer Isaac Collins (1746–1817) and Rachel Budd (1750–1805) who moved from Burlington County, New Jersey, to New York City in 1796. Mary married Isaac T. Longstreth in 1808. In 1826, their daughters Mary Anna and Susan Longstreth opened a school in Philadelphia that continued for more than thirty years. Mary's sister Susannah Collins (1781–1876) taught at the Nine Partners' School before her marriage to Richard Morris Smith in 1810.

Collection of Mr. and Mrs. David Jon Greenwood.

Fig. 329. *Hannah Coffin/ 12ᵗʰ moᵗʰ 23ᵈ 1805.* Silk on linen; 14¾" x 17½". Although Hannah failed to name her school, her sampler is a typical example from the Nine Partners' Boarding School. For related pieces naming the school between 1801 and 1805, see Krueger, *Gallery,* Fig. 44; Ring, *Treasures,* Fig. 52; and *A&AW,* December 27, 1985, 94. Another was worked on green linsey-woolsey by Lydia Mitchell in 1810 (private collection). Hannah Coffin (1795–1824), the daughter of Shubael Coffin (1739–1817) and his second wife, Sarah Olney (1756–1841), was born in Nantucket but moved with her family to Clinton, Dutchess County, New York, about 1804. Hannah died unmarried.

Nantucket Historical Association, Fr 87-3.

Fig. 330. *Sarah R Hicks Boarding School Nine Partners/ 1808*. Silk on linen; 12⅝″ x 17⅜″. A modest array of typical geometric half medallions was worked at the Nine Partners' School by 1803, if not earlier (B&C, Pl. CVII). Sarah R. Hicks (1793–1835) was tenth among the eleven children of the Quaker minister Elias Hicks (1748–1830) and Jemima Seaman (1750–1829) of Jericho, New York. Sarah married Robert Seaman (1792–1870) in 1814. Elias Hicks was the Quaker leader whose doctrines instigated the separation of American Quakers into two opposing factions in 1828. They were later referred to as Orthodox and Hicksite Quakers. *Private collection.*

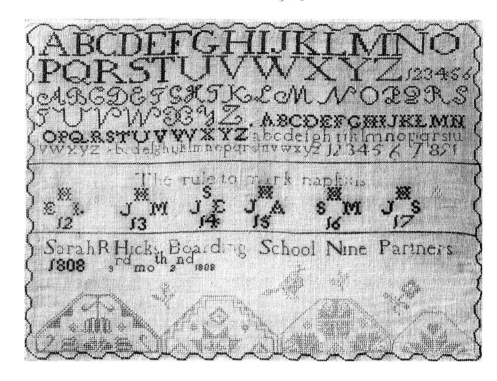

Fig. 331. *Jane Titus Nine Partners Boarding School 1ˢᵗ month 11ᵗʰ 1827*. Silk on linen; 15¼″ x 16½″. Jane's sister Hannah Titus (b. 1810) worked a nearly identical sampler in the same year (private collection). Here the lettering, geometric half medallions, and small cross-stitched motifs are characteristic of English Quaker work as well as samplers from the Delaware Valley; therefore, this sampler would be difficult to assign to a specific region if its origin was not given. Obviously, much older girls were attending the Nine Partners' School in the 1820s than when the school opened. Jane Titus (1807–1881) was the daughter of Henry Titus (1784–1872) and Phebe Titus (1786–1865) of Glen Cove, New York. *Private collection.*

Fig. 332. *Elizabeth Quinby Sampler Westchester 11 of 2 Month 1811.* Black and blue silk on linen; 18⅞" x 14⅞". Elizabeth also worked a plain marking sampler and gave her age as nine in 1808. Her family belonged to the Purchase Monthly Meeting, and she no doubt attended the school in Westchester that was administered by the Purchase Preparative Meeting. Her sampler reveals that "the rule to mark napkins" was not exclusive to the Nine Partners' Boarding School. Elizabeth Quinby (1799–1869) was the daughter of James Quinby (1759–1799) and Hannah Underhill (1769–1846) of Westchester, which is now a part of the Borough of the Bronx. She married Charles R. Underhill (1796–1861) in 1819.
Collection of the Underhill Society of America, Inc.

Fig. 333. The Nine Partners' Boarding School after a drawing by student Alexander H. Coffin, 1820. This former store and inn of the 1760s was lengthened to ninety-nine feet and accommodated boys and girls in well-divided quarters. The basement was the dining room, the second floor and attic served for lodging, and the former store area on the west end became the schoolroom.
Haviland Records Room, Archives of the New York Yearly Meeting of the Religious Society of Friends, New York City.

fragist. In 1812, her instructress Deborah Rogers married Jacob Willets, who had entered the school on the day it opened, and he became the head teacher on his eighteenth birthday in 1806.[7] In 1819 they moved to Nantucket.

A number of children had been accepted from other meetings by 1814 when ten-year-old Richard Hallett Townsend of Baltimore came to the school where his mother had been a teacher, and he left a fascinating account of the four happy years he spent there. Richard recalled the pleasures of swimming in Philip Hart's pond in summer, and skating on it in winter, and he remembered a day so cold that "even with our two stoves in the schoolroom," classes were suspended so they could crowd together in smaller quarters. The boys saw little of the girls except on Sunday afternoons when a meeting was held in the girls' schoolroom.[8]

Richard Townsend visited the school in 1827 but found no familiar faces there. It was very much reduced in size, having been adversely affected by the schism in ideology that finally divided the Friends in 1828. When the separation occurred, the Nine Partners' School remained with the orthodox branch while the Hicksites opened a school at Mechanic under the direction of former Nine Partners' teachers Jacob and Deborah Willets. By 1850, less than one half of the students were Friends' children, and after 1853, the Nine Partners' School was no longer administered by the New York Yearly Meeting. Its facilities were leased to various individuals until its final closing in 1864.[9]

---

7. Jacob Willets (b.1788) wrote a widely used arithmetic book and also published a geography and atlas. Deborah Rogers (1789–1870) was from Marshfield, Massachusetts.

8. Richard H. Townsend, *The Book of Remembrance* 2 (1835), 4. Typescript, Friends' Historical Library of Swarthmore College.

9. James H. Smith, *History of Dutchess County, New York* (Syracuse, N.Y.: D. Mason and Co., 1882; reprint, Interlaken, N.Y.: Heart of the Lakes Publishing, 1980), 326–7.

Map Samplers of Pleasant Valley

Working maps on silk, linen, or wool was a fairly common practice at British girls' schools during the last quarter of the eighteenth century.[1] It served the dual purpose of teaching geography and embroidery, and exquisitely worked maps, particularly of the British Isles, survive in considerable numbers.[2] In England of the 1780s, maps were being commercially printed on the ground material for embroidery. Even Quaker teachers who normally discouraged needlework "that is thought purely ornamental" evidently felt that the geography lessons linked to these pieces would justify their creation.[3]

By 1775, maps were also being worked in America,[4] and a few map samplers have survived from every region of the early Republic. Nevertheless, American map embroidery was relatively rare, and only two recognizable groups of American map samplers are presently known.[5] These are the maps of Maryland (Figs. 559–562) and maps on silk that are attributed to a girls' boarding school in Pleasant Valley, Dutchess County, New York.[6]

In keeping with the close kinship of New York nineteenth-century samplers to English work, New York schools also produced more map samplers than schools in other regions, but only the maps of Pleasant Valley compose an easily recognized group.[7] The majority of these pieces depict the two hemispheres (Fig. 334). Girls also worked the state of New York,[8] the United States (Fig. 335), North

---

1. Some English maps are said to date from much earlier. See Colby, 125–36.

2. For English maps naming schools, see Huish, 95; and Anne Sebba, *Samplers: Five Centuries of a Gentle Craft* (New York: Thames and Hudson, 1979), 72, 74.

3. The policy for needlework at the York School was expressed by Sarah Grubb, whose mother, Esther Tuke, established the school for girls in 1785 (Sturge and Clark, *The Mount School* [1931], 10).

4. Frances Brenton's map in B&C, Pl. XXIX; for the identity of its maker see Ring, *Virtue*, 57, n. 69. Nancy Shippen's mother requested that she work a map at Mrs. Rogers' school in Trenton in 1777 (Armes, *Nancy Shippen* [1935], 41. Also, Ann Smith (1774–1813) from Barbados worked a map in Philadelphia in 1787, which is described by Roberdeau Buchanan in *Genealogy of the McKean Family of Pennsylvania* (Lancaster, Pa.: Inquirer Printing Co., 1890), 127. See also *ANTIQUES*, March 1990, 610.

5. Two maps of 1809 are known from the Quakers' Frankford School near Philadelphia (a location now within the city), and more will probably appear. See B&C, Pl. XCII. One by Sarah Rodman of New Bedford, Massachusetts, is in the Antiquarian House, Plymouth.

6. Pictorial embroideries on silk are not generally called samplers, but embroidered maps have been consistently known as samplers regardless of the ground material and whether or not they were signed and dated.

7. For a divergent example of 1822, see *Early Arts and Crafts of the Susquehanna Valley* (Binghamton, N.Y.: Roberson Center, 1982), Fig. 111; also, Sandra Brant and Elissa Cullman, *Small Folk, A Celebration of Childhood in America* (New York: E. P. Dutton in association with the Museum of American Folk Art, 1980), Fig. 192.

8. Caroline Patten's *State of New York*, 1806, is in the Adriance Library, Poughkeepsie; Helen M. Livingston's, 1806, is in the author's collection. An exquisite small, unsigned map of Europe, worked in the same technique, is in the Schenectady Museum, 78.17.68. It descended in a local family and was probably worked in Pleasant Valley.

America (Fig. 336), and the Western Hemisphere (Fig. 337). Continents or countries are usually outlined with chenille, all lettering is worked in hair-fine black silk, and shorelines are edged with blue paint. A worked and painted ribbonlike banner may identify the subject of the map, and the maker often included her name, the name of her hometown, and the date, as in Figure 334. Known examples date from 1803 until 1824, and an advertisement in the *Poughkeepsie & Constitutional Republican* of June 7, 1803, relates to their origin:

BOARDING SCHOOL AT
Pleasant Valley

ANN SHIPLEY, AGNES DEAN, AND
PHEBE SHIPLEY.

Respectfully inform their friends and the public, that they have this day opened a BOARDING-SCHOOL for Female Education, at Pleasant-Valley, near Poughkeepsie; where GIRLS from six years of age and upwards, will be boarded and instructed in different branches of learning, on the following terms, viz.

Reading and Plain Sewing.   at 20 Dols. per Quarter
Grammar, Writing, Arithmetic, and most
kinds of Needle Work ...   25   "   "
Geography, Working Maps, the
Use of the Globes &c.   30   "   "

One quarter's advance with each scholar will be expected. Strict attention will be paid, not only to the education, but to the morals and behavior of those pupils who may be placed under their care.

N. B. Books and Stationery will be provided free of expense.
Pleasant-Valley, 6th mo. 1st, 1803[9]

The trio of women who started this school were related to each other and all were members of the Religious Society of Friends. Ann Shipley (1760–1854) was the widow of Morris Shipley (1754–1795) whose father emigrated from Staffordshire, England, to Philadelphia in 1750.[10] When finishing his education in Kendal, England, Morris fell in love with his first cousin, and in 1779 they eloped to Gretna Green in Scotland. They returned to her home in Uttoxeter where their four children were born, and eventually they were again accepted into the Society of Friends. About 1784, Morris resumed business with his father in Philadelphia and traveled between England and America until 1795 when his family joined

---

9. Also in Poughkeepsie's *Political Barometer* of June 7, 1803. See front endpapers.
10. Hinshaw, *Encyclopedia of American Quaker Genealogy* (1926–1950), 2:649. William Shipley (1723–1793) arrived in Philadelphia from Uttoxeter, England, without his wife and two children who died on the voyage. In 1752 he married Jael Morris (d.1765).

Fig. 334. *BETSEY MELLEN/ ATHENS/ 1810.* Silk, chenille, and paint on silk; 17¾" x 21½". Betsey worked the most popular map pattern at the Pleasant Valley school. Polly Platt also named *Athens* on a similar map of 1809 (Ring, *Treasures,* Fig. 53). Maria Merritt's map of 1817 is illustrated in *Early American Life,* April 1984, 44. See Susanna Hart's embroidered hemispheres (but disregard the date) in SPB Sale 3438, November 18, 1972, Lot 646. Ann Townsend's hemispheres of 1807 are in the Dutchess County Historical Society; Elizabeth Thorn's of 1817 are in the Columbia County Historical Society. Betsey Mellen was probably Elizabeth Mellen, the daughter of David Mellen and Jane Ostrander, who was baptized at the Dutch Reformed Church in Kinderhook, Columbia County, New York, on January 18, 1796.
Staten Island Historical Society, gift of Miss Martha E. Ostrander, 1976, 5112.

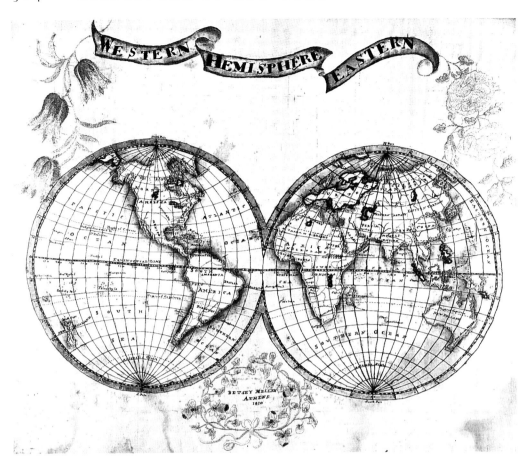

him in Abington, Pennsylvania.[11] Shortly thereafter, they moved to New York where Morris Shipley died in 1795.[12] At about this time, Ann's sister Alice Shipley Abbatt arrived in New York with her husband, Robert Abbatt, and their six children,[13] and in 1799, both families moved to Clinton, Dutchess County, New York. Ann soon became the treasurer of the Oswego Monthly Meeting and a recognized minister, and her son William married Phebe Comstock of Hudson, New York, in January 1803. In the meantime, her brother-in-law, Robert Abbatt, purchased property in Pleasant Valley and built a grist mill and a cotton mill; and in October of 1802, his daughter Agnes became the wife of Israel Dean of Clinton.

These families were educated, prosperous, and well acquainted with influential Quakers in both England and America. So Ann Shipley, with her niece Agnes Abbatt Dean, and her new daughter-in-law Phebe Shipley, was well qualified to open a boarding school modeled on English prototypes, and the school she established

---

11. Unpublished Shipley family genealogy supplied by Mrs. Jeanette Shipley Michener of Newtown, Pennsylvania, in 1988.

12. Hinshaw, *Encyclopedia,* 3:286. Morris Shipley's will was proved on November 20, 1795 (Surrogate's Office, City of New York, 14:323–4).

13. Merchant Robert Abbatt became a naturalized citizen in New York on March 14, 1797 (*NYGBR* 97, no. 1 [1966]: 4).

Fig. 335. *UNITED STATES/ Cecilia Lewis/ 1809.* Silk, chenille, and paint on silk; 14″ x 18″. A nearly identical map was worked by H. Cockburn in 1808 (Worcester Art Museum), and an undated one by Ann Scott Mann can be found at the Newport Historical Society. In 1809, Ann E. Colson worked a more complete example by extending the St. Lawrence River to the edge of her silk (Sotheby's Sale 5622, October 24, 1987, Lot 325). Ann Colson also painted a map of the hemispheres in 1809 (private collection). This sampler maker may have been Cecilia Goold Lewis (bapt. March 22, 1792), the daughter of Francis Lewis and Elizabeth Ludlow of Flushing, Queens County, New York. *State Historical Society of Wisconsin, 1984, 294.*

is believed to have produced the map samplers considered here.[14] "Working maps" was specifically mentioned in their first advertisement and again in 1805 and 1806.[15] Obviously Ann or Agnes was experienced with map embroidery on silk. Agnes Abbatt's name does not appear on the eighteenth-century enrollment list of Esther Tuke's boarding school for young ladies on Trinity Lane in York, England, but she was probably familiar with the maps being made there. Like the Pleasant Valley maps, they were worked "upon white silk in which the shape of each county was defined . . . in chenille, whilst the names of the counties and of the chief towns were worked in silk."[16] Two Shipley girls from Uttoxeter attended the York School in 1802, and it is very likely that Ann Shipley was acquainted with Esther Tuke and her school's curriculum, as was the English Quaker Martha Routh, who advised the founders of the Nine Partners' School at an earlier date.

Ann and Phebe Shipley's association with the school was severed by June 12, 1805, when an advertisement in Hartford's *Connecticut Courant* announced that "the BOARDING SCHOOL for Female Education of Pleasant Valley, near Pough-

---

14. The school may have been located on eight acres purchased by Ann Shipley from Daniel D. Dean of Beekman on June 15, 1801, for £300. It was described as "land in the town of Clinton west side of road leading from Poughkeepsie through Pleasant Valley to Timothy Beadles . . . runs by a small piece of land . . . on which a school house is now built" (Dutchess County Deed Book 17, 174). Pleasant Valley was incorporated in 1813.

15. *Connecticut Courant,* Hartford, June 12, 1805; *Poughkeepsie Journal & Constitutional Republican,* July 15, 1806.

16. Sturge and Clark, *The Mount School* (1931), 11.

Fig. 336. *NORTH AMERICA/ Silvia Grinnell,* c.1804. Silk, chenille, and paint on silk; 20⅜″ x 23¾″. Silvia's map is strikingly similar to the map of North America published August 12, 1804, by R. Wilkinson in London. This likely source was discovered by Judith N. Lund. The only divergence is Silvia's straight northern boundary for the Louisiana Purchase, which was not finalized until years later. Sarah Willis (1794–1874), also of New Bedford, worked a nearly identical map (Harbeson, opp. 94), as did Anna Maria Schuneman of Catskill, New York (Kassell, *Stitches in Time* [1966], 39). Silvia also worked a map of the United States, much like Figure 335 (Whaling Museum, 82.39.2). Silvia Grinnell (1791–1844) was the daughter of shipmaster Cornelius Grinnell (1758–1850) and Syliva Howland (1765–1837), a lifelong Quaker of New Bedford, Massachusetts. In 1819 Silvia married William Tallman Russell (1788–1842).

Whaling Museum, New Bedford, Massachusetts, 82.39.1.

keepsie, will in future be conducted by Robert Abbatt and Agnes Dean." This may have been Robert Abbatt, Jr., since Robert Abbatt, Sr., was busy with his cotton factory. Possibly the younger Abbatt daughters, Mary and Ann, also helped in the school, since Agnes soon had several children. In the fall of 1807, Ann Shipley, with her son William, his wife Phebe, and their children, returned to New York City.[17]

In the meantime, Pleasant Valley was prospering as a textile manufacturing center,[18] and samplers indicate that this was the most productive period of the boarding school. Robert Abbatt was much involved with the Union Mills and the Pleasant Valley Manufacturing Company, but disaster struck this enterprise on January 27, 1815, when the mills burned. In 1817, Robert and Alice Abbatt moved to New York City, and they were soon followed by their daughter Agnes with her husband, Israel Dean, and their six children. Robert Abbatt died in 1826, and in 1830, his widow and two sons sold his remaining "parcel of land" in Pleasant Valley.[19]

The fate of the Pleasant Valley Boarding School after the departure of its founders is unknown. Various references suggest that it continued into the 1820s, and two samplers support this belief. One is a beautifully preserved and unquestionably related example dated 1821, although it is atypical for having place names lettered in ink. Another typical although poorly executed map of the hemispheres was worked by Lucy C. Berry in 1824.[20]

---

17. Ann Shipley (1760–1854) was the daughter of Joseph Shipley (1721–1778) and Hannah Ecroyd (1724–1793) of Uttoxeter. Her daughter Hannah (c.1782–1805) married Robert Bowne in 1802; daughter Mary (b.1783) married William Ferris Pell in 1802; son Morris (b.1784) married Ann Eddy in 1808. In 1831 Ann Shipley went to Ohio and died in Cincinnati, as did her son William in 1837.

18. Frank Hasbrouck, ed., *The History of Dutchess County, New York* (Poughkeepsie: S. A. Mathieu, 1909), 420.

19. Dutchess County Deed Book 48, 196.

20. In the Adriance Library, and the C-H.

Fig. 337. *Mary M. Franklin Pleasant Valley 1808*. Silk, chenille, paint, and ink on silk; 20⅜″ x 23¾″. Mary's elegant rendition of the Western Hemisphere is the only known example of this form from the Pleasant Valley Boarding School. Mary Franklin has not been identified.

Winterthur Museum, 57.552A.

Female Association Schools

A charming group of small samplers known as "Female Association" samplers has survived from several New York City schools operated by Quaker women. The delicate work of Lucy Turpen and Ann Hayden (Figs. 338, 339) illustrates their most typical form. Between 1815 and 1826, children often made them as gifts for members of the Female Association,[1] and they were usually signed with the name of the Female Association School where they were made.

In 1798, a group of prominent Quaker ladies banded together for "the Relief of the Sick Poor" of New York City, and they later initiated plans for a school for needy children.[2] The first school under the direction of this Female Association opened for boys and girls in June 1801, but the enrollment was later limited to girls. The second school commenced classes in Henry Street on February 18, 1812, with Mary I. Morgan as preceptress. The third school opened on January 8, 1815, and the fourth on July 7, 1817, with Isabella Morgan as the teacher. Early members of the Association included Ann Shipley and Agnes Abbatt (who later taught in Pleasant Valley). They probably resumed their membership after returning to New York City some years later. Also much involved was Sarah Collins, the daughter of Isaac Collins and the elder sister of Mary (Fig. 328).[3]

In addition to basic subjects, the girls were taught all types of practical stitchery, and the students of School No. 3 had completed 271 pieces of needlework just three months after it was opened. Sixteen samplers were among the items listed.[4] Most of the samplers known today name either School No. 2 or School No. 3. Like Lucy Turpen, other girls who attended the Female Association schools probably became teachers, and a number of New York samplers bear some resemblance to the ones shown here.[5] The Female Association continued to supervise these schools until 1845 when their jurisdiction was transferred to the Public School Society.[6]

---

1. Examples of 1815 and 1826 are in the PMA, the Nantucket Historical Association, and the DAR. See also *ANTIQUES,* September 1977, 392.

2. Bourne, *History of the Public School Society of the City of New York* (1873), 652–3. Also, in 1797, Mrs. Isabella Graham, with her daughter Joanna Bethune and twenty-eight other ladies, established the Society for the Relief of Poor Widows with Small Children in New York City, where they taught young children to read and sew. Elizabeth Bayley Seton was treasurer until 1804; there were also many Quaker members. (*The Westchester Historian,* Westchester County Historical Society 62, no. 4 [Fall 1986]: 100.)

3. Ibid., 653–5.

4. Ibid., 654. This list appears in Krueger, *Gallery,* 13.

5. Traces of Female Association influence appear on a sampler naming the *New York Orphan Asylum* in 1821 (Schenectady Museum, 76.40.1).

6. Bourne, *History,* 657.

Fig. 338. *For Jane B. Haines,/ a member of the Female Association./ By Lucy Turpen aged 11 years./ Female Association school No 3,/ New York 1815.* Silk on linen; 7⅝″ x 7⅛″. Lucy worked her sampler for Jane Bowne Haines (1790–1843) of Long Island who married Reuben Haines III (1786–1831) of Philadelphia, the grandson of Margret Wistar (Fig. 373). Jane's brother Robert married Ann Shipley's daughter Hannah, and her sister Hannah married Benjamin Collins, the brother of Mary (Fig. 328). Obviously Jane kept her affiliation with the Association after her marriage in 1812. Lucy Turpen later taught at New York's African Free School where her "amiable disposition and faithful, as well as successful discharge of her duties, rendered her greatly esteemed, both by her pupils and by the trustees." Her capabilities were credited to her training at a Female Association School, for these schools were regarded as "models for similar establishments." (Charles C. Andrews, *History of the New York African Free Schools* [New York: Mahlon Day, 1830], 21). Lucy Turpen later moved to Ohio.

Wyck Charitable Trust, Philadelphia, 88.564.

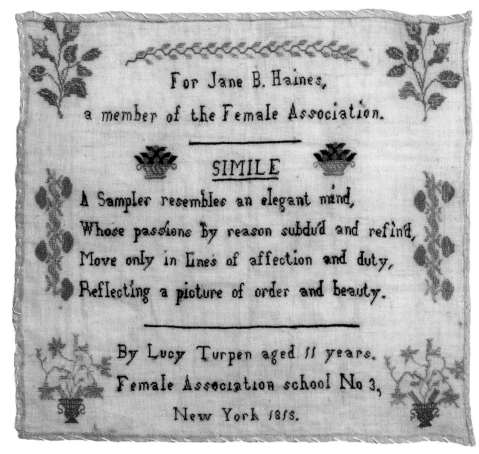

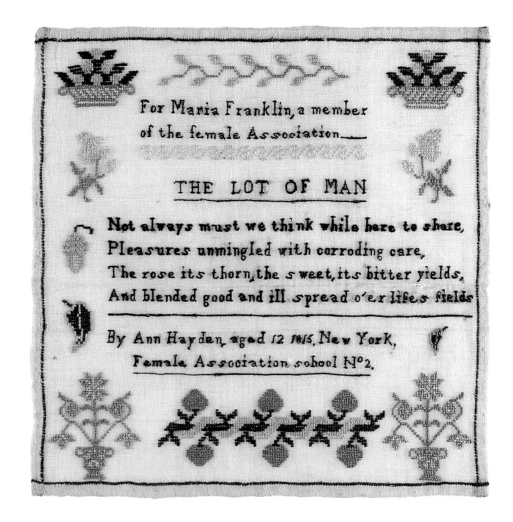

Fig. 339. *For Maria Franklin, a member/ of the female Association/ By Ann Hayden, aged 12 1815, New York./ Female Association school No. 2.* Silk on linen; 7¼″ x 7⅛″. For an 1820 example from the same school, see Krueger, *Gallery*, Fig. 77. Maria Franklin (1787–1867) was the daughter of prominent New Yorker Thomas Franklin (1762–1830) and Sarah Polhemus (1764–1791). Her paternal grand-mother was Deborah Morris (1736–1787) of Philadelphia. Sampler maker Ann Hayden is unidentified.

Author's collection.

Mourning Embroideries of Albany

The earliest and most beautiful print-work embroideries to survive from Federal America were worked in Albany by daughters of the most prominent families of this region; yet the schools of their origin remain tantalizingly elusive. These are all mourning pieces that range in date from about 1801 to about 1820, and there are two major recognizable groups. Within each there are many variations, as well as occasional pieces that will not fit precisely into either group, and obviously this type of mourning piece was favored by a number of Albany teachers.

The earliest and largest group of Albany memorials is predominantly print work (Figs. 340, 341, 343) with a few related pieces in colored silks (Fig. 342). Dated examples range from 1801 to 1805, and the latest known death date on a monument within this group is August 19, 1804. Possibly the latest recorded piece is a memorial by Emily C. Avery who was born on July 2, 1793.[1] While the embroidery technique remained reasonably constant between 1801 and 1805, the patterns and painted figures reflect the work of two different hands. One type is represented here by the Lansing and Beeckman memorials, and their patterns are attributed to the artist and engraver Henry W. Snyder because his characteristic signature is found on the Beeckman memorial (Figs. 341, 341a).[2]

Henry W. Snyder was born in New York City on December 23, 1784, and he died on April 19, 1864. He was the son of William Snyder who went from Holland to Virginia, and is listed as a shopkeeper at 112 Chatham Street in New York directories from 1795 until 1797. William Snyder purchased property on Market Street in Albany in 1795, when Henry was probably an engraver's apprentice in New York, but he must have joined his father in Albany around 1800. Snyder's work in Boston publications of 1807 through 1816 suggests that he moved there shortly after the Beeckman-type memorials were drawn, but he was again in Albany when the first city directory was published in 1813. From 1821 until 1832, Snyder was the Chamberlain (treasurer) of the city of Albany, and in 1826 he was the architect of the Albany Alms House. He moved to Utica, New York, in the early 1830s, and he died there, as did his brothers, cabinetmaker Rudolph (1778–1861) and chairmaker Jacob (1781–1863). Snyder was evidently a precocious craftsman and artist, for when the Beeckman memorial was worked, he was eighteen years old, and he was only sixteen when Catharine Lansing made her memorial.[3] There is, however, no evidence that this pattern drawer was a differ-

1. Dickensen death of *19ᵗʰ August 1804* (cited Fig. 340); see Avery in Ring, *Treasures,* Fig. 152.
2. David McNeely Stauffer, *American Engravers upon Copper and Steel* (New York: The Grolier Club, 1907), 256, 493–4.
3. His activities closely paralleled the work of John R. Penniman (1782–1841) who was painting Willard clock faces at the age of thirteen (*ANTIQUES,* July 1981, 148).

A MOURNING PIECE   *BY CATHARINE LANSINGH.*

Fig. 340. *A MOURNING PIECE/ BY CATHARINE LANSINGH* inscribed on the glass; *C L/ 1801* worked in the lower right corner; and dedicated on the plinth: *In Memory of/ Elsie, Wife of M^r. A Lansing/ Ob.^t March 1.st 1796. AE.^t 38^{yrs} & 23 Days.* Black and brown silk, pencil, and ink on silk; 17½" x 22¼". A virtually identical embroidery was dedicated to John Demarest (SPB, Halpert Collection, Sale 3572, November 15, 1973, Lot 238). Another, dedicated to a Dickensen infant, is illustrated in *ANTIQUES,* August 1981, 248. These pieces have plinths like that in the memorial worked by Margaret Ten Eyck (1791–1853) in 1805, which closely resembles the Beeckman memorial signed by Snyder (Swan, *Guide,* 92). Catharine Lansing (1783–1867) was the daughter of Abraham A. Lansing (1752–1822) and his first wife, Elsie Van Rensselaer (1758–1796). In 1796, Catharine attended the Moravian Seminary for Young Ladies in Bethlehem, Pennsylvania, as did her sister Arietta in 1798. Catharine married her first cousin Philip P. Van Rensselaer (1783–1827) in 1804; her second husband was John Fay, Jr. *Author's collection.*

ent Snyder. He obviously had access to the now-unknown design source for the Gothic church that appears in Figure 341 as well as in countless other examples of schoolgirl art on silk, paper, and velvet from both New York and Massachusetts.

Snyder's basic composition for the Beeckman memorial is similar to that of others within this group that were evidently worked at the same school, but drawn by a different hand as early as 1801 (Fig. 343). Their most conspicuous difference is in the style of the large trees and the size of the mourners. The characteristic trees of the Snyder type are willows with slender trunks, and deciduous trees with light and airy foliage (Fig. 341), while the Yates embroidery (Fig. 343), and those related to it, have willows with heavy trunks and branches, and deciduous trees with dense foliage arranged in tiers.[4] The Yates type is closely related to two identical memorials painted on canvas. They are inscribed at the base in a similar manner, and they have the same arrangement of church, roadway, and trees—the one at the left with tiered foliage, and at right, a willow with a heavy trunk and branches. Also, as in the embroideries, they have exceptionally diminutive figures. Both are dedicated to Peter Van Vechten (1780–1797) and his cousin Judith Van Vechten (1785–1797) of Albany.[5]

---

4. For others, see SPB Sale 4076, February 1, 1978, Lot 214; Blackburn, *Cherry Hill* (1976), Fig. 153; Barclay family memorial in the New York State Museum, Albany, 83.18.2; anonymous memorial in the Shelburne Museum (recorded in DAPC).

5. Schorsch, *Mourning Becomes America* (1976), Pl. 3/172.

Fig. 341. *Sacred to the Memory of Iohn Jac Beeckman, Maria his Wife & Daughters Deborah Sarah & Eve* worked on the silk beneath the picture; signed on the silk at right *Snyder Dlt*; and at left beneath the glass *Margery M'Leod*, who may have been the teacher, c.1803. Black and brown silk, paint, and ink on silk; 20″ x 25″. Attributed to Margarietta Beeckman (1787–1850), the only granddaughter of John Jac Beeckman

of possible age to have worked this memorial. She was the daughter of his eldest son, Jacob Beeckman (1761–1817), and Ann McKinney (1764–1834), and they lived in Schenectady. Margarietta Beeckman married Stephen Rowan (c.1787–1835) in 1804, and they had ten children. See similar patterns in Swan, *Guide*, 92, and *MAD*, February 1991, 9-F. *Albany Institute of History and Art, 1909.11.1.*

Fig. 341a. Lower right corner of the Beeckman mourning piece showing the signature of *Snyder Dlt* that has been embroidered. The monuments also have embroidered inscriptions for John Jac Beeckman (1733–1802) and his wife and daughters, who died within the years 1791–1794. The pattern is believed to have been drawn by Albany engraver Henry W. Snyder.

Fig. 342. *WORKED BY ELIZA STARR. ALBANY 1802* inscribed on the glass. Silk, paint, and ink on silk; 14½" x 22¼". Although worked in colors, this memorial is closely related to the Beeckman type of mourning pieces while its church is the same one pictured in the Yates embroidery (Fig. 343). The monuments are dedicated to Eliza's mother, Elizabeth Starr, who died June 28, 1801, aged forty-four, and her brother who died August 2, 1801, aged twenty-one. The figures no doubt represent Eliza C. Starr (1790–1845) and her sister, Hannah Starr (c.1778–1858), the only daughters of Benajah Starr (1750–1825) and Elizabeth (1756–1801). This family moved from Danbury, Connecticut, first to Salem, New York, and then to Schenectady, where Elizabeth died. Benajah remarried, but his five children died unmarried.
Private collection; photograph courtesy of Christie's.

Almost nothing is known of the schools that may have produced Albany's earliest mourning pieces. The first important and enduring academy in Albany was established by an act of the Common Council in 1780, and George W. Merchant of Philadelphia became headmaster.[6] This school was generally known as Merchant's Academy. It was housed in private dwellings, and was not officially incorporated until 1813. Girls as well as boys are believed to have attended the Academy,[7] but there is no evidence of a schoolmistress teaching accomplishments, and during the 1790s, at least ten families of the Albany area sent their daughters to the Moravian Seminary for Young Ladies in Bethlehem, Pennsylvania. However, by 1799, a Mr. and Mrs. Samuel Lilly were keeping boarding schools for boys and girls in Albany. In an advertisement datelined December 26, 1799, they informed their patrons that their "Academies" would open on January 6, and they again advertised their "Albany Boarding School" on December 30, 1800.[8] Their further identity and the duration of their schools are unknown.

Another school that may have existed as early as 1801 was kept by a Mrs. Bell in 1804,[9] and in 1806, Frances Wilson was there as a boarder. Frances was the

6. Merchant (1756–1830), was a German named Koopman, who had Anglicized his name. (*Collections of the History of Albany* [Albany: Joel Munsell, 1867], 2:16.) Merchant's wife was Elizabeth Spencer (c.1759–1814).
7. Maria Gansevoort Melville (1791–1872), the mother of Herman Melville, attended this school (Alice P. Kenney, *The Gansevoorts of Albany* [Syracuse, N.Y.: Syracuse University Press, 1969], 172).
8. *The Albany Centinel,* January 3 and December 30, 1800.
9. No Bell advertisements have been found, but in *The Albany Gazette,* October 25, 1804, dancing master M. O'Duhigg planned to commence his school "at Mrs. BELL'S for ladies. . . . It has not been determined if this was the Mrs. Bell teaching in Harrisburg, Pa., in 1799 (see Krueger, *Gallery,* 19).

daughter of Scotsman Dr. William Wilson (1756–1828) and Mary Howey (1753–1801) of Clermont, New York. Wilson was the private physician for the family and employees of Chancellor Robert R. Livingston (1746–1813), and his daughter Polly married Livingston's son, Alexander, who died at the age of twenty-three. On January 22, 1806, Frances Wilson wrote from Albany to her sister in Germantown, New York, with a candid description of life at Mrs. Bell's school:

> I wish you and some of the family would write me very often, and tell me what you are doing. I just been making a hearty breakfast [on] dry bread and tea, while you had Something good for yours. Our daily fare here is bread and Apple-sauce for breakfast, dirty beef for dinner and bread and apple-sauce for supper after which by way of digestion, we go to the hotel and dance till bed time, then we march up in order to dreary bed-chambers as cold as Chastity herself. My mourning piece is done, & I intend working one for our sister Mary in Memory of Alexander. My Toilette Cushion is almost done. I intend giving that to her too.[10]

The duration of Mrs. Bell's school is unknown. If Frances Wilson's mourning pieces could be found, they might reveal that the Bell school was the source of the earlier Albany work.

The second group of Albany memorials is also dominated by print work. The typical monuments are classical, urn-topped obelisks upon plinths, and they are shaded by thin, lofty willow trees with visible, uplifting branches. The mourners' faces are usually painted in colors (Figs. 344, 346), although in some cases they appear to have been painted by different hands, and variations in the style of embroidery suggest that the artist drew patterns for more than one school. Within this group, the earliest recognizable example is a memorial to Leonard Gansevoort (1751–1810), depicting his Whitehall mansion.[11]

In the summer of 1810, Albany artist Ezra Ames is known to have painted three "fancy pieces" and two "mourning pieces" for "Mrs. Tompson," and his account book reveals that he occasionally did this type of work as late as 1819.[12] A portrait by Ames with a mourning vignette in the background (Fig. 345) strongly suggests that he was the artist for the Gourlay type of memorial (Fig. 344). Two of these memorials picture actual buildings (Whitehall, and the Dutch Reformed

---

10. Wilson Letters (privately owned). Frances Wilson (c.1790–1879) attended School No. 1 in Clermont between 1796 and 1800 (Wilson Papers, Clements Library, University of Michigan). In 1809 she married merchant Fyler Dibble (d.1844), and they lived in Clermont and New York City.

11. Worked by his granddaughter Hester Ten Eyck (1796–1861), c.1811; unlocated but illustrated in Bennett, *The People's Choice* (1980), 28. Possibly the latest example is the memorial by Christian Monteath (b.1805) with a death date of July 29, 1816 (Groft, *The Folk Spirit of Albany* [1978], Fig. 93); or the work of Eliza McMillan (1805–1837), Skinner Sale 1446, May 30, 1992, Lot 178.

12. Bolton and Cortelyou, *Ezra Ames of Albany* (1935), 53, 171. Thompson students mentioned were the Misses Briton, Little, and Bassett.

Fig. 343. Anonymous mourning piece embroidered beneath the picture *Sacred to the Memory of Ann Mary Yates* and inscribed on the plinth *A. M. Y./ ob 23d Nov. 1794*, c.1801. Silk, paint, and ink on silk; 17″ x 24½″. A very similar memorial but with a different church was made by a girl of the Van Vranken family and dated 1801 (Groft, *The Folk Spirit of Albany* [1978], Fig. 95). It and the Yates embroidery have the basic format of the Beeckman memorial and similar inscriptions on the silk, but with heavier trees and weepers that are smaller in proportion to the monuments. Ann Mary Helms Yates (1749–1794) was the wife of Peter Waldron Yates who was a lawyer in Albany. They had one son and eight daughters. Donor information indicates that the embroiderer married a Peirce. Probably this was worked by Engeltie (Angelica), the eighth child, who was born July 12, 1786. *Albany Institute of History and Art, gift of Katherine V. V. Peirce, 1922.1.*

Church in Fig. 344), and the meetinghouses found on many other pieces may have been local churches.

Because Ames was painting patterns for schoolmistress Catharine Thompson, who taught between 1804 and 1816, it is likely that she was responsible for some of the memorials within this group. "Mrs. Thompson," having received "her education in England and France," advertised the opening of her "BOARDING and DAY SCHOOL" in *The Albany Gazette* of November 15, 1804. In May of 1805, her school was in the "airy and commodious house formerly occupied by Mrs. TURPIN," where she would teach "Reading, English and French Grammar, plain Sewing, Ornamental Needle-work on Muslin, Tambouring, Embroidery, Filligree, Chenille, point and cloth works, . . . " and Mr. J. Thompson would teach "Writing, Arithmetic, and Geography."[13]

Between 1805 and the publication of Albany's first city directory in 1813, many schools were advertised, but of those, only Catharine B. Thompson's Young Ladies' School at 38 Columbia Street and John Nugent's young ladies' seminary appeared in the directory of 1813. Catharine disappeared from the directory after the entry of 1816. However, her promising new school in South Carolina was soon dissipated by an epidemic, and in 1818 she married a merchant. The obituaries of *The Albany Gazette* included the following on October 4, 1819: "At Beaufort, South Carolina, on the 24th ult. after a few days illness, of the prevailing fever, the celebrated and learned Mrs. Milne, formerly Miss Catharine B. Thomp-

---

13. *The Albany Gazette,* May 9, 1805. J. Thompson was probably Catharine's brother John (b.1782). Catharine (b.1780) was the daughter of Alexander B. Thompson and Elizabeth Ann Wicks of Rhinebeck.

Fig. 344. Anonymous mourning piece with plinth inscribed *IN MEMORY of/ Julia Louisa Gourlay,/ Died 25ᵗʰ April 1813/ Aged 2 years 10/ Months & 29 Days*, c.1814. Silk, chenille, paint, and ink on silk; 18¾″ x 22½″. In the background is the Dutch Reformed Church of Albany, which was built in 1715 and destroyed in 1806. This was evidently copied from an 1806 engraving by Henry W. Snyder after Philip Hooker. The figure, urn-topped obelisk, and tall, scrawny willow tree all distinguish this group of Albany memorials. The similarity of the willow to an example painted by Ezra Ames (Fig. 345) strongly suggests that he was the artist for this group of memorials. This piece is attributed to Annatie (d.1828) or Maria Gourlay (d.1825), eldest of the seven daughters born to Albany iron founder James Gourlay (1770–1862) and Helen Bromley (1773–1850), and the sisters of Julia Louisa.
Albany Institute of History and Art, U1978.151.

Fig. 345. Detail from the portrait *A Daughter of Elkanah Watson* by Ezra Ames (1768–1836), Albany, New York, 1818. The lofty but somewhat spare willow tree in this painting resembles the willows in Figures 344 and 346. For the full painting, see Schorsch, *Mourning Becomes America* (1976), Fig. 49/171.
The Art Museum, Princeton University, Y 1970-2.

Opposite: Fig. 346. *M. SMYTHE* inscribed on the glass, and with initials of a thirteen-year-old child and three infants on the monuments, but undated, c.1816–1818. Black and brown silk, paint, and ink on silk; 15¾″ x 20½″. For related pieces, see Groft, *The Folk Spirit of Albany* (1978), Fig. 93, and SPB, Garbisch Sale I, No. 3595, January 24, 1974, Lot 192. This memorial was also in the first Garbisch Sale, Lot 199, and it then had part of a New York City newspaper and a page from an account book on the back, both dated 1818, along with the name Margaret Fryer Smythe, in some unknown form. In 1803, Charles Smythe (c.1783–1844) and Margaret Fryer (d.1823) were married in Albany's Saint Peter's Episcopal Church, and their two daughters named Catherine were baptized there in 1804 and 1820. *The Albany Argus* recorded the death of their daughter Margaret, aged seven, in December 1830, and she was survived by four brothers (will of her grandfather Isaac I. Fryer, May 6, 1831 [Albany County Will Book 7:256]). Although no evidence has been found, it was possibly an earlier daughter named Margaret who worked this embroidery, and the figures may represent M. Smythe and her mother. The original backing of the frame is lost, and the identity of its maker remains undetermined.
Private collection; photograph courtesy of Christie's.

son, of this city." The last directory listing for John Nugent's School was in 1815.

Another artist who may have contributed to the Albany memorials was Louis Lemet (c.1779–1832) who appeared in Albany by 1804 and advertised the opening of a "DRAWING-SCHOOL" in *The Albany Gazette* of June 26, 1806. Lemet was a crayon portraitist and engraver who was associated with St. Memin at an earlier date. In 1809, he bought the looking-glass store of John P. Boue, and in 1810 he advertised that for those "who may please to favor him with the framing of NEEDLE WORK, he offers to PAINT THE HEAD GRATIS."[14] He worked in Albany until about 1828.

Although various women continued to advertise schools for girls in Albany during the late teens and early twenties of the nineteenth century, none have left identified evidence of their teaching, and the vogue for print-work memorials evidently ended before 1825.

---

14. *The Albany Gazette,* supplement of March 27, 1809; advertisement in *The Albany Register,* January 20, 1810, and illustrated in Norman S. Rice, comp., *New York Furniture Before 1840* (Albany: Albany Institute of History and Art, 1962), 59.

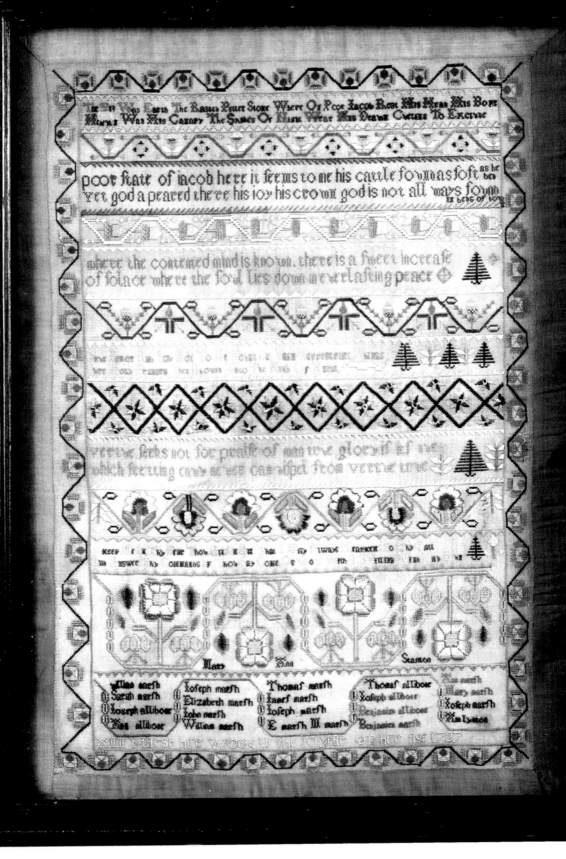

NEEDLEWORK OF PENNSYLVANIA

Philadelphia's Opulent Embroidery

On October 27, 1682, William Penn (1644–1718), a wealthy Englishman and devout Quaker, disembarked from the *Welcome* at New Castle, on the Delaware River, and proceeded to take formal possession of the vast lands granted to him by King Charles II. Penn called this land *Pennsylvania* (Penn's Woods) in honor of his father and systematically laid out the city soon to be known as Philadelphia (City of Brotherly Love). The rapid growth and remarkable success of his colony may be explained in one word: *tolerance*. It was not only promised by Penn, it was practiced, and it attracted large numbers of his countrymen. Penn also promoted his colony in the Low Countries of Germany, since he admired German industry, and the German Reformers were in harmony with his beliefs.[1] Letters from early Pennsylvania settlers impressed hoards of central Europeans whose lives had been continually disrupted by political and religious conflicts. Despite the risks, many of these oppressed people forsook their ancestral homeland for the promise of peace and a reasonable hope of prosperity.[2]

Penn's "Holy Experiment" found Philadelphia approaching the size of Boston by 1730,[3] and the arts of its people were developing the distinctive styles that would characterize this area for a century to come. The "plainness" favored by Penn and his followers affected dress in a noticeable way, but the artifacts of Pennsylvania became lavishly elegant and exuberantly decorative. They reflect the blending of different cultures, and, especially during the Federal period, this also became evident in the needlework.

Fig. 347. *ANN MARSH her WORK IN the 10 year OF her Age 1727.* Silk on linen with silk ribbon border; 15″ x 11″; original deep, black-painted frame of the period. Within five columns, Ann included many Marsh and Allibone family names; also *Ann Lynton,* and above the columns, *Mary Ann Stanton.* Ann Marsh (1717–1797) was born in England to Joseph Marsh, a skinner and glover, and Elizabeth Allibone (1683–c.1741). She remained single, and like her mother, she taught needlework to the daughters of prominent Philadelphians. Based on the documentation for Figure 359, and other comparisons, Figures 353–359 and 361–362 are attributed to her instruction; and probably she taught Amy Lewis, Figure 366.
Collection of Lydia Willits Bartholomew.

---

1. References to Penn's mother being from the Low Countries have been refuted. She was Margaret Jasper, probably Anglo-Irish, and first married to Nicasius Van der Schuren. She married William Penn in January 1643/44.

2. For concise comments on the blending of English and European cultures, see Garvan and Hummel, *Pennsylvania Germans: A Celebration of Their Arts 1683–1850* (1982), 99–102.

3. In 1730, Boston had 13,000 people; Philadelphia 11,500 (Bridenbaugh, *Cities in the Wilderness* [1938], 303).

Philadelphia and its environs produced three important groups of samplers during the colonial period, as well as a characteristic type of pictorial embroidery, and their basic styles remained popular throughout the eighteenth century. Beginning with the earliest Pennsylvania needlework, flowers and foliage dominated the patterns rather than buildings, people, or animals, and this preference continued until the last major samplers of importance were worked in the 1840s.

BAND-PATTERN SAMPLERS

Philadelphia's earliest identifiable group of samplers is now composed of thirteen pieces worked between 1725 and 1740, and their thoroughly English patterns were in keeping with current fashions in London. Conventionalized floral band patterns persisted from the seventeenth century, but long inscriptions were in vogue, and by 1727 these samplers consistently had an all-enclosing border. This surrounding vine of Indian pinks is essentially the same on twelve pieces, and it appears as a band pattern at the top and bottom of the earliest dated piece by Sarah Logan (Fig. 348). Many of the motifs on these samplers are identical in design and coloring, and their verses are often repetitious. Nine examples include the same acorn band pattern, and nine pieces also have a geometric diamond band pattern that appears to be unique to this group in America.[4] Even more consistent is a stylized floral band pattern found on all thirteen samplers (Fig. 347a). Each girl, except Ann Wilkinson (Fig. 350) and Elizabeth Hudson, worked tiny pine trees for line-end designs, and all but Elizabeth Rush included information about their families, or columns of family names, which usually included grandparents, parents, siblings, and other relatives. Therefore, most of the sampler makers can be positively identified.[5]

These distinctive samplers were known to collectors by 1921,[6] but the first piece to evoke serious study was the prime example worked by Ann Marsh, whose teaching career received attention even before her sampler was published in 1969 (Fig. 347).[7] Speculation about *her* teacher was aroused by the two uniden-

4. It appeared in a German pattern book of 1529 (*ANTIQUES,* February 1991, 370). For eight samplers not illustrated here: Ann Robins, 1730, and Sarah Howell, 1731 (B&C, Pls. CX, CXI); Mary Morris, 1727 (Schiffer, 19); Elizabeth Rush, 1734 (Swan, *Guide,* 33); Elizabeth Hudson, 1737 (Hornor, *The Story of Samplers* [1971], Fig. 26); Ruth Biles, c.1725, and Prudence Dunbar, 1740 (Ring, *Treasures,* 36); Mary MacColloch, 1740 (SPB Sale 4148, July 8, 1978, Lot 149).

5. Unidentified is Prudence Dunbar (b.c.1729) who was probably the daughter of David Dunbar and Sarah Crowell.

6. B&C, 395.

7. Schiffer, "American Needlework" (1969), 105. Thomas Woody recorded Ann's teaching in *Early Quaker Education in Pennsylvania* (1920), 73; he also illustrated a page from her school account book in *A History of Women's Education in the United States* (1929, reprint, 1974), 1:200. John Marshall Phillips (1905–1953), Curator of the Mabel Brady Garvan Collection at Yale University, and a collateral descendant, attempted to enlarge upon her history (George Norman Highley Papers, CCHS). In 1968, Schiffer was the first to publish much of her needlework. "Ann Marsh—18th Century Needlewoman" was presented by Sandra Downie at the Irene Emery Roundtable on Museum Textiles in 1975 (*Proceedings,* Textile Museum, Washington, D.C., 1976).

Fig. 348. *sarah logan her/ work in the 10/ year of her age/ in the year 1725* inscribed in the lower arcade at far right. Silk on wool; 12" x 9". In the other sections, from left to right, she worked *Sarah logan/ was born 9 of th 8ᵐᵒ 1715 15 mi/ after 4 in the af/ter noon; william logan/ was born ye 14 of/ ye 3ᵐᵒ 1718 30 mi/ after 5 in ye morn; this work in han/ my friends may hav/ when i am dead an/ laid in grave.* Sarah (Sally) Logan (1715–1744) was the eldest child of James Logan (1674–1751) and Sarah Read (d.1754), who were married in Philadelphia on December 9, 1714. Sarah married Isaac Norris (1701–1766), and their Fairhill estate was between Stenton and the city. Sarah died shortly after the birth of her fourth child. Her portrait is shown in Myers, *Hannah Logan's Courtship* (1904), 9. For the sampler of her niece and namesake, see Figure 369. *Fairmount Park Commission, Loudoun Mansion, Philadelphia, 89.499.*

Fig. 347a. Band pattern of stylized carnations and rosebuds from Ann Marsh's sampler of 1727. It appears on thirteen pieces worked between 1725 and 1740; also on the samplers of Rebecca Jones, 1750 (Fig. 353), Sally Wister, 1773 (Fig. 354), and Mary Hollingsworth, 1785 (Schiffer, 33). Between 1823 and 1838 it was worked on samplers naming *Sarah Boone* or *Sarah L. Boone*, a Berks County Quaker schoolmistress. See Catharine Weidner's 1838 sampler (acc. no. 57.14) in the Historical Society of Berks County, Reading.

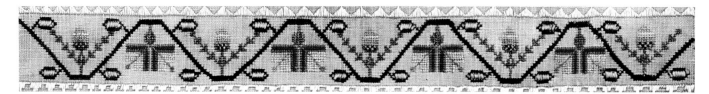

Fig. 349. Sampler inscribed *Richard Sandiford Elizabeth Sandiford MS 1731.* Silk on linen; 16½″ x 8¾″. This is the earliest known example within this group to include an alphabet. It is attributed to Margaret Sandiford, the eldest daughter of Richard Sandiford (d. 1725) and Elizabeth Walter of Barbados, British West Indies, who was evidently educated in Philadelphia. This sampler descended with the possessions of Ann Marsh. *Collection of Lydia Willits Bartholomew.*

tified female names on her sampler, but the recently discovered Logan and Trotter samplers (Figs. 348, 351) made it possible to solve the mystery of her mistress: Ann was taught by her mother. This fact helps to explain Philadelphia's enduring needlework styles from the 1720s to the 1790s. Elizabeth Marsh was the schoolmistress who established the trends in Philadelphia's elegant schoolgirl embroidery, and her daughter Ann maintained them. Teaching the daughters of James Logan probably enhanced the reputation of Elizabeth Marsh, but surely her artistry impressed all the illustrious families who became her patrons.

James Logan, the father of Sarah, whom he called Sally, was among Philadelphia's most prominent citizens, and at times, the most powerful man in the Colony. He came as secretary to William Penn and was attorney to the Penn family. He eventually served as provincial commissioner of property, business agent for the Proprietors, mayor of Philadelphia in 1723, president of the Council from 1736 to 1738, and governor of Pennsylvania. He was also a successful landowner and energetic merchant, dealing in a vast variety of imported goods as well as materials from the Indians.

Logan's Ledger of 1720–1727 relates mostly to his business negotiations, but occasional references to household expenses offer clues to the education of his children from 1723 through 1727. The "Schoolmaster" or "Mistress" was often unnamed, but on July 26, 1723, Joan Humphries was listed as having been paid £9-2-6 "in full for Schooling."[8] She was possibly a governess to Sally and Billy who were then seven and five years old. She came to the colony from Middlesex County, England, in 1707, and had formerly "lived in Wm Penn's family."[9] Payments to Sally's "Mistress" in December of 1723, and March and September of 1724, indicate that she was then attending school. Logan finally named the teacher on August 28, 1727, when he wrote: "Elizabeth Marsh for Sally and Hanah's Schooling 8-2-8¼."[10] She also appeared earlier in Logan's business accounts, for on May 5, 1725, the year of Sally's sampler, the ledger included "Elizabeth Marsh to acct of haberdashery £9-16-8¼."[11] A cross-reference with the household accounts suggests that Elizabeth may have received haberdashery supplies in exchange for teaching. Like many women of this period, she probably combined shopkeeping with teaching and sold the goods for the works she taught. At this time the Logan family was living in the city, for the building of their Germantown mansion known as Stenton was not completed until 1730.

Elizabeth Marsh, Philadelphia's premier schoolmistress, was born on August 1, 1683, in Worcester County, England.[12] She was the daughter of Joseph Allibone,

8. James Logan's Ledger, 147. Manuscripts, HSP.
9. *Abstracts from the Record of Certificates received at the Monthly Meeting of Philadelphia from 1685–1758,* 522. HSP. "Joan Humphries (schoolmistress)" also heads a 1721 business account in Logan's Ledger, 129.
10. Logan Ledger, 165, 191, 268.
11. Ibid., 230. Haberdashery is defined as men's furnishings, or, particularly in Britain, as notions (ribbons, lace, thread, needles, etc.), and in the eighteenth century it also applied to milliners' supplies.
12. *Digested Copy of the Registers of Births of the General Meeting of Herefordshire, Worcestershire and Wales from 1635–1837* (Philadelphia: Genealogical Society of Pennsylvania, 1908).

Fig. 350. *Ann Wilkinson Her Work Finished In The 13ᵗʰ/ Year Of Her Age 1734.* Silk on wool; 15″ x 12″. Ann's recently discovered sampler combines typical characteristics with several band patterns and motifs previously unknown to this group. Ann Wilkinson (1721–1759) was the daughter of Philadelphia shipcarver and stonecutter Anthony Wilkinson (c.1698–1765) and Elizabeth. She married mastmaker Thomas Cuthbert (1713–1781) at Christ Church on May 19, 1744, and nine of their ten children reached adulthood. Beneath the Ten Commandments in verse, Ann's sampler records the deaths and previously unknown ages of her grandparents, Gabriel and Ann Wilkinson, in addition to naming her parents, paternal aunts and uncles, and siblings. It also corrects her baptismal record at Christ Church, given as "27 October 1721, ae 4 years" but it must have been "ae 4 weeks"; and it consequently proves that she was born after rather than before her brother Brian, as was formerly believed. (See Eunice Story Eaton Ullman, "The Gabriel Wilkinson Family," *PGM,* XXVI, 2 [1969], 61.)
Private collection.

a carpenter, and Ann (probably Ann Allen), and in 1681 and 1683 her father was imprisoned for refusing to pay the tithe and for worshipping as a Friend.[13] On September 8, 1711, Elizabeth married Joseph Marsh in Hallow, Worcester County,[14] and the births of their four children were recorded in *The Worcestershire Monthly Meeting Records:* Benjamin, February 21, 1713; Ann, November 7, 1714 (evidently transcribed in error for 1717); Mary, November 19, 1719; and Joseph, February 14, 1723.[15] Elizabeth was forty years old in 1723, and she was no doubt an experienced schoolmistress before she embarked for America. No record of the family's migration to the colony has been found. Presumably Elizabeth came to Philadelphia in the spring or summer of 1723 and was the unnamed "Mistress" paid by James Logan in December of that year. In any case, Logan's Ledger, Trotter's Receipt Book (Fig. 352), and Ann Marsh's embroideries (Figs. 347, 373) provide convincing evidence that Elizabeth was responsible for the eleven related band samplers worked before 1740, and also for Margret Wistar's sconces of 1738 (Fig. 374). Possibly Ann, then twenty, was already teaching with her mother in 1738. Judging by the location of Elizabeth's patrons, the Marsh family was probably living in or near an area bound by Chesnut, Race, Front, and Third streets.

In 1734, Joseph and Elizabeth Marsh acquired property on the west side of the

13. Highley Papers, CCHS.
14. *IGI* for Worcester County, England.
15. *Digested Copy of the Registers of Births.*

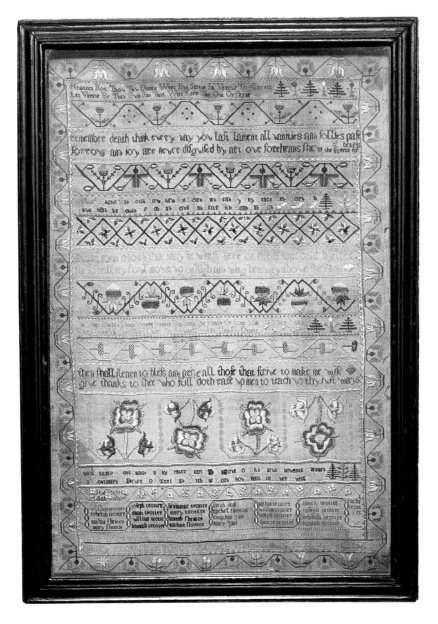

Fig. 351. *Mary Trotter Her Work in The 8 Year of Her Age IN the Year 1735.* Silk on linen; 16¾" x 10⅞"; sewn to the backboard of its original deep, black-painted frame of the period. In six and one half columns of names, Mary Trotter listed many relatives and numerous siblings. Mary (c.1727–1803) was the daughter of Joseph Trotter (1697–1770) and Dinah (Shenton) Shelton (1694–1769). Her father, a prosperous cutler and ironmonger, was a member of the Pennsylvania Assembly from 1739 to 1756. On August 17, 1751, Mary married David Bacon (1729–1809), a Philadelphia hatter. They had ten children.

Private collection.

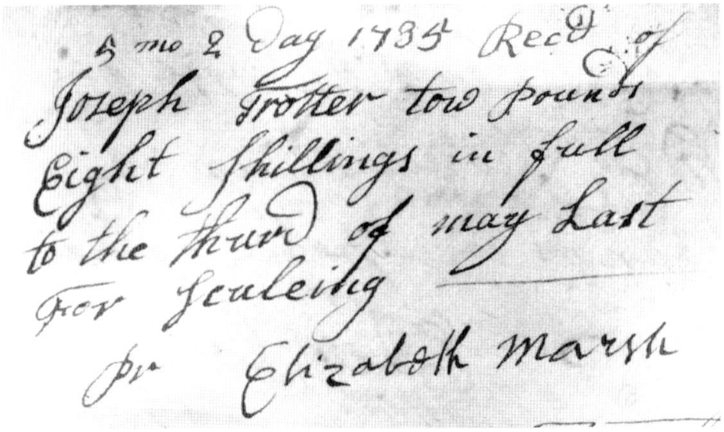

Fig. 352. An entry in Joseph Trotter's Receipt Book, dated "5 mo 2 Day 1735" and signed by schoolmistress Elizabeth Marsh. Actual size. It records payment of "tow pounds Eight Shillings in full to the thurd of may Last For Sculeing." All entries are in the same hand, with signatures of the recipients. Similar receipts were signed by Elizabeth in payment for schooling on June 2, 1737, and July 4, 1738.

Thompson Collection, No. 83, Manuscripts, Historical Society of Pennsylvania.

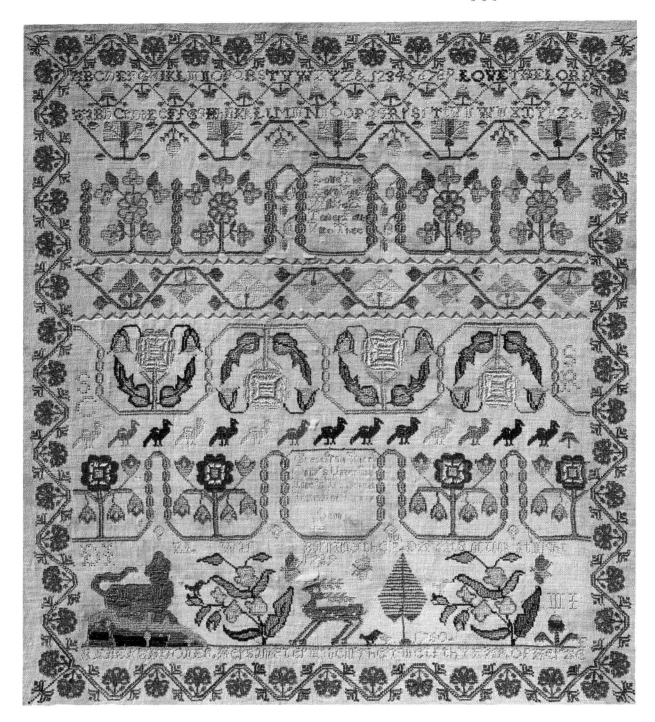

Fig. 353. *REBEKAH JONES HER SAMPLER made in the twelfth year of her age/ 1750; also, RI was born July the 7ᵗʰ Day at 8 oclock at night/ 1739*. Silk on linen; 13″ x 11⅝″. Despite a different border, Rebecca's sampler bears close kinship to earlier band-pattern samplers. It includes three typical band patterns, including the pervasive alternating carnation and rosebud design (Fig. 347a). Also, like Sarah Logan (Fig. 348), Rebecca included the exact time of her birth, and the same opening maxim. Her work is enlivened by birds and animals, while her two sprigs of naturalistic flowers herald the forthcoming patterns in compartmented samplers. Although her mother was a schoolmistress, she most likely made this sampler under the instruction of Ann Marsh. Rebecca Jones (July 7, 1739–April 15, 1818) was the only daughter of William Jones and Mary Porter (1707–1761). For Rebecca's white-work sampler, see Figure 364.

Friends Historical Association Collection, Atwater Kent Museum— The History Museum of Philadelphia, 87.35.1004.1.

Schuylkill River, and a mortgage of November 1738 named their three living children: Benjamin, Ann, and Mary. Elizabeth Marsh died sometime between this transaction and the payment of their loan in January 1742, and her husband and children survived her.[16] Elizabeth probably died in 1741, for she was most likely responsible for the two 1740 samplers within the group considered here. Nothing more is known of Joseph Marsh and his son, Benjamin. In 1744 Mary Marsh married Othniel Tomlinson of Salem, New Jersey, and before his death in 1756, they moved to Concord, Chester County, Pennsylvania. In 1760, she married the twice-widowed Aaron Ashbridge (1712–1776). Mary's only child, Mary Tomlinson (1747–1800), married Samuel Hibberd (1743–1793), and they had seven daughters.

Ann Marsh never married and taught school in Philadelphia until at least 1792 (Figs. 361, 362). Her school account book of 1763–1778 belonged to a descendant of her sister in the 1950s,[17] and another of 1772–1789 is now at the Historical Society of Pennsylvania. During the Revolutionary period, Ann was teaching Emlens, Herbensons, Howells, Mifflins, Reads, and many other children from Philadelphia's influential families, including Sally Wister (Fig. 354), Deborah Norris, and Nancy, the daughter of General Cadwalader.[18] Like her mother, she had no need to advertise her school, but why her name is absent from the city's first directories of 1785 and 1791 is unexplained. Ann must have been lonely in 1794 when she wrote the following to her widowed niece of Willistown, Chester County: "If you have Room i should be glad to Come and live with thee for Company but how i shall get my things up i dont know."[19] Obviously the move was accomplished, for Ann made her will in Willistown on August 17, 1795, and she devised either fifty or one hundred pounds to each of Mary Hibberd's seven daughters,[20] as well as furniture, silver, and linens. The inventory of her personal estate totaled £1,209-19-1½ in addition to £1,054-10-1½ in cash and bonds.[21]

Ann Marsh continued the band-pattern sampler style of her mother, and it surely influenced other teachers such as Mary Askew (Fig. 542), Mary Shaw,[22] and

16. Philadelphia Deeds, Book F 10, p. 328; H 15, p. 176. There is no evidence that the Marsh family lived on this property.

17. George Norman Highley to Elizabeth Taylor Scott, August 6, 1976 (Highley Papers, CCHS).

18. Marsh account book, 1772–1789, and Ann Marsh receipt to Mrs. Norris, December 20, 1774. Norris Papers, 7:11 (HSP). It was the nine-month-old infant Ann (nicknamed Nancy) Cadwalader (1771–1850) who sat on the famous card table in the 1772 family portrait by Charles Willson Peale. The table and portrait are now in the PMA. See ANTIQUES, May 1984, 1122. Nancy's needlework skills may have helped her in later life. She married Robert T. Kemble in 1796 but subsequently lost her fortune and kept a small school in New York. Her only child, Mary Dickinson Kemble, worked as a governess before marrying William H. Sumner of Boston. (Wainwright, Colonial Grandeur in Philadelphia [1964], 153–4.)

19. Photostat of Ann's letter, Highley Papers, CCHS.

20. Ann Marsh's influence appears in samplers by Mary Hibberd's granddaughters, Mary and Elizabeth Evans. They named Willistown schoolmistress Sarah Shaw, and one is dated 1812 (Bartholomew collection).

21. Estate No. 4590, Chester County Court House.

22. In 1796, Hannah Minshall worked a sampler in the early band-pattern form and named Mary Shaw, who was probably her teacher (private collection). This may have been Mary Shaw, widow and seamstress in the Philadelphia directories of 1795–1800.

Fig. 354. *SARAH WISTERS WORK 1773*. Silk on linen; 11¼″ x 9⅞″. Sarah Wister (1761–1804), called Sally, was the daughter of Philadelphia merchant Daniel Wister (1738–1805) and Lowry Jones (1742–1804), who were of German and Welsh descent, respectively. Sally attended the school kept by Quaker schoolmaster Anthony Benezet in 1777. She was also taught by Ann Marsh from 1774 until 1776, and surely during the previous year when she worked this sampler, with its typical border and band patterns in the early style. In 1778, her sampler attracted the attention of the dashing Virginian Captain Alexander Spotswood Dandridge. Sally noted that he "observ'd my sampler, which was in full view. Wish'd I would teach the Virginians some of my needle wisdom; they were the laziest girls in the world" (Myers, *Sally Wister's Journal* [1902], 158–9). Sally later wrote poetry and contributed to the *Port Folio* under the nom de plume of Laura (Ibid., 40). She died unmarried. *Philadelphia Museum of Art, gift of Sally Wister Ingersoll Fox, 75-128-1.*

possibly the mother of Rebecca Jones. Mary Porter Jones was the widow of a mariner who was lost at sea, and she kept a small school in Drinker's Alley.[23] Rebecca's sampler (Fig. 353) may have been worked at her mother's school, but its pattern, technique, and inscriptions strongly suggest that it was made under the instruction of Ann Marsh. Mary Jones is known to have sought the best possible education for her daughter, and she may have been sent to Ann's school before attending the girls' school of Anthony Benezet.

Rebecca's conversion to the Society of Friends occurred shortly thereafter, despite the disapproval of her Anglican mother, and she became a recognized Quaker minister by 1760. She also assisted her mother in teaching, and after her mother's death in 1761, Rebecca continued to teach for a livelihood. She was joined by Hannah Cathrall (1736–1806) and in 1774, Catharine, the daughter of Margret Wistar Haines (Fig. 374) was among their pupils.[24] They kept the school in Drinker's Alley for twenty-three years, but Rebecca's firm commitment to "plainness" precluded instruction in ornamental needlework.[25] Thereafter Rebecca devoted her time to the Society of Friends, traveled in England, and was active in planning the Westtown School. Rebecca Jones was the Friends' most renowned female minister in early America. Her recently discovered sampler proves that she was born on the evening of July 7, 1739, rather than July 8 as stated in most published biographies. It confirms the records of her christening at Christ Church on "25 July 1739," aged "2 wks & 4 day."

———————

23. Mary Porter (1707–1761), born in Barbados, was the daughter of Thomas Porter (b.1683) and Elizabeth Westbury, who were married at Christ Church, Barbados, January 29, 1706. Mary married William Jones in Philadelphia's Christ Church on February 23, 1729. Her son Daniel (1730–1771) later lived in Mt. Holly, New Jersey, where he was an innkeeper and warden of St. Andrews Church (*IGI*; see also Allinson, *Memorials of Rebecca Jones* (1849).

24. Letter from Margret Haines to Catharine Haines, 1774 (Wyck Papers, Series II, Box 8, Folder 7, American Philosophical Society, Philadelphia).

25. Allinson, *Memorials,* 17.

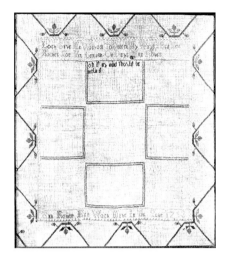

Fig. 355. *Ann Flower Her Work Made In The Year 1753.* Silk on linen; 11⅝″ x 9⅞″. Ann's unfinished sampler is the earliest known instance of this compartmented form in Philadelphia, and it is interesting to see that the name and date were completed before the most intricate part of the pattern was undertaken; also, that Susanna Head and Lydia Speakman signed their samplers with exactly the same wording, although Ann worked the capital letters and date in eyelet stitches (Figs. 357, 358). Ann Flower (1743–1778) was the daughter of Enoch Flower (1703–1773) and Ann Jones (1711–1775) of Philadelphia. In 1765, Ann married Samuel Wheeler (1742–1820), a master blacksmith and ironworker. They had five children. *Collection of Anne Flower Cumings Dybwad.*

COMPARTMENTED VERSE AND FLOWER SAMPLERS

Although narrowly bordered band samplers remained in favor at Philadelphia schools throughout the eighteenth century, by the 1750s a distinctive compartmented style had been introduced. Within a deeply arcaded floral border, these samplers are divided into nine or twelve equal sections, which are alternately filled with wonderfully naturalistic floral bouquets and tightly worked pious inscriptions. The earliest evidence of this style is found in the unfinished sampler begun by Ann Flower in 1753 (Fig. 355),[1] and in 1760, Mary Webb completed an exquisite example (Fig. 356). As yet, no samplers of this type have been recorded from the 1770s, but Susanna Head's magnificent piece with twelve sections was made in 1781 (Fig. 357), and obviously under the same instructress who taught Lydia Speakman in 1785 (Fig. 358). It is now reasonably certain that these girls were instructed by Ann Marsh, for Mary Cooper's work of 1789 descended with a notation that Ann Marsh was her teacher (Fig. 359). Ann Marsh probably introduced this style, but it was continued by other teachers late in the century, for Sarah Hoopes dated her sampler two years after the death of Ann Marsh (Fig. 360).

Two newly recognized Philadelphia forms are close contemporaries of the later compartmented samplers. They are attributed to Ann Marsh's school because of similar embroidery and the kinship of their makers to Miss Marsh's pupil Mary Cooper. Most spectacular are the delicate pictorial samplers made by Sarah Cooper and Hannah Firth in 1792 (Figs. 361, 362), while Sarah's cousin Hannah Cooper worked a verse-filled oval beneath similar swags in 1791.[2]

These embroideries were made by a group of wealthy and well-acquainted Quaker girls from across the Delaware River who attended Ann Marsh's school at the same time. They probably remained friends throughout life, for Hannah Firth married Isaac Cooper Jones, who was the first cousin of Hannah Cooper and a third cousin of Sarah and Mary Cooper. Isaac C. Jones was a successful merchant much involved in the China trade, and he died a highly esteemed Philadelphian at the age of ninety-five. Hannah was also remembered as "the impersonation of good nature and genial hospitality." They lived in a large house on Arch Street but entertained most elegantly at Rockland, their country seat on the Schuylkill River.[3]

1. Ann was nine or ten years old when she abandoned this sampler, but in 1768 she completed a splendid rendition of the Flower arms, which is nearly identical to Figure 377 (with her prayer book cover and a twenty-seven-page sketch book, it is now in the Winterthur Museum).

2. *ANTIQUES,* December 1989, 1341.

3. *Recollections of John Jay Smith* (Philadelphia: J. B. Lippincott Co., 1892), 271.

Fig. 356. *Mary Webb Her Work in the/ Thirteenth year of her age 1760* and naming *Joseph Webb Edith Webb NW.* Silk on linen; 17″ x 15″. At left center Mary worked the verse begun by Ann Flower (Fig. 355), and her flowers are worked in the minute tent stitches found on later pieces within this group. Her border is similar to the deeply arcaded border on Mary Hollingsworth's 1785 band sampler (Schiffer, 33), which includes the stylized band pattern (Fig. 347a) favored by the Marsh teachers. The format of her sampler also resembles the white work of Amy Lewis, 1759 (Fig. 366). Mary Webb (April 2, 1747–1833) was the daughter of Joseph Webb (1722–1753), a house carpenter of Philadelphia, and Edith Way (1727–1772). Her father's ledger for the years 1744 to 1753 is in the Joseph Downs Collection, Winterthur Museum Library, No. 2158. In 1763, Mary's widowed mother married Nathan Hussey (d.1775), a shopkeeper of York, Pennsylvania. Mary was married on May 28, 1771, at the York Meeting, to Joseph Updagraff (1726–1801), and they had nine children. *Private collection.*

Fig. 357. *Susanna Head Her Work Made In The Year 1781.* Silk on linen; 18¼″ x 12¼″. Susanna's sampler is the most elaborate example of this Philadelphia form. The style, stitches, and the red and black coloring of her inscriptions appear to characterize the lettering on later work from Ann Marsh's school, and they support attributions of other pieces, such as a modified compartmented sampler by Ann West, 1787, which also has a cross border with several floral motifs identical to Susanna's work (*ANTIQUES*, December 1989, 1339). Susanna Head (1766–1845) was the daughter of Philadelphia merchant John Head (1723–1792) and his second wife, Elizabeth Hastings (d. 1770). Susanna married William Sansom (1763–1840) in 1788. Their daughter, Eliza H. Sansom (1789–1870), worked a modest sampler in 1801 with a large rendition of the Roman alphabet.
Collection of George Vaux.

Fig. 358. *Lydia Speakman Her Work Made In The Year 1785* and with the names *Townsend Speakman* and *Hannah Speakman*. Silk on linen; 20½" x 17"; original deep mahogany frame. Several of the flowers in Lydia's border are identical to those on Susanna Head's sampler, and the style of her signature is also the same. Lydia worked a borderless band-pattern sampler with similar flowers when she was eight years old in 1784 (Hershey Museum of American Life, Hershey, Pennsylvania). Lydia Speakman (1776–1857) was the daughter of Townsend Speakman (1743–1793) and Hannah Carver (1754–1833). Her father came from Reading, England, to Philadelphia in 1771, and became a druggist at No. 18 South Second Street. He died in the yellow fever epidemic. In 1794, Lydia married John Hart (c.1767–1834), who had become her father's apprentice at the apothecary shop in 1782. He continued to work as a druggist, and they had thirteen children, including two sets of twins.

Collection of Katherine Y. Downes.

Fig. 359. *Mary Cooper's Work Made in The Y^r 1789.* Silk on linen; 18″ x 16½″; original deep frame. Mary named her parents, her sister Sarah, and included the initials of three brothers. Inscribed on the sampler's backboard is this statement: "Mary Cooper's Work/ done at Ann Marshs school/ Philadelphia." Mary also worked a pictorial silk embroidery entitled *Spring* and based on a print from James Thomsons' *Seasons* (New Jersey State Museum). A nearly identical piece was made by Isabella Hall (1777–1816). See Rumford, *American Folk Paintings* (1988), 375. Mary Cooper (1776–1869) was the eldest daughter of Samuel Cooper (1744–1812) and Prudence Brown (1739–1822). Her father was a prominent citizen of Camden, New Jersey, and owned the ferry rights at Cooper's Point. Mary married Richard Matlack Cooper (1768–1843) in 1798, and they lived on Cooper Street in Camden. Her husband became president of the State Bank of Camden, a judge of the Gloucester County Courts, and a United States Congressman, 1829–1833. They had eleven children.
Winterthur Museum, 87.36.

Fig. 360. *Sarah HOOPes/ DauGhter OF Abr/am/ ANd SUSaNNa Hoo/PeS/ Her WOrK doN/ IN The 14th Year OF/ Her AGe 1799.* Silk on linen; 16½″ x 13¾″. Sarah Hoopes (1785–before 1833) was the eldest daughter of shoemaker Abraham Hoopes (1755–1806) and Susanna McNees (1752–1833) of Newtown, Delaware County, Pennsylvania. She died unmarried.
National Museum of American History, Smithsonian Institution; gift of Mrs. W. H. Hoopes, 203959.

Fig. 361. *Sarah Cooper Her Work Made In The Year 1792*. Silk and coiled metal on linen; 18¾″ x 17¾″; original deep walnut frame. Sarah's style of lettering and her minute tent stitches on sheer linen closely resemble the work of her sister Mary (Fig. 359), and her sampler is therefore attributed to Ann Marsh's Philadelphia school. In 1814, Sarah Cooper (1779–1835) married, as his second wife, Henry Hull (1765–1834) of Stanfordville, New York. He was a farmer and merchant, and like his father, Tiddeman Hull, a minister in the Society of Friends. Their children were Samuel Cooper Hull (1818–1868) and Mary Prudence Hull (1820–1841), who both died unmarried.
Author's collection.

Fig. 362. *Hannah Ffirth Her Work Made In The Year 1792*. Silk on linen; 17½″ x 15″. Hannah was surely a classmate of Sarah Cooper (Fig. 361). The condition of her sampler reflects near destruction in a recent fire. Hannah Firth (1778–1854) was the daughter of Ezra Firth (1745–1779) and Elizabeth Carpenter (1751–1779) of Lower Penns' Neck, Salem County, New Jersey. In Woodbury, New Jersey, on April 20, 1797, Hannah married Isaac Cooper Jones (1769–1865), and they had ten children. See Hannah's silk embroidery (Fig. 410).
Collection of Laura Riegel Cook.

WHITE-WORK SAMPLERS

The most unique samplers produced in America are the Dresden-work samplers made in Philadelphia during the second half of the eighteenth century, since their floral patterns appear to have neither foreign nor American counterparts.[1] They were evidently preceded by lacy cut-work samplers (Figs. 364, 366), which were also peculiar to this region in America, although they were widely worked in Europe. Whether English or German teachers originated the fashion for white-work samplers in Philadelphia remains unknown, but they reflect the influence of much earlier European sampler embroidery.

A signed sampler with needlepoint lace survives from the reign of Elizabeth I,[2] and the earliest-known signed and dated white-work sampler has *Mary Quelch 1609* worked in hollie point much like the signatures in Figures 363, 367.[3] A 1618 German sampler also has cut-work panels with needlepoint lace,[4] and this technique was used on many signed and dated English samplers throughout the seventeenth century.[5] No Dresden-work samplers are known in Britain,[6] but the English form most closely related to Philadelphia cut work evidently emerged in the 1720s.[7] These linen on linen samplers usually have squares and circles of cut work with needlepoint lace and hollie-point insertions (Fig. 363), and over the centuries the terminology for this needlemade lace has become increasingly confusing. Collars were described as "Hollie worke" in the inventories of Mary Stuart (1542–1587),[8] but it is not known if this referred to the knotted lace stitch used for insertions on the samplers in Figures 363 through 367 and called "hollie point" by today's textile scholars.[9] It is generally believed that hollie point is a corruption of "Holy point," which referred to the needle lace on church work depicting scriptural subjects during the Middle Ages and which first appeared on garments in the early seventeenth century.[10] It is perhaps more likely that this term was derived from the pattern being formed by leaving holes in the rows of buttonhole stitches that created the filling and therefore described as "holy" (holey) point.[11] Its extreme delicacy raises doubt that it was widely used for church laces during the Middle Ages.[12]

---

1. White-work Dresden samplers were made in Scandinavia, and a piece dated 1678 survives in Stockholm (Swain, 80).

2. Ashton, Fig. 2. This sampler with Elizabeth's royal arms was presumably worked before her death in 1603.

3. Swain, 88, Pl. 54.

4. Ashton, Fig. 64.

5. Ibid., Figs. 8, 9, 21, 30.

6. Swain, 80.

7. Colby, 178, Figs. 102, 105.

8. Palliser, *A History of Lace* (1875), 289.

9. King, Figs. 37–39; Swain, 125, 126, Pl. 55; Caulfeild and Saward, *The Dictionary of Needlework* (1882; reprint, 1972), 253–6.

10. Colby, 178; Caulfeild and Saward, *Dictionary*, 253.

11. Swain, 87.

12. Earnshaw, *A Dictionary of Lace* (1982), 80.

Fig. 363. *MARY BROWN 1732* worked in hollie point at right center. England. Silk and linen on linen; 8¾" x 8¾". For similar English examples, see Colby, Figs. 102, 105. Seventeenth-century European white work is illustrated in King, Figs. 61, 62.
Cooper-Hewitt, National Museum of Design, Smithsonian Institution, 1981-28-80.

The cut work illustrated here (Figs. 363–367) is believed to have been variously described by eighteenth-century American teachers as nun's work, cut work, or point work. Perhaps the first colonial woman to advertise instruction in this technique was "Martha Gazley, late from Great Britain" who offered to "Teacheth . . . Nuns-work Philligree and Pencil Work upon Muslin" in *The New-York Gazette* of December 13/21, 1731. A decade later, schoolmistress Martha Logan specifically mentioned "tent and cut work" in Charleston's *South Carolina Gazette* of March 27, 1742. However, no Philadelphia teachers had advertised cut work when Rebecca Jones worked her small sampler in 1751 (Fig. 364). She was then eleven or twelve years old and had already completed a decorative silk embroidered sampler (Fig. 353).

"Dresden work" is better understood than many of the obsolete terms describing techniques from the eighteenth century, since it has been consistently applied to drawn work in which no threads are removed and the design is created by pulling the ground material with embroidery stitches.[13] Boston women were evidently the earliest to mention Dresden work in American newspapers. Instruction in Dresden work was offered by Elizabeth Murray, Elinor and Mary Purcell, and Bridget Suckling in March, May, and July of 1751, respectively,[14] and it was probably in Boston that Rachel Leonard fashioned her initials and *1752* amid the Dresden work of her shawl (Fig. 368). In 1759, Mrs. Anderson was the first

13. Margaret H. Swain, letter of June 17, 1986.
14. *The Boston Evening-Post,* March 25 and May 6, 1751; *The Boston Gazette, or Weekly Journal,* July 2, 1751.

Fig. 364. *1751/ REBE/KAH/ JONES* worked in the rectangle on the second row. Linen on linen (cut work with buttonhole stitches and hollie-point insertions); actual size. This is now the earliest known signed and dated white-work sampler made in America. Worked by Rebecca Jones (July 7, 1739–April 15, 1818) at the age of eleven or twelve, it was probably made under the instruction of her mother, Mary Porter Jones (d.1761), who kept a school at her home in Philadelphia during the 1740s and 1750s. It does not display the perfection of her earlier sampler (Fig. 353).
Friends Historical Association Collection, Atwater Kent Museum—The History Museum of Philadelphia, 87.35.1004.2.

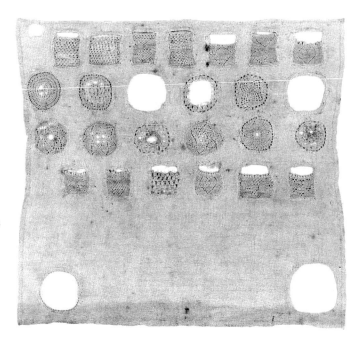

Fig. 365. Cut-work sampler by Rebecca Jones, c.1751. Linen on linen; 7⅞″ x 8½″. Probably this was a practice piece made before the dated example that bears Rebecca's name (Fig. 364).
Friends Historical Association Collection, Atwater Kent Museum— The History Museum of Philadelphia, 87.35.1004.3.

Fig. 366. *Amy Lewis Her Work 1759* and with *Amy/Lewis* worked in hollie point at left of center. Silk and linen on linen over silk; 6″ x 6″. The composition of Amy's cut-work sampler resembles the compartmented embroidery of Mary Webb (Fig. 356). Attributed to Amy Lewis (1741–1762), the only child of linen draper William Lewis (d.1754) and Hannah (d.1762) of Haverford, Pennsylvania.

Germantown Historical Society, 83-257.

Philadelphia schoolmistress to mention "all Manner of Berlin or Dresden NEEDLEWORK,"[15] and other teachers soon joined her. Eighteenth-century American examples of this delicate work survive principally in garments, especially infant clothing, except for samplers from Philadelphia,[16] and twenty-one examples made between 1763 and 1796 are considered here.[17]

The earliest Philadelphia Dresden-work sampler known today was worked by fourteen-year-old Sally Logan. It survives in the most elaborate original frame found on an American sampler (Fig. 369).[18] Her family's Quaker convictions obviously did not restrain the elegance of their lifestyle. Sally grew up at Stenton, the mansion in Germantown that was completed in 1730 by her grandfather,

15. *Pennsylvania Gazette,* April 12, 1759.

16. One atypical example of unknown origin is signed *Frances Walker 1788* (photograph files at MESDA).

17. Pieces not illustrated here: Jane Humphreys, 1771, Mary Clark, 1789, Martha Cogill, 1763, and Mary Smith, 1783 (B&C Pls. XXXVI, XXXVII, and described, 38, 76); Susannah Razor, 1783, Mary Jackson, 1788, and Catharine Knorr, 1788 (*ANTIQUES,* February 1974, 360; December 1984, 1425; and December 1989, 1339); R. Hughes, 1784, Frances Paschal, 1788, and I G, 1790 (Schiffer, 29, 31); Elizabeth Lehman, 1790 (Garvan, *The Pennsylvania German Collection* [1982], 277); Elizabeth Mason, 1786 (National Museum of American History, Washington, D.C., 71679); Lydia Sheward, 1796 (C-H, 1981-28-158); Peggy Hollingsworth, c.1789 (Museum of the City of New York, 58.318.41); EF, 1795 (Art Institute of Chicago, 28.192); Catherine Matilda Brothers (b.c.1762), New Brunswick Museum, Saint John, New Brunswick, Canada, 42027; and MS, 1795 (*MAD,* July 1992, 14B), now in the Winterthur Museum, 92.65.

18. The completely original appearance of Sally's sampler is marred by a textile conservator's white spacer, which shows within the edge of the frame.

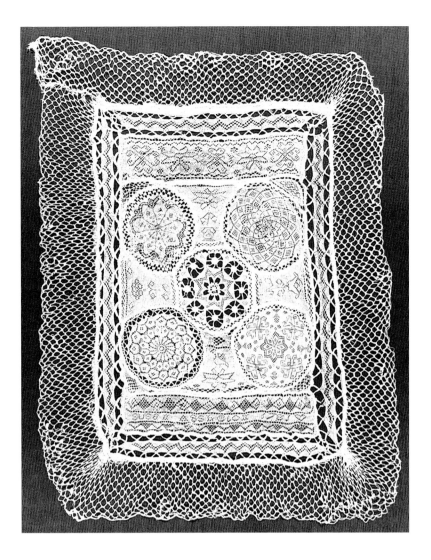

Fig. 367. *Susan Assheton 1781* worked in hollie point. Cut-work and hollie-point sampler with netted border; linen; 11″ x 8¼″ overall. A nearly identical sampler, except for the border; was worked by Sarah Keen in 1762 (Swan, *Plain & Fancy*, Fig. 19). Susan Assheton (1767–1834) was the daughter of Dr. Ralph Assheton (1736–1773) and Mary Price (1743–1795), and she was christened in Philadelphia's Christ Church. She died unmarried. See "Susan Assheton's Book," *PMHB* 55 (1931): 174–86.
San Antonio Museum Association, gift of Miss Katherine McKnight, 66-117-32.

James Logan (1674–1751). Like her brothers, she was probably taught by Anthony Benezet before he resigned from the girls' school in the summer of 1766.[19] Upon her marriage to Thomas Fisher in 1772, her father provided furnishings for her household that were made by Thomas Affleck and carved by James Reynolds.[20] Their home life, however, was soon disrupted by the Revolution, for Sally's husband, a conscientious Quaker, was banished to Winchester, Virginia. Her letters to Thomas reveal her good education and appealing personality. Fortunately, Sally's sampler survived these chaotic times and today it remains with her descendants.

No other Dresden-work samplers are known to survive in the condition of Sally Logan's. Nearly unaltered is Susanna Meyer's work (Fig. 371), but the cerise-colored silk of its backing was replaced by a conservator. Its faded ribbon border is intact and the original cerise color is known because part of the ribbon was covered by the sanded gold liner of its frame. There is little question that

19. Benezet was teaching Logan sons William and James from 1753 to 1755 (Logan family accounts, Journal Book B, 1752–1755, at Stenton). He resigned from the girls' school temporarily because of ill health (Brookes, *Friend Anthony Benezet* [1937], 42).
20. Logan also bought earthenware for Sally from Daniel Drinker (*William Logan's Waist Book, 1769–1773*, entries of April 2 and June 1, 1773. Manuscripts, HSP).

Fig. 368. The border of a kerchief initialed *R L* and dated *1752*. Dresden work, button-hole, chain, and double back stitches in cotton and linen threads on white India muslin. Worked by Rachel Leonard (1727–1805) of Norton, Massachusetts. See her canvas-work coat of arms dated *1740* (Fig. 65).
Museum of Fine Arts, Boston, gift of Mrs. Susan Hedge Davis, 12.193.

Fig. 368a. Detail of Rachel Leonard's ker-chief with initials *R L.*, worked with cotton.

these samplers were framed upon completion and mounted against a colored ground to enhance their patterns. However, several pieces that have been in mu-seums for many years were separated from their frames long ago and textile con-servators usually remounted them on white. In some cases, original ribbon borders, once thought to be later additions, were removed.

There are a number of variations among the nineteen Dresden-work samplers available for comparison, at least in photographs. All except two include cut-work circles (Fig. 371), five have the name worked in hollie point, five still have some form of ribbon border, and five others have some circles edged with ribbon.[21] Eleven are all white except for ribbon embellishments, seven pieces have the names worked on net, and four are so similar in both their signatures and pat-terns that they are certain to have been made at the same school (Fig. 371). Also of common origin are five pieces of the 1790s with floral borders worked in col-ored silks (Fig. 372). However, the teachers remain unknown, and because the embroiderers of these samplers did not give their ages, their positive identity is usually impossible to determine unless some family history accompanied their work.

---

21. This number includes Mary Smith's of 1783, which is clearly described in B&C, 76.

Fig. 369. *Sarah Logan/ 1766* worked in a hollie-point panel beneath the basket. Linen and cotton on linen with a blue silk backing and blue ribbon border; 14″ x 12½″. Sally's sampler is exceptional for its fourteen cut-work circles and an alphabet worked in hollie point with two versions of the letters *M* and *N*. Many similarities suggest that the same instructress taught Jane Humphreys in 1771 (B&C, Pl. XXXVI). Sarah Logan (November 6, 1751–January 25, 1796) was the daughter of William Logan (1718–1776) and Hannah Emlen (1722–1777). On March 17, 1772, she married Thomas Fisher (1741–1810), who was a founder of the Westtown School and its first treasurer; he was also a manager of the Pennsylvania Hospital and a charter member of the American Philosophical Society. They had six children. Sarah was the niece of Sarah Logan (Fig. 348).
Privately owned.

Fig. 370. *MARY BABB 1783* worked in a hollie-point panel below the basket. Linen, cotton, and silk on linen with silk ribbon surrounding seven cut-work circles; 9¼″ x 10¼″. Mary worked five sprays of flowers and the stems from her basket in colored silks. The description of Mary Smith's sampler of 1783 suggests that it was much like this, and Mary Clark's sampler of 1789 has similar ribbons, as does Catharine Knorr's of 1788.

Cooper-Hewitt, National Museum of Design, Smithsonian Institution, 1974-42-12.

Fig. 371. *Susanna Meyer Her Work/ 1787*. Linen on linen with silk ribbon border; 18¾" x 17½". Susanna's ribbon border was once a bright cerise color. The Mason, Knorr, and Lehman samplers have very similar patterns and signatures. The Hollingsworth sampler is also similar and lacks cut-work circles, but has a hollie-point signature. These pieces date from 1786 to 1790 and were surely worked at the same school.
Author's collection.

Fig. 372. *MARY JONES/ 1795.* Silk and cotton on linen with gold leaf; 15¼″ x 13¼″. Mary's sampler is lavishly embellished with colored silks as are several others within this group. The closest counterparts to this example are signed *I*

G 1790 (Schiffer, 31) and *E F 1795* (Art Institute of Chicago). *Metropolitan Museum of Art, bequest of Barbara Schiff Sinauer, 1984.331.22.*

PICTORIAL EMBROIDERIES

At an early date the elegance of Philadelphia's pictorial embroidery suggested the grandeur that would characterize Philadelphia furniture of the mid-eighteenth century. When New England girls had scarcely begun to work fishing ladies with crewels on canvas, the young ladies of Philadelphia were already creating exquisite silk embroideries on silk (Figs. 373, 374), and their teacher was conscious of the craze for East India styles. A smiling sun beneath billowing clouds survived from the baroque pictures of the seventeenth century,[1] but naturalistic flowers upon a mounded hillock were in keeping with the fashionable Indo-Persian designs of the period.[2] Compared to the lifestyle of the English gentry, the prosperous Philadelphians may have fitted Defoe's description of "the middle sort who live well,"[3] but to most of their fellow colonists, Philadelphia of the 1730s was an impressive metropolis, and the quality of its schoolgirl embroidery paralleled its growing sophistication.

The Philadelphia girls who worked incredibly intricate band-pattern samplers in the 1720s were well prepared to undertake delicate flower arrangements on silk when they reached their mid-teens (Fig. 373), while some pieces were impeccably executed by much younger children, such as Margret Wistar, who worked a pair of sconces at the age of nine (Fig. 374). Although pastoral scenes and various episodes from print sources were occasionally chosen, flowers worked with lustrous silks on silk moiré taffetas appear to have been Philadelphia's most popular form of pictorial needlework during the eighteenth century, and the preference for picturing flowers continued in Pennsylvania through the first half of the nineteenth century (Figs. 518–521).

As with samplers, the works of the precocious Ann Marsh are among the earliest extant examples of Philadelphia pictorial embroidery (Fig. 373). The heavier frame suggests that Ann's picture is older than the same pattern worked by Margret Wistar in 1738 (Fig. 374). Ann was twenty years old and possibly already teaching when Margret worked her pair of sconces, and it is conceivable that Margret was her pupil. It is, however, far more likely that Ann and Margret were each taught at an early age by Ann's mother, Elizabeth Marsh.

Between January 1987 and January 1992, four remarkable Philadelphia silk embroideries emerged. They were made by Elizabeth Flower, Mary Flower, and Ann Whitebread (Figs. 377–380), and their subjects are relatively uncommon to Philadelphia work. Only one example of arms from this region was previously known, and it was worked by Ann Flower, the sister of Elizabeth (Fig. 377). No Philadelphia pastoral scenes had been published before the appearance of Mary

---

1. See Cecilia Woodward, "A Sequence of Early Needlework," *ANTIQUES,* April 1926, 237–44.
2. For other Philadelphia examples, see Swan, *Guide,* 75; Skinner Sale 1120, November 1, 1986, Lot 244; Fawdry and Brown, 69.
3. Christopher Hibbert, *The English, A Social History* (New York: W. W. Norton & Co., 1987), 308.

Fig. 373. Silk embroidery by Ann Marsh, c.1730. Silk on silk with silk ribbon border; 17½" x 10½"; original walnut frame. In addition to Margret Wistar's embroideries (Fig. 374), an unknown girl worked a similar piece initialed *A L* (Winterthur Museum). For another silk embroidery and sundry other pieces by Ann Marsh, see *ANTIQUES*, December 1984, 1422.
Private collection.

Fig. 374. *Margret Wistar her Work/ in the 9 year of her age 1738.* Silk on silk satin with linen border; 15⅝" x 8¾"; one of a pair of silk embroideries framed as sconces in deep walnut frames of the period and attributed to the school of Elizabeth Marsh. Margret Wistar (1728/29–1793) was the daughter of Caspar Wistar (1696–1752) and Catherine Jansen (1703–1786). Her father was a button manufacturer, merchant, and founder of the Wistarburgh Glassworks in Salem County, New Jersey. Margret married Reuben Haines I (1727–1793), and they both died in the yellow fever epidemic. They had five children. In 1752, Margret's sister Sally (1738–1815) worked a pair of small pictures with birds in flowering trees on a silk moiré taffeta ground (Swan, *Plain & Fancy,* 80, and *Guide,* 90). For the samplers of Margret's granddaughter, Ann Haines, see Figures 427–430.
Wyck Charitable Trust, Philadelphia, 88.1939.

Fig. 375. *Mary King 1754* inscribed beneath the leopard's extended right foot. Silk, metallic threads, and beads on silk moiré; 18¼″ x 24⅛″. Mary's brilliant embroidery on a gleaming gold ground is one of the most impressive of Philadelphia's pictorial silk embroideries. Four related pieces, possibly from the same school, have animals worked on a cream-colored ground. (See Christie's Sale, May 31, 1986, Lot 62, and January 21, 1989, Lot 469; also, catalogue of The Philadelphia Antiques Show, April 1993, 65). Another is in the Winterthur Museum. This needleworker may have been the Mary King who married William Turner in Philadelphia on June 29, 1767; or possibly she was Mary, daughter of the joiner John King (d.1767) and Margareth Smith, who married John Hollman. *Winterthur Museum, 66.978.*

Flower's in 1987 (Fig. 379), and it has now been joined by Ann Whitebread's shepherd (Fig. 378). Even more exceptional is Mary's hunting scene (Fig. 380), which was thought to represent a specific group of local hunters until its English print source was discovered.[4]

The Flower pictorial embroideries, made when the three sisters were between the ages of twenty and twenty-four, were all exquisitely worked and elegantly framed. Elizabeth, Ann, and Mary Flower were the great granddaughters of Enoch Flower (1635–1684) who was appointed Philadelphia's first schoolmaster by William Penn and the Provincial Council of Pennsylvania. Their father, Enoch Flower, styled himself a joiner in his will, but evidently he was a most successful businessman.[5] In 1732, he was a prominent charter member of the "Colony on Schuylkill," an organization of sportsmen whose members were a "frolicsome lot of the best social set."[6] Enoch Flower married Ann Jones at the Philadelphia Meeting House on December 24, 1736, and they had nine children between 1737 and 1749, but five died in infancy. Perhaps Enoch was too sociable and frolicsome, since he was disowned by the Friends in 1744.[7] It is interesting to note that his daughter Ann worked a handsome Irish-stitched cover for the Church of England's

---

4. I was informed of this print source by John Hays of Christie's, New York, who discovered it with the assistance of Susan Mayor of Christie's, London.

5. The inventory of his estate was appraised at £1,695-14 (Philadelphia Administration, 1773, File 27, Book H, 112).

6. Lippincott, *Early Philadelphia* (1917), 303–4.

7. Hinshaw, *Encyclopedia of American Quaker Genealogy* (1926–1950), 2:525.

Fig. 376. *Sarah Hinchman 1768*. Silk on silk; 9½″ x 8½″.
Sarah Hinchman (c.1756–1797) was the daughter of Isaac
Hinchman and Lettice Woolston (c.1729–1780) who were
married in 1753. Sarah became the wife of James Ash
(1750–1830) in Philadelphia's Christ Church on May 18,
1771, and died shortly after the birth of her seventeenth
child, who lived until 1880. Surviving with her needlework is her child-size, curly-maple chest on frame, with
the inscription beneath the bottom drawer "Sarah Hinchman her Drawers/ bought about the year 1760" (William
MacPherson Hornor, *Blue Book Philadelphia Furniture*
[Philadelphia, 1935], Pl. 62).
Private collection.

Book of Common Prayer, which was given to her by her father in 1765,[8] the year
she was disowned because of her marriage, out of Meeting, to the non-Quaker
Samuel Wheeler. However, in 1777, she received a certificate to the Gwynedd
Monthly Meeting with her sisters, Elizabeth and Mary.[9] Apparently Enoch was
also reinstated since upon his death in 1773, he was buried in the Friends'
Ground in Philadelphia's Middle District.[10] In 1775, Ann Jones Flower was sur-
vived by Enoch, her "helpless son" who was "sufficiently provided for in the dis-
tribution of his Father's estate," and by her three daughters, Elizabeth, Ann, and
Mary. To each daughter she devised a house and lot "left to her by her father John
Jones," and she equalized their value with bequests of money.[11]

A close contemporary of the Flower sisters was Anne Whitebread, but few
facts are known of her life. She is said to have been sent from abroad to a school
in Philadelphia in order to thwart a romance with a suitor unacceptable to her
parents.[12] He followed her, however, and in 1771 they were married. Anne died
in 1772 and was survived by one child, whose descendants preserved her needlework (Fig. 378).

8. Bookcover and title page illustrated in Christie's Sale, May 28, 1987, Lot 113.
9. Hinshaw, *Encyclopedia,* 2:525.
10. *Philadelphia Monthly Meeting Births and Burials 1688–1829,* HSP.
11. Will of Ann Flower, 1775, Philadelphia Wills, File 119, Book Q, 138. Ann Flower was the daughter of
John Jones (1677–1742) and Elizabeth Fox (1686–1742).
12. Historical information was attached to the back of this embroidery by a family member in Doylestown,
Pennsylvania, on September 27, 1948. It led to the reliable identification of the maker.

Fig. 378. Pictorial embroidery attributed to Anne White-bread, c.1768. Silk on silk moiré with linen tape visible on the sides; 13½" x 9¾". Anne Whitebread was born in England, or possibly in the West Indies, and attended an unknown school in Philadelphia. On January 24, 1771, she married William Bellamy in Philadelphia's Christ Church. Anne died following the birth of her daughter Mary Anne, who was born on June 24, 1772. Mary Anne Bellamy married Michael Cress of Bucks County, Pennsylvania, and her mother's embroidery remained with her descendants until at least 1948.
Private collection; photograph courtesy of Sotheby's.

Fig. 377. "Elizabeth Flower, November 1765" inscribed on the backboard. Silk with silver and gold metallic threads on silk moiré; 11½" x 12¾". This coat of arms depicts the arms of the Flower family of Wiltshire, England. Elizabeth skillfully worked a double cypher in gold beneath her shield, in the same manner found on an almost identical coat of arms worked by her younger sister Ann in 1763 (Swan, *Guide*, 137). Elizabeth Flower (1742–1781) was the fourth child of Enoch Flower and Ann Jones and the second to survive infancy. She was thirty-five years old when she married druggist Christopher Marshall, Jr. (1740–1806) in 1777, and she died four years later. On the backboard of this embroidery are the initials "EMS" for her daughter Elizabeth Flower Marshall who married Christopher Slocum in 1806.
Collection of Mr. and Mrs. E. J. Nusrala.

Fig. 379. "Mary Flower her Work done in the Year 1764" inscribed on the backboard. Silk, paint, and mica on silk moiré; 16¾" x 20½". In 1767, Mary worked a high chest cover in brightly colored wools with a green fringe and measuring 19½" x 40". It is owned by a descendant of her sister Ann. Mary Flower (1744–1778) was the daughter of Philadelphia joiner Enoch Flower (1703–1773) and Ann Jones (1711–1775). She died unmarried.
Collection of Eddy G. Nicholson.

Fig. 380. *Mary Flower 1768* is inscribed on the linen edging beneath the sanded gold mat, and "Mary Flower her Work in the Year 1768" is written on the backboard. Silk on silk with the ground fully embroidered; 16¼″ x 20½″. Mary's composition was derived from one of the many editions of *The Chace* engraved by Thomas Burford after James Seymour. First published in 1754 as a mezzotint in sets of four, this print was reissued a number of times, and pirated by other London printsellers who published it as line engravings in reverse to the mezzotints. One of their prints was probably the source for Mary Flower's embroidery, or her pattern may have been reversed from an original edition. See *ANTIQUES,* February 1991, 380.
Collection of Eddy G. Nicholson.

Fig. 381. *Hannah Maris 1791.* Silk on silk; 14″ x 11½″. Hannah was twenty-one years old when she worked this silk embroidery. An unsigned piece of almost identical design is recorded at MESDA, and another by Elizabeth Jones is privately owned. Hannah Maris (b.1770) was the daughter of George Maris (1737–1803) and Jane Foulke (1735–1807) of Montgomery and Chester counties. She married John Wilson on March 8, 1796. For her sampler of 1786, see Schiffer, *Arts and Crafts of Chester County, Pennsylvania* (1980), 175.
Collection of Margaret B. Schiffer.

Fig. 382. *Mary Seckels Work 1786.* Silk on linen; 20″ x 19″. Mary's exuberant scene is in striking contrast to earlier Philadelphia samplers, and no prototype for her composition has been found. Ann Buler worked the same pattern in the same year (B&C, Pl. XXXIII), and conspicuous similarities reveal that Mary's schoolmistress also taught Maria Grotz (Fig. 383). Mary Seckel may have been the Mary, born about 1776, to Laurence Seckel (1747–1823) and his first wife, Barbara Chrystler. Their Mary married Adam Guier, Jr. (1775–1832), in 1796 and they lived in Kingsessing. Laurence Seckel was one of the managers of the Pennsylvania Hospital, a trustee of the Young Ladies Seminary, and a founder of Philadelphia's Saint John's Evangelical Lutheran Church.
Collection of Dr. and Mrs. Raymond L. Candage, Jr.

Fig. 383. *MARIA GROTZ WORK 1789.* Silk on linen with shirred ribbon border and rosettes; 21½″ x 19¾″; survived in its original deep, Philadelphia frame until the 1970s. On this remarkable sampler, Maria pictured the peaceable kingdom with the appropriate verse:

Rise Crown'd With Light Imperial Salem Rise
Exalt Thy Tow'ry Head And Lift Thy Eyes
The Lambs With Wolves Shall Graze The Verdant Mead
And Boys In Flowry Bands The Tiger Lead
The Steer And Lyon At One Crib Shall Meet
And Harmless Serpents Lick The Pilgrims Feet

The unidentified Maria may have been a daughter of George Grotz, a breeches maker at 7 North Fourth Street, Philadelphia, in 1791.
Private collection.

Philadelphia in the Federal Period

When the Revolution was over, the daughters of Philadelphia's elite were still being taught exquisite needlework by Ann Marsh, but more women began teaching accomplishments to middle-class girls than ever before, and fanciful pictorial samplers emerged in the 1780s. Two striking compositions represent a little-known Philadelphia form that may become an important group (Figs. 382, 383).

SAMPLERS WITH MANSIONS AND TERRACED GARDENS

Presently known in great numbers are the stepped-terrace samplers (Fig. 384), and variations of this type were worked at many different schools from the 1790s until about 1830. Although first popular in Philadelphia, this ultimately became a dominant style of the Delaware Valley with recognizable subgroups springing up in both Pennsylvania and New Jersey.[1] At present, the earliest-known group was made under the tuition of Mary Coeleman Zeller, whose school was discovered because Mary Snowden worked *Philadelphia* and *M Zeller* on her sampler in 1806 (Fig. 388).

Mary Zeller's patterns are easily recognized by airy, asymmetrical motifs that float in random arrangement above her balanced terraces and lend a feeling of ebullient spontaneity to her compositions. Her tree-lined stepped terraces are usually surmounted either by a black and orange castle (Figs. 384, 385) or by a Georgian mansion with a pediment (Fig. 388), or occasionally by only a large vase of flowers.[2] A milk cow and a shaggy goat are often included, but the most consistent identifying motif is one or more renditions of the Agnus Dei, found in Johann Sibmacher's pattern book *Newes Modelbuch In Kupffer gemacht* of 1604 (Fig. 386). The stag worked on these and other Pennsylvania samplers was probably derived from Sibmacher's pattern as well (Fig. 387), although perhaps indirectly. While his book is the earliest known source of these patterns, they were often reprinted by others, and Mary Zeller may have been working from a pattern book, or from earlier embroideries, when she drew designs for her students. The motifs she favored definitely reflect German influence. For example, the well

---

1. See B&C, Pls. LXVII, LXXXIII. The latter, by Margaret Kerlin, 1801, is particularly English in concept, and despite saying *Wrought in Burlington,* it was catalogued as English when the A. W. Drake Collection was exhibited at the Cincinnati Art Museum, January 9–30, 1909; Krueger, *Gallery,* Figs. 53, 58; Sotheby's, Kapnek Collection, Sale 4531Y, January 31, 1981, Lots 169, 170.

2. Elizabeth Snyder's sampler of 1803 in PB, Haskell Sale, Part Six, February 16, 1945, Lot 1145.

Fig. 384. *Ann Heyl Her Work Made In The Year 1789*. Silk on linen; 21⅝" x 18½". Ann's sampler is now the earliest example attributed to Mary Zeller's school. She worked the typical Agnus Dei (Lamb of God), and her "Sibmacher" stag is almost identical to the pattern (Fig. 387). A closely related sampler by Elizabeth Stine, 1793, has a shirred ribbon border and rosettes (Edmonds, Fig. 13). Ann Heyl (c.1779–after 1860) was fifth among the seven children of Johannes Heyl (1750–1788) and Anna Maria Stricker, who were married at the German Reformed Church in Philadelphia on September 18, 1771. Ann married Philadelphia confectioner David Seeger (1767–1830), and they were childless.
Private collection.

Right: Fig. 385. *Catharine Goodman Her Work Made In The 13th Year Of Her Age March 29th*, c.1803. Silk on linen; 17¼″ x 22¼″. Catharine's goat, her cow, and all her little sheep seem to be watching *The Angel Retrieving Peter Out of Prison*. It was probably Catharine who removed the date of her sampler in later life. She has not been identified. Her border and other motifs relate to the 1803 sampler of Elizabeth Snyder (see footnote 2).
Location unknown; photograph courtesy of Sotheby's.

Left, above: Fig. 386. Johann Sibmacher (d.1611), *Newes Modelbuch In Kupffer gemacht* (Nurnberg, 1604), Pl. 26. Etching, 5⁵⁄₁₆″ wide. The Agnus Dei or Lamb of God is a Christian symbol known since the fourth century. This form had appeared by the thirteenth century and was worked on seventeenth-century European samplers. It is seldom found on American work.
Metropolitan Museum of Art, Harris Brisbane Dick Fund, 1929.

Left, below: Fig. 387. Johann Sibmacher, *Newes Modelbuch In Kupffer gemacht*, Pl. 28, 5⁵⁄₁₆″ wide. A stag of slightly different form appears in Sibmacher's 1597 pattern book, Pl. 16. European patterns were often printed in this manner from the sixteenth to the eighteenth century; later, both hand-drawn and printed examples were used by Pennsylvania Germans (see Fig. 452).
Metropolitan Museum of Art, Harris Brisbane Dick Fund, 1929.

house in Figure 384 can be found on German work and on other American samplers made under German instruction.[3] Also, Ann Heyl's fruit tree is common to Dutch and German samplers, and the three-towered castle was perhaps an adaptation from German prototypes.[4]

Mary Zeller (1743–1818), born Maria Coeleman, was probably the daughter of

---

3. For an 1804 Moravian example from Salem Academy, see *ANTIQUES,* September 1984, 438; for an example on another form of stepped-terrace sampler, see Ring, *Treasures,* Fig. 65; also, on an 1830 sampler of Reading, Pennsylvania, in Schiffer, 80.
4. Possibly inspired by a three-towered structure common to German samplers; see Figures 446, 450; also Hersh, *Samplers of the Pennsylvania Germans* (1991), 94–5.

Fig. 388. *Mary Snowden Her Work Done in The 16th Year Of Her Age Philadelphia A D 1806. M Zeller.* Silk on linen; 24″ x 23″. Mary Snowden worked a more realistic mansion than those on the earliest examples, and, most importantly, she named her teacher. For a similar piece of 1806 with its original frame, see *ANTIQUES,* January 1987, 84. Another of 1808 is in the Schiffer collection. Mary Snowden (b. June 16, 1791) was the daughter of Philadelphia carpenter Thomas Snowden (c.1768–1831) and Rachel (b.c.1767). She was baptized at the Second Presbyterian Church with four younger children in 1803.
Private collection.

Fig. 389. *Margaret Hopple Daughter of George &/ Catharine Hopple Her Work done In/ the 12 Year of her age In Hannah/ Keegan's School in the Year/ 1791.* Silk on linen; 20¼″ x 17⅞″. In addition to pious verses, Margaret also worked many family names. The Philadelphia directory of 1793 listed George Hopple as a "butcher 383 No. third St." His will, proved in 1803, called him a victualler. He was survived by his wife and seven children. Margaret's marriage and death dates have not been found.
Photograph courtesy of the Museum of Early Southern Decorative Arts.

Jacob and Maria Coeleman who were the godparents of her son Jacob Zeller.[5] Where she was born is unknown, but she married Johann George Zeller in Philadelphia's First Reformed Church on October 13, 1768, and by 1778, she had given birth to one son and four daughters.[6] Mary was a widow with only two girls in her household in 1790,[7] and the Philadelphia directory of 1791 listed her as a schoolmistress at 31 Coates Alley. By 1793 she was located at 119 North Third Street, and directories described her as a "teacher" or a "teacheress" at this address through 1810. In 1811 and 1814 she was listed as a milliner, and in 1817 the listing was Zeller and Coleman, milliners. Evidently she taught or sewed for a livelihood during most of her long widowhood. Mary died on December 30, 1818, "after a long and painful illness;" and the funeral was to be from her residence at 119 North Third Street.[8] She had lived close to her son, Jacob, who was a bookbinder at 121 North Third Street.

Unlike the Zeller patterns, the 1791 stepped-terrace sampler by Margaret Hopple includes balanced motifs and many family names (Fig. 389). Margaret named *Hannah Keegan's School* and surrounded her composition with an Indian pink border characteristic of earlier band-pattern samplers. Little is known of Hannah Walker Keegan. She was born in Philadelphia in 1749, and married Joseph Keegan at St. Michael's and Zion Lutheran Church on December 28, 1769.[9] She was evidently a widow before 1791,[10] and she appeared in the city directories as a schoolmistress in Hoffman's Alley from 1794 through 1797, but no later references to her have been found. Despite the names Walker and Keegan, her marriage in the Lutheran Church strongly suggests that she was of German descent. As yet, only one other sampler can be confidently attributed to her school.[11]

Among the many types of Philadelphia samplers with castles on a hill, one survives in remarkable numbers (Figs. 390, 393). It shares motifs with Philadelphia's distinctive house and garden samplers, which feature strolling couples in plumed hats (Figs. 391, 394). At present, the red mansions with checkered foundations are known to date from between 1796 (Fig. 390) and 1830 (Fig. 393), while the house and garden form appeared by 1798, if not earlier (Fig. 391), and was worked until at least 1834.[12] Examples of both types often include the same

---

5. *Records of the First Reformed Church of Philadelphia,* Collections of the Genealogical Society of Pennsylvania (Philadelphia, 1903), 75:399, HSP.

6. Mary's children were Maria, b.1769; Jacob, b.1772; Maria, b.1774; Cathrina, b.1776; and Elizabeth, b.1778 (Ibid.).

7. United States Census of 1790.

8. *Poulson's American Daily Advertiser,* Philadelphia, December 31, 1818.

9. *Pennsylvania Vital Records* (1983), 2:51, HSP.

10. The Philadelphia directory of 1785 names "Peter Keggan blacksmith Sugar Alley" and in 1791 it lists "Susannah Keckan widow 70 Sugar Alley." This was probably Hannah Keegan. She was listed as "Hannah Keegan schoolmistress Hoffman's Alley" in 1794 and as "widow schoolmistress" in 1796.

11. The undated work of Henrietta Maria Howell, aged nine (Brooklyn Museum, 32.240). Fanny Wilson's 1795 family record above a stepped terrace bears some resemblance to the Hopple sampler (Krueger, *Gallery,* Fig. 36). A piece similar to Fanny's was worked in 1793 by Abigail Jones (b. December 11, 1764), the daughter of Samuel and Elizabeth (collection of Dr. and Mrs. Donald M. Herr).

12. Sampler signed *Letitia A. Blegler Philadelphia Dec 1 1834* (Old Deerfield, Inc.).

Fig. 390. *Catharine Lapps work done in the 13th year of her age Philadelphia Jan 18th 1796. Silk on linen; 19″ x 21″.* Catharine's mansion was probably an adaptation from the same source that inspired the castlelike buildings on samplers made at Mary Zeller's school (Fig. 384). The central figures with plumed hats relate to those in Figures 391 and 394. Mary Geyer worked a very similar sampler, also in 1796 (*ANTIQUES,* December 1989, 1342), as did Mary Hofecer in 1798 (Sotheby's Sale 5282, February 1, 1985, Lot 352). Catharine Lapp was born September 24, 1783, and baptized Catharina at St. Michael's and Zion Lutheran Church. She was the daughter of Michael Lapp and Margareta. He was a baker at 82 South Fourth Street.
Collection of Mr. and Mrs. E. J. Nusrala.

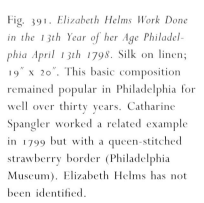

Fig. 391. *Elizabeth Helms Work Done in the 13th Year of her Age Philadelphia April 13th 1798. Silk on linen; 19″ x 20″.* This basic composition remained popular in Philadelphia for well over thirty years. Catharine Spangler worked a related example in 1799 but with a queen-stitched strawberry border (Philadelphia Museum). Elizabeth Helms has not been identified.
Collection of Margaret B. Schiffer.

Fig. 392. *Mary Orr Her Work In/ The 9ᵗʰ Year Of Her age/ 1806.* Silk on linen; 16½″ x 15¼″. Mary's striped basket, owl, and animals are found on many examples of both the mansion and the house and garden types, and her spindly legged sheep are seen in Figure 393. Mary Orr (b.c.1798) may have been the Mary Orr who married Thomas Allen at Philadelphia's Third Presbyterian Church on November 7, 1822. *Collection of Ann Bauer.*

Fig. 393. *Margaret Kramar/ 1830.* Silk on linen; 17½″ x 24¼″. Margaret's mansion and animals are essentially the same as those worked in 1806 (Fig. 392). A very similar sampler by Cecilia Kelter, 1829, formerly in the collection of Mrs. Bradbury Bedell, is now in the Vassar College Library. Margaret Kramar was probably the Margaretha Kramer born to Henry Kramer and Dorothy Sanderson on September 3, 1816, and baptized at Philadelphia's Dutch Reformed Church. *Philadelphia Museum of Art, Whitman Sampler Collection, gift of Pet Inc., 69-288-161.*

Fig. 394. *Jane McFarlan Her Work Done In The Year 1814.* Silk on linen; 22½″ x 21½″. Jane's black basket is similar to the one in Figure 392, while her house and garden are nearly identical to those worked by Ann Major in 1812 and Mary Ann Hoover in 1818. (Skinner Sale 773, October 30, 1981, Lot 184; and *ANTIQUES,* December 1989, 1343). Also, for another Philadelphia group, c.1825–1830 with some related motifs, see Edmonds, Fig. 57; and Sotheby's Sale 4338, February 2, 1980, Lot 1306. Jane McFarlan was born to William and Elizabeth McFarlan on January 19, 1802, and baptized at Philadelphia's Second Presbyterian Church on December 25, 1804. Her father was a coachmaker on Union Street.
Author's collection.

striped baskets, figures with plumed hats, couples that seem to be crossing swords, spindly legged sheep, awkward rabbits, similar birds, and the same borders. The significance of the foreign-looking red mansion and its great popularity in Philadelphia is unexplained. No European prototypes have been found, but it may have evolved from the checkered structure on the Zeller samplers.[13] It was occasionally replaced by a Georgian house with keystone windows and fanlights together with the other typical motifs.[14] In the meantime, the house with fence, trees, and strolling couples remained faithful to the earliest renditions, and it is likely that both types originated at the same school.

Despite the enduring designs and the consistent embroidery technique found on these samplers, no Philadelphia schoolmistress is known to have taught steadily between 1795 and 1830, nor has a teacher been found with a daughter who may have continued her school. Like Mary Zeller, the instructress probably kept a day school and taught the daughters of local craftsmen and shopkeepers who lived in the vicinity of her home. Philadelphia's first city directory of 1785 listed sixteen schoolmistresses, and four of these were still teaching in 1800, but they did not appear in the 1805 directory.[15] Two teachers, Miss Elizabeth Jones and the widow Mary Thompson, were listed from the late 1790s until 1817, but it is not known if they kept dame schools or taught accomplishments to older girls. Throughout the early nineteenth century there was a continuous succession of advertisements for girls' schools in Philadelphia newspapers. Many of those who advertised appeared in the directories only briefly, or not at all, and it is difficult to know if they actually commenced the schools they proposed. Yet groups of samplers clearly reveal that many Philadelphia women taught embroidery in a consistent style for a number of years.[16] They were no doubt well known to their neighbors, but only samplers with documentation can identify them now.

---

13. For this building in a different composition but with many similar motifs, see Christie's Sale, October 13, 1983, Lot 114; ANTIQUES, March 1989, 622.

14. Ring, Treasures, Fig. 64.

15. They were Sarah Baker, Isabella Fenton, Elizabeth Irvine, and Sarah Price.

16. A growing group of samplers with balanced patterns in the English style now date from between 1829 and 1833. They name D. H. Mundall's Seminary, including the address at 101 South Fifth Street, Philadelphia (for Charlotte Edmonds, 1830, see Butterfield & Butterfield, San Francisco, Sale 4633G, March 20, 1991, Lot 87); similar is the work of Sophia Fox, 1829, in the Brooklyn Museum, 32.283; Victorine Delacroix, 1833, is listed in B&C, 386. Mrs. Deborah H. Mundall taught earlier in Delaware. Samplers by Mary Leland Howley, 1823, and Ann Jane Couper, 1824, name DHM Seminary New Castle (private collections). Philadelphia directories list Mrs. Mundall's seminary from 1828 through 1842. She died in 1850 (Philadelphia Wills, Book 25, p. 26).

PHILADELPHIA EAGLES AND
E. BRUNELL'S SCHOOL

In 1816, or perhaps earlier, a spectacular sampler style emerged in Philadelphia, and its most conspicuous feature is a noble American eagle. Some of its motifs, such as angels holding a cartouche, eight-pointed stars, giant butterflies, and awkward rabbits, had been known before, but in Maria Bolen's work (Fig. 396) a giant American eagle sweeps down and hovers above a prim brick house, while in the foreground, disinterested people and animals amble about the lawn amid towering plants. Here is Philadelphia in the fortieth year of the Declaration of Independence, and the bold eagle seems to have descended from the heavens and crowded itself into this tranquil scene of a gentleman's country seat. Except for the eagle, this sampler has a decidedly English aura with its tiny, meticulously worked motifs on a fine woolen ground.

Surprisingly, an English sampler of 1795 (Fig. 395) has many motifs identical to those worked by Maria Bolen and another Philadelphia girl in 1823 (Fig. 397). The maker of the English sampler is not specifically named, but in a pair of angel-held cartouches, much like Maria Bolen's, are the names *Elizabeth Brunnell* and *Andrew Brunnell,* and it appears that the Philadelphia teacher must have been aware

Fig. 395. *An East View of Liverpool Lighthouse and Signals on Bidston Hill. Anno Domini 1795* and with the names *Elizabeth Brunnell* and *Andrew Brunnell.* Silk on wool; 19¼" x 21". This finely worked English sampler contains many motifs that appear on the other samplers pictured here.
Cooper-Hewitt, National Museum of Design, Smithsonian Institution, 1974-42-10.

Fig. 396. *Maria Bolen Her Work 1816.* Silk on wool; 20⅛″ x 19″. The upper half of Maria's sampler closely resembles English work. The eagle appears to have been added after the basic pattern was nearly completed, since it invades the border and crowds the house. Each cartouche with flanking angels is identical in design to those in Figure 395, as are many other small motifs, including four awkward rabbits like the one at lower right in the English sampler. These strange little animals also appeared on other Philadelphia samplers at an early date. The disproportionate scale of the figures and plants in the foreground and their random arrangement add American informality to the composition of this wonderfully appealing enigma. Maria may have been the Maria Bolen baptized at St. Mathew's Lutheran Church in Philadelphia on March 24, 1802, but nothing more is known of her.
Collection of Mrs. Theodore H. Kapnek, Sr.; photograph courtesy of The Magazine Antiques.

of this sampler or others very much like it. By 1825, however, the surroundings of the impressive eagle have changed, and none of the earlier English elements are conspicuous in the work of Margaret Moss (Fig. 398). Her sampler reflects the freedom of form and lack of constraint that characterize American work. Two years later, Rebecca Skinner worked essentially the same pattern (Fig. 399) and named the *E Brunell School.* Indeed, the appearance of this sampler would seem to confirm a relationship between the Bidston Hill sampler of 1795 (Fig. 395) and the Philadelphia teacher, but E. Brunell has not been identified. It seems significant, however, that an Andrew Brunell first appeared in the Philadelphia directory in the year 1816. He is described as a rigger, and over the years he became a mariner, a ship carpenter, a shopkeeper, and in 1859, the year of his death, he was listed as "Andrew Brunell gent. 1344 Columbia Ave." The following year his widow, Mary Brunell, was selling trimmings at the same address.

Fig. 397. *Margret/ Tshudy/ 1823.* Silk on linen; 22″ x 24″. Although it lacks the eagle, Margret's sampler is closely related to Maria Bolen's and it also contains many of the motifs found in Figure 395. However, its striped vases suggest the influence of Philadelphia's mansion and garden samplers. This sampler maker may be the Margaret Tshudy who married John McGinnis at St. Joseph's Church in Philadelphia on July 28, 1831.
Collection of Wendell and Elisabeth Donaghy Garrett.

No record of an E. Brunell in Philadelphia has appeared, but it is logical to assume that this teacher was a woman, possibly named Elizabeth. The uncommon Brunnell (Brunell) name on both the English and American samplers, in addition to the similar motifs, strongly suggest that this teacher was an Englishwoman in some way related to the Elizabeth and Andrew Brunnell of the sampler. Possibly E. Brunell was Andrew's mother or his first wife and had this sampler in her possession when they settled in Philadelphia. It is also possible that Elizabeth and Andrew Brunnell were a sister and brother who came to Philadelphia together. Her failure to appear in the directories would not be unusual if she boarded with others.

The Brunnell sampler of 1795 was in the collection of Eva Johnston Coe, but her scrapbooks do not reveal where she purchased it.[1] If it was found in Philadelphia, or nearby, the connection would seem irrefutable. Nevertheless, despite the inexplicable circumstances, there is little doubt that Maria Bolen, Margaret Tshudy, Margaret Moss, and an unknown girl worked their samplers at E. Brunell's school, as did Rebecca Skinner.

---

1. The scrapbooks are in the C-H.

Fig. 398. *Margaret Moss/ Aged 11 Years/ 1825* and inscribed in the opposite cartouche, *Elizabeth Wiert/ Aged 80 Died/ 1825.* Silk on linen; 27″ x 25½″. Margaret worked the most pleasing composition within this group and improved the eagle with a banner inscribed *E Pluribus Unum.* She included the same cartouches but with the angels above them; also eight-pointed stars, large butterflies, and the long-tailed sheep seen in the upper tier of the English sampler. Margaret Moss is unidentified, as is the maker of a very similar sampler whose name has worn away (Ring, *Treasures,* Fig. 67). *Cooper-Hewitt, National Museum of Design, Smithsonian Institution, 1974.42.8.*

Fig. 399. *Rebecca/ Skinner/ Aged Ten/ Years 1827/ E Brunell School.* Silk on linen; 25½″ x 25⅛″. Rebecca's sampler is now so faded that it is difficult to see the many small motifs in common with the English sampler. She also placed uncommon paired hearts below the flag at left. In 1824 Rebecca worked a related sampler with a house and figures below an eagle and five alphabets but it has not been found (B&C, 223). Rebecca Swain Skinner (November 13, 1816–March 1, 1909) was the daughter of painter and glazier William Skinner (1789–1835) and Esther Fowler (1783–1864) of Philadelphia. She married Robert D. Wilkinson (1813–1868), a Philadelphia hatter, on August 26, 1837. They had ten children. *Gloucester County Historical Society, Woodbury, New Jersey, 32.125.*

Fig. 400. *Respectfully presented to Michael and Margaret Weaver by their affectionate/ daughter Ann Margaret in the 13th year of her age 1816/ Philadelphia December 24ᵗʰ.* Silk on linen; 16¾" x 17½". Ann's basket floats above the tablet beneath it. Elizabeth Weckerly (Krueger, *Gallery,* 52) and Margaret Hetzel (PMA, 69.288.133) worked their baskets in a similar position in 1817 and 1818. As in Figures 401 and 402, later examples usually have the basket resting on the tablet. Ann Margaret Weaver (1804–1878) was the daughter of Michael Weaver and Margaret Kurtz. Her father was a ship chandler and ropemaker. In 1825 they lived at Germantown and Frankford roads. Ann married Joseph Baker at St. Michael's Evangelical Church in Germantown on April 19, 1826. In 1897, Ann's daughter, Emily M. Baker, gave the sampler to her niece.
The Valentine Museum, Richmond, Virginia, V.75.279.9.

PRESENTATION SAMPLERS

Ann Margaret Weaver signed her sampler *Respectfully presented to Michael and Margaret Weaver by their affectionate daughter Ann Margaret in the 13ᵗʰ year of her age 1816,* and above her basket she thoughtfully added *Philadelphia December 24ᵗʰ* (Fig. 400). Ann Margaret's work is now the earliest recorded example within a group commonly called Philadelphia presentation samplers, and their standard pattern remained popular until 1839 (Fig. 404) or perhaps later. At least fifteen closely related examples are known. Although one pictures a house rather than a basket, and six signed examples lack the presentation inscription, their basic patterns are easily recognized.[1] Of the thirteen samplers that include a verse, nine girls

---

1. Elizabeth Sickfrits, 1824, with a house, is in the C-H. For those with no presentation: Mary Ann Stevenson, 1829, in *The Clarion,* Spring/Summer 1986, 8; Mary Ann Boyd, 1831, in Ring, *Treasures,* 42; and Christina Margaret Lieb's of 1825 is in a private collection.

worked the poem that begins, "Jesus permit thy gracious name to stand/As the first efforts of a youthful hand," as seen in Figures 402 and 404. There is no doubt that these samplers were made under the same instructress, but they have left no clues to the school that produced them.

The possible significance of naming *Philadelphia* or *Kensington* on the samplers has been considered. There is, however, no evidence that this applied to the location of the school but only that three "Kensington" sampler makers named the section of the city where they lived. Directories indicate that at least four Philadelphia women taught school during the entire twenty-four-year period spanned by these samplers, and two were definitely teaching accomplishments to young ladies. Most prominent among these was Mrs. Deborah Grelaud, whose boarding school existed between 1806 and 1849. Also, Mrs. Adelaide LeBrun's Seminary was open from 1816 until 1839. Two other women were described as "teacher" or "tutoress" throughout this long span of time, but nothing is known of their schools. Mrs. Eliza Martien (or Martin) was a teacher at 16 or 38 Church Alley from 1808 through 1839, while Miss Anna Sanders kept school at 73 North Seventh Street from 1808 until 1851.

The basket worked by Ann Haas in 1827 (Fig. 403) is nearly identical to the baskets in the presentation samplers and was probably made under the same instructress. Ann's work shows no trace of Quaker influence, and the Germanic castle adds to the possibility that the Grelaud or LeBrun seminaries may have produced the presentation pieces. It is also possible that one of the above-mentioned teachers was German, for many names were Anglicized upon arrival in America.

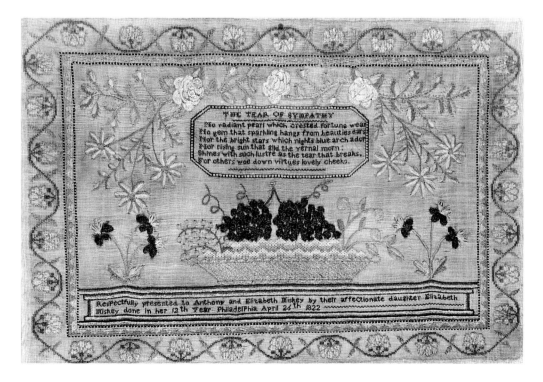

Fig. 401. *Respectfully presented to Anthony and Elizabeth Miskey by their affectionate daughter Elizabeth/ Miskey done in her 12th Year Philadelphia April 26th 1822.* Silk and wool on linen; 17″ x 24″. Elizabeth's sampler closely resembles 1821 examples by Eliza Fegenbush and Elizabeth Kline, who both omitted the presentation and their parents' names (Sotheby's Sale 5755, October 22, 1988, Lot 191; *ANTIQUES,* October 1990, 692). Elizabeth Miskey (c.1810–1832) was the daughter of Anthony Miskey (c.1757–1839) and Elizabeth Smith (1780–1837). Her father was in the glass business with his twin brother and left a sizable estate. Elizabeth Miskey Devenny had two children before her death at the age of twenty-two. *Cooper-Hewitt, National Museum of Design, Smithsonian Institution, 1941-69-71.*

Fig. 402. *Mary Murphy's work done in the 13*th/ *year of her age Kensington 1830.* Silk and wool on linen; 16½″ x 17¼″. Kensington, a northeasterly part of Philadelphia, was also named by Catharine Rihl in 1820 (Winterthur Museum) and Martha N. Hewson in 1830 (Harbeson, opp. 60). This sampler maker was probably the Mary Murphy who married cordwainer Henry Mathias at the First Presbyterian Church of Kensington on May 19, 1836.

Location unknown; photograph courtesy of Sotheby's.

Fig. 403. *Ann Haas's Piece made in the 11*th *year of her age/ Anno Domini MDCCCXXVII.* Silk on linen; 17½″ x 16½″. Ann's basket with its queen-stitched strawberries and typical presentation flowers and grapes suggests that it was made at the same Philadelphia school as the presentation pieces. Also, its Germanic building and the style of dating indicate that the teacher may have been German or French. Ann Haas (c.1817–1894) was the daughter of Philadelphia oak cooper John Haas (d.1860) and Elizabeth. They lived at Third and Race streets. On March 4, 1846, Ann married James P. Robinson (c.1817–1891) of Salem County, New Jersey. Her sampler went from her granddaughter to the Gloucester County Historical Society in 1923.

Gloucester County Historical Society, Woodbury, New Jersey, 23.36.

Fig. 404. *Respectfully Presented to Adam and Elizabeth Kandle by their affectionate daughter Eliza M Kandle/ in the 18th year of her age 1839.* Wool on linen; 22½″ x 22¾″. Elizabeth's work reveals that a remarkable consistency was maintained in these patterns for at least twenty-three years, and her verse appears on eight other examples within this group. Materials, however, had changed from predominantly silk to all wool. Eliza Kandle has not been further identified.
Philadelphia Museum of Art, Whitman Sampler Collection, gift of Pet Inc., 69.288.208.

SAMUEL FOLWELL: HIS PATTERNS
AND PAINTING ON SILK

Fig. 405. Samuel Folwell
(March 10, 1764–November
25, 1813), self-portrait,
c.1810. Paint on paper;
4″ x 3″.
*The New-York Historical
Society, 38684.*

Pictorial embroidery on silk was popular in Philadelphia from the 1730s until the post-Revolutionary period, so it is not surprising that there was an early transition from the rococo style to neoclassicism in this largest of American cities with its keen interest in fashions from abroad. Yet it was not the newly arrived French or English drawing masters or embroiderers who initiated the style for lustrous urns and temples. Instead it was a native-born craftsman who managed to fan the flames of fashion and promote his patterns and his wife's embroidery school until their output became the largest body of neoclassical silk embroidery to survive from Federal America.[1]

Samuel Folwell (Fig. 405) was a methodical artist of moderate ability but relentless energy who supported himself by teaching drawing, cutting profiles, painting miniatures, working in hair, engraving, and in particular by drawing and painting on silk for his wife's embroidery school as well as others. The enormous popularity of his patterns and his wife's instruction is especially remarkable since Philadelphia during this period was virtually inundated with semi-impoverished French refugees from both France and Santo Domingo who sought to support themselves by instructing young ladies in various artistic accomplishments.[2]

Samuel Folwell was twenty-two years old when he advertised as a miniature painter, hair worker, and engraver in Philadelphia's *Pennsylvania Packet* of June 10, 1786, and he continued to give his address at Laetitia Court in advertisements of 1788, 1789, and 1793.[3] He also solicited business in Charleston, South Carolina, in the spring of 1791, saying that "Specimens of his likenesses, mourning devices, fancy pieces, etc . . ." could be seen in Charleston at 29 Elliot Street. In August, Folwell was again in Philadelphia, and in March of 1793 he announced the opening of "A Drawing School for Young Ladies" where instruction would include "Painting upon Sattin, Ivory or Paper. . . ."[4] It was probably in 1793 that Samuel married Ann Elizabeth Gebler (1773–1824), a daughter of the German blacksmith Gottfried Gebler (d.1814) and Catharine, for their first child, Susanna, was born in 1794. Samuel and Elizabeth may have commenced working together as pattern

1. In addition to work on silk, Folwell's patterns were occasionally worked and painted on linen or cotton. On linen is *CALLIOPE AND CLIO* after his drawing for the *Philadelphia Repertory* of May 5, 1810 (*ANTIQUES,* February 1981, 421), now in a private collection. For a piece of 1811 on cotton, see Sotheby's Sale 5622, October 24, 1987, Lot 321. Both were analyzed by Dorothy McCoach.
2. Folwell's most consistent competitor was the English drawing master James Cox (1751–1834), working in Philadelphia by 1790.
3. *Pennsylvania Packet,* Philadelphia, March 26, 1788; July 9, 1789; and March 6, 1793, as recorded in Prime, *The Arts and Crafts in Philadelphia, Maryland, and South Carolina* (1932), 9–12. In 1797, Richard Folwell, printer, resided at 2 Laetitia Court; only widow Folwell was there in 1798, while Samuel had moved to 14 Moravian Alley (Philadelphia directories).
4. *Charleston City Gazette and Advertiser,* March 7, 1791; *Pennsylvania Packet,* March 6, 1793 (Prime, *Arts and Crafts,* 11–12).

Fig. 406. *SACRED TO FRIENDSHIP* worked on the temple, and *E H* with *H W* on the plinth, c.1798. Silk and paint on silk; 16″ x 20″. The subject matter and the painting suggest that this is an early example drawn and painted by Samuel Folwell. Two other early pieces are entitled *Shepherdess of the Alps* (for the work of Margaret Randolph, c.1796, see Sotheby's Sale 5746, September 10, 1988, Lot 302; the other at HSP; see also Schorsch, *Mourning Becomes America* [1976], 16/108). This example is attributed to Hannah Wallis (1781–1859), who included the initials of her cousin and classmate Elizabeth Hollingsworth. Both girls are known to have been attending a Philadelphia girls' school when this piece was worked. Hannah was the daughter of Samuel Wallis (1731–1798) and Lydia Hollingsworth (1744–1812) of Philadelphia. She married William Miller (d.1827) in 1816. For her mother's sampler of 1759, see *ANTIQUES*, February 1974, 356.
Daughters of the American Revolution Museum, Washington, D.C., 87.30.

drawer and embroidery teacher between Susanna's death in 1796 and Godfrey's birth in 1799.[5] The painting on several embroideries of the 1790s appears to be Samuel's work, but it is impossible to know if these earliest examples reflect Elizabeth's instruction (Fig. 406). One of the first to resemble pieces usually attributed to her school is "The Parting of Hector and Andromache," worked by Margaret Thackara in 1799.[6]

The death of Washington in December of 1799 gave a fortuitous boost to Folwell's career by providing the ultimate popular hero for the styles he already espoused. He signed the exquisite memorial painting in Figure 407, and drew countless adaptations for embroidery, in addition to the historical, Biblical, mythological, and allegorical subjects that were often copied from English prints. Many of the embroideries are of a monumental size unequaled elsewhere in America. Folwell must have constructed extraordinarily large standing frames for the creation of such dazzling decorations, and working them would have required

---

5. Anita Schorsch, "A Key to the Kingdom," *Winterthur Portfolio* 14, no. 1 (Spring 1979): 46. The Folwells had Godfrey Gebler on March 31, 1799; Courtland Frederick on August 2, 1801; Ann Elizabeth on July 7, 1803; Samuel on September 7, 1805; and Rebecca Eliza on March 28, 1808 (Records of the First Reformed Church of Philadelphia, HSP).

6. Owned by descendants of the maker. For similar figures and temple, see *ANTIQUES*, February 1981, 423.

Fig. 407. Mourning picture signed *S. Folwell philad^{ia} Pinx^{t}*, c.1800. Paint on silk; 20½" x 24". Inscribed on the plinth *SACRED/ TO THE MEMORY/ OF THE/ ILLUS-TRIOUS/ WASHINGTON/* beneath a small oval inscribed *THY/ LOSS WE ER/ SHALL Mourn;* and on the banner *The/ Deeds/ of/ Washington.* Folwell's Washington memorial patterns for needlework closely resemble this painting. The stance of Liberty differs slightly as her head rests on her hand in the embroideries (Figs. 408, 409). A similar monument, crossed trees, cascading flowers, sprigs of plants in a mounded landscape, and this style of lettering are all standard elements of Folwell mourning patterns. A number of Folwell's needlework compositions are also in this shape with a wide border of embroidered or painted flowers.
Private collection.

both considerable space and exceptional skill in handling materials, which often included heavy metallic braids and fringes, spangles, and glass beads. Despite relatively little advertising after 1800, the volume of Folwell's work reveals that he was well patronized, and similar compositions painted by other hands suggest that he willingly sold his designs to other teachers.[7] In 1805, Folwell again sought work in Charleston, advertising drawings on silk and satin for young ladies that reflected "the newest fashions in the first schools of Philadelphia and all other capital towns in America. . . ."[8]

"Mr. SAMUEL FOLWELL, Limner" died at noon on November 26, 1813, "in the 49th year of his age." His funeral took place in his home on Dock Street, and

7. For patterns like Figure 409, but worked at another school, see Ring, *Treasures,* Fig. 161, and Eliza Gravenstine's work of 1807 in the *Philadelphia Antiques Show Catalogue* (1988), 34. Davida Deutsch attributes the painting on these pieces to Raphaelle Peale (lecture, "New Fashion for Mourning in the Decorative Arts," Williamsburg Antiques Forum, February 8, 1990). For other Folwell-type compositions painted by unknown hands, see *ANTIQUES,* February 1982, 479; *The Needle and Bobbin Club Bulletin* (1925), Fig. 12 (this piece is now at Stratford Hall); and the *Old Print Shop Portfolio,* April 1951, 191. Crude renditions of the composition in Figure 408 were also worked on silk and painted on silk and velvet (SPB, Garbisch, Sale 3637, May 8, 1974, Lot 4).

8. *The Charleston Times,* April 24, 1805, as quoted by Deutsch in *ANTIQUES,* September 1985, 526. Mrs. Deutsch also reveals Folwell's prolific production of memorial jewelry and the kinship of his compositions to his embroidery patterns. For more on Folwell and likely proceedings at his school, see *ANTIQUES,* February 1981, 416–17, 420–3; October 1986, 646–7; and March 1989, 616, 620, 624.

Fig. 408. Anonymous Washington memorial with glass initialed *E T,* c.1800–1805. Silk, paint, ink, and paper on silk; 22½″ x 26½″; original and characteristic Philadelphia frame. Above the printed portrait applied to the plinth is the inscription *SACRED TO/ THE MEMORY OF THE/ ILLUSTRIOUS/ WASHINGTON* and on the urn *THY/ LOSS WE E'R SHALL/ MOURN.* Except for the position of Liberty's arms, the configuration of this embroidery is similar to the painting (Fig. 407). For another embroidery more closely related to the painting, see *ANTIQUES,* November 1987, 916. This pattern, with a dejected soldier and the composition in Figure 409, represent Folwell's most typical Washington memorial designs. *Collection of Mr. and Mrs. George P. Valluzzo; photograph courtesy of Sotheby's.*

Fig. 409. Anonymous Washington memorial, c.1800–1805. Silk, paint, and ink on silk; 21½″ x 27⅝″. Inscribed on the plinth *SACRED/ TO THE MEMORY OF/ THE/ ILLUS-TROUS/ WASHINGTON* and on the urn *G W.* This Folwell composition, more than any other, was occasionally painted by other hands. Possibly it was derived from a still undiscovered print. *National Museum of American History, Smithsonian Institution; gift of Eleanor and Mabel Van Alstyne, 256396.*

Fig. 410. *H.J./ INNOCENCE & FRIENDSHIP/ 1804* inscribed on the glass and *SACRED TO FRIENDSHIP* inscribed on the plinth. Silk, chenille, paint, and ink on silk; 21³⁄₁₆″ x 27⅛″. This composition and its many variations were among Folwell's most popular patterns. Another example, also entitled *Innocence and Friendship,* was worked by Mary P. Paul of Philadelphia and has real straw on the thatched roof of its cottage. Also, both the faces and hands of its figures are painted (see *The Museum* [quarterly of the Newark Museum] 19, nos. 3 and 4 [1967]: 40). Hannah Firth Jones (1778–1853) worked this piece when she was twenty-six years old, seven years after her marriage to Isaac Cooper Jones, a Philadelphia dry goods merchant. Her embroidery demonstrates that young matrons patronized Mrs. Folwell's embroidery school in order to create an impressive decoration. (See also Hannah's sampler of 1792, Fig. 362.)
Allentown Art Museum, gift of Mrs. William P. Hacker, 82.31.3.

he was buried in the German Presbyterian Cemetery.⁹ He left Elizabeth with five young children, and from 1814 through 1819 she was listed in Philadelphia directories as Elizabeth or Eliza Folwell, "widow, teacher and embroiderer." Shortly before Samuel's death, her only advertisement appeared in a Philadelphia paper (Fig. 411). Apparently at a very early age Folwell's son Godfrey (1799–1855) began to draw patterns and paint them in the style of his father. They are occasionally difficult to distinguish from Samuel's work. By 1819, Godfrey Folwell appeared in the Philadelphia directory as "G. Folwell teacher of fancy drawing," and although signed pieces by his father have not been found, at least two embroideries are known to bear Godfrey's signature. He copied many of the prints favored by his father, but a favorite of his own appears to have been a scene from Sir Walter Scott's *The Lady of the Lake,* first published in 1810 (Fig. 418). However, Godfrey Folwell soon abandoned this career and worked as a silver chaser, first in Baltimore, and finally in Philadelphia.

The most surprising circumstance concerning the Folwells is their evident lack of significant competition in producing elegant silk embroideries when girls' schools of every description were seeking patronage in Philadelphia, and while others in that vicinity were advertising in local papers. A well-established board-

---

9. *Poulson's American Daily Advertiser,* Philadelphia, November 27, 1813; Registration of Philadelphia Deaths 1803–1860, microfilm, HSP.

Mrs. E. FOLWELL,

INTENDING to resume her former SCHOOL OF EMBROIDERY, takes this method of informing her friends and the public in general, she will commence as soon as she has a certain number of Young Ladies engaged. Mr. FOLWELL, being a Master of Drawing, those Ladies under her tuition will have a double advantage in shading, which is all the merit of the picture.

E. F. flatters herself those Ladies who were pleased to patronise her before, will now have the goodness to recommend her to such of their acquaintance as may wish to send their daughters.

The terms will be eight dollars per quarter for whole days and five dollars for half days. Any person wishing to engage will please to apply at No. 1 Ransted Court, above Chesnut, in Fourth street.

sept 18   d6t

Fig. 411. Elizabeth Folwell's only known advertisement appeared in *Poulson's American Daily Advertiser,* Philadelphia, on September 18, 1813.
American Antiquarian Society.

Fig. 412. Anonymous embroidery inscribed on the glass *WANDERING SHEP-HERDESS,* c.1800–1805. Silk, metallic thread, and paint on silk; 18¼″ x 22½″. The figures here exemplify Folwell's characteristic style of painting. The sea also has his typical choppy waves. For an almost identical composition, see *ANTIQUES,* March 1988, 623.
Private collection.

ing school for girls was kept by Ann Brodeau who came from England in 1775,[10] and the 1790s brought a number of new rivals: Mrs. Capron, "lately from Elizabeth Town," but educated in Paris, appeared in Philadelphia in 1793[11]; the aggressive and artistic Catherine Groombridge (c.1760–1837) also came from England with her artist husband, William Groombridge (1748–1811), in 1793[12]; and no mistress of a French boarding school had more prestigious supporters than Marie Rivardi whose seminary opened in 1802[13]; while Madame Grelaud taught successfully from 1806 until 1849.[14] There is ample written evidence that these women and a great many others were teaching accomplishments to girls in Philadelphia between 1800 and 1820, but no characteristic silk embroideries can now be associated with their schools.

10. *The Pennsylvania Gazette,* December 6, 1775. The 1790 census recorded twenty-seven females in her household.

11. *The Philadelphia Gazette and Philadelphia Daily Advertiser,* May 3, 1793.

12. In *Poulson's* of October 1, 1800, Mrs. Groombridge advertised her Columbia House Boarding and Day School with appreciation for encouragement after "more than seven years in Philadelphia." In the summer of 1794 she taught embroidery and drawing to Nelly Custis ("Washington's Household Account Book 1793–1797," *PMHB* 30, no. 3 (1906): 315.

13. Mary Johnson, "Madame Rivardi's Seminary in the Gothic Mansion," *PMHB* 104, no. 1 (January 1980): 3–38. Rivardi also advertised a school in New Orleans in August 1802 (Woody, *A History of Women's Education in the United States,* 1:298). For a silk embroidery from Mrs. Rivardi's school, see Christie's, October 1, 1988, Lot 262.

14. Lucy Lee Bowie, "Madame Grelaud's French School" (June 1944), 142–53.

ANN HUTCHINSON.
1806.

Fig. 414. *THE LITTLE COTTAGERS BY A H 1806* inscribed on the glass. Silk, chenille, and paint on silk; 20″ x 27¼″. Folwell's custom of painting arms and legs white but leaving faces and necks unpainted is especially conspicuous in his pictures of the cottagers. Ann Hutchinson probably worked this embroidery and its companion piece of her family (Fig. 413) before her seventeenth birthday on September 20, 1806. *Allentown Art Museum, gift of Elizabeth M. Wistar, 86.36.2.*

Opposite: Fig. 413. *ANN HUTCHINSON 1806* inscribed on the glass. Silk, chenille, and paint on silk; 20¼″ x 25¾″. Ann's embroidery belongs to a group of family portrait pieces that are the most personal and charming examples of Folwell's work, and were surely the most expensive. Ann Hutchinson (1789–1848) was the daughter of Mahlon Hutchinson (1754–1836), a Philadelphia merchant, and Sarah Palmer (b.1757). She married Dr. John Craig Heberton (1790–1829) on May 8, 1817. Pictured from left to right: Ann's grandmother Sarah Walker Palmer (1729–1808), her brother John Palmer Hutchinson (1787–1875), her mother, her brother Randal Hutchinson (1795–1851), Ann, her sister Sarah Hutchinson (b.1785), her brother Benjamin Palmer Hutchinson (1797–1876), her father, and her eldest brother, Mahlon Hutchinson, Jr. (1781–1862). Ann's and her sister's fashionable Empire gowns are in marked contrast to the Quaker styles worn by their mother and grandmother.
Allentown Art Museum, gift of Elizabeth M. Wistar, 86.36.1.

Fig. 415. Ann Hutchinson Heberton, self-portrait, c.1830. Oil on canvas; 30⅛″ x 25¼″.
Allentown Art Museum, gift of Elizabeth M. Wistar, 86.36.3.

Fig. 416. Embroidered picture attributed to Eliza Macpherson, c.1819; silk, chenille, metallic threads, and paint on silk; 27⅝″ x 33½″; original frame, probably by Earps and Co. of Philadelphia, working 1814 to 1825. The pattern and painting are attributed to Godfrey Folwell (b.1799), and the composition was derived from a print entitled *Lady Elizabeth Grey imploring of Edward IV the restitution of her deceased Husbands Lands forfeited in the dispute between the Houses of York and Lancaster*. It was engraved by William Wynne Ryland after a painting by Angelica Kauffmann and published in London, March 4, 1780. For the print and an example painted by Samuel Folwell in 1809, see Ring, *Treasures*, 98. A magnificent example painted by Samuel and worked by Sophia B. Lybrand, 1812, is now at Gore Place, Waltham, Massachusetts. For another, by Godfrey, see Schiffer, 103. This embroiderer was probably Elizabeth Macpherson (July 17, 1806–March 11, 1820), the daughter of General William Macpherson (1756–1813). He married in 1802, as his second wife, Elizabeth White, the daughter of Bishop William White. Eliza was baptized at Philadelphia's Christ Church on October 2, 1806, and worked this piece when she was thirteen years old. Her father was a Major in the Revolution and highly esteemed by George Washington (*PMHB* 5, no. 1 [1881]: 88–92).
White House Collection, 961.10.1.

Fig. 417. Anonymous, uninscribed Biblical embroidery usually entitled *The Ascension,* c.1810. Silk, chenille, and paint on silk; 25½″ x 33″. Attributed to Samuel Folwell, although it is evident that both Samuel and his son Godfrey painted pieces with this composition, which was no doubt derived from a print. The Winterthur Museum owns an example signed by Godfrey (*ANTIQUES,* October 1986, 646–7). A similar piece naming *Mary C. Kreider, 1818,* is in the PMA. The figure at far left appears in three other Biblical embroideries of identical form. A privately owned one, dated 1812, is called *The Nativity;* others are entitled *The Adoration of the Christ Child.* One is in the St. Louis Art Museum (*ANTIQUES,* February 1972, 383); the other, dated 1811, in PB, Haskell Sale VI, No. 634, February 17, 1945, Lot 1536.
Private collection.

Fig. 418. Anonymous embroidery depicting *The Lady of the Lake,* c.1819. Silk, chenille, metallic thread, and paint on silk; 25½″ x 32″. Attributed to Godfrey Folwell. For a similar piece signed by him, see *ANTIQUES,* October 1986, 646.
Private collection; photograph courtesy of Sotheby's.

Fig. 419. *E P POLK   THE COTTAGERS   1804* inscribed on the glass. Silk, chenille, and paint on silk; 25¾″ x 33½″. For this composition Folwell surely copied an English print, a section of which (the girls by the cage) occurs on a printed textile (an example is in the Allentown Art Museum). This vignette was worked alone on an English pictorial silk embroidery (Richard A. Bourne Co., August 23, 1983, Lot 191). Eliza Newell of New Castle, Delaware, worked *The Cottagers* in 1804 (Kenmore, Fredericksburg, Virginia). Her rendition is nearly identical to this embroidery—more so than Ann Hutchinson's (Fig. 414). Elizabeth Peale Polk (1786–1874) was the eldest child of the artist Charles Peale Polk (1767–1822) and Ruth Ellison. She was named for her paternal grandmother, a sister of Charles Willson Peale. She died unmarried. Her embroidery descended in the family of her nephew William Stewart Polk (1827–1917), son of her brother David. *Collection of Mr. and Mrs. Rudolph Ellis Carter.*

The popularity of Mrs. Folwell's school is emphatically demonstrated by the embroidery in Figure 419. Between 1791 and 1793 the young Charles Peale Polk (1767–1822) solicited business as a portrait painter in Baltimore and advertised a "Drawing School . . . for the Tuition of young Ladies, in that ornamental necessary Art,"[15] but despite having this artist for a father, and numerous Peale cousins who were artists, Elizabeth Peale Polk worked one of Folwell's popular patterns at Elizabeth Folwell's embroidery school when she was eighteen years old. The number of Folwell embroideries now identified offers convincing evidence that working an impressive picture at Mrs. Folwell's school must have been a craze of considerable proportion with the affluent schoolgirls and young women of Philadelphia between 1800 and about 1820. Along with all this productivity, Elizabeth Folwell gave birth to five children between 1799 and 1808.

---

15. *Maryland Gazette,* Baltimore, May 24, 1791; *Baltimore Daily Repository,* May 3, 1793 (Prime, *Arts and Crafts,* 30, 52).

Fig. 420. Thomas Clark, *Front View of Westtown Boarding School*, c.1805. Watercolor on paper; 8″ x 9″. Although it lacks the fanlight in the pediment, this view closely resembles many embroidered versions of the building. Thomas Clark of Woodbury, New Jersey, entered Westtown School at age sixteen in July 1805 and departed in March 1806. This building was 110 feet long and 60 feet deep; completed in 1799, it was demolished in 1887. *Westtown School.*

Westtown School

The Friends' Westtown Boarding School in Chester County, Pennsylvania, has been in continuous operation since May 6, 1799, and a wealth of schoolgirl needlework has survived from its first fifty years of existence. Following its inception, Westtown quickly became the most respected Quaker boarding school within this stronghold of Quaker culture, and both its procedures and its needlework were widely copied by its students and others who opened schools in this region during the early nineteenth century.

The need for such a school was clearly outlined by Owen Biddle in 1790 when he published *A Plan for a School . . . similar to that at Ackworth, in Yorkshire, Great-Britain, varied to suit Circumstances of the Youth Within the Limits of the Yearly-Meeting for Pennsylvania and New Jersey.* It was proposed to the Philadelphia Yearly Meeting in 1792, and in 1794 forty-seven men and seven women were appointed to the School Committee. After careful study of English schools and much deliberation about the location, the building was finally erected on 600 acres of farmland in Westtown Township (Fig. 420). By the close of 1799, about one hundred boys and one hundred girls were in residence at Westtown.[1]

Girls' studies at Westtown were essentially the same as for boys except for less emphasis on arithmetic, and girls spent one-third of their time in the sewing room. However, their instructress helped with their spelling lessons while they sewed. The majority of samplers worked at Westtown were either plain and prac-

---

1. The first superintendents were Richard and Catharine Hartshorne of Rahway, New Jersey, who served one year. The first teachers for the girls were Elizabeth Bellerby and Phebe Cox (Dewees, *Centennial History of Westtown Boarding School* [1899], 43, 46).

Fig. 421. *INFORMATION* about Westtown Boarding School issued by the Philadelphia Yearly Meeting on April 11, 1799. The demands for plain clothing were strictly enforced. Hannah Albertson of Plymouth, Pennsylvania, wrote to her parents on July 29, 1799, "They have made a rule we are not to wear calico pockits, nankeen mittens, nor white under petticotes." (Hole, *Westtown Through the Years, 1799–1942* [1942], 47.)
Westtown School.

INFORMATION

For Parents, and others inclining to fend Children for Education to Friend's boarding fchool at West-Town.

It is agreed by the committee of the Yearly Meeting that the School be opened for the admiffion of twenty children of each fex on the fixth day of the fifth month next. The firft twenty of each fex on the lift to be firft admitted.

Applications for admiffion of Children (none of which are to be allowed under eight years of age) muft be made either to the *fuperintendent at the School or to the Treafurer for the time being, who, in cafes which appear doubtful, are to confult as many of the committee as can with leaft inconvenience be collected. The Superintendent is to forward to the Treafurer fuch applications as fhall be made to him and agreed to ; the Treafurer on receipt of fixteen dollars (the price of one quarters tuition and boarding,) together with a notification of the name and age, alfo the certificate of a Phyfician that the child is in health and particularly free from fores or infectious diforders, fhall grant a bill of admiffion. A like fum is to be paid to the Treafurer on the entrance of every fucceeding quarter, and confidered the property of the Inftitution whether the child ftay the time out or not.

No child is to be admitted for lefs than twelve months ; and two months notice is to be given to the Superintendent by any Parent or Guardian propofing to remove a child or children from the School.

No children fhall leave the houfe without permiffion from the Superintendent ; and fhould any be taken away by Parents or Guardians without fuch permiffion, their places fhall be confidered as vacant, and they not re-admitted but upon renewed application and fatisfactory conceffion. No child is to be brought to the Inftitution nor taken away therefrom on the firft day of the week.

The children are to bring with them the following articles of cloathing.

BOYS	GIRLS	
Six fhirts,	Six fhifts,	Three Frocks or Habits,
Four pocket Handkerchiefs,	Three fhort gowns,	Four aprons,
Four pair of ftockings,	Six neck handkerchiefs,	Four pocket handkerchiefs,
Two pair of fhoes,	Two pair of pockets,	Three night caps,
Two hats,	Four pair of ftockings,	Two pair of fhoes,
Two fuits to confift of coat }	Two worfted upper petticoats,	Two linnen under petticoats,
waiftcoat and trowfers or breeches, }	One flannel do.	Bonnets, cloak, and mittens,

The girls are alfo to bring with them a pair of Sciffors, Thread-cafe, Thimble, Work-bag and fome plain fewing or knitting to begin with.

Each child to bring alfo a large and fmall tooth comb and cloaths bag, which latter as well as their cloaths to be marked with the Initials of their name and the number of their bill of admittance. If the cloathing be not fufficiently plain as to colour or fhall require much wafhing it fhall be returned, but if the *make* only be exceptionable it will be altered and the expenfe charged. All the cloathing fent, to be ftrong and fubftantial. Remnants, the fame as the cloaths fent with the children, will be acceptable to repair them.

To prevent inconvenience the Parents or Guardians are not to fupply their children with money, or printed books. Such of the latter as are judged proper for them will be furnifhed by the Committee.

4th Month, 11, 1799.

*The prefent Superintendent is Richard Harfhorne and the Treafurer Thomas Fifher.

tical exercises in marking and darning (Figs. 423, 425, 428), or pious verses enclosed by simple borders. Westtown's undulating vine-and-leaf border (Fig. 429) soon became popular at Quaker schools throughout the Delaware Valley and persisted on more elaborate samplers worked at many schools during the 1820s and 1830s. Except for a darning sampler (Fig. 425), the school's most typical embroideries are represented here by the work of one girl (Figs. 427–430). The ten-year-old orphan Ann Haines (Fig. 431) was the granddaughter of Margret Wistar Haines (Fig. 374). Her father was expelled from meeting for fathering her out of wedlock and died shortly thereafter. Ann was strongly attached to Hannah Marshall Haines, the widow of her uncle Caspar Haines. She wrote to Hannah about working on "wristbands" and "threadcases," and offered "to do a shirt for thee if thou wilt send it."[2] Except for schooling or travel, Ann lived her entire life at Wyck, where she was much engaged in the family's activities and affectionately known as Cousin Ann.

It has been said that "some of the most proficient" Westtown students

---

2. Ann Haines to Hannah Haines, 4 New-Bank Street, Philadelphia, December 9, 1806, and January 13, 1807. In 1811, Ann was attending the Briar Cliff School in New York, and wrote to Hannah Haines on April 7, 1811, mentioning her "much loved preceptress S Marriott." (Wyck Papers, Series II, Box 25, Folder 366, American Philosophical Society, Philadelphia.) This was Susanna Marriott (c.1768–1857) who came from Marsden, Lancashire County, England, in 1793, and kept the school in Westchester County, New York, at least from 1810 to 1811. In 1820 she began teaching in Aurora, New York, where she wielded great influence and was much beloved. (Emily Howland, *Historical Sketches of Friends in Cayuga County, New York* [Auburn, N.Y.: Cayuga County Historical Society, 1882; reprint, Ithaca, N.Y., 1964], 14–15.)

Fig. 422. Profile of a perky Hannah Hunt (November 14, 1786–1829), the first girl admitted to Westtown School, c.1800. Paint on paper; height 4″. Hannah was the daughter of John Hunt (1753–1836) and Rachel Gibbons (1760–1845) of Darby, Pennsylvania. She entered the school on May 6, 1799, and departed on May 5, 1800. According to custom, she was assigned No. 1 in the girls' school and this number identified her accounts and possessions. Her cap may be the type required for Westtown girls over fourteen (Dewees, *Centennial History of Westtown Boarding School* [1899], 70), although Hannah departed at age thirteen. She is said to have been of "medium size, handsome, with dark blue eyes, brown hair, pretty complexion, a bright, cheerful and affectionate disposition and very conscientious." On January 8, 1806, she married Hugh McIlvain (1775–1838) and they had nine children. (*The Westonian* VII, no. 6 [June 1901]: 101–2.) *Westtown School.*

were "allowed to stitch views of the School, to be framed and exhibited as pictures."[3] There is little reliable evidence of this practice, however. While a number of embroideries depict the school building, such as the splendid side view of the school by *R B M* (Fig. 432), none can be positively assigned to the period of the maker's attendance. Within a few years after the establishment of Westtown School, many of its former students were employed as teachers by Monthly Meetings throughout the Delaware Valley. Their Westtown education surely contributed to the wide conformity found in nineteenth-century Quaker samplers of this region, and they were probably responsible for most of the sampler views of Westtown School (Figs. 531, 538). The majority of these young women taught briefly before marriage, and they were generally engaged with agreements like that of twenty-one-year-old Rachel Hunt. She was to teach at the Friends' Brick School in Chester Township, New Jersey, for the sum of two dollars per scholar, provided that no less than twenty were enrolled. She was told to instruct in "reading, writing, sewing, marking and grammar if the employers desire it. To commence 4th mo. 27th, 1812. Each employer to pay his equal dividend for fire wood according to the number of schollars sent; she finding quills and ink."[4] Eventually Rachel married David Roberts, and they were superintendent and matron of Westtown School from 1858 to 1861.

The most unique objects produced by Westtown schoolgirls are the stuffed silk globes, which usually have continents outlined in silk, and silk-embroidered longitudes and latitudes, with other elements either painted or inked (Figs. 434, 435). Surviving globes range in date from Ruth Wright's example of 1815,[5] to about 1844 (Fig. 435).[6] Eight globes are in the Westtown School collection, and many others are in museums and private collections.[7]

Schools that emulated Westtown School and its needlework proliferated in the Delaware Valley well into the 1830s. Some were boarding schools such as the Pleasant Hill Boarding School in Byberry Township, which was opened by John Comly, a former Westtown teacher, and his wife, Rebecca Budd. She was among the first students at Westtown and also taught there before her marriage in 1803.[8] This school and many others are named on samplers that are closely related to Westtown work.

3. Hole, *Westtown Through the Years, 1799–1942* (1942), 101.

4. James C. Purdy, *Moorestown and Her Neighbors* (Moorestown, N.J.: Historical Society of Moorestown, 1976), 79. Customary hours of teaching were 8 until 4, "allowing one hour at noon" during November through March; otherwise, 8 until 5:30 with two hours at noon.

5. Swan, *Plain & Fancy*, 60–1; for another of 1818, see Skinner Sale 1434, March 21, 1992, Lot 1.

6. Routine sewing classes ended in 1843. The last sewing teacher was Rebecca McCollin, employed from 1834 to 1843. Less formal instruction continued for girls who requested it. The Girls Merchandise Book, 1840–1847, reveals that the father of Sarah R. Sheppard (Fig. 435) was charged for "sewing room" expenses of .74 in October of 1843 and .33 in 1847, while sewing expenses for other girls continued into the 1850s. (Letter from Alice B. Long, Westtown School Curator, January 27, 1987.)

7. The Chester County Historical Society; the Monmouth County (New Jersey) Historical Society; the Mercer Museum; the DAR; the Los Angeles County Museum; and the Minneapolis Institute of Arts.

8. Rebecca Budd was the niece of Rachel Budd (the wife of Isaac Collins) and also the first cousin of Mary Collins (Fig. 328).

Fig. 423. *WESTTOWN SCHOOL/ Mary French 6th mo 27th 1800.* Silk on linen; 12½" x 10½". Mary's exquisitely worked sampler is one of the earliest and finest surviving examples of the bell-decorated, cut-cornered form derived from Ackworth prototypes. She also stitched ligatures in the identical order used by Candia Power (Fig. 424). This basic style continued in the area into the 1820s. An example from the North School in Philadelphia is dated 1821 (*ANTIQUES*, December 1989, 1341). Mary French (1786–1870) of Westfield, Burlington County, New Jersey, entered Westtown School in December 1799 and remained one year. She was the only child of Robert French, Jr. (1749–1811), and Hannah Warrington (1760–1786). She married Josiah Roberts (1783–1841) in 1808. Teachers Mary Cowperthwaite and Atlantic Matlack were among the witnesses at their wedding. They had four children.

Historical Society of Moorestown, New Jersey, 77-7-2.

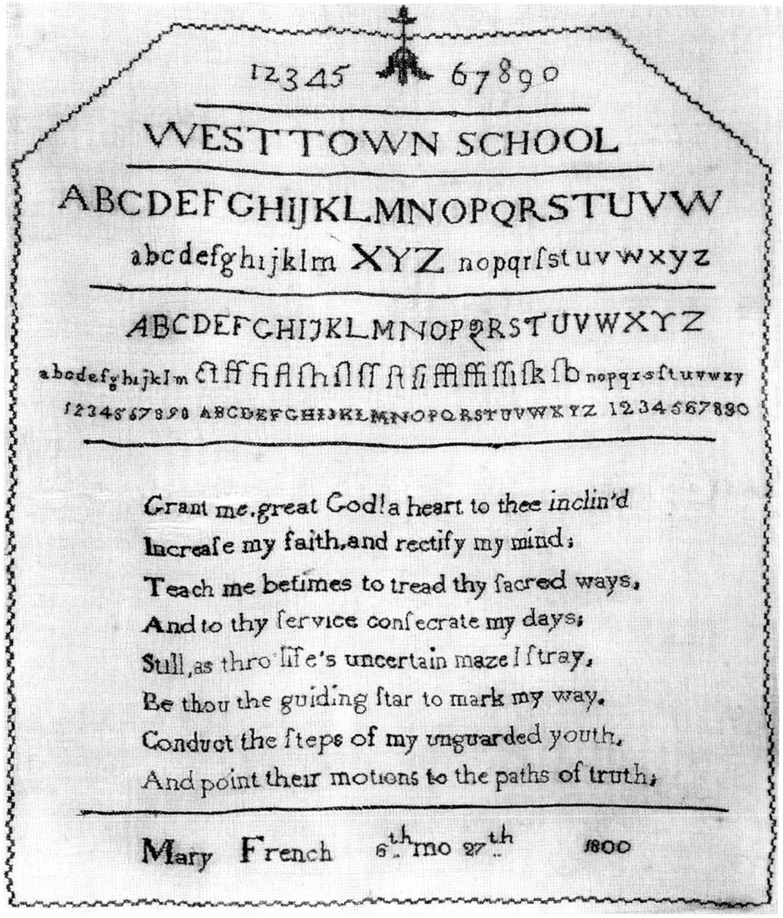

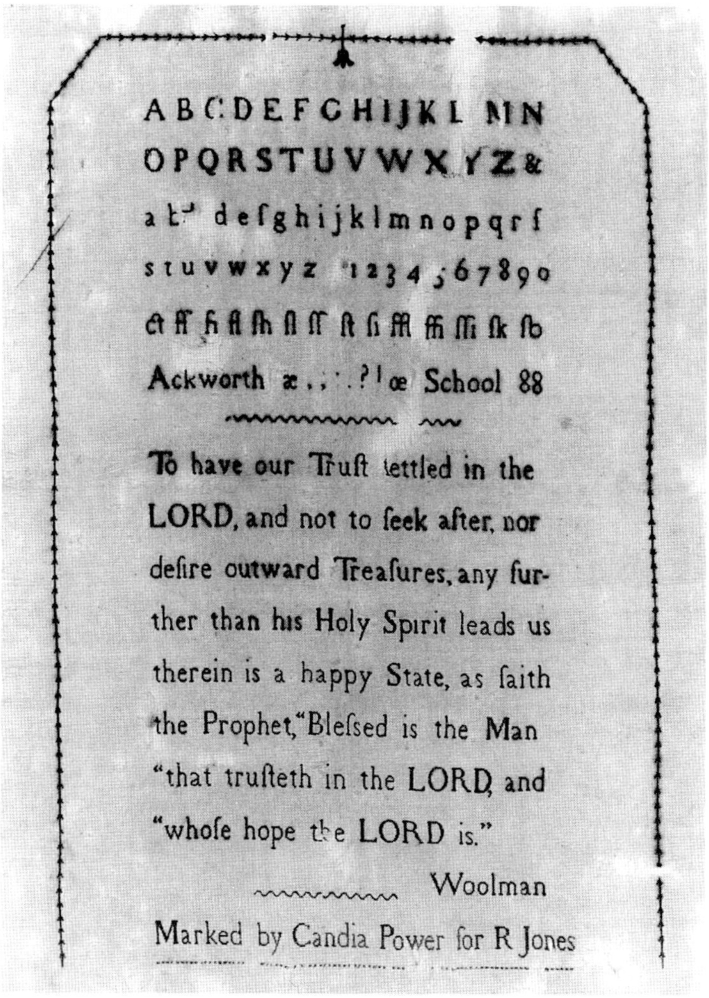

Fig. 424. *Marked by Candia Power for R Jones/ Ackworth . . . School/ 88.* Silk on wool; 14½" x 10½". Candia quoted a passage that appeared in *Serious Considerations on Various Subjects of Importance* by John Woolman (London, 1773), 385. John Woolman (1720–1772) was the revered Quaker preacher and friend of Rebecca Jones (1739–1818) to whom this sampler was given by Candia Power, who attended the Ackworth School from 1785 to 1788. Candia's sampler indicates that the Roman-style alphabet and rows of ligatures were common to English Quaker work before they appeared in America, and that patterns from Ackworth School unquestionably influenced the teachers at the Westtown School.

Westtown School, 59.

Fig. 425. *Mary Canby/ Weston School/ 1813.* Cream cotton on green linsey-woolsey; 9¼″ x 9″. This characteristic Westtown darning sampler has cross-stitch, pattern darning, and chain stitch to simulate knitting (in center). The earliest known Westtown darning samplers are three small white-on-white pieces worked by Phebe Downing of Downingtown, Pennsylvania, in 1801. Earlier darning samplers were made elsewhere in this region. Sarah Richardson's is dated 1799 (Friends' Historical Library of Swarthmore College). Mary Canby (1798–1890) of Wilmington, Delaware, was the eleventh child of Samuel Canby (1751–1832) and Frances Lea (1757–1814), and the first cousin of Frances Canby (Fig. 543). She entered Westtown School in June 1812, attended one year, and returned for another year in 1814. In 1824 she married John W. Tatum.
Westtown School, 513.

Fig. 426. *WESTTOWN SCHOOL/ Rachel Ellis/ 1801.* Silk on linen; 11″ x 13½″. Rachel's unembellished border appears to have been a forerunner of the more popular vine-and-leaf border seen in Figure 429. For an earlier plain oval from Westtown School, see Ruth James' sampler of 1800 in Krueger, *Gallery,* Fig. 41. Rachel Ellis, from Muncy, Lycoming County, Pennsylvania, entered Westtown School at the age of ten in May 1799 and left in October 1801. See her marking sampler of 1800 in *ANTIQUES,* December 1984, 1426.
Westtown School, 571.

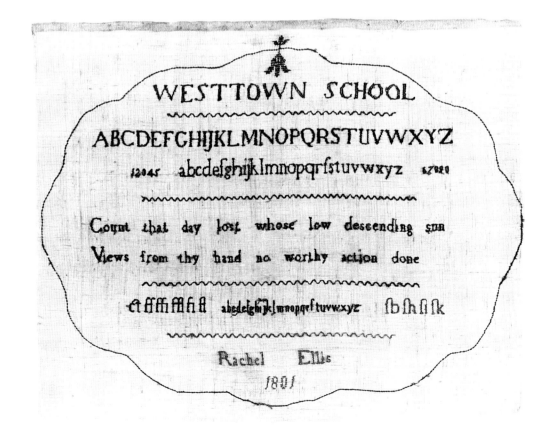

Fig. 427. *Ann Haines*, c.1804. Silk on linen; 10¼″ x 15″. Ann's random arrangement of medallions, sprays of flowers, and other small motifs with various initials is typical of both English and American Quaker samplers of the early nineteenth century. The earliest-known Westtown sampler with geometric motifs was worked by Hannah Price in September 1800 (Schiffer, 43).
Wyck Charitable Trust, Philadelphia, 88.561.

Fig. 428. *Ann Haines*, c.1803. Silk on linen; 14″ x 10½″. This basic alphabet sampler is probably the first piece Ann worked after entering Westtown School. Similar pieces survive in large numbers and they often name *Westtown, West Town,* or *Weston.*
Wyck Charitable Trust, Philadelphia, 88.562.

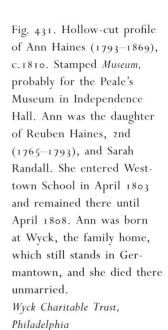

Fig. 431. Hollow-cut profile of Ann Haines (1793–1869), c.1810. Stamped *Museum,* probably for the Peale's Museum in Independence Hall. Ann was the daughter of Reuben Haines, 2nd (1765–1793), and Sarah Randall. She entered Westtown School in April 1803 and remained there until April 1808. Ann was born at Wyck, the family home, which still stands in Germantown, and she died there unmarried.
Wyck Charitable Trust, Philadelphia

Fig. 429. *West-Town Boarding School./ Ann Haines. / 1806.* Silk on linen; 10¾″ x 13¾″. The vine-and-leaf border seen here, probably original to Westtown, was used in 1802, if not earlier (*ANTIQUES,* December 1981, 1310). For pieces from other schools, see Figure 547; also B&C, Pl. XCIV. Ann's *Extract* was probably the last sampler she worked at Westtown.
Wyck Charitable Trust, Philadelphia, 88.552.

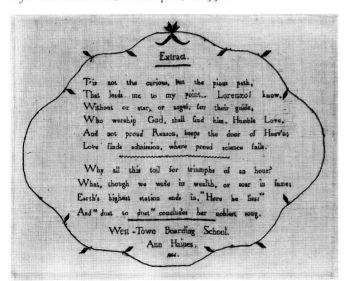

Fig. 430. *Ann Haines 1804.* Silk on linen; 12½″ x 13¾″. Ann's sampler is typical of Quaker work in the Delaware Valley, and similar pieces were made in Pennsylvania, New Jersey, and Delaware from 1800 until about 1835. See Figure 314; also B&C, Pl. XCIV.
Wyck Charitable Trust, Philadelphia, 88.563.

Fig. 432. *R B M/ July 1837/ Weston Boarding School House.* Silk on linen; 18″ x 18″. This remarkable side view of the Westtown School resembles earlier watercolors and appears to be an accurate rendition. The tiger, ostrich, peacock, burro, and reindeer lend a Victorian feeling to the composition, but the rose sprays, eight-pointed stars, and swan are in the traditional Quaker style. Its maker is unknown. *Collection of Margaret B. Schiffer.*

Fig. 433. *FRIENDS' BOARD-ING SCHOOL, WEST-TOWN, PA. On Stone by J. T. French; Lith. of T. Sinclair, 79 S. 3rd St. Phila.,* c.1840. 11¹⁄₁₆″ x 15¾″. This front view of the Westtown School building was portrayed on many samplers with varying degrees of accuracy. The facade had seventeen windows on three floors, with basement windows partly showing, and four dormers. *Westtown School.*

FRIENDS' BOARDING SCHOOL, WEST-TOWN, PA.

Fig. 434. Terrestrial globe by Rachel Burrough in its original protective box, c.1822. Silk, paint, and ink on silk; 5¾″ in diameter. Rachel Burrough (1805–1865) was the daughter of Joseph Burrough and Martha Davis of Evesham, New Jersey. She entered Westtown School in 1821. In 1833, she married Charles Coles (1807–1839). Before attending Westtown School, Rachel worked a sampler that names the *Chesterford School*. See her sister's Chesterford School rendition of the Westtown School in B&C, Pl. XCV.
Collection of William C. Coles, Jr.

Fig. 435. Terrestrial and celestial globes made by Sarah R. Sheppard, c.1844. Silk, paint, and ink on silk; approximately 4¾″ in diameter. These pieces are exceptional for the gold-colored silk ground of the terrestrial globe and the colorfully painted signs of the zodiac on the celestial globe. Sarah was enrolled at Westtown in October 1843 and departed in April 1844. She probably returned, for there were charges to her father in 1847. Her school number was 915. Sarah Richards Sheppard (1832–1906) was the daughter of Benjamin Sheppard and Mary R. Saunders (1799–1873) of Greenwich, New Jersey. She married George W. Thorp (1830–1920) of Frankford, near Philadelphia, and had five sons.
Monroe County Historical Association, Stroudsburg, Pennsylvania, 42.26.1 and 46.26.2.

Chester County Samplers

Chester County was one of the three original counties established under William Penn's charter in 1682 and its population remained predominantly English throughout the eighteenth century. This county was noted for its prosperous farms and fine craftsmanship and by 1790 its population was approaching thirty thousand. In 1825, Anne Royall (1769–1854) left a glowing account of her visit there:

> I knew not which to admire most, the appearance of the country, or the neat plump Quaker and his wife. . . . They seemed to be the happiest people on earth, health on their cheeks, contentment on their contenance. . . . West Chester is a most delectable spot . . . I found more taste, talent and refinement in West Chester, in proportion of the number of inhabitants, than in any town, without exception, I have visited.[1]

The earliest-known Pennsylvania sampler to name the school of its origin was worked in 1765 by Lydia Hoopes at Mrs. Hollis' School in Goshen Township, Chester County[2] but few eighteenth-century samplers can be confidently assigned to Chester County because children of the county's affluent families often attended Philadelphia schools. By the nineteenth century, Chester County had many schools in addition to the Westtown School, and they have left an abundance of samplers. However, the majority are typical Quaker samplers of the Delaware Valley, and their place of origin cannot be determined without the identity of the child or her teacher.

Perhaps the earliest distinctive Chester County form was begun by a woman whose initials were *E W,* and they appear on three similar samplers of 1804 (Fig. 436).[3] This schoolmistress probably taught in East Bradford Township, where the sampler makers lived, and she may have been teaching earlier, for a sampler of 1800 is unquestionably related to the three that bear her initials.[4] The delicacy of her designs, a balanced format, and almost flawless execution reveal that she was teaching in the best English tradition, and although her students were Quaker girls, Quaker motifs are not conspicuous. The basic style of these finely worked samplers was continued under the instruction of Hannah C. Carpenter (Fig. 437)

1. Anne Newport Royall, *The Black Book I* (Washington, D.C., 1828–1829), 321.
2. Schiffer, 24–5. See page 467 of this book, footnote 2.
3. For Sarah Strode's sampler of 1804, see *ANTIQUES,* December 1984, 1431. A sampler by Sidney Jefferis (1790–1882) is initialed *E W* (Edmonds, Fig. 41). Another by Ann Jefferis, 1804, is described in B&C, 180.
4. Sampler of Hannah White, born December 19, 1786, the daughter of John and Elizabeth (Edmonds, Fig. 40).

Fig. 436. *Lydia Jefferis s Work Aged/ fourteen years/ 1804,* and with the initials *E W* for her teacher. Silk on linen gauze; 20¼″ x 17⅜″. This and several related examples (see Fig. 437) include verses based on the 137th Psalm, beginning "By Babels streams we sat and/ wept/ When Sion we thought on/ In midst thereof we hang'd our/ harps/ The willow trees upon." Lydia Jefferis (1789–before 1812) named her parents, grandparents, brothers, and sister. She was the daughter of Emmor Jefferis (1760–1813), a farmer, and Charity Grubb (1762–1836) of East Bradford Township. On December 12, 1805, she married George Worth (1785–1833). She left two sons who both died in 1825.

Chester County Historical Society, 1981.527.

and perhaps other teachers as well. It is likely that "E W" instructed Hannah Carter Carpenter. However, the twenty-two-year-old Hannah was evidently teaching when she worked her impressive sampler in 1811, since her initials are found on a similar sampler made by her cousin Lydia Carter in the same year. Sarah Carpenter named Hannah as her "preceptress" in 1819,[5] and Mary Graves was twenty-six years old when she worked an enormous sampler, recording on it that she had *done this work with Hannah C. Carpenter in . . . 1824.* The similar sampler of Hannah T. James was most likely made under Hannah's instruction (Fig. 439).

By 1813 some of the delicate design elements found on the Carpenter samplers were combined with a unique form of willow tree (Fig. 440), and during the 1820s these willows often flanked central pots with tall rose trees, which were also common to this region (Fig. 441). E. B. Harvey, who instructed Hannah Hatton, was Elizabeth Brinton (1791–1846), the daughter of William Brinton (1756–1832) and Deborah Darlington (d.1840). On November 22, 1810, she married Alban Harvey (1789–1826) of Birmingham Township, Chester County; they had seven children, four of whom died young. Their son, William, married Maria, the sister of Elizabeth's student Hannah Hatton. Elizabeth taught from 1821 or earlier, through 1827, and possibly until September 1837 when she married William Levis (1782–1849).

One of the largest and most easily recognized groups of Chester County samplers is represented by Mary Hibberd Garrett's work (Fig. 442). Mary and three other girls named *E. Passmore* as their preceptress in 1820 and many similar sam-

---

5. Carter, 1811, and Carpenter, 1819, are in the CCHS.

Fig. 437. *Hannah Carpenter was born/ the 28ᵗʰ of the 2ⁿᵈ mo. 1789./ and done this work in the year/ 1811.* Silk on sheer linen; 27½" x 26". Hannah's hollow-cut profile is impressed with the word *Museum*, a mark used by the Peales in Philadelphia. The watercolors probably depict Hannah's home at left and possibly her cousin Lydia Carter's stone house at right, which was probably her mother's childhood home. For Lydia's similar sampler, see *ANTIQUES*, December 1984, 1432. Hannah Carter Carpenter (1789–1863 or 1870) was the daughter of schoolmaster William Carpenter (1761–1797) and Rachel Carter (b.1761) of West Bradford, Chester County. Samplers attributed to Hannah's instruction date from 1811 to 1826. In 1860 she was a seamstress and living in West Bradford with her sister Lydia, the wife of John Worth. His brother George Worth married Lydia Jefferis (Fig. 436). *Chester County Historical Society, NS188.*

plers were made until the mid-1830s.[6] Elizabeth Passmore is known to have been teaching in East Goshen in 1824,[7] and the similar samplers could normally be confidently attributed to her teaching. However, H. Matlack, the daughter of William Matlack of East Goshen, also worked this typical form in 1824 and named *Catharine Richard* in the space reserved for the preceptress.[8] Catharine Richard may have been teaching with Elizabeth Passmore, or possibly she continued the school. Her name has not been found again, nor has Elizabeth Passmore been further identified. Nevertheless, it is reasonable to believe that Elizabeth Passmore originated the local custom of surrounding the names of deceased family members with black silk rather than stitching their names in black in the more customary manner.[9]

There is no evidence that Chester County schools produced large, neoclassical silk embroideries like those worked at the Moravian seminaries or favored by the patrons of Philadelphia's Samuel Folwell. However, during the 1830s, their students created exceptionally large pictorial samplers such as Mary Caley's (Fig. 443). In elaborate mahogany frames, these pieces became major decorations in the front halls or the family parlors of Chester County homes.

---

6. See Rachel Denn Griscom's 1821 sampler in Krueger, *Gallery*, Fig. 83; Esther Hibberd's 1824 sampler is in Skinner Sale 1126, March 21, 1987, Lot 288; Mary Louisa Thomas, 1832, appears in *ANTIQUES*, December 1984, 1430. For variations of the style, see the sampler of Orpah Lewis, 1825, in Sotheby's Sale 5551, January 28–31, 1987, Lot 1096; also Elizabeth M. Konkle's sampler of 1828 in Sale 5622, October 24, 1987, Lot 289.

7. She is named as a teacher in the Chester County Commissioner's records of 1824, now at the CCHS.

8. CCHS.

9. For an English example of 1762 with the deceased father's name stitched in black, but misinterpreted as the maker's, see Huish, Fig. 34.

Fig. 438. *Elizabeth Hibbards Work per/ formed in the 15ᵗʰ year of her age 1813. Silk on linen with ribbon border; 18½" x 23".* Elizabeth's sampler is closely related to those initialed *E W* (Fig. 436), and also to the work of Hannah C. Carpenter who may have instructed her (Fig. 437). Elizabeth Hibbard (1798–1840) was the daughter of William Hibbard (1770–1849) and Jane Williamson (1772–1851) of East Goshen, Chester County. She died unmarried. In 1824, Elizabeth's sister Esther (1818–1896) worked a sampler much like Mary Hibberd Garrett's (Fig. 442), probably under the instruction of Elizabeth Passmore (see footnote 6). Elizabeth was Mary Garrett's second cousin. *The State Museum of Pennsylvania, Pennsylvania Historical and Museum Commission, 45.8.2.*

Fig. 439. *Hannah T James/ 1826. Silk on sixty-two-count linen gauze with thirty-two cross-stitches to the inch; 22¾" x 24½".* In its size, composition, and border, Hannah's work is much like the 1824 sampler of Mary Graves, who named Hannah C. Carpenter as her instructress (Schiffer, 61). Hannah Townsend James was the daughter of Joseph James (1784–1822) and Mary Townsend. Her father was a farmer in Thornbury, Delaware County, but he died accidentally when she was thirteen years old, and where she was living in 1826 is unknown. In Philadelphia, on March 6, 1834, she married Thomas Harlan Mercer (1806–1853). They lived on a farm in Westtown Township, Chester County, and had eight children. *Chester County Historical Society, NS50.*

Fig. 440. *Sibilla Ways/ work 1813.* Silk on linen; 24½" x 24½". Sibilla named grandparents, parents, and siblings, with deceased grandparents appropriately in black. Her willow trees are evidently unique to Chester County but the school of their origin is unknown. Susanna Palmer worked similar trees in 1816 (PMA). Sibilla Way (1801–1866) was the daughter of Joseph Way (1769–1839) and Leah Taylor (1770–1851) of Pennsbury Township. On December 6, 1826, she married Ephraim Baily (1803–1837), a farmer, and they had two children.
Chester County Historical Society, NS6.

Fig. 441. *Hannah Hattons work/ done in the year/ 1827* and with the name *E B Harvey Preceptress.* Silk on linen; 21½" x 25¼". Hannah's trees are definitely related to those in Figure 440, but there is little likelihood that both girls were taught by Elizabeth Brinton Harvey. A related sampler was worked by Elizabeth Smith, also in 1827 (PMA, 69-288-246), and Elizabeth's sister, Lydia Smith, named *Elizabeth B Harvey Preceptress* on her sampler of 1821 (private collection). Hannah Hatton (1812–1895) was the daughter of Samuel Hatton (1787–1833) and Sarah Martin (1792–1882). In 1827, her father was a wool manufacturer in Birmingham, Delaware County. Hannah married Garrett Hoopes (1804–1848), a farmer, on March 14, 1833, and had three children. In 1855, she married Amos McNelly (1819–1889).
Chester County Historical Society, NS73.

Fig. 442. *Mary H. Garretts'/ Work 1820.* Silk on linen gauze with ribbon border; 22″ x 27½″. Mary named her teacher, her parents, and her grandparents, with the names of those deceased surrounded by black. This treatment appears to be peculiar to Chester County, and may have originated with Mary's acknowledged instructress, *E. Passmore* of East Goshen Township. In 1820, E. Passmore's name was also worked on the samplers of Elizabeth Phebe Smedley (CCHS); Sarah H. James (Harbeson, opp. 52); and Mary Ann Simcos (private collection). Mary Hibberd Garrett (1805–1831) was the daughter of Josiah Garrett (1776–1856) and Lydia Hibberd (1777–1842) of East Goshen. She died unmarried, aged twenty-five. *Location unknown; photograph courtesy of* The Magazine ANTIQUES.

Fig. 443. *Mary Caley/ 1837.* Silk and chenille on linen with ribbon border; 24⅝″ x 27″. As in the samplers naming *E. Passmore,* Mary Caley surrounded her dead sister's name with black and placed her verse in a grapevine enclosure. Mary Caley (b. 1821) was the daughter of Samuel Caley (1790–1870) and Ann Phillips (1794–1844) of Newtown Square, Delaware County. She married Amos Lukens in 1850 and Thomas P. Baynes in 1883. *Chester County Historical Society, NS65.*

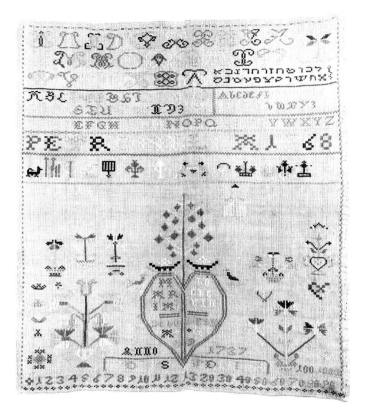

Fig. 444. Sampler signed *PETRONELLA 1768* and with the birthdate of its maker, *ANNO 1737*. Silk on linen; 16¼″ x 14″. This was worked by Maria Hocker (1737–1791), a member of the Ephrata Cloister, which was a communal society established in Lancaster County in 1732 by the German Pietist Conrad Beissel (1691–1768) and a group of religious celibates. Maria, known as Sister Petronella, was the daughter of Ludwig and Margaret Hocker. Her father, called Brother Obed, was a schoolteacher at the Cloister, and Maria is believed to have taught needlework. This may account for her sampler being worked at the age of thirty-one. Her unusual alphabets were derived from a German pattern book of about 1722 (*ANTIQUES*, February 1991, 370, 374–5). A printed compilation of Beissel's hymns was beautifully illuminated by Sister Petronella (HSP).
Historical Society of Pennsylvania, Z.13.29.

Samplers of the Pennsylvania Germans

Despite the large migration of German settlers to Pennsylvania during the late seventeenth and early eighteenth centuries, German influence on Pennsylvania samplers of the colonial period is imperceptible, and any early evidence of their sampler embroidery is rare (Fig. 444). Such a void does not reflect an absence of this cultural tradition, for just as in England, the working of samplers was an established part of a girl's education among the Dutch and Germans during the seventeenth century and earlier. Rather, it reflects the failure of the earliest Pennsylvania Germans to establish schools for their children where girls were taught by women.[1] This probably stemmed from both an agrarian lifestyle and the diversity of the Protestant Reformers who came from central Europe. To name but a few, there were Mennonites, Moravians, Schwenkfelders, Lutherans, Calvinists, Dunkards, Sabbatarians, and Anabaptists. It has been said that during the 1740s there were fifteen different religious groups in Germantown, and forty-five

---

1. Basic primary subjects were usually taught to boys and girls by men at church-directed schools. Some scholars believe that "The German was always more concerned with his future daughter-in-law's industrious habits and domestic duties than with her personal beauty or mental accomplishments." (Woody, *A History of Women's Education in the United States* [1929; reprint, 1974], 1:183.) See also Earle, *Child Life in Colonial Days* (1899), 71–2.

Fig. 445. *MAGDALENA LAUBACH/ 1791*. Wool on linen; 15⅞"
x 16½". Directly below the end of her second alphabet,
Magdalena worked the *OEHBDDE* device. She enclosed her
work in a narrow border similar to those occasionally found
on German samplers. Magdalena Laubach was the daughter of
John Laubach and Anna Catharina of Pikeland Township,
Chester County. They belonged to the German Reformed
Church. Magdalena married Conrad Acker.
Chester County Historical Society, NS37.

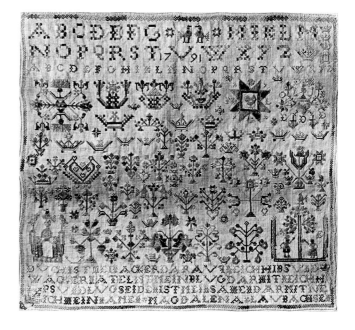

in southeastern Pennsylvania.[2] When the Moravian leader Count Zinzendorf was
in Germantown in 1742, he attempted to unite some of these people with the
Moravians but with slight success. Among the German settlers at this time, only
the Moravians appear to have been dedicated to educating girls as well as boys,
though the absence of any characteristic Moravian needlework from their schools
of the colonial period remains unexplained. Other Germans who sought advanced
education for their daughters evidently availed themselves of English instruction,
which hastened their acculturation into the dominant English society.[3]

As elsewhere in America, educational opportunities for Pennsylvania girls increased notably during the 1790s. Many German women were then teaching in
their communities, and they taught sampler embroidery in the traditions of the
European regions from which they came. Like German work of the seventeenth
and eighteenth centuries, Pennsylvania German samplers are often crowded with
a variety of cross-stitched motifs in borderless, random arrangements, and like
those from northern Germany, these samplers are usually almost square.[4] This
type can seldom be assigned to specific German sects, but exceptional flower motifs distinguish a group of samplers made by the Schwenkfelder girls between
1794 and 1817 (Figs. 446–448).[5]

The Schwenkfelders came to Pennsylvania from Silesia in the 1730s and settled

---

2. John B. Frantz, "Schwenkfelders and Moravians in America," in Peter Erb, ed., *Schwenkfelders in America*
(Pennsburg, Pa.: Schwenkfelder Library, 1987), 104–5.

3. For instance, Caspar Wistar's daughter Margret (1729–1793), who was taught by Elizabeth Marsh (Fig.
374).

4. German samplers are often much more elaborate than Pennsylvania pieces, and like Dutch samplers, some
were horizontal at a very early date. The majority of Pennsylvania Germans were Protestant, and the cru-
cifix and instruments of the passion that characterize the long, vertical eighteenth-century samplers from the
Catholic regions of southern Germany are seldom found in Pennsylvania. For early German samplers and
related foreign examples see Hersh, *Samplers of the Pennsylvania Germans* (1991), 24–42.

5. In their recent study of 424 Pennsylvania German samplers, Tandy and Charles Hersh have identified a

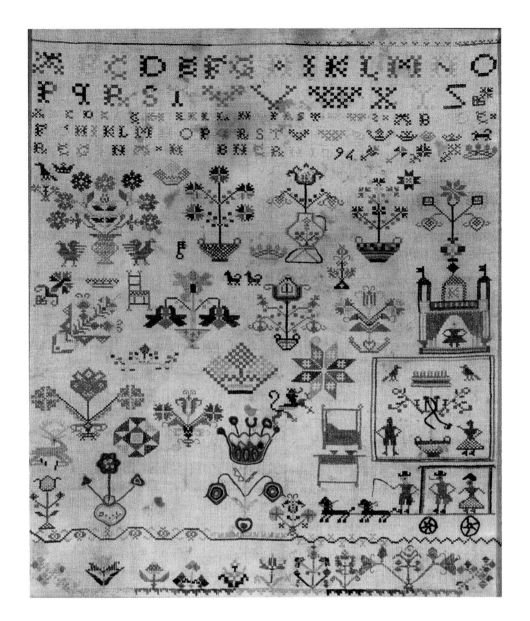

Fig. 446. *REGINA HUBNER 1794.* Silk on linen; 23½" x 18". Regina worked a variety of typical German motifs. However, the elaborate crown to the left of her eight-pointed star, and the tulip directly below it, appear to be characteristic of Schwenkfelder instruction and occur on samplers by other girls of her community. The typical cross-stitch predominates, but she also used chain, satin, eyelet, and stem stitches. Regina Hubner, or Heebner (1777–1862), was the daughter of George Heebner (1744–1783) of Worcester Township, and his second wife, Anna Schubert (1749–1784). In 1796, she married the Reverend John Schultz (1772–1827), a farmer and Schwenkfelder minister in Hereford Township, Berks County. They had thirteen children.
Schwenkfelder Library, Pennsburg, Pennsylvania, 79.3.

Fig. 447. Sampler dated *1801* with the initials *SK* and *CS.* Silk on linen; 13" x 13¼". This sampler was made by Christina Schultz (1782–1819), the eldest daughter of the Reverend Melchior Schultz (1756–1826) and Salome Wagner (1761–1835). The initials *SK* were probably for her future husband, for on June 6, 1802, Christina married Samuel Kriebel (1776–1841). Melchior Schultz, a minister and farmer, lived in the house now known as the Peter Wentz Farmstead on Schultz Road in Worcester, which was used as Washington's headquarters during the battle of Germantown in 1777. Schultz acquired the property in 1794. Christina's sister, Maria Schultz (1785–1811), worked an almost identical sampler in 1801 (Goschenhoppen Folklife Museum), and her youngest sister worked the sampler in Figure 448.
Schwenkfelder Library, Pennsburg, Pennsylvania, 80.37.

Fig. 448. *ROSINA SCHULTZ 1817*. Silk on linen; 20½″ x 18¾″. Rosina's sampler lacks the chain-stitched flowers made by her sister (Fig. 447), but she included several versions of the checker-board crowns and various other similar motifs. Rosina Schultz (1798–1872) married Melchior Kriebel (1790–1868) in 1820, and they had six children.

Schwenkfelder Library, Pennsburg, Pennsylvania, 80.58.

mostly in Montgomery County near Philadelphia. Their beliefs were inspired by Caspar Schwenkfeld (1490–1561), and they were much like the Quakers in their religious philosophy. Christopher Schultz (1718–1789) was the foremost leader of the Schwenkfelders in Pennsylvania during the eighteenth century, and it was he who instigated the establishment of Schwenkfelder schools in 1764.[6] Their eighteenth-century school records, however, mention neither girls nor any instructress. Only the samplers reveal that women were teaching in the 1790s. The similarity of the examples in Figures 446 and 447 suggests that the same woman kept a school at least from 1794 through 1801, probably in Worcester Township, Montgomery County, known as the Lower District of the Schwenkfelders.

The samplers in Figures 445, 449, and 453 each include a familiar European heart and crown motif known in the seventeenth century.[7] Possibly of Pennsylvania origin, however, are its surrounding letters, *OEHBDDE,* which represent the major syllables in the epigram *O Edel Herz Bedenk Dein End* (O noble heart, consider your end). This motif with seven branches emanating from the heart and interspersed with the letters is known on Pennsylvania samplers dating at least from 1791 (Fig. 445) until the close of the sampler-making era (Fig. 453). It was particularly popular with the Mennonites although certainly not exclusive to them.[8]

number of cohesive groups of samplers that they assign to specific sects and regions. Such distinctions usually reflect school instruction. They insist, however, that Pennsylvania German samplers were worked at home, although this is contrary to European tradition and the convictions of most sampler scholars.

6. *Schwenckfeldiana* 1, no. 3 (Norristown, Pa.: The Schwenckfelder Church, September 1943): 6–9.

7. Notice one version on the German sampler of 1663, Fig. 8.

8. This design appears on Pennsylvania German hand towels made between 1799 and the 1860s. See Gehret, *This Is The Way I Pass My Time* (1985), 205–11.

The Mennonites were among the earliest German immigrants to Penn's colony, and under the leadership of Francis Daniel Pastorius (1651–1719/20), they established themselves at Germantown in 1683. By 1710, Swiss Mennonites were also in Lancaster County. Although vastly outnumbered by Lutheran and Reformed immigrants from Germany, sects such as the Schwenkfelders, Mennonites, and Moravians have left more discernible evidence of their needlework heritage than have their more dominant brethren.

Rather than samplers in a purely German style, Pennsylvania German girls often worked samplers with a curious blend of German and Quaker motifs. Under Quaker instruction, they even worked German patterns within English-style borders, like Catharine Fretz, who named schoolmistress *Debby Ely* on her sampler of 1820. Debby Ely also taught Catharine's cousin Mary Landes, another Mennonite girl, who worked typical Quaker motifs on a sampler of 1817 and named her instructress.[9] Quaker teacher Deborah Ely (b.c.1795) was the daughter of Joseph Ely (1772–1846) and Martha Williams. She taught from 1816 until 1824 in Plumstead Township, Bucks County,[10] and she probably held classes in the Deep Run Meeting House, southwest of Hinkletown. It was built in 1806 and used for both German and English schools for twenty-five years.[11]

With the exception of Catholic motifs, many typical German patterns are found within flowing borders edged with ribbons and rosettes (Fig. 450, 451, 453),[12] and the most naïve and colorful are usually thought of as "Pennsylvania Dutch." Somewhat surprisingly, this designation is often accurate, since it is now known that many more German women were teaching accomplishments than have been recognized in the past. German women responsible for important groups of Pennsylvania samplers include Mary Coeleman Zeller of Philadelphia, Mary Endress Ralston of Easton, Catharine Welshans Buchanan of Marietta, and Elizabeth Hains Mason of Kutztown. Mrs. Jemima Hartzell, who is credited with a wonderfully folksy group of samplers from the Pittsburgh area, was probably also of German descent.[13] Newly recognized is Philadelphia schoolmistress Salome Schneider (Fig. 451),[14] and not to be forgotten is Ann Elizabeth Gebler Folwell, who produced the largest group of silk embroideries, in both size and number, to survive in America.

9. For the sampler by Catharine Fretz (1805–1889) and the 1817 work of Mary Landes (1798–1884) see Hersh, *Samplers of the Pennsylvania Germans*, 236 and 59, respectively.

10. Plumstead School Records, courtesy of Joel Alderfer of the Mennonite Historians of Eastern Pennsylvania.

11. J. C. Wenger, *History of the Mennonites of the Franconia Conference* (Telford, Pa.: Franconia Mennonite Historical Society, 1937), 200. I am indebted to Dorothy McCoach for knowledge of Deborah Ely and her students.

12. Occasionally the nearly square spot-motif samplers of northern Germany also have decorative embroidered borders and ribbon embellishments.

13. *ANTIQUES*, February 1981, 411, Fig. 15, and 419, Pl. XV. Probably made under German instruction in Reading is a group of samplers, c.1812–1831, and often initialed *MT* for the teacher. See Schiffer, 80; also *MAD*, June 1991, 15-A, top right.

14. Joan Stephens kindly called my attention to the 1798 sampler of Hannah Haas, who named *SALOME SNIDER*.

Fig. 449. *ELISABET KRIEBEL 1830.* Silk on linen; 22⅛″ x 22⅛″. Elisabet worked a central motif between birds that is strikingly similar to the upper left motif in Figure 446. She also included many designs used by her mother (Fig. 447), and her aunt (Fig. 448), as well as the *OEHBDDE* device. Elisabet Kriebel (1812–1891) was the daughter of Samuel Kriebel and Christina Schultz. Her father was a miller near Cedars, Pennsylvania.
Philadelphia Museum of Art, gift of J. Stogdell Stokes, 28-10-92.

Fig. 450. *LYDIA • YEAKLE • HER • W1799.* Silk on linen with ribbon border; 20½″ x 19″. Lydia's sampler includes a remarkable combination of motifs. The Indian pink border appeared on Philadelphia's earliest band samplers and endured throughout the eighteenth century. The Biblical spies were worked in England, New England, New York, Charleston, the Netherlands, and Germany, but seldom in the Delaware Valley. Peacocks were popular in Britain as well as northern Europe, but her castle motif is truly Germanic. The tree-lined stepped terrace, of unknown source, appeared in Philadelphia in the 1780s and spread through the Delaware Valley, while the birds near the baskets were usually favored by Quakers. Also, the nearly balanced arrangement reflects English taste. Lydia Yeakle (1783–1845) lived near Philadelphia, where she was probably instructed by a German woman. She was the daughter of Christopher Yeakle (1757–1843) and Susanna Kriebel (1761–1830). In 1807, she married David Schultz (1779–1851), a farmer in Upper Hanover Township, Montgomery County.
Schwenkfelder Library, Pennsburg, Pennsylvania, 80.59.

Fig. 451. *ELISABETH/ GRIEGER/ 1797.* Silk on linen with silk ribbon border and rosettes; 24½″ x 20¾″. Elisabeth included her birthdate, *2/ FEB/RUARIUS/ 1787,* and named her parents, *NICOLAUS GRIE/GER* and *SOPHIA/ GRIEGER.* It is uncertain if *MARGARETHA* (top right) was Elisabeth's middle name or the first name of her teacher *SALOME SCHNEIDER* (second line, right). Nearly identical is a *1797* sampler by Elizabeth Simon of Philadelphia, who also named *SALOME SCHNEIDER* (PMA, 1984-130-1); and Hannah Haas stitched *SALOME SNIDER* on a closely related piece of 1798 (Sotheby's Sale 5282, February 1, 1985, Lot 448). Elisabeth Grieger was baptized in Philadelphia's St. Michael's and Zion Lutheran Church on March 4, 1787. Her sampler heralds an emerging group made under a German preceptress in Philadelphia. A similar border and various motifs sugggest that Salome Schneider also taught Lydia Yeakle (Fig. 450).

Collection of Joan Stephens; photograph courtesy of Sotheby's.

Fig. 452. Sampler pattern for SARAH SCHULTZ 1827. Ink and paint on paper; 15½" x 12½". In Pennsylvania, as in Germany, sampler patterns were often recorded on hand-drawn graph paper and later on printed paper. This custom was eventually used commercially for Berlin wool-work patterns.
The Reading Public Museum and Art Gallery, 50-26-1.

Fig. 453. *Fanny Nisley A Daughter of Martin Nissley and Anna/ Nissley is Born the 3 day of December 1821 Rapho is my Station/. . . Fanny/ Nissley her Sampler worked in the 18th year of her age in/ the year of our Lord. Rapho Township Lancaster County/ and State of Pennsylvania. November the 18th 1839 AD.* Cotton on linen with silk ribbon; 22¼" x 21". Fanny worked typical German motifs, including the crowned heart with the letters *OEHBDDE,* but their symmetrical arrangement and her border suggest English influence. Fanny was the daughter of Martin Nissley and Anna Bomberger. For an 1836 sampler and an 1839 hand towel by Fanny, and two samplers by her sisters, see Gehret, *This Is the Way I Pass My Time* (1985), 70–1.
Philadelphia Museum of Art, Whitman Sampler Collection, gift of Pet Inc., 69-288-145.

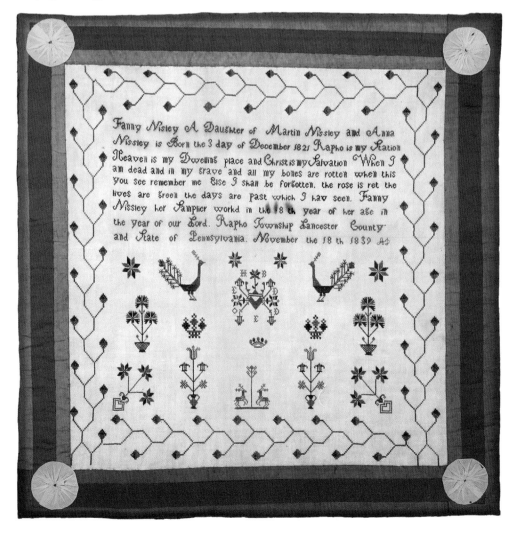

Samplers of the Susquehanna Valley

THE BRATTEN SISTERS

Fig. 454. Profile of Martha
Taylor, c.1803.
Winterthur Museum, 91.7.

A wonderfully appealing and cohesive group of samplers was produced in Lancaster, York, and Dauphin counties between 1797 and 1838. Today, they are generally known as samplers of the Susquehanna Valley. The earliest recorded pieces belonging to this group were worked at a school in Lancaster opened by Mrs. Leah Galligher early in the year 1797. Possibly their patterns were influenced by the compartmented designs that were popular in Philadelphia during the second half of the eighteenth century (Figs. 355–360). Martha Taylor (Fig. 454) signed the earliest-known sampler from Leah Galligher's school, dated March 2, 1797, and in 1799, another student recorded the births and marriages of Leah and Rachel, the twin daughters of George and Sarah Bratten, who both kept schools with their husbands in Lancaster (Fig. 460).

Leah and Rachel Bratten were born near Wilmington, Delaware, in 1764, but by 1778, if not earlier, the Bratten family was living in Derry Township, Cumberland County, Pennsylvania.[1] Leah and Rachel were the youngest of George Bratten's six daughters and obviously they must have had advanced instruction in ornamental needlework, possibly in Philadelphia, or perhaps in Lancaster. How it happened that they both married schoolmasters is unknown, but it is unlikely that they met their husbands during their school days, for they married at the ages of twenty-seven and twenty-nine. The "Parson SteVonson" who married them was probably Matthew Stephens who was the Presbyterian pastor in Derry and Wayne townships from 1786 until 1794.[2] George Bratten was a widower when he died in Wayne Township, then Mifflin County, in 1797, and his will directed that his four older daughters should each receive a new Bible, but he left "Thirty pounds apiece to my two Daughters Rachel and Leah."[3]

Leah, the wife of Francis Galligher and later of Isaac Maguire, may have established the pervasive sampler style that spread throughout this region; in any case, the patterns she favored between 1797 and 1826 were either closely copied or

1. Aimee Appleby, comp., *Listing of Inhabitants in 1778, Cumberland County, Pennsylvania* (Laughlintown, Pa.: Southwest Pennsylvania Genealogical Services, 1983), 2. The area where the Bratten family settled became Mifflin County in 1789.

2. *The Centennial Memorial of the Presbytery of Carlisle* (Harrisburg: Meyers Printing and Publishing House, 1889), 1:450–1. Leah and Rachel were baptized by William McKennan, pastor of the Red Clay Creek Presbyterian Church, Mill Creek Hundred, Delaware, from 1755 to 1809 (J. Thomas Scharf, *History of Delaware, 1609–1888* [Philadelphia: L. J. Richards & Co., 1888], 2:920).

3. Mifflin County Wills, Lewiston, Pennsylvania, 1:115. George Bratten named sons Edward and George, and daughters Elizabeth James, Isabel Stalford, Sarah Burr, and Jean Weburn.

Fig. 455. *Martha Taylor a Daughter of James and/ Elizabeth Taylor s Was Born in Septem/ 29 1785 and Made this Sampler in the 12/ year of her age in Mrfs Galligher s School/ in the year of our LORD 1797 March 2/ Martha Taylor is my/ name Lancaster is/ my Habitation Octor/ara is my dwelling place & christ is/ my Salvation.* Silk on linen; 17⅛" x 17⅝". Martha worked her sampler before Leah Galligher advertised the opening of her school in May 1797. Surprisingly, she also worked a plain sampler naming the school in 1798.
Winterthur Museum, 91.5.

Fig. 456. *Elisabeth Taylor a Daughter of James/ and Elisabeth Taylor was born in/ October 8 1789 and Made this/ Sampler in Mrfs Galligher s School in/ the 9 year of her age in the Year . . . / this is Doctor Hands House,* c.1798. Silk on linen with ribbon border; 17⅝" x 18⅛". Elisabeth pictured the home of Edward Hand (1744–1802), a Lancaster physician. Revolutionary officer, and member of the Continental Congress. His 1792 house is now known as Rockford Plantation. Elisabeth, the sister of Martha (Figs. 454 and 455), married Davis Beaumont.
Winterthur Museum, 91.6.

Fig. 457. *Mary Walker/ Made this sampler in the 16ᵗʰ year of/ her age in Mrfs Galligher School under her/ Directions in the year of Our LORD 1797/ Decemb.* Silk on linen with silk ribbon border; approximately 18½″ square. Mary named *Lancaster* as her *Habitation,* and her sampler is a supreme example of Leah Galligher's Lancaster style. Mary may have been assisting Leah before her departure for Harrisburg in 1802, and possibly she continued with Leah's students, for three closely related samplers of 1803 name *Mary Walkers School* (Fig. 461). No trace of Mary's birth or marriage has been found, but most likely she was the mother of Mary Walker Reed (b.c.1812)

who married cabinetmaker Henry Swentzel (1808–1887) in Lancaster's Trinity Lutheran Church on October 9, 1832. Her sampler descended in their family to its present owner. After teaching as Mary Walker, she was probably the Mary Reed who advertised a school in 1807, and perhaps the same Mary Reed whose name appears on samplers of 1824 (Fig. 462). A Mrs. Mary Reed died in Lancaster on August 27, 1832, in her fiftieth year (*Lancaster Journal,* August 31, 1832). Her age corresponds to the age of this sampler maker.
Collection of Barbara Abrams.

Fig. 458. *Ann Susanna Riddle a Daughter of/ John and Barbara Riddles Was bor/ FebuarY 17 1788 and Made this/ Sampler in Mrfs Gallligher s School/ by her Direction in the 11 year of/ her age in the year of our LORD/ 1798.* Silk on linen; 15¼″ x 15¼″. The doors of Ann's church are open or unworked, and this is typical of samplers made at Leah Galligher's school. It also occurs on an 1802 example worked by Mary Snodgrass at Leah's school in Harrisburg. Dolly Sheller worked a sampler with the same church in 1800. Ann Susanna Riddle married John Weaver and died before her father, John Riddle (c.1757–1827). She had three children.
Collection of Dr. and Mrs. Donald M. Herr.

modified in various ways by other teachers for many years (Figs. 461, 462, 469).[4] Leah Galligher advertised the opening of her school for "Young Girls" in the *Lancaster Journal* of April 21, 1797, and offered "to teach them spelling & reading, also all kinds of plain sewing, knitting and Working of Lace if required." In March 1800, Francis and Leah placed a joint advertisement, saying that "they have rented a House from Mr. HUMES, in the north end of Queenstreet, and intend to open School . . . the 7th of April next," where they would teach "the several branches of Literature, in both Schools, as heretofore."[5]

In 1800, Dolly Sheller made a sampler much like Ann Riddle's (Fig. 458), and Leah was probably teaching Dolly early in 1802 when she worked the piece that appears to be a forerunner of the most striking style to develop in this region—samplers depicting figures with real hair and varied metallic embellishments (Fig. 460). However, at this time, Leah's career in Lancaster was coming to a close. On March 10, 1802, in an advertisement headed "CAUTION," Francis Galligher renounced all responsibility for Leah because she "has absconded from my bed and board."[6] This and other accusations by Francis led to a long and bitter retort addressed "To the Public" by Leah's brother George Bratten:

> Francis Galligher and his wife Leah . . . so far as they are legally competent to do so, have dissolved the bands of Matrimony . . . before Judge Kuhn. On the part of Francis Galligher, the separation was voluntary, and was confessedly owing to no fault of his wife; but to his own incapacity, and long-continued UNMANLY deception . . .
>
> We are not willing further to expose the particulars of Francis Galligher's infamous conduct; . . . but . . . any continuance of his attacks on the character of our Relation . . . shall call forth from us . . . the real circumstances which have given rise to this Separation.[7]

Leah evidently left Lancaster for Harrisburg shortly after this incident, since a sampler typical of her instruction names *Harrisburgh in the year of our Lord 1802.*[8]

---

4. Ann Eshleman (b.1807) of Strasburg worked a related sampler at the *Isabella Sampler School* in 1822, as did Maria Kindig and Anna Maria Crise at Catherine Peterman's school in 1820 and 1834 (all in private collections). Examples from Mary Reed's school: Mary Bissikumner's is in the Winterthur Museum; Sophia Meylin worked two—one is illustrated in Ring, *Treasures,* Fig. 79, and one is in the North Museum, Franklin and Marshall College, Lancaster; Anna Mary Stormbach's is in a private collection.

5. *The Intelligencer & Weekly Advertiser,* Lancaster, March 19, 1800.

6. Ibid., March 10, 1802.

7. Ibid., March 17, 1802. Francis Galligher arrived in New Castle, Delaware, from Ireland in August 1784. He was granted citizenship in June 1798 (Petition 18, naturalization records, Lancaster County Historical Society). He died in Hempfield Township on December 24, 1809, aged sixty (*Lancaster Journal,* December 30, 1809).

8. Sampler of Mary Snodgrass (Ring, *Treasures,* 46). Elizabeth Hoover's elaborate sampler of 1803 displays Leah's typical "Harrisburg" style and names *Harrisburgh* and *Mrs Leah Bratten school* (collection of Amy Finkel). Tabitha Deem's 1808 sampler names *Harrisburgh* but no teacher (recorded at the Smithsonian). It relates to the work of Cassandanna Hetzel, 1823 (*ANTIQUES,* April 1975, 690).

Right: Fig. 460. *Dolly Sheller/ is my name and/ Dolly Sheller made/ this lady Lancaster/ 1802.* Silk, hair, coiled metal, spangles, and paint on linen with ribbon border; 9½″ x 8″. This is the earliest known example of the striking pictorial samplers from this region. Dolly was probably one of the last girls to be taught by Leah Galligher in Lancaster. Her undulating shirred ribbon-on-ribbon border is also typical of Lancaster County and may have originated with Leah Galligher. Dorothea (Dolly) Sheller (1791–1867) was the daughter of John and Rosanna Sheller. On May 4, 1813, she married John Wind (c.1783–1858).
Collection of Margaret B. Schiffer.

Fig. 461. *Catherine Shindle a Daughter of Peter/ and Elisabeth Shindle Was born Nov/ 22 1790 and Made this Sampler in/ the 13 year of her age in Mary Walk/ers School in the year of OUR/ LORD 1803 October 18.* Silk on linen; 16½″ x 16½″. Two similar samplers of 1803 name *Mary Walker's School* (Hornor, *The Story of Samplers* [1971], Fig. 32; Sarah Long's is in a private collection), but the identity of this teacher is uncertain. She was probably the Mary Walker who attended Leah Galligher's school in 1797 (Fig. 457). Peter Shindle (1760–1849) was a tavernkeeper and tobacconist in Lancaster. The family lived in a two-story stone house on the corner of North Queen and Orange streets. Catherine died unmarried in 1873.
Location unknown; photograph courtesy of Sotheby's.

Fig. 462. *Sophia Shindel a Daughter of Jacob and Catharine/ Shindel was born Febuary 21 st 1812 and made this/ sampler in the 13th Year of her age in Mary Reeds/ School in the year of our Lord 1824.* Silk on linen with ribbon border; 12" x 18". Four other samplers naming this school are dated 1824 (see footnote 4). This schoolmistress was perhaps the former Mary Walker, although it is possible that she was the widow Mary Dehuff Reed (1761–1829). On May 12, 1807, a Mary Reed advertised "a School in the east End of Kingstreet; where she teaches as formerly, Spelling, Reading, and Writing; Needlework of all kinds, and plain Sewing" (*Intelligencer & Weekly Advertiser,* Lancaster).
Philadelphia Museum of Art, Whitman Sampler Collection, gift of Pet Inc., 69.288.301.

The Oracle and Guardian is said to have described Leah's school on the corner of Walnut and Front streets about 1804, but this entry has not been found.[9]

On June 15, 1805, Harrisburg's *Oracle of Dauphin* reported the following: "Married, in Cumberland county, on Saturday last, mr. Isaac Meguier, to Mrs. Galaugher, both of this town." In 1806, *Leah Meguier's School* was named on Rachel Geiger's sampler (Fig. 463), and on September 18, 1806, Leah's son John Bratten Armstrong Maguire was born. Her second son, William, was born September 17, 1809, but lived less than two months. Sarah Maguire was born January 8, 1811, and son Isaac Collins Maguire on July 10, 1812, when Leah was forty-eight years old.[10]

Despite the demands of these babies, the most elaborate samplers to name Leah's school were worked between 1806 and 1812. In *The Oracle* of May 2, 1813, "ISAAC MAGUIRE, BOOT & SHOEMAKER" announced his new location on Locust Street and mentioned that "Mrs. Maguire will likewise continue her school as usual, in teaching all kinds of needlework, music and the first rudiments of common education." The Maguires never owned property in Harrisburg, and they lived and worked in various rented houses. In the fall of 1815, "MRS. MAGUIRE" informed her friends "that she had returned from the country, and resumed her school . . . in Mulberry Street,"[11] and historian William Henry Egle has left the following account of her activities at about this time:

9. Egle, *Notes and Queries* [1894–1901; reprint, 1970], annual vol. 1900, 98.

10. *Records of the Zion Lutheran Church, Harrisburg, Pa., Baptisms, 1795–1816.* Photostat, Genealogical Society of Pennsylvania, 1925, HSP. *Presbyterian Graveyard Records of Harrisburg,* in the Dauphin County Historical Society.

11. *The Oracle of Dauphin,* Harrisburg, November 18, 1815.

She was a lady of considerable taste in dress. She used to give her scholars one or two parties in the year, and among other entertainments she played the fiddle and encouraged the young folks to dance, which was thought to be very fine, as after a dance or two they were regaled with a glass of lemonade and a slice of gingerbread. On such occasions, she made more than an ordinary display of accoutrements in the article of personal adornment. At one time she appeared in a bright yellow silk dress, black silk stockings and red slippers, with the very fantastical head-dress of that day, composed of every variety of flowers and ribbons of different colors, and as she was not blessed with any great extent of personal charms, she had the satisfaction of making a very grotesque if not appropriate appearance for a staid matron of 53. She . . . had a few years before become the wife of Isaac McGuire, a very amiable, quiet, orderly citizen, who never fancied the trouble of a dispute with his better half, and therefore quickly submitted as a kind, good soul and vassal, subject to all her whims and oddities.[12]

On March 20, 1819, under the heading "Mrs. M'Guire's School, For young Misses," Leah indignantly stated in *The Oracle,* "Reports have been circulated that . . . Mr. M'Guire's family were about moving to the western country . . . such reports are entirely without foundation and . . . the school will be continued at the old stand, in Mulberry street. . . . Terms of tuition for reading, writing & c. 2 dollars and 50 cents per quarter, and for grammar & c. with Needle work 3 dollars per quarter." In October of 1820 her "DAY SCHOOL" was located on Second Street,[13] and newspaper reports of 1821 reveal that Leah was paid $33.40 for teaching poor children.[14] The last advertisement to offer the joint services of the Maguires appeared in *The Oracle of Dauphin* on April 6, 1822, and the latest known sampler to name *Mrs. Leah Meguiers School* was made by Leah Schreiner in 1826 without any pictorial motifs.[15] Leah lost her nineteen-year-old son on July 24, 1826, and she died on February 1, 1830.[16] Isaac Maguire died in his seventieth year on March 10, 1846, and left a widow named Susan Allen Maguire (c.1785–1870) whom he had married in 1834.[17]

After Leah Galligher's departure from Lancaster, her sister Rachel continued to

---

12. Egle, *Notes and Queries,* 98. Unfortunately Egle (1830–1901) gave no source for this information, but much of his material was derived from early newspapers.

13. *The Oracle of Dauphin,* September 23, 1820.

14. *Pennsylvania Intelligencer,* Harrisburg, March 9, 1821.

15. Leah Schreiner, the daughter of Michael and Mary, born in Lancaster County, April 18, 1809 (privately owned). Ann Ireton Simon named *Leah Meguier* in 1823. Her alphabets and long inscriptions are surrounded by a queen-stitched border (recorded in DAPC, 85.637). In 1823, Priscilla Selzier named *Leah Meguier* on an alphabet sampler of 3⅝" x 15" (Berks County Historical Society). Also, an Irish-stitched pocketbook has ribbon-bound inner flaps embroidered with an alphabet and signed *Margaret Deebler her pocketbook was Made in Mrs Leah Meguiers school in Harrisburg In The year 1818* (*MAD,* December 1989, 11-E).

16. Presbyterian graveyard records in the Dauphin County Historical Society, Harrisburg, and the *Pennsylvania Intelligencer, and Farmers' and Mechanics' Journal,* Harrisburg, February 4, 1830.

17. *Democratic Union,* Harrisburg, March 18, 1846.

Fig. 463. *Rachel Geiger a Daughter of Henry and/ Rachel Geiger was born October the 18 in/ Mifflin County Waynetownship in the/ year of our LORD 1785 and Made this/ Sampler in Harrisburgh in Mrs. Leah/ Meguiers School A. D. 1806./ Catherine Rhodes a Daughter of Henry/ and Rachel Geiger was born in Dauphin/ County near Harrisburgh the 6 day of/ December in the year of our LORD 1783.* Silk, hair, coiled metal, spangles, and paint on gauze over linen; 16″ x 17½″. Rachel was twenty years old when she worked this sampler. It is exceptional both for its rendition of the Virgin Mary nursing her child and for

Rachel's reference to the birth of her sister who was then married. Rachel Geiger (1785–1852) was the daughter of Henry Geiger (d.c.1785) and Rachel Wakefield (1761–1825). In 1788, Rachel's mother moved to Harrisburg and before 1800 she married the widower James Johnston. Rachel married Robert Johnston, a son of her stepfather, and they had two daughters who evidently died young. In her will of 1852, Rachel's nephew, Joseph Rhodes, was her principal beneficiary and her sampler belongs to one of his descendants. *Privately owned.*

Fig. 464. *Elizabeth Fin/ney a Daugh/ter of Samuel/ and Anne Fin/ney was born/ in Hanover/ Dauphin Coun/ty September/ 11 in the year of/ our Lord 1791/ and made this/ Sampler in/ Harrisburg in/ Mrs. Leah Me/guier's School/ in the year of/ our Lord 1807.* Silk, hair, coiled metal, spangles, metallic braid, and paint on linen gauze, with ribbon border; 20″ x 22″. Elizabeth's pattern was evidently derived from the print in Figure 465. *Collection of Margaret B. Schiffer.*

Fig. 465. *SPRING/ Printed & Sold by B. Plen/ Philad.ᵃ,* c.1800. Hand-colored etching; 10⅝″ x 8⅞″. One of a set of four with verses from James Thomson's *Seasons.* Similar but more sophisticated series were published in London by R. Sayer and J. Bennett in 1783 and by Laurie and Whittle in 1794, but with *Spring* in reverse to this composition. *Photograph courtesy of Sotheby's.*

Fig. 466. *Catharine Boas a Daughter of John and Susannah/ Boas was born in Reading April 15 in the year/ of our Lord 1797 and Made this Sampler/ in Harrisburgh in Mrs Leah Meguier s School/ in February 20 in the year of our Lord 1812.* Silk, coiled metal, and paint on linen with ribbon border; 20″ x 20″. Fourteen-year-old Catharine was no doubt a classmate of nineteen-year-old Barbara Baner who worked an elaborate sampler with similar corner motifs in the same year (Edmonds, frontispiece). The latest pictorial sampler to name *Leah Meguier* is dated 1825 (B&C, Pl. XCVII); now at C-H, 1941-69-119. *Location unknown; photograph courtesy of Sotheby's.*

teach there with her husband, William Armstrong. They were located in a house "Opposite the Rev. H. Muhlenberg's" in 1805 where "Mrs. *ARMSTRONG* teaches, as usual, spelling, reading, writing, plain sewing, sampler work, spriging, flowering on muslin and sattin, rug work, and setting in lace."[18] This excerpt is from their first Lancaster advertisement, but Ann Herbst's sampler reveals that Rachel was teaching in Lancaster in 1801 (Fig. 467). Only four samplers from the Armstrong school have been recorded, and their pictorial format appears to reflect the common schooling received by Rachel and Leah Bratten (Fig. 468). In December 1813, the Armstrongs announced that their school would commence on January 3, 1814,[19] and thereafter nothing is known of them. The census of 1810 indicates that the Armstrongs had a daughter between the ages of ten and sixteen, and three children under the age of ten, but they were not in Lancaster in 1820. William Armstrong may have been the William who advertised a school in Harrisburg's *Oracle of Dauphin* on March 23, 1822. In the Lancaster *Intelligencer* of January 12, 1822, Sarah R. Armstrong described "her intention to return" to Lancaster and open a school for young ladies "at the house of George Messersmith in Queen-street" where she would teach "Reading and Writing, plain Sewing, Embroidery, with other fine Needle-work; and Music." Most likely she was a daughter of Rachel Armstrong and named Sarah Rachel for her grandmother and her mother. Instead, she may have been related to the John D. Armstrong who advertised a school in the Lancaster *Intelligencer* of September 28, 1816.

18. *The Intelligencer & Weekly Advertiser,* Lancaster, April 16, 1805. See front endpapers.
19. Ibid., December 25, 1813.

Fig. 467. *Ann Herbst daughter of Henry/ & Elisabeth Herbst was born the/ 10ᵗʰ of August in the year of our/ Lord 1792 and made this Sampler in/ the 9ᵗʰ year of her age in Mrs. Ar/mstrongs School A D 1801/ Ann Herbst is m/y name Lancast/er is my Habitati/on King Street is my dwelling place.* Silk on linen; 18½″ x 18½″. Ann's work is the earliest-known sampler from Rachel Armstrong's school. It more closely resembles the early work from her sister Leah's school (Fig. 455) than the later pieces (Fig. 468) made under her own instruction (see the 1808 and 1813 samplers by the Rine sisters in B&C, Pl. LXXXIV; and Schiffer, 59). Ann included a recognizable rendition of Lancaster's Trinity Lutheran Church, which was basically completed in 1766. When the steeple was added in 1794, it was the second tallest structure in North America. *Heritage Center of Lancaster County, Lancaster, P88.6.*

Fig. 468. *Phebe Bratton Daughter of James and/ Isabella Bratton was born March 13 1783/ and made this Sampler in Mrs. Armstrongs/ school Lancaster in the year of our Lord/ 1805.* Silk and paint on sheer linen; 16″ x 16¼″. Phebe was twenty-two years old when she worked this sampler and was probably living with the Armstrongs. She was the daughter of James Bratton and Rachel Armstrong's sister Isabella Bratton (or Bratten), who later married Alexander Stalford and died before 1804. *Winterthur Museum, 70.98.*

CATHARINE WELSHANS BUCHANAN

Samplers with figures having real hair, and several with designs similar to those on the Maguire samplers from Harrisburg, name the closely connected communities of *Wrightsville, Marietta, Maytown,* and *Columbia* from the year 1812 until 1838. The majority of these pieces were made under the instruction of Catharine Welshans Buchanan whose name appears as *Mss Welchans* on a sampler of 1812 (Fig. 469) and as *Mrs. Buchanan* on samplers dated from 1819 to 1828. Figures 470–472 reflect her typical style, and they make possible the attribution of many others to the Buchanan school. The close relationship of the Welshans-Buchanan patterns to those used by Leah Maguire in Harrisburg reveals that Catharine must have been very familiar with work from the Maguire school, and quite possibly she attended Leah's school in Harrisburg.

Catharine Welshans (Mrs. Buchanan) was born on May 5, 1792, and christened at the First Reformed Church in York. She was second among the seven children of the gunsmith Joseph Welshans and Sabina Wolf, who were married on November 6, 1785. By 1806, Joseph was living in Wrightsville, Hellam Township, and he is said to have walked from Wrightsville to Maytown (crossing the Susquehanna River from York to Lancaster counties) every other Sunday to play the organ in Maytown's Reformed Church.[20] There is no evidence that the family had links to Maytown at that time except for Mary Hamilton's sampler naming *Mss Welchans School* in Maytown in 1812 (Fig. 469). The close similarity of the Hamilton sampler to the 1819 work of Mary Fitz (Fig. 470) offers convincing evidence that the twenty-year-old Catharine was teaching needlework in Maytown, and it was evidently there that she met her husband.

On June 5, 1813, a Lancaster paper reported that the Reverend John Armstrong had performed the marriage of James G. Buchanan of Maytown to Miss Catharine Welshans, daughter of Joseph Welshans, Esq., of Hellam Township, York County.[21] James Galbraith Buchanan (1784–1848) was a saddler in Maytown where he owned a two-story log house with a barn on High Street. It appears, however, that he and Catharine moved to Wrightsville shortly after their marriage, for their daughter Juliet was born there on November 13, 1814, and another child, Sarah, was born in 1817.[22]

Why Catharine taught school during the early years of marriage and motherhood remains unexplained (Fig. 470). She never advertised, and possibly she taught only embroidery. The name of James G. Buchanan is absent from the tax records of Donegal Township, Lancaster County, from 1819 until 1824; thereafter the Buchanans' move to Marietta is confirmed by Eliza Blanchard's sampler of

20. *Biographical Annals of Lancaster County, Pennsylvania* (J. H. Beers & Co., 1903), 1135.

21. *The Intelligencer & Weekly Advertiser.* They were married on May 20, 1813.

22. Both were christened at the nearby Kruetz Creek Reformed Church, with Catharine's father and her grandmother Magdalene Welshans as sponsors.

Fig. 469. *Mary Hamilton a Daught/er of John and Catharine/ Hamilton was born in/ County Antrim February/ the 1 in the year of our/ Lord 1794 and made this/ Sampler in Maytown in/ Mss Welchans School in/ the year of our Lord 1812.* Silk, metallic thread, hair, and paint on linen; 17½″ x 16½″. Bolton and Coe published this teacher's name as "Mrs. Welchans," but it was actually *Miss* Welshans, and she was Miss Catharine Welshans who became Mrs. Buchanan in 1813. Notice the close relationship of this sampler to the work of Mary Fitz (Fig. 470).
Cooper-Hewitt, National Museum of Design, Smithsonian Institution, 1970-28-17.

Fig. 470. *Mary Fitz a Dau/ghter of Jacob and/ Susana Fitz was/ Born in York Coun/ty September the/ 24 1807 and made/ This Sampler in V/ Wrightsville in Mrs./ Buchanans School in the Year 1819.* Silk, hair, metal, and paint on linen with ribbon border; 16½″ x 17½″. As in the buildings on samplers from the Leah Galligher Maguire school, the doorway of the house is unworked. However, the central scene differs from the typical Maguire format. The Fitz family lived in Hellam Township, York County. In 1823, Ann Osborn worked the same bench and similar ladies within a naturalistic floral border and named *Mrs. Buchanan,* who was probably still in Wrightsville (Sotheby's Sale 5156, January 27, 1984, Lot 476).
Cooper-Hewitt, National Museum of Design, Smithsonian Institution, 1941-69-26.

1825 (Fig. 472). During the next decade many girls worked similar pieces that named neither the teacher nor the town, but they can be confidently attributed to Catharine Buchanan's school because of their related patterns and overall embroidery technique.[23]

In 1836, for unknown reasons, Christian and Juliana Fritz Roth granted property on High Street in Marietta to Reuben Welshans (1795–1878) in trust, for the use of his sister Catharine Buchanan.[24] According to the census of 1850, Catharine was then a widow with no occupation, and in her household were her daughter Juliet (1814–1890), her son Joseph (1821–1861), a merchant, and Mary Buchanan, aged twenty, who was possibly her youngest daughter.[25] Catharine died intestate on May 25, 1852, and she is buried near her children and grandchildren in the Marietta Cemetery.[26]

In 1819, when Catharine Buchanan was a young matron teaching in Wrightsville, Sarah McCardell (1791–1863), still single and one year older, was teaching directly across the Susquehanna River in the larger town of Columbia. Sarah's students also worked garden scenes and beguiling figures with real hair (Fig. 474), and another sampler that bears her name shows kinship to the work of Phebe Ann House (Fig. 475).[27] Sarah McCardell may have continued to teach after her marriage to the wealthy miller Jacob Shenk (1785–1842), or her style was closely copied by another instructress.

Beginning in the early 1820s, an unknown schoolmistress in York initiated a distinctive type of mourning sampler (Fig. 476). These pieces are seldom signed and dated, but a consistent type of tree and mourner was maintained for at least ten years, and the trees resemble those worked on the later samplers from Mrs. Buchanan's school.[28] A number of women were keeping private schools in York during this period, but no York sampler naming a schoolmistress has been found.[29]

---

23. Mary Ann McKinney's memorial is at the San Antonio Museum Association. Elizabeth Ann Spangler's memorial of 1830, and Eliza C. Libhart's sampler of 1832 are in private collections. Elizabeth Stackhouse's memorial of 1834 belongs to the Lancaster County Historical Society.

24. Mentioned in a deed of November 10, 1859, whereby Catharine's son Joseph transferred this property to Juliet Buchanan (Lancaster County Deed Book W, 8:592).

25. Ibid. Mary evidently died before 1859, for in the above-mentioned deed, Joseph and Juliet were named as Catharine's *only* children.

26. James G. Buchanan (1784–1848) is buried beside his mother in the Donegal Presbyterian Church graveyard.

27. Sarah Ann Boyer's sampler in Edmonds, Fig. 43. Also related is a sampler by Eliza Roberts, 1829 (Christie's East Sale 6195, September 30, 1968, Lot 89). Another by Luranah Moore, 1831, names the *Wagon town school* (private collection).

28. A similar tree occurs on an 1830 sampler naming *East Hempfield Township Lancaster County*. It is attributed to the Buchanan school because of its resemblance to another atypical example that named the school in 1828. See Krueger, *Gallery,* Figs. 101, 104.

29. George R. Prowell, *History of York County* (Chicago, 1907), 1:724–5.

Fig. 471. *Eliza Ann Cochrans Work Made in Marietta in/ Mrs. Buchanans School in the year of our Lord 1826.* Silk, hair, and paint on gauze over linen with ribbon border; 19¼" x 19¼". At present, Eliza Ann's fishing scene appears to be a unique example from the Buchanan school, but the familiar garden bench and floral border relate it to many other pieces. Several Cochran families lived in Marietta but Eliza Ann has not been identified.

Collection of Beatrice and Henry Blatner.

Fig. 472. *Eliza I Blanchards work made in/ Marietta in Mrs. Buchanan s School/ in the year of our Lord 1825.* Silk, hair, and paint on gauze over linen; 16″ x 16¼″. The monument is dedicated to Elizabeth Blanchard who died February 26, 1823.

Little girls in peach-colored dresses were also worked by Mary Ann Lucy Gries in 1826 (Ring, *Treasures,* 47). *Collection of Joan Stephens.*

Fig. 473. *Elizabeth Terry s work made in Marietta A.D. 1836.*
Silk, hair, wire, and paint on linen with ribbon border; 17½"
x 19". The death of three infants is recorded on the plinth.
For an almost identical memorial made *in Maytown in the year
1838,* see Fawdry and Brown, 104. There is little doubt that
they were both worked under Catharine Buchanan's instruction. Elizabeth Terry (1822–1844) was the daughter of George
W. Terry (1792–1838), a shoemaker, and Elizabeth Haines
(1792–1870) of Maytown. She died unmarried and is buried
with her parents in the Maytown Reformed Church yard.
*Abby Aldrich Rockefeller Folk Art Center, Williamsburg, Virginia,
62.604.1.*

Fig. 474. *Jane Hylands work/ done in the year 1819 Columbia lancaster/ County Pennsylvania Sarah McCardell, Tutoress.* Silk, hair, and metallic thread on linen; 17″ x 20¾″. Jane Simpson Hyland (c.1805–1892) lived in Columbia most of her life and died unmarried at her sister's home in West Chester. Sarah McCardell (1791–1863) was the daughter of James Terrance McCardell of Conestoga. She married Jacob Shenk (1785–1842). *Chester County Historical Society, NS1.*

Fig. 475. *Phebe Ann House's work/ 1825.* Silk, wool, and spangles on linen with a spangled ribbon border; 21¼″ x 24″. For a nearly identical sampler of the same year, see Schiffer, 72. Phebe Ann House (1813–1890) was the daughter of John House, a Quaker, and Esther Staman of Washington Boro. She married Benjamin Taylor Davis (1809–1844) in 1836 and had three daughters. In 1849, she married Joseph Lamborn. *Privately owned.*

Fig. 476. Memorial sampler with plinth inscribed *In Memory/ of George/ C. Stoher/ Departed/ this life in the 71th Year of/ his age 1821*, c.1822. Silk and paint on linen; 19½" x 17½". This sampler represents an easily recognized group worked in York, c.1821–1833. An almost identical piece, and dedicated to the same man, is in the Historical Society of York County; also, a very similar memorial is signed *Charlotte Koons s work York 1821* (Skinner Sale 1196, March 26, 1988, Lot 166). Another example, c.1833, belongs to the Dauphin County Historical Society.
Collection of Mr. and Mrs. R. W. Weesner.

Fig. 477. *Susanna. Vogle. song.s Work. made in. the 9th. Year. of. her. age. York. Pennsylvania. 1831.* Silk and paint on linen; 17" x 17¼". The arrangement of the *Hymn* and its border is found on Sarah Holland's sampler naming *York* in 1830 (Dauphin County Historical Society). These samplers are obviously related to York mourning samplers like Figure 476. Susanna Voglesong (b.1822) was the daughter of Daniel Voglesong and Susan, of York.
The Pennsylvania Farm Museum of Landis Valley, Pennsylvania Historical and Museum Commission, F74.4.1.

Fig. 478. *Mary Stoy The Daughter of William and Mary/ Stoy Her Work Done In The 12th Year Of her age/ At Mrs Hoff School/ In 1821.* Silk and paint on linen with silk and paint on appliquéd silk, and silk ribbon border; 13½" x 15½". The garland around the lady's head, and the flowers in her hand and in her basket, suggest that she may have been copied from a figure representing Spring or Summer. Maria Magdalena Stoy was born in Lebanon on September 5, 1810. She was the fourth child and fourth daughter of Wilhelm Stoy and Anna Maria Jungst. Little is known of the Stoy family but probably they were living in Lebanon in 1821, for Mary's sister Sarah was married there on January 27, 1825.
Location unknown; photograph courtesy of Sotheby's.

The Towering Ladies of Lebanon

In 1821, Mary Stoy worked a giant lady beside a modest house, thereby introducing the nineteenth century's most beguiling counterparts to the bewitching works of Marblehead (Fig. 478). Mary named her teacher, *Mrs Hoff,* as did Lavinah Britenbach in 1828 (Fig. 481). Samplers reveal that this woman taught for at least ten years, probably in or near Lebanon, where most of her students have been located,[1] but her identity is undetermined. She may have been the widow Margaret Hoff who lived in Lebanon with two young sons and a teenaged daughter in 1820.[2] However, no references to a schoolmistress named Hoff have been found in Lebanon, or in Lancaster or Reading, where Hoff families also resided.

Like Matilda Filbert's rendition of Liberty (Fig. 482), the people portrayed in these samplers were most likely inspired by prints and placed in the teacher's preferred surroundings, which have many elements of design and technique in common. Of the six samplers with figures, all but Rebecca Smith's probably unfinished piece have painted faces as well as pink ribbon ruching with rosettes, and three have survived in their original mahogany frames (Figs. 478–480).

It is entirely possible that the teacher responsible for this group was aware of the earlier pictorial samplers of the Susquehanna Valley, but her patterns reveal no specific traces of influence from the Armstrong-Galligher-Meguier schools. Another embroidery with a giant lady towering over a house was worked by Martha Vastine of Coatesville, Chester County, in 1812, but no link to the painted ladies of Lebanon has been found.[3]

---

1. Information from Family Files at the Lebanon County Historical Society.
2. United States Census of 1820 for Lebanon County, Pennsylvania. Ages of family members indicate that this Margaret Hoff was not the woman of that name shown in Lancaster in the United States Census of 1830. A Margaretha Hoff was sponsor at the baptism of Margaretha Rosina Hoff, daughter of Jacob and Maria, on September 15, 1822 (unpublished records of the First Reformed Church in Lebanon, 1764–1851, in the Lebanon County Historical Society). Fig. 481, naming Hoff, was discovered by Mary Jaene Edmonds.
3. *ANTIQUES,* December 1984, 1433.

Fig. 479. *Elizabeth Karch 1822.* Silk and paint on linen with silk ribbon border; 11½" x 9½". The green and white striped lawn is similar to Mary Stoy's work, but the heads are painted directly on the linen ground. Elizabeth Karch (b. 1806), the second child of George Karch (b. 1782) and Anna Maria Beyer, was baptized at the Evangelical Lutheran Church in Lebanon. She married David Shirk in 1826.
Private collection; photograph courtesy of Edwin and Sheila Rideout.

Fig. 480. *Maria B Greenawalt 1822.* Silk, paint, and paper on linen with pink ribbon border; 9½" x 11⅜". The harpist has a paper sash, and paper was also applied to the hem of her dress. Her painted head has black hair, a white face, and a bright red spot on her cheek. Maria Barbara Greenawalt (1810–1888) was the daughter of Lebanon tanner Leonard Greenawalt (1777–1855) and Catharine Pool (1780–1850). She died unmarried.
Location unknown; photograph courtesy of Sotheby's.

Fig. 481. *Lavinah Britenbach The Daughter Of/ John And Elizabeth Britenbach Her/ Work Done In The* 10th *Year Of Her Age/ At* Mrs *Hoff School 1828.* Silk and paint on linen with paint on appliquéd silk and silk ribbon border; 18″ x 18″. John (b.c.1790) and Elizabeth Sheetz Britenbach (b.c.1788) lived near Myerstown in Jackson Township, where he was a prosperous farmer and tanner. Evidence of Lavinah Britenbach's marriage to Henry Beerbower is found in the baptismal records of the Trinity Tulpehocken Reformed Church in Jackson Township, where their daughter Lavinah was baptized in 1850.
Collection of Elizabeth Clark Olson.

Fig. 482. *Matilda Filbert Her Work in* th *12*th *Year of Her age/ 1830.* Silk, chenille, and paint on linen, with paint and spangles on appliquéd silk, and silk ribbon border; 22½″ x 17″. Small portions of new ribbon have been added to the border. The green ground was in straight rows (see Fig. 483) but was pulled into waves when tacked to a stretcher. Matilda's composition was inspired by the print in Figure 484. Her leafy basket has unusual two-toned or shaded fruit, which also appear in Figure 483. Marie Matilda Filbert (1818–after 1872) was the daughter of John Filbert (1777–1857) and Anna Maria Leiss (1781–1865) of Womelsdorf, Berks County. She married Augustus Leiss (d.1860), and they had three daughters.
Author's collection.

Fig. 483. *Rebecca Smith/ Her Work 1831*. Silk on linen; 14½″ x 14″. Absence of both paint (including no feet) and a ribbon border suggest that Rebecca's sampler is unfinished. Its vivid colors indicate that it probably was not framed until recently. Rebecca Smith was possibly the daughter of Joseph Smith (1795–1862), a weaver of Annville, and Barbara Neu (1798–1865). She married Henry Craiglow in 1833. *Location unknown; photograph courtesy of* The Magazine ANTIQUES.

Fig. 484. *LIBERTY. In the form of the Goddess of Youth; giving Support to the Bald Eagle.* Stipple engraving by Edward Savage after his life-size, now-lost painting; 22⅞″ x 14¹¹/₁₆″. Published by Savage in Philadelphia, June 11, 1796.
Worcester Art Museum, Worcester, Massachusetts.

The Moravian Embroideries of Bethlehem

Everyone ought to receive a universal education.
—John Amos Comenius (1592–1670)[1]

Fig. 485. Baroness Benigna Zinzendorf de Watteville (1725–1789); copy of the original portrait by Valentine Haidt (1700–1780) now in Herrnhut, Saxony, East Germany. Oil on canvas; 23⅜″ x 18⅞″. Benigna was the foundress of the Moravian Seminary and the eldest daughter of Count Nicolaus Ludwig von Zinzendorf (1700–1760), who planned the first Moravian settlement in America. In 1746 she married John, Baron de Watteville, who succeeded her father as head of the Moravian community. She died in Saxony. She is pictured in the typical close-fitting, blue-ribboned cap of the Moravian matron. Single women had pink ribbons, and widows wore white.
Moravian Academy, Upper School, Bethlehem.

The Moravians in America followed the philosophy of their famous educator, Bishop Comenius. Consequently, the first widely acclaimed girls' boarding school in the United States was the Moravian Seminary for Young Ladies in Bethlehem, Pennsylvania. This school traced its beginning to Ashmead House in Germantown where the sixteen-year-old Countess Benigna (Fig. 485) began teaching Moravian girls in 1742.[2] By 1749 it had found a permanent home in Bethlehem, and it was opened to the daughters of non-Moravians in 1785.

The first non-Moravian boarder was Elizabeth Bedell from Staten Island, New York, who entered the school on May 21, 1786, and by 1789 "so many applications had been received . . . that the authorities were greatly concerned that the [Seminary] building . . . would not be able to contain them."[3] At this time the age for admission was eight to twelve, and many girls were permitted to remain until the age of sixteen. Charges of £20 per year were payable quarterly in advance and covered board and common schooling, which consisted of reading, writing, grammar, history, geography, arithmetic, plain sewing, and knitting.[4] Instruction in fine needlework and other accomplishments was offered at extra cost, and even a transgression of the rules such as speaking at meals except to the tutoress could increase one's bill by a one cent fine per offense. Nevertheless, attendance at this costly school continued to grow, and in the summer of 1797, Principal Jacob Van Vleck had to notify patrons that no new admissions could be considered for the following year and a half.

Possibly the best account of life at the Young Ladies' Seminary during its earliest years was written by twelve-year-old Amelia Blakely to her brother Harry on August 16, 1787:

1. As quoted in *Bethlehem of Pennsylvania, The First One Hundred Years, 1741 to 1841* (Bethlehem, Pa.: Bethlehem Chamber of Commerce, 1968), 142.
2. The Countess Benigna taught in Germantown and Bethlehem before returning to Europe in 1743. She helped with the permanent establishment of the school in Bethlehem in 1749, and returning in 1784, she participated in plans for the acceptance of non-Moravian girls, which was officially announced on October 2, 1785. (Mabel Haller, *Early Moravian Education in Pennsylvania* [Nazareth, Pa.: Moravian Historical Society, 1953], 16. Also, information from Rebecca H. Heck, Archivist, Moravian Academy, February 5, 1987.)
3. Haller, *Early Moravian Education*, 24.
4. Reichel and Bigler, *A History of the Rise, Progress and Present Condition of the Moravian Seminary for Young Ladies* (1874), 83, 84.

Fig. 486. A Christmas
celebration at the Moravian
Seminary, 1801. Watercolor
on paper; 6½″ x 13¾″.
Attributed to Anna Maria
Kliest (1762–1821) by the
Reverend Vernon Nelson,
Archivist. Kliest was an art
teacher and the principal
tutoress at the Seminary
from 1788 until 1805 when
she married John Gambold
(1760–1827) and moved to
the Indian Mission in Georgia. The scene depicts the
basement of the second
Seminary building occupied
from 1790 through 1815,
and destroyed in 1857. The
boarding students face the
stage, wearing frilled cam-
bric caps known as the
English cap. Moravian girls
and teachers sitting against
the wall wear close-fitting
Moravian caps. The monu-
ment is inscribed *The Word/
was made/ Flesh* and relates
to passages used in the
Christmas play of 1801
(*Bethlehem Diary,* Moravian
Archives).
Moravian Archives, Bethlehem.

My dear Harry,

On the 8th of May, Papa and I left Baltimore for this place, tarried about a week in Philadelphia, and on the 15th arrived here. It is 54 miles north of Philadelphia.

The nunnery, as Papa calls it, is a large pile of stone buildings, about four hundred feet in length, has 47 windows in one story, in which there live about two hundred females.

In the apartment where I reside, at the boarding school for Misses, there are about thirty little girls of my age. Here I am taught music, both vocal and instrumental; I play the guitar twice a day—am taught the spinnet and forte-piano;—and some times I play the organ.

We rise at six, and after combing our heads, and washing we retire for prayers, to a little chapel, which is part of this building, and which is con- secrated to the use of our school. . . . This chapel no man or boy ever en- ters. At seven we go to breakfast, at eight school begins, in which we are taught reading and grammar, both English and German, for those who chose; writing, arithmetic, history, geography, composition, &c. till eleven; when we go into a large chapel, which also joins this house, and where there is an organ. Here we see three gentlemen,—the person who delivers a short lecture on divinity and morality—the organist, who plays a hymn, in which we join with our voices—and the boys' schoolmaster. In this meeting the boys attend with us. At three quarters after eleven we dine; and at one school begins. In the afternoon we are taught needle-work, tambour, draw- ing, music, &c. till three, when school is out after which we walk, or di- vert ourselves as we please, at six we sup, then play on some musical instrument, or do as we please, till half after seven, when we retire for evening prayers; at eight we go to bed. We all sleep in a large chamber, with windows on both sides at which a lamp burns during the whole night. After we are in bed, one of the ladies, with her guitar and voice, serenades us to sleep.

On Sundays divine service is performed in the great chapel, where the whole society, men women and children meet. Their preaching is some times in German. They sing enchantingly, in which they are joined with the bass-viols, violins and an organ. To call the people into the chapel four French horns are blown, with which you would be delighted.

We have a bell that rings to call us to school, dinner, children's meetings, &c. there is a large clock, the hammer of which strikes upon this bell. This clock strikes not only the hours, but the quarters, and to a minute regulates our different employments. . . .

On one side of our house, runs the Minorcas-creek, on another the river Lehigh, on the banks of which, are laid out the most beautiful walks, planted with locust, willow, Bass and other trees. Our gardens delight the eye, as well as please the palate. . . .

We have two ladies of the first education, who teach in the school, another who teaches music, and a gentleman who examines, and corrects in grammar and music.[5]

Amelia received "private Instruction in fine Needle Work, drawing &c. for 3 months" but her handiwork has not been found.[6]

During the 1790s, the Moravian Seminary was already famous for exquisite ornamental needlework, and the beauty of the silk embroideries produced there was praised by a host of both foreign and American visitors. It reflected the skill of the Single Sisters of the Moravian sect, who also made a variety of appealing embroidered objects to sell to visitors.[7]

No distinctive samplers survive from Bethlehem, nor has a unique group of silk embroideries been identified from the eighteenth century. However, Moravian origin is often revealed by their preference for central motifs placed on irregular islands of embroidered ground that seem suspended within the unworked and unpainted silk rather than filling the lower section of the silk with embroidery (Figs. 487, 488, 600). This style persisted from about 1788 until the 1820s. It also occurs on embroideries worked at the Moravian girls' schools in Lititz, Pennsylvania, and Salem, North Carolina,[8] a consistency that no doubt resulted from the frequent interchange of teachers between these institutions. The earliest-known

---

5. *Connecticut Courant*, Hartford, April 28, 1788. Amelia Louisa Blakely (1775–1794) was the second non-Moravian girl to attend the seminary. She was the daughter of Baltimore merchant Joseph Blakely and Sarah (c.1753–1787). She died in Barbados. For her poetical entry in the pupils' "Journal" of June 4, 1789, see Haller, *Early Moravian Education*, 243.

6. The Girls' Seminary Ledger of 1782–1789, 156 (Moravian Archives, Bethlehem).

7. The Single Sisters of the Moravian sect have occasionally been misleadingly described as "the nuns of Bethlehem," but celibacy was never practiced by the Moravians. Theirs was a communal society in which all children were required to live and be educated in their appropriate "choir."

8. For Salem Academy work, see Figure 574; also *ANTIQUES*, September 1974, 434–42.

Fig. 487. Silk embroidery worked by Susan Bagge, c.1788. Silk and chenille on silk; 8¼″ x 6¾″. Susan's exquisite strawberry plant may be the earliest identified student embroidery from the Seminary in Bethlehem. In the characteristic Moravian manner, it is an object on a floating island of ground. Susanna Elisabeth Bagge (1775–1850) was the daughter of the joiner and Moravian minister, Nicolaus Lorenz Bagge (d.1789), and Susan Elisabeth Birstler (d.1778) of Bethabara, North Carolina. In 1789, her father was pastor in Hebron, Pennsylvania. Susan married the Reverend Johann Frederick Stadiger (1775–1849) on April 26, 1802. In 1808, Stadiger became the warden in Bethlehem.
Collection of Mr. and Mrs. William B. Leckonby.

Fig. 488. Pictorial embroidery by Frances Thacker Burwell, c.1794. Silk on silk; 16⅝″ x 13⅝″. Frances entered the Seminary in January 1793 and departed June 6, 1794. In December 1793, she purchased six ounces of embroidery silk and one-fourth yard of "Sattin" for a total of two pounds and fourteen shillings (Seminary Ledger, 1792–1796, 235). On March 1, 1794, she was charged one pound, two shillings, and ten pence for "making up sundry articles" (Ibid., 323). Frances Thacker Burwell (1781–1864), was the daughter of Major Nathaniel Burwell and Martha Diggs (1759–1842) of King William County, Virginia. She married Colonel Lewis Harvey.
Botetourt County Historical Society, Fincastle, Virginia, 966-50-10; photograph courtesy of the Museum of Early Southern Decorative Arts.

Fig. 489. Pictorial embroidery by Eliza Kortright, c.1814. Silk and metallic thread on silk; 19″ x 20½″. This composition is characteristic of Moravian work, and a number of closely related pieces survive from the seminaries in Bethlehem, Lititz, and Salem, North Carolina. An almost identical example was worked in Bethlehem, c.1818, by Lucy B. or Ann B. Corbin of Williamsburg, Virginia (recorded at MESDA). Urns upon monuments did not necessarily denote mourning and were often inscribed as tokens of respect or affection (see also vol. I, xii). Eliza Kortright (b.1802) entered the school June 6, 1814, and on September 30 she was charged $2.47 for satin and the drawing of a "frame piece," having purchased a "set of embroidery silk" for $8.87 in June (Day Book F, 196). Eliza was the daughter of John Kortright (d.1810) and Catherine Seaman Kortright (1774–1861). Her father's sister Elizabeth was the wife of President James Monroe. Her mother became the wife of Brockholst Livingston, Judge of the U.S. Supreme Court. Eliza married Nicholas Cruger.
The New-York Historical Society, 1910.34.

example of this type was worked by Susan Bagge (Fig. 487) who entered the Seminary in the fall of 1785 and was one of five Moravian girls boarding there before the school was opened to outsiders. The motherless Susan was ten years old when her father, a Moravian minister, was transferred to Pennsylvania from Bethabara, North Carolina. She was officially recorded as a student in the newly organized Seminary in 1787 and remained there through 1789. The student "Journal" recorded Susan's narrow escape from injury on November 21, 1788, when "in the evening Susan Bage sat spinning, and growing sleepy, her flax caught fire."[9] Susan taught at the Seminary from 1797 until her marriage in 1802.

The Seminary account books in the Moravian Archives contain charges for each girl's attendance and indicate that the teachers mounted the embroideries, and that either a teacher or an ornamental artist drew the patterns and painted them. Painted faces on the memorials of 1810 to 1813 appear to be the work of two different hands, but the artists have not been identified. They may have been Benedict Benade, who was being paid for painting in 1808 and 1809, and Mary Salome (Sally) Meinung, an instructor in drawing and painting from 1808 to 1810.[10]

---

9. "Extracts from the Journal of Daily Events, kept by the younger Pupils of the Bethlehem Boarding School, 1788 and 1789," Reichel and Bigler, *History,* 66.
10. Day Book E, 98, Moravian Archives, Bethlehem. For an account of ornamental artist Christohof Benedict Benade (1752–1841) of Nazareth and Filetown, see Charles M. Sandwick, Sr., *Jacobsburg, A Pennsylvania Community and Its People* (Nazareth, Pa.: Jacobsburg Historical Society, 1985), 25–7, 105–6.

Fig. 490. Palemon and Lavinia, embroidered by Hester or Sarah Witman, c.1810.
Silk, spangles, and paint on silk; 14¾″ x
15″. Frame labeled by "Charles N. Robin-
son/ No. 36 Chesnut Street, Philadelphia"
(working at this address 1823–1849). This
scene was derived from the print in Figure
491, and the same figures were worked in
Lititz (Fig. 500). Probably from the Bethlehem Seminary is a similar rendition
painted on silk (SPB, Garbisch Part II, Sale
3637, May 8, 9, 1974, Lot 172). Hester
(b.1795) and Sarah Witman (1797–1885)
were the daughters of William Witman, Jr.
(1772–1828), and Mary Green
(1771–1835) of Reading, Pennsylvania.
They entered the Seminary in August 1809
after it was noted that they "have had
smallpox, measles, and whooping cough."
They were to be instructed in all branches
and have one dollar a month for pocket
money (see back endpapers for their
itemized expenses). Hester married Dr.
John Bodo Otto of Reading; Sarah married
David Otto of Philadelphia.
Author's collection.

Fig. 491. A scene from the poem "Autumn." Drawn by William Hamilton, engraved by Lawson, and published in *The Seasons, with the Castle
of Indolence Poems* by James Thomson (1700–1748). Printed by Budd &
Bartram, for Thomas Dobson, at the Stone House, No. 41 South
Second Street, Philadelphia, 1804. Image: 4¼″ x 3⅛″. This represents
the moment when Palemon recognizes that Lavinia, a gleaner in his
field, is the long-sought daughter of his friend Acasto. These figures
were widely copied in needlework, and this engraving probably appeared in other editions of Thomson's *Seasons*. It was the inspiration for
the decoration on an 1818 whiteworked bedcover at the Abby Aldrich
Rockefeller Folk Art Center (81.609.3), and its figures with different
backgrounds occur on Lititz embroideries.
The Library Company of Philadelphia.

Fig 493. Mourning piece by Mary Eliza Sevier, c.1813. Silk, chenille, spangles, and paint on silk; 15⅝″ x 13⅛″. Occasionally the trees in this pattern were combined with the monument and weeper in the Maxwell memorial (Fig. 492). See Schorsch, *Mourning Becomes America* (1976) Fig. 62/207. Mary Eliza entered the Seminary on October 8, 1810, and departed in January 1814. She purchased silk and satin for a framed piece each year of her attendance but probably this memorial to her mother was her most elaborate work. On March 13, 1813, she was charged $3.77 for gold spangles, silk, and work on a framed piece (Day Book F, 147). Mary Eliza Sevier (1799–1884), of Burlington County, New Jersey, was the daughter of John Sevier, Jr. (1766–1845), and his second wife, Rebecca Richards (d. before 1809), and the granddaughter of John Sevier, first governor of Tennessee. In 1819, she married Joseph William Throckmorton (1794–1883) of Monmouth County, New Jersey. He became a Philadelphia merchant.

Moravian Academy, Upper School, Bethlehem.

Fig. 492. *M. B. Maxwell* in the smaller reserve on the plinth and in the larger one *Sacred to the/ MEMORY/ of my beloved brother/ CHARLES SHIELD MAXWELL,* c.1812. Silk, metallic thread, spangles, paint, and ink on silk; 12¾″ x 9¾″. Margaret Maxwell worked the Seminary's most frequently found mourning pattern. The characteristic border, which appears to be spangled tape, is actually chain-stitched. Similar pieces are in the Baltimore Museum, the Brooklyn Museum, the Museum of the City of New York, and the collections of Old Salem, Inc. Margaret B. Maxwell (1798–1850) entered the Seminary in June 1811 and attended through June 1812. This piece was probably made in the spring of 1812 and took three months to complete. On March 31, 1812, there were charges for "Sattin & drawing a Frame Piece 2.54½" and on June 30, "Work on a Frame Piece 50cts/ Silver Thread & spangles 87cts Painting $1" (Day Book F, 23). Margaret was the daughter of Robert Maxwell of Middletown, Delaware.

Newport Historical Society, 01.172.

Fig. 494. *E.B./ 1813* inscribed on the glass and on the plinth *To the/ MEMORY/ of my beloved father/ JOHN BOLLER.* Silk, chenille, spangles, paint, and ink on silk; 29″ x 24″. Eliza Boller attended the Seminary from April 1810 through March 1813. Charges from June 30, 1812, to March 31, 1813, probably pertain to this piece: "Silk & Work on a Frame Piece 2.49/ Cash for making up fine Needlework .13/ silk and work on Frame Piece .39/ Cash for spangles & Work on a Frame 1.11 Painting 1″ (Day Book F, 37). Eliza was also paying two dollars for every three months' instruction in fine needlework. Eliza Boller (1799–1891) was the daughter of John J. Boller (1774–1808), who emigrated from the Palatinate in 1793, and Anna Catherine Eckel (1780–1847) of Philadelphia. She married Charles H. Baker on December 8, 1815. Eliza's 1813 copy book of Moravian music is at HSP. *Allentown Art Museum, gift of Mrs. William P. Hacker, 79.80.63.*

Fig. 495. *Mary Ritter* embroidered on the silk and with the inscription *God/ be merciful unto/ you & bless/ You!/ Ps 67.1*, 1824. Ribbon, silk chiffon, silk, and chenille on silk; 6¼" x 8¾". A victory wreath in ribbon work was one of the most popular patterns at Moravian schools in the late 1820s and 1830s. This and Figure 497 have intricate ribbon-work flowers with only two chiffon roses. The majority of later and larger pieces are dominated by chiffon or crepe work (see Figs. 502, 504). In 1824, Mary's account was charged with eight months' instruction in "Ribbon Work, $8.61/ Ribbon work materials 4.49/ Drawing Pattern 1.25" (Bill Book H, 502, Moravian Archives). Mary Ritter (b.1808), the daughter of Jacob Ritter of Philadelphia, entered the Seminary, with her sister Eliza, in September 1822 and attended until September 1824.
Annie S. Kemerer Museum, Bethlehem, 61.K.360.

Fig. 496. Third home of the Young Ladies Seminary in Bethlehem. Paint on silk; actual size. Built in 1748 as the Single Brethren's House, this building was first occupied by the students and staff of the Seminary on November 10, 1815. At 1 P.M. the procession of boarding pupils, day scholars, and teachers, numbering 132, entered their new quarters while the trombones played "The Lord bless thy going out and thy coming in." Since 1786, 965 boarders had attended the school. Many belonged to the most illustrious families of America. Among them were the daughters of General Greene in 1788, the daughters of Chief Justice John Jay in 1794 and 1796, and a grandniece of George Washington in 1796.
M. and M. Karolik Collection, Museum of Fine Arts, Boston, 39.242.

An easily recognized type of mourning embroidery became popular in Bethlehem about 1809 (Figs. 492–494).[11] Their solidly worked willow leaves are a distinctly Moravian technique, which also appears on embroideries from Linden Hall (Fig. 501). More exclusive to Bethlehem is a chain-stitched border decorated with clusters of tiny spangles (Figs. 490, 492, 494).[12] Eliza Boller's mourning embroidery is presently the largest and most impressive piece belonging to this dominant group of Bethlehem memorials (Fig. 494), and its typical Philadelphia frame retains the remnants of an indecipherable Philadelphia framer's label.

In addition to working mourning pieces and other subjects in silk on silk, the Seminary students could undertake tambour work, worsted work, artificial flower making, beadwork, velvet painting, Japanning, and ebony work, but no products of these courses are known to be distinctively Moravian. The handwork most peculiar to Moravians in America was called "Ribbon work" when it was introduced

---

11. For examples, c.1809–1810, see *ANTIQUES*, September 1983, 548.
12. For Seminary embroideries of allegorical figures recognizable by this border, see the work of Rebecca Davis, 1816, in SPB, Haskell, Part 4, Sale 599, November 8, 1944, Lot 145; and SPB, Garbisch I, Sale 3595, January 23, 24, 1974, Lot 185.

Fig. 497. Ribbon-work wreath attributed to Eliza Rice, c.1825. Embroidered on the silk *Der Herr segne/ und behute dich* (The Lord bless and keep you). Ribbon, silk chiffon, silk, and chenille on silk; 7½″ x 10¼″. Except for its black silk ground, this is nearly identical to the work of Eliza's older classmate Mary Ritter (Fig. 495). Eliza entered the Seminary in March 1822 and remained two years. Her account (in Bill Book H, 226) includes charges for Drawing and Music but none for Ribbon work. Therefore this wreath was probably made in 1825, as Eliza's name appears on Charles F. Seidel's list of girls attending the Moravian school for day scholars in 1825 (information from the Moravian Museum provided by Dorothy McCoach). Eliza Rice (1812–1852), a Moravian girl, was the daughter of Joseph Rice and Anna Salome Heckewelder of Bethlehem. She married W. B. Luckenbach in 1830. *Moravian Museum, Bethlehem, A24.*

to the Seminary curriculum late in 1822. Actually, these floral compositions are combinations of silk chiffon with ribbon, chenille, and silk embroidery (Figs. 495, 497), and today they are commonly called crepe work. Instruction in "Ribbon work" cost three dollars for three months, and it did not become popular at the Seminary until the middle of 1824. By 1825, however, about half the students were paying the fee to learn ribbon work, and "under the able instruction of Sister Polly Blum, this branch was pursued by successive pupils for upwards of twenty years."[13] It was under her direction that the pupils created a monumental crepe-work wreath for presentation to Mrs. John Quincy Adams in 1826. It can now be seen at the Adams National Historic Site in Quincy, Massachusetts.[14]

As an adjunct to the Seminary, the Moravians also had a day school for local girls. These students are not listed in the records of the boarding school. Therefore the embroideress of a recognizable and signed Bethlehem piece is not always easily identified.

During the twentieth century the Moravian's venerable school for girls in Bethlehem has undergone several moves and reorganizations. Now coeducational, it is known as the Moravian Academy.

---

13. Reichel and Bigler, *History*, 200. According to Reichel and Bigler, crepe work was brought from Germany to Bethlehem by visitors to the Church Synod in Herrnhut and introduced at the Seminary in 1818. Yet girls' account books show no charges for this before 1822. A map on silk with a crepe and ribbon-work border was made at the Female Model School, Kildare Place, Dublin, Ireland, in 1817 (Henry Ford Museum, 92.0.106).

14. For this and other Moravian schoolgirl art, see *Art & Antiques*, November–December 1980, 78–83; also, Schiffer, 105–21.

Fig. 498. Pictorial embroidery by Rebecca Anderson, c.1811. Silk, chenille, spangles, and paint on silk; 18½" x 17¼"; original frame bears the earliest-known Philadelphia label of S. Kennedy, 72 Chesnut, dated Sept. 11, 1812. (For Kennedy data, see *ANTIQUES,* May 1981, 1186.) Rebecca's classmate, Catharine Kapp, worked the same pattern in 1811 (Schiffer, 108). Rebecca and Catharine were probably instructed by Salome Tschudy, who taught music and embroidery from March 1811 until March 1813 (Linden Hall records, courtesy of Patricia T. Herr). Rebecca Anderson (b.c.1799) of Salem, New Jersey, was the daughter of John Anderson and Hannah Thompson. Her mother married (second) Leonard Sayre who then lived in Cincinnati. Rebecca entered the Lititz school, aged eleven, in 1810. Her uncle Dr. Benjamin Archer (husband of her mother's sister Rachel) was responsible for her bills, and her embroidery descended in his family.

Salem County Historical Society, Salem, New Jersey, P231.

The Moravian School in Lititz

The girls' school known today as Linden Hall Seminary began on May 24, 1748, as a school for Moravian children in Warwick Township, Lancaster County,[1] and upon moving to Lititz in 1766, the girls were taught separately in the Sisters' House that is now called the Castle.[2] The school began admitting non-Moravian girls in 1794, and it still continues on its original site in Lititz.[3] It became known as Linden Hall in 1838 when basswood saplings from Berlin, Germany, were planted beside the school building.

Like the school's philosophy and its daily routine, the embroideries from Lititz are closely related to those of the Moravian Seminary in Bethlehem. For instance, their silk pictures often have willow trees with solidly stitched leaves as seen in Susan Winn's embroidery (Fig. 501) and as are common to Bethlehem memorials (Figs. 492–494). The earliest known examples may be the most difficult to distinguish, for the exchange of both teachers and craftsmen employed by these in-

---

1. For a complete account of this school, see Mabel Haller, *Early Moravian Education in Pennsylvania* (Nazareth, Pa.: Moravian Historical Society, 1953), 83–113.

2. Ibid., 91–2. Because of the Revolutionary War, the school was closed from May 31, 1775, until October 1784.

3. Ibid. Nine-year-old Margaret Marvel of Baltimore, the first non-Moravian boarder, was enrolled on September 7, 1794. For a broadside describing terms and conditions of the boarding school in 1809, see De-Pauw and Hunt, *Remember the Ladies* (1976), 100.

stitutions resulted in needlework so similar it cannot be assigned to either school unless confirmed by enrollment records.[4] Nevertheless, by 1817, if not earlier, two identifiable characteristics had developed in Lititz. One is the unique practice of including a grotto or rocks worked in chenille with dark outlines as found in Figures 501 to 503. Many such pieces have a dark brown or black solidly worked chenille border heavily decorated with fanciful spangles and metallic threads (Figs. 501, 503).

The teacher who originated the identifiable features of Lititz work remains unknown, but the chenille rocks and spangled chenille borders were worked through the 1820s, and at least four different artists painted the figures on the embroideries. It is now evident that many pieces of 1815 and 1816 were drawn and painted by Samuel Reinke,[5] including the Hanson and Winn embroideries (Figs. 499–501). In a letter of August 8, 1815, Sarah Ann Hanson informed her father "that we have had our pieces of embroidery painted, by a gentleman from Nazareth, whom Mr. Freeauf (the principal) engaged to do this work for us."[6] Lititz school records of June 30, 1815, reveal that Samuel Reinke was paid two dollars for painting Sarah Ann's "Moses in the Bulrushes" (Fig. 499). In December of 1815 he charged twenty-five cents each for drawing large pieces for Sarah Ann Hanson and Susan Winn, and these were painted in April 1816 for two dollars and three dollars, respectively (Figs. 500, 501).[7] Also in 1815, Reinke drew a pattern for Mary I. McKaleb, another Lititz student who worked the same Moses pattern within an oval, and above paired cornucopias identical to those worked by Eliza Kortright in Bethlehem (Fig. 489).[8] This indicates that Reinke drew patterns and painted pieces for both schools. The disproportion of the figures in the Hanson and Winn embroideries, as well as in the Annan memorial (Fig. 502), may reflect either the original drawing or the student's interpretation of it, since the needleworker embroidered around the appropriate spaces for painting.

The majority of Lititz embroideries from the 1820s have figures much like Nancy Dunlap's work (Fig. 503) and their easily recognized little people are now

4. Bethlehem enrollment records for the boarding scholars are reasonably complete and published in Reichel and Bigler, *A History of the Rise, Progress and Present Condition of the Moravian Seminary for Young Ladies* (1874). Lititz enrollment records are unpublished.

5. Samuel Reinke (1791–1875), born in Lititz, was among the first students at the Moravian Theological Seminary in Nazareth. He taught at Nazareth Hall (the Moravian boys' school), 1813–1817, and was principal of the Lititz School from 1824 to 1826. (Haller, *Early Moravian Education*, 78, 96.) Particularly interesting are his *Twelve Views of Churches, Schools and Other Buildings, erected by the United Brethren in America*, with brief descriptions annexed.

6. Correspondence, Linden Hall Archives. At this time Reinke and ornamental artist Benedict Benade were both in Nazareth. Benade's name occurs in Lititz records of 1813 under "Embroid Acct." I am indebted to Patricia T. Herr for knowledge of the Hanson letter, references to Reinke and Benade, and the Lititz records in the Moravian Archives in Bethlehem; also to Mrs. Ridgely Cropf, Alumnae Secretary, who provided enrollment information.

7. Lititz School Journal D, 1814–1818, 79, 137, 177, payments to Samuel Reinke. Moravian Archives, Bethlehem.

8. See the McKaleb work in Skinner Sale 902, May 27, 1983, Lot 188; also *Moses* embroideries in *A&AW* (August 17, 1984), 13; and Ronald Bourgeault's *Northeast Auctions*, August 4, 5, 1990, Lot 601.

Fig. 499. Pictorial embroidery inscribed on the silk *Moses and the Egyptian Princess/ Sarah A. Hanson fecit,* c.1815. Silk, chenille, spangles, paint, and ink on silk; 18″ x 14⅝″. Sarah's embroidery, painted by "a gentleman from Nazareth," reveals the style of artist Samuel Reinke. Sarah Ann Hanson (c.1801–before 1828), with her sister Emeline (b.c.1802) entered the Lititz school in 1814. They were the daughters of Benjamin Hanson (d.1829) and Martha Hynson of Chestertown, Kent County, Maryland. Sarah Ann married Thomas Jarvis Jones, Jr., in 1818.
Private collection; photograph courtesy of the Museum of Early Southern Decorative Arts.

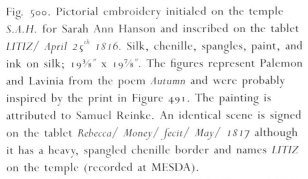

Fig. 500. Pictorial embroidery initialed on the temple *S.A.H.* for Sarah Ann Hanson and inscribed on the tablet *LITIZ/ April 25ᵗʰ 1816.* Silk, chenille, spangles, paint, and ink on silk; 19⅜″ x 19⅞″. The figures represent Palemon and Lavinia from the poem *Autumn* and were probably inspired by the print in Figure 491. The painting is attributed to Samuel Reinke. An identical scene is signed on the tablet *Rebecca/ Money/ fecit/ May/ 1817* although it has a heavy, spangled chenille border and names *LITIZ* on the temple (recorded at MESDA).
Private collection; photograph courtesy of the Museum of Early Southern Decorative Arts.

attributed to ornamental artist Peter Lehn Grosh (1798–1859).[9] Also typical of this later Lititz group are scenes with churches painted in the backgrounds and angels hovering in the sky. By the mid-1820s, crepe and ribbon work was often included in these pictorial compositions (Fig. 502). A number of crepe-work wreaths survive from the 1830s, although seldom with the brilliant original coloring found in the farewell gift to Charles F. Kluge (Fig. 504).

9. The artist was discovered by Patricia T. Herr (letter of February 19, 1992). Her history of the Lititz school embroidery will be published in *ANTIQUES* of February 1993.

Fig. 501. *Erected by/ Susan Winn* inscribed on the plinth beneath the epitaph *Sacred to the Memory of/ my dear Sister/ CAROLINE WINN,* c.1816. Silk, chenille, spangles, paint, and ink on silk; 18⅞″ in diameter. Susanna Bolland Winn (b.1801) and her sister Elizabeth Anne (b.1803) entered the school in 1815. They were the daughters of Baltimore flour merchant John Winn (c.1751–1831), born in Yorkshire, England, and Susanna. The girl at right wears a necklace with the initials *S W.* The other figures may represent her mother, her sister Elizabeth, and brother Perry Nelson Winn. Their sister Caroline was born in March and died in June 1806. In December 1824, Susan married John Renolds of Frederick County, Maryland. *National Museum of American History, Smithsonian Institution; gift of Albert Adsit Clemons, 148588.*

Fig. 501a. Detail of Winn memorial with painting attributed to Samuel Reinke. Notice the disproportionate size of the head and arm in the figure of Susan, at right. This also occurs in Figure 499.

Fig. 502. Anonymous mourning embroidery inscribed *In Memory/ of my/ Sister/ Mary Jane Annan,* c.1824. Silk, chenille, crepe, ribbon, paint, and ink on silk; 21ʺ x 21ʺ. Characteristic chenille-worked rocks confirm the Lititz origin of this embroidery. Also from Lititz is a very similar documented example (Swan, *Guide,* 102) worked in 1819 by Mary Sarah Downing (1803–1876) of East Caln Township. The Winterthur Museum owns a similar composition painted by Charles Graeff while a student at Nazareth Hall, the Moravian boys' school in Nazareth.
Collection of Edward Grosvenor Paine.

Fig. 503. *NANCY DUNLAP/ LITIZ 1823/ SACRED,/ To the Memory of my/ beloved Mother,/ SARAH DUNLAP*. Silk, chenille, spangles, metallic thread, paint, and ink on silk; 13⅜″ x 12″. Nancy's memorial is the most typical Lititz form of the 1820s. Ann Dunlap, called Nancy, was the daughter of James Dunlap and Sarah of Allen, Cumberland County, Pennsylvania. She entered the school in 1823.
Collection of Dr. and Mrs. Donald M. Herr.

Fig. 504. Crepe-work wreath inscribed *A TOKEN OF/ Affectionate Regard/ from the teachers of/ LITIZ SEMINARY,* c.1836. Crepe, ribbon, silk, chenille, and ink on silk; 17¾″ x 16¾″. Written on the back "A Farewell gift to C. F. Kluge upon his retirement as principal of Linden Hall, made by one of them." Charles F. Kluge (1801–1880) was the principal of Linden Hall from 1830 until 1836 and the principal of Nazareth Hall from 1839 to 1844.
Moravian Archives, Bethlehem, no acc. no.

Fig. 505. Unsigned sampler by Emeline Eagles, c.1834. Silk and wool on linen; 18″ x 20½″. Inscribed on the back: "This sampler was made by our Mother Emeline Eagles Wyckoff Born in Easton Pa. in 1820. She went to Miss Ralston Private School. The teacher drew one flower at a time. Mother shaded it and worked it. She started it when she was twelve years old & finished it when she was fourteen." Related examples were made by *Mary Anna Curtain Easton 1830* (*Early American Life,* February 1984, 46, 47) and *Fredericka Amalia Hutter,* c.1830 (recorded in DAPC). Emeline Crane Eagles (1820–1901) was the daughter of Easton saddler Alexander Eagles (d.1840) and Margaret Crane (1794–1878). After her father's death, her mother moved to the Stroud mansion in Stroudsburg where she kept a hotel called the Mansion House. In June 1847, Emeline was married there to Jacob L. Wyckoff (1815–1887) of Mendham, New Jersey. The mansion is now the home of the Monroe County Historical Association. *Monroe County Historical Association, Stroudsburg, Pennsylvania, 73.V.1.*

Samplers of the Lehigh Valley

EASTON SAMPLERS AND MARY RALSTON'S SCHOOL

Mrs. Mary Ralston may have set the trend in eastern Pennsylvania for large samplers featuring impressive buildings surrounded by heavy floral borders worked in wool. Emeline Eagles' sampler was made under her instruction between 1832 and 1834 (Fig. 505), and therefore, a number of similar samplers are now attributed to her teaching (Figs. 506, 507).[1] Also, related motifs suggest she was responsible for earlier pictorial samplers which are unique in having their architectural elements outlined with cotton thread (Figs. 509–513).[2] Pieces now attributed to Mary Ralston's recently discovered school were worked from 1813 through 1834, and several later examples were almost certainly made under her influence if not under her instruction. Although a number of women kept schools in Easton dur-

1. In 1984, Agnes Webb was the first to recognize that Emeline Eagles' sampler was the key to a group of samplers worked at Mary Ralston's school. The research was begun by Mrs. Vertie Knapp, then Curator of the Monroe County Historical Association.

2. This technique was recognized by Dorothy McCoach, a textile conservator in Bethlehem. She has generously shared her research pertaining to this group of embroideries.

ing the early nineteenth century, no others are known to have taught there consistently for such a long period.[3]

Mary Ralston was born in Philadelphia on November 1, 1772, and baptized Maria Dorothea Endress at Saint Michael's and Zion Lutheran Church. She was third among the seven children of Johann Zacharias Endress (1726–1810), a brewer from Lowenstein-Wertheim, who arrived on the ship *Chance* in 1766, and married, as his second wife, the widow Anna Maria (Henrici) Sansfelt (d.1798). Endress quickly amassed a considerable fortune and extensive property in Philadelphia but as an active patriot he suffered severe losses during the Revolution. When the British occupied the city, he moved his family to Northampton County, but they returned in 1778, and he was determined to reestablish his business. During the following decade, he achieved some success, but new financial difficulties forced him to move to Elkton, Maryland, in 1789. He later lived with family members in Lancaster and died at Mary Ralston's home in Easton in 1810.[4] Despite the turmoil of the Revolutionary period, this well-educated man provided a good education for his children. His son, Christian F. L. Endress (1775–1827), graduated from the University of Pennsylvania in 1790, and from 1801 until 1815 he was the much respected and influential pastor of Easton's Lutheran Church.[5] No records of Mary's education have been found, but attendance at Philadelphia schools no doubt made possible her career as a teacher and the successful management of her affairs during a long widowhood.

Mary Endress married Isaac Ralston, a native of Northampton County, at the First Reformed Church of Lancaster on November 1, 1799, and their only child, Mary Ann Endress Ralston, was born December 16, 1802.[6] Details of Isaac Ralston's death are unknown, but Mary commenced teaching in a rented room in Easton's Union Academy building sometime between 1805 and 1810,[7] and about 1812, she opened a private girls' school in her home in Easton. In that year she bought property on Fermor Street, just opposite the Academy building,[8] and taught there until she moved to Spring Garden Street in 1829 (Fig. 508). Mary was assisted by her daughter, and in January of 1835, they were among several teachers of private schools who were chosen to receive pupils from district schools on special terms.[9]

Mary Ralston evidently retired from teaching in the early 1840s, and having

3. Estoy Reddin, ed., *Two Hundred Years of Life in Northampton County, Pa.* (Easton, Pa.: Northampton County Bicentennial Commission, 1976), 89–93.

4. Don Yoder, ed., *Pennsylvania German Immigrants, 1709–1786* (Baltimore: Genealogical Publishing Co., 1980), 207–8, 276–87.

5. Preston R. Laury, *The History of the Allentown Conference of the Ministerium of Pennsylvania* (Kutztown, Pa.: Kutztown Publishing Co., 1926), 133.

6. Isaac was the son of James Ralston and Sallie King (Egle, *Notes and Queries* [1894–1901; reprint, 1970], 316–18).

7. Reddin, *Two Hundred Years*, 90.

8. Northampton County Deed Book B4, 118. Christian Endress et ux to Mary Ralston, recorded June 23, 1814. Property on the west side of Fermor Street; 24 feet on street, 70 feet deep.

9. Uzal W. Condit, *The History of Easton, Pennsylvania* (Easton, Pa.: G. W. West, 1885), 381.

Fig. 506. *Catharine Shimer December 15th 1829.* Silk, cotton, and wool on linen; 16½″ x 17¾″. Within this group, Catharine's sampler is now the earliest example to include wool. As with most signed examples from Mary Ralston's school, an exact date is given, and, in keeping with earlier practice, the windows of the buildings are outlined with three-ply S-twist cotton thread. Also, in the characteristic Ralston manner, the linen ground is sewn to a cotton muslin backing. Catharine Shimer (1815–1904) was the daughter of Easton miller Abraham Shimer (1785–1859) and Margaret Leidy. She married John Schweitzer Oberly (1809–1887) and had six children.
Private collection.

sold her Easton property, she moved with her daughter to Lehighton, about thirty-two miles from Easton. Mary was deeply devoted to her daughter, and when Mary Ann died unmarried in 1845, Mrs. Elizabeth Shewell Lorraine Swift (1795–1872) wrote a touching poem about her loss, which was published in Easton newspapers and elsewhere.[10] When reporting Mary Ralston's death in Lehighton on April 13, 1850, the *Easton Democrat and Argus* observed that she "had resided in this place, where for many years she conducted a female school. Her many moral and social virtues made a lasting impression upon the affections of this community."[11]

Recognizable samplers from Mary Ralston's school are now emerging with amazing frequency, and because of the length of her teaching, it appears likely that they may eventually be one of Pennsylvania's largest groups of embroideries. Her school, however, should not be confused with the *Easton School* named on samplers of 1813, 1822, and 1827. This was a Quaker school in Burlington County, New Jersey (see Figs. 538, 539).

10. Ethan Allen Weaver, comp., *Poets and Poetry of the Forks of the Delaware* (Germantown, Pa., 1906), 265.
11. Issue of April 18, 1850. In her will of November 10, 1847, Mary Ralston requested that she be buried in Philadelphia's Laurel Hill Cemetery and that Mary Ann be moved there (Carbon County File 108). This request was honored by her executors.

Fig. 507. *Sarah Dawes Aged 12 years,* c.1830. Silk, wool, and silk-embroidered velvet appliqué on linen; 21¼″ x 30¼″. Sarah's name and age are hidden by the frame. The same mansion appears on a very similar unsigned sampler, which also has silk-embroidered black velvet for the centers of several flowers. Another magnificent undated example is signed *Mary Ann Innes/ Easton* (both in private collections). Sarah Dawes (d.1854) was the daughter of Joseph Dawes (d.1861), an Easton millstone maker, and Susanna Yohe (1781–1833). She married Levi Bennett (1815–1876) and had three children.
Northampton County Historical Society, Easton, Pennsylvania, 73.V.1.

208 Spring Garden Street · Easton · Pennsylvania
circa 1812.

Fig. 508. House on Spring Garden Street, Easton, drawn by Joseph A. Galantino, 1980. Built by Samuel Sitgreaves about 1812, this house was sold to Mary Ralston by his executors in April 1829, and she kept her school here until she sold the property to Sarah Maxwell in May 1835. The samplers in Figures 505–507 were no doubt worked here.
Photograph courtesy of Jay A. Miers, Sr.

Fig. 509. *Maria Green Easton/ Aged 16. Years May. 3ᵈ. 1813.* Silk and cotton on linen; 13³⁄₁₆″ x 13³⁄₈″. Characteristics of this early group are the layered format with small buildings, the evergreen trees with the trunk extending into the foliage, an irregular vine border, and the practice of outlining windows and other architectural elements with white cotton thread. The earliest known example was worked by Maria's sister Elizabeth (1800–1878) and dated *February 22ᵈ 1813* (Allentown Art Museum). Maria Green (1797–1865) was the daughter of Benjamin Green (1770–1852) and Elizabeth Trail (1777–1816) who lived at Fourth and Spring Garden streets in Easton. She married Enoch S. Clark of Monroeville on November 21, 1818.
Private collection.

Fig. 510. *Sarah Wagener Aged 12 Years 1813.* Silk and cotton on linen; 12¼″ x 12³⁄₈″. In every way, Sarah's work is typical of this early Easton group. Sarah Wagener (1800–1873) was the daughter of David Wagener (1770–1854) and Rosanna Beidleman (1775–1848). In 1823 she married bricklayer Joseph Howell (1798–1889), and they had ten children.
Northampton County Historical Society, Easton, Pennsylvania, 43.V.1.

Fig. 511. *Susan Barnet/ 1814.* Silk and cotton on linen; 13½″ x 13½″. Susan worked the most intricate example within this early Easton group. The covered bridge was no doubt the bridge over the Delaware River between Easton and Phillipsburg, New Jersey. Designed by Cyrus Palmer of Newburyport, Massachusetts, it was begun in 1794 and completed in 1806. Susan's grandfather Henry Barnet was a member of the bridge commission. Susan's sister Eliza Barnet (1796–1867) worked a sampler in 1814 much like Maria Green's (Fig. 509), and her sampler, and those of Maria and Elizabeth Green, have frames identical to Susan's. Susan Barnet (1798–1852) was the daughter of Easton tanner William Barnet, Sr. (c.1757–1829), and Elizabeth Stone. In 1822, she married John M. Hoeber (d.1832), a merchant of Butzville. They had two children.
Moravian Historical Society, Nazareth, Pennsylvania, 1181.

Fig. 512. *Elizabeth Herster Easton June 22ᵈ/ 1821.* Silk and cotton on linen; 14″ x 18″. This is the earliest-known sampler within this group to have the heavy floral border typical of later examples from Mary Ralston's school, but it is worked in silk rather than wool. The outline use of cotton continues, and the tree at left resembles those on the samplers of 1813 (Figs. 484, 485). Elizabeth Herster (1809–1885) was the daughter of George Herster (1788–1819) and Susanna Mixsell (1793–1865) of Easton. She married John Tindall (1807–1886) on March 12, 1834, and they had three daughters.
Private collection.

Fig. 513. *A. M. Kisselbach January 9ᵗʰ 1822.* Silk, cotton, and linen on linen; 10½″ x 12″. Here the small houses resemble those worked by Susan Barnet (Fig. 511), and the border is much like Elizabeth Herster's (Fig. 512). Anna Maria Kisselbach (b.1807) was the daughter of Easton tax collector Christian Kisselbach (1789–1848) and Elizabeth. She worked an alphabet sampler naming *Easton* in 1821 with a band pattern related to the borders on Easton samplers of 1813 (private collection).
Northampton County Historical Society, Easton, Pennsylvania, no acc. no.

ELIZABETH MASON AND THE
SAMPLERS OF KUTZTOWN

The colorful samplers of Kutztown first received recognition in 1915 when the work of Helena Kutz (Fig. 514) was illustrated in the *Centennial History of Kutztown* with firm documentation by its maker that it was worked at Mr. Mason's school under the instruction of Mrs. Mason. Former students recalled that William Mason married a "lady from Pricetown" shortly after his arrival in Kutztown, and that they had three children during the years that they kept the school.[12]

The "lady from Pricetown" was Elizabeth Baish Hains Mason (1797–1875), the fifth and youngest child of Philadelphia cabinetmaker Adam Hains (1768–1846) and Margaret Baish (d.1855). Her father is now famous in the field of American decorative arts for his superb labeled pembroke table in the collection of the Winterthur Museum.[13] The son of Heinrich and Anna Catharine Hahns, he was born in Philadelphia on February 28, 1768. His father was the proprietor of the Spread Eagle Tavern, and by about 1789, father and son had Anglicized their names to Henry and Adam Hains. In 1791, Adam married Margaret Baish, the daughter of Philadelphia cordwainer Martin Baish, and the city directory of 1793 describes him as a cabinetmaker at 135 North Third Street. In the year of Elizabeth's birth, the removal of his "cabinet manufactory" to 261 South Market Street was announced in *The Pennsylvania Journal* on May 18, 1797.

What prompted Hains to leave Philadelphia is uncertain. The city directory of 1799 described him as a cabinetmaker at 261 High Street (also known as Market Street) and as a grocer at this address in 1802, but by 1803 he and his wife had disposed of their inherited Philadelphia real estate and soon thereafter moved to Berks County. Elizabeth was then about six years old and whether or not she later attended Philadelphia schools is unknown. The possibility is suggested, however, by her will of 1869 wherein she devised "to my daughter Mary M. H. Smith my embroidered picture representing Rebecca at the well."[14] It is conceivable that this was a Berlin wool-work picture made in later life, but more likely it was a pictorial silk embroidery worked during her girlhood, and therefore it was probably made while attending a Philadelphia school or possibly one in Harrisburg.

Even though Philadelphia was scarcely farther from Pricetown than Easton was, it is also possible that Elizabeth Hains attended Mary Ralston's school in Easton. In any case, she was probably acquainted with Mrs. Ralston through her parents who would surely have known the Endress family in Philadelphia. The German families of Henry Hains and Zachariah Endress both lived in the vicinity of Vine and Third streets and both were members of Saint Michael's and Zion Lutheran

---

12. *Centennial History of Kutztown . . . 1815–1915* (Kutztown, Pa.: Kutztown Publishing Co., 1915), 97.

13. Carl M. Williams, "Adam Hains of Philadelphia," *ANTIQUES,* May 1947, 316–17.

14. Berks County, Pennsylvania, Wills 13:127.

Fig. 514. *Helena Kutz her/ Work in the 11ᵗʰ Year/ of her age 1842.* Wool and silk on linen; 16¼″ x 19¼″. Depicted here is the Old Saint John's Union Church in Kutztown, a frame building used by the Lutheran and Reformed congregations from 1791 until it was replaced by a brick church in 1876. Across White Oak Street, at the intersection of Walnut Street, is the Franklin Academy, which was erected in 1835–1836 and survives today as a private residence. This school was incorporated in 1838, and continued for about twenty years. It was intended to be a nonsectarian advanced school for boys, and there is no evidence that girls were admitted. Helena Kutz (1831–1925) was the daughter of Benjamin Kutz (1806–1871) and Sarah Sittler (1806–1892). She married Jonathan Biehl (1827–1888).
The Kutztown Area Historical Society Museum, no acc. no.

Church where Adam Hains and Mary Endress were baptized in 1768 and 1772. The teaching careers of Mary Ralston and her daughter had drawn to a close before the earliest-known sampler from Elizabeth Mason's school was made, but it is reasonable to assume that Elizabeth Mason was aware of the needlework from Mary Ralston's long-lasting school in Easton, which was then an important Delaware River community and trade center.

The schoolchildren of Kutztown remembered William Mason as an excellent teacher who had a library and sold books, but some "were afraid of him because he seemed so gay and stylish and spoke English while we spoke only German."[15] The 1850 census of Berks County reveals that Mason was then teaching in Reading and that his children were born between 1829 and 1837. No marriage date has been found for William Mason and Elizabeth Hains, but he probably commenced teaching in Kutztown about 1827 or 1828 and departed before 1850. The records of Christ Episcopal Church in Reading include the baptism of their third child, "Mary Margaret Mason, the daughter of William and Eliza Baish Mason of Kutztown," which took place on August 5, 1837.[16] Mason is believed to have left

---

15. *Centennial History,* 97. William Mason (b.1801) was the son of Allen Mason and Esther Scarlet of Robeson Township, Berks County.

16. *Records of Christ Episcopal Church, Reading, Berks County, Pennsylvania, 1825–1850* (Salt Lake City, Utah: The Genealogical Society, 1947), 23.

Fig. 515. *Mary Butz/ her Work/ In 1842.* Wool and silk on linen; 17¼″ x 24⅛″. Mary worked the largest and most elaborate rendition of Old Saint John's Church and the Franklin Academy. For another example by an eight-year-old girl in 1841, see Ring, *Treasures,* 49. Mary Butz (1829–1913) was the daughter of Egedus Butz (1805–1890) and Elizabeth Bieber (1810–1877). She married David Kemp.
Collection of Joan Stephens.

Kutztown because the prosperity of his school declined after the opening of the Franklin Academy in 1835.[17]

Adam Hains left his entire estate to his wife, and in her will of June 8, 1846 (proved 1855), Margaret Baish Hains devised "unto the sole and separate use of my daughter Eliza married to William Mason the sum of one thousand dollars."[18] In 1869, Elizabeth Mason bequeathed to her husband their house and land on Elm Street in Reading, for his lifetime, and named her two sons as executors.[19]

---

17. *Centennial History,* 97.
18. Berks County Wills 10:296.
19. Ibid., 13:127.

Fig. 516. *By E B Mason Catharine Reeser her Work In 1842.* Wool and silk on linen; 22″ x 25½″. Elizabeth Mason evidently wanted this lavish composition to be recognized as her original design. Nearly identical pieces signed with her name were worked by Caroline E. Bieber in 1843 (Skinner, October 6, 1979, Lot 137), and by Catharine Graeff with unknown date (private collection).
Private collection.

THE LEHIGH VALLEY STYLE

A number of spectacular samplers of the Lehigh Valley cannot be confidently assigned to specific schools. They often bear some resemblance to Ralston work as well as to embroideries from Elizabeth Mason's school in Kutztown (Figs. 514–516), and to a signed example from Esther Hudders' school in Catasauqua (Fig. 519). The samplers in Figures 517 and 518 fall into this category.

Of special interest is the sampler of Sarah Ann Dreisbach (Fig. 517), for three others were almost certainly worked under the same instructress during a ten-year time span. Sarah Ann Graffin signed a nearly identical piece with the same blue building and the same verse in 1839. In 1829, Elizabeth Wilson Horner used silk and cotton in the Ralston manner, and Elizabeth Mary Kern dated a similar composition *June 29, 1830.*[20] Each example includes the distinctive tree with multicolored diamond-shaped leaves that is found in a related form on the Kisselbach sampler of 1822 (Fig. 513). These four girls all lived in or near the Scotch settlement at Bath, which was almost equidistant between Easton and Catasauqua.

One noteworthy teacher, who may have been responsible for many samplers from this region, has thus far been linked to just a single example (Fig. 519). However, its quality and the length of her teaching career suggest that she directed the work on many of the bold and brilliantly colored samplers of the Lehigh Valley. Esther Pritchard Hudders (1807–1887), the daughter of Amos Pritchard and Louisa Blakslee, was born in Waterbury, Connecticut, but she grew up near Springville in Susquehanna County, Pennsylvania, where she attended the Montrose Academy.[21] She was teaching school in Highland Township, Chester County, when she met John Hudders (1812–1881), a wheelwright and a native of Columbia. They were married September 8, 1833, and shortly thereafter they moved to the "Irish Settlement" near Bath, where John managed a farm for his uncle, James Clyde. In 1837, he opened a wheelwright shop in South Easton, but with little success, and they returned to the Irish Settlement in 1842. They were childless, and with her sister, Betsy Pritchard, Esther taught in Bath from 1842 until 1847. By 1847, both John and Esther Hudders were teaching, and in 1849 they settled permanently in Catasauqua where they became respected educators. Esther instructed girls in sewing and embroidery as well as in more advanced subjects, and she was regarded as a "woman of great intellectual force and ability."[22]

---

20. The Horner sampler belongs to the Northampton County Historical Society and is recorded at DAPC; the others are privately owned.

21. Susquehanna Academy in Montrose was chartered in 1816 and opened in 1818. The name was changed to the Montrose Academy around 1850, and in 1857 it became a normal school.

22. James L. Laux, *History of the Public Schools of Catasauqua* (Catasauqua, Pa.: Alumni Association of Catasauqua Schools, 1914), 52–7.

Fig. 517. *Sarah Ann Dreisbach November 18th 1838.* Wool on linen; 17½″ x 25″. Sarah Anna Dreisbach (1822–1909) was the daughter of Jacob Dreisbach, Jr. (1794–1825), a tanner, and Magdalina Bleim (1798–1861) of Lehigh Township. She married Augustus Getz (1820–1870). They lived in Bethlehem and had five children.

Moravian Museum, Bethlehem, 1025.

Fig. 518. *Maria Meyer April 22th. 1841 South Whitehall. AK.* Silk and wool on linen; 14″ x 14″. The heart-shaped centers of Maria's flowers also appear on a sampler worked by Maria Esther Eberhard, c.1840, at the Lehigh County Historical Society. Maria Meyer (b.1825) was the daughter of George Meyer (1790–1865) and Rebecca Gangwehr. She married Joseph Diehl in 1842 and William Burger in 1847. *Private collection.*

Fig. 519. *Paulina C. Roth/ Work'd this in 1850.* Wool on linen; 17″ x 19⅛″. Paulina named her teacher *Esther Hudders* and included the names of her parents. Paulina Catharine Roth (b.c.1834) was the daughter of Joseph Roth and Mary of Catasauqua.

Allentown Art Museum, 80.04.

Fig. 520. *Leah Young daughter of Joseph and Mariah C/ Young wrought this sampler in the year 1847* and she named *Mary Tidball* at the end of a four-line verse. Wool and linen on linen; 25¾″ x 24¾″. Like the Borland sisters, Leah worked two red hummingbirds. Leah, the eldest child of Joseph and Mariah Catherine Young, was born in Ohio about 1831. Between 1836 and 1840, she moved with her parents and three younger children to Nottingham, Washington County, and later to Peters Township.
Private collection.

Western Pennsylvania Samplers

Big, bold flowers and exotic trees characterize a striking group of large samplers worked in Washington County during the final years of the schoolgirl needlework era (Figs. 520, 521). Abagail Higbee worked the earliest known example in 1838 and *Mary A McCosh* was evidently her teacher.[1] Four girls named *Mary Tidball* or *Mary T* on samplers of 1840 and 1847, suggesting that Mary McCosh may have become Mary Tidball between 1838 and 1840. Probably she also taught Jane Gibson, who worked related flowers and birds above a homey red brick house in 1852.[2]

Most of these sampler makers were the daughters of farmers in Peters Township, but schoolmistress Mary Tidball has not been identified. She may have been the Mary Tidball who joined a newly formed Christian Church in Peters Township about 1839, as did Obadiah Higbee, father of the sampler maker Abagail Higbee.[3] The exuberant sampler patterns offer no convincing clues to the origin or background of this schoolmistress, but her scholars named their parents in the style favored from New Jersey to the Susquehanna Valley of Pennsylvania.

---

1. Eleven-year-old Abagail Higbee named her parents, Obadiah and Sarah Higbee. See *The Sampler Engagement Calendar, 1993* (East Lyme, Connecticut: S. & C. Huber, 1993), 40.
2. Joseph and Isabella Gibson are named on Jane's sampler, now in a private collection. Where the Gibson family lived is unknown.
3. Boyd Crumrine, ed., *History of Washington County, Pennsylvania* (Philadelphia: L. H. Everts & Co., 1882), 895.

Fig. 521. *Elizabeth Borland daughter of Andrew and Elizabeth/Borland wrought this sampler in the year 1847* and *Mary Tidball* was her instructress. Wool and linen on linen; 26⅛″ x 25″. Three Borland sisters worked samplers with Mary Tidball. Rebecca, aged eleven in 1840, placed a red house amid bold flowers and trees within Leah Young's border (Fig. 520). See *A&W,* March 1, 1991, 174. Margaret A. was sixteen when she worked a piece similar to Elizabeth's sampler in 1847 and named *Mary T* (DAPC). Each girl included two hummingbirds. Elizabeth (b.c.1833) was the daughter of Andrew Borland (1793–1860) and Elizabeth McClure. She married J. R. McClure, and Margaret A. married John Bell. *Private collection.*

NEEDLEWORK OF
NEW JERSEY

Nᴇᴡ Jᴇʀsᴇʏ was first settled by the Dutch, on the Hudson River (at Bergen and Hoboken), and the Swedes, along the Delaware River, but it was ceded to the English in 1664 and named in honor of one of its proprietors, Sir George Carteret, a native of the Island of Jersey. A Quaker colony was established in West Jersey in the 1670s, and the province was divided into East and West Jersey from 1674 until 1702 when New Jersey became a united royal colony. It was administered by the governor of New York until 1738 and maintained two capitals, Burlington and Perth Amboy, until 1790.

Samplers of New Jersey

In a survey of samplers conducted by the Massachusetts Society of the Colonial Dames of America in 1920, entries from New Jersey were outnumbered only by those of Massachusetts.[1] In their subsequent publication by Bolton and Coe, forty-six eighteenth-century New Jersey samplers are described, including the earliest recorded example to name a schoolmistress.[2] On her sampler of 1743, Hannah Foster of Evesham Township, Burlington County, clearly stated that *Elizabeth Sullivan taught me.* Like many Quaker girls of that region, the fifteen-year-old Hannah named her parents and grandparents, as well as four sisters.[3] Hannah's teacher

Fig. 522. *Mary Antrim/ 1807.* The date appears in calligraphy on paper at the top of the original frame. Silk and painted paper on linen; 17″ x 16¾″. A related piece, without the lady rider, was worked by Mary Shreve in 1807 (Burlington County Historical Society). Attributed to Mary Antrim (1795–1884), the daughter of weaver John Antrim (1766–1849) and Sarah Rogers (1772–1815) of Burlington Township. She married Isaac Davis (1796–1884) in 1819, and they lived in Bordentown. *Author's collection.*

---

1. B&C, iii.
2. Probably of Chester County origin is an alphabet sampler measuring 8¾″ x 4⅛″ and signed *IW AW/ WROUGHT BY/ ANN WALTERS/ TAUGHT BY MARY/ BROWN 1731/ RW IW EW* (collection of Joan Stephens).
3. Hannah Foster, the daughter of William Foster and Hannah Core, was one of twelve children. Her mother was a minister in the Society of Friends and attended the New York Yearly Meeting with Rebecca Jones in 1770 (Amelia Mott Gummere, *The Journal and Essays of John Woolman* [Philadelphia, 1922], 538).

Fig. 523. *Charlotte Hough/ Daughter of/ Samuel and Susan/nah Hough Aged/ 10 Years 1799 Sarah Shoemaker.* Silk on linen; 16⅜″ x 14¾″. Charlotte's work is the latest example among six samplers that name schoolmistress *Sarah Shoemaker* between 1786 and 1799. Two unlocated pieces naming *Sarah Shoemaker* are listed in Bolton and Coe (43, 77). For the earliest recorded example, see Krueger, *Gallery,* Fig. 30. Charlotte Hough (1789–1844) was the daughter of Samuel Hough and Susannah Newbold who lived at Meadow Farm, near Juliustown, Burlington County. Charlotte died unmarried as did her eldest sister, Elizabeth Hough (1778–1861), who named *Sarah Shoemaker* on a sampler of 1794 (privately owned). *Collection of Joan Stephens.*

was Elizabeth Sampson Sullivan (1713–1755), a young Englishwoman by birth, who had recently become a widow (for the second time) as well as recently becoming a Quaker. She had survived an incredible series of hardships during a tumultuous life. Yet undaunted, "she settled steadily to the business of school-keeping, with which and her needle, she maintained herself handsomely" even while traveling as a Quaker minister.[4] Her teaching career, however, was relatively brief, for on September 14, 1746, she married Aaron Ashbridge (1712–1776), a prosperous farmer of Chester County, Pennsylvania. Yet she did not rest from her ministry, and she died nine years later while on a preaching mission in Ireland. In 1760, Ashbridge married the widow Mary Marsh Tomlinson, the sister of Philadelphia schoolmistress Ann Marsh (see Figs. 347, 373).

The only eighteenth-century New Jersey schoolmistress presently known through tangible evidence of her teaching is Sarah Shoemaker, whose name appears on six samplers worked between 1786 and 1799, and some of these are known to have been made by Burlington County girls (Fig. 523). These samplers, however, are not noticeably similar, and pieces lacking Sarah Shoemaker's name probably remain unrecognized. She is said to have taught in Pemberton by Bolton and Coe, though heirs of the Hough sampler makers believe she taught in Julius-

---

4. "Some Account of the Life of Elizabeth Ashbridge," an autobiography edited by William Evans and Thomas Evans, *The Friends Library* (Philadelphia, 1840), 4:10–24.

town. Unless she worked as a governess, it now seems most likely that she taught in Mount Holly during the 1790s. She was probably the same Sarah Shoemaker accepted from Northern Philadelphia by the Mount Holly Monthly Meeting in September 1789, along with the Joseph Earl family who had moved from Upper Springfield;[5] and in 1797, Sarah Shoemaker's name was worked on Esther Earl's sampler.[6]

Although needlework from their schools is now unknown, other eighteenth-century New Jersey teachers have received recognition. Among them was Mrs. Rogers in Trenton who taught the daughters of prominent Philadelphians while the British occupied that city during the Revolution. Nancy Shippen was with Mrs. Rogers in 1777 when her mother advised her that "Your Pappa thinks you had better work a pr of ruffles for General Washington if you can get proper muslin." She also urged her not to "offend Miss Jones by speaking against the Quakers."[7] Whether or not this was the much beloved Rebecca Jones is now uncertain. Another notable Trenton schoolmistress was Madame Mary Dunbar (1732–1808) who taught three generations of Trenton girls. Among her students were several daughters of the Quaker printer Isaac Collins (1746–1817). They entered her school at the age of three and continued until the age of thirteen when they were enrolled at Trenton Academy, of which their father was an original proprietor.[8] The daughter of Susanna Collins (1781–1876) recalled Madame Dunbar's success in teaching needlework: "My mother at the age of seven years, had completed a set of six fine linen shirts for her father, all made by her own little fingers. She used to tell how pleased her parents were when she took them home, and how every hem and buttonhole was examined and commended."[9] Isaac Collins later moved to New York and his younger children attended the Nine Partners' Boarding School. His daughter Susanna taught there before her marriage to Richard Morris Smith in 1810.

Among the most appealing of New Jersey samplers is a small group made by Burlington County girls at an unknown school between 1804 and 1807 (Figs. 522, 524, 525). The girls who worked these samplers are believed to have lived in the vicinity of Burlington, Wrightstown, or Mount Holly, but it is unlikely that they could have walked to the same day school. They probably attended a boarding school, perhaps in Mount Holly or Burlington.

---

5. Mount Holly, Burlington County, New Jersey, Monthly Meeting Minutes 1776–1827, 143–4.

6. B&C, 43.

7. A. Shippen to Nancy Shippen (1763–1841), September 22, 1777 (Armes, *Nancy Shippen: Her Journal Book* [1935], 40–1).

8. Trenton Academy (1782–1884) was organized in February 1781. James Burnside was the first teacher. Girls were admitted, but there was no preceptress. In 1787, John Mease from Philadelphia was employed and Mrs. Mease was permitted to use the unfurnished room in the Academy for her girls' school. About 1800, the Academy leased the Brick School House on the Presbyterian Church grounds for the girls' school, but the preceptress is unknown (William L. Dayton, *Historical Sketch of The Trenton Academy* [Trenton, 1881], 16, 28). Eliza Hazard named *Trenton Academy* on her sampler of 1812 (Old Barracks Museum, Trenton).

9. *Reminiscences of Isaac and Rachel (Budd) Collins with an Account of Some of their Descendants* (Philadelphia, 1893), 39–42.

Fig. 524. *Mary Bowker 1804.* Silk and painted paper on linen; 16½″ x 16½″. Mary's lady on a horse has a painted paper head, and her pattern for the dress and hat was almost identical to the one used by her classmates Ann Stockton (Fig. 525), Ann Folwill (Brant and Cullman, *Small Folk* [1980], 117), and Nancy Platt (B&C, Pl. LIX). Mary Bowker (c.1790–1875) was the daughter of Joseph Bowker (d.1802) and Mary Lame, and they lived in Mt. Holly. Mary married Charles Brown and had two daughters. *Collection of Thomas E. Rock.*

Fig. 525. *Ann Stockton 1804.* Silk and painted paper on linen; 16½″ x 16½″. Several Ann Stocktons lived in the Springfield and Mt. Holly area, so this sampler maker cannot be identified. She was probably a sister or a cousin of Lydia Stockton, who worked a similar undated sampler (part of the Alexander W. Drake Sale, American Art Galleries, New York, March 12, 1913, Lot 764; illustrated in *The Delineator*, September 1903, 304). *Private collection.*

Burlington Academy in the town of Burlington was organized in 1794 and it continued as an English and classical school for thirty years, but little is known of its program for girls or of the women who taught there. Advanced needlework instruction must have been available in 1806 since the Academy's name appears on a pictorial silk embroidery of that date.[10]

The broadside in Figure 526 describes Mrs. Staughton's school in Burlington, but the date of its establishment and its exact duration remain unknown. Maria Staughton was the wife of the English-born Baptist minister William Staughton, who arrived in Bordentown in 1796 and became associated with an academy founded by Burgess Allison.[11] About 1801, he moved to Burlington where he founded Burlington's First Baptist Church, which he served until 1805. His wife's school was most likely discontinued that year since he was pastor of Philadelphia's First Baptist Church between 1805 and 1811, and on weekday afternoons he taught history, geography, and natural philosophy at Madame Marie Rivardi's Seminary for Young Ladies.[12]

Contemporary with Mrs. Staughton's school, but also of short duration in New Jersey, was a school kept by a seemingly sophisticated but transient schoolmistress named Mrs. Hopkins who kept her boarding school for young ladies in Trenton, Bordentown, and Bloomsbury (now part of Trenton) between 1802 and 1805.[13] In *The True American* of April 22, 1805, she described her school's examination, and named the ten young ladies who were awarded silver medals by "the Rev. Dr. Smith (president) and the Rev. Dr. Hunter (professor of mathematics) at the College of Princeton, the Rev. Dr. Allison of Bordentown, and Richard Stockton, Esq. of Princeton," whom she thanked for their "delicately judicious distribution of the honors." This was Elizabeth J. Hopkins (Mrs. Thomas Hopkins), who opened a school at 200 South Front Street in Philadelphia in November of 1805,[14] and she appeared as Mrs. Hopkins in Philadelphia directories from 1809 until 1811. Probably she was the Mrs. Hopkins teaching in Frederick, Maryland, in 1812, but she was again in Philadelphia in 1818.[15]

At the same time, other New Jersey schools were operating with less fanfare and more lasting results. Woodbury Academy in Woodbury, Gloucester County, was built with the proceeds of a lottery in 1791 and on land given by Joseph Bloomfield, later governor of New Jersey. The Reverend Andrew Hunter, a Presbyterian minister, was the first preceptor, and both Captain James Lawrence

10. *ANTIQUES*, February 1974, 362.
11. William Staughton was born in Warwickshire, England, and came to the United States in 1793.
12. Mary Johnson, "Madame Rivardi's Seminary in the Gothic Mansion," *PMHB* (January 1980), 12–20.
13. *The True American*, Trenton, April 18 and October 17, 1803; March 26 and October 22, 1804. Mr. and Mrs. Thomas Hopkins kept this school. See Thomas Hopkins, *Stockton versus Hopkins* (Philadelphia: printed for the author, 1808), in the Library Company. This relates to the dismissal of Mary F. Stockton, daughter of Richard Stockton, from the Hopkins' School in Trenton. I am indebted to Tessa Cadbury for this information.
14. *Poulson's American Daily Advertiser*, Philadelphia, November 13, 1805.
15. MESDA craftsmen records, Maryland, 45791; *Aurora General Advisor*, Philadelphia, January 1, 1818.

Fig. 526. Broadside for Mrs. Staughton's Boarding School in Burlington, with a description of the subjects taught and the terms, c.1804, 3¼″ x 4⅞″. As was often the case, the girls were expected "to find their own beds and bedding."

The New-York Historical Society.

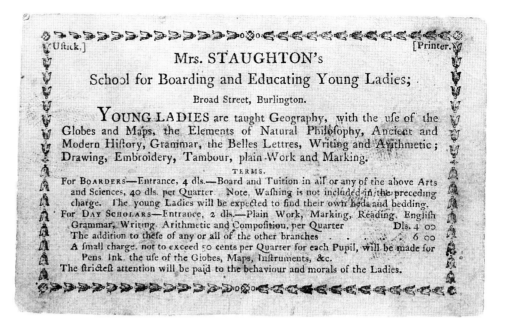

Fig. 527. *Wrought by Ruth Brown/ daughter of Job and Elizabeth Brown./ 5th month./ 1806/ Woodbury Academy.* Silk on linen; 21½″ x 21¼″. Ruth's unusual pattern is meticulously worked and her border of fine tent stitches is reminiscent of Philadelphia samplers (Figs. 361, 362). Ruth Brown (d.1830) was the eldest daughter of Job Brown (d.1831) and Elizabeth Allen (d.1832), who were married at the Salem Friends Meeting in 1790. They lived in Woodbury, where Ruth died unmarried.

New Jersey State Museum, Trenton, New Jersey, 88.11.1

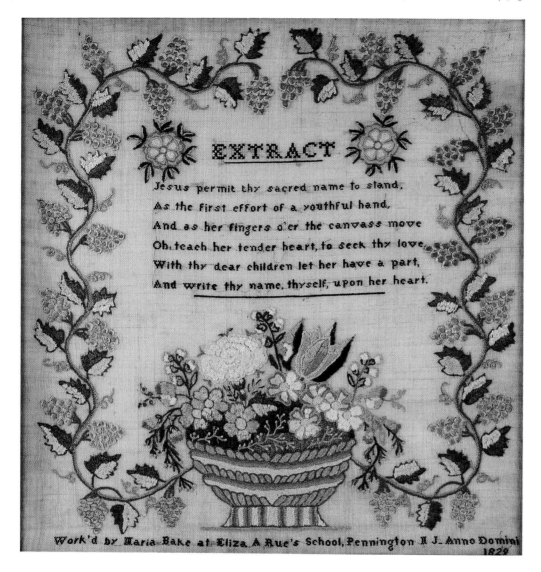

Fig. 528. *Work'd by Maria Bake at Eliza A Rue's School, Pennington NJ. Anno Domini/ 1829.* Silk on linen; 16" x 17". A grapevine flowing from a basket and enveloping an *Extract* is a repetitious feature of samplers from Eliza Rue's school. Two typical examples are in the New Jersey State Museum, and for another, see Allen, *Family Record,* Fig. 127. Maria Bake (1813–1890) was the daughter of Pierson Bake (1790–1866) and Hannah Eccles (1793–1861) of Pennington. She married Woolsey Blackwell on September 29, 1839, and they had three children. *Collection of Joan Stephens.*

(1781–1813) of "Don't give up the ship" fame, and naval hero Stephen Decatur (1779–1820) were once students there.[16] The school was still functioning in 1837.

Nothing is known of a preceptress at Woodbury Academy, but obviously an exceptionally talented woman was teaching in 1806 when Ruth Brown worked her superb sampler (Fig. 527). Ruth's border suggests that her mistress was taught by Ann Marsh, as her delicate work in tent stitch resembles that of Philadelphia samplers (Figs. 361, 362). Regardless of the school's Presbyterian affiliations, the style of dating reveals that this teacher was a Quaker, or she deferred to the fact that Ruth was.

A recognizable group of samplers from Pennington, New Jersey, was made under the instruction of Eliza A. Rue, who taught there during the 1820s and

---

16. Thomas Cushing and Charles E. Sheppard, *History of Gloucester, Salem, and Cumberland Counties, New Jersey* (Philadelphia: Everts & Peck, 1883), 176–7.

Fig. 529. *Matilda Johnston's work wrought/ in the year of our Lord 1838.* Silk on linen; 20½″ x 17″. Matilda named no school or town and not even her age is there to help in her identification. Yet the design and workmanship of her sampler clearly reveal that she must have been taught by Eleanor T. Stephens, probably in Cream Ridge, or possibly at some other location. *Private collection.*

Fig. 530. *Elizabeth E Woodwards work wrought in the/ Year of our lord 1832 under the tuition of/ Eleanor T Stephens Cream Ridge Seminary.* Silk on linen; 20½″ x 17″. The distinctive style of the flowers in this sampler makes it possible to recognize other work from Eleanor T. Stephens' school, such as the sampler in Figure 529. Elizabeth E. Woodward (c.1820–1865) was the daughter of Nimrod Woodward and Catherine of Cream Ridge, Monmouth County. In 1839 she married William Henry Hendrickson (c.1813–1899) of Middletown. They had three children.

Author's collection.

probably much later. This teacher's patterns featured lush baskets of fruit or flowers with heavy grapevines enclosing an extract, and pieces relating to Maria Bake's sampler (Fig. 528) are easily identified. Though often undated, they usually include a record of the maker's parents and siblings. Schoolmistress Eliza A. Rue (1797–1854) was the daughter of the Reverend Joseph A. M. Rue (1751–1826), who was descended from Huguenots of Monmouth County, and Elizabeth Liscomb (1760–1845) of New York. Rue was the Presbyterian pastor in Pennington from 1785 until 1826, and it was most likely after his death that Eliza undertook teaching. Neither she nor her sister Sarah (1790–1852) married, and they are buried in the Pennington Presbyterian churchyard with their parents.

Another group of New Jersey samplers can usually be recognized just by the style of the embroidered flowers and a few minor pictorial motifs (Figs. 529, 530). Several such pieces name the preceptress *Eleanor T. Stephens,*[17] and *Cream Ridge Seminary* also appears on two examples (Fig. 530). This teacher evidently taught from 1827 until 1838 (probably in Cream Ridge, which is near Freehold in Monmouth County), but she remains unidentified. This and the two preceding groups of identifiable New Jersey samplers are known only in small numbers, and at present the state's sampler heritage is dominated by Quaker work from Burlington County.

---

17. Mary Ann Hollinshead, 1827 (Krueger, *Gallery,* Fig. 100); Sarah T. Wikoff's sampler is identical to that in Figure 530 (Pioneer History Museum, Salt Lake City); and Armenia Hutchinson, 1833 (Hunterdon County Historical Society, Flemington, New Jersey). The latter were called to my attention by Mary Jaene Edmonds and Frances K. Faile, respectively.

Fig. 531. *Sarah Jessup/ Evesham School/ 1813.* Silk on linen with ribbon border; 23½″ x 18½″. Sarah's splendid view of the Westtown School was worked under the instruction of Atlantic Matlack, a former Westtown scholar, who kept the Evesham School in the summer of 1813. Sarah's classmate Martha Davis (b.1799) worked an almost identical sampler, including the same verse (private collection), and Martha's cousin Lydia Burrough worked this pattern at the Chesterford School in 1814 (B&C, Pl. XCV). These cousins later attended the Westtown School. Sarah Wilkins Jessup (1801–1861) was the daughter of John Jessup (1773–1826) and Deborah Wilkins (1779–1807). In 1822 she married Joseph Borton (1800–1868).
Collection of Allis B. Borton.

Quaker Samplers of Burlington County

The Quaker schools of Burlington County produced New Jersey's largest group of important samplers and they can be recognized by many common characteristics in both design and technique. Among the appealing pictorial examples that feature buildings, three major variations have emerged (Figs. 531–533, 535). The earliest known group includes pieces naming the *Evesham School 1813* (Fig. 531),[1] and the *Chesterford School 1814.* This type usually has an extract or verse within a vine-and-leaf border. The building is enclosed in an oval formed by an arched sky and a curving front fence with willow trees at either end; swans and sheep are on the lawn, and beyond the gate a straight walk leads to the door of an unmistakable rendition of the Westtown Boarding School in Chester County, Pennsylvania.

The two other principal types name no schools. A loftier Westtown School building and a verse in a floral wreath appear on pieces from the 1820s (Figs. 532,

1. For a similar but unsigned example of questionable date (said to be 1812), see Christie's East Sale 6195, September 30, 1986, Lot 88. It has spangles worked on the curving sky, as does another with a five-bay house, by Ruth Edwards, 1824 (private collection).

Fig. 532. *Kiziah Sharps/ Work wrought A D 1825/ K S the daughter of Isaac Sharp/ And Hannah Sharp his wife was/ Born the 12th day of the 12th mth.* Silk on linen with ribbon border; 23¼" x 23". Three samplers almost identical to Kiziah's were worked in 1823, 1826, and 1830. The earliest is initialed A M M, probably for the teacher (see footnote 2). Kiziah Sharp (b.1810) was the daughter of Isaac Sharp and Hannah Garwood of Medford. She married Allen Prickitt (1812–1886).
Private collection.

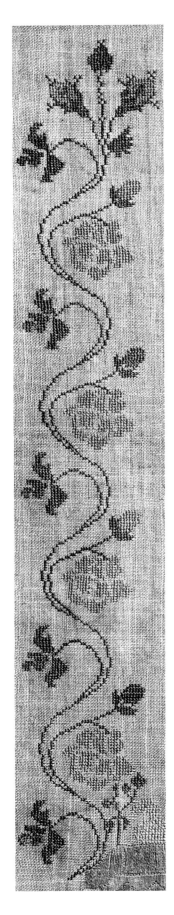

533). These usually have small figures as well as birds and animals beside the building and some have an oversized rooster.[2] A third style, also from the 1820s, has a large five-bay or three-bay house on a fenced mound with the inscription beneath a grapevine garland. On the lawn a giant rooster towers above a man with a gun aimed at a fox amid peaceful sheep and swans (Fig. 535). All examples have backgrounds crowded with typical Quaker motifs, but the most consistent identifiable motif of the Burlington County Quaker samplers is a rose-vine border in which a leaf tendril on one side and a rosebud stem on the other give the appearance of a double vine. Variations, as in Figures 533 and 534, occur in the stitchery of this border, but the cross-stitched style is by far the most common.[3] Samplers related to the three most impressive "building" types occur with a number of recognizable variations and name the Evesham School (Figs. 534, 536), among others in Burlington County and nearby communities.[4]

The Evesham School was established at Upper Evesham (now Medford) in 1784,[5] but the School Trustees' Minutes of 1801 reveal that no women had yet been employed, since they note the desirability of hiring a female who "might teach needlework and obviate the necessity of girls going from such schools, to others, to learn that art."[6] Thereafter the Minutes include scattered references to women teaching for brief periods of usually three to five months. This offers an explanation for the occurrence of identical sampler patterns that name different schools. The Friends schools in Burlington County were day schools with an often changing succession of men and women teachers. Minutes indicate that the frequently unnamed "mistress" seldom taught at the same school for two consecutive years, particularly before 1820.

At present, samplers naming the *Evesham School* are dated 1807, 1813, and 1820, and these dates correspond to three of the five years from 1805 through 1820 when a woman was teaching this school for part of a year. The Evesham Monthly Meeting Minutes of July 30, 1807, state that "A mistress hath been employed one quarter & visited by women trustees." Evidently twelve weeks was long enough for Jane Haines to work her sampler, which is said to have been

---

2. Nearly identical to Figures 532 and 533 are Sarah Ann Hartman, 1823 (Krueger, *Gallery*, Fig. 88); Hannah Austin, 1827 (PB Haskell, Part Five, December 1944, Lot 788); and Ann Reed, 1830 (privately owned). Closely related are Rachel Braddock, 1823 (Brooklyn Museum) and Jemima Braddock, 1828 (PMA). Hartman, Reed, and Rachel Braddock worked the *Friendship* verse in Figure 533.

3. At left, the typical border worked by *Mary W. Cooper/ 1814* (see footnote 14). This border is not totally exclusive to New Jersey and occasionally occurs elsewhere. It is known as a side border on 1829 and 1831 samplers from the East Land School, Little Britain, Lancaster County, Pennsylvania. For one, see *ANTIQUES*, December 1984, 1429.

4. Eleanor Page pictured the Westtown School but named the *Cross Roads School* in 1818 (Monmouth County Historical Society); Mary Hollinshead Risdon named the *Poplar Grove School* in 1814 (Brant and Cullman, *Small Folk* [1980], 118); the *Brick School 1822* and the *West Chester School 1817* are named on samplers at the Moorestown Historical Society. The latter has been mistakenly assigned to Pennsylvania (B&C, 386).

5. Woody, *Quaker Education in the Colony and State of New Jersey* (1923), 185. The name Medford was not in general use until about 1815 (*Medford, Pioneer Township* [Medford, N.J.: Medford Historical Society, 1975], 90–2). Cross Roads was the seat of government for the large township of Evesham.

6. Woody, *New Jersey*, 189.

Fig. 533. *Anna Braddock the daughter of/ William Braddock & Anna his wife/ A B work wrought in the 14th year/ Of her age 1826.* Silk on linen; 22⅛" x 26". Anna's sister, Jemima Braddock, also worked this lofty version of the Westtown School building on a sampler at the age of twelve in 1828. Anna

Braddock (b.c.1813) was the daughter of William Braddock (d.1851) and Anna Rogers of Evesham Township. She may have been the Anna Braddock who married James H. Moore in 1833. She was named Anna Summers in her father's will. *Collection of Joan Stephens.*

Fig. 534. *Esther Gardiner, Evesham School, 1813.* Silk on linen with ribbon border, 22″ x 18¼″. Esther was no doubt also instructed by Atlantic Matlack, and her sampler was placed in a mahogany veneered frame identical to the one on Sarah Jessup's work (Fig. 531). Another classmate was Ann Rogers whose 1813 *Evesham School* sampler was exhibited at the Cincinnati Art Museum in 1909. It was Lot 856 in the Alexander W. Drake Sale at the American Art Galleries in 1913, where its catalogue description would also fit Esther's sampler: "Poplar and willow trees, sheep and cattle in foreground. Graceful border of flowers and leaves. Sampler finished with border of quilled satin ribbon. Mahogany frame of the period." Ann Rogers went to Westtown School with her classmate Martha Davis in 1817. Esther Gardiner (1795–1852) was the daughter of Joseph Gardiner (b.1764) and Mary Wilkins. They lived on a farm near the Evesham Meeting House. Esther died unmarried.

Collection of Esther Thomas Woodward.

much like the work from Westtown School.[7] Early in 1813 "Atlantic Matlack opened school which was superintended by Women Trustees during its continuance which was nearly 5 months."[8] Obviously Atlantic Matlack was responsible for the patterns worked at the Evesham School in 1813 (Figs. 531, 534), and she may have originated the striking vignette of the Westtown School worked by Sarah Jessup with a vine-and-leaf enclosed extract reminiscent of Westtown. This is not surprising, for the twenty-one-year-old Atlantic Matlack had entered Westtown School at the age of eighteen on May 2, 1810, and attended until April 18, 1811. She was the daughter of Moorestown blacksmith Reuben Matlack and Elizabeth Coles. It is also possible that she attended the same Moorestown school where Martha Heuling worked a view of Westtown School on her sampler in 1806.[9]

The Westtown School was a logical subject for sampler embroidery at Quaker schools, since it was an impressive structure housing a much respected institution that many Quaker children aspired to attend.[10] In 1814, Lydia Burrough (b.1800)

7. The sampler of Jane Haines, 1807, is listed in B&C, 166, and on 385, dated 1808. On page 374 it is mistakenly dated 1808 with the name *Julia*. A Jane Haines from Evesham entered Westtown School in September 1809, aged fifteen (Westtown Archives).

8. Evesham Preparative Meeting School Trustees Minutes 1795–1840, April 26, 1813 (Friends Historical Library of Swarthmore College).

9. See Martha Heuling's sampler in B&C, Pl. XCIII and 172. Atlantic Matlack (1791–1826) probably attended the Brick School near her home, where her father was a member of the school committee (Woody, *New Jersey*, 215–17). Atlantic moved to Philadelphia in 1816, married William Thomas (d.1856) in 1818, and died following the birth of her fifth child.

10. At least 261 Burlington County girls had attended Westtown School by 1830, and the majority of samplers that picture Westtown School were made at Burlington County Quaker schools.

Fig. 535. *Martha C Hootons work/ wrought in the 13 year of her/ age 1827.* Silk on linen with ribbon border; 23″ x 24½″. Martha's impressive sampler is the most famous example from New Jersey. It was widely exhibited and illustrated before 1910 as part of the Alexander W. Drake Collection (Huish, 103). It was also in the Theodore H. Kapnek Collection until 1987. Elizabeth Evans worked a very similar sampler with a three-bay house in 1826 (*ANTIQUES,* September 1978, 557).

Another, without the grape garland, was worked by Rachel Haines in 1830 (partly illustrated in *Colonial Homes,* February 1987, 82). In 1830, Rebecca Slim worked the same building and added a giant mouse beside the roosters, sheep, and swans upon her lawn (Eva Johnston Coe's Scrapbook I, 74, at the C-H). Martha C. Hooton's identity has defied discovery. *Private collection; photograph courtesy of Sotheby's.*

Fig. 536. *Hannah Gardiner/ Evesham School/ 1820.* Silk on linen with ribbon border; 22⅝″ x 18″. Hannah worked the border most commonly seen on Quaker samplers of Burlington County. Her instructress was Elizabeth Borton. Hannah Gardiner (1808–1886) was a sister of Esther (Fig. 534). She married Josiah B. Evans of Haddonfield. *Collection of B. Franklin Blair.*

worked a view of the Westtown School while attending the Chesterford School,[11] and it is almost identical to Sarah Jessup's rendition (Fig. 531). Although no records naming the schoolmistress have been found, this offers convincing evidence that Atlantic Matlack was teaching at the Chesterford School in 1814. The location of the Chesterford School has been given as Chester County, Pennsylvania,[12] when, in fact, it was on the road to Camden in what is now Maple Shade, Burlington County, which was within walking distance of Atlantic Matlack's home. The school was kept in a one-room red brick building constructed by Joseph Burrough (the father of Lydia) on a lot he donated for school use in 1811.[13] Lydia and her sister Rachel both left samplers naming the Chesterford School, and they later attended Westtown School where Rachel worked the globe in Figure 434.

Elizabeth Borton taught at the Evesham School for six months in 1820, when

11. B&C, Pl. XCV.

12. Ibid., 386.

13. Edith Cutler, *Maple Shade, A Story of Three Hundred Years, 1682–1982* (Maple Shade, N.J.: Maple Shade Historical Society, 1983), 16. The Chesterford School was still functioning in 1847. Today the building houses the Maple Shade Historical Society. I am indebted to William C. Coles, Jr., for the identification and history of the Chesterford School.

Fig. 537. *Mary Crispin,s work/ wrought in the 11th year/ of her age,* c.1829. Silk on linen with ribbon border; 23" x 23". Mary's house and lawn are identical to Martha Hooton's (Fig. 535), but she omitted the people, and unlike other examples within this group, this sampler includes alphabets. Mary Crispin (c.1819–1910) has not been fully identified.
Burlington County Historical Society, Burlington, New Jersey, 58.5.2.

Hannah Gardiner worked the sampler in Figure 536.[14] The style of the grapes above Hannah's extract resemble those worked by Martha Hooton and suggest that she also was taught by Elizabeth Borton in 1827 (Fig. 535). The Evesham School had no mistress in 1827, although Rebecca H. Engle taught there in 1826, Amy Haines in 1828, and Amy Sykes in 1830 and 1831.[15] All three were Westtown alumnae.

In 1813, when girls at the Evesham School were working elegant views of the Westtown School (Fig. 531), a more simplified version of the same building was being made at the nearby Easton School (Fig. 538).[16] Heretofore assigned to Easton, Pennsylvania, this school was a Friends' school of the Haddonfield Quarter in Evesham Township, and it commenced classes in a newly completed building in 1803. The daughters of Cyrus Moore and Obadiah Engle named the school on

---

14. Evesham Trustees Minutes, December 28, 1820. Probably the same as *Elizabeth Barton, preceptress* on a sampler naming the *Pleasant grove School* in 1814, and worked by Mary W. Cooper with the typical rose-vine border (detail illustrated). A nearly identical sampler names *Laurelgrove School/ Hannah Barton, preceptress/ 1814* (both privately owned). The latter is listed in B&C, 126, 387.

15. Evesham Trustees Minutes, November 28, 1826–February 2, 1832.

16. The *Easton School* was named by Catharine Withcim in 1813 and Hannah E. Moore in 1822 (B&C, 198, 243, 386). The Moore sampler was Lot 941 in the Drake Sale at Anderson Galleries, New York, on March 12, 1913.

Fig. 538. *Eliza Moore/ Easton School/ 1813*, and with the initials *C. M., M. M., and E. C.* for the maker's parents and her schoolmistress. Silk on linen; 18⅞″ x 16⅞″. Eliza's building appears to be a simplified rendition of the Westtown School. Her instructress was Elizabeth Conrow from Moorestown who entered Westtown School in November 1807, and in 1812 and 1813, she taught at the Friend's Easton School, near Lumberton, in Evesham Township, Burlington County. Sarah Mingin also worked a sampler naming the Easton School in 1813 and including the initials *E. C.* (Stephens collection). Eliza Moore (b.1797) was sixth among the eleven children of Cyrus Moore (1760–1842) and Mary Austin (b.1764). She married John Engle. *Northampton County Historical Society, Easton, Pennsylvania, 46.V.1.*

Fig. 539. *Sarah Ann Engle/ Easton School/ E. B./ 1827*. Silk on linen with green ribbon border; 25¼″ x 23″. The Minutes of the Easton Preparative Meeting did not name the schoolmistress at the Easton School in 1827. The initials E. B. could stand for Elizabeth Borton. Abigail Borton kept the school in 1825, Lucy Page in 1830, and Martha Warrington in 1831 to 1832. All three were former Westtown scholars. Sarah Ann Engle (1812–1879) was ninth among the ten children of Obadiah Engle (1763–1843) and Patience Cole (1771–1844). She entered Westtown School in December 1829, and in the year 1834 she taught at the Easton School. (Woody, *Quaker Education in the Colony and State of New Jersey* [1923], 199.) Sarah Ann married Barclay Haines (b.1812) on November 12, 1835. *Private collection.*

Fig. 540. *Rachel Evans/ Pine Grove School/ 1813.* Silk on linen; 16⅝″ x 15″. Rachel's sampler is entirely typical of Quaker work from the Delaware Valley but it could be assigned to no specific area if she had not named her school, which was in Evesham Township. Rachel Borton Evans was the daughter of Jacob Evans (b.1755) and his second wife, Rachel Borton (1774–1844). Rachel's sister Syllania worked a sampler naming the Pine Grove School in 1809. *Collection of Joan Stephens.*

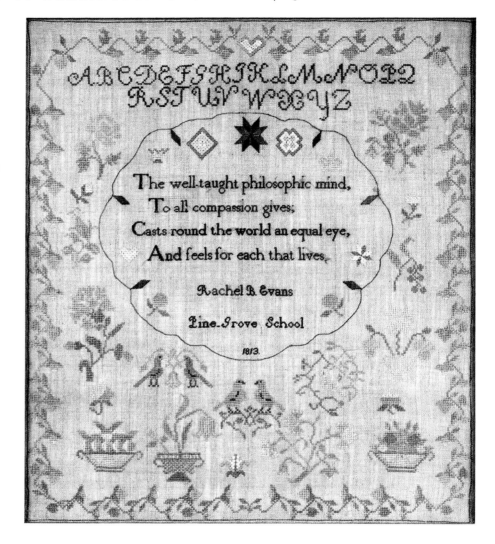

their samplers (Figs. 538, 539), and both men served as trustees of the Easton School which continued through 1870.[17] The location of the Pine Grove School has also met with confusion in the past (Fig. 540).[18] Pine Grove was located east of present-day Medford, in Evesham Township, and the school first opened on December 3, 1792, under the tuition of John Atkinson. Among its teachers were Mary Cowperthwaite, from 1805 to 1809, and Abigail Bradford in 1821.[19] Jacob Evans, the father of sampler makers Rachel and Syllania Evans (Fig. 540), and his son-in-law, Jacob Roberts, both served as trustees of the Pine Grove School, which continued at least until 1830.[20]

17. Woody, *New Jersey,* 194–9.
18. In B&C, 155, a sampler was described as follows: "Tullania Evans. 1809. Pinegrove School. 9 yrs. Born October 6, 1799. Daughter of Jacob and Rachel Evans." On page 387 it was assigned to Charles City County, Virginia. The name *Syllania* was misread, for the maker was the sister of Rachel Evans (Fig. 540), and she was named for her paternal grandmother, Syllania Gaskill Evans. She married Jacob Roberts (c.1798–1855).
19. *Proceedings, Centennial Anniversary, 1809–1909,* Friends' Cropwell Preparative Meeting House, Marlton, New Jersey.
20. Woody, *New Jersey,* 208–11.

Fig. 541. *Tuition by / C A Washington / INGEBER R VANDVER'ˢ / Work in the 12th year / of her age 1829.* Silk, chenille, and appliqued painted velvet on linen, with inscription worked in brown linen; 18¾″ x 18¼″. A nearly identical anonymous piece of 1829 names *Wilmington, Del* (described in Vandever object report, WM). Schoolmistress Catherine A. Washington (c.1791–after 1870) was the daughter of John Washington (d.1833) and Mary Elizabeth. She was born in Philadelphia but from 1805 until 1818 her father kept the Cross Keys Tavern on the Kennett Road (now the northeast corner of Delaware Avenue and Adams Street, Wilmington). By 1850 Catherine was living in the household of her brother, John Henry Washington, a Wilmington basket maker. Ingeber Robinson Vandever (b.1818) was the daughter of Peter Vandever and Ellen Lomax. Vandever succeeded John Washington as keeper of the Cross Keys Tavern and also served as sheriff of New Castle County. Ingeber married Louis Askew and died in Cincinnati.

Winterthur Museum, 90.73.

NEEDLEWORK OF

DELAWARE

Delaware was named after England's Lord de la Warr (1577–1618) by a Virginia sea captain, and although its first settlers were Dutchmen and Swedes, its enduring cultural legacy began with its inclusion in William Penn's vast land grant of 1682. The "Three Lower Counties" had a separate legislative assembly by 1704, but Delaware was ruled by Pennsylvania's governors until the Revolution. In 1787, it was the first state to ratify the Constitution.

The surviving needlework from Delaware is in keeping with the dominant Quaker styles of the Delaware Valley, and the colony's first long-lasting school was established by Friends on Quaker Hill, near Wilmington, in 1748.[1] Few samplers of colonial Delaware are known today, and the women who taught are unidentified, but several teachers of the early Federal period have been recorded, and two samplers of the 1780s include the name of an instructress. The earliest was worked by Ann Tatnall of Wilmington in 1786 (Figs. 542, 544), and she named Mary Askew as her preceptress. Ann's sampler is remarkably similar to Philadelphia's earliest band-pattern samplers. It also includes two of their typical verses, which suggest that Mary Askew was originally from Philadelphia or was taught there. Also attributed to her school is the somewhat simpler sampler made by seven-year-old Frances Canby in the same year (Fig. 543).

Schoolmistress Mary Askew (c. 1743–1825) was most likely the Mary Jones who married William Askew at Wilmington's Trinity Church on April 3, 1765. The record of his death has not been found, but her school was probably the result of early widowhood. On September 24, 1789, Mary married, as his third wife, the elderly widower Vincent Bonsall (d. January 10, 1796), who had mar-

---

1. Wilmington, on the banks of the Christina River, was first called Willingtown after English merchant Thomas Willing who settled there around 1731. Governor George Thomas named the town of Wilmington after Spencer Compton, Earl of Wilmington, in 1739. William Shipley, an English Quaker, was then its most influential citizen. (John A. Munroe, *History of Delaware* [Newark: University of Delaware Press, 1979], 57–8.)

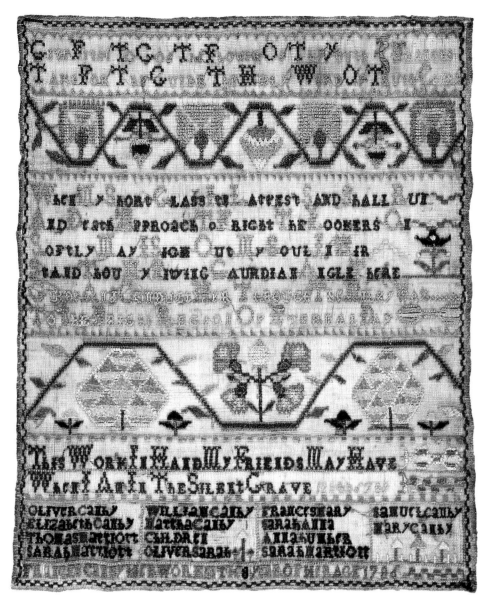

Fig. 543. *Frances Canby Her Work In the 8 year Of Her Age 1786.* Silk on linen; 12″ x 9½″. The similarity of this sampler to the work of Ann Tatnall suggests that Frances was also instructed by Mary Askew. Frances Canby (1778–1833) was the daughter of William Canby (1748–1830) and Martha Marriott (1747–1836) of Wilmington. In 1804 she married Benjamin Ferris (1780–1867), and they had ten children.
Winterthur Museum, 82.284A.

Fig. 542. *Ann Tatnall Her Work Done In The 12 Year Of Her Age 1786 Mary Askew.* Silk on linen; 17″ x 12½″. Ann's sampler relates conspicuously to Philadelphia samplers worked from the 1720s through the 1740s and suggests that her teacher, Mary Askew, was copying her own girlhood embroidery. In the typical Philadelphia fashion, Ann named grandparents, parents, and other family members. Ann Tatnall (1775–1816) was the daughter of Joseph Tatnall (1740–1813) and Elizabeth Lea (1744–1805) of Wilmington. In 1794, she married Thomas Sipple (1765–1798) and in 1800, John Bellah (1777–1824). She had one daughter by Sipple and five children by Bellah.
Photograph from American Samplers *by courtesy of the Massachusetts Society of the Colonial Dames of America.*

ried his first wife before 1747. Mary was certainly well acquainted with Frances Canby's family, for when Bonsall died, Samuel Canby, the uncle of Frances, was coexecutor of his will, and when Mary died at the age of eighty-two in 1825, Frances Canby's husband, Benjamin Ferris, was the executor of her will.[2] A contemporary of Mary Askew was schoolmistress Abigail Giles, whose name was worked on the 1788 sampler of Susannah James of New Castle County, a sampler described by Bolton and Coe in 1921. They also remarked on this sampler's similarity to the 1798 work of Mary James of New Castle County, and this may mean that Abigail Giles continued to teach for at least ten years.[3]

Another important teacher was Wilmington's Mrs. Elizabeth Way (1738–1798), who kept a respected girls' school on Second Street in the 1790s. She was known as "a celebrated teacher of needlework," and also as "a disciplinarian of the old school," because she resorted to the use of necklaces of burrs or morocco spiders to correct the slouch of those who stooped. Elizabeth Way's maiden name remains unknown, although she is said to have been well acquainted with the artist Benjamin West in her youth.[4] Her husband was Joseph Way (b.1728), the uncle of Mary Webb (Fig. 356), and they had three children. Their son John (1762–1833) became Judge of the Court of Common Pleas, but Mrs. Way's last days were darkened by the loss of her daughter Sarah (1764–1798) and her son Joseph (1768–1797) in the yellow fever epidemic.

In Wilmington's *Delaware Gazette* of June 7, 1796, Miss H. Brown proposed opening a school "at her house on Shipley-street" for the instruction of young ladies in the "art of DRAWING, TAMBOURING, PAINTING, MAKING OF LACE, FILLEGREE, ARTIFICIAL FLOWERS & c." No other subjects were mentioned, and the duration of her school is unknown. In the same paper of February 4, 1797, Mrs. Chappell advertised "EDUCATION" at her seminary and offered subjects similar to Miss Brown's. She urged "speedy application" or she would "return to England . . . as before intended."[5] In the meantime, Deborah and Polly Thelwell, the daughters of Wilmington schoolmaster John Thelwell (c.1732–1812), were teaching from the late eighteenth century until some years after their father's death.[6] Also, Miss Elizabeth Montgomery (1778–1863), better known for her reminiscences of Wilmington, kept a girls' school there during the early nineteenth century, and at least one silk embroidery from her school has been identified.[7]

Fig. 544. Undated profile of Ann Tatnall (1775–1813) of Wilmington. Her father, Joseph Tatnall, was a successful miller who entertained Washington and Lafayette during the Revolution. He was the first president of the Bank of Delaware and became one of the nation's richest men. The sampler of Ann's aunt, Elizabeth Tatnall, aged eleven in 1755, is among the earliest known examples by a Delaware girl, and the sampler of her daughter, Eliza Tatnall Sipple (1795–1865), was worked at the Southern Boarding School in 1804. Both are described in B&C (78, 222). In 1830, Eliza Sipple married Marriott Canby (1787–1866), the brother of Frances Canby (Fig. 543). *Historical Society of Delaware.*

---

2. Notice in the *American Watchman* of August 23, 1825.

3. B&C, 55, 379.

4. Elizabeth Montgomery, *Wilmington Reminiscences of Familiar Village Tales, Ancient and New* (Philadelphia: T. K. Collins, Jr., 1851; reprint, Cottonport, La.: Polyanthos, 1971), 239–40.

5. In the *Delaware Gazette* of February 19, 1796, John Chappell advertised for "One or two Girls, as apprentices to the tambour and sattin-stitch business, likewise making child-bed linen, etc." This was probably the Mr. and Mrs. John Chappell who appeared in Baltimore in 1801.

6. B&C, 378–9.

7. See footnote 4. Elizabeth Montgomery was teaching at Market and Eighth streets in 1814. She was the daughter of Hugh Montgomery (c.1750–1780) and Rachel (c.1750–1825). For *Hector Taking Leave of Andromache* by her student Katharine Wallace, 1818, see *ANTIQUES,* April 1975, 690.

Wilmington's most successful girls' boarding school of the early nineteenth century opened on April 1, 1811, under the supervision of Joshua Maule and Eli Hilles (Fig. 545). Although Maule and Hilles were Quakers, their Wilmington Boarding School was nonsectarian, and because of experienced, capable management, it was well patronized by pupils from near and far, but particularly from the South. Maule died in 1812, and Eli's brother Samuel forsook his nearby boys' school and joined his brother at the girls' school. It was housed in the Matthew Crips mansion, which was built in 1797 on the east side of King Street, between Seventh and Eighth.

Eli (1783–1863) and Samuel Hilles (1788–1873) were born in West Chester, Pennsylvania, but they grew up in Brownsville in western Pennsylvania. Both brothers taught at the Westtown School between 1806 and 1811, and in 1821, Samuel married Margaret Hill Smith (1786–1882) of Burlington, New Jersey, who had entered the Westtown School in August 1800 and again in 1807. It is therefore not surprising that samplers from the Wilmington Boarding School are so closely related to the work from Westtown (Figs. 546, 547). In 1818, the Hilles brothers built a fine new six-story brick school building at the northeast corner of Tenth and King streets. Eli retired from teaching in 1828, being much involved in business and civic enterprises, and in 1832, Samuel and Margaret Hilles became the first superintendent and matron at the Haverford School, now Haverford College. Thereafter the boarding school was supervised by John M. Smith, Dubre Knight, and others until the 1850s.[8]

At present, there are two distinctive sampler styles from nineteenth-century Delaware. The earlier form, seen in Figures 548 and 549, had emerged at the Southern Boarding School by 1803 and was continued at the nearby Camden School in 1806.[9] The Southern Boarding School existed from April 1801 until 1805 at Duck Creek Crossroads (near Smyrna), and it was under the direction of the Friend's Duck Creek Meeting of the Southern Quarter.[10] However, when space was available, children of nonmembers were admitted. A number of samplers name this school, but the majority have cross-stitched sprays of flowers in the most typical Quaker manner and could not be recognized if the school's name were not included.

The second, more pictorial, form of sampler was worked in Lewes, Delaware, in 1806, 1808, and 1823 (Figs. 550–552). The examples from 1823 name *Mrs. Bowers School Lewes,* but she has not been identified. The only Bowers recorded in

---

8. Samuel E. Hilles, *Memorial of the Hilles Family, more particularly of Samuel and Margaret Hill Hilles* (Cincinnati, 1923), 13–14. Dubre Knight (d. 1868) and his wife, Jane W. Edwards Knight, were the superintendent and matron of Westtown School from 1861 to 1868. Jane W. Edwards entered Westtown School as a student in April 1831.

9. For these samplers and another from the Southern Boarding School, see "Delaware Samplers" by Susan B. Swan in the *Delaware Antiques Show Catalogue* (December 1985), 52–7, Figs. 3, 4, 5.

10. William C. Dunlap, *Quaker Education in Baltimore and Virginia Yearly Meetings With an Account of Certain Meetings of Delaware and the Eastern Shore Affiliated With Philadelphia* (Philadelphia, 1936), 290–7.

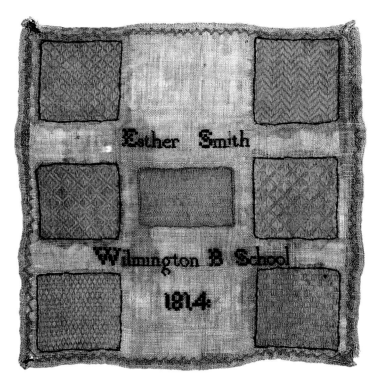

PROSPECTUS
OF THE
Wilmington Boarding School.

THE subscribers think it proper to inform their friends and the public in general, that they have concluded to open a BOARDING SCHOOL for GIRLS within the Borough of Wilmington, in a high, healthful, pleasant and retired situation, where are comfortable and convenient accommodations for the purpose. It is presumed that such an institution will not be unacceptable, when we reflect, that several seminaries for female education have been lately discontinued; and that the literary improvement of females is a subject which has been much neglected, to the evident loss of society.

The girls intrusted to their care will be considered in every respect, as a part of their family; and as the number of pupils is not to exceed fifty it will be in their power, and it is their design to pay particular attention to their instruction in the branches they contemplate teaching; which are, Spelling, Reading, Writing, Arithmetic and Book keeping; Geography with the use of Maps and Globes; Astronomy, Natural Philosophy and the Elements of Botany and Chemistry: Also the English and French Grammar, History and Composition. A proper attention will also be paid to instruct the girls in plain Needle work.

Scholars will be admitted for any time not less than three months; and the terms are, one hundred and thirty dollars per annum, to be paid in quarterly instalments and each payment in advance, with the addition of five dollars per Quarter for those who study French.

Stationary, &c. will be furnished at the School at the customary prices.

The morals, health, and comfort of the scholars, will receive a particular and interested attention.

N. B. It is desirable that the scholars may not be supplied with white or very light coloured apparel, on account of extra washing: It is hoped also that parents and others will be particularly careful to send no child under the effect of any infectious disease

School to open the first of the 4th mo next.— Subscriptions will be received by JOHNSON and WARNER, and EMMOR KIMBER, Philadelphia; and by JOSHUA MAULE, Wilmington

Joshua Maule,

Eli Hilles.

Fig. 545. "PROSPECTUS OF THE Wilmington Boarding School" as published in *Poulson's American Daily Advertiser*, Philadelphia, December 21, 1810. "The subscribers . . . have concluded to open a BOARDING SCHOOL for GIRLS within the Borough of Wilmington . . . to open the first of the 4th mo. next." In addition to academic subjects "a proper attention will also be paid to instruct the girls in plain Needle work."
The Library Company of Philadelphia.

Fig. 546. *Esther Smith/ Wilmington B School/ 1814.* Cotton, wool, and silk on linen; 10″ x 9¾″. The arrangement of Esther's darning sampler is much like that in the work from Westtown School (Fig. 425), but her border and the black outline around six sections is atypical. Her classmate Mary Gill worked the most usual form (B&C, Pl. LXIX). In 1818, Mary L. Browning worked a more ambitious piece with nine examples of darning rather than the usual seven (Swan, "Delaware Samplers" [1985], 54), as did Elizabeth B. Culin in 1820 (Winterthur Museum).
The Metropolitan Museum of Art, bequest of Mabel Herbert Harper, 57.122.49.

Fig. 547. *Wilmington Boarding School/ Martha Newbold/ 1818.* Silk on linen; 11½″ x 13½″. Martha worked an undulating vine-and-leaf border in the style of the Westtown School, and her crisp, clear embroidered lettering is flawless. This may have been the Martha Newbold who was teaching in Woodbury, New Jersey, in 1826 (receipt at the Gloucester County Historical Society). However, three girls named Martha Newbold entered the Westtown School—in 1805, 1808, and 1824—(the last aged twenty-one), so it is impossible to identify the Woodbury teacher.
Collection of Joan Stephens.

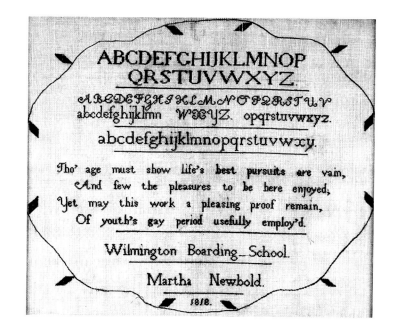

Fig. 548. *Ann B Stockly/ Southern Boarding School Delaware 1803.* Silk on linen; 14″ x 13″. Ann's composition appears to be unique to this school. For another of the same year, see Krueger, *Gallery,* Fig. 49. Each example of 1803 includes the maker's birthdate and her parents' names. Ann B. Stockly (b.1791) was third among the six children of Charles Stockly (1757/58–1805), a well-to-do planter of Accomack County, Virginia, and his second wife, Ann Taylor (d.1802). Thompson Holmes, husband of Ann's eldest sister, became guardian of the Stockly orphans in 1805. They went to William H. Coxon's school; Ann also had a singing master (Orphans' Accounts, Accomack County, Virginia, 1805–1819, Document 2, 115). Her youngest brother, Ayres, eventually resided in Smyrna, Delaware.
Collection of Geraldine Duclow.

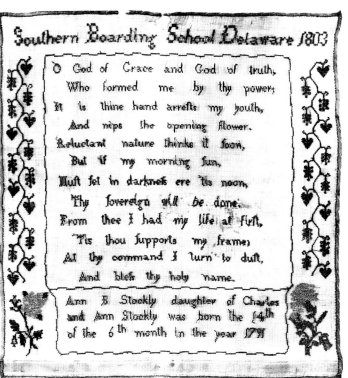

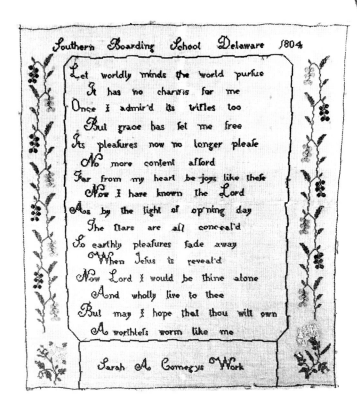

Fig. 549. *Sarah A. Comegys Work/ Southern Boarding School Delaware 1804.* Silk on linen; 14¾″ x 12⅞″. Sarah failed to name her parents, but the maker is believed to have been Sarah Allie Comegys (b.c.1790), the daughter of John Comegys (b.1756) and Elizabeth (1763–1832). She married John Turner of Baltimore in 1815, and they had three children.
Delaware State Museums, Dover, 54.215.

Fig. 550. *Ellon Roades/ her work/ Sept-r 16th/ 1808.* Silk on linen; 16½″ x 17½″. The pine trees, gazebo, and diagonal enclosures with initials relate Ellon's sampler to the later Lewes pieces (Figs. 551, 552) and to the 1806 sampler of Sarah Art (Swan, "Delaware Samplers," Fig. 7). Ellon Roades (b.1793) was the daughter of Hinman Roades (b.1765) and Margaret Thompson. She married Burton Stockley (1797–1861) at the Lewes Presbyterian Church on January 20, 1818.
Delaware State Museums, Dover, 78.54.

the 1820 census of Sussex County was George Bowers, aged between twenty-six and forty-five with a wife under twenty-seven. They lived in Lewes, close to the West and Waples families, but they do not appear in the Delaware census of 1830. Perhaps the schoolmistress was the mother of George Bowers but lived with other family members.

Fig. 551. *Elizabeth H Waples/ work don in Mrs Bowers'/ school Lewes May 30th/ 1823.* Silk on linen; 18½" x 20¾". Elizabeth's family record includes the births of twelve children and the deaths of five, and she added the death of her father in 1828. Elizabeth Waples (b.1811) was the daughter of Woolsey Waples (c.1776–1828) and Nancy W. Kollock of Lewes. She married David C. Hazzard at the Lewes Presbyterian Church on August 23, 1831.
Delaware State Museums, Dover, 63.596.

Fig. 552. *Margaret Howard/ Wests' work done in/ Mrs Bowers' school/ Lewes April 28th/ 1823.* Silk on linen; 18½" x 19½". Despite different borders, Margaret's work is very similar to that of Elizabeth H. Waples (Fig. 551), and they were no doubt classmates. Margaret Howard West (1814–1842) was the daughter of Lewis West and Elizabeth Howard of Lewes. She married Presbyterian minister Cornelius Hopkins Mustard on May 13, 1834, and had four children (two survived her) before her death at age twenty-eight. *Privately owned.*

NEEDLEWORK BY MARYLAND AND DELAWARE GIRLS

Fruit and Flower Samplers

AN IMPRESSIVE and entirely cohesive group of samplers was worked between 1811 and 1835 by girls from Maryland, Delaware, and possibly Pennsylvania. These samplers characteristically have a very wide, all-enveloping fruit and flower border, which rises from a center basket or a large rose and encloses a sharply defined center panel. Within it are one to four alphabets, a verse, and the maker's name and date, usually above a solidly worked scene containing a central tree flanked by paired sheep or rabbits and large butterflies. Three examples from 1811 are less elaborate than those illustrated here, and each has a tree centered in its lower border and a central vase of flowers in the upper border,[1] but their relationship to later pieces is unmistakable. Between 1816 and 1820, the most enduring variations of the basic pattern were fully developed (Figs. 554, 555) and in 1835 Eliza J. Benneson worked essentially the same pattern used by Ann E. England in 1820 and Margaret Hall in 1823 (Figs. 555, 553).[2]

None of the recorded examples within this group has survived with a clue to its origin. The first to receive recognition was the stunning large sampler by Ann E. England, and she is among the few sampler makers to be fully identified. Two earlier samplers were made in 1815 and 1818 by girls of Harford County, Maryland, but their home towns and the names of their parents remain unknown.[3]

---

1. The 1811 samplers of Mary Ann M. and Eliza Holtzbecher are illustrated in Sotheby's Sale 5809, January 27, 1989, Lots 1104, 1105 (the Holtzbechers lived near White Clay Creek, New Castle County, Delaware). *Mary Johnsons'/ work Anno Domini/ 1811,* recorded in DAPC, is said to be of Chester County origin.

2. In 1835 Eliza Ann O'Martin worked a border similar to Susanna Holland's (Fig. 554), but without the pineapples, and included a deeper, asymmetrical scene with a house and man (owned by Bihler and Coger Antiques about 1968).

3. Abigail Jane Garrett (1803–1890) omitted the scene and the date from her sampler. It is said to have been

Fig. 554. *Susanna M Holland/ 1816.* Silk on linen; 20¾″ x 16⅝″. Abigail Jane Garrett worked a similar basket and large grapes in 1815 (see footnote 3) and Elizabeth V. Bell's sampler of 1819 is nearly identical (DAPC). Susanna M. Holland is unidentified.

Baltimore Museum of Art, gift of Mrs. Francis White from the collection of Mrs. Miles White, Jr., 73.76.327.

Fig. 555. *Ann E England/ 1820.* Silk on linen; 25″ x 20″. Ann Eliza England (1805–1827) was the eldest child of Joseph England (1763–1828) and his second wife, Eliza Boulden. Her father was a farmer and miller and lived on White Clay Creek in Mill Creek Hundred, New Castle County, Delaware.

Private collection; photograph courtesy of Sotheby's.

Fig. 556. *Eliza J. Benneson/ 1835.* Silk on linen; 26″ x 22½″. Eliza's alphabets and her decorative motifs are remarkably similar to those worked by Ann England (Fig. 555), and leave no doubt that these girls were taught by the same instructress.

Cooper-Hewitt, National Museum of Design, Smithsonian Institution, 1941-69-254.

Most of the sampler makers have relatively common English names, and because they did not include their ages on their work, only a few reasonably certain attributions have been possible.

These samplers do offer strong evidence that they were made at the same long-lasting school, or under the instruction of one woman who taught at various locations. However, likely schools capable of producing such sophisticated embroideries between 1811 and 1835 are uncommon. Schoolmistress Susannah Travers and the Misses Rookers kept schools during the proper period in Baltimore, as did Deborah Grelaud and several others in Philadelphia, and during these years there were many teachers who were continually moving about, but distinctions in their needlework have not been recognized. The Quaker schools of long duration, such as Westtown and the Wilmington Boarding School, did not produce this type of work, and the samplers bear no hint of Quaker instruction. None of the appropriate names appear on the enrollment records of Saint Joseph's Academy, although the Sisters of Charity own an example given by a descendant who thought it was made there,[4] and these girls did not attend the Moravian schools in Lititz or Bethlehem. In 1921, Margaret Hall's sampler was recorded by Bolton and Coe, but this group of samplers was unrecognized until well after the England sampler appeared in 1977. Most likely emerging examples will soon offer an explanation of their origin.[5]

worked when she was twelve and lived in Harford County, Maryland (MESDA records). Eliza M. Brown's sampler of 1818 resembles pieces from 1811. It lacks a solidly worked scene but has large pineapples in the side borders. Eliza may have been the Eliza M. Brown who married Elijah B. Rodgers in 1830; they were both of Harford County (Maryland Historical Society).

4. Ann Blany's sampler of 1819 is much like Susanna Holland's (Fig. 554). It was presented to Saint Joseph's Academy by Milton Markland in 1971.

5. Gary W. Parks, Director of the Packwood House Museum, Lewisburg, Pennsylvania, is working on the history of this group. He has kindly shared the identity of the Holtzbecher sisters.

WROUGHT BY MARY C. FINLEY, ST. JOSEPH'S, MAY 6, 1830.

Fig. 557. *WROUGHT BY MARY C. FINLEY ST. JOSEPH'S, MAY 6, 1830,* inscribed on paper beneath the picture. Dedicated on the plinth to Mary's grandmother *Mrs. JANE FINLEY/ Who died on the 21st of July 1814. Aged 68.* Silk, chenille, paint, and ink on silk with ink on paper; 20¼″ x 24″. Mary's memorial includes the most frequently found features of Maryland's largest and most easily recognized group of embroideries. Samplers and silk embroideries from Saint Joseph's Academy, the Catholic girls' school founded by Saint Elizabeth Ann Seton, date from 1812 (Fig. 576) until about 1840. Although they often lack evidence of Catholic instruction, memorials worked by Catholic girls usually have a cross and I H S painted on the characteristic urn shown here (see Fig. 578). Mary Culbertson Finley (1814–1891) entered the Academy in 1829. She was the daughter of James Finley (1776–1849) and Adaline Ottalie Reeser (1785–1875), who moved from Chambersburg, Pennsylvania, to Baltimore after their marriage. They were Presbyterians. Mary married Alexander Wray (1803–1861), who came from Ireland about 1820; they had two daughters.
Private collection.

NEEDLEWORK OF
MARYLAND

MARYLAND WAS the fourth English colony to be established in what is now the United States. In 1632, Cecil Calvert, the second Lord Baltimore, received by charter from Charles I all the lands north of Virginia to the fortieth parallel, and under the leadership of the Proprietor's brother, Leonard Calvert, a successful settlement was established at St. Mary's City in 1634. The Calverts were Catholics, but they favored tolerance toward all Christians. However, throughout the colonial period, the degree of religious tolerance in Maryland fluctuated with the changing monarchs and attitudes in England, and Maryland Catholics were soon outnumbered by Protestant denominations. Nevertheless, Maryland is the only state where recognizable needlework has survived from a Catholic school.

Annapolis was founded by Puritans from Virginia in 1648, and it soon became the colony's principal town as well as its capital in 1695. No samplers are known from the first century of colonization in Maryland, but there is little question that they were being worked there at an early date. In 1679, Frances, the wife of Thomas Redly, was paid 210 pounds of tobacco from the estate of George Beckwith for "Samplers worke done to the Orphants of Beckwith . . ." and surely this indicates that she had been teaching his daughters.[1] The seventeenth-century interest in worked furnishings is conspicuous in the 1688 inventory of William Stevens of Somerset County, which included a quantity of "Turkey worke" and "Needle worke" furnishings, and a "Chamber called the Wrought Chamber."[2] Perhaps of Maryland origin were the "3 old Samplers" listed in John Rolph's Kent County inventory of 1723.[3]

---

1. *Maryland Prerogative Court, Inventories and Accounts*, April 20, 1679, 6:50 (MESDA records). This is the only known reference to a specific woman teaching sampler embroidery in seventeenth-century America.
2. Ibid., 1688–1692, 10:56–60.
3. Ibid., October 16, 1723, 9:358. I am indebted to Martha W. Rowe for calling these inventories to my attention.

Among the first to advertise a girls' school in Maryland were Mary Ann March and her daughter in Annapolis. In March of 1751, they were prepared to "Teach young Misses, all sorts of Embroidery, Turkey Work, and all Sorts of rich Stitches learnt in Sampler work, at Ten Shillings a Quarter."[4] Annapolis papers carried similar advertisements throughout the eighteenth century, but the duration of these schools and the products of their instruction are now unknown. Maryland colonial samplers are rare, and as yet, no characteristic Maryland sampler style of the eighteenth century has emerged.[5]

Map Samplers of Maryland

Opposite:

Fig. 558. *Samuel Lewis, The State of Maryland, From the Best Authorities, 1795/ Engraved for Carey's American Edition of Guthrie's Geography improved./ W. Barker, sculp.;* 11⅛″ x 16⅝″. The unique configuration of Kent Island offers convincing evidence that the basic patterns for the map samplers were derived from this map. Some diverse wording and county boundaries may have been taken from the 1795 Dennis Griffith *Map of the State of Maryland* and the 1796 *Map of the States of Maryland and Delaware* by J. Denison (see Edward C. Papenfuse and Joseph M. Coale III, *Atlas of Historical Maps of Maryland, 1608–1908* [Baltimore: Johns Hopkins University Press, 1982], 45–53). The Lewis map was widely copied and plagiarized, and teachers may have used other editions that had variations or additions. *Maryland Historical Society.*

Six samplers depicting the state of Maryland comprise the earliest group of maps worked in America. While their differences suggest origins at several schools, their basic patterns were all derived from the Samuel Lewis map of 1795 (Fig. 558). Presumably these maps were worked in or near Maryland, but the schoolmistress who initiated this region's unusual interest in map embroidery remains unknown. There seems little doubt that she was an English-trained teacher who was keeping a boarding school, since the earliest example of 1798 (Fig. 559) is nearly identical to another of 1799,[6] and the girls who made them lived in widely divided counties. Also, both maps were worked on wool in a shaded cross-stitch often found on English map samplers of the late eighteenth century.[7]

Relatively few Maryland boarding schools of 1798 and 1799 are known today, and the most successful women teachers, who had no need to advertise, may be totally forgotten. However, the Maryland gentry's patronage of Philadelphia schools indicates that respected Maryland academies offering advanced accomplishments were scarce. In 1798 and 1799, the Falconar and Ogle daughters could have been studying at Mrs. Mansell's well-established girls' school in Chestertown. This teacher was "Lately from LONDON" when she first advertised her "ACADEMY and BOARDING-SCHOOL for YOUNG LADIES" in the *Maryland Journal & Baltimore Advertiser* of December 1, 1786, where she mentioned instruction in "all Kinds of Needle-Work in Silk and Worsted, Darning and Embroidery." Sarah Mansell was soon patronized by the Ridgelys of Delaware, and she was recognized for needlework that was "very Handsome & well done."[8] Her school was

---

4. *The Maryland Gazette,* Annapolis, March 27, 1751.
5. Among the earliest is a 1738 band sampler by Mary Clare Carroll (1727–1781) of Annapolis, now in the Mount Clare Museum, Carroll Park, Baltimore.
6. Map by Mary Ogle (1786–1814), the daughter of James Ogle (1753–1800) and Mary Biggs (b.1756); she married Richard Elder. Her map is in the Maryland Historical Society.
7. For an English map of 1780 in the same style but on a linen ground, see King, Fig. 46.
8. Mabel Lloyd Ridgely, ed., *The Ridgelys of Delaware & Their Circle* (Portland, Me.: The Anthoensen Press, 1949), 49. A bill from William Mansell to Mrs. Ridgely, March 1, 1787, is illustrated on page 50.

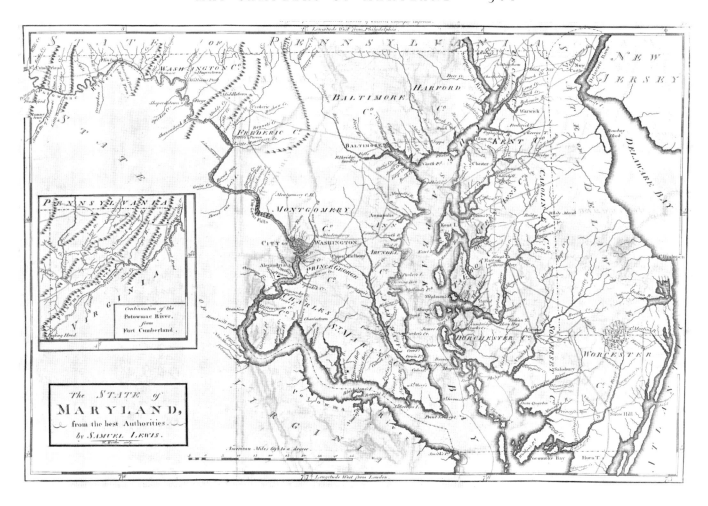

unusual for its comparatively long duration of at least fifteen years in the same place.[9] Another likely boarding school for the Falconar and Ogle girls was opened in Baltimore in 1795 by Mrs. Lacombe, a French lady who was assisted by "Mrs. Beck from London." This school continued in Baltimore through 1801.[10] Mrs. Mather's background is unknown, but she was also teaching "fancy needlework" at her young ladies' boarding school in Baltimore in 1798 and 1799.[11]

H. Potts is the only Maryland map embroiderer who signed her work with a location, and it was not in Maryland (Fig. 560). Presumably she worked her map in Virginia although she may have attended a Maryland school and given her home location as did the New York girls who worked maps at the Pleasant Valley boarding school a few years later (Figs. 334, 337). Two other examples depart from a rounded cartouche for the title and signature, and Hariot Beall even omitted her

---

9. *Herald and Eastern Shore Intelligencer,* Easton, Maryland, January 19, 1802.

10. *Herald and Norfolk & Portsmouth Advertiser,* Virginia, September 28, 1795; Baltimore city directory of 1800–1801. The 1800 census recorded nine young girls in Mary Lacombe's Baltimore household. She was again teaching in Baltimore in 1809 (*Baltimore Evening Post,* July 22, 1809). In 1820 she was living in Baltimore's twelfth ward (U.S. census), and died in Baltimore in 1827 (Baltimore County Court House, Probate Records Book 12, Folio 365).

11. *Columbian Mirror and Alexandria Gazette,* Alexandria, Virginia, May 23, 1799.

Fig. 559. *A/ Map/ of/ Maryland/ E(?) Falconar/ 1798.* Silk on wool; 20¾" x 30". A very similar map was worked in 1799 by Mary Ogle of Frederick County, Maryland. The maker of this map belonged to the Falconar family of Kent County, Maryland. The map pattern worked by both girls was essentially derived from the Lewis map (Fig. 558), but they named a *Part of Virginia* in the manner found on the Dennis Griffith map. This girl named *Washington* and *Annapolis* but ignored Baltimore, although Mary Ogle included it. *Maryland Historical Society, gift of Mrs. Francis H. Jencks and Miss Delia Pleasants,* 59.34.1.

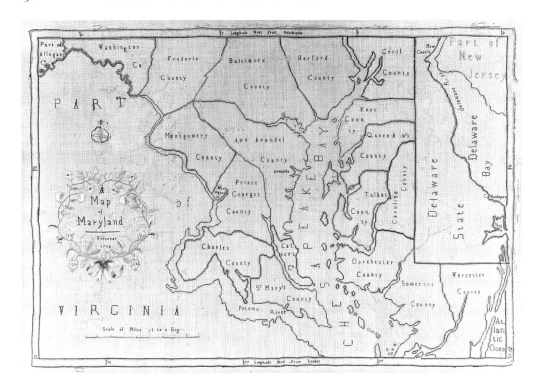

date (Fig. 561). However, the similarity of her map to another worked by Elizabeth Susannah Bowie in 1800 suggests that these girls may have been classmates at a boarding school. The Bowies lived in Prince George's County,[12] while Hariot was a George Town girl.[13] It was sixteen years later when Mary Stevens worked her considerably more sophisticated map on silk (Fig. 562), but in size and pattern it closely resembles the Falconar map, although Mary named many more towns, islands, and rivers.

Except for the Stevens map, there is little likelihood that these samplers were made under the tuition of any of the three women of this region who followed the uncommon practice of advertising instruction in map embroidery between September 1799 and October 1810. Mrs. O'Reilly was the first to mention embroidered maps in her extravagant advertisements of 1799 and 1800. Mr. and Mrs. O'Reilly had arrived in Baltimore in 1799 and described themselves as "natives of Europe" when they announced their proposed boarding school in September of that year.[14] The following spring they commenced teaching at 51 South

12. Elizabeth Susannah Bowie (b.1785) married Joseph Howard of Anne Arundel County in 1809. In 1956, her sampler belonged to Mrs. Maurice Thompson of Chevy Chase, Maryland. It was exhibited at the Maryland Historical Society and pictured in *The Baltimore American,* January 15, 1956.
13. According to B&C, 126, Harriet Beall of Georgetown also worked "A Chart of the World" in 1801.
14. *The Telegraph and Daily Advertiser,* Baltimore, October 10, 1799. According to the advertisement, they had just come from Europe, but like Mr. and Mrs. Chappell, they may have worked elsewhere in America. In 1802, Robert O'Reilly gave up his boys' school to devote himself entirely to the girls' school (*Telegraph and Daily Advertiser,* February 13, 1802). His name was not mentioned in Mrs. O'Reilly's Alexandria advertisements.

Fig. 560. *THE/ STATE/ of/ MARYLAND/ H Potts/ Alexandria/ 1799.* Silk on linen; 14″ x 17¼″. This work is simpler than the large pieces worked on wool (Fig. 559), but it is clearly based on the Lewis map (Fig. 558). H. Potts may have been taught by Betsy Lunt, who advertised in *The Times and Alexandria Advertiser* on February 24, 1798, and offered instruction in "Plain Needle Work, Fancy Work and Drawing." This sampler maker could have been Hannah Potts who married Enoch Best in Loudon County, Virginia, on November 1, 1806. *Maryland Historical Society,* 67.10.1.

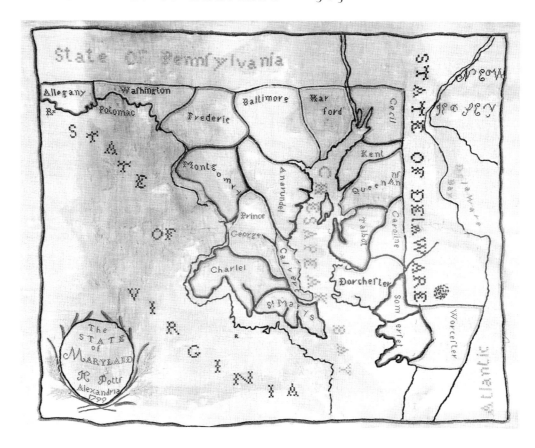

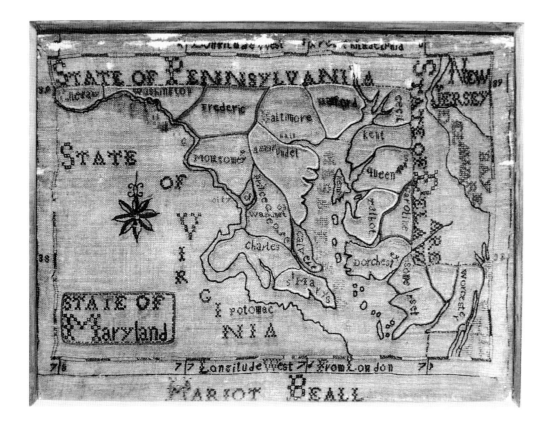

Fig. 561. *STATE OF/ MARYLAND/ HARIOT BEALL,* c.1800. Silk on linen; 13″ x 17½″. Hariot's map is clearly related to another worked by Elizabeth Susannah Bowie in 1800 (privately owned). Both girls worked their title in a rectangle much like the Lewis map (Fig. 558), and they strictly adhered to its lettering. Despite the prominence of the Beall family, Hariot has not been identified. *Private collection; photograph courtesy of Sotheby's.*

Street, but in April of 1800, they were "In a very healthful and pleasant situation, corner of Church Street and St. Pauls' Lane," and they described their curriculum as follows:

> Young Ladies will be taught French and English grammatically . . . Writing and Arithmetic; History, Geography and the use of the Globes; Music, Drawing, and all kinds of work, viz. Embroidery in chenilles, gold, silver, silks, &c. comprising figures, historical and ornamental, landscapes, flowers, fruit, birds, &c. maps wrought in silks, chenilles, gold, &c. print work in figures or landscapes; cloth work in fruit, birds, flowers, &c. filagre and varnishing in vases, pyramids, baskets, tea cadees, epergnes, &c. grotto and shell work, artificial flowers, tambour and Dresden, cross stitch, tent stitch, tapestry, &c. bugle and pearl work; painting on velvet, gauze, silk, vellum, &c. with many other elegant accomplishments too numerous to mention. . . . Grown up ladies will be taught any of the above accomplishments by the lesson.[15]

Mrs. O'Reilly listed the subjects she taught in exactly the same manner when she advertised a school in Alexandria in 1804,[16] but she had evidently departed from that town when Mrs. Edmonds arrived there in 1810 and offered to teach "Embroidery in chenilles, gold, silver and silk. Maps wrought do. . . ."[17] Later that year, Mrs. Maria Anne Dunlap, "HAVING been engaged in the tuition of youth for some years past," was then prepared to teach "Embroidery, Tambour, Marking, Working Maps, plain work, &c. &c." in addition to the basic subjects.[18]

Maryland maps resembling the elegant work described by Mrs. O'Reilly and Mrs. Edmonds have not been found. These women must have been aware of the local interest in map embroidery when they first commenced teaching in this region, and therefore included it in their advertisements. If their schools actually produced maps on silk embellished with gold and silver threads, these may now be unidentified and looked upon as English.

---

15. *Federal Gazette and Baltimore Daily Advertiser,* April 1, 1800; *The Telegraph and Daily Advertiser,* July 1, 1800.

16. *Alexandria Advertiser and Commercial Intelligencer,* November 20, 1804. Between 1814 and 1818, Mrs. O'Reilly taught in Petersburg and Richmond, Virginia (MESDA Craftsmen File Nos. 27117, 27118).

17. *Alexandria Daily Gazette,* March 6, 1810. Julia F. Edmonds taught in York County, Virginia, in 1809 and Norfolk in 1818 (MESDA Craftsmen File Nos. 54860, 10297). In *Poulson's American Daily Advertiser* of March 21, 1827, she advertised a school in Philadelphia, having been "long and successfully engaged as an instructress of female youth in Alexandria."

18. *Alexandria Daily Gazette,* October 2, 1810.

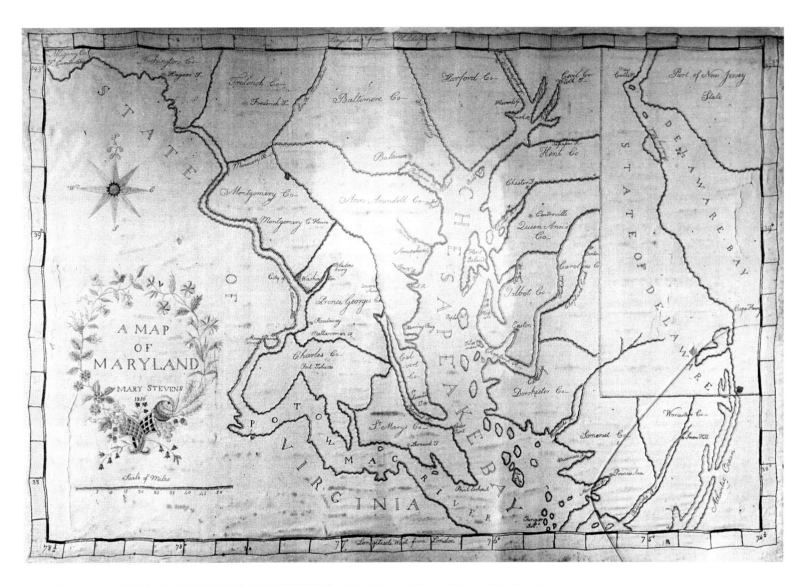

Fig. 562. *A MAP/ OF/ MARYLAND/ MARY STEVENS/ 1816.* Silk on silk; 21½″ x 31¾″. Mary's floral cartouche and compass resemble those on Mary Ogle's map of 1799, and her map is close to the same size. However, she named the *State of Virginia* and more closely copied the lettering of the Lewis map. Mary Stevens (1799–1866) lived in Talbot County, Maryland. *Location unknown; photograph courtesy of The Museum of Early Southern Decorative Arts.*

Building Samplers of Baltimore

The artistic rendering of gentlemen's country seats was a conceit of the young Republic, but it was especially conspicuous in the city of Baltimore, which experienced an unparalleled surge of growth and prosperity during the early nineteenth century. Today the most famous evidence of this fashion survives on Baltimore's painted furniture, but a local preference for depicting impressive buildings also resulted in Maryland's most interesting group of samplers.[1] Appealing samplers with colorful houses, probably of imaginary form, were being made by Baltimore girls in 1798.[2] In 1804, however, Lydia Miller worked twin town houses that are clearly akin to the decorations on John and Hugh Finley's high-style furniture, and at precisely the same time (Fig. 563).[3] This was evidently the beginning of a trend that would reach full flower in the 1820s, when "building" samplers became the fashion at a number of Baltimore schools.

It was perhaps an enterprising ornamental artist, already engaged in painting furniture, who first sketched elegant mansions or public buildings on linen for a schoolmistress. Or it may have been imaginative teachers who chose to combine a little whimsy with reality in designing decorative samplers. The latter seems more likely. It was not a newcomer just copying a print, but someone who knew local customs when they placed gatekeepers with large keys at the ends of the hospital (Fig. 570), or embellished neat brick houses with pairs of towering church belfries, which were the tallest structures in the town (Figs. 573, 574).

Little is known of the women teaching accomplishments in Baltimore when Lydia Miller worked two samplers with pairs of town houses in 1803 and 1804. The Baltimore directory of 1803 listed nine schoolmistresses, John Chappell's boarding school, and Mr. and Mrs. O'Reilly's ladies' academy, but of these, only Mrs. Gover, Mrs. Chappell, and Mrs. O'Reilly were definitely teaching ornamental needlework.[4] Catharine Groombridge arrived from Philadelphia in the fall of 1804, and newspaper advertisements of her curriculum rivaled in extravagance those of the O'Reilly's, who were then moving to Alexandria.

---

1. They first received attention when Elisabeth Donaghy Garrett published Mary Ann Craft's unusually accurate rendition of Saint Patrick's Church in *ANTIQUES,* April 1975, 699–700.

2. In 1798 a handsome house beneath a painted paper eagle was worked by seven-year-old Ann Clair Tinges, daughter of Baltimore clockmaker Charles Tinges (MESDA, 3574).

3. Colwill, *Francis Guy, 1760–1820* (1981), 75–85.

4. Sarah Gover, schoolmistress, in the directory of 1803, was Mrs. Brown when she advertised instruction in ornamental needlework in Baltimore's *American & Commercial Daily Advertiser* of January 25, 1809. Mrs. Chappell, earlier in Wilmington, advertised in Baltimore in 1801 (Ibid., August 11, 1801). She was probably the Mrs. Chappell in Chestertown in 1806 (MESDA Craftsmen File No. 50130), and the same woman teaching at 47 North Gay Street, Baltimore, in 1827 (*American & Commercial Daily Advertiser,* August 30, 1827).

Fig. 563. *Lydia Miller her work/ Baltimore/ June the 22ᵈ 1804/ aged 9 Year.* Silk on linen; 20½" x 17¼". Although of different shape, Lydia's buildings bring to mind the twin town houses of the Buchanan family, which are painted on the skirt of an elegant pier table in the Baltimore Museum of Art. On a sampler of 1803 Lydia worked similar houses with five-bay facades for each major structure. Lydia Miller of Baltimore (b.c.1795) was the great, great grandmother of the donor, Elizabeth Elliott Lamb Reyes. An unquestionably related sampler of 1804, although without buildings, was worked by eight-year-old Elizabeth Coates, the daughter of Francis Coates and Charlotte Linton (see *The Luminary,* newsletter of MESDA, vol. 12, no. 2 (Fall 1991): 2, 3. *Chester County Historical Society, NS96.*

The best remembered long-lasting girls' school in Baltimore of the Federal period was first advertised on July 22, 1808, by "M & S Rooker" who mentioned that they had "very recently left England" where they had "conducted a school of the first respectability in the environs of London."[5] This school soon became the enterprise of Mary (1785–1868), Harriet (1790–1876), and Rebecca Rooker (1793–1862) who came from England with their parents about 1807.[6] The Misses Rookers' English Seminary for Young Ladies appeared in Baltimore directories from 1810 until 1833, and the last listing was Miss Rooker's Academy on Lombard Street, near Sharp, in the directory of 1835–1836. In 1811, Mary Rooker married John Norris (1774–1829), a miller of Harford County, and they had five children, but after his death she resumed teaching with her sisters.[7] Harriet left the school in 1834 when she married the widower Basil Crapster (b.c.1787), a

---

5. *American & Commercial Daily Advertiser.*

6. Their second advertisement was headed "English Seminary, Miss Rookers" (*Federal Gazette & Baltimore Daily Advertiser,* October 5, 1808). They were among the twenty-one children of the Reverend James Rooker (1754–1828) and Mary Berry (1761–1812). After his wife's death, Rooker became pastor of the Presbyterian Church in Germantown, Pennsylvania.

7. Thomas M. Myers, *The Norris Family of Maryland* (New York, 1916), 33–4; *American & Commercial Daily Advertiser,* December 30, 1829.

Fig. 564. *Elizabeth Ireland's*
performance at Mrs Lyman's/
Baltimore May 22^d 1819 AD.
Silk on linen; 24½" x 27¼".
Elizabeth's work is now the
earliest of Baltimore's large
architectural samplers and
the only one to name an
instructress. This sampler
maker may have been
Elizabeth Martha Ireland
(b.1799), the daughter of
John Ireland, Associate
Rector of Saint Paul's
Church, and Joanna Giles.
Author's collection.

planter of Anne Arundel County.[8] As yet no samplers from the Misses Rookers'
school have been identified, and only two silk embroideries can be confidently attributed to their teaching. Both are worked predominantly in heavy chenille.[9]

Baltimore's large building samplers possibly evolved from the more typical
sampler format of 1804 to architectural records in needlework by 1819 (Fig.
564). The Mrs. Lyman who taught Elizabeth Ireland may have figured in this transition, but the style flowered in the 1820s without a trace of Mrs. Lyman's name.
The Mrs. Lyman of the sampler was probably the "Eleanor Lyman schoolmistress
Montgomery St" in the directory of 1814–1815.[10] This Eleanor Lyman was the
daughter of Robert and Mary Ricks, and she was probably born before 1780. On
September 3, 1799, Eleanor Ricks was married to Joseph Lyman by the Reverend
John Ireland in Baltimore's Saint Paul's Church, and she was a bride of sixteen

---

8. *Baltimore American,* July 29, 1834.

9. For Rebecca Rooker's embroidery, see *ANTIQUES,* April 1975, 701. A shepherdess by Jane Schardel has
glass inscribed *English Seminary Baltimore Md. 1816* (private collection). A Biblical embroidery possibly from
this school is illustrated in Wheeler, *The Development of Embroidery in America* (1921), opp. 76.

10. The 1822–1823 directory listed "Mary Liman, teacher Barre, s side E of Sharp." She did not appear
again. The directories, although helpful, are not fully reliable records of residency. Many long-time inhabitants never appeared or were listed sporadically.

Fig. 565. *Ann Barrieres wor[k] October fifth 1820.*
Silk on linen; 17½″ x 16¾″. Ann's classmate
was no doubt Mary Helen Gallagher, who
worked a very similar sampler in 1820 (Peale
Museum, Baltimore). Their fenced houses, and
upturned garlands partly framing a four-line
verse, appear to be simplified versions of the
center section of Elizabeth Ireland's sampler
(Fig. 564). Ann Barriere (1811–c.1888) was the
daughter of Joseph Barriere (d.1847) and Jane.
Her father was a sea captain in 1814, and a
grocer on South Charles Street in 1824. In 1838
Ann married Gibbons Moore (b.c.1814), a
farmer of Anne Arundel County.
Maryland Historical Society, 68.28.1.

Fig. 566. *Ann Amanda Ashum s
Work finished in her 9th year March
13th 1832.* Silk on linen; 15″ x
18½″. Ann's sampler is somewhat
more exuberant than Ann Barriere's (Fig. 565), but their
patterns were essentially the
same. Susan Mary Clyce
(1818–1892) of Lexington,
Virginia, was probably at school
in Baltimore when she featured a
gazebo within similar surroundings on her sampler of 1833
(privately owned). Ann Ashum
(c.1824–1901) was the daughter
of ship pilot Alexander Ashum
(1787–1859) and Permelia Lynch.
In 1832 they lived on Bond Street
near Gough. Ann married James
Atwell, and later became the
third wife of Thomas H. Spencer
(1810–1878).
Collection of Charles S. Booz, Jr.

Fig. 567. *Mary Davis Baltimore March the 13th 1826.* Silk, chenille, and paint on linen; 30″ x 38½″. Mary's bow knot is nearly identical to the lower one worked by Elizabeth Ireland (Fig. 564), while her palm tree suggests kinship to the Wigart and Smith samplers (Figs. 568, 569). Mary gave no age to help distinguish her from the many Baltimore girls named Mary Davis.
Metropolitan Museum of Art, bequest of Barbara Schiff Sinauer, 1984.331.10.

Opposite:
Fig. 569. *Margaret Smith's Work Finished in the Eleventh Year of her Age./ November 12th 1827.* Silk on linen; 17″ x 21″. Margaret's sampler is definitely related to Sarah Ann Wigart's work (Fig. 568) and nearly identical to an undated example by Charlotte Coates Boyd (Edmonds, Fig. 64). All three samplers have similar animals in raised work. Margaret Ellen Smith (1817–1848) was among the eleven children of Dennis A. Smith (b.c.1781) and Rebecca (b.1784), the daughter of Job Smith. In 1827 they lived on West Baltimore Street east of Green Street. Margaret was married to John Ingersoll of New Orleans on July 26, 1836, and died at Tesheevah Plantation in Yazoo County, Mississippi.
Private collection.

Fig. 568. *Sarah Ann Wigarts work finished Nov' 1ˢᵗ A D 1826.* Silk and wool on linen; 26″ x 27″. Early records of this sampler say that it depicts the Rectory of St. Paul's Church, but aside from its five-bay building with a pediment, there is little to support this belief, since the rectory (which still exists) had a gabled roof and dependencies, and its windows were not arched. The distinctive foliage on the tree at left also appears on other samplers picturing this building, including a similar pattern with a three-bay version of this house worked by Mary Louisa Horn (1834–1923) of Baltimore in 1846 (Historical Society of Carroll County). Similar leaves also appear on the tree to the right of Elizabeth Ireland's house (Fig. 564). Several Wigart families lived in Baltimore but Sarah Ann has not been identified. *Maryland Historical Society, 70.20.1*

days when Joseph Lyman died.[11] No records of a second marriage or of her death have been discovered.

Three groups of Baltimore building samplers can now be identified, and they probably originated at only two schools.[12] The bow knots on the Ireland and Davis samplers are remarkably similar (Figs. 564, 567), and this may mean that Mrs. Lyman was responsible for the mansions with palm trees, which now compose a group of at least four related pieces (Figs. 567–569). More significant is the central section of Elizabeth Ireland's sampler, for it is essentially the same pattern worked in simpler form from 1820 until 1832 (Figs. 565, 566). These samplers suggest that Mrs. Lyman continued to teach during the 1830s.

Modified versions of the Barriere-type pattern (Fig. 565) soon appeared elsewhere, however. In 1830, a very similar house behind a straight fence with an identical "eyeglass"-shaped gate was worked by Frances Bush, who named *St. James First African P E Church School in Baltimore* on a floral sampler of 1832, and both samplers are believed to have been made there.[13]

The third group includes five enormous samplers. Worked between 1822 and 1840, they depict the Baltimore Hospital and a twin-towered building (Figs. 570, 572–574). Despite the differences of being embroidered in silk or wool, the obvious similarity of their black gates links these samplers to the same instructress. The four identified sampler makers lived in or near the Old Town section of the city and within possible walking distance of the only schoolmistress known to have taught from 1822 through 1840. Mrs. Susanna Travers' "young ladies seminary 70 High st ot" was listed in Baltimore directories of 1812 and 1837–1838, although other nearby addresses also appeared in the intervening years, and her last listing was "young ladies seminary 67 S High st" in 1840–1841.[14] Mrs. Travers may have been the Susan Travers who married John Travers in Dorchester Parish on April 24, 1806. The census of 1820 records two boys, five girls, and three adult women in her household.

Just as in Philadelphia, Baltimore's dominant sampler styles cannot now be associated with the better-known women who taught there during the Federal period, and they were evidently made under the instruction of teachers who have received no recognition in the histories of their community.

11. Bill and Martha Reamy, *Records of St. Paul's Parish* 1 (Baltimore: The Protestant Episcopal Church Records . . . 1801–1825), 132.

12. In addition to the Baltimore samplers discussed here, B&C listed four that may be related: Mary Ann Armstrong, 1824, 123; Martha Ann Cooper, 1826, 143; Mary Ann Kennedy, 1823, 184; and Ann Woodward, 1824, 244. They illustrated the mansion house worked by Eliza Rebecca Picket (1815–1890) in 1825, Pl. LXXXI. Eliza was a milliner until her marriage in 1843 to hatter Ephraim Price (1808–1884). Her samplers are in the Peale Museum, Baltimore. See the 1824 Armstrong sampler in *MAD*, February 1990, 16-C.

13. Both at the Maryland Historical Society. Baltimore's free black population was the largest of any city in the United States. See Bettye Gardner, "Antebellum Black Education in Baltimore," *Maryland Historical Magazine* 71, no. 3 (1976): 360–6.

14. The directories give no occupation for Susanna Travers in 1824, nor do they list her in 1827 and 1829, but there is little doubt that she was there, for her address was 37 High Street in 1824 and 1831.

Fig. 570. *Ann Maria Krebs Aged 10 Years November 14 1822.* Silk on linen; 20¾″ x 27½″. Ann Maria's reasonably accurate view of the Baltimore Hospital has the type of black iron gate and sections of fence that were favored by her teacher for at least eighteen years. In the 1820s, an unknown girl worked a large but quite different view of this building with cheerful bouquets in the upper windows and called it the *Baltimore Hospital* (*ANTIQUES,* January 1962, 117). Anne Royall visited the hospital in 1824 and observed that "The gate is locked day and night, and a man duly stationed on the inside, to open it for those who apply for admittance, for which they pay him 12½ cents" (Anne Royall, *Sketches of History, Life, and Manners, in the United States* [New Haven, 1826], 192). Ann Maria Krebs (1812–1837) was the daughter of victualler Jacob Krebs (1774–1867) and Caroline Rowe, who lived at the southeast corner of Gough and Eden streets. She married Alexander Nicholson in 1832 and had one son.
Private collection.

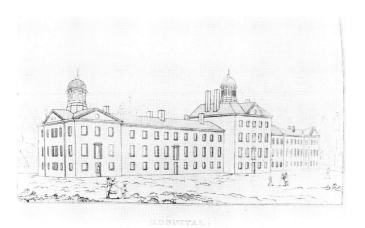

Fig. 571. View of the Baltimore Hospital from an illustration by John Hazelhurst B. Latrobe (1803–1891) in *Pictures of Baltimore* by Fielding Lucas, Jr. (Baltimore, 1832). In 1797 Jeremiah Yellott donated to the state a seven-acre lot for a lunatic asylum and general hospital. The brick building had a four-story center section measuring 64 by 56 feet, and two three-story wings, each 120 by 36 feet. It was built by Baltimore County and demolished about 1870.
Maryland Historical Society.

Fig. 572. *Margery Jane McGuire Aged 10* with *Ann* and *McGuire* inscribed in the circles above, and *Maryland Hospital* above the gate, c.1840. Wool on linen; 25″ x 25″. Margery's somewhat narrowed hospital lacks birds atop tall steeples at either end, but it is basically like the Krebs building (Fig. 570), with the same striped base, a related gate, and similar iron insertions in the brick wall. Margery Jane McGuire has not been identified.

Author's collection.

Fig. 573. *Elizabeth Friedenwald Aged 11 Years in 1838* and with the initials *J F* and *M F* in the circles above. Wool on linen; 24″ x 25″. Elizabeth, usually called Betsey, worked a twin-towered mansion with the same window arrangement found on an 1829 version of the building by Elizabeth Blyden (Edmonds, Fig. 65), but it lacks the pediment and fancier doorway. However, its gate and fence definitely resemble those in the earlier work, while the motifs jutting in from the upper corners relate to a similar treatment in the lower corners of the Krebs sampler (Fig. 570). Betsey Friedenwald (1824–1894) was born in Hesse-Darmstadt, Germany, to Jonas Friedenwald (1803–1893) and Merle Bar Stern (1794–1871), who came to Baltimore in 1832. Her father was a clothier, and in 1838 they lived on Bond Street south of Shakespeare. Betsey married Moses Wiesenfeld (1819–1871) in 1841.

Collection of Mr. and Mrs. Philip Kahn, Jr.

Fig. 574. *Martha Jane Smith Aged 10*, c.1840. Wool on linen; 22½″ x 24″. Martha worked golden-topped twin towers exactly as they appear on the Elizabeth Blyden example of 1829. They may be likened to the twin steeples of the First Presbyterian Church, which dominated the Baltimore skyline from 1791 until 1859, but otherwise, none of the twin-towered sampler buildings resemble the church. Martha's building has ball-topped corner pilasters like the earlier work, a striped base like the Krebs hospital (Fig. 570), and her iron gate is typical. Martha Jane Smith (1829–1900) was the daughter of shoemaker Richard Smith, whose shop and home were at 24 Thames Street. She married John A. Thompson (1823–after 1898) on November 8, 1848. *Maryland Historical Society, 73.78.23.*

Saint Joseph's Academy

Fig. 575. Elizabeth Ann
Bayley Seton (1774–1821)
by Charles Balthazar Julien
Fevret de Saint-Memin,
1797. Pen and engraving on
paper; 2″ in diameter.
Elizabeth Ann was a daughter of Dr. Richard Bayley
(1745–1801) and Catherine
Charlton (d.1777). Known
as Betty Bayley, she was a
society belle of New York
when she married William
Magee Seton (1768–1803),
scion of a shipping empire,
on January 25, 1794. His
death and financial disaster
left her the destitute mother
of five children by 1804.
Corcoran Gallery of Art,
Washington, D.C., 76.15.

The needlework pictures from Saint Joseph's Academy comprise the largest group of recognizable embroideries from a Catholic girls' school in the United States, and they reflect the career of America's most famous Catholic woman, Saint Elizabeth Ann Seton.[1] After teaching briefly in New York City and in Baltimore, she established her school for girls in Emmitsburg, Maryland, in 1809. Directed by the Sisters of Charity, it continued as Saint Joseph College until 1972.

Elizabeth Ann Bayley Seton (Fig. 575) was born an Episcopalian in New York City, and it was after marriage and widowhood that the young mother of five was converted to Catholicism at the age of thirty. She then undertook teaching as a means of support, but distrust of her newly adopted religion thwarted her teaching efforts in New York, and being assured of greater acceptance among the Catholics of Baltimore, she moved there in June of 1808. She was keeping a small school on Paca Street and had been joined by four other pious women when she embraced the ideology of the French Daughters of Charity of Saint Vincent de Paul. In 1809, she and her companions took the vows of this order, adopted a habit, and established the Sisters of Charity in America.[2] Samuel Sutherland Cooper, a recent Catholic convert, admired the endeavors of these women, and, on the condition that they move to Emmitsburg, he offered to fund the opening of a girls' boarding school. Thus it came about that Elizabeth Seton and her entourage journeyed into the wilderness fifty miles from Baltimore in the summer of 1809.

The founders of this school endured a rugged beginning in a run-down farmhouse, but their first building, a log structure, was ready for use in February of 1810 (Fig. 576). It was named Saint Joseph's House, but after it was sheathed and painted, it was generally known as the White House and it became the most popular subject for the students' pictorial embroideries during the 1820s (Fig. 577).[3] It was also painted in the background of the majority of mourning pieces worked

<hr />

1. Elizabeth Seton became the first American-born saint of the Catholic Church. She was beatified by Pope John XXIII on March 17, 1963.

2. Elizabeth Seton was inspired by the principles of the French Sisters of Charity, but the American Sisters of Charity were not affiliated with the French order until 1850.

3. A view of this building was also worked at the New York Orphan Asylum kept by the Sisters of Charity in 1819 (Sisters of Charity, Mount Saint Vincent-on-Hudson), and possibly others were worked under their direction elsewhere. An anonymous view of Saint Joseph's House and the Dubois Building, c.1840, but similar to the one in Figure 580, descended in a Quebec family and was probably worked at the Ursuline Academy (Christie's, January 20, 1990, Lot 546). This suggests that an engraving or lithograph of these buildings once existed. However, Sister Cecilia O'Conway, one of Mother Seton's original group, later become an Ursuline in Quebec, and her sister, Mrs. O'Madden of Philadelphia, taught needlework at the Ursuline Academy around 1840. I am indebted to Joyce Taylor Dawson of Ontario for this information.

during this period (Figs. 557, 578). Less common are embroidered renditions of the Dubois Building, the school's second major building, erected in 1826 (Fig. 580).[4]

It is not known whether Elizabeth Seton or one of her colleagues initiated the relatively uncommon practice of picturing the Academy's buildings in embroidery or paint. She is said to have helped a homesick Mary Jamison work her sampler in 1812 (Fig. 576), but the majority of known silk embroideries were made after her death in January 1821.[5] In 1820, because of advancing tuberculosis, Mother Seton relinquished her guidance of the Academy to Sister Margaret George, who served as directress until 1847.

As with other Catholic girls' schools, the working of pictorial silk embroideries continued longer at Saint Joseph's Academy than was customary at other schools, and while the mourning embroideries of the 1830s depart from the earlier form, some repetitious elements in their compositions usually offer clues to their origin (Fig. 582). Through the names on the epitaphs, their makers may often be identified in the enrollment records kept by the Sisters of Charity in Emmitsburg.[6]

Fig. 576. *Mary Jamisons work at saint Joseph's school 13 July 1812* and with the verse *Live Jesus live and let it be/ My life to die for love of thee.* Silk and chenille on linen; 10¼" x 18½". This early view of Saint Joseph's House reveals the log construction, which was later covered by clapboards. It accommodated thirty-two paying boarders by 1813. Another unmistakable sampler view of this building must have been erroneously entitled and dated in later years (B&C, Pl. LXV). A related sampler was made by Rebecca May Walker. It belongs to the Sisters of Charity, Emmitsburg.
Saint Joseph's Provincial House Archives, Emmitsburg, Maryland, no acc. no.

---

4. This building was named for Jean Dubois (1764–1842), a French émigré and Sulpician priest who founded Mount Saint Mary's College for Catholic men near Emmitsburg in 1808. Its early buildings sheltered Mother Seton and her companions when they reached Emmitsburg in 1809. Jean Dubois became the Bishop of New York in 1826.

5. Between 1809 and 1821, nineteen members of Mother Seton's community died (including two of her daughters), most of them from tuberculosis.

6. For more about the school's history and other embroideries, see *ANTIQUES*, March 1978, 590–9.

Fig. 577. Saint Joseph's Academy by Elinor Theresa Kelly, 1826. Silk, chenille, and paint on silk; 16¼″ x 22½″. Elinor's accurate and frequently found view of Saint Joseph's House belongs to Maryland's most impressive group of pictorial embroideries. Here, the front door is open to the visitors approaching in a carriage, and in the left background, the village of Emmitsburg nestles beneath the mountains. Saint Joseph's House still exists although by 1850 an addition had altered the symmetry of its facade, and it has survived two moves. Elinor Kelly was the daughter of John Kelly and Elizabeth Fitzsimmons of Pittsburgh. Her name and the date appear on the frame of her embroidery. She was no doubt the Ellen Kelly listed in the enrollment records of 1826. *Collection of Joan Stephens.*

Fig. 578. Anonymous memorial inscribed on the urn *I H S* and on the plinth *IN/ Memory/ of/ ANDREW CAPPEAU/ who/ departed this life/ August 18th/ 1818/ Aged 11 months and 11 days,* c.1827. Silk, chenille, paint, and ink on silk; 19¾″ x 23½″. On the hillside at left are the early buildings of Mount Saint Mary's College, a two-mile distance from the Academy. At far right is Saint Joseph's House and the Dubois Building. Attributed to Margaret Ann Cappeau, the eldest daughter of dry goods merchant Joseph Cappeau (1769–1855) and Sarah Galloway of Baltimore. Margaret entered Saint Joseph's Academy in 1826. On October 1, 1833, she married William H. Savage. Margaret's sisters, Mary, Cecilia, Frances, and Sarah, also attended the Academy. *Saint Joseph's Provincial House Archives, Emmitsburg, Maryland.*

Fig. 579. Anonymous mourning embroidery inscribed on the plinth *Sacred/ to the/ Memory/ of/ MARY LINDSAY./ Who died May 14th 1823./ aged 3 years.* c.1828–1832. Silk, chenille, paint, and ink on silk; 20¾″ x 23¼″. The practice of painting the Academy buildings and local scenery on memorials evidently ended about 1830 although student paintings depicted the expanding campus of the 1840s (*ANTIQUES*, March 1978, 599). The Lindsay view was probably derived from a drawing book, but the monument, trees, and style of painting relate to earlier work. The embroiderer may have been Sarah or Ellen Lindsay, enrolled at the Academy in 1828, or Sarah Lindsay, who entered in 1831. The backboard bears the label of *WILLIAM SHERMER/ No. 30, ARCH STREET,/ PHILADELPHIA,* a framer at this location from 1828 until 1849. *Author's collection.*

Fig. 580. Needlework picture of Saint Joseph's Academy by Mary Reanald McDonald, c.1831. Silk, chenille, and paint on silk; 18¼″ x 23¼″. Mary's embroidery depicts Saint Joseph's House and the once red Dubois Building, which has faded to a cream color. This large building housed an unprecedented enrollment of 167 boarding students in 1831. It was demolished in 1964.
Saint Joseph's Provincial House Archives, Emmitsburg, Maryland.

Fig. 581. Mary Reanald McDonald, c.1840–1845. Oil on canvas; 30″ x 25″. Mary McDonald, who worked the embroidery in Figure 580, was from Ebensburg, Cambria County, Pennsylvania. She joined her sister Alice at the Academy in 1831. Eventually they both became Sisters of Charity. Mary joined the Order in 1846.
Saint Joseph's Provincial House Archives, Emmitsburg, Maryland.

Fig. 582. Anonymous memorial with monument inscribed *Sacred/ to the/ Memory/ of/ FRANCES BAECHTEL/ Born/ February 1ˢᵗ 1805/ Died/ April 1ˢᵗ 1837/ Aged 32 years/ 2 months,* and with a smaller gravestone inscribed *IN/ Memory of/ David Baechtel,* c.1837. Silk, chenille, paint, and ink on silk; 16⅜″ x 25¾″. A verse on the monument discloses that the maker was the daughter of Frances Baechtel, and the work is attributed to Henrietta Baechtel who entered the Academy in 1837. A very similar memorial, to members of the de Roldos family, was probably worked by Antoinette de Roldos who was enrolled in 1835 (Monmouth County Historical Association, Freehold, New Jersey). Another memorial of similar composition, dedicated to Elizabeth A. Beelen, was sold in Sotheby's Sale 5746, September 10, 1988, Lot 277. It was probably worked by Elizabeth Beelin, a student at the Academy in 1833. Henrietta B. Baechtel (1823–1894) was the daughter of Samuel Baechtel (1793–1846) and Frances (1805–1837). They lived at White Oak Forest, near Hagerstown, and her father was one of the largest landowners in Washington County, Maryland. In 1844, Henrietta married Joseph B. Loose (1810–1884), and they lived in Hagerstown. Of their children, one son survived her.
Author's collection.

Fig. 583. "An Accessit of Excellence in the Second Class of Catechism Obtained by Miss Mary Leret Nichols." from the "Sr: Superior St: Joseph's. July 2d 1828." Paint and ink on paper; 4″ x 5″. Colorful certificates as well as printed rewards of merit were given to Academy students for proficiency in different branches of learning, and this custom continued into the late nineteenth century. By 1868, "gold medals and crowns" were being awarded and excellence in "Plain Needlework, French embroidery, and Silk Embroidery" was still individually recognized (Catalogue of Saint Joseph's Academy, 1868–1870).
Saint Joseph's Provincial House Archives, Emmitsburg, Maryland.

Worked by Catharine F. Queen. Academy of the Visitation. Georgetown. D.C. 1799.

Fig. 584. *Worked by Catharine F. Queen. Academy of the Visitation, Georgetown, D.C. 1799* inscribed in ink on silk beneath the picture, but probably at a later date. Silk, paint, and ink on silk; 16″ x 18″. Catharine's work and Figure 585 may have been attempts to depict the "two handsome Dwelling Houses" with a "large fish pond" that were advertised by John Threlkeld in the George Town *Sentinel* of June 25, 1799. This property, measuring 180 by 192 feet, was purchased by Mary de la Marche in 1800. The school continues at this location, which is now 35th and P streets in the District of Columbia. The Sisters were grazing their cows on this land until World War II. Catharine F. Queen (1788–1872) was the daughter of Joseph Queen (1754–1802) and Ann Edwardina Jerningham (1761–1814) of Upper Marlboro, Prince George's County. On April 14, 1817, Catharine married Robert Boone (1790–1861). They lived in Frederick, Maryland, and had one son.

NEEDLEWORK OF THE DISTRICT OF COLUMBIA

Embroideries known to have been worked in the District of Columbia are relatively rare, although the Visitation Convent and at least three women advertised girls' schools in the federal city before the government moved there in the fall of 1800. The first was Ann Vidler who commenced teaching on the first Monday in May of 1797,[1] but from these early schools, only the work from the Young Ladies' Academy in George Town (Visitation Convent) has been identified.

The Young Ladies' Academy, George Town

George Town was established at the fall line of the Potomac River by a vote of the Maryland Assembly in 1751, and it was the major tobacco port of the region when George Washington chose this area for the nation's new capital in 1791. George Town then became a part of the District of Columbia, but as an established town, like Alexandria, it was permitted to govern itself while the city of Washington was under the jurisdiction of Congress. This situation continued until 1871 when it was absorbed by the city, and the spelling of its name was changed to Georgetown.[2]

Also in 1791, the country's first Catholic college was opened in George Town, and its president assisted three French nuns in establishing a girls' school near the college in 1798. Known today as the Georgetown Visitation Preparatory School, it is the oldest Catholic girls' school in continuous existence within the original

---

1. *Washington Gazette,* April 22, 1797.
2. Eleanore C. Sullivan, *Georgetown Visitation since 1799* (Baltimore, 1975), 34, 87–8.

Republic,[3] and its opening was announced in *The Columbian Mirror and Alexandria Gazette* on November 1, 1798.

A New Academy
FOR YOUNG LADIES

George Town, September 15

MESDAMES De La Marche, Chevalier and Le Blond de la Rochefoucault, formerly members of the monasteries of St. Claire at Touts, and Amiens in France, respectfully inform the public that their New Academy will be fit for the reception of boarders and day scholars against the first of October next. . . .

The branches which are to complete their system of instructions are sewing, embroidery, writing, arithmetic, geography, and the English and French languages taught grammatically by well qualified professors. . . . The other liberal accomplishments, such as music, drawing, and dancing, will also be taught in the academy by eminent professors. . . .

The Boarders must have a correspondent in the neighbourhood to supply their other necessaries, and answer for the payment of the quarters. They are to bring with them a knife, fork and spoon, their bedstead and complete bed furniture, with this necessary observation, that the disposition of the sleeping rooms will not admit of beds larger than between 5 and 5½ feet by 2–2½.[4]

These French noblewomen had been tossed on the sea of misfortune since the French Reign of Terror began in 1792. They sought refuge in Charleston, Baltimore, New Orleans, Havana, and again in Baltimore, and finally in George Town, where Father DuBourg, president of the Catholic college, encouraged them to open a girls' school in a nearby rented house. In 1799, they moved to a better rented house, which they soon bought.[5] Shortly thereafter they were joined by three pious Catholic ladies from Philadelphia.[6] However, the lifestyle of sackcloth and sandals favored by the Frenchwomen, known as the Poor Clares, proved to be too austere for the Philadelphians, and in 1800 they moved into a separate house. It is now believed that the French nuns occupied the blue house shown in the embroideries (Figs. 584, 585), while the American ladies kept the school in the brick building, but there is little doubt that the school was their joint enterprise.

Mother de la Marche died in 1804, and her Poor Clare companions returned

---

3. The Carmelite Order was established in Port Tobacco, Charles County, Maryland, in 1790, but the nuns did not teach. They moved to Baltimore in 1831 and kept a school for girls from 1831 until 1851. A Biblical silk embroidery in the Baltimore Museum of Art is inscribed on the glass "*SUSAN HINKLE—CHRIST at the WELL. CARMELITE ACADY.*"

4. See front endpapers for a complete copy of this ad.

5. Sullivan, 48–9.

6. Ibid. The ladies were Alice Lalor, Mrs. Maria McDermott, and Mrs. Sharpe.

Fig. 585. Embroidered picture inscribed on the back "This is a picture of Georgetown Convent about the year 1800 made by Eliza Jaimeson of Charles County, Md." Silk and paint on silk; 13″ x 18″. Eliza Jameson (c.1786–1853) was the daughter of Walter Jameson (c.1760–1814) and Theresa Edelin (1765–1812). She died unmarried. *Georgetown Visitation Convent, no acc. no.*

to France. In the meantime, the three pious American ladies were joined by other Catholic women, and with the help of Bishop Leonard Neale (1747–1817) they were officially accepted into the French Order of the Visitation in 1817.[7] The school then became the Academy of the Visitation, but the samplers reveal that the new name did not immediately come into general use (Figs. 587, 588).

In 1824 Anne Royall visited the Convent and observed that "All denominations send their children to this seminary, which is much celebrated for its salutary regulations . . . the pupils must conform to a uniform dress, which is a brown frock and black apron in school, and a white dress on Sunday."[8] In 1829, after a visit from President Andrew Jackson, the courtesy was returned, and the young ladies marched in a line to the President's house. "It was an interesting spectacle. The uniform was snow white, blue cape, bonnets trimmed with blue ribbon, each lady carrying a parasol."[9]

No early enrollment records survive from the Academy nor is there a reference to the first teacher of needlework. The samplers in Figures 586 and 587 are rare for their obvious Catholic emblems, which are seldom found on work from Catholic schools in the eastern United States.[10]

Like many other schools of the early nineteenth century, the Academy of the Visitation had an annual examination and exhibition after which prizes for excellence were awarded, and girls from the junior and senior classes were chosen as queens for the day and crowned with wreaths (see Fig. 601). In 1828, the awards were presented by President John Quincy Adams.[11]

---

7. Ibid., 64. There were thirty-eight Sisters in December 1817.

8. Anne Royall, *Sketches of History, Life, and Manners, in the United States* (New Haven, 1826), 179, 181.

9. As described in the *Richmond Enquirer* and quoted in Sullivan, 80.

10. B&C, 156, describes the 1802 sampler of Teresia Fenwick of Saint Mary's County, Maryland, which is said to have a Calvary cross and to name the instructress *Eleanor Morland*. Catholic motifs are also known on Louisiana samplers, including a piece signed *FAIT PAR LOUISE/ CELESTE BABIN AUX ATTAKAPAS/ 1819.* Attakapas was the Indian name for St. Martinsville (Acadian House Museum, St. Martinsville).

11. Sullivan, 77–8.

Fig. 586. *Elenor Durkee her work done at the/ Young Ladies Academy Georg/Town A. D 1810 in the 10ᵗʰ Year of her age.* Silk on linen; 21″ x 15¾″. The nine-year-old Elenor created a modest monstrance for her cross and framed it with the words *love to H/IM/ and you.* Below her signature she centered another cross above the letters *IHS,* and beneath her trees she worked *CEDAR GROVE.* Elenor Durkee was probably from Baltimore. *The Baltimore American* of September 22, 1820, recorded the marriage of "Henry Green and Eleanor Durkee both of Baltimore."
Philadelphia Museum of Art, Whitman Sampler Collection, gift of Pet Inc. 69-288-216.

Below: Fig. 587a. Mary Rose Boarman worked hearts suspended within a golden monstrance above a flower-draped monument with the inscription *VENI LUMEN CORDIUM.*

Fig. 587. *Mary Rose Boarmans' work done/ at the Young Ladies Academy George/ Town A. D. 1818. in the 14ᵗʰ year of her/ age.* Silk on linen; 21⅝″ x 16½″. This flawlessly worked sampler, with its Catholic symbolism, was worked one year after the school became the Academy of the Visitation. Closer communication with the French Order may have introduced new Catholic motifs for the samplers. A Mary Rose (b.c.1805) has not been found among the many Boarmans of Maryland.
Georgetown Visitation Convent.

Fig. 588. *Eleanora Neale's/ work done at the/ Young Ladies/ Academy George/ Town A. D. 1823.* Silk on linen; 20½″ x 15⅜″. A sampler of similar design and with the same parrot was worked by eleven-year-old Eleanor Waring, who also named the *Young Ladies Academy George Town* in 1819 (Sotheby's Sale 5622, October 24, 1987, Lot 303). This sampler maker was probably Eleanora Neale (1808–1845), the daughter of Henry A. Neale, Sr. (d.1844), of Charles County (see back endpapers for her expenses). In 1827, she married, as his second wife, James Henry Neale (1802–1872).
Georgetown Visitation Convent, no. acc. no.

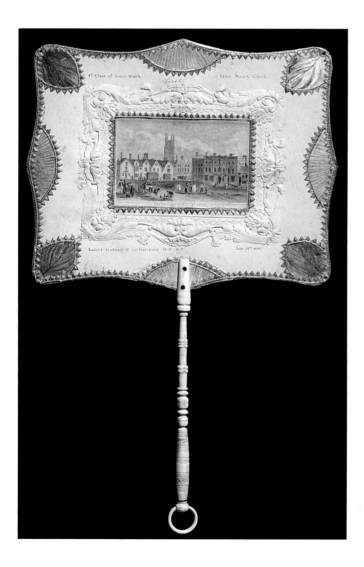

Fig. 589. A reward of merit in the form of a hand screen. Inscribed in ink "1st Class of Lace-work/ Miss Nancy Clark/ Ladies Academy of the Visitation G. T. D. C./ July 28th 1830." Paint and gold metallic paper on embossed cardboard; 7″ x 8¾″ with an ivory handle, 7¾″.
Georgetown Visitation Convent.

Fig. 590. *Julia Ann Crowley/ Washington City the 14th of April 1813.* Silk and chenille on linsey-woolsey; 20½″ x 18⅜″. The neat brick building may be the Academy where this sampler was worked. Julia Ann Crowley was probably the daughter of Washington ship carpenter Timothy Crowley, who lived near the Navy Yard bridge. Julia married Thomas Fitten, also a ship carpenter, on June 28, 1820.
Daughters of the American Revolution Museum, Washington, D.C., 63.11.

Samplers of Washington City

A small but appealing group of samplers was worked in Washington between 1810 and 1813, and is best represented by Maria Boswell's sampler with its glorious original colors (frontispiece). The first to investigate the history of these Washington City samplers was Elisabeth Donaghy Garrett, and she published Julia Ann Crowley's sampler (Fig. 590) with Martha Ensey's nearly identical counterpart worked on linen in the same year.[12] Mrs. Garrett pointed out that the Crowley and Ensey families lived near the Navy Yard and that their daughters may have at-

---

12. *ANTIQUES,* April 1975, 694–8.

Fig. 591. *Charlotte Clubb/ Washington City July 20th 1813*. Silk on linen; 20″ x 17½″. Charlotte's pattern is suggestive of Philadelphia work, but the bow-tied enclosure for her name definitely relates it to the three examples that picture the building with a bell tower. Probably similar to this sampler is the work of Julia O'Brien who named *Washington City* in 1812. Bolton and Coe describe her "Large brick house with garden" below a four-line verse and enclosed in a rose-and-tulip border. Charlotte Clubb has not been positively identified. Most likely she was the daughter of Elizabeth Clubb, who lived close to the Boswells in the Fifth Ward of the city in 1820.

American Museum in Britain, Claverton Manor, Bath, 59.237.

tended the school in a nearby brick academy building, which was burned by the British on August 27, 1814. Knowledge of the Boswell and Clubb samplers (frontispiece, Fig. 591) has reinforced the probability that the sampler makers walked to the Navy Yard school, since they also lived in that vicinity.[13] An earlier sampler by Julia Ann Crowley has recently emerged, which names the *Washington Navy Yard February th 10th 1810* (Fig. 592). It certainly supports the likelihood that the samplers were worked at the academy building near the Navy Yard, and the pieces depicting the cupolated building probably portray its appearance.

The border of the "Navy Yard" sampler is common to Philadelphia work (like Fig. 391). Its red mansion with white stringcourses and a checkered base also suggests that the Washington Navy Yard schoolmistress either came from Philadelphia or was educated there. An undated sampler in the Philadelphia Museum of Art was worked by eight-year-old Nancy Cooper who pictured a house and spindly legged sheep that are remarkably similar to Charlotte Clubb's, although other elements of the composition are quite different.[14]

Two other samplers of unknown origin name *Washington*,[15] and in her autobiography, Mrs. Julia A. Tevis described the samplers worked at a school kept by Mr. and Mrs. Simpson in Georgetown in 1813: "The girls at this school wrought the most elaborate samplers with a variety of stitches, and bordered them with pinks, roses, and morning glories, and sometimes, when the canvas was large enough, with the name and age of every member of the family."[16] Perhaps the best-known Washington seminary was kept by Miss Lydia English, who attended the Moravian Academy in Lititz and taught in Washington from 1826 until 1861.[17] At least one sampler dated 1831 is known from this school, and a surviving catalogue of pupils covers the years 1826 through 1831.[18]

13. I am indebted to Jean Taylor Federico and the late Michael W. Berry for knowledge of the Boswell sampler and the sampler makers' places of residence.

14. PMA, 69-288-86.

15. Charlotte Sutherland, 1809 (Krueger, *Gallery*, Fig. 60); Maria Brightwell, 1827 (*Winter Antiques Show Catalogue*, New York, 1976, 66). One sampler is known to name *Miss Bootes's Seminary, Georgetown*, c.1834 (*MAD*, July 1991, 31-F).

16. *Sixty Years In a School-Room: An Autobiography of Mrs. Julia A. Tevis, Principal of the Science Hill Female Academy* (Cincinnati: Western Methodist Book Concern, 1878), 84.

17. Thomas Froncek, ed., *An Illustrated History of the City of Washington* (New York: Alfred A. Knopf, 1977), 138–9. The 1850 U.S. census for the District of Columbia lists Lydia S. English, aged fifty, and forty-seven females in her household along with their ages and birthplaces.

18. Gloria Seaman Allen discovered the catalogue and is doing research on the history of this school.

Fig. 592. *Julia Ann Crowley/ Aged 10 years. the 14th/ of Decr 1809./ Washington Navy Yard February th 10th 1810.* Silk on linen; 21⅜″ x 17¾″. Julia's recently discovered sampler joins a group of five that name *Washington City*, one of which is her own work (Fig. 590).
Colonial Williamsburg Foundation, 1991-25.

NEEDLEWORK OF VIRGINIA AND THE SOUTH

Jamestown, Virginia, established in 1607, was the first permanent English settlement in America, and the United States census of 1790 found Virginia the most populous state of the young Republic.[1] However, South Carolina's Charles Town,[2] founded in 1670, became the largest and wealthiest English settlement south of Philadelphia, and it developed a high degree of sophistication and culture at an early date.

The *South Carolina Gazette* commenced publication in Charles Town on January 8, 1732, and on February 15, 1734/35, Mrs. Phillipene Henning advertised her school in Church Street where "Young Ladies will be taught French and English, also all sorts of Needle-work to perfection." This was the beginning of a continuous series of advertisements for girls' schools that appeared in the colonial papers of Charles Town and Williamsburg, Virginia, and they rival in number the notices of teachers in Boston and Philadelphia newspapers of the same period. Just as in the North, needlework was paramount among the subjects offered by the southern schoolmistress, but there the analogy ends.

Although southern samplers exist in considerable numbers,[3] they are scarce in comparison to those from the regions north of Maryland, a fact partly explained by the educational practices of an agrarian society. In the south the children in a family were often taught at home by a male tutor, while some families organized subscription schools and hired schoolmasters to teach in convenient locations.[4]

Fig. 593. *Eliz^th Boush Workd this Peice at E. Gardners 1768 9*. Silk on silk; 19½″ x 11½″. Elizabeth's rendition of the Sacrifice of Isaac was probably derived from Gerard de Jode's *Thesaurus Sacrarum Historiarum Veteris Testamenti* (Antwerp, 1585), 1:25. Elizabeth was the only daughter of Samuel Boush III (d. 1784) of Norfolk, an ardent American patriot who saved the *Records of Norfolk County* from destruction by the British. Her embroidery is the earliest-known American needlework picture to name the school of its origin. *Museum of Early Southern Decorative Arts, 2847.*

---

1. The total population of the five southern states was only slightly less than the total population of the eight northern states, but 35.6% of the southern population was Negro, and this was about nine-tenths of all the Negroes in the United States.
2. Officially Charleston after 1783.
3. B&C recorded ten eighteenth-century Charleston samplers, six worked between 1734 and 1774. This exceeded the number of colonial pieces from New York. Ten other eighteenth-century samplers were recorded from Virginia and father south.
4. Spruill, *Women's Life and Work in the Southern Colonies* (1938; reprint, 1972), 193–6.

Fig. 594. *E/LIZaBeth Gibbes her sampler Being/ 9 years OLD IVLY the 31 1729.* Wool on linen; 19¼″ x 8⅝″. Elizabeth worked the Apostles' Creed and the Lord's Prayer, and having accomplished this tedious task, she left her pictorial section unfinished. Her work may be the earliest-known sampler from the South. Elizabeth Gibbes (1720–1739) was the daughter of Benjamin Gibbes (1681–1721) and his second wife, Amarinta Smith. They lived in Charles Town, where Elizabeth married Joseph Izard (1715–1745) in 1738 and died before her nineteenth birthday.
Private collection; photograph courtesy of the Museum of Early Southern Decorative Arts.

Samplers, however, other than the simplest sort, were the products of formal instruction at schools kept by women. Of course, well-to-do families also had governesses, but their patterns were not reproduced in sufficient numbers to characterize an area. While only eight northern towns produced recognizable styles in samplers and pictorial embroideries during the colonial period,[5] it is nevertheless perplexing that not one pervasive pattern is known from schools of the colonial South.

The duration of the schools kept by the many women who advertised is often impossible to determine, but the teachers responsible for the embroideries of Elizabeth Hext and Elizabeth Boush (Figs. 595, 593) are known to have taught for several years, and these pieces should have counterparts. Schoolmistress Mary Hext was a young woman with three small children when her husband, Amias Hext, died in 1723.[6] She was probably already well established as a teacher before December 18, 1740, when the following notice appeared in the *South-Carolina Gazette:*

> Whereas by the late Fire in *Charlestown,* the Subscribers House was burnt down; This is to give Notice, that she has now taken a convenient airy House very suitable for the Reception of young Misses to board. Any Person or Persons in the Country may have their Daughters boarded and taught in a true and faithful Manner, at a reasonable Price, by *Mary Hext.*

In August of 1741, Mary Hext informed her patrons "that young Misses might be boarded and taught Needle Work, of all sorts . . . Writing, Arithmetick, Dancing and Musick is also taught by Masters well qualified, who give due Attendance in the same House of Col. Samuel Prioleau in Friend street, Charles-Town."[7]

---

5. Boston, Salem, Haverhill, and Newbury/Newburyport, Massachusetts; Newport, Rhode Island; Norwich, Connecticut; New York; and Philadelphia.

6. A. S. Salley, Jr., "Hugh Hext and Some of His Descendants," *The South Carolina Historical and Genealogical Magazine* 6, no. 1 (January 1905): 29–40. Amias Hext, planter of Colleton, devised one-third of his estate to his wife, Mary. The inventory of May 13, 1724 totaled £1860, including eleven Negroes, livestock, furniture, etc. Charleston County, South Carolina *Wills,* 58:327, 390 (MESDA records).

7. *South Carolina Gazette,* August 6, 1741 (see front endpapers). Providence Hext, a sister of Elizabeth, was married to Samuel Prioleau, Jr., but mention of the house probably identifies Mary's school's location rather than indicating that she lived with this family.

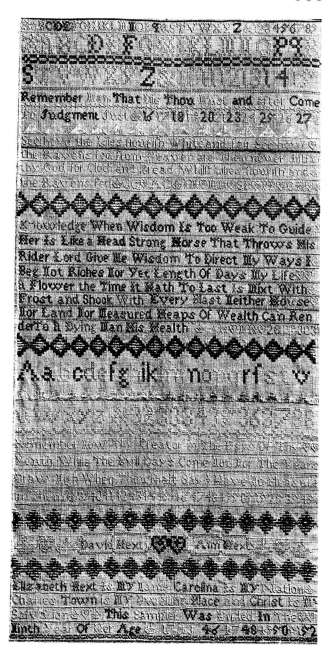

Fig. 595. *Elizabeth Hext Is My Name Carolina is My Nation/ Charles Town is My Dwelling Place and Christ is My/ Salvation This Sampler Was Ended In The/ Ninth Year of Her Age 1743.* Silk on linen; 17″ x 8⅜″. Elizabeth worked three alphabets and numerals to number 52; also a number of familiar maxims and the *Epigram on Providence* by John Hawkins of Boston. Her parents, *David Hext* and *Ann Hext,* are named beside paired hearts, and both hearts and crowns are repeatedly used as line-end motifs. Elizabeth Hext (1735–1769) was fifth among the five daughters of David Hext (d.1754) and Ann Hamilton (d.1754) of Charles Town. She married Robert Williams, Jr., in 1755.
The Liberty Corporation, Greenville, South Carolina; photograph courtesy of Sotheby's.

Mary again advertised her school in November of 1743, and probably she taught until her marriage to the widower John Dart in April 1746. Dart died in 1754, leaving a sizable fortune, so it is doubtful that Mary resumed teaching. Mary's birthplace, schooling, and maiden name are unknown, but there is little doubt that she taught Elizabeth Hext, the daughter of her deceased husband's brother.

Even before Elizabeth Boush's embroidery appeared (Fig. 593), the extraordinary advertisement of her Norfolk teacher had attracted attention (Fig. 596).[8]

---

8. Woody, *A History of Women's Education in the United States 1* (1929; reprint, 1974), 284–5; Spruill, *Women's Life,* 200.

Schoolmistress Elizabeth Gardner left no clues to the identity of her parents or her place of birth. She first advertised her school in Norfolk on March 21, 1766, and on November 25, 1769, she married Freer Armston (b.1738), a soap boiler from Leicestershire, England. Possibly Elizabeth taught until 1774 when the Loyalist Armstons prepared to leave the colony. They finally joined Lord Dunmore and the British fleet in December of 1775, and after much misery, they reached England safely in August 1777.[9]

An intensive search for Virginia samplers is under way at Colonial Williamsburg, and a Williamsburg group from the 1790s has been discovered (Fig. 598), together with a number of potential groups from the nineteenth century.[10] One group of four related samplers is represented here by the work of Mary Calloway White who named *James Town* in 1834 (Fig. 599). These pieces are unusual in having central scenes painted on the linen ground. Their similar patterns and materials suggest that they were made under one instructress between 1817 and 1834. The earliest, of 1817, names *Richmond,* as does its undated counterpart. Another names *Chesterfield Co. Va. Oct the 1st 1833.*[11] Possibly these were made under a teacher who moved about, or each girl identified her home town rather than the location of her school.

Mary White's sampler calls attention to the first girls' school in Prince Edward County, which was opened in 1817 in Jamestown (a village on the Appomattox River that no longer exists). A lottery provided the funds to erect a school building and Mrs. Mary R. Cowardin was the first preceptress.[12] During the previous year, Mrs. Cowardin had taught at the Pridesville Female Seminary in Amelia County, and an advertisement for this school described her "superior mental attainments" and "long experience in her profession."[13] Whether or not Mrs. Cowardin was teaching in Jamestown when Mary White made her sampler is now unknown. Mary's father was the headmaster of the Jamestown school during the early 1830s,[14] but the school's duration is undetermined.

The most successful girls' boarding school in the South opened in 1804 when the Moravians of Salem, North Carolina, decided to accept outsiders. They had established a school for their female children in 1772, and Salem Academy and College is now the oldest girls' school in continuous existence within the original Republic. This school found it necessary to publish notices discouraging applicants, rather than to entice them, for its popularity often exceeded its

9. British Public Record Office; Virginia Survey Report No. 2391. For more about Elizabeth Boush and Elizabeth Armston, see MESDA *Journal* 3, no. 2 (November 1977): 1–23.

10. This study was begun by Kimberly A. Smith, Assistant Textile Curator at Colonial Williamsburg. See the MESDA *Journal* 16, no. 2 (November 1990): 30–101.

11. The samplers of Mildred Malone, 1817, and Flora Virginia Homes are in the Valentine Museum, Richmond; see Amanda A. Bowles, 1833, in Krueger, *Gallery,* Fig. 108.

12. Herbert Clarence Bradshaw, *History of Prince Edward County, Virginia* (Richmond: The Dietz Press, 1955), 162.

13. *The Richmond Enquirer,* December 16, 1815.

14. Bradshaw, *History,* 163, 746.

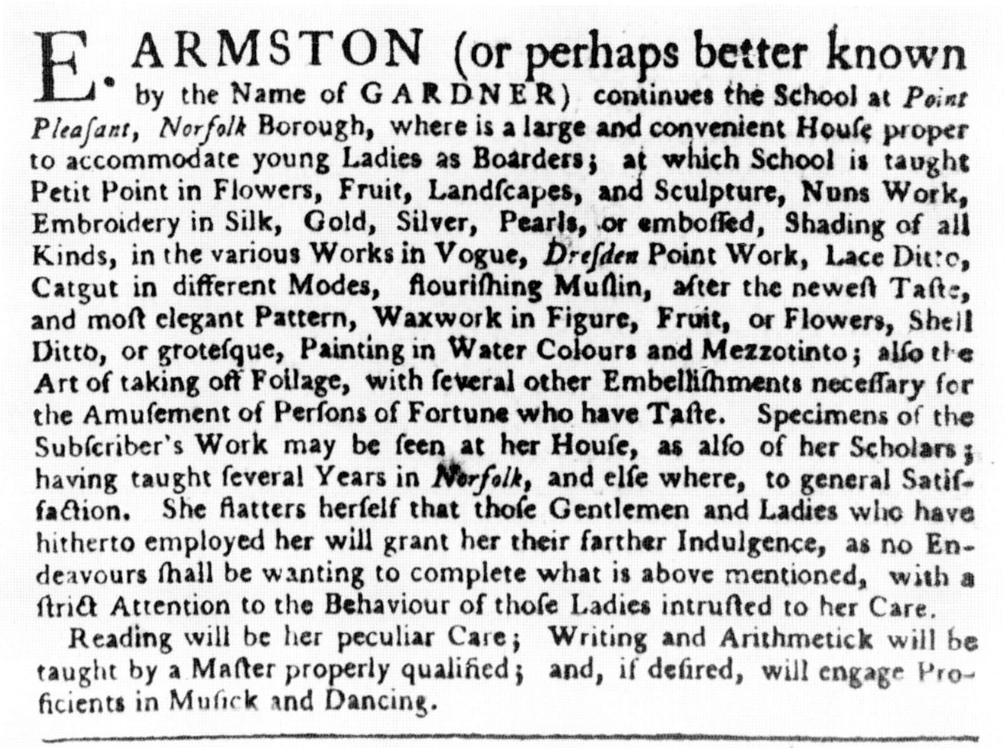

E. ARMSTON (or perhaps better known by the Name of GARDNER) continues the School at *Point Pleasant*, *Norfolk* Borough, where is a large and convenient House proper to accommodate young Ladies as Boarders; at which School is taught Petit Point in Flowers, Fruit, Landscapes, and Sculpture, Nuns Work, Embroidery in Silk, Gold, Silver, Pearls, or embossed, Shading of all Kinds, in the various Works in Vogue, *Dresden* Point Work, Lace Ditto, Catgut in different Modes, flourishing Muslin, after the newest Taste, and most elegant Pattern, Waxwork in Figure, Fruit, or Flowers, Shell Ditto, or grotesque, Painting in Water Colours and Mezzotinto; also the Art of taking off Foilage, with several other Embellishments necessary for the Amusement of Persons of Fortune who have Taste. Specimens of the Subscriber's Work may be seen at her House, as also of her Scholars; having taught several Years in *Norfolk*, and else where, to general Satisfaction. She flatters herself that those Gentlemen and Ladies who have hitherto employed her will grant her their farther Indulgence, as no Endeavours shall be wanting to complete what is above mentioned, with a strict Attention to the Behaviour of those Ladies intrusted to her Care.

Reading will be her peculiar Care; Writing and Arithmetick will be taught by a Master properly qualified; and, if desired, will engage Proficients in Musick and Dancing.

Fig. 596. Elizabeth Gardner Armston's advertisement for her young ladies' boarding school in Norfolk, as it appeared in *The Virginia Gazette*, Williamsburg, February 20, 1772.
Courtesy of the Museum of Early Southern Decorative Arts.

Fig. 597. Elizabeth Boush (c.1753–before 1810) by John Durand, 1769. Oil on canvas; 30″ x 25″. Elizabeth's portrait was painted the year she completed her Biblical embroidery (Fig. 593), and her flowers may be artificial ones made under the instruction of Elizabeth Gardner. In 1772, Elizabeth married Champion Travis (d.1810), and they had seven children. Their last home was in Williamsburg. It is now called the Travis House and belongs to the Colonial Williamsburg Foundation.
Colonial Williamsburg Foundation, 1982-271.

Fig. 598. *Ann Pasteur Maupin Her/ Sampler October The Twentieth Ninety One In/ The [Eleventh] Year Of/ Her Age.* Silk on linen; 16″ x 11⅛″. Ann's sampler is finely worked with reversible stitches, and two similar undated pieces are known. B&C (53) unquestionably described another by Sarah Hornsby. This piece also bears kinship to a Virginia example of 1761. See MESDA *Journal* 16, no. 2 (November 1990): 46–55. Ann Pasteur Maupin (1781–before 1856) was the daughter of Williamsburg harnessmaker Gabriel Maupin (1737–1800) and his second wife, Dorcas Allen (b.1745). Elizabeth Boush (Fig. 597) and her husband were godparents to Ann's sister, Mildred (b.1777). Ann married Norborne Booth Beall in 1799. *Colonial Williamsburg Foundation, 81-161.*

facilities.[15] Certainly needlework survives from Salem Academy, but unless labeled, it cannot be easily distinguished from Pennsylvania Moravian work (Fig. 600).

Although no recognizable silk embroideries are known from Charleston, they were surely being worked there,[16] and Philadelphia's Samuel Folwell was obviously aware of a market for his patterns when he traveled to the South seeking patronage. In 1818, carver and gilder Peter Fiche advertised his services and informed the ladies "he has constantly on hand a selection of handsome engravings which will be loaned to them for copying, free of expense, on condition that they will have their copies framed by him."[17] As elsewhere, Charleston teachers were no doubt copying popular prints for embroidery patterns, and finished work was placed in expensive frames.

While much southern needlework is waiting to be discovered, along with the history of the women who taught there, *The Crowning of Flora* (Fig. 601) vividly reveals that southern girls were learning to be ladies in the same ceremonious manner practiced in Boston and Philadelphia.

---

15. The first of a number of such notices appeared in *The Raleigh Star* of May 7, 1813. See front endpapers.
16. For a silk embroidery worked in Charleston about 1789, see *ANTIQUES*, February 1991, 368, Pl. I.
17. *Courier*, Charleston, October 22, 1818.

Fig. 599. *Mary Calloway White/ James Town Nove/mber 22 1834.*
Wool and paint on linen; 19⅝″ x 15⅝″. Mary Calloway White
was the daughter of William White (1776–1842) and Polly
Price. In the 1830s they lived in Jamestown, Prince Edward

County. Mary's father was headmaster of a girls' school where
Mary no doubt worked this sampler.
Museum of Early Southern Decorative Arts, M3199.

Fig. 600. Mourning embroidery by Minerva Heard, Salem Academy, c.1823. Silk, chenille, ribbon, paint, and ink on silk; 19⅞″ x 22¼″. In the typical Moravian manner, Minerva created a "floating island" on the silk, and above a slab inscribed *AAH/ Departed/ June 3/1822,* she surrounded her memorial verse with newly fashionable ribbon work. Another Academy student worked a nearly identical memorial dedicated to an infant brother, *M W,* who died in 1805 (private collection). Minerva Ann Heard (b.1806) was born in Morgan County, Georgia, to Abram A. Heard (1769–1822) and Nancy Coffee. Her home was in Calhoon, McMinn County, Tennessee, when she entered the Academy on May 3, 1822. She departed April 17, 1824. Minerva came to the school with her personal slave, who cared for her clothing, etc. In 1829, she married, as his second wife, Pryor Lea of Knox County, Tennessee.

Old Salem, Inc., Winston-Salem, North Carolina, 3664.

Fig. 601. *The Crowning of Flora: Raleigh Female Academy* by Jacob Marling (1774–1833), 1816. Oil on canvas; 30⅛" x 39⅛". This remarkable painting of a ceremony at the Female Academy in Raleigh, North Carolina, fits the descriptions of similar events held at countless girls' schools in both the North and South during the early nineteenth century. For a full account of its recent identification, see the essay by Davida Deutsch in *The Luminary, Newsletter of the Museum of Early Southern Decorative Arts* 9, no. 2 (Summer 1988). *Chrysler Museum, Norfolk, Virginia, gift of Edgar William and Bernice Chrysler Garbisch, 80.181.20.*

Fig. 602. *Eliza/ Waterman's/ Work. 1788.* Providence, Rhode Island. Silk and hair on linen; 14″ x 12″. Eliza labeled her building *the State House* and worked a fairly accurate rendition of this 1762 structure which still exists. Hers is one of the most elegant eighteenth-century samplers to survive from Mary Balch's school, and her nine figures have real hair. Elizabeth Waterman (1777–1870), called Eliza, was second among the thirteen children of Rufus Waterman (1746–1829) and Hannah Sprague (c.1752–1833). Her father was a prosperous manufacturer and cotton-mill owner in Providence. Eliza outlived all her siblings and died unmarried.
Private Collection; photograph courtesy of the Rhode Island Historical Society.

ACCOMPLISHMENTS
BECOME
AMERICAN ART

SAMPLERS HAD SCARCELY ceased to be a standard part of a girl's education when they became of interest to antiquarians, and their history was considered by Fanny Bury Palliser when she wrote *A History of Lace* in 1864.[1] A decade later, collecting early American artifacts was accelerated by Centennial exhibitions, and by the 1880s collecting schoolgirl embroidery was well underway in both England and America. Samplers were especially popular with collectors for several unique reasons: the majority were worked by children aged six to fourteen years, and they were usually signed and dated; also, they were never created to be sold, had seldom been altered, and were consistently genuine.

In both England and America, the first well-known collectors were men. In 1896, Andrew W. Tuer's *History of the Hornbook* included a chapter on samplers with illustrations from his collection. Collector Marcus B. Huish was instrumental in organizing a sampler exhibition at the Fine Arts Society in London in 1900, and his *Samplers and Tapestry Embroideries* (1900) became the first book devoted solely to these subjects. Another collector, Mrs. R. E. Head, wrote about samplers for *Connoisseur* of March 1902, and she was already lamenting their rising prices. In 1913, a revised edition of the Huish book included a section on American samplers, which was largely derived from an article by Alice Morse Earle in *The Century Magazine* of March 1912.[2] She reminded collectors that "It would have been comparatively easy in past years to gather a collection of samplers in this country; but it will be easy no longer; for, like all other 'antiques,' they are now sought for by dealers, and cherished with exceptional jealousy by rustic owners." Despite her dire predictions, collecting was encouraged by Mrs. Earle. Between

---

1. On page 5 she recorded the reference to a sampler in the household account book of Elizabeth of York, 1502, but Huish was evidently unaware of this in 1900 and 1913.
2. Published after the death of Alice Morse Earle (1851–1911).

Fig. 603. Alice Morse Earle (1851–1911) was the daughter of Edwin Morse and Abigail Clary of Worcester, Massachusetts. In 1874 she married Henry Earle of Brooklyn, New York. Her interest in early American life and artifacts was shared by her sister Frances Clary Morse, who was also an author and antiquarian. Mrs. Earle was survived by three of her four children.
American Antiquarian Society.

1891 and 1903 she wrote sixteen books about early American life and artifacts, and samplers were not neglected. Collectors have searched in vain for Polly Coggeshall's Bristol, Rhode Island, sampler, which Earle illustrated in 1899.[3] Polly was the sister of Patty (Fig. 221).

The sampler collection of Alexander Wilson Drake (1843–1916) was featured in *The Delineator* of September 1903, and in 1911 Alice Earle called it the finest collection in America.[4] Drake was born in New Jersey and became an important engraver and art director in New York City, where he was among the founders of both the Grolier Club and the Aldine Club. His samplers were shown at the Art Association of Indianapolis in 1905, the Corcoran Gallery in Washington in 1908, and the Cincinnati Art Museum in 1909. In 1913 the Drake Collection was auctioned at the American Art Galleries in New York where 2039 lots included 303 samplers, but only three were illustrated in the catalogue. Martha C. Hooton's New Jersey sampler (Fig. 535), the most widely published sampler in the collection, sold for $57. (In 1987 it brought $44,000 at Sotheby's.)[5] A Newport sampler of 1795, despite poor condition, was sold to the Metropolitan Museum of Art for $80.[6]

In 1909, attention was called to another important collection when sixty samplers belonging to George Arthur Plimpton (1855–1936) were exhibited at Teachers' College of Columbia University. Plimpton was the New York publisher who made Ginn & Company the best-known textbook firm in the world. He also formed the world's largest collection of educational books and manuscripts, and America's largest collection of hornbooks, all of which eventually went to Columbia University. His samplers, however, remained with his family until they were auctioned at Skinner Galleries in 1986.[7]

Many important collections were begun by American women before 1920, and a number of these now form the nucleus of museum collections. An early enthusiast was Mrs. Bradbury Bedell, née Emmeline Reed (1853–1920), of Philadelphia, who collected both American and foreign samplers (Figs. 288, 532, 553). Her collection of 167 framed pieces was a bequest to the Vassar College Library in 1920.[8] Her sister-in-law, Miss Margaret S. Bedell of Catskill, New York, had similar interests, and her samplers, mostly of European origin and numbering more than one hundred, went to the Brooklyn Museum upon her death in 1932.

Mrs. Virginia Bonsal Purviance White (1870–1955) lived in Baltimore and began collecting in the 1890s. Her samplers were given to the Baltimore Museum

3. Earle, *Child Life in Colonial Days* (New York: Macmillan, 1899), 334. Reproduced in Ring, *Virtue,* Fig. 107.
4. *The Century Magazine* 83, no. 5 (March 1912): 685. *The Delineator* article of 1903 was called to my attention by Mary Jaene Edmonds.
5. Sale 5551, January 31, 1987, Lot 1056.
6. See Ring, *Virtue,* Fig. 19, or Huish, *Samplers and Tapestry Embroideries* (1913), Fig. 46.
7. Sale 1098, May 30, 1986.
8. Called the Martha Reed Collection in honor of her niece, a Vassar alumna. All pieces listed in B&C are not at Vassar because some were given to members of her family. Unlocated now is the Chesterford School sampler, Pl. XCV.

of Art by her daughter-in-law in 1973 (Figs. 210, 276, 554). Mrs. Emma Blanxious Hodge (1862–1928) was a Chicago collector whose samplers were exhibited at the Art Institute of Chicago in 1914, and she wrote about samplers for the *Bulletin of the Minneapolis Institute of Arts* when her collection was shown there in April 1921.[9] She owned pieces of great importance, which were illustrated by Bolton and Coe (Pls. XXV, CVI, CIX), but their location was unknown when the remnants of the collection were sold at Sotheby's on February 2, 1980.[10]

Possibly the foremost connoisseur among early sampler collectors was Eva Johnston Coe (1866–1941), who co-authored *American Samplers* (1921). Mrs. Coe's father was one of the founders of the Metropolitan Museum of Art and its first president. However, upon her death, her superb collection, consisting of about three hundred pieces, went to the Cooper-Union (now the Cooper-Hewitt Museum), and in keeping with her wishes, her daughters' samplers eventually joined hers.[11]

Interest in samplers grew rapidly during the teens of the twentieth century. Dwight M. Prouty, curator at the Society for the Preservation of New England Antiquities, mounted an impressive exhibit of needlework in the spring of 1913. It included at least sixty-five framed samplers, and Mrs. Thomas A. Lawton loaned a large album with 187 samplers sewn to its pages. Also displayed were needlework pictures and embroidered coats of arms.[12] Appreciation of samplers had been equally high in Providence since an early date, and probably reflected awareness of work from Mary Balch's school. In 1920 the Rhode Island Historical Society sponsored a loan exhibition consisting of 334 embroideries. Among them were stunning eighteenth-century samplers from Newport and Providence, and the Society had the foresight to photostat the most important pieces.

In the meantime, the Massachusetts Society of the Colonial Dames of America was conducting a remarkable survey of samplers with the help of members throughout the country, and in 1921 they published their monumental study called *American Samplers*. This book by Boston's Ethel Stanwood Bolton and New York collector Eva Johnston Coe was reviewed in the first issue of the magazine *ANTIQUES*, January 1922, in which the editor, Homer Eaton Keyes, chided the authors for having neglected two important collections. They did fail to mention the collection of the New Hampshire Historical Society, but the usually careful Homer Keyes simply overlooked the entries belonging to New York collector Mabel Herbert Harper (1880–1957).

Mrs. Lathrop Colgate Harper was better known as Mabel Herbert Urner, whose newspaper column called "Helen and Warren" was syndicated throughout this country and abroad for thirty years. She and her book dealer husband were

Fig. 604. Alexander Wilson Drake (1843–1916), engraver, artist, author, and collector, was born near Westfield, New Jersey. He studied in New York, and in 1870 he was the art director for *Scribner's Monthly*, which became *The Century Magazine* in 1881. Drake married three times and was survived by two daughters. *The Grolier Club.*

9. *Bulletin* 10, no. 4 (April 1921): 25–8.

10. Sale 4338, Lots 1302–38.

11. For Coe samplers see Figs. 10, 50, 76, 123, 128, 140, 162, 282, 287, 395, 398, 401, 469, 470, and 556.

12. See *The Christian Science Monitor,* May 3, 1913. From the Lawton Collection are Figs. 75 and 279.

Fig. 605. *Susanna,/ Leak,/ Aged 12/ Years/ 1826.*
Silk on wool; 12½" x 12¾". English collector
Andrew W. Tuer prized this sampler for its
depiction of a horn book, and late in her life he
met its maker. It appears in *History of the Horn-*
book, Vol. II (1896) 259, with its print source (by
Godby after Metz) as the frontispiece. The print,
entitled *The School,* is above a verse by Isaac
Watts. Various versions of this composition are
known. See Ring, *Treasures,* Figure 1.
Author's collection.

avid collectors of samplers, books, and many other things. Alice Van Leer Car-
rick wrote about her samplers for *Country Life* of December 1924, where they appeared in glowing color. Upon her death, Mrs. Harper left eight hundred
samplers, mostly of foreign origin, to the Metropolitan Museum of Art.

The first notable company collection was formed by the Whitman Chocolate
Company which commenced business in Philadelphia in 1842. Walter P. Sharp
was president of the company in 1912 when he created an assorted box of choco-
lates with packaging inspired by his grandmother's sampler. It soon became the
best-selling box of candy in America, and the Whitman Company began collecting samplers. In 1969 when the collection was given to the Philadelphia Museum
of Art,[13] it consisted of more than fifteen hundred pieces from many nations.

After the 1920s, collecting continued but scholarly interest in samplers sub-
sided. A lone exception was Nancy Graves Cabot. She recognized that the colonial fishing lady and her companions in canvas work were the products of Boston
boarding schools, and she pointed out their relationship to samplers of the same
period in *The Magazine ANTIQUES* of July 1941. Although Bolton and Coe were
aware of regionalism in American samplers, no one else expanded their studies
between the 1920s and the 1960s.

During this period, Abby Aldrich Rockefeller was the best-known collector
who actually liked mourning embroideries, which had generally been misunder-

---

13. A gift of the parent company, Pet Inc. Eight Whitman samplers are illustrated here.

stood and scorned by collectors, including Alice Morse Earle.[14] Undaunted by the unappreciative, Mrs. Rockefeller boldly hung Rhode Island memorials along her staircase at Bassett Hall in Williamsburg. Another exceptional admirer of memorials was Miss Ethel Frankau, a vice president of Bergdorf Goodman in New York.[15]

During World War II collecting lagged, but in 1944 and 1945 a remarkable auction of American antiques took place at Parke-Bernet Galleries in New York. It required six sales and twenty-eight sessions to disperse the collection of Mrs. Jonathan Amory Haskell, née Margaret Riker (1864–1942) of Red Bank, New Jersey, and New York City. Hers was said to have been the largest collection of Americana ever brought together by one person, and it included many samplers and embroidered pictures. Laura Hyde's spectacular Connecticut sampler (Fig. 234) went to the Metropolitan Museum for the relatively high price of $130. A similar example (Fig. 233) brought $9,000 at auction in 1983, and it was considered a sleeper.

Attitudes changed in the 1960s. In 1964 Averil Colby wrote the most thorough book ever to appear on English samplers, and in 1968 Margaret Schiffer offered important information in *Historical Needlework of Pennsylvania*. During the 1970s, even mourning embroideries gained wider acceptance, and this was partly stimulated by dispersal of folk art from the Halpert and Garbisch collections.[16] The latter, in particular, included a wealth of memorials, most of which had been purchased and stored, but never displayed.

The year 1966 saw the appearance of the most zealous sampler collector of the second half of the twentieth century. This was Philadelphia businessman Theodore H. Kapnek. In about ten years he assembled a collection of samplers that rivaled or surpassed the quality of earlier collections, and it soon filled the walls of a home already rich in antique furniture, porcelains, and miniature furniture. In 1979, he bought from the heirs of Mrs. Thomas A. Lawton of Rhode Island the important sampler collection she had formed before 1920, consisting of about two hundred pieces. He kept the most colorful work and sold the rest to others.

Ted Kapnek died in August 1980, and when his collection was auctioned at Sotheby's on January 31, 1981, needlework prices changed for all time.[17] Five samplers in the Kapnek Sale sold for more than $20,000 each, and 172 lots ex-

14. Mrs. Earle called mourning embroideries "decadent successors of the significant heraldic embroideries of early years," which indicates that she also mistook heraldic embroideries for mourning devices (Earle, *Child Life,* 327).

15. *ANTIQUES,* November 1946, 315.

16. SPB, Halpert, Sale 3572, November 15–16, 1973; Garbisch, Sale 3595, January 23–24, 1974; Sale 3637, May 8–9, 1974; and Sale 3692, November 12, 1974. Illustrated here from the Garbisch Sales: Figs. 81, 86, 281, 342, 346, and 522.

17. A sampler sold in 1974 for $3,750 (Fig. 522) held the auction record until one sold for $5,700 in 1980 (Fig. 141). SPB, Garbisch III, Sale 3692, November 12, 1974, Lot 72; C. G. Sloane & Co., Sale of June 5–8, 1980.

ceeded $641,000. It was clear that folk art collectors were looking at samplers as never before.

New records were set in 1987 when a Philadelphia silk embroidery (Fig. 380) sold at Christie's in January for $187,000, and one week later a sampler (Fig. 602) commanded $192,500 at Sotheby's. This figure was surpassed in June when Ruthy Rogers' sampler (Fig. 147) brought $198,000 at Skinner's, and her work maintains the auction record for a sampler.[18] Schoolgirl art, however, soared to a new level in 1989 when a painting on silk (Fig. 606) sold at Christie's for $374,000.[19]

Despite rising prices and growing enthusiasm for collecting samplers, major collections are still being given to museums. In 1981, the bequest of Gertrude M. Oppenheimer added about five hundred samplers from many nations to the already impressive collection at the Cooper-Hewitt Museum, and the choice American samplers owned by Barbara Schiff Sinauer were a bequest to the Metropolitan Museum in 1984.

People collect samplers for a variety of reasons. Some buy them simply as "homey" accessories to antique furniture in bedrooms and children's rooms. The knowledgeable needlewoman may be attracted to intricate stitchery and skillful technique most likely to be found in samplers that are early and foreign. Choice seventeenth-century pieces are still available. Some collections are confined to pieces from one state, or even one county; others seek a variety of styles in alphabets or concentrate on special verses. However, the majority of collectors choose samplers for their visual impact as decorations. A variety of stitches is usually less important than a lively naïveté, and childlike imperfections are apt to be more appealing than flawless execution. This often contributes to the preference for American samplers over English ones and the correspondingly higher prices. Connoisseurs want samplers or pictorial embroideries of good color and condition that fit into the historical context of their time. Very unique or puzzling pieces are generally avoided. Increasingly enlightened collectors often seek examples of the most outstanding schools of work, which offer an overview of the trends in schoolgirl needlework during the colonial and Federal periods. Consequently, many meaningful collections have been formed in recent years. Indeed, after a century of collecting, these lovingly wrought works of American girlhood have achieved appreciation quite beyond the wildest expectations of the mistresses or their makers.

---

18. Christie's, January 24, 1987, Lot 110; Sotheby's Sale 5551, January 31, 1987, Lot 1050; Skinner Sale 1156, June 6, 1987, Lot 182.
19. Christie's, June 3, 1989, Lot 181.

Fig. 606. Anonymous painting of Aurora. Probably Boston, c.1820. Paint and gilded paper on silk, with a printed paper label inscribed *"Hail, bright Aurora, fair Goddess of the Morn!/ Around thy splendid Car, the smiling Hours submissive wait attendance, ascend—and/ reillume the face of Nature with thy refulgent beams, & from the Arch of Heaven banish night."* 21″ x 24½″. The frame bears the label of STILLMAN LOTHROP/ LOOKING GLASS SHOP/ No. 71. MARKET STREET, BOSTON, working at this address 1818–1822. Four very similar paintings are known and two are attributed to girls born in 1797 and 1798 (see Rumford, *American Folk Paintings* [1988], 225–226, 239–241, 256). Probably from the same school is a depiction of Naiad (Christie's Sale of January 26, 1991, Lot 177).
Private Collection.

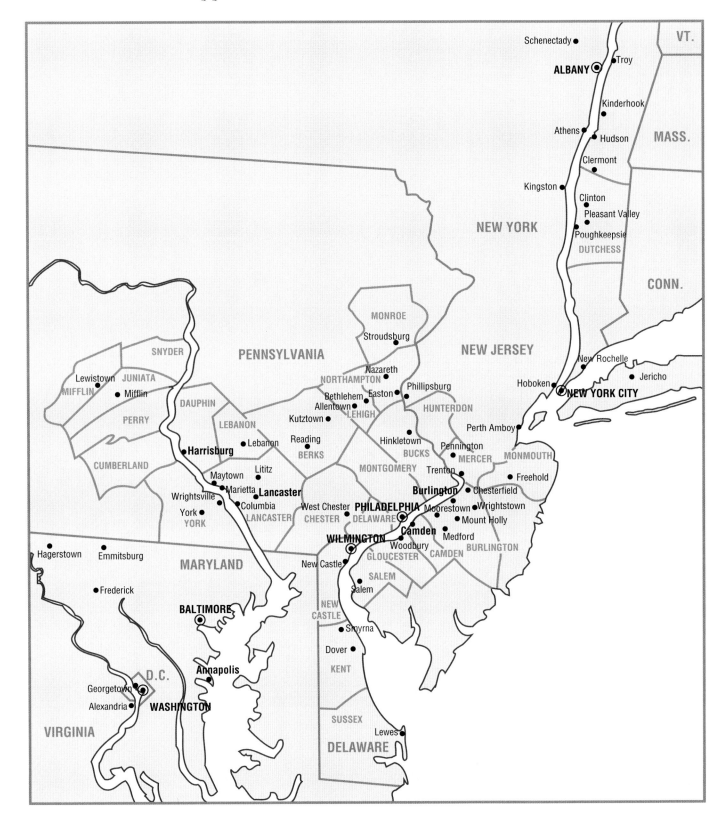

Richmond

Williamsburg

NORFOLK

VIRGINIA

Salem

Raleigh

NORTH CAROLINA

New Bern

SOUTH CAROLINA

GEORGIA

CHARLESTON

Beaufort

SAVANNAH

Appendix

PMA   Philadelphia Museum of Art, Philadelphia, Pennsylvania.
RIHS   Rhode Island Historical Society, Providence, Rhode Island.
SPNEA   Society for the Preservation of New England Antiquities,
                       Boston, Massachusetts.

PUBLICATIONS

Allen, *Family Record*   Allen, Gloria Seaman. *Family Record: Genealogical Watercol-
                          ors and Needlework.* Washington, D.C.: DAR Museum,
                          1989.

ANTIQUES   *The Magazine ANTIQUES.* New York: Brant Publications.

A&AW   *Antiques And The Arts Weekly.* Newtown, Conn.: The Bee
                          Publishing Company.

Ashton   Ashton, Leigh. *Samplers, Selected and Described.* London &
                          Boston: The Medici Society, 1926.

B&C   Bolton, Ethel Stanwood and Eva Johnston Coe, *American
                          Samplers.* Boston: Massachusetts Society of the Colonial
                          Dames of America, 1921.

The Clarion   *The Clarion, America's Folk Art Magazine* (The Museum of
                          American Folk Art quarterly). New York. Renamed
                          Folk Art, fall 1992.

Colby   Colby, Averil. *Samplers.* London: B. T. Batsford, 1964.

Edmonds   Edmonds, Mary Jaene. *Samplers & Samplermakers.* New
                          York: Rizzoli/Los Angeles County Museum of Art,
                          1991.

EIHC   *Essex Institute Historical Collections* (Essex Institute quar-
                          terly). Salem, Mass.: Essex Institute.

Fawdry and Brown   Fawdry, Marguerite and Deborah Brown, *The Book of Sam-
                          plers.* New York: St. Martin's Press, 1980.

Harbeson   Harbeson, Georgiana Brown. *American Needlework.* New
                          York: Coward-McCann, 1938.

Huish   Huish, Marcus B. *Samplers and Tapestry Embroideries.*
                          London: Longmans, Green, and Co., 1913.

IGI   *International Genealogical Index of the Church of Jesus Christ of
                          the Latter Day Saints.* Salt Lake City, Utah.

King   King, Donald. *Samplers.* London: Her Majesty's Stationery
                          Office, 1960.

Krueger, *Gallery*   Krueger, Glee F. *A Gallery of American Samplers: The
                          Theodore H. Kapnek Collection* (exhibition catalogue).
                          New York: E. P. Dutton in association with the Museum
                          of American Folk Art, 1978.

Krueger, *New England*   Krueger, Glee. *New England Samplers to 1840.* Sturbridge,
                          Mass.: Old Sturbridge Village, 1978.

MAD   *Maine Antique Digest* (a monthly newspaper). Waldoboro,
                          Maine: Maine Antique Digest, Inc.

NEHGR   *The New England Historical and Genealogical Register* (New
                          England Historic Genealogical Society quarterly).
                          Boston, Mass.

NYGBR   *The New York Genealogical and Biographical Record* (The New
                          York Genealogical and Biographical Society quarterly),
                          New York.

PGM   *The Pennsylvania Genealogical Magazine (The Genealogical So-
                          ciety of Pennsylvania biannual).* Philadelphia. Issues irreg-
                          ular between 1895 and 1948 and known as *Publications
                          of the Genealogical Society of Pennsylvania.*

PMHB   *The Pennsylvania Magazine of History and Biography* (The His-
                          torical Society of Pennsylvania quarterly). Philadelphia.

Ring, *Treasures.*   Ring, Betty. *American Needlework Treasures: Samplers and Silk
                          Embroideries from the Collection of Betty Ring.* New York:
                          E. P. Dutton in association with the Museum of Amer-
                          ican Folk Art, 1987.

Ring, *Virtue*   Ring, Betty. *Let Virtue Be a Guide to Thee: Needlework in the
                          Education of Rhode Island Women, 1730–1830* (exhibition
                          catalogue). Providence: The Rhode Island Historical So-
                          ciety, 1983.

Schiffer   Schiffer, Margaret B. *Historical Needlework of Pennsylvania.*
                          New York: Charles Scribner's Sons, 1968.

Swain   Swain, Margaret H. *Historical Needlework: A Study of Influ-
                          ences in Scotland and Northern England.* London: Barrie &
                          Jenkins, 1970.

Swan, *Guide.*   Swan, Susan Burrows. *Winterthur Guide to American Needle-
                          work.* A Winterthur Book/Rutledge Books. New York:
                          Crown Publishers, Inc., 1976.

Swan, *Plain & Fancy*   Swan, Susan Burrows. *Plain & Fancy: American Women and
                          Their Needlework, 1700–1850.* New York: Holt, Rinehart
                          and Winston, 1977.

AUCTION HOUSES

Christie's   Christie, Manson & Woods International, Inc., New York.
Christie's East   A division of Christie, Manson & Woods, Inc., New York.
PB   Parke-Bernet Galleries, Inc., New York.

Skinner   Skinner, Inc., Bolton, Massachusetts.
Sotheby's   Sotheby's, New York.
SPB   Sotheby Parke Bernet, Inc., New York.

All auction house publications cited are for Americana sales.

Bibliography

Allen, Gloria Seaman. *Family Record: Genealogical Watercolors and Needlework.* Washington, D.C.: DAR Museum, 1989.

Allinson, William J., comp. *Memorials of Rebecca Jones.* Philadelphia, 1849.

Andrews, Charles C. *History of the New-York African Free-Schools from Their Establishment in 1781, to the Present Time.* New York: Mahlon Day, 1830.

Armes, Ethel, ed. *Nancy Shippen: Her Journal Book.* Philadelphia: J. B. Lippincott, 1935.

Ashton, Leigh. *Samplers, Selected and Described.* London and Boston: The Medici Society, 1926.

Barnard, Henry. *Normal School, and Other Institutions, Agencies, and Means Designed for the Professional Education of Teachers.* Hartford: Case, Tiffany and Company, 1851.

————, ed. *The American Journal of Education.* 14 vols. Hartford, 1856–1864.

Barrett, Walter. *The Old Merchants of New York City.* Vol. 3. New York: Thomas R. Knox & Co., 1885.

Benes, Peter. *Old-Town and the Waterside: Two Hundred Years of Tradition and Change in Newbury, Newburyport, and West Newbury, 1635–1835* (exhibition catalogue). Newburyport, Mass.: Historical Society of Old Newbury, 1986.

————. *Two Towns, Concord & Wethersfield: A Comparative Exhibition of Regional Culture 1635–1850* (exhibition catalogue). Vol. 1. Concord, Mass.: Concord Antiquarian Museum, 1982.

————, ed. *Families and Children: Annual Proceedings of the Dublin Seminar for New England Folklife, 1985.* Boston: Boston University, 1987.

Bennett, Allison P. *The People's Choice: A History of Albany County in Art and Architecture.* Albany: The Albany County Historical Association, 1980.

Bentley, William. *The Diary of William Bentley, D.D.* 4 vols. Salem, Mass.: Essex Institute, 1905–1914. Reprint. Gloucester, Mass.: Peter Smith, 1962.

Berkin, Ruth, and Mary Beth Norton, eds. *Women of America: A History.* Boston: Houghton Mifflin, 1979.

Bethune, Joanna Graham. *The Life of Mrs. Isabella Graham.* New York: John S. Taylor, 1839.

Blackburn, Roderic H. *Cherry Hill: The History and Collections of a Van Rensselaer Family.* Albany: Historic Cherry Hill, 1976.

Bolton, Charles Knowles. *Bolton's American Armory.* Boston: F. W. Faxon Co., 1927.

Bolton, Ethel Stanwood, and Eva Johnston Coe. *American Samplers.* Boston: Massachusetts Society of the Colonial Dames of America, 1921.

Bolton, Theodore, and Irwin F. Cortelyou. *Ezra Ames of Albany.* New York: New-York Historical Society, 1935.

Bourne, William Oland. *History of the Public School Society of the City of New York.* New York: George Putnam's Sons, 1873.

Bowditch, Harold. "Early Water-Color Paintings of New England Coats of Arms." *Publications of the Colonial Society of Massachusetts* 35 (December 1944): 173–210.

Bowen, Helen. "The Fishing Lady and Boston Common." *ANTIQUES* 4, no. 2 (August 1923): 70–3.

Bowen, Richard LeBaron. "The Scott Family Needle Work." *Rhode Island Historical Society Collections* 2, no. 1 (January 1943): 11–21; 2, no. 2 (April 1943): 49–57.

Bowie, Lucy Lee. "Madam Grelaud's French School." *Maryland Historical Magazine* 34, no. 2 (June 1944): 141–8.

Bowne, Eliza Southgate. *A Girl's Life Eighty Years Ago: Selections from the Letters of Eliza Southgate Bowne.* Introduction by Clarence Cook. New York: Charles Scribner's Sons, 1888.

Brant, Sandra, and Elissa Cullman. *Small Folk, A Celebration of Childhood in America.* New York: E. P. Dutton in association with the Museum of American Folk Art, 1980.

Branton, Harriet. "Sarah Foster Hanna and the Washington Female Seminary." *Western Pennsylvania Historical Magazine* 61, no. 3 (July 1978): 221–31.

Brecht, Samuel Kriebel, ed. *The Genealogical Record of the Schwenkfelder Families . . .* Pennsburg, Pa.: The Board of Publication of the Schwenkfelder Church, 1923.

Bridenbaugh, Carl. *Cities in the Wilderness: The First Century of Urban Life in America, 1625–1742.* New York: Ronald Press, 1938.

Brookes, George S. *Friend Anthony Benezet.* Philadelphia: University of Pennsylvania Press, 1937.

Cabot, Nancy Graves. "Another Needlework Picture." *The Magazine ANTIQUES* 45, no. 6 (June 1944): 300–1.

———. "Engravings as Pattern Sources." *The Magazine ANTIQUES* 58, no. 6 (December 1950): 476–81.

————. "Engravings and Embroideries." *The Magazine ANTIQUES* 40, no. 6 (December 1941): 367–9.

————. "The Fishing Lady and Boston Common." *The Magazine ANTIQUES* 40, no. 1 (July 1941): 28–31.

Carpenter, Charles H., Jr., and Mary Grace Carpenter. *The Decorative Arts and Crafts of Nantucket.* New York: Dodd, Mead & Co., 1987.

Caulfeild, Sophia Frances Anne, and Blanche C. Saward. *The Dictionary of Needlework: An Encyclopedia of Artistic, Plain and Fancy Needlework.* London, 1882. Reprint. New York: Crown, 1972.

Caulkins, Frances Manwaring. *History of Norwich, Connecticut: From Its Possession by the Indians, to the Year 1866.* Hartford: Case, Lockwood and Co., 1866. Reprint. Chester, Conn.: Pequot Press, 1976.

Channing, George G. *Early Recollections of Newport, R.I. from the Year 1793 to 1811.* Providence: A. J. Ward, Charles E. Hammett, Jr., 1868.

Claussen, W. Edmunds. *Wyck: The Story of an Historic House 1690–1970.* Philadelphia: privately printed, 1970.

Colby, Averil. *Samplers.* London: B. T. Batsford, 1964.

Colwill, Stiles Tuttle. *Francis Guy, 1760–1820.* Baltimore: Maryland Historical Society, 1981.

Cowles, Julia. *The Diaries of Julia Cowles.* Edited by Laura Hadley Moseley. New Haven: Yale University Press, 1931.

Crowninshield, Frances Boardman, ed. *Letters of Mary Boardman Crowninshield 1815–1816.* Cambridge, Mass.: Riverside Press, 1905.

Darusmont, Frances Wright. *Views of Society and Manners in America.* New York: F. Bliss and E. White, 1821.

Davidson, Mary M. *Plimoth Colony Samplers.* Marion, Mass.: The Channings, 1974.

The Decorative Arts of New Hampshire: A Sesquicentennial Exhibition. Concord, N.H.: The New Hampshire Historical Society, 1973.

DeCou, George. *Burlington: A Provincial Capital.* Philadelphia: Harris and Partridge, 1945.

Demos, John. *A Little Commonwealth: Family Life in Plymouth Colony.* New York: Oxford University Press, 1970.

DePauw, Linda Grant, and Conover Hunt. *Remember the Ladies: Women in America 1750–1815* (exhibition catalogue). New York: Viking Press in association with the Pilgrim Society, 1976.

Deutsch, Davida Tenenbaum. "John Brewster, Jr., An Artist for the Needleworker." *The Clarion* 15, no. 4 (Fall 1990): 46–50.

————. "Needlework Patterns and Their Use in America." *The Magazine ANTIQUES* 139, no. 2 (February 1991): 368–81.

————. "The Polite Lady: Portraits of American Schoolgirls and Their Accomplishments, 1725–1830." *The Magazine ANTIQUES* 135, no. 3 (March 1989): 742–53.

————. "Samuel Folwell of Philadelphia: An Artist for the Needleworker." *The Magazine ANTIQUES* 119, no. 2 (February 1980): 420–3.

————. "Washington Memorial Prints." *The Magazine ANTIQUES* 111, no. 2 (February 1977): 324–31.

Deutsch, Davida Tenenbaum, and Betty Ring. "Homage to Washington in Needlework and Prints." *The Magazine ANTIQUES* 119, no. 2 (February 1981): 402–19.

Dewees, Watson W. and Sarah B. *Centennial History of Westtown Boarding School: 1799–1899*. Philadelphia: Sherman & Co., 1899.

Dexter, Elizabeth Anthony. *Colonial Women of Affairs*. Boston: Houghton Mifflin, 1924.

Dwight, Elizabeth Amelia. *Memorials of Mary Wilder White*. Edited by Mary Wilder Tiletson. Boston: Everett Press, 1903.

Dyer, Elisha. "The Old Schools of Providence." *Narragansett Historical Register* 5, no. 1 (July 1886): 220–40.

Earle, Alice Morse. *Child Life in Colonial Days*. New York: Macmillan, 1899.

————. *Home Life in Colonial Days*. New York: Grosset & Dunlap, 1898.

————. "Samplers." *The Century Magazine* 83, no. 5 (March 1912): 676–85.

Earnshaw, Pat. *A Dictionary of Lace*. Shire Publications, Ltd., 1982.

Edmonds, Mary Jaene. *Samplers & Samplermakers*. New York: Rizzoli/Los Angeles County Museum of Art, 1991.

Egle, William Henry, ed. *Notes and Queries Historical, Biographical and Genealogical relating chiefly to Interior Pennsylvania*. Harrisburg, Pa., 1894–1901. Reprint. Baltimore: Genealogical Publishing Co., 1970.

Emery, Sarah Anna. *My Generation*. Newburyport, Mass.: Moses H. Sargent, 1893.

————. *Reminiscences of a Nonagenarian*. Newburyport, Mass.: William H. Huse & Co., 1879.

English Samplers at the Fitzwilliam. Cambridge: Fitzwilliam Museum, 1984.

Erb, Peter, ed. *Schwenkfelders in America*. Pennsburg, Pa.: Schwenkfelder Library, 1987.

Fairbanks, Jonathan L. et al. *Paul Revere's Boston: 1735–1818* (exhibition catalogue). Boston: Museum of Fine Arts, Boston, 1975.

Fairbanks, Jonathan L., and Robert F. Trent. *New England Begins: The Seventeenth Century*. 3 vols. Boston: Museum of Fine Arts, Boston, 1982.

Fawdry, Marguerite, and Deborah Brown. *The Book of Samplers*. New York: St. Martin's Press, 1980.

Field, June. *Collecting Georgian and Victorian Crafts*. New York: Charles Scribner's Sons, 1973.

Flynt, Suzanne L. *Ornamental and Useful Accomplishments: Schoolgirl Education and Deerfield Academy, 1800–1830* (exhibition catalogue). Deerfield, Mass.: Pocumtuck Valley Memorial Association and Deerfield Academy, 1988.

Franklin, Ruth B. "Some Early Schools and Schoolmasters of Newport." *Bulletin of the Newport Historical Society* 96 (January 1936): 13–31.

Frost, J. William. *The Quaker Family in Colonial America*. New York: St. Martin's Press, 1973.

Gaines, Edith. "Collectors' Notes: More Quillwork and Waxwork." *The Magazine ANTIQUES* 97, no. 2 (February 1970): 272–4.

—————. "Quillwork: American Paper Filigree." *The Magazine ANTIQUES* 78, no. 6 (December 1960): 562–5.

Gardiner, Dorothy. *English Girlhood at School: A Study of Women's Education through Twelve Centuries*. London: Oxford University Press, 1929.

Garrett, Elisabeth Donaghy. "American Samplers and Needlework Pictures in the DAR Museum, Part I: 1750–1806." *The Magazine ANTIQUES* 105, no. 2 (February 1974): 356–64.

—————. "American Samplers and Needlework Pictures in the DAR Museum, Part II: 1806–1840." *The Magazine ANTIQUES* 107, no. 4 (April 1975): 699–701.

—————. *At Home: The American Family 1750–1870*. New York: Harry N. Abrams, 1990.

—————. "The Theodore H. Kapnek Collection of American Samplers." *The Magazine ANTIQUES* 114, no. 3 (September 1978): 540–59.

Garvan, Beatrice B. *The Pennsylvania German Collection*. Philadelphia: Philadelphia Museum of Art, 1982.

Garvan, Beatrice B., and Charles F. Hummel. *Pennsylvania Germans: A Celebration of Their Arts 1683–1850*. Philadelphia: Philadelphia Museum of Art, 1982.

Gehret, Ellen J. *This Is The Way I Pass My Time*. Birdsboro, Pa.: The Pennsylvania German Society, 1985.

Giffen, Jane C. "Susanna Rowson and Her Academy." *The Magazine ANTIQUES* 98, no. 3 (September 1970): 436–40.

The Great River: Art & Society of the Connecticut Valley, 1635–1820 (exhibition catalogue). Hartford: The Wadsworth Atheneum, 1985.

Griffin, Frances. *Less Time for Meddling: A History of Salem Academy and College 1772–1866*. Winston-Salem, N.C.: John F. Blair, 1979.

Groft, Tammis Kane. *The Folk Spirit of Albany* (exhibition catalogue). Albany, N.Y.: Albany Institute of History and Art, 1978.

Hackenbroch, Yvonne. *English and Other Needlework Tapestries and Textiles in the Irwin Untermyer Collection*. Cambridge, Mass.: Harvard University Press for the Metropolitan Museum of Art, 1960.

Hanley, Hope. *Needlepoint in America*. New York: Charles Scribner's Sons, 1969.

Harbeson, Georgiana Brown. *American Needlework*. New York: Coward-McCann, 1938.

Harris, Estelle. "The Genealogical Sampler." *Daughters of the American Revolution Magazine* 60, no. 12 (December 1926): 713–22.

Hawke, David Freeman. *Everyday Life in Early America*. New York: Harper & Row, 1988.

Head, Mrs. R. E. "A Collection of English Samplers." *Connoisseur* 2 (March 1902): 164–70.

———. "A Collection of Needlework Pictures." *Connoisseur* 1 (November 1901): 154–61.

———. *The Lace and Embroidery Collector.* London: Herbert Jenkins, 1921. Reprint. Detroit: Gale Research Company, 1974.

Hersh, Tandy and Charles. *Samplers of the Pennsylvania Germans.* Birdsboro, Pa.: The Pennsylvania German Society, 1991.

Hinshaw, William Wade. *Encyclopedia of American Quaker Genealogy.* 6 vols. Ann Arbor: published by the author, 1926–1950.

"History in Needlework." *Historical New Hampshire* (April 1946): 9–13.

Hitchings, Sinclair. "Thomas Johnston." *Boston Prints and Printmakers 1670–1775.* Boston: The Colonial Society of Massachusetts, 1973.

Hole, Helen G. *Westtown Through the Years, 1799–1942.* Westtown, Pa.: Westtown Alumni Association, 1942.

Hopkins, Samuel. *Memoirs of the Life of Mrs. Sarah Osborn.* Worcester, Mass.: Leonard Worcester, 1799.

Hornor, Marianna Merritt. *The Story of Samplers.* Philadelphia: Philadelphia Museum of Art, 1971.

Hughes, Therle. *English Domestic Needlework 1660–1860.* London: Lutterworth Press, 1961.

Huish, Marcus B. *Samplers and Tapestry Embroideries.* 2nd ed. London: Longmans, Green, and Co., 1913.

Images of Childhood (exhibition catalogue). New Bedford, Mass.: Old Dartmouth Historical Society, 1977.

Jarman, T. L. *Landmarks in the History of Education.* London: Cresset Press, 1951.

Johnson, Mary. "Antoinette Brevost: A Schoolmistress in Early Pittsburgh." *Winterthur Portfolio* 15, no. 2 (Summer 1980): 151–68.

———. "Madame Rivardi's Seminary in the Gothic Mansion." *Pennsylvania Magazine of History and Biography* 104, no. 1 (January 1980): 3–38.

Jones, C. R. *Memento Mori; 200 Years of Funerary Art and Customs of Concord, Massachusetts* (exhibition catalogue). Concord, Mass.: Concord Antiquarian Society, 1967.

Jones, Mary Eirwen. *British Samplers.* Oxford: Pen-in-Hand Publishing Co., 1948.

Jourdain, M. *The History of English Secular Embroidery.* New York: E. P. Dutton and Co., 1912.

Kassell, Hilda. *Stitches in Time: The Art and History of Embroidery.* New York: Duell, Sloan and Pearce, 1966.

Kendrick, A. F. *English Embroidery.* London: G. Newnes, 1905.

———. *English Needlework.* London: A. C. Black, 1933.

———. "Tudor Embroideries." *Connoisseur* 99 (March 1937): 145–52.

Kettell, Samuel. *Specimens of American Poetry with Critical and Biographical Notices in Three Volumes.* Vol. 1. Boston: S. G. Goodrich, 1829.

King, Donald. "The Earliest Dated Sampler." *Connoisseur* 149 (April 1962): 234–5.

————. *Samplers*. London: Her Majesty's Stationery Office, 1960.

Krueger, Glee F. *A Gallery of American Samplers: The Theodore H. Kapnek Collection* (exhibition catalogue). New York: E. P. Dutton in association with the Museum of American Folk Art, 1978.

————. "Mary Wright Alsop 1740–1829 and Her Needlework." *The Connecticut Historical Society Bulletin* 52, nos. 3–4 (Summer/Fall 1987): 124–228.

————. *New England Samplers to 1840*. Sturbridge, Mass.: Old Sturbridge Village, 1978.

Lambert, Miss. *The Hand-Book of Needlework*. New York: Wiley and Putnam, 1842.

Larcom, Lucy. *A New England Girlhood: Outlined from Memory*. Cambridge, Mass., The Riverside Press, 1889.

Lesley, Susan I. *Memoir of the Life of Mrs. Anne Jean Lyman*. Cambridge, Mass., 1876.

Levey, Santina M. "English Embroidered Cabinets of the Seventeenth Century." *The Magazine ANTIQUES* 139, no. 6 (June 1991): 1130–9.

Lippincott, Horace Mather. *Early Philadelphia: Its People, Life & Progress*. Philadelphia: J. B. Lippincott Co., 1917.

Little, Nina Fletcher. *Little by Little: Six Decades of Collecting American Decorative Arts*. New York: E. P. Dutton, 1984.

Llanover, Lady Augusta Hall, ed. *The Autobiography and Correspondence of Mary Granville, Mrs. Delany*. London: R. Bentley, 1861.

Lockridge, Kenneth A. *Literacy in Colonial New England*. New York: W. W. Norton, 1974.

MacLear, Martha. *The History of the Education of Girls in New York and New England, 1800–1870*. Washington, D.C.: Howard University Press, 1926.

McEntee, Sister Mary Bernard. *The Valley: A Narrative of the Founding and Development of Saint Joseph's Academy, High School, College and Alumnae Association, 1809–1972*. Emmitsburg, Md.: Saint Joseph College Alumnae Association, 1972.

Meulenbelt-Nieuwburg, Albarta. *Embroidery Motifs from Old Dutch Samplers*. New York: Charles Scribner's Sons, 1974.

Miner, George L. "Rhode Island Samplers." *Rhode Island Historical Society Collections* 13, no. 2 (April 1920): 41–51.

Myers, Albert Cook, ed. *Hannah Logan's Courtship*. Philadelphia: Ferris & Leach, 1904.

————, ed. *Sally Wister's Journal*. Philadelphia: Ferris & Leach, 1902.

Nason, Elias. *A Memoir of Mrs. Susanna Rowson*. Albany: Joel Munsell, 1870.

Nevinson, John L. *Catalogue of English Domestic Embroidery, of the Sixteenth & Seventeenth Centuries, Victoria and Albert Museum*. London: His Majesty's Stationery Office, 1950.

————. "John Nelham, Embroiderer." *Bulletin of the Needle and Bobbin Club* 65, nos. 1 and 2 (1982):17–19.

Northend, Mary Harrod. *Memories of Old Salem Drawn from the Letters of a Great-Grandmother.* New York: Moffatt, Yard and Co., 1917.

Norton, Arthur O. *The First State Normal School in America: The Journals of Cyrus Peirce and Mary Swift.* Cambridge, Mass.: Harvard University Press, 1926.

Norton, Mary Beth. *Liberty's Daughters: The Revolutionary Experience of American Women, 1750–1800.* Boston: Little, Brown and Co., 1980.

Nylander, Jane. "Some Print Sources of New England Schoolgirl Art." *The Magazine ANTIQUES* 110, no. 2 (August 1976): 292–301.

Palliser, Fanny Bury. *A History of Lace.* 3rd ed. London: Sampson Low, Marston, Low & Searle, 1875.

Parker, Rozsika. *The Subversive Stitch.* London: Women's Press, 1984.

Patten, Ruth. *Interesting Family Letters of the Late Mrs. Ruth Patten, of Hartford, Conn.* Hartford: D. B. Moseley, 1845.

Patten, William. *Memoirs of Mrs. Ruth Patten, of Hartford, Conn. with Letters and Incidental Subjects.* Hartford: P. Canfield, 1834.

Patterson, Jerry E. *The City of New York.* New York: Harry N. Abrams, 1978.

Payne, Francis G. *Guide to the Collection of Samplers and Embroideries.* Cardiff, Wales: National Museum of Wales and the Press Board of the University of Wales, 1939.

Pike, Martha V., and Janice Gray Armstrong. *A Time to Mourn: Expressions of Grief in Nineteenth Century America* (exhibition catalogue). New York: Museums at Stony Brook, 1980.

Pond, Jean Sarah. *Bradford, A New England Academy.* Bradford, Mass.: Bradford Academy Alumnae Association, 1930.

Prime, Alfred Coxe. *The Arts and Crafts in Philadelphia, Maryland, and South Carolina: 1721–1785.* Topsfield, Mass.: Wayside Press, 1929.

———. *The Arts and Crafts in Philadelphia, Maryland, and South Carolina: 1786–1800.* Series Two. Topsfield, Mass.: Wayside Press, 1932.

Reichel, William C., and William H. Bigler. *A History of the Rise, Progress and Present Condition of the Moravian Seminary for Young Ladies at Bethlehem, Pennsylvania, With a Catalogue of Its Pupils 1785–1858.* 2nd ed., rev. and enl. Philadelphia: J. B. Lippincott, 1874.

Reynolds, Ronna L. *Images of Connecticut Life.* Hartford: Antiquarian & Landmarks Society of Connecticut, 1978.

Ring, Betty. *American Needlework Treasures: Samplers and Silk Embroideries from the Collection of Betty Ring.* New York: E. P. Dutton in association with the Museum of American Folk Art, 1987.

———. "The Balch School in Providence, Rhode Island." *The Magazine ANTIQUES* 107, no. 4 (April 1975): 660–71.

———. "For Persons of Fortune Who Have Taste: An Elegant Schoolgirl Embroidery." *Journal of Early Southern Decorative Arts* 3, no. 2 (November 1977): 1–13.

————. "Heraldic Embroidery in Eighteenth-Century Boston." *The Magazine AN-TIQUES* 141, no. 4 (April 1992): 622–31.

————. *Let Virtue Be a Guide to Thee: Needlework in the Education of Rhode Island Women, 1730–1830* (exhibition catalogue). Providence: The Rhode Island Historical Society, 1983.

————. "Mary Balch's Newport Sampler." *The Magazine ANTIQUES* 124, no. 3 (September 1983): 500–7.

————. "Maryland Map Samplers." *Maryland Antiques Show Catalogue.* Baltimore: Maryland Historical Society, 1986.

————. "Memorial Embroideries by American Schoolgirls." *The Magazine ANTIQUES* 100, no. 4 (October 1971): 570–5.

————. "Mrs. Saunders' and Miss Beach's Academy, Dorchester." *The Magazine ANTIQUES* 110, no. 2 (August 1976): 302–12.

————. "Needlework Pictures at Bassett Hall." *The Magazine ANTIQUES* 121, no. 2 (February 1982): 476–82.

————. "Needlework Pictures from Abby Wright's School in South Hadley, Massachusetts." *The Magazine ANTIQUES* 130, no. 3 (September 1986): 482–93.

————. "Peter Grinnell and Son: Merchant-Craftsmen of Providence, Rhode Island." *The Magazine ANTIQUES* 117, no. 1 (January 1980): 212–20.

————. "Print Work: A Silk-wrought Deception." *Theta Charity Antiques Show Catalogue.* Houston: Houston Alumnae of Kappa Alpha Theta, 1980.

————. "Saint Joseph's Academy in Needlework Pictures." *The Magazine AN-TIQUES* 113, no. 3 (March 1978): 592–9.

————. "Salem Female Academy." *The Magazine ANTIQUES* 106, no. 3 (September 1974): 434–42.

————. "Samplers and Pictorial Needlework at the Chester County Historical Society." *The Magazine ANTIQUES* 126, no. 6 (December 1984): 1422–33.

————. "Samplers and Silk Embroideries of Portland, Maine." *The Magazine ANTIQUES* 134, no. 3 (September 1988): 492, 512–25.

————. "Schoolgirl Embroideries: A Credit to the Teachers." *Worcester Art Museum Journal* 5 (1981–82): 18–31.

Roscoe, Theodore Swan. *History of Derby Academy 1784–1984.* Hingham, Mass.: Trustees of Derby Academy, 1984.

Rumford, Beatrix T., ed. *American Folk Paintings: The Abby Aldrich Rockefeller Folk Art Center Series II.* Boston: Little, Brown and Co., 1988.

Schaffner, Cynthia V. A., and Susan Klein. *Folk Hearts: A Celebration of the Heart Motif in American Folk Art.* New York: Alfred A. Knopf, 1984.

Schiffer, Margaret B. "American Needlework." *The Delaware Antiques Show Catalogue.* Wilmington: Junior Board of the Delaware Division, Wilmington Medical Center, 1969.

————. *Arts and Crafts of Chester County, Pennsylvania.* Exton, Pa.: Schiffer Publishing, 1980.

————. *Historical Needlework of Pennsylvania*. New York: Charles Scribner's Sons, 1968.

Schipper-van Lottum, M. G. A. *Over Merklappen Gesproken ... De geschiedenis van de Nederlandse merklap vooral belicht vanuit Noord-Holland*. Amsterdam: Wereldbibliotheek, 1980.

Schorsch, Anita. *Mourning Becomes America: Mourning Art in the New Nation* (exhibition catalogue). Clinton, N.J.: Main Street Press, 1976.

Scott, Barbara. "Madame Campan." *History Today* 23, no. 10 (October 1973): 683–90.

Scott, Kenneth. "Needlework Samplers and Mourning Pictures as Genealogical Evidence." *National Genealogical Society Quarterly* 67, no. 3 (September 1979): 167–74.

Semi-Centennial Catalogue of the Officers and Students of Bradford Academy 1803–1853. Cambridge, Mass.: Metcalf and Co., 1853.

Seybolt, Robert Francis. *The Private Schools of Colonial Boston*. Cambridge, Mass.: Harvard University Press, 1935.

Sibley, John Langdon, and Clifford K. Shipton. *Biographical Sketches of Those Who Attended Harvard College . . . (1690–1770)*. 17 vols. Boston: Massachusetts Historical Society, 1873–1975.

Sigourney, Lydia H. *Letters to My Pupils with Narrative and Biographical Sketches*. New York: Robert Carter & Brothers, 1860.

————. *Lucy Howard's Journal*. New York: Harper & Brothers, 1858.

Silsbee, M. G. D. *A Half Century in Salem*. Cambridge, Mass.: Riverside Press, 1887.

Smith, Helen E. *Colonial Days and Ways*. New York, 1900.

Smith, Kimberly A. "The First Effort of an Infant Hand: An Introduction to Virginia Schoolgirl Embroideries, 1742–1850." *Journal of Early Southern Decorative Arts* 16, no. 2 (November 1990): 30–101.

Smith, Thelma M. "Feminism in Philadelphia, 1790–1850." Pennsylvania Magazine of History and Biography 68, no. 3 (1944): 243–68.

Some Pictures and Samplers from the Collection of Lady St. John Hope. Cambridge, England: University Press, 1949.

Sprague, Laura Fecych, ed. *Agreeable Situations: Society, Commerce, and Art in Southern Maine, 1780–1830*. Kennebunk, Me.: The Brick Store Museum, 1987.

Spruill, Julia Cherry. *Women's Life and Work in the Southern Colonies*. 1938. Reprint. New York: W. W. Norton & Co., 1972.

Stoudt, John Joseph. *Early Pennsylvania Arts and Crafts*. New York: A. S. Barnes, 1964.

Studebaker, Sue. *Ohio Samplers: Schoolgirl Embroideries 1803–1850* (exhibition catalogue). Lebanon, Ohio: Warren County Historical Society, 1988.

Sturge, H. Winifred, and Theodora Clark. *The Mount School, York, 1785–1814, 1831–1931*. London: J. M. Dent & Sons, 1931.

Sullivan, Eleanore C. *Georgetown Visitation since 1799*. Baltimore, 1975.

Swain, Margaret H. *Figures on Fabric: Embroidery Design Sources and Their Application.* London: Adam and Charles Black, 1980.

——. *Historical Needlework: A Study of Influences in Scotland and Northern England.* London: Barrie & Jenkins, 1970.

——. "John Nelham's Needlework Panel." *Bulletin of the Needle and Bobbin Club* 65, nos. 1 and 2 (1982): 3–16.

Swan, Susan Burrows. "Delaware Samplers." *The Delaware Antiques Show Catalogue.* Wilmington: Junior Board of the Medical Center of Delaware, 1985.

——. *Plain & Fancy: American Women and Their Needlework, 1700–1850.* New York: Holt, Rinehart and Winston, 1977.

——. "Recent Discoveries about Philadelphia Samplers." *The Magazine ANTIQUES* 136, no. 6 (December 1989): 1334–43.

——. *Winterthur Guide to American Needlework.* A Winterthur Book/Rutledge Books. New York: Crown Publishers Inc., 1976.

Synge, Lanto. *Antique Needlework.* Dorset, England: Blandford Press, 1982.

Tarrant, Naomi E. A. *The Royal Scottish Museum Samplers.* Edinburgh: Her Majesty's Stationery Office at HMSO Press, 1978.

Townsend, Gertrude. "An Introduction to the Study of Eighteenth Century New England Embroidery." *Bulletin of the Museum of Fine Arts, Boston* 39, no. 232 (April 1941): 19–26.

——. "Notes on New England Needlework before 1800." *Bulletin of the Needle and Bobbin Club* 28, nos. 1 and 2, (1944): 2–23.

Vanderpoel, Emily Noyes, comp. *Chronicles of a Pioneer School from 1792 to 1833, Being the History of Miss Sarah Pierce and Her Litchfield School.* Cambridge, Mass.: University Press, 1903.

——. *More Chronicles of a Pioneer School from 1792–1833, Being Added History on the Litchfield Female Academy Kept by Miss Sarah Pierce and Her Nephew, John Pierce Brace.* Cambridge, Mass.: University Press, 1927.

Vincent, Margaret. *"May Useful Arts Employ My Youth."* The Hope R. Hacker Sampler Collection in the Allentown Art Museum. Allentown, Pa.: Allentown Art Museum, 1987.

Wace, A. J. B. "English Domestic Embroidery, Elizabeth to Anne." *Bulletin of the Needle and Bobbin Club* 17, no. 1 (1933): 12–36.

Wainwright, Nicholas B. *Colonial Grandeur in Philadelphia.* Philadelphia: Historical Society of Pennsylvania, 1964.

Walton, Karin-M. *Samplers: Catalogue of the Collection of Samplers in the City of Bristol Museum & Art Gallery.* Bristol, England: City of Bristol Museum & Art Gallery, 1983.

Wardle, Patricia. *Guide to English Embroidery, Victoria and Albert Museum.* London: Her Majesty's Stationery Office, 1970.

Watts, Isaac. *Horae Lyricae, Poems Chiefly of the Lyric Kind in Three Books.* London: John Clark, 1722.

Wheeler, Candace. *The Development of Embroidery in America*. New York: Harper & Bros., 1921.

Winslow, Anna Green. *Diary of Anna Green Winslow, a Boston Schoolgirl of 1771*. Edited by Alice Morse Earle. Boston: Houghton Mifflin, 1894.

Woody, Thomas. *Early Quaker Education in Pennsylvania*. New York: Teachers College, 1920.

———. *A History of Women's Education in the United States*. 2 vols. New York: Science Press, 1929. Reprint. New York: Octagon Books, 1974.

———. *Quaker Education in the Colony and State of New Jersey*. Philadelphia: University of Pennsylvania, 1923.

Wyatt, Sophia Hayes. *Autobiography of a Landlady of the Old School*. Boston: published by the author, 1854.

Index

The majority of women's names are listed under schoolmistresses or embroiderers, and the latter includes the dates of their work if known. Additional family names may appear in captions for the embroiderers. Bold-faced type indicates an illustration.

PHOTOGRAPHIC CREDITS

The author wishes to thank the many fine photographers who are unnamed here but were responsible for photographs from various institutions credited in the captions, in addition to the following:

Douglas Armsden, 273; David Behl, 147; Barry Blau, 392; E. Irving Blomstrann, 245; David J. Bohl, 83, 83a, 130; Susan Boice, 93; Barbara Borders, 209, 463; Boynton Photography, 202; Will Brown, 548; Donald H. Byerly, 420, 421, 422, 424, 425, 426, 433, 552; Cathy Carver, 95, 204, 283; Hal Cohen, 124; Robert Corrigan, 476; Joseph Crilley, 526, 527; Herbert L. Crossan, 296; Francis Doyle, 97, 215; George Fistrovich, 437, 440, 443; Rick Gardner, 72; Brenda Gilmore, 220; Jeff Goldman, 565, 568, 571, 574; Ralph Grabiner, 553; Melvin L. Gurtizen, 454, 455, 456; Jud Haggard, 12, 25, 115, 146, 164, 227, 308, 361, 394, 490, 530, 542, 547, 564, 572, 582; John Harkey, 196, 207, 602; Alfred Harrell, 223, 360; Alan Harvey, 27, 28, 160, 192, 193, 197, 270; Hayman Studio, 471; Helga Photo Studio, 18, 20, 31, 31a, 62, 69, 70, 71, 75, 84, 86, 88, 89, 94, 96, 106, 109, 114, 126, 127, 134, 136, 138, 143, 144, 145, 150, 153, 156, 158, 159, 161, 171, 172, 175, 176, 177, 178, 181, 182, 185, 203, 205, 211, 222, 228, 241, 250, 251, 259, 260, 261, 263, 264, 265, 266, 271, 272, 274, 275, 278, 279, 280, 281, 285, 286, 288, 292, 299, 299a, 300, 301, 302, 317, 318, 328, 330, 331, 332, 338, 347, 347a, 348, 349, 350, 353, 358, 364, 366, 369, 373, 376, 381, 384, 388, 391, 396, 397, 399, 403, 406, 407, 412, 423, 427, 428, 429, 430, 431, 432, 434, 435, 442, 460, 462, 464, 474, 483, 485, 486, 493, 495, 497, 498, 504, 505, 506, 508, 512, 513, 514, 517, 518, 524, 525, 529, 531, 532, 534, 536, 537, 538, 555, 557, 563, 576, 578, 580, 581, 583, 584, 585, 587, 588, 589; George Henderson, 199; Hi-Tek Photo, 549, 550, 551; G. R. Hockmeyer, 339, 605; John T. Hopf, 65, 419; William N. Hosley, Jr., 247; Scott Hyde, 10, 35, 36, 50, 76, 123, 128, 140, 154, 162, 398, 469, 556; Hans Kaczmarek, 351; Bob Kolbrener, frontispiece, Vol. II; Eric Long, 7, 104, 129, 151, 184, 472, 523, 528, 533, 540, 577; Benjamin Magro, 289, 290; Jennifer Mange, 163; Ken McKnight, 293; Richard Merrill, 139; Allen Mewbourn, 86, 87, 100, 110, 219, 277, 297, 340, 371, 482, 522, 579; Lori Minor, 246; Munroe Studio, 79; Michael Nedzweski, 121, 142; Frank Newbould, 313; Gene Ogami, 190, 481; Panaro & Prettyman, 566; Henry E. Peach, 183; Ken Pelka, 22, 287, 395, 470; Luigi Pellettieri, 377, 380; Terry Pommett, 165, 166, 167, 168, 329; Clive Russ, 102; Schopplein Studio, 355; Dan Sellers, 15, 516; Tony Senior, 312, 315; Mark Sexton, 92, 108, 116, 122, 157, 304, 305; Richard A. Siciliano, 213; Richard Straus, 187, 409, 501; Duane Suter, 569, 570; Robert Walch, 195, 322, 362, 417, 446, 447, 448, 450, 458, 487, 507

A NOTE ON THE TYPE

The text of this book was set in a typeface named Perpetua, designed by the British artist Eric Gill (1882–1940) and cut by the Monotype Corporation of London in 1928–1930. Perpetua is a contemporary letter of original design, without any direct historical antecedents. The shapes of the roman letters basically derive from stone cutting, a form of lettering in which Gill was eminent. The italic is essentially an inclined roman. The general effect of the typeface in reading sizes is one of lightness and grace. The larger display sizes of the type are extremely elegant and form what is probably the most distinguished series of inscriptional letters cut in the present century.

Composition and separations by North Market Street Graphics, Lancaster, Pennsylvania
Printed and bound by Arcata Graphics, Kingsport, Tennessee

Back endpapers:

Bills and Receipts for Schooling

Elizabeth Marsh to Joseph Trotter, May 2, 1735. See Fig. 351.

Thompson Collection, No. 83, Historical Society of Pennsylvania.

Receipt to James Vaux (one of the executors of Caspar W. Haines, dec'd) from the Westtown school treasurer for the expenses of Ann Haines, May 6, 1806. See Figs. 427–431.

Wyck Papers (Series V/B205/F52), American Philosophical Society, Philadelphia.

Convent of the Visitation to Henry Neale. Expenses for his daughter Eleanora, March 1823. See Fig. 588.

The Visitation Convent, Washington, D.C.

Ann Marsh to Mrs. Norris "for your daughter Debby," December 20, 1774.

Norris Papers (Vol. 6, 119), Historical Society of Pennsylvania.

Mary Ralston to the Reverend Mr. Hetch, May 1, 1840.

Northampton County Historical Society, Easton, Pennsylvania.

Boarding School in Bethlehem to William Witman for Hester and Sarah Witman, December 30, 1809. See Fig. 490.

Private Collection.

Receipt for expenses of Julia A. M. Pickens at the Salem Female Boarding School, August 23, 1809.

Salem Academy and College, Winston-Salem, North Carolina.

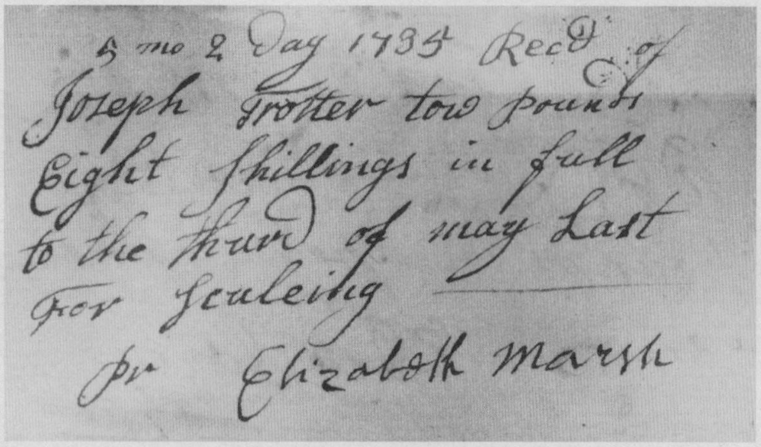

5 mo 2 Day 1735 Rec'd of
Joseph Trotter tow pounds
Eight shillings in full
to the third of may Last
for Scaleing ————
pr Elizabeth Marsh

September 4 1774 Mrs Norris
one Quarter Schooling her your
december 20 1774
Rec'd the Above in full

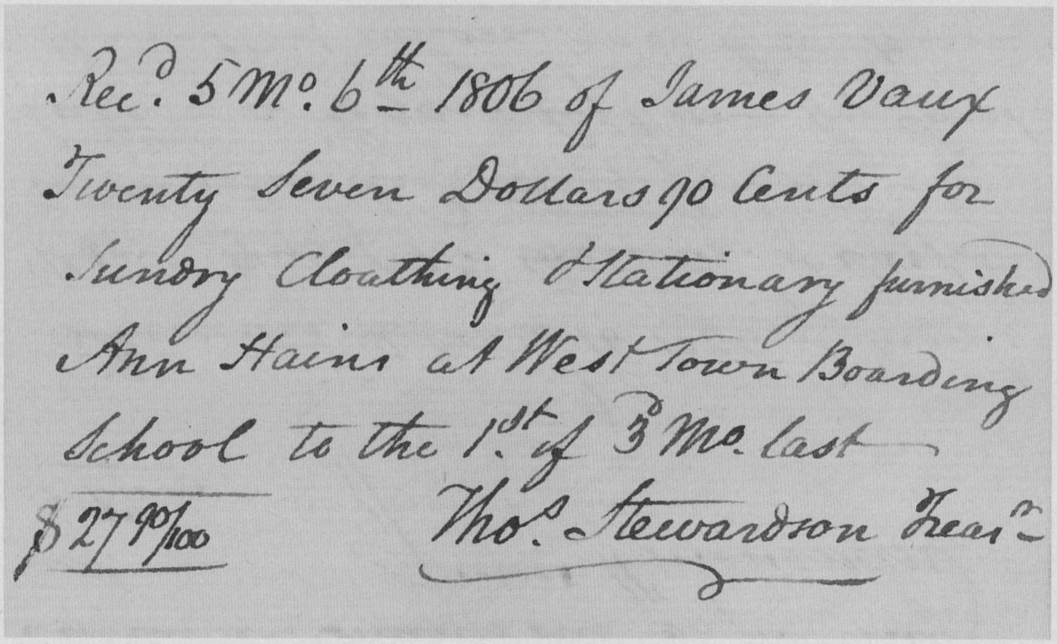

Rec'd 5 Mo. 6th 1806 of James Vaux
Twenty Seven Dollars 90 Cents for
Sundry Cloathing & Stationary furnished
Ann Hains at West Town Boarding
School to the 1st of 3 Mo. last ————
$ 27 90/100   Thos. Stewardson Treasr

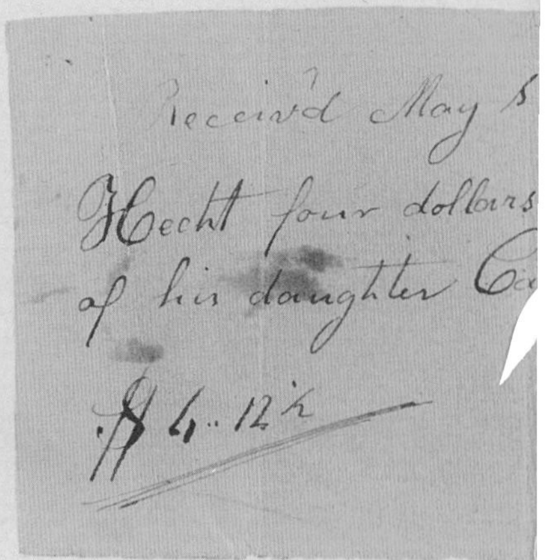

Receiv'd May 5
Hecht four dollars
of his daughter C——
$ 4. 12½

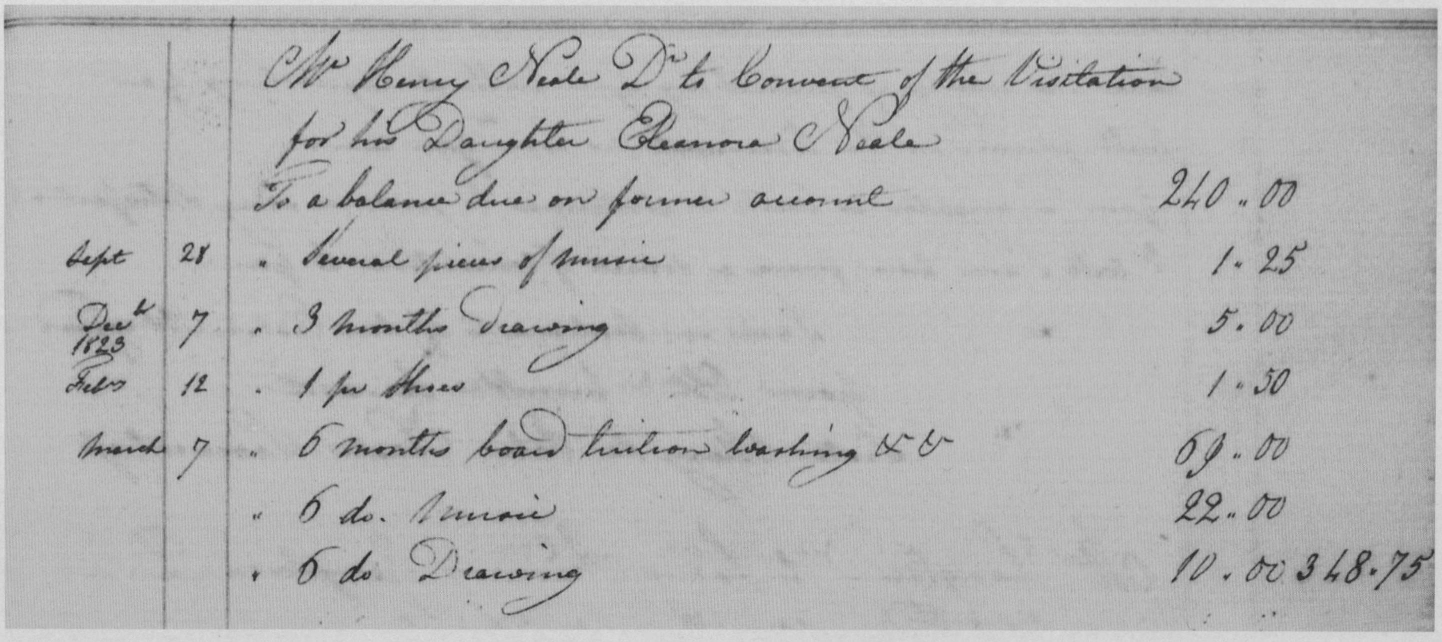

		Mr Henry Neale Dr to Convent of the Visitation for his Daughter Eleanora Neale	
		To a balance due on former account	240 . 00
Sept	28	Several pieces of music	1 . 25
Decr 1823	7	3 months drawing	5 . 00
Febr	12	1 pr Shoes	1 . 50
March	7	6 months board tuition washing &c	69 . 00
		6 do. Music	22 . 00
		6 do Drawing	10 . 00 348 . 75